KNOWLEDGE ORGANIZATION, INFORMATION SYSTEMS AND OTHER ESSAYS

PROFESSOR A. NEELAMEGHAN FESTSCHRIFT

KNOWLEDGE ORGANIZATION, INFORMATION SYSTEMS AND OTHER ESSAYS

PROFESSOR A. NEELAMEGHAN FESTSCHRIFT

Edited By:
K.S. Raghavan
K.N. Prasad

Assisted By:
S.K. Lalitha

Published By:

Ess Ess Publications

4837/24, Ansari Road
Darya Ganj
New Delhi-110 002

For:

Ranganathan Centre for Information Studies
Chennai and Bangalore
2006

ISBN: 81-7000-458-6

Rs.1125/-

Published by:
Ess Ess Publications
4837/24, Ansari Road, Darya Ganj, New Delhi-110 002
Tel: 011-23260807, 51563444 Fax: 011-51563334
E-mail: info@essessreference.com
url: www.essessreference.com

For:
Ranganathan Centre for Information Studies

Printed in India at:
Printline, New Delhi

CONTENTS

PROFESSOR A. NEELAMEGHAN FESTSCHRIFT COMMITTEE

FOREWORD

Propelled by professional pride and enthused by the desire to capture the rapidly emerging innovations in the field of Information Science and Technology, a group of eminent and senior professionals established the Ranganathan Centre for Information Studies (RCIS) in July 1993 on the occasion of the centenary celebrations of Dr. S.R. Ranganathan. Its key objectives are promotion of education, training, research, advisory services including project design and implementation in information studies, informatics and telematics and the dissemination of research results. Besides organizing seminars and conferences on state of art developments, RCIS launched the quarterly journal, *Information Studies* with Prof. A.Neelameghan and Prof. S. Pathasarathy as editors. The information profession owes a great deal of debt to the untiring dedication of Prof. Neelameghan in steering this land mark journal for more than a decade containing original contributions on a range of issues relating to the scientific, technological, policy and professional aspects of the discipline of information studies.

Beginning from his early association with Dr. S.R. Ranganathan in 1962, his contributions to research in the area of Knowledge Organization have been acclaimed worldwide. His close association with a number of United Nations Agencies and International Organizations in formulating information strategies and programmes for developing countries from the early Seventies, when the power of Information Sciences for socio-economic development was just beginning to be appreciated, brought him world-wide commendations. In 1974 he was elected Chairman of the International Advisory Committee of UNESCO/UNISIST. He also served the UNESCO/General Information Program as Project Coordinator of the UNESCO/UNDP Postgraduate Training Course for Science Information Specialists in Southeast Asia. Even after his retirement in 1986, Prof. Neelameghan continue as a consultant and resource specialist for a number of International organizations such as WHO, UNIDO, IDRC (Canada) and UNESCO. His focus on National Information Policy and Planning, Education for Information and Development Communication has resulted in remarkable impact not only on the field of information science but also on raising the awareness of practitioners. He continues to be active in the field, both on his own and through the Sarada Ranganathan Endowment for Library Science, Bangalore.

RCIS is indeed privileged to bring out the Festschrift Volume, containing invited contributions from eminent scholars and professionals from around the world in honour of Prof. Neelameghan. Beyond the efforts to create special tools and techniques for information organization in the current era of revolutionary changes in the field of Information Science and Technology, special attention is needed for Knowledge Organization, a field close to the heart of Prof. Neelameghan. I am confident that the seminal contributions of very many distinguished experts in this field will help researchers to address the emerging challenges and opportunities in fostering a Knowledge Society.

12th August 2005

M. Anandakrishnan
Vice-Chairman, RCIS

PREFACE

In bringing out this volume of essays, we wish to honour a distinguished teacher and one of the most eminent information scientists of our time.

Prof. A. Neelameghan was born on 3rd July 1926, in the Walthamstow Mansion Annexe in Ootacamund (Udhagamandalam), Nilgiris, Tamil Nadu. Dr. C. Rangachari, the famous doctor from Chennai, was in attendance. He was the last of the seven children to his parents. Only he and the first born survived childhood. The year he was born saw the flowering of the *Kurinji* that spreads a carpet of blue flowers on the mountain slopes every twelve years or so. Hence his name '*Neelameghan*'. His father was pioneering cultivation of vegetables, etc. on the hillside, protecting his orchards against wild boars, foxes and wolfs. The mother and the baby, not yet one year old, moved to his uncle's home in Damal village near Kancheepuram. In 1929, they joined the father in Mahe, a former French Colony in North Malabar, Kerala.

His first schooling was in a Catholic Convent and then at the College Mahe de Labourdonnais (now Jawaharlal Nehru High School). He matriculated with top honours in 1943 and was admitted to the Madras Christian College, Tambaram. He graduated in 1947 majoring in physics. Dr. Hemalata Iyer in her paper based on interview sessions with Professor Neelameghan recounts his further career.

During his professional career beginning in the early 1950s, Professor Neelameghan distinguished himself by providing innovative information services in different types of institutions; assisted in the planning and development of educational programmes in Information Studies in India and in other developing regions of the world; taught in these schools and programmes; organized and conducted over a hundred workshops and training courses. He has a large family of students, spanning from Fiji and Papua New Guinea in the Far East through many countries in Asia, Africa and Arab States, to Latin America and the Caribbean in the West. He is credited with the introduction of courses in information and communication technologies and informetrics in the training of library and information professionals in developing countries in the 1970s and 1980s. Dr. John Rose describes his services with UNESCO in his paper.

The impact of Professor Neelameghan's work in different branches of library and information science and more particularly in the area of knowledge organization is so well recognized in the information world that it does not require comment in this introduction.

Besides being an eminent teacher, Professor Neelameghan is a researcher to the core. His theoretical contributions to the epistemological foundations of knowledge organization by way of identifying and defining new modes of formation of subjects, his search for multi-disciplinary evidence in support of Dr. S.R. Ranganathan's postulate of 'Absolute Syntax' to help formulate universals in the structure of indexing languages, his work on the need for a theoretical basis for U.D.C., his research into developing a typology of lateral semantic relations, his work on the application of the principles of the 'General Theory of Classification' in designing databases are but a few examples that stand testimony to this.

Prof. Neelameghan's range of knowledge and work are indeed very wide and varied; and in each one of the areas that he has worked on he has left his footprints. Interestingly in bringing out this volume we realized that different groups within our profession and outside know him for his significant contributions to their area of work and operation! LIS educators and planners acknowledge his inputs to curriculum design and design of doctoral programmes in LIS; persons who have worked with him in various international organizations that he has been associated with remember him for his significant inputs in planning information systems and information policy issues; professionals outside LIS know him for what he has done to help them in designing and developing effective systems for managing data and information in their own working environment especially for his pioneering efforts in the applications of the text retrieval software CDS/ISIS for creation and management of non-bibliographic databases. His pragmatic approach to the creation of information bases for user groups in different institutions (e.g. Hospitals, NGOs, religious missions) has won for him wide acclaim and a large number of friends and admirers among non-LIS professionals. In research, he always emphasized the importance of precision and would never allow a method of data collection to shape our research problem and approach. He firmly believes that research improved practice, planning and decision-making and also teaching.

PREFACE – Raghavan; Prasad

Professor Neelameghan's career and work has by no means been confined to the field of library and information science in the narrow sense. As a consultant for UN. IDRC and several other international organizations and more particularly as a senior officer of UNESCO, his contributions to development communication, and information policy issues especially in the developing countries of Asia, Africa, Arab States and Latin America have been substantial. Even after his formal retirement from UNESCO, his services have been sought both within and outside the country.

He has authored over 600 papers of which more than 250 are research papers, several with Dr. S.R. Ranganathan and with colleagues in the Documentation Research and Training Centre, and researchers in India and abroad. He has also authored, coauthored and/or edited some 25 books and conference/seminar volumes; prepared course materials for open university programmes, such as those of IGNOU; prepared a large number of technical reports to governments and institutions in India and abroad following advisory and technical assistance missions undertaken to various countries on behalf of or at the invitation of international organizations.

He continues to provide technical assistance and advise to institutions and maintains virtual collaboration with other researchers in information studies in India and abroad. His present research interests include, among others, knowledge organization, concept relationships, and multilingual multicultural thesauri. He has special interest in medical history and historiography.

Given this, planning the contents of this volume was indeed a difficult task. Surely it is very difficult, in a volume such as this, to include papers on every facet of work of the individual whom we seek to honour, who has made contributions to such a wide range of areas as Professor Neelameghan has. We decided that the volume should therefore have only invited contributions. The papers in this volume represent only a cross section of the facets of our broad discipline to which Prof. Neelameghan has made significant contributions.

The papers that were received were categorized into a few broad areas:

- Knowledge Organization;
- Interoperability, Digital Library and Information Retrieval;
- Knowledge Management in Specialized Areas;
- Information Society; and
- The Person and Associated Organizations.

As is to be expected, *Knowledge Organization* is the dominant theme and there are as many as ten papers in the area. Papers in this section and those in the section on *Interoperability* and *Digital Library* represent some of the current areas of research and discussions. The papers in the section on *Knowledge Management in Specialized Areas* focus on information systems developed in different domains to provide information support to end users of such systems. Incidentally, Professor Neelameghan has been associated with most of these. The papers in the section on *Information Society* highlight the changing paradigm and its implications. The papers in the section on *The Person and Associated Organizations* highlight his contributions to organizations and institutions with which he has been associated as well as to the discipline as a whole. As is to be expected there are a couple of brief write-ups that are purely personal reminiscences.

We are grateful to the authors of all the papers and members of the festschrift volume committee for their valuable contributions. We express our sincere thanks to Dr. M. Anandakrishnan for the Foreword.

Bangalore
24.08.2005

K.S. Raghavan
K. N. Prasad

TOWARDS A FUTURE FOR KNOWLEDGE ORGANIZATION

Ingetraut Dahlberg

Discusses the origin and evolution of the Information Coding Classification (ICC); its theoretical basis, and structure and advantageous attributes for organizing knowledge. Pleads that the considerable work already done on the system should be taken up and developed by interested research groups through collaborative effort. Concludes with some thoughts on the future of knowledge organization for information retrieval and other applications

1 A LOOK INTO OUR COMMON HISTORY

The 1972 Conference of the International Federation for Documentation (FID) at Budapest, led to two remarkable decisions regarding our beloved field of classification. It was decided: 1) to move the leadership of the FID/Classification Research Committee (FID/CR) from Denmark to India with Prof. A. Neelameghan as its chair, and 2) to establish a "Broad System of Ordering" (BSO) according to the resolutions of UNESCO's UNISIST Programme of 1971 (UNESCO, 1971) by a special Subgroup of FID/CR and members of FID's Central Classification Committee (concerned with the UDC revision work). This Subgroup acted from 1973-1974 under the name FID/SRC (Subject Reference Code) and delivered two rather opposing suggestions (from the two different parties of this group) in 1974 to a so-called Expert Meeting, which decided to leave the elaboration of the final version of the BSO to a 3-Man-Panel headed by Eric Coates[1]. The meetings of FID/SRC had been co-sponsored by UNESCO and were held at the FID Headquarters in The Hague. Fortunately through this co-sponsorship Prof. Neelameghan was frequently invited to participate in the meetings. I was also asked to participate in the work of this group and contributed to it my collection of names of subject fields and its systematisation, which I had started already in 1972 as a project of the German Documentation Society,

Frankfurt (Dahlberg, 973). When in Sept.1974 the FID/SRC Group was dissolved, I continued my work on the elaboration of a universal classification system of subject/knowledge fields on the theoretical basis, which I had first outlined in my doctoral dissertation written in 1972-1973 (Dahlberg, 1974). And since in 1975-76 I was given the opportunity to propose a new universal classification system on the basis of the subject fields taught at German universities (a work for the German Association of Universities - Hochschulverband) I could also check my theoretical insights included in this system of knowledge fields with the reality and practical needs of university teaching fields.

The result of my theoretical and practical work of these past years was presented for the first time in December 1977 during the 11th Sarada Ranganathan Endowment Lectures in Bangalore, India, and it was only through the question of one of the participants of this one-week-seminar, about how I would name the new universal system, that I thought about it and subsequently called it 'Information Coding Classification – ICC'. Surely Prof. Neelameghan will remember as he kindly edited the publication resulting from this seminar (Dahlberg, 1978) (5). He will also remember that I had invited him to join the Editorial Board of '*International Classification*', started in the Spring of 1974 and renamed as '*Knowledge Organization*' by the ISKO[2] Conference of 1992 at Madras, India.

2 THE NECESSITY OF DEFINITIONS

Already in 1973 it occurred to me that it was necessary to base the terms denoting subject fields on definitions of the respective concepts and therefore I established a huge card-file and listed in it all the definitions, which I found to a given name of a subject field in four encyclopaedias and about 500 special glossaries or dictionaries. This took a number of years, actually until 1978 and was partly supported by the German Research Association (DFG).

The knowledge gained from the project of the Hochschulverband and later-on from the definitions improved the further elaboration of the ICC tremendously as every definition naturally sets out the hierarchy and scope of a concept supplying thus 'automatically' also its necessary context. Very important was also the help coming from the correspondence with a large number of German professors during the time of the two projects. On the other hand I realized that they were not able to understand my way of grouping and arranging the concepts of subject fields – but this will become clear later on.

3 A SHORT INTRODUCTION INTO THE THEORETICAL BASIS AND OUTLINE OF THE ICC[3]

First of all it needed a theory of the concept. This I had already anticipated in my dissertation but made clearer in my presentation at the 1975 FID/CR Conference in Bombay (Dahlberg, 1975). Concepts can be defined as being *Knowledge Units having been* synthesized *from the necessary statements about any referent (which yield the characteristics of a concept) and being represented / verbalized by a name, a term, or a code of some kind*[4]. The elements of the ICC are the concepts representing object areas, subject groups and subject fields. I distinguish between concepts of being, concepts of form (facets) and combinations of both, that is, the subject concepts.

The main classes of the ICC are not disciplines or bundles of disciplines but ontical objects determining their respective areas. Thus the 9 main ontical areas of the ICC are the following:

1 Form and structure area
2 Energy and matter area
3 Cosmos and earth area
4 Bio-area
5 Human area
6 Socio-area
7 Economic and technical area
8 Knowledge and information area
9 Metaphysical and cultural area

Fig. 1: The "Main classes" or ontical areas of the Information Coding Classification (ICC)

As it appears there is a tri-partition in the sequence forming: (1) the conditions for living beings 1-3, (2) the living beings: 4-6, and (3) material, intellectual and metaphysical products of living beings: 7-9.

Each one of these areas constitutes a level necessary for the next area. Thus the areas build up on each other, they presuppose each other[5]. In order to systematize the subject groups possible in each area, I decided to introduce the following stereotype sequence of aspects, actually facets, and called it *Systematifier*. This device can of course also be applied to the subdivision of each subject field occurring in a subject group.

The Systematifier distinguishes the following sequence of concepts of form/facets, again to be split into 3 parts, as follows:

1	Theory and general constituting concepts of an area, subject group or field
2	Objects as well as systems of objects and parts of objects
3	Activities and processes exerted onto or by the objects
4	Specialties evolving out of facets 1-3
5	Specialties evolving out of facets 1-3
6	Specialties evolving out of facets 1-3
7	Influences from other areas and fields on the subject of facets 1- 3
8	Applications to other areas and fields from the subject of facets 1-3
9	Synthesis and environment of the knowledge of 1-3 socially applied, as e.g. its teaching and didactics, information and documentation on the subject group or field, etc.

Fig. 2: The Systematifier for the Subdivision of Components of a Subject Area or a Field

This sequence resembles in a way the idea of a facet formula, which is meant to represent the concepts in a statement (e.g. title of a book) on any subject. Ranganathan (1933, 1963; 1967) had developed his faceted Colon Classification from the observation, that the activity facet, expressed by verbs in such statements needs different complements in different fields. But he also looked for a general formula, his "absolute syntax" for application in each subject field. Actually the "absolute syntax" relates to the 2-3 necessary items of a sentence, namely Subject, Predicate and - also but not always - Object. With the *Systematifier* outlined above I introduced the elements of such a general formula as the components of every subject area or field and by this giving each facet concept a position in the general position plan of the system which characterizes the kind of concept so-to-speak automatically. Thus 'Theory' is always at position 1, 'Objects' are always at position 2, etc. And since I used for the whole system only the numbers from 1-9 on each level, the codes for each subject area and subject field can very easily be used and memorized.

In his book of 1975 (Neelameghan, 1975) and recently in a paper with K.S. Raghavan (Neelameghan and Raghavan, 2004) A. Neelameghan speaks of "Seminal Mnemonics" which he defines as "*Identification at the near seminal level, of similar subsets or groups of ideas in subject domains and deriving a similar pattern of organization of the subsets in different domains*". The Systematifier can indeed be understood as such a tool for mnemonics. It was developed by analyzing all the subject groups included in the ICC and thousands of subject fields and finding their respective components. However, it depended also on the development or 'maturity' of a subject group or field, if all positions were occupied by concepts and classes of concepts[6].

Compared with the facet formula of the Colon Classification (PMEST = Personality, Matter, Energy, Space and Time) the ICC seems to lack first of all the facet "Matter". But it was found that this form concept refers to the varying attributes of either the object facet 2 or the activities facet 3 or even to the entire subject group. Therefore such varying attributes must be introduced as special sub-facets of the facets named. If they characterize entire fields, their position would be under the respective facets 4, 5, and 6. With respect to the Time and Space Facets the ICC holds for these concepts relevant places in geography and history. From there they also can be combined with any other subject field needing such dimensional concepts.

In 1991 I added to the matrix of the ICC (*see* Fig.3) a so-called 'zero-layer' which contains the general form concepts. These are the pure categories of form, applicable, if elaborated, in any statement with the subject concepts where needed. They should not be regarded in their vertical line as absolute determiners of the contents of this line.

	1	2	3	4	5	6	7	8	9
0 General Form Conc.	01 Theories Principl.	02 Object Component	03 Activity Process.	04 Property Attribut.	05 Persons or cont.	06 Institut. or cont.	07 Technol. Product.	08 Applicat. Determin.	09 Distrib. Synthesi
1 FORM & STRUCTURE AREA	11 Logic	12 Mathematics	13 Statistics	14 Systemology	15 Organization	16 Metrology	17 Cybernetics (Contr. & automat.)	18 Standardization	19 Testing & monitoring
2 ENERG & MATTER AREA	21 Mechanics	22 Physics of matter	23 Gen. & ech. physics	24 Electronics	25 Physical chemistry	26 Pure chemistry	27 Chemical technol.& engg.	28 Energy sci.& technol.	29 Electrical engg.
3 COSMO & GEO-REA	31 Astronomy & astrophysics	32 Astronautics & space research	33 Basic geosciences	34 Atmosphere sci. & tech.	35 Hydrospher. & oceanol sci. & tech.	36 Geological sciences	37 Mining	38 Materials sci.& metallurgy	39 Geography
4 BIO-AREA	41 Basic biol. sciences	42 Microbiology & cultivation	43 Plant biology & cultivation	44 Animal biology & breeding	45 Veterinary sciences	46 Agriculture & horticulture	47 Forestry & Wood sci.& technol.	48 Food science & technol.	49 Ecology & envi ronment
5 HUMAN AREA	51 Human biology	52 Health & theoretical medicine	53 Pathology & medicine	54 Clinical medicine & cure	55 Psychology	56 Education	57 Profession, labor, leisure	58 Sports	59 Household & homelife
6 SOCIO-AREA	61 Sociology	62 State & politics	63 Public admini stration	64 Money & finances	65 Social aid, social politics	66 Law	67 Area Planning Urbanism	68 Military sci. & tech.	69 History
7 ECONOMICS & TECHNOLOGY AREA	71 Gen.& natl. economics	72 Busines economics	73 Technology in general	74 Mechanical & precision engg.	75 Building	76 Commodity sci. & technol.	77 Vehicle sci. & technol.	78 Transport technol.& services	79 Utilities & service econom.
8 SCIENCE & INFORMATION AREA	81 Science of science	82 Information sciences	83 Informatics, computer science	84 Information in general	85 Communication sci.	86 Mass communication	87 Printing & publishing	88 Communication engg.	89 Semiotics
9 CULTURE AREA	91 Language & linguistics	92 Literature & philology	93 Music & musicology	94 Fine arts	95 Performing arts	% Culture. sci.i.n.s.	97 Philosophy	98 Religion & secret teachings	99 Christian Religion

Fig. 3 Network of Knowledge Groups

4 A LEXICON OF KNOWLEDGE FIELDS

In continuing our 'history': So far, until 1979, some 7500 German terms out of a collection of 12500 terms denoting subject fields together with their definitions, synonyms and sometimes also English equivalents were selected and subsequently entered into a card file and later on into computer using the systematic arrangement of the ICC. Unfortunately the *Lexicon of Knowledge Fields* which was to be generated on the basis of this input could never be published for two reasons. On the one hand we were lacking funds for the final edition and on the other hand – while waiting for the funds - we were already busy with another project, the elaboration of the huge *Classification and Indexing Bibliography*, published so far in 3 volumes (Dahlberg, 1982-85) S. Seetharama (from DRTC, Bangalore) had helped us with the indexing of this work in 1981. We had hoped to resume the work on the Lexicon later on and publish it in systematic and alphabetical order, but time ran out and, very important, took all our time and energy. Looking at this problem from the point of view of today's globalization, an updated version and its publication seems to become really important in order to have a tool for mutual understanding of the contents of subject fields between the different nations of this world. The material has not been lost; it is still with me in the basement of my house and waits for somebody interested in its updating and publishing.

5 TERMINOLOGY AND CLASSIFICATION

The huge field of terminology as the science of the adequate naming and definition of concepts can equally be based on the Concept Theory mentioned above. And indeed, the well-known engineer, the late Prof. Eugen Wüster who started the science of terminology at about the same time as Dr. Ranganathan developed his first edition of Colon Classification in the beginning of the thirties of the past century, was one of my 'forerunners' in developing the theory of concepts with the theories of kinds of concepts, kinds of characteristics, kinds of conceptual relationships and kinds of definitions. Wüster's approach (Wuster, 1966) was taken over by the German terminology standards as well as pertinent ISO Recommendations. It looks to me that it would become a most necessary and fruitful exercise for terminologists and classificationists of all nations, if they would find a chance to collaborate in the establishment of conceptual terminology and classification systems according to the principles established through the ICC structure and its element position plan. For just as we need to know how things operate in the material world in order for us to construct and handle them properly, I think we should also be able to understand the relationships of what we know and speak about and show them not only in semantic graphs as this was done by linguists, but by coherent structures which refer to the world of Beings/Entities and their Attributes and Activities in Space and Time. It is my dream that a time will come when terminologists and classificationists will join and work together towards this goal of seizing the knowledge of mankind step by step in the network of an enlarged ICC system of knowledge fields and their specific items.

6 INSIGHT COMES FROM RECOGNITION AND UNDERSTANDING

Any defined concept which is inter-subjectively accepted is a knowledge unit in our world of apprehension. And the rules of systematization of such knowledge units/concepts and classes of concepts for the purpose of constructing, displaying and using conceptual classification and terminology systems should therefore be taught, not only in the schools of library and information science but also in the schools of higher education. A German theologian and philosopher, Paul Tillich (Tillich, 1923), once stated in 1923 (by referring to the necessity of recognizing and understanding):

> "*Recognition occurs where something is established as a necessary item in a context (as an association of concepts). A single item in its isolation is no object of recognition. Where there is no comprehensive context, one may well look at things, but will not understand them*" (My translation, I.D.)

In other words, the context which a definition and thus also a classification system (which is a definition system) can provide by its hierarchical and other relationships is a necessary precondition for everybody to apprehend the items of our world of thoughts. Knowledge, after all, is the understanding of relations. Therefore, and notwithstanding those who would rather speak of 'Knowledge

Management' as this seems to suggest that one knows how to handle knowledge, I still think that next to many other activities in our field of Knowledge Organization a highly important activity would be the establishment of very concisely elaborated systems of knowledge units/ concepts in the sense of the old broad Elsinore definition (Atherton, 1965) ("establishing relationships between semantic units") (Dahlberg 1996) according to a common theoretical basis as given with the ICC. If only those '*in power*' would start to recognize their responsibility (not only toward the scientific society) for this and begin with the necessary '*homework*' and associate with those who have the same in mind! This has been my 'preaching' for a long time but nobody seems to care. And perhaps this paper, again, will not find the persons to take up the challenge. But I use this opportunity to repeat my desire again, especially as many of us have given up thinking along these lines when facing the terrific possibilities of computer handling of words and texts. But they forget the fact that concepts can be expressed in numerous ways. There is, according to R. Fugmann (Fugmann, 1985), no way of predicting the many possibilities of how people might have expressed their thoughts in natural language, not to speak of possible other natural languages.

The way toward this goal could also be pursued if one would start to establish a switching system of the six existing universal classification systems on the basis of the ICC to be utilized as the 'black box' in the switching mechanism. The methodology for this was already outlined in papers of the Washington and Lille ISKO Conferences (Dahlberg, 1996 and Dahlberg, 1998). It will not be an easy task but it would lead the way out of the conceptual and terminological confusion which still prevails worldwide. And it would provide a tool to the scientific community which could help in understanding and using our knowledge of yesterday, today and tomorrow in the most pertinent way.

7 ADVANTAGES OF AN ONTICALLY AND CATEGORICALLY ORDERED STRUCTURE OF KNOWLEDGE UNITS

Here I would like to refer to the advantages of using a structure and the principles guiding a scheme like the ICC. Therefore, am listing 10 of them for policy considerations and possible actions in the future.

7.1 Easy Recognition of Position of System Elements (Concepts, Classes)

In the *Information Coding Classification* – ICC, the vertical pillar of the areas of being and the horizontal structure of the form categories are holding vigorously together, just like the strong beams of a stable crane, the subject groups and their element positions and form by this a matrix which permits everyone to see on first sight, where which subjects can be found.

7.2 Usability of a Decimal Notation to Reflect the Hierarchy

As the ICC has 9 levels of being and in each subject group also 9 aspect areas/facets, it was possible to use a decimal notation for the 81 system positions of subject groups and also all their subfields on the next levels. By this the hierarchical relationships can also be shown very clearly and explicitly.

7.3 Combinability of Concepts with Each Other Facilitated by the Notation

Indeed all concepts of this matrix may be combined in a given case and by the ease of the decimal notation any concept combination can therefore also be represented by a combined notation. At the same time the meaning of the form categorical system positions are made visible. This will become also self-evident in representing inter- and trans-disciplinary, multi-, pluri-, and syndisciplinary concepts (Dahlberg, 1994).

7.4 Definability of Concepts According to their form Categories/Facets Facilitates the Search for Concepts

The order of the concepts according to form categories or facets on the basis of their definability as elements of such categories facilitates their searchability and traceability and thus excludes errors in finding the correct system positions of a concept.

7.5 The High Degree of Order in the System Favours Memorizability

By the definability (6.4) according to categories a high degree of order is included in the system which facilitates the extensive use of the system by its inbuilt mnemonics as well as when using it in the machine.

7.6 Representational Predictability and Representational Fidelity

These two further concepts used by R. Fugmann in his principles for indexing (Fugmann, 1985) can be applied here too since contents and syntax of the system are - by its consistently used structure on all levels of hierarchies - very easy to recognize and to predict and should permit its use without misunderstanding.

7.7 Computerizability

Because of the simplicity of notation and its inbuilt facets, computerization should be achieved easily.

7.8 User-friendliness and Further Development of the System

As the facets in the system are arranged in such a way that a newcomer to the system will quickly be able to recognize, at which system positions he/she might find certain concepts and subjects, the system not only facilitates its use but also its further development.

7. 9 Compatibility

The possibility of correlating the system with other universal systems is given and would – if used in the Internet with the function of a switching system – facilitate the direct access to the concepts and classes of other universal systems, if once the necessary correlating work is done (*see also* 20 and 21).

7.10 Universality of the System

As all the ontical areas of our world are included in the ICC together with their possible aspects, the system can be used as a universal system with regard to its contents, its possible applications and also with respect to the users of all countries.

8 TOWARDS A FUTURE FOR KNOWLEDGE ORGANIZATION

When exactly 30 years ago my dissertation with the proposal of a new universal classification system – as shortly outlined above – was published and when also in the spring of 1974 the journal *International Classification* was started, we were full of hopes that something could be moved with respect to overcoming the thinking along the lines of the past as expressed in the six existing universal classification systems with their discipline-based structures and their weaknesses outlined in (Dahlberg, 1974). But except for the only colleague who read and understood my concern and aims, namely, Dr. Giliola Negrini and her team from Rome, who started to develop subject groups according to the principles utilized in the ICC[7] there was almost nobody else to get interested in this new approach of mine. Of course, the thesaurus construction development started already in the sixties of the past century and its slow movement towards faceted classification[8] should not be forgotten as an example of indeed a very remarkable new direction in the development of new approaches. But the old systems found their revisors and they are all still eagerly active with their revision work and the oldest system from 1876 in use worldwide is now on the way to its 23rd edition, still based on the same main classes as in its beginning, as if we were still thinking in 19th century terms. How come? A friend of mine would comment: "The inertia of matter must have prompted to the sluggish brain to stick to what you have, lest to lose orientation"!

Nobody would suggest that there is no development – the revision work on these systems testifies to it -, but the interest of the majority of the young computer specialists, as much as they started to recognize our problems and labelled them by their own terminology with terms like 'is-a' and 'has-a' for the generic and partitive relationships, their "domains" for subject-fields, their "topic maps" for facet analysis and their "ontologies" for classification systems, etc. has apparently not been noticed by the "revision workers". And they are apparently neither willing to read our literature nor to make any move toward trying to understand what librarians and information scientists have taken the trouble to try and solve these problems their life long.

Thus, what is the future for knowledge organization in the sense of an organized enterprise in seizing our knowledge units as proposed above, i.e. that terminologists and classificationists try together to elaborate field by field the definitions of terms and bringing them into the systematic frame of e.g. the ICC, so that a coherent whole be achieved, comprising all the relationships which concepts may enter into, outside of their own field of reference? This is, by the way, another reason why the work so far done e.g. in the field of terminology with its elaboration of concept systems, has to my knowledge not found the necessary resonance in the scientific world: it has failed in the necessary representation of conceptual relationships of the concepts of one subject field with those of another one included in the same universal system. In a paper at the 1994 Bratislava ISKO Conference on Environmental Knowledge Organization I showed by the ICC-matrix, how all concepts of the Environment Subject Group (here under the synthesis group of the bioarea 4, i.e. under 49) were related to all the other subject areas of the ICC. Thus the notation of these concept-combinations evidences these relationships too and profits in its extension from the contents (the characteristics) of the related pertinent concepts (see 26).

In these days - our world is facing a terrific change in almost every respect. Many people are afraid of catastrophes and terror and by that very fear will even attract such evil through their own thoughts. They are more concerned with themselves and how they can survive in the disaster around us, monitored every day on the screens of our TV sets, than thinking and acting positively and trusting God our Creator and lovingly heavenly Father. As long as this continues I do not see a chance for the necessary collaboration between librarians, information scientists, and terminologists, not to speak of hard scientists and technicians venturing to identify and organize the concepts of our knowledge in the way outlined. However, it is not only my hope but even my firm belief that times will change and that people will change and reconsider the hitherto lost values and begin seriously to collaborate with each other obeying thereby God's will as expressed in the double commandments of JESUS CHRIST: "*Love God above all and thy neighbour as yourself*". Although it may still take some time until this happens, but the probability that it will happen can be evidenced by the fact that already very many people now are on the way to remember the old forms of spirituality or embark on new searches. This will surely also bring together all those sharing this new interest and the feeling of responsibility for the wonderful values and virtues which mankind possesses indeed. Here I would also like to refer to the 35 spiritual healing powers within everybody, which were revealed already through Hildegard of Bingen (1098-1179) to be revived again.

Therefore I do foresee also a future for a true knowledge organization activity – not just today, but surely tomorrow when mankind has made the necessary step towards a truly new society of brothers and sisters.

END NOTES

1. Their work was completed in 1978 and presented at the FID-Conference in Edinburgh, Sept.1978. (2)
2. ISKO =International Society of Knowledge Organization
3. A more elaborate explanation can be found in (5)
4. For this see also (7) and (8).
5. This theory of levels of our knowledge had been introduced by the British philosopher Feibleman (1965)(9) and the German philosopher Nicolai Hartmann (1964)(10). Their "Laws of the levels" are described and included in (4).
6. For an example of the application of the systematifier in the field of Knowledge Organization please see the Classification System (Outline) of the current bibliography on this field in the quarterly journal *Knowledge Organization*
7. See among her many papers presented at ISKO conferences e.g. (23) and (24),
8. See the Thesaurofacet of Jean Aitchison (25)

REFERENCES

1. UNESCO (1971). *UNISIST Study Report on the feasibility of a world science information system* by the United Nations Educational, Scientific and Cultural Organization and the International Council of Scientific Unions. Paris: Unesco, p. 161.

2. BSO (1978). *Broad system of Ordering*. Schedule and Index. 3rd rev. The Hague,Paris: FID and Unesco, p. 102+82.

3. Dahlberg, I (1973). *Projekt Ordnungssystem der Wissensgebiete*. Phase I. Materialsammlung (Project Order system for knowledge fields. Phase I: Collection of items. Frankfurt: Deutsche Gesellschaft für Dokumentation. p. 228.

4. —. (1974) *Grundlagen universaler Wissensordnung*. Probleme und Möglichkeiten eines universalen Klassifikationssystem des Wissens. (Foundations of universal organization of knowledge. Problems and possibilities of a universal classification system of knowledge). München. Verlag Dokumentation. p. 384.

5. —. (1978) *Ontical structures and universal classification*. Bangalore: Sarada Ranganathan Endowment for Library Science. p. 76.

6. —. (1975) *On the theory of the concept.* Paper. 3rd Int.Study Conf.on Classification Reseach, Bombay 6-11 Jan. 1975.

7. —. (1978) A referent-oriented analytical concept theory for INTERCONCEPT. *Int.Classif.* Vol. 5(3); p.142-151

8. —. (1995) Conceptual structures and systematization. *Int.Forum Inf.Doc*. Vol. 20(3); p. 9-24.

9. Feibleman, J.K (1965). The integrative levels in nature. Brit.J.Philosophy of Science 1954. Reprinted in Kyle, B.: Focus on information. London. *Aslib*. p. 27-41.

10. Hartmann, N. (1964) Der Aufbau der realen Welt. Grundrisse der Allgemeinen Kategorienlehre. (The structure of the real world. Foundations of a General Science of Categories). 3.ed. Berllin, *deGruyter*. p. 579.

11. Ranganathan. S.R. (1963) *Colon Classification*. Madras-London 1933. 6th ed with amend. p. 450

12. —. (1967) *Prolegomena to library classification*. 3rd. Ed. Bombay, p. 640.

13. Neelameghan, A. (1975) *Presentation of ideas in technical writing*. New Delhi: Vikas Publ.

14. —; Raghavan, K.S. (2004) *Seminal mnemonics in knowledge organization*. Paper to be published. p. 18.

15. Dahlberg, I. (1982-1985) *International Classification and Indexing Bibliography* (ICIB). Frankfurt: INDEKS Verlag (now Ergon Verlag, Würzburg), 3 vols.

16. Wüster, E. (1966) *Internationale Sprachnormung in der Technik* (International Standardization of language in technology). 1932? 2nd ed. Bonn: Bouvier Verlag, p. 470.

17. Tillich, P. (1923) *Das System der Wissenschaften nach Gegenständen und Methoden.* (The system of the sciences according to objects and methods). Göttingen: Vandenhoek & Ruprecht, P. 167.

18. Atherton, P. (Ed.) (1965) FID/CR *Committee on Classification Research.* Proc. of the 2nd Int.Study Conf., Elsinore, 14-18 Sept.1964, Copenhagen: Munksgaard. p. 563.

19. Fugmann, R. (1985) The Five-Axiom-Theory of information supply. *J. Amer. Soc. Inform. Sci.* Vol. 36(2); p. 116-129 (esp. p.121 and 123)

20. Dahlberg, I. (1996) Library catalogs in the Internet. Switching for future subject access. *Advances in Knowledge Organization.* Vol. 5; p. 155-164

21. —. (1998) Classification structure principles. Investigations, experiences, conclusions. *Adv. in Knowledge Org.* Vol. 6; p. 80-88

22. —. (1994) Domain interaction: Theory and practice. *Adv. in Knowledge Org.* Vol. 4; p. 60-71

23. Negrini, G. (1992) Systematization of science and technology research. **In**: *Cognitive Paradigms in Knowledge Organization.* 2nd Int. ISKO Conf. Madras 1992. Bangalore: Sarada Ranganathan Endowment for Libr.Sci. p. 293-307

24. —; Zozi, P. (2002) Ontological analysis of literary work of art. **In**: *Challenges in Knowledge Represntation and Organization for the 21st Century.* Proc. 7th Int.ISKO Conf. Granada 2002. Würzburg: Ergon Verl. p. 67-73

25. Aitchison, J. (1969) *Thesaurofacet.* A thesaurus and faceted classification for engineering and related subjects. Whestone, Leicester: English Electric Co. p. 25+491

PROFESSOR NEELAMEGHAN'S CONTRIBUTION TO THE ADVANCEMENT AND DEVELOPMENT OF CLASSIFICATION IN THE CONTEXT OF KNOWLEDGE ORGANIZATION

Nancy J. Williamson

Presents a brief overview of Prof. A. Neelameghan's works/contributions more particularly to classification and knowledge organization, based on papers abstracted in Library and Information Science Abstracts and Information Science Abstracts, since the early 1960s when he joined Dr. S.R. Ranganathan at the Documentation Research and Training Centre, in Bangalore. Concludes "Following the path of Neelameghan's research and publication we get a picture of how certain aspects of knowledge organization have developed with particular emphasis on the importance and impact of faceted classification in that development. The result is an outstanding contribution to the history, development and application of the facet model developed by Ranganathan, affirmed at the Dorking Conference in 1957 and seemingly reaffirmed" in the present analysis in 2003.

1 INTRODUCTION

An examination of citations from Professor Neelameghan's research and publications in *Library and Information Science Abstracts* (148 citations) and in *Information Science Abstracts* (117 citations) provides clear evidence of a highly prolific author, teacher and researcher in the field of knowledge organization. A more detailed scan of the titles and abstracts published between 1968 and 2004 reveals very significant development in his research from a fairly narrow focus on classification in his early work through increasing depth and breadth in various aspects of knowledge organization. Following in the footsteps of S.R. Ranganathan, over nearly four decades he has become a classification theorist, educator, and researcher of considerable eminence. The theory and principles of faceted classification and their application in numerous contexts is one of the most significant factors in the development of modern information retrieval systems. Neelameghan's work has become a very important factor in keeping Ranganathan's theories alive and well.

Library and information science owes much to Neelameghan and his colleagues, to the Dorking Conference of 1957, and to the work of the Classification Research Group (CRG) in the UK. Together they have advanced the cause of faceted classification over the past 47 years and pointed the way to the future. Neelameghan himself was extremely fortunate to have had close association with S.R. Ranganathan in the faculty of the Documentation Research and Training Centre (DRTC). Moreover, while he has continued his association with the DRTC in Bangalore, his influence has been felt not only through his writings but also in his role as visiting lecturer and scholar in numerous institutions across the world, including some in South America, United States, Canada, Africa, Asia, and Europe.

It would be impossible to do justice to all of the many facets of Neelameghan's work in one short article. Instead this paper provides a brief overview and enlarges on a few aspects of his work that appear to be significant milestones in his research and publication.

2 AN OVERVIEW

Given his involvement in the DRTC and the close association with Ranganathan, it is not surprising that Neelameghan's earliest concentration focused on classification – specifically on the expansion of the *Colon Classification (CC)*. In this capacity he was involved in the expansion and development of numerous depth classification schedules to accompany *CC*. These expansions covered a wide range of subjects including such topics as: air vehicle wing production (Neelameghan, 1970a), food technology (Neelameghan, 1970c), banking (Neelameghan, 1971a), and international trade (Neelameghan, 1971b). While *CC* was his primary interest, it is not surprising that he took a serious look at its merits in conjunction with the *Universal Decimal Classification (UDC)* since the idea of a faceted system had its origins in Ranganathan's early contact with *UDC* (Neelameghan, 1971c).

Early in his research (Neelameghan, Venkataraman, 1968) he came to the realization that a freely faceted classification system would be highly amenable to computer application. This phase of his investigation began with simple manipulation of class numbers (Neelameghan, 1969) and over the years has led to more complex issues such as the computer simulation of the classification process (Neelameghan 1972a); and computer applications in online searching (Neelameghan, Carino, 1983). Ultimately his interests have lead to research in the areas of knowledge discovery (Neelameghan, Iyer, 2003) and knowledge engineering (Haravu, Neelameghan, 2003).

While Neelameghan has never wavered from his interest in the *Colon Classification*, he has expanded the application of its principles into research with information technology. The essential basis for all of his work has been the Ranganathan model of the theory and principles of knowledge organization. A landmark article explaining this is his "Research in library classification". There he states that the "essential basis for research in library classification is the study of the structure and development of the universe of subjects" (Neelameghan, and Gopinath, 1967). This is based on two parameters: the user and the subject as embodied in documents. It sets the stage for his own work, in which his understanding of the foundations for a good document retrieval system is classification that is based on a resilient design methodology and a holistic approach, supported by Ranganathan's five laws of library science as the basic guiding principles for library classification.

2.1 The universe of Subjects

With this background, the core of his research focuses on the "universe of subjects" and radiates from that point. A search of 'Neelameghan' and 'subject' in *Information* Science *and Technology Abstracts (ISTA)* retrieves 47 citations. Of these, 28 citations were determined to be on aspects of 'subject' per se. Nine citations were for versions of depth classification schedules developed for *CC*, and the remaining 10 citations were on other related topics. The 28 articles on 'subject' per se represent a significant portion of Neelameghan's published output, evidence that this is the core and foundation of his work. In these articles he provides an in-depth analysis of the nature of 'subject' from a variety of angles that include definition, arrangement and structure. The universe of subjects is portrayed as an infinite continuum, multi-dimensional, turbulent in nature, and dependent on the context. Further, he sees classification work as belonging to Ranganathan's three planes –the idea plane, the verbal plane and the notational plane. The "universe" itself divides into primary basic subjects (e.g. Generalia, Science (general), Mathematics, Fine arts, Psychology, etc.) as found in *CC* and similar to the main classes in *DDC, UDC* and other universal systems. Such classes may occur in various ways (Neelameghan and Gopinath, 1967). These include: by fission, by fusion or the creation of interdisciplinary subjects (e.g. psycholinguistics), and by distillation (i.e. by distilling out a topic and combining it with other topics). The latter are often action topics that diverse subjects have in common (e.g. the term 'management' in combination with various disciplines such as physical laboratory management, business management, and records management). Among other modes identified are: clustering, and agglomeration, or the collecting together of entities into larger masses, which are without cohesion among the components (e.g. Mathematical Sciences, Biological Sciences) (Neelameghan, 1973a).

Another characteristic of subjects is change. Neelameghan addresses the problem of change in both the intellectual and technological senses. Over time, subjects go through the process of the natural evolution of terminology, division into new subjects and interdisciplinary relationships with other subjects both new and old. At the same time there has been the impact of new technology on the design and development of computerized document finding systems that present new challenges and new possibilities. In this latter context he views 'subject' as a system and investigates the design of document finding systems via the systems approach (Neelameghan, 1972c).

2.2 Relationships and the Universe of Subjects

Other research on the universe of subjects focuses on the nature and problems of structure and arrangement of subjects and their component parts. With respect to structure, among the issues are helpful order and hierarchical and non-hierarchical (i.e. associative) relationships. In his study of non-hierarchical relationships he used a semi-mechanical method of generating the RTs in a thesaurus resulting in the identification of different kinds of relations – including facet relations, phase relations, and coordinate relations (Neelameghan, 1975a).

2.3 Neelameghan and Information Technology

Neelameghan came early to a connection between cataloguing and classification and the computer. Much of this early work was experimental and practical, with implications for the design of computerized retrieval systems. At the beginning, he focused on experiments with the use of the computers in synthesizing class numbers (Neelameghan, Venkataraman, 1968) a task in which the *Colon Classification* could be expected to perform well. Then he compared the results with traditional processes. In another experiment, he also prepared a computer simulation of step-by-step procedures used in the process of classifying (Neelameghan 1972a). While classification is deemed to be an intellectual process, it was revealed that there are a number of steps that are clerical in nature and can therefore be accomplished more efficiently and quickly, by machine. Ultimately this led to the design and demonstration of the advantages in the use of faceted analytico-synthetic systems in document finding (Neelameghan, 1968) i.e. online retrieval. As his research developed he took on increasingly greater challenges. Beyond the simple operation of synthesizing numbers there was the concern of helpful order or the sequencing (Neelameghan, 1973b) of the components of an idea (i.e. compound subjects). Using the "wall-picture principle" he examined the assumption that in a compound subject the syntax of facets should parallel *Absolute Syntax.* The helpfulness of this principle is demonstrated and an analogy drawn with trends in the development of the theory of syntax and generative grammar of natural language. The possibility is raised for the conversion from one language into another based on a common syntax.

In other pioneering work, the implications for interface between the user and the computer were investigated. Reader-computer dialogue was examined using two methods for aiding the user in searching. One method was the display for the user of parts of the classification schedules and the relevant index terms. The second method was the display of a permuted subject index (POPSI, a relative of PRECIS) together with the related catalogue records. All of these experiments had implications for the design of computerized catalogues and other document finding systems (Neelameghan, 1972b).

2.4 Recent Contributions to Research

As time has advanced and technology has become more sophisticated, Neelameghan has broadened his horizons beyond classification per se into the field of knowledge organization in general. This has been increasingly so since the beginning of the 21st century, as evidenced by a culmination and bringing together, of all the aspects of his research – classification, the systems approach, hierarchical and non-hierarchical relationships, and the universe of subjects. One important factor in this is the development in information and communications technologies enabling almost seamless access to vast amounts of information worldwide and the ability to download large quantities of this information to personal desktop computers. He identifies needs in three areas of concern: the need to filter and select the most relevant information, the need to be able to organize the retrieved information, and the need to assist in computer-user interaction. Neelameghan, Prasad (2002) address the second and third of these concerns by looking at the complementary roles of subject classification and thesauri – two systems that have much in common with each other - one (thesauri) on the verbal plane and the other (classification systems) on the notational plane. Both can be seen as having roles in the mapping of concepts, in indicating relationships in a particular context, in designing and using user-interfaces, in vocabulary management at the input stage, in the search and retrieval stages, and in the designing of classification and indexing tools. (Neelameghan, Prasad, 2002) All of this is seen in the context of the analytico-synthetic methodology of Ranganathan. The article emphasizes structure and relationships and gives particular attention to a particularly troublesome area – lateral or non-hierarchical associative relationships, with 29 types of such relationships identified. In a recent study (Neelameghan and Satish, 2004) the following domains of application semantic relations, particularly lateral relations, were noted:

- Design of classification schemes, thesauri and other vocabulary control devices;
- Design and Development of Databases;
- Development of Appropriate Search Strategies for Information Retrieval in a variety of environments;
  - Web browsing, web searching
  - Searching and browsing textual and image databases
- Web design and development particularly establishing the basis for creating hyperlinks in Hypertexts, hypermedia, etc documents
- Systems analysis and software engineering;
- Text semantics, lexical cohesion; and
- Natural language processing

Interestingly the above mentioned domains of applications were reported in conference proceedings and periodicals devoted to different areas, such as the following:

Artificial intelligence	Memory and cognition
Text analysis, summarization	Experimental psychology
Linguistics	Learning
Computational linguistics	Hypermedia
Natural language processing	Information retrieval
Knowledge organization	System studies

Obviously, then, different categorizations of relations among concepts are possible in the different domains. "It is, therefore, useful to develop a theory of conceptual relations based on a generalization and logical abstraction of the prevalent ideas and practices among different disciplinary groups." As a first step in a paper under publication (Neelameghan, Raghavan, 2004) attempt a more elaborate study contributing to categorizing semantic relations more particularly lateral relations.

In Neelameghan's recent writings he has entered a new phase, the bringing together all aspects of his research in the context of the digital environment (Neelameghan, 2002a). In doing so, he points out the importance of three factors: first, the usefulness of adopting the faceted model in defining subject classification systems as affirmed at the Dorking conference in 1957; secondly, the significance of the fact that the PMEST framework, applicable to a BS (Basic Subject) or isolate, has stood the test of time and developments in the universe of subjects; and thirdly, the importance of the analytico-synthetic methodology as the basis for designing and applying schemes for subject classification. He also observes that "increasingly, non-faceted type general classification schemes are changing to faceted structure to the extent possible" (Neelameghan, 2002b). This is certainly true of such schemes as *UDC* and to some extent *DDC*. Further, he notes that classification schemes in specialized fields are frequently adopting the faceted model. In this environment, Neelameghan also recognizes the importance of using a variety of subject access tools in complementary roles. The various tools can provide for different uses of a system – mapping of concepts, designing and using user-interfaces, vocabulary management and designing subject classification and indexing tools (Neelameghan, Prasad, 2002). Using Unesco's WINISIS software (Neelameghan, 2002c) at the Sarada Ranganathan Endowment for Library Science (SRELS) in Bangalore, the authors describe how subject classifications and thesauri can perform different functions and how they can be linked together so that a user can move from one to the other. He sees this approach as being particularly important with interdisciplinary topics (e.g. natural resources). Such support would provide a wider perspective of the subject and would be useful in formulating search expressions in retrieval. For more comprehensive information users would be able to revise mapping of interrelations among both hierarchical and lateral concepts.

Based on his earlier experience of structuring and representing complex objects/subjects, such as those going with motor vehicle production engineering, and food technology (see Neelameghan, 1992, 1997), Neelameghan has shown the applicability of Ranganathan's generalized facet structure framework for describing different entities, his examples include description of institution, bird, medicinal plant, and folk dance, and suggests that a metadata framework can be derived from the generalized facet structure model for describing objects consistently (Neelameghan, Asundi, 2001).

Finally, in his most recent research Neelameghan has moved into a new phase of research. Using the case study method, Havaru and Neelameghan (2003) examine the application of text mining to the development of knowledge-based products. Using two approaches they examine, first of all, the steps and processes used in the planning, designing, and development of a multilingual, multi-media CD product as a possible tool for users who are international and intercultural. Secondly, they investigate the application of natural language processing software in text mining. In doing so, they demonstrate that it is possible to link concepts in a processed text to a related thesaurus, glossary or classification scheme and suggest that the features of a faceted scheme can enhance the usefulness of text mining and data mining. Again using the case study method, Neelameghan and Iyer (2003) investigate various ways that information organization can assist with knowledge discovery in non-bibliographic databases.

Dr. Ranganathan's concept of seminal mnemonics in knowledge organization and presentation of ideas has been commented on by Subramanyam (1976) and Beghtol (2001) and applied by Neelameghan (1970a, 1975b). Based on more recent studies Neelameghan and Raghavan (2004) have examined seminal mnemonics from human cognitive process angle.

Following the path of Neelameghan's research and publication we get a picture of how certain aspects of knowledge organization have developed with particular emphasis on the importance and impact of faceted classification in that development. The result is an outstanding contribution to the history, development and application of the facet model developed by Ranganathan, affirmed at the Dorking Conference in 1957 and seemingly reaffirmed in the above analysis in 2003.

REFERENCES

1. Beghtol, Clare (2001). Relationships in classificatory structure and meaning. ***In:*** *Relationships in the organization of knowledge*, ed. by Carol A. Bean and Rebecca Green. London: UK: Kluwer Academic Publishers.
2. Haravu, L. J. and Neelameghan, A. (2003). Text mining and data mining in knowledge organization and discovery: The making of knowledge-based products. *Cataloging & Classification Quarterly Vol.* 37(1/2); p. 97-114.
3. Neelameghan, A. (1967). Research on the structure and development of the universe of subjects. *Library Science with a Slant to Documentation. Vol.* 4 (4); p. 336-355.
4. —. (1968). Design of the document finding system: General features. *Library Science with a Slant to Documentation.* Vol. 5 (4); p. 303-316.
5. —. (1969) Formulation of isolate numbers by computer using the devices of Colon Classification. *Library Science with a Slant to Documentation.* Vol. 6 (2); p. 141-190.
6. —. (1970a). Seminal mnemonics as a pattern for system analysis. *Library Science with a Slant to Documentation.* Vol. 7; Paper P.
7. —. (1970b). Air vehicle wing production: Depth classification version of CC. *Library Science with a Slant to Documentation. Vol.* 7(1); p. 46-80.
8. —. (1970c). Food technology: Depth classification version of CC. *Library Science with a Slant to Documentation. Vol.* 7(3); p. 209-288.
9. —. (1971a) Banking: Depth classification version of CC. *Library Science with a Slant to Documentation. Vol.* 8(1); p. 43-67.
10. —. (1971b). International trade: Depth classification version of CC. *Library Science with a Slant to Documentation. Vol.* 8 (3); p. 249-278.
11. —. (1971c) Search for a theoretical basis for UDC: A postscript to the Herceg-Novi Symposium *Library Science with a Slant to Documentation. Vol.* 8(4); p. 303-322.
12. —. (1972a). Computer simulation of some steps in classifying: Built-in features of a theory-based scheme for classification. *Library Science with a Slant to Documentation.* Vol. 9(4); p. 499-522.
13. —. (1972b). Specification of subject of reader's query: Reader-computer dialogue. *Library Science with a Slant to Documentation.* Vol. 9(4); p. 636-656.
14. —. (1972c). Systems approach in the study of attributes of the universe of subjects. *Library science with a Slant to Documentation.* Vol. 9(4); p. 445-472.

15. —. (1973a). Basic subject. Library Science with a Slant to Documentation. Vol. 10(2); p. 149-157.

16. —. (1973b). Basic subjects and their arrangement: A summary. *Library Science with a Slant to Documentation.* Vol. 10(2); p. 207-221

17. —. (1975a). Non-hierarchical associative relationships: Their types and computer-generation of rt links. In Documentation Research and Training Centre. Indian Statistical Institute. *Seminar on thesaurus in information systems, Bangalore, India, 1975 December 1-5.* Bangalore: DRTC.

18. —. (1975b). *Presentation of ideas in technical writing.* New Delhi, Vikas Publishing House

19. —. (1992). Application of Ranganathan's general theory of knowledge classification I designing specialized databases. *Libri.* Vol. 42(3); p. 202-226.

20. —. (1997). *S.R. Ranganathan's postulates and normative principles: application in specialized databases design, indexing and retrieval.* Bangalore, India: Sarada Ranganathan Endowment for Library Science.

21. —. (2002a) Classification in the digital environment. *Information Studies.* Vol. 8(1); p. 1-8.

22. —. (2002b) Systems perspective of subject representation architecture: S.R. Ranganathan's model revisited. *Information Studies.* Vol. 8(4); p. 205-220.

23. —. (2002c). WINISIS-based information handling tools from SRELS. *Information Studies.* Vol. 8(2); p. 71-82.

24. —. and Carino, P.B. (1983). Training in computer applications and on-line search for students of library science. *UNESCO Journal of Information Science, Librarianship and Archives Administration.* Vol. 5(1); p. 12-22.

25. —. and Gopinath, M.A. (1967) Research in library classification. *Library Science with a Slant to Documentation.* Vol. 4(4); p. 356-381.

26. —. and Asundi, Ashok Y. (2001). A metadata framework for description of objects derived from the generalized facet structure for subject analysis and synthesis. *Digital Libraries: Dynamic landscapes for knowledge creation, access and management. The 4th International Conference of Asian Digital Libraries, Bangalore, December 10-13, 2001....Conference papers,* p. 192-308/Edited by Shalini R. Urs, T.B. Rajashekar, and K.S. Raghavan.

27. — and Iyer, H. (2003). Information organization ~~to~~ assist knowledge discovery: Case study with non-bibliographic databases. *Cataloging & Classification Quarterly.* Vol. 37 (1/2); p. 115-130.

28. —. and Prasad, K.N. (2002) Digitized schemes for subject classification and thesauri: Complementary Roles. *Information Studies.* Vol. 8 (1); p. 25-42.

29. —. and Raghavan, K.S. (2004). *Seminal mnemonics in knowledge organization*. Paper to be published. 2004. p. 18.

30. —. and Satish, Komalavalli (2004). Knowledge diffusion in clusters of web-based communities: a case study. IADIS WBC04 International Conference on Web Communities, Lisbon, Portugal, 24-26 March 2004, Paper 11.

31. —. and Venkataraman, S. (1968). Use of computer for the synthesis of class numbers: A case study with a freely faceted version of Colon Classification. *Library Science with a Slant to Classification.* Vol. 5(4); p. 359-388.

32. Subramanyam, K. (1976). Seminal mnemonics in classification. *International Classification.* Vol. 3(1); p. 16-18.

KNOWLEDGE ORGANIZATION SYSTEMS OVER TIME

S. Seetharama

Presents an overview of the concepts, techniques and tools of knowledge organization. Knowledge Organization Systems (KOS), such as, authority files, glossaries, dictionaries, subject headings lists, classification schemes, taxonomies, categorization schemes, thesauri, semantic networks, ontologies, etc are involved in organizing, retrieval and dissemination of information. Specifically, KOS are useful in Users Needs Assessment, Database(s) creation, Online systems, OPAC and for generation of information services and products. Practical experiences suggest that new information systems to access a wider range, quantity, and forms of information and enable provision of a variety of information services and products to meet the needs of people, KOS can perform functions even in an electronic/digital environment as efficiently and effectively as in a traditional library environment. Hence, it is necessary that information professionals and computer-scientists work in an integrated manner to enhance information handling operations in electronic/digital libraries.

0 PREAMBLE

I had the good fortune of being a student and later, a colleague of Prof. A. Neelameghan. It was he who guided me and smoothened the rough edges of mine so that I could function efficiently and effectively as an information professional. As a teacher he brought a fresh approach in teaching the various subjects and had the ability of viewing and presenting the subject from different perspectives. He would often mislead (!) me during my depth classification project to provoke my thinking process and to test whether I had the courage of conviction in what I did or believed (in the sequence of quasi-isolates, for example!). It is these actions of his that helped me in my professional career. Prof. Neelemeghan's sincerity, commitment and dedication to work are exemplary. I offer my salutations to him and wish that he continues to make available his expertise and services to the library and information profession for many more years.

1 INTRODUCTION

'Knowledge organization for the sake of knowledge organization' is a myth. To the librarian and information professional, knowledge organization (KO) has always been and will continue to be a specific purpose-oriented activity, the purpose being to organize the documents/information in a collection or their surrogates in a database, assist users in browsing; formulating search expressions, presenting information services and products to users in forms and formats convenient to the target user(s). Essentially, KO is an intellectual process of organizing information and/or information sources to provide access facilitating information retrieval and dissemination.

KO is a natural phenomenon in all human beings. Perhaps, it starts at an early stage – when a newborn identifies the mother from others as well as when they grow up and start playing sorting and matching games. This ability is developed as one progresses in life largely by observing and comparing new experiences with earlier experiences – by understanding relations among different concepts, recognizing patterns among relations followed by understanding the foundational principles underlying the patterns representing knowledge, the principles being universal and completely context independent. In other words, KO is an inherent characteristic of human beings. Evidence of this can be seen in Aristotle's categorization of knowledge into groups. In the 17th century, Francis Bacon and the editors of the encyclopedia pondered ways to organize growing bodies of knowledge and their disciplines (Groli, 2004)

However, by the end of the 19th century and in the early part of the 20th century, formal systems to organize knowledge embodied in documents of library collections were developed: Library of Congress classification and subject headings, Melvil Dewey's Decimal Classification, the Universal Decimal Classification, S. R. Ranganathan's Colon Classification, Bliss' Bibliographic Classification, etc., are well known examples. Thus, Cronin's (1985) comment that "Librarians were the first to bring some discipline and order to information management with their classification and cataloguing schemes/codes" is justifiable. Nevertheless, it has been argued in recent times that with automation of information retrieval, it is possible to dispense with traditional classification methodologies. But remember that KO underlies all thinking; thus, it would be prima facie surprising if it found no place in information systems of the future.

2 DEFINITIONAL ANALYSIS

In discussing about KO, it would be helpful to define and delimit the use of the terms and consider some of the resulting implications. This is especially true because the meaning of terms depend on the context in which they are used.

2.1 Information

Information is some meaningful message recorded in conventional or non-conventional media and stored and processed by systems and services with a view to providing a more or less permanent memory of the message and their discussion with users.

An unconventional definition, however, states that information is: what we take in from outside to feed our knowledge so that we can function successfully and achieve our aims.

It is what is necessary and what is available in a given situation for a purpose.

2.2 Information Management

Information Management (IM) is one of the buzz terms of the present age of library science/information science/archives and record management. It is a term that has come to significance as a consequence of the greatly increased interest in Information Technology. Two ideas, therefore, come together in the concept of IM: information as an important economic resource and IT as a tool for its effective management.

On the other hand, Lynda Woodman comments that "IM is all about getting the right information, in the right form, to the right person, at the right cost, at the right time, in the right place, to take the right action". This sounds quite familiar- a re-enunciation or implication of Ranganathan's Five Laws of Library Science. Based on Tonche Ross survey (1994), Best (1996) defines IM "as the effective production, storage, retrieval and dissemination of information in any format and on any medium to support (Institutional) business objectives".

From the above, one can infer that IM covers the whole spectrum of information, handling activities, technology and its role in information handling as well as various management activities and practices in institutions.

2.3 Knowledge Management

Knowledge management (KM) is "the discipline of enabling individuals in an organization to collectively create, acquire, share, evaluate and leverage knowledge to achieve the corporate mission of an organization" Sveiby (1997) defines KM as "the systematic, explicit and deliberate building, renewal and application of knowledge to maximize an enterprise's knowledge-related effectiveness and returns from its knowledge assets". It aims at producing actionable knowledge that individuals can use to create organizations in which the search for valid knowledge, a commitment to personal responsibility and stewardship, and a dedication to effective action and learning are paramount. In addition, KM also aims at facilitating innovation and enhancing the quality of decision-making. In other words, KM is a systematic way of leveraging information and expertise to improve organizational innovation, responsiveness, productivity and competency (Pradeep, 2001).

2.4 Knowledge Organization System

A knowledge organization system (KOS) is intended to encompass all types of schemes for organizing information and promoting KM and includes classification schemes, knowledge maps, subject headings, semantic networks, ontologies, glossaries, term lists, etc. The purpose of KOS is:

- To organize materials for the purpose of retrieval and to manage a collection for user to be able to identify an object of interest whose existence is not known;
- To guide the user through a discovery, process whether browsing or direct searching whether through themes on a webpage or site search engine; and
- To allow the organizers to answer questions regarding the scope of a collection and what is needed to "round it out.

2.5 Knowledge Map

A knowledge map points to knowledge sources but does not contain them. Knowledge maps typically point to people as well as to documents and databases. The purpose of these maps is to show people in the organization where to go when they need expertise. In an organization, every employee has a "mini map" in his/her head about his/her own expertise and place, to where he/she goes to get questions answered. An "Organizational knowledge map" can be created by combining the "mini maps' and adequate search facilities are to be provided for accessing by users. This knowledge repository should record meaningful concepts, categories and definitions, processes, actions and sequences of events, the linkages away from them, etc, and should be indexed.

2.6 Classification

In simple terms, classification is placing like things together. It has been described as a process of division/sorting the entities of a universe into sub-aggregates on the basis of a preferred characteristic or putting like entities into the same sub-aggregate and unlike entities into different sub-aggregate. It has also been described as a process of division of a universe into groups plus that of arranging the groups into a definite sequence i.e., ranking. Classification involves the process of representation of the thought content by a class number with the sole objective of facilitating storage, retrieval and dissemination of information.

3 KNOWLEDGE ORGANIZATION SYSTEMS OVER TIME

Knowledge Organization and KOS have been in existence from time immemorial. While Aristotle and his followers were great systematizers of the domains of knowledge in their time, Bacon, Hobbes, Kant, Hegel, Comte, Ampere, Spencer had their own schemes of classes of knowledge.

3.1 Traditional Library Era

Perhaps, formal systems to organize knowledge have been developed by librarians in the 19th century in order to manage collections of books on different subjects. Classification schemes like DDC, LC, etc were developed to arrange and store books on particular locations on the shelves. In this process, an APUPA pattern of arrangement was possible by assigning appropriate class numbers to books on closely related subjects. But, then there was the problem of multi-focal books with each focus demanding a separate location. This was taken care of by providing multiple access points beyond the limits of a single location through assigning of Subject Headings. Ranganathan termed this relationship between classification and cataloguing as 'Symbiosis'.

The next milestone in KO was the arrival of the faceted approach of Ranganathan and consequent development of the analytico-synthetic Colon Classification. This brought about a fundamental change in KO – a truly flexible and expressive way of classifying and retrieving information.

The application of facet analysis and structured representation of data/information in mechanized informational storage and retrieval systems can be seen in:

- Object Oriented Database Design using a faceted approach is the report on an information retrieval system on internal combustion Engine by Kinze Tanabe
- Use of faceted schemes of classification, such as, UDC in computerized system as exemplified in the work of Freeman and Atherton; Schneider's design of information systems to support cancer research; GREMAS system described by Fugman; classification and indexing aspects of BNB, the British Technology Index, Development of PRECIS, the Thesaurofacet, Computer-assisted method for synthesis of faceted class numbers, etc.

3.2 Electronic/Digital Era

While librarians were the first to bring some discipline and order to information management with their classification schemes and cataloguing codes, in recent times, it is being argued that with automation of information retrieval, it is possible to dispense with techniques of knowledge organization, in particular classification. This is rather a strange argument as in the electronic/digital era, only the form of documents has changed from physical to electronic/digital form, but not the content. In other words, whether, the documents are books, periodicals, websites, computer files, manuscripts, etc, they still have a "content" which still needs to be analyzed to facilitate access, retrieval and dissemination -- i.e. KOS would still be needed in the electronic/digital era. More attention is now being paid to applying the methods and techniques of KO developed by librarians to organizing digital information sources with necessary modifications. This is exemplified by the fact that terms such as "Electronic libraries/Digital libraries/ Virtual libraries" are being used currently realizing the affinity of modern technologies with traditional library concepts. This was foreseen by Ranganathan, Vickery and some others as can be seen in their writings.

Though it is true that IT has provided facilities for new forms of indexing, searching including full text searching, there are some problems as a word taken out of a text can be misleading. Hence, the use of KOS like selected keywords, subject headings, classification schemes, thesauri become necessary to facilitate effective and efficient information access and retrieval even in computer-based systems.

The success of search engines/Internet directories has been largely due to their own semantic schemas used to organize information. For example, the success of the Google search engine shows that automatic analysis of links in a complex hypertextual environment can achieve relatively more precise results. It has also been reported that some online directories use library KOSs: For example:

- BUBL LINK Catalogue of Internet Resources;
- Librarian's Index to the Internet; and
- Scorpion Project, which is a part of the large CORC initiative by the Online Computer Library Centre (OCLC).

KOSs have also migrated from print to electronic media with necessary changes to work in the web environment. A case in point are the indexing and abstracting services — where the shift has been from print–only products to print and online services as well as CD-ROM products and now the Web. In a similar manner, publishers like Academic Press and Elsevier involved in the production of electronic products and online services have developed their own KOS to provide bibliographical records linked to the full text of the documents. Elsevier's website has a subject categorization scheme to provide access to individual websites of its more than 2000 titles. Also several websites have experimented with principles of KOSs, particularly faceted classification, to facilitate retrieval from their databases.

At this point, we may mention two projects aimed at applying faceted indexing to digital documents. They are:

1) FATKS: Facet Analytical Theory in Knowledge Systems for Humanities. http://www.ucl.ac.uk/fatks at university of college, London; and
2) Faceted Subject Indexing System for application to web documents in Thailand (Devadason et al, 2002).

4 USEFULNESS OF KOS: SOME EXAMPLES

4.1 Subject Index

Information storage and retrieval systems find it useful to provide alphabetical indexes as a means of fast access to the information contained in the databases. The subject indexes may be part of an inverted file (author, title, subject, etc) or a separate file. The helpfulness of the subject index entries to users depends in a large measure on how adequately the subject content (ideas) of each document (if a bibliographical database or the data about the entity described (if an object-oriented database) has been analyzed and represented precisely and comprehensively by the index terms. In this work, the analytico-synthetic procedure can be useful as already indicated above. Chain procedure is one such technique based on the analytico-synthetic methodology (Ranganathan, 1967). Further, POPSI or Postulate-based Subject Indexing explicitly uses facet – analysed subject strings based on the General Theory of Knowledge organization of Ranganathan, to derive pre-coordinated index entries.

4.2 Database Creation

Neelameghan (1997) has shown how the normative principles of KO are useful in designing databases – e.g. in the preparation of the Field Definition Table (FDT), a pre-requisite for database creation, KOS principles have a role to play. He has presented several examples of databases in which the theories, principles and techniques of concept categorization, classification & knowledge organization, and the analytico-synthetic approach, as well as those of methods of vocabulary control and natural language indexing developed for organizing and retrieving are also helpful in designing non-bibliographic object databases (ODBs). Each database forms a component of a group of databases serving the needs of an institution or user group; such a group of databases includes bibliographical databases, referral databases (e.g. profile of institutions, experts, etc., often integrated into a single database) and other non-bibliographical databases. All the databases were developed using Micro-CDS-ISIS software.

4.3 Online Systems

Svenonius (1983) identified some uses of KOS/classification in online retrieval systems:

- To improve recall and precision and to save the time of user in formulating search expression and in searching;
- Perspective classification can be used to contextualize the meaning of vague search terms, enabling the computer to simulate in part the negotiation of a search request carried on by reference librarians;
- Use of traditional classification in online systems is to provide a structure for meaningful browsing;
- To provide a framework for representation and retrieval of non-bibliographic information;
- Automatic classification can be used to collocate citations in ways not possible in manual systems, e.g., by similarity of linguistic features;
- Classification can be used to achieve compatibility of retrieval languages by;
- Serving as a mediating or switching language; and
- In brief, KOS/classification has such an important place in online systems that we should prepare for a resurgence of interest in both its theory and practice.

4.4 OPAC

A similar line of thinking can be seen in the work of Stephen Walker (1991), Liu and Svenonius (1991), Nohr (1991), Watanabe (1994) who have used classification techniques in OPAC searching. Similarly, Library of Congress Subject Headings List, Rules for Subject Cataloguing (RSWK), Thesaurus, and Keyword Indexing have been used for subject search and retrieval in OPACs.

5 INFORMATION SERVICES GENERATION

5.1 Role of KO

To state that KO has a role in the generation of information services is to say the obvious. If one were to analyse the different steps involved in the generation of information products/services, it will become evident that KO has several roles to play - it may be in relation to the user's interests profile construction, document profile construction, arrangement and presentation of information, database creation, etc.

5.2 Study of Users' Needs

In the planning, design and development of library and information services, it is absolutely necessary to study the information needs of users. While it is easy in the case of specialists in particular disciplines, it is difficult in the case of planners and decision-makers whose functions are more task-oriented than discipline-oriented. Therefore, an alternative approach is to use a model or Reference Framework according to which planning and decision making programmes can conceptually be analyzed into different phases, sub-tasks, activities, etc, and the information support needed identified for each of these. When this analysis is done (which is essentially based on KO/classification in one sense), it would be possible to select/extract relevant data and information from different sources/ databases and repackage them into relevant subsets for convenient use at the different stages of planning work.

5.3 Reference Framework

Some of the uses of Reference Framework, which is a KO technique, are:

- Facilitates identification/determination of the total view of the interest of the target group as well as the specific components of the interest area and their inter-relationships (mapping);
- Useful in the precise definition of the information product and their contents; determination of priority areas and weighting; and division of areas of work – literature search, extracting, abstracting, etc. – among members of a team. Cooperation is possible as the framework can define precisely the work areas;
- Useful in information organisation, i.e., in the actual production of the text of the product (with necessary headings and sub-headings) which would match with the information needs of users;
- Helpful in information repackaging, that is, orientation of information to the needs of a particular group of users;
- Preparation of profiles of users;
- Generation of anticipatory and repackaging services;
- Facet analysis of reader's questions for providing reference service;

- Designing of databases, determining the contents of records in the files, etc.;
- For assessing the availability of data/information by identification of the strengths and weakness and thus initiating action to fill the gaps;
- Helpful in resource-sharing in relation to acquisition and production of information products among a group of libraries, information centres, etc.; and
- Useful in comparative studies, etc.

6 INFORMATION CONSOLIDATION PRODUCTS

At the Tata Energy Research and Documentation and Information Centre, Mumbai, Ranganathan's postulates and principles as enunciated in his General Theory of Knowledge Organisation have been applied in the preparation of the following information packages (Seetharama, 1992, 1997, 1999).

- Biogas Technology: An Information Package;
- Cook stove Technology: An Information Package; and
- Wind Pump Handbook.

7 CONCLUSIONS

From the foregoing account, it is clear that Knowledge Organisation Systems like authority files, glossaries, dictionaries, gazetteers, Subject headings, classification schemes, taxonomies, categorization schemes, thesauri, semantic networks, ontologies, etc are involved in organising, retrieval and dissemination of information. Specifically KOS are useful in Users Needs Assessment, Database(s) creation, Online systems, OPAC and for generation of information services and products. With the growing applications of IT to information handling operations, doubts have been expressed as to the need for and role of KOS. However, evidence available suggests that new information systems to access a wider range, quantity, and forms of information and enable the provision of a variety of information services and products to meet the needs of people to cope with changes taking place in the environment, KOS can perform functions even in an electronic/digital environment as efficiently and effectively as in a traditional library environment. Hence, it is necessary that information professionals and computer-scientists work in a collaborative manner to enhance efficiency and effectiveness of information handling operations in electronic/ digital libraries.

BIBLIOGRAPHICAL REFERENCES

1. Best, David P. (1996). Ed. *The Fourth Resource: Information and its management*. Aslib, Gower, Hampshire.
2. Cronin (B) (1985). Ed. *Information Management: from strategies to action*. Aslib, London.
3. Devadason, F.J, Intaraksa (Neelawat), Patamawongjariya (P), Desai (Kavita) (2002). Faceted indexing based system for organising and accessing Internet resources. Knowledge Organisation. Vol. 29; p. 65-77.
4. Groli, C. *Is there a role for traditional knowledge organisation systems in the Digital Age*. http://eprints.rclis.org/archive/00001415/01/kos-role.htm
5. Liu, S and Svenonius, E. (1991). DORS: DDC Online Retrieval System. *Library Resources and Technical Services*. Vol. 35; p. 359 –75.
6. Neelameghan, A. (1997). S. R. Ranganathan's General Theory of knowledge Classification in designing, indexing and retrieving form specialized databases. *LibSc*. Vol. 34; p. 3-53.
7. Nohr, H. (1991). Classification as the basis of a subject cataloguing component in an OPAC. Demands on elements and structure. *Bibliotheksidients*. Vol. 25; p. 664 – 670.
8. Ranganathan, S R. (1967). *Prolegomena to Library Classification*. Edn. 3, Bombay. Asia Publishing House.
9. Seetharama, S. (1997). *Information Consolidation and Repackaging*. Ess Ess Publications, New Delhi
10. —. (1999). Role of Classification in an Electronic Era. *VUJIS*. Vol. 4; p. 1-15.
11. —. (1992). Role of Classification in information service generation. *Lib Sc*. Vol. 29; p. 109–18.
12. Svenonius, E. (1983). Use of Classification in Online Retrieval. *Library Resource Technical Service*. Vol. 27; p. 77-80.
13. Walker, S. (1991). Views on classification as a search tool on a computer. **In** *Computers in Libraries. 1991. Proceedings of 5th Annual Conference*, London, p. 130–139.
14. Watanabe, T. (1994). An experimental OPAC system using NDC & to improve subject access. Toshookan Kai. *The Library World*. Vol. 46; p. 164 – 176.

THE FACET CONCEPT AS A UNIVERSAL PRINCIPLE OF SUBDIVISION

Clare Beghtol

Facet analysis has been one of the foremost contenders as a design principle for information retrieval classifications, both manual and electronic in the last fifty years. Evidence is presented that the facet concept has a claim to be considered as a method of subdivision that is cognitively available to human beings, regardless of language, culture, or academic discipline. The possibility that faceting is a universal method of subdivision enhances the claim that facet analysis as an unusually useful design principle for information retrieval classifications in any field. This possibility needs further investigation in an age when information access across boundaries is both necessary and possible.

1 INTRODUCTION

In 1948, the Scientific Information Conference invited the Royal Society to establish a standing committee on the topic of a subject classification in science. When the Royal Society realized the complexity of this request, it asked the library community to contribute its expertise to the enterprise, and, as a result, the Classification Research Group was formed in February 1952 (CRG 1953). In response to the invitation to study subject classification in science, the CRG published a comprehensive memorandum that provided a logical and cogent argument for the use of faceted classification for all kinds of information retrieval (CRG 1955).

The Group was determined to start from first principles. Its objective was "to review the basic principles of bibliographic classification, unhampered by allegiance to any particular published scheme" (CRG, 1955). To this end, the Group analyzed the process of information retrieval into four steps, i.e.:

1. Identifying the exact subject of the search,
2. Locating this subject in a guide which refers the searcher to one or more documents,

3. Locating the documents, and
4. Locating the required information in the documents. (CRG, 1955).

Of these, the first two are the province of an information retrieval system and the last two are the province of the searcher. These two initial steps can be carried out by various types of system, and the CRG concluded that a classified file with an index would be the most efficient and effective kind of system. However, the question of how to construct the best kind of classification for the purposes of information retrieval remained. The Group reasoned that experience had shown that an enumerative classification system based on the idea of the tree of knowledge subdivided into finer and finer groups could not accommodate the needs of information retrieval because:

A simple tree of knowledge cannot satisfactorily represent the generic relations between terms. A type of schedule is needed which allows a given genus to be subdivided in more than one way to give several sets of subclasses, each of which is a homogeneous group of collateral species. Such a schedule is in fact a faceted classification (CRG, 1955).

The Group believed, in addition, that the weaknesses of the information retrieval classifications available at the time derived from their lack of adherence to the principles they espoused. The Group credited S.R. Ranganathan with developing the principles and techniques of facet analysis, and they agreed with him that a provisional set of basic categories was needed They disagreed, however, with his hypothesis of five fundamental categories for all of knowledge. Instead, they believed that careful study of different subject fields might yield fundamental categories that could be generalized to other subject fields.

The CRG's 1955 memorandum on faceted classification marked the beginning of a vast literature on facet analysis and faceted classification for information retrieval. The fiftieth anniversary of this memorandum is approaching, and it seems useful to examine some of the streams of research that have come out of discussions of facets. The overall purpose of this paper is to consider the implications of the possibility that facet analysis may be a fundamental cognitive ability of human beings. Such a multi-disciplinary investigation can provide insight into a number of areas of information studies. In particular, it can reveal the importance of facet principles for applications designed to make knowledge organization useful for information retrieval in a globalized information environment.

2 ORIGINS AND DEVELOPMENT OF FACETS IN KNOWLEDGE ORGANIZATION AND INFORMATION RETRIEVAL

In the literature of information retrieval, a facet is "the totality of sub-classes based on a single train of characteristics of a main class.... A facet carries the same name as the train of characteristics to which it is related" (Ranganathan, 1950). S.R. Ranganathan is generally credited with coining this term and with leading and championing the development of applications of the concept for use in bibliographic classification systems. Nevertheless, at least one other claim to the term and its particular meaning was made by Cordonnier, who stated that he used the term with the same meaning in 1933 (Cordonnier, 1961). Ranganathan apparently did not use the term with that meaning until 1944 (Satija, 1992).

Regardless of the exact origin of the term in the bibliographic classification literature, the influence of facet theory, facet analysis of documents undergoing classification, analytico-synthetic methodology, and synthetic notations is undeniable. In addition to the usage of the terms and the development of their applications to document classification in the various editions of Ranganathan's *Colon Classification*, the major bibliographic classifications have all benefited both theoretically and practically from the facet concept. The recent editions of the *Dewey Decimal Classification* (DDC), the *Universal Decimal Classification* (UDC), and the second edition of the *Bliss Bibliographic Classification* (BBC2) are all indebted to the facet concept and to its various ramifications. In addition, the use of facets in electronic applications is becoming widespread. For example, a DDC-based catalogue using facet techniques has been produced (Tinker, Pollitt, O'Brien, and Braekevelt, 1999) and BBC2 has been advocated as a model for faceted classification in a digital environment (Broughton 2001). In addition, researchers in other fields are using facet analysis as the basis for vocabulary control and content management systems (Doyle 2003; Fast, Leise and Steckel 2002 – 2004).

3 GROUPING AND SUBDIVIDING: A COGNITIVE UNIVERSAL

The cognitive ability to create groups of things and/or ideas appears to be available to all human beings. This strong claim about human cognition has been assumed in many studies in many disciplines and explicitly studied in many others, and this view is apparently seldom challenged. Less studied and presumably less understood is the extent of the universality of the methods that may be used to subdivide these groupings usefully for some explicit purpose. Working on the assumption that semantic and lexical universals are also cognitively universal, Goddard and Wierzbicka (1994) studied a large number of languages to discover these kinds of linguistic commonalities. They were able to identify eight categories of semantic and lexical universals across a large number of languages. These were:

1. Substantives: I, YOU, SOMEONE, SOMETHING, PEOPLE;
2. Mental Predicates: THINK, SAY, KNOW, FEEL, WANT;
3. Determiners and Qualifiers: THIS, THE SAME, OTHER, ONE, TWO, MANY, ALL;
4. Actions and Events: DO, HAPPEN, TO/IN;
5. Meta-Predicates: NO, IF, CAN/COULD, LIKE, BECAUSE, VERY;
6. Time and Place: WHEN, WHERE, AFTER, BEFORE, UNDER, ABOVE;
7. Taxonomy and Partonomy: KIND OF, HAVE PARTS; and
8. Evaluators and Descriptors: GOOD, BAD, BIG, SMALL (1994).

The interesting category for our purposes is "Taxonomy and Partonomy: KIND OF, HAVE PARTS." It is noteworthy that taxonomy and partonomy are two types of classificatory subdivision of a group, and Goddard and Wierzbicka have apparently felt no need to justify the assumption of the prior existence of the ability to make groups. Taxonomy and partonomy have been studied extensively in a number of fields, and some of their implications for bibliographic classification systems were discussed by Beghtol (2000). Of particular interest here is that it has been shown that subdivision into parts and subdivision into kinds are not mutually exclusive (Beghtol 2000; Tversky 1989).

Are facets a universal cognitively available method of subdividing a group? Kwasnik (1999) identified four structural principles that have been widely used for devising classification schemes and that can all be used for information retrieval and for knowledge discovery. These four structural principles are hierarchies, trees, paradigms and facet analysis. Hierarchies and trees are both based on the general idea of different levels of classifiable entities. *Hierarchies* are usually considered to be appropriate for genus/species relationships of some thing (e.g., *is-a* relationships), and *trees* are usually considered to be appropriate for other kinds of relationships involving different levels of the thing (e.g., the organization chart of a corporation). Paradigms involve establishing the presence or absence of some entity in a matrix with two axes and establishing the nature of the entity at the intersection of two axes. Facets, as we have seen, involve subdividing a group on the basis of some appropriate and useful characteristic of division. All these structural methods warrant study in their own right, but here we focus on facets and facet analytical techniques. It should be noted also that these four structural principles are not entirely mutually exclusive and in addition that more than one of them can be used in a single classification system. Three examples that help position facets as a cognitive available method of subdivision are given. These are 1) Facets and the Hierarchical Tree of Knowledge; 2) Facet Analysis in Two Unrelated Disciplines; and 3) Facets in Naïve Classifications for Knowledge Discovery.

3.1 Facets and the Hierarchical Tree of Knowledge

Often, the idea of a hierarchical structure and the idea of a tree structure are not clearly distinguished from each other, and hierarchies are often depicted as trees in various kinds of branching diagrams. The inadequacy of trying to encompass knowledge in one tree-like hierarchical arrangement has been the subject of discussion in the literature of bibliographic classification at least since the publication of James Duff Brown's *Subject Classification* in the late nineteenth and early twentieth centuries. Brown's view was that "the departments of human knowledge are so numerous, their intersections so great, their changes so frequent, and their variety so confusing, that it is impossible to show that they proceed from one source or germ" in the way that a tree grows from a seed (Brown, 1914). Similarly, Broadfield remarked that "the only tree that could meet the requirements of logic would be the one whose trunk ended at the first ramification, and whose branches produced sub-branches only once, and so on as far as the last twig; in which also every coordinate set of branches or sub-branches issued from exactly the same point in the parent stem" (Broadfield, 1946). Ranganathan, too, rejected the tree metaphor for depicting the world of knowledge: For in the true Tree of Knowledge, one branch is grafted to another at many points. Twigs too get grafted in a similar way among themselves. Any branch and any twig are grafted similarly with one another. The trunks too become grafted among themselves. Even then the picture of the Tree of Knowledge is not complete. For the Tree of Knowledge grows into more than three dimensions. A two dimensional picture is not easily produced. There are classes studded all along all the twigs, all the branches, and all the trunks (Ranganathan, 1965).

Like the CRG, as discussed above, these classificationists were dissatisfied with one of the most pervasive classificatory structures that are intuitively available to human beings. Similarly, there is a general dissatisfaction with the display of classification systems as trees in branching diagrams (Beghtol 1997). Ranganathan tried to modify the hierarchical tree satisfactorily by linking it specifically to the banyan tree, which has a primary trunk and a number of secondary trunks. He produced two illustrations of banyan trees to show their complexity. In one illustration, the banyan tree is shown upside down (Ranganathan, 1965) and in the other illustration it is shown right side up (Ranganathan, 1967). Neither of these hierarchical depictions proved intellectually satisfactory to him, but he continued to use the tree structure in diagrams, presumably because it offered a convenient method of showing subdivisions, whether they are genus/species subdivisions or faceted subdivisions. For example, he used hierarchical diagrams to illustrate facet principles in three figures in *Prolegomena to Library Classification* (Ranganathan, 1967). In each of these figures, the highest level was Agriculture, subdivided by three facets. In one figure, for example, the three facets were "by area", "by problem" and "by utility," and these were subdivided in turn on the second level of hierarchical division by appropriate faceted subdivisions. The figures illustrate different ways of subdividing a whole ("Agriculture") and the different results that would occur if different initial subdivisions were used. In these cases, a hierarchy subdivided by faceted subdivisions was used. The example demonstrates that the claim that hierarchical and faceted subdivisions in classification systems are mutually exclusive is invalid. Thus, we cannot say that a classification system is either faceted or hierarchical with the implication that a system cannot be both faceted and hierarchical. It seems possible, then, that the facet method of subdivision is a lexical and semantic universal in the same way that taxonomy and partonomy are.

3.2 Facet Analysis in Two Unrelated Disciplines

Evidence that facet principles may be cognitively available to all human beings can be found in the concurrent discovery of the facet principle in two separate disciplines. Louis Guttman in Israel began to use facet principles for social science research, primarily survey research, at about the same time that Ranganathan in India began to use facet principles for bibliographic classification (Beghtol 1995a). The uses each of these researchers found for the same principles of facet analysis and analytico-synthetic methods contrasted with each other both in subject matter and in the kind of reasoning used in each of the two fields. Guttman used the analytico-synthetic method to create "mapping sentences" (Beghtol 1995b) that could be used to ensure that all the combinations of the variables in some research project had been fully investigated. In addition, he was able to create "laws" for social research by generalizing the mapping sentences in various projects to create a method of establishing these laws inductively. In addition, Guttman developed statistical methods based on facet analysis. These statistical methods spread throughout the social sciences and are still in use today. In Library Science, Ranganathan used the analytico-synthetic method to structure bibliographic classification systems in such a way that any document topic would be expressible in the system. In contrast to Guttman, Ranganathan reasoned deductively from his Five Laws of Library Science to arrive at the rationale for using facet structures in bibliographic classification systems. The discovery of facet principles in these two contrasting research areas at the same period and the contrasting uses of the same facet principles that could be made by these two researchers provide some empirical evidence for the cognitive availability of facet analysis as a method of subdividing a whole.

3.3 Facets in Naïve Classifications for Knowledge Discovery

Bibliographic classification systems are developed for the general purpose of information retrieval, and they may be used in either manual or electronic environments. Classifications for knowledge discovery are developed for the purpose of creating new knowledge and new ways of developing knowledge, and they are often created by scholars and researchers in various disciplines. These classifications may be called "naïve" classifications because they are developed by people who have no particular training or interest in classification for information retrieval. One example of classification for knowledge discovery was discussed above in the case of the Guttman's use of facet principles and analytico-synthetic methodology. Guttman analyzed social science research variables into mapping sentences and then synthesized the variables into specific research projects. In this way, all possible combinations of the variables could be used for research. This method is analogous to Ranganathan's method of ensuring that all possible combinations of document topics could be accommodated in bibliographic classification systems if they are needed.

The general purpose of naïve knowledge discovery classifications is to advance research in the discipline. Previous research has hypothesized that some of the specific goals of naïve classifications are to: 1) discover gaps in knowledge; 2) fill gaps in knowledge; 3) reconstruct historical situations and evidence; 4) facilitate integration and communication of findings; 5) suggest revisions or amplifications of accepted classifications (Beghtol 2004). Naïve classificationists often intuitively use facet techniques to develop their classifications, and the categories they create are recognizable as facets even though the authors use different terminologies for the concept. Examples of these other terminologies are "systematic tabulation" (Ré 1980), "analytical types" (Marchese 1984), and "constellations" (Hodson 1980). This terminological inconsistency does not conceal the similarity of the ideas in all these areas. In these cases, the authors have particularly praised their classifications because of their analytico-synthetic capabilities. For example, Altman called facets the "dimensions" of social research and pointed out that the method was "capable of including variables with any combinations of values on these dimensions" (Altman, 1967).

4 CONCLUSIONS AND FURTHER RESEARCH

Ranganathan articulated and developed the facet concept for bibliographic classification systems, and the examples above show that he may have used a cognitive universal that can be further exploited in the present era of the globalization of information. In this regard, we might adopt and expand Ranganathan's concept of seminal mnemonics as an explanatory principle that can account for the use of facets in many kinds of research areas and projects. The theoretical basis for seminal mnemonics has been described by Subramanyam (1976) as arising from Hindu thought about the relationship between perception and intuition. As a first step, we may then relate seminal mnemonics to the kinds of symbolic classification explicated by Needham (1979). Both Subramanyam and Needham emphasize the substrata of human consciousness that underlie the perceptual level of human experience. The possibility that we may discover more cognitively available methods of subdivision through the study of seminal mnemonics and symbolic classification strengthens the argument that universal methods of subdivision exist and may not be restricted to taxonomy, partonomy and facet analysis. Study of these universal methods would be appropriate for efforts at creating knowledge organizations across the many boundaries of information retrieval. In addition, these methods are not mutually exclusively and can be used fruitfully to complement each other. These complementarities are also worthy of study.

5 ACKNOWLEDGEMENT

This research was partially supported by the Social Sciences and Humanities Research Council of Canada grant number 410-2001-0108.

REFERENCES

1. Altman, I. (1967). "Choice points in the Classification of Scientific Knowledge." In *People, Groups, and Organizations*, pp. 47-69. Edited by B.P. Indik and F.K. Berrien. New York: NY: Columbia University, Teachers College Press.

2. Beghtol, C. (2004). "Classification for Information Retrieval and Classification for Knowledge Discovery: Relationships between 'Professional' and 'Naïve' Classifications." *Knowledge Organization*, in press.

3. —. (2000). "A Whole, Its Kinds, and Its Parts." In *Dynamism and Stability in Knowledge Organization*. Proceedings of the 6th International ISKO Conference, 10-13 July, Toronto, Canada, pp. 313-319. Edited by C. Beghtol, L.C. Howarth, and N. J. Williamson. Würzberg

4. —. (1997). "Graphic Representations of Hierarchical Systems: Preliminary Study." *Advances in Classification Research*, vol. 7. Proceedings, 7th American Society for Information Science (ASIS) Special Interest Group for Classification Research (SIG/CR) Classification Research Workshop, Oct. 20, Baltimore, MD, pp. 22-43. Edited by P. Solomon. Medford, N.J.: Learned Information.

5. —. (1995a). "'Facets' As Interdisciplinary Undiscovered Public Knowledge: S.R. Ranganathan in India and L. Guttman in Israel." *Journal of Documentation*, 51(3): 94-114.

6. —. (1995b). "Mapping Sentences and Classification Schedules As Methods of Displaying Facets." *Advances in Classification Research*, vol. 6. Proceedings, 6th ASIS SIG/CR Classification Research Workshop, Oct. 8, Chicago, Ill., pp. 1-12. Edited by R.P. Schwartz, *et al.* Medford, N.J.: Learned Information.

7. Broadfield, A. (1946). *The Philosophy of Classification*. London: Grafton.

8. Broughton, V. (2001). "Faceted Classification as a Basis for Knowledge Organization in a Digital Environment: The Bliss Bibliographic Classification as a Model for Vocabulary Management and the Creation of Multi-Dimensional Knowledge Structures." *The New Review of Hypermedia and Multimedia* 7: 67-102.

9. Brown, J.D. (1914). Subject Classification for the Arrangement of Libraries and the Organization of Information, with Tables, Indexes, etc., for the Subdivision of Subjects. 2nd rev. ed. London: Grafton.

10. Cordonnier, G. (1961). "Metalanguage pour les traductions d'intercommunications entre hommes et son adaptation dans le domaine des machines pour recherches documentaires. In *Information Retrieval and Machine Translation*, pp. 1091-1138, part 2. Edited by A. Kent. New York: Interscience Publishers.

11. CRG. (1955). "The Need for a Faceted Classification as the Basis of all Methods of Information Retrieval." *Library Association Record* 57 July: 262-268.

12. –. (1953). "Classification Research Group." Signed by B.C.V. *Library Association Record* 55 June: 187-188.

13. Doyle, B. (2003). "The Classification and Evaluation of Content Management Systems." The Gilbane Report 11(2): 2-13. http://www.gilbane.com/artpdf/GR11.2.pdf , accessed March 25, 2004.

14. Fast, K.; F. Leise and M. Stekel. (2002-2004). "All about Facets and Controlled Vocabularies." http://www.boxesandarrows.com/archives/all_about_facets_controlled_vocabularies.php , accessed March 25, 2004.

15. Goddard, C. and Wiezbicka, A. (1994). "Introducing Lexical Primitives." In *Semantic and Lexical Universals: Theory and Empirical Findings*, pp. 31-54. Edited by C. Goddard and A. Wierzbicka. Amsterdam: John Benjamins.

16. Hodson, F.R. (1980). "Cultures as Types? Some Elements of Classification Theory." *Institute of Archaeology Bulletin* 17: 1-10.

17. Kwasnik, B. (1999). "The Role of Classification in Knowledge Representation and Discovery." *Library Trends* 48(1): 22-47.

18. Marchese, R.T. (1984). "Material Culture and Artifact Classification." In *American Material Culture: The Shape of Things Around Us*, pp. 11-24. Edited by E. Mayo. Bowling Green, OH: Bowling Green State Univ. Popular Press.

19. Needham, R. (1979). *Symbolic Classification*. Santa Monica, CA: Goodyear Publishing Co.

20. Ranganathan, S.R. (1950). *Classification, Coding, and Machinery for Search.* UNESCO/NS/SL/3. Paris: Unesco.

21. —. (1965). *The Colon Classification*, Rutgers Series on Systems for the Intellectual Organization of Information, vol. 4. Edited by S. Artandi. New Brunswick, N.J.: Graduate School of Library Science, Rutgers the State Univ.

22. —. (1967). *Prolegomena to Library Classification.* 3rd ed. New York, NY: Asia Publishing House.

23. Ré, P. (1980). "My Drawings and Paintings and a System for their Classification." *Leonardo* 13: 94-100.

24. Satija, M.H. (1992). "Ranganathan and Classification: A Chronology 1924-1992." *International Classification* 19(1): 3-6.

25. Subramanyam, K. (1976). "Seminal Mnemonics in Classification." *International Classification* 3(1): 16-18.

26. Tinker, A J, A.S. Pollitt, A. O'Brien, and P.A. Braekevelt. (1999). "The Dewey Decimal Classification and the Transition from Physical to Electronic Knowledge Organization." *Knowledge Organization* 26 (2): 80-96.

27. Tversky, B. (1989). "Parts, Partonomies, and Taxonomies." *Developmental Psychology* 25(6): 983-995.

FACET ANALYSIS AS A KNOWLEDGE MANAGEMENT TOOL ON THE INTERNET

Kathryn La Barre
Pauline Atherton Cochrane

In 2001, a group of information architects involved in designing websites, and knowledge management specialists involved in creating access to corporate knowledge bases appeared to have re-discovered facet analysis and faceted classification. These groups have been instrumental in creating new and different ways of handling digital content of the Internet. Some of these practitioners explicitly use the forms and language of facet analysis and faceted classification, while others seem to do so implicitly. Following a brief overview of the work and discussions on facets and faceted classification in recent years, we focus on our observations about new information resources which seem more in line with the Fourth law of Library Science ("Save the time of the reader") than most library OPACs today. These new developments on the Internet point to a partial grasp of a disciplined approach to subject access. This is where Ranganathan and Neelameghan's approach needs to be reviewed for the new audience of information system designers. A report on the work undertaken by us forms a principal part of this paper.

1 PRELIMINARY NOTE

For Pauline Atherton Cochrane, the senior author (i.e. older) of this festschrift paper to honour A. Neelameghan - it has been a half-century since I first heard of the Five Laws of Library Science, espoused by S. R. Ranganathan. As a student at the University of Chicago, Graduate Library School, I met Professor Ranganathan on my birthday in 1959 – an auspicious occasion, because he lectured on facet analysis and I still have my notes! His research and teaching and that of his students and colleagues influenced the rest of my career. So much of my research and teaching reflects their point of view, their focus on canons and principles based on theory derived from practice. Any critical reviews I ever made also reflected their views. Even to this day as we now look to the websites on the Internet for examples of improved access to "information stores" the canons and principles provide essential guidance.

This paper will focus on observations we two have been making about new information resources which seem more in line with the Fourth law of Library

Science ("Save the time of the reader") than most library online library catalogues (OPACs) today. This may point the way to improvements of OPACs so that more traditional information stores (e.g. libraries) will finally live up to our stated goal, "Books are for use". Underlying these new developments on the Internet seems to be a partial grasp of all that is involved in this disciplined approach to subject access. This is where Ranganathan and Neelameghan's approach needs to be reviewed for this new audience of information system designers. The new technologies allow for easy vocabulary updates and user information item influences and design features – so much easier than the constrictive catalogue and classification systems in the paper libraries of the last century.

The main part of the paper is a report on the work in progress undertaken by the younger author with some guidance from the older author. We are pleased to share it with Neelameghan and the readers of this book. We encourage you to send comments on our observations.

2 INTRODUCTION

The need for mutable and responsive information organization and access structures is continually reinforced. The dynamic nature of the universe of knowledge reflects the increasingly complex interrelationships, which Ranganathan and Neelameghan commented on so long ago. The use of the postulational approach in database design and the continuing importance of facet analysis for searching the Internet (Neelameghan, 1992, 2002) can impact the discussions of faceted web interface design (Rosenfeld and Morville, 2002). Facet analysis (FA) has come to be regarded as an ideal tool for searching and organizing documents in electronic environments. As a theoretically-grounded approach to information system design, the use of FA has the potential to result in versatile access and organizational structures in OPACs or on the Internet that are well-suited to the needs of the task at hand while remaining equally accessible to novices and experienced searchers alike.

In 1999, Ellis and Vasconcelos issued what was to become a clarion call by invoking the words of Ingwersen and Wormell (1992) and others in the 1992 issue of *Libri* commemorating Ranganathan's birth centenary. These voices joined with the voices of others across the years in a crescendo now impossible to ignore, a reminder of the continuing relevance of the work of Ranganathan, Neelameghan, and others who never lost sight of the importance of facet analysis and the postulational approach to faceted classification as described in the *Prolegomena* (Ranganathan, 1967) and in the Colon Classification, 7th ed. (Ranganathan and Gopinath, 1989). Figure 1 provides an overview of literature and prevailing topics through the years that has kept this theory foremost in the minds of many in our discipline.

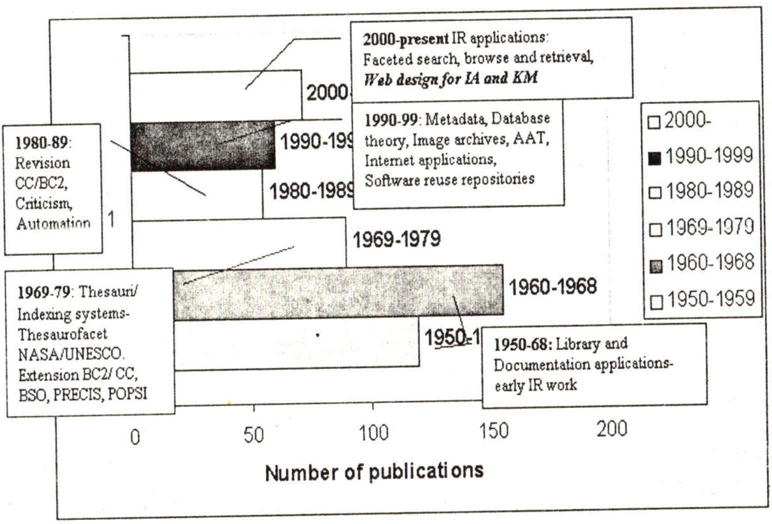

Fig. 1: Distribution of core publications/topic themes relating to application of facet analysis and faceted classification 1950-present.

3 OVERVIEW

In 2001, a group of information architects charged with designing websites, and knowledge management specialists charged with creating access to corporate knowledge bases seemingly re-discovered facet analysis and faceted classification. This group of practitioners has been instrumental in creating new and different ways for people to engage with the digital content of the Internet. Some of these practitioners explicitly use the forms and language of facet analysis and faceted classification, while others seem to implicitly mimic the forms. (Refer to Appendix 1 for examples of such discussions.) Granted, simple use of forms and language is by no means incontrovertible evidence that the resultant organization and access structures use the Postulational approach to faceted classification as theoretical underpinnings. However, such elements may be indicative of the use of underlying theory, and may serve to indicate areas in which the organization and access structures may be improved or strengthened by the consistent application of existing theory. Such a situation may also reveal novel areas of practice that may well serve to inform or to augment existing theory. The research in progress described in this paper intends to follow Neelameghan's advice (1992) to use Ranganathan's postulates and principles of the General Theory of Knowledge Classification as criteria for assessing and evaluating the Internet applications described by these information architects. The research in progress described in this paper seeks to answer the following research questions:

4 RESEARCH QUESTIONS

1. What types of access and organizational structures are used in websites?
2. What is the evidence that there is use of the postulational approach to facet analysis and faceted classification in website construction and design of website search tools?
3. In what ways do the products of those Web designers who make explicit claims to utilize or be informed by facet analysis or faceted classification conform to or depart from the theory as described by Ranganathan?

4.1 Research Overview

Given the frequency with which the terms facet, and faceted classification appear in discussions and on websites, it would seem that FA/FC has broad crossover appeal. Internet documents and discussion lists hosted by Knowledge Management (KM) specialists, and Information Architecture (IA) firms dominate the top results of a Google search using the phrases "faceted classification" or "facet analysis". The Faceted Classification Discussion (FCD) List, created December 2002, provides a forum for academic and business researchers interested in practical and theoretical discussions of FA/FC. Often, attempts to find common ground are hampered by the task of translating practice into language that is understandable to all participants. Statements like these are seductive:

- Faceted classification [is] one of the most powerful, yet least understood, methods of organizing information" (Merholz, 2001, online); and
- Faceted classification serves up multiple 'pure' classification schemes rather than a single 'motley' Taxonomy" (Rosenfeld and Morville, 2002).

Questions abound. What is FC? Where does the blogger or Web designer - someone with a casual interest in this latest hot topic - turn to find out more about the topic? Who holds the keys (or maps) to the kingdom? The first three sites that turn up on a Google search for faceted classification are:

- Phil Murray's website, KMConnection, geared for Knowledge Management (KM) enthusiasts [http://www.kmconnection.com/DOC 100100.htm];
- Peter Merholz's extensive discussion of "Innovation in classification" (2001) at peterme.com; and
- The Faceted Classification Discussion List (FCD) [http://www. poorbuthappy.com/fcd/] moderated by Peter Van Dijck, creator of XFML and Phil Murray, founder of KMConnection.

References to scholarly articles about FA and FC in the Library and Information Science literature are slowly beginning to appear in lists of Web links and Web logs alike.

Table 1: Brief timeline for discussions of faceted classification on websites

September 2001	Peter Merholz posts a discussion of faceted classification "Innovation in classification" on his weblog.
January 2002	Travis Wilson launches FacetMap, a software tool designed to assist in the creation of faceted displays.

March 2002	Phil Murray posts a series of essays and lists of references about faceted classification on his website KMConnection
April 2002	Extensive discussion about faceted classification on a listserv created for Information Architects by SIG/IA (American Society for Information Science and Technology – Special Interest Group/Information Architecture).
May 2002	Peter Van Dijck creates XFML. Extensible Faceted Mark-up Language as an extension of XML.
July 2002	Rosenfeld and Morville publish the *Information Architecture for the World Wide Web*, 2nd ed. with a discussion of faceted classification in information architecture
December 2002	Van Dijck/Murray establish the Faceted Classification Discussion List for academics and practitioners interested in the subject

At the recent American Society for Information Science and Technology Information Architecture Summit, (ASIST-IA Summit) in Austin, Texas (March 2005), several speakers discussed faceted classification: how to make one (Leise, Rice, and Warner, 2005), its use on the website for the Government of Canada (Marleau and Alberts, 2005), creating faceted interfaces (Mulder, 2005), as a browsing mechanism at Yahoo (McKennon and Baker, 2005), as the framework for the controlled vocabularies at the BBC website (Hanley, 2005) and at ProQuest (Farnum, 2005). In fact, the term *facets* as a central component of information architecture appeared in a remarkable number of presentations. Attendees seemed eager to learn more about facets, facet analysis and faceted classification. These sessions were well attended, leaving one curious to know whether there is substance behind the elaborate presentations and theory underpinning the website designs and software applications that were discussed at the conference. It would seem that this group of practitioners is using facet analysis in various ways.

4.2 Current uses of facet Analysis and Faceted Classification on the Internet

Applications that claim to utilize FA or FC are as varied as the available definitions for these terms. There are several general categories of applications: Faceted metadata and data modelling or management applications can involve software or website features such as faceted search (FS) or faceted browsing (FB).

Faceted metadata is a common application. Peter Van Dijck's (2004, online) XFML: [http://xfml.org/] provides "an open XML format for publishing and sharing hierarchical faceted metadata and indexing efforts between websites." The main idea behind XFML is to provide support for automatic links between websites with related content (*See*: Mark Pilgrim's excellent tutorial http://diveintomark.org/archives/2002/12/03/this_is_xfml). Other applications support *data modelling or management* such as Travis Wilson's FacetMap [http://facetmap.com], "created to let users browse complex metadata while retaining a simple, familiar, menu interface." FacetMap consists of software that allows the browsing of visual data in a number of different formats by facets or conceptual categories. Similar to FacetMap but lacking the visualization and modelling features are *search and browsing systems* software that provides faceted search and browsing: Endeca [http://endeca.com], and Adiuri's Waypoint products [http://www.adiuiri.com] are two examples. Websites which are often cited as exemplars of faceted design include: Epicurious the "world's greatest recipe collection" [http://eat.epicurious.com/], and Wine.com [http://wine.com/]. The reasons for this are not clear, but they are the most frequent illustrations of FA/FC on KM and IA lists and Weblogs and commonly appear in presentations during the last four years of the IA Summit (ASIST, 2005; Denton, 2003; Merholz, 2001; Morville, 2001; Park, 2001; Rayborn, 2004; Rosenfeld, 2002; Van Dijck, 2004; T. Wilson, 2004).

More traditional conceptualizations of FA and FC exist alongside these other applications. FATKS: Facet analytical theory in managing knowledge structure for humanities [http://www.ucl.ac.uk/fatks/] created a faceted classification system and easily automatable indexing tool for the humanities (Broughton, 2003). Other projects include the Facet Project (Tudhope, 2003) [http://www.glam.ac.uk/soc/research/hypermedia/facet_proj/], which tested the efficacy of faceted thesauri for retrieval of multimedia collections. Hearst's Flamenco project [http://bailando.sims.berkeley.edu/flamenco.html] which, by exposing faceted metadata, allows users to expand and organize search strategies in collections of art and architectural images, and Pollitt's work with Interactive Information Retrieval [http://poseidon.hud.ac.uk/external/research/CeDAR/dorking.htm], based on a facet analytical approach that utilizes post-coordinated searching and a faceted thesaurus to generate different views of search results.

Table 2: Examples of websites and software applications

Epicurious (recipe website)	http://www.epicurious.com
Wine.com (wine shop)	http://www.wine.com
Siderean software	http://www.siderean.com
Endeca software	http://www.endeca.com
Adiuri systems	http://www.adiuri.com

5 RESEARCH DESIGN

Given the diverse understandings and variety of applications that claim to apply FA/FC, an investigation of the use and utility of facet analysis is timely. This study intends to uncover different types and kinds of practice and may provide the potential for discovery, new developments that may augment the traditional application of the postulational approach to faceted classification. The first step is the development of a framework for analysis of websites that utilize FA/ FC. This framework for analysis relies on Ranganathan's postulates and principles and provides scaffolding for future efforts in development across various applications beyond websites. It is anticipated that one result of the website analysis will be the creation of a set of design guidelines that highlights commonalities and differences among FA/FC applications on the Internet.

6 WEBSITE ARCHITECTURE

The creation of website architecture involves the processes of structuring, organizing and labelling information in such a way that a visitor to a website can find what is sought. A properly constructed website may have four basic components (Rosenfeld and Morville, 2002):

- System of organization;
- Search system;
- Navigation system; and
- Labelling system.

These are important distinctions, which may not be self-evident. More easily understood are the differences between the labelling system and the search system. Labelling systems are forms of representation that serve to provide context, describe content, present navigation options, or index terms. Labels are in use on buttons and navigation bars of a website (2002). Search systems are another ubiquitous website component. Most websites have a text box so that site visitors can search for desired information. Metadata and indexing are often important aspects of a website's search system (2002) but will not be captured during the data collection, though their obvious presence will be noted.

Less clear are the distinctions between the organizational and navigation systems. The organizational system is the foundation of a website and is composed of organizational schemes and structures. An organizational scheme defines "the *shared characteristics* [italics added] of content items and influences the logical grouping of those items." Telephone books use *alphabetical organization*, and TV programming guides use *time* as an organizational scheme (2002). Other familiar schemes may concentrate on more ambiguous characteristics of information, such as topic, or task. The organizational structure "defines the *types of relationships* [italics added] between content items and groups" (2002). Rosenfeld and Morville here refer to hierarchies which may be evident when viewing a site map. Hypertext is another example of an organizational structure which is nonlinear, but provides access or pathways to information (2002).

Navigation systems are often embedded in the content of the site where they provide context and flexibility. Embedded navigational systems may be global (providing navigation for the site as a whole), local (providing navigation for a small part of a website) or contextual (linking to specific page document or object). Navigational systems may also be supplemental, and include stand-alone components of a website such as sitemaps, indexes and guides (Rosenfeld and Morville, 2002).

Rosenfeld and Morville make a distinction between search and browsing systems on websites, but urge designers to integrate these components in ways that allow users to easily jump between the two (Rosenfeld and Morville, 2002). In the language of the practitioners who explicitly invoke the language or forms of facets, faceted (or guided) navigation and browsing and faceted searching are central to the applications they create. Two categories of website components are of interest to the present study, browsing and search aids. Browsing aids, such as site-wide navigation, or local navigation, site maps and tables of content, and search aids, such as the search interface and presentation of search results are the website components that will be analyzed for use of facet analysis.

The current research revisits the same territory as earlier research which examined 75 e-commerce sites for evidence of faceted approaches (Adkisson, 2003). For the present study, a sample of 1000 websites, drawn from the Open Directory Project (DMOZ.org) will be analyzed. Each site will be captured by printing the first page, search page, results page, and sitemap.

Wireframes will also be created for each site. A wireframe is a representation of a website which is free of graphics and allows the site architecture to be displayed more clearly. This is an example of a wireframe for the website epicurious.com, an often-cited example of faceting in website design. This wireframe demonstrates page components and the flow through three layers (home page to browse page to result page) of the site:

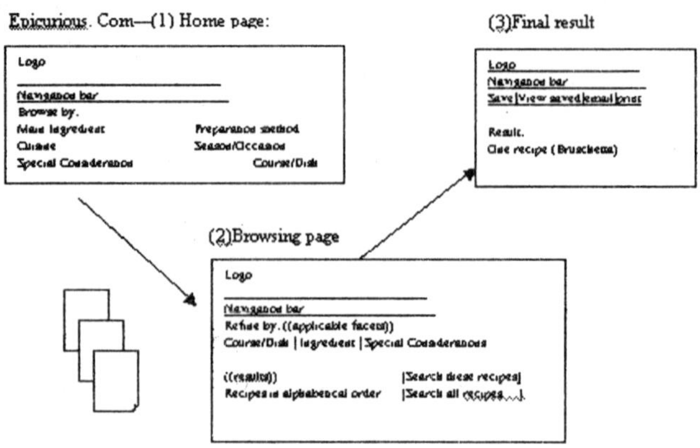

This wireframe example demonstrates the use of FA for browsing. On the home page (1) a visitor may browse the site by ingredients, preparation or other categories (or facets). The browse link takes a visitor to the browsing page (2) where the query may be refined using applicable categories (facets) or the visitor may choose from a recipe result set that is in alphabetical array. The choice of a specific recipe leads the visitor to the final result page (3).

After collecting website components and creating wireframes, a group of 20 Information Architects who claim to use facet analysis or faceted classification in construction and design of websites will be interviewed in order to determine their attitudes and current levels of understanding about faceting. During the interviews, descriptions of current applications of FA/FC will be collected. It is expected that the analysis of these descriptions will help to support the creation of a set of prevailing principles which govern current use of facets within this community of website designers. These principles can then be compared to the evaluative criteria embedded in Ranganathan's postulates and principles of the General Theory of Knowledge Classification. Those which are of special interest in the present research as indicated by Ranganathan's *Elements* (1962) and the *Introduction to the 7th edition of the Colon Classification* (1989) are outlined below:

Table 3: Ranganathan's dynamic 'Guiding Principles' for the present research

- Postulates

    Five fundamental categories (PMEST)

    Three planes of work (Idea, Verbal, Notational)

- Canons

    Parsimony; Symmetry

    Possibly: Currency, Consistent sequence, Enumeration, Context, Reticence, Relativity, Mnemonics, Phase relation, Classic Device

7 CONCLUSIONS

Developments of FA/FC on the Internet and its relevance to OPAC design should not be a huge leap of faith. Access to library catalogue information (author, title, subject, etc.) is now part of the "faceted metadata" developments. Access to index vocabulary structures (thesauri, *FAST*-Faceted Access to Subject Terminology, *ClassWeb* at the Library of Congress, etc.) will be improved if the FA/FC systems on the Internet are used as models. Classified catalogues were first tested online (AUDACIOUS) using UDC in the mid-1960s but were never widely accommodated in OPAC design. Other innovations: beyond "keyword searching" need to be incorporated into OPACs soon or all information seeking, even for library holdings, will move to access systems like the Google Print™ program which is soon to have *full text* libraries online (http://www.google.com/intl/en/ press/pressrel/print_library.html).

REFERENCES

1. Adkisson, H. (2003). *Use of faceted classification*. Web design practices. Retrieved 2 February 2005, from http://www.Webdesignpractices.com/navigation/facets.html

2. ASIS&T. (2005). *Crossing boundaries: Sixth Annual ASIS&T Information Architecture Summit*. March 3-7, 2005. Montréal, Quebec, Canada. Handouts and Proceedings. Silver Spring, MD: ASIS&T and Information Architecture Institute.

3. Ellis, D. and Vasconcelos, A. (1999). Ranganathan and the Net: Using facet analysis to search and organise the World Wide Web. *Aslib Proceedings*. Vol. 51(1); p. 3-10.

4. Farnum, C. (2005). Making the most of controlled vocabularies in search interfaces. Presentation at the *Sixth Annual ASIS&T Information Architecture Summit. March 3-7, 2005*. Montréal, Quebec, Canada.

5. Hanley, M. (2005). Change, influence, and IA at the BBC. Presentation at the *Sixth Annual ASIS&T Information Architecture Summit. March 3-7, 2005*. Montréal, Quebec, Canada.

6. Ingwersen, P. and Wormell, I. (1992). Ranganathan in the perspective of advanced information retrieval. *Libri* Vol. 42(3); p. 184-201.

7. Leise, F.; Rice, S. and Warner, A. (2005). Developing a faceted classification. Presentation at the *Sixth Annual ASIS&T Information Architecture Summit. March 3-7, 2005*. Montréal, Quebec, Canada.

8. Marleau, Y. and Alberts, I. (2005). Faceted classification in the government of Canada: Toward a global approach to information architecture. Presentation at the *Sixth Annual ASIS&T Information Architecture Summit. March 3-7, 2005*. Montréal, Quebec, Canada.

9. McKennon, W. and Baker, B. (2005). One size does not fit all: A story of faceted browse at Yahoo! Presentation at the *Sixth Annual ASIS&T Information Architecture Summit. March 3-7, 2005*. Montréal, Quebec, Canada.

10. Merholz. P. peterme.com. Retrieved 1 June, 2004 from, http://www.peterme.com/archives/00000063.html Posted: 09/23/2001.

11. Mulder, S. (2005). The faceted interface: PC Connection case study. Presentation at the *Sixth Annual ASIS&T Information Architecture Summit. March 3-7, 2005*. Montréal, Quebec, Canada.

12. Neelameghan, A. (1992). Application of Ranganathan's general theory of knowledge classification in designing specialized databases. *Libri.* Vol. 42(3); p. 202-226.

13. —. (2002). Classification in the digital environment. *Information Studies.* Vol. 8(1); p. 1-8.

14. Ranganathan, S. R. (1945/1960/1962). *Elements of library classification.* New York: Asia Publishing.

15. —. (1967). *Prolegomena to library classification.* Madras: Asia Publishing House.

16. —. and Gopinath, M. A. (ed.) (1989). *Colon Classification Edition 7.* Bangalore: Sarada Ranganathan endowment for library science.

17. Rosenfeld, L. and Morville, P. (2002). Faceted Classification. *Information architecture for the World Wide Web.* Sebastapol, CA: O'Reilly. p. 204-208.

APPENDIX 1

Current Discussions of Facets on the Internet

In 2001, the topic of facets and faceted classification began to spread across the Web and was a subject of discussion at the ASIST - IA Summits.

Discussion lists:

- sigia-l [http://www.info-arch.org]
- facetedclassification list [http://finance.groups.yahoo.com/group/ facetedclassification/]
- Topicmap mail [http://www.infoloom.com/mailman/listinfo/topicmapmail
- SWAD: Europe Thesaurus Activity - RDF representations for thesaurus data
- public-esw-thes@w3.org [http://www.w3.org/2001/sw/Europe/reports/thes/]

Websites:

- Community Infrastructure for Information Architects[http://www.info-arch.org]
- Asilomar Institute for Information Architecture AIfIA [http://www.aifia.org],
- Boxes and Arrows: The design behind the design [http://www.boxesandarrows.com]

Excerpts from discussions:

Lists of references:

> "Lately I've been hearing a lot about **Faceted Classification**. I'm not sure who was the first to coin it but it's a navigation method that seems to work very well when you have a large list of items you need to classify and browse." (Long list of references and examples). Park, N. 11-28-01. Strange Systems: http://www.strangesystems.net/archives/ 000002.php "So, I went looking for the article that would explain faceted classification in a language that I could understand." Snowdeal, E. C. 6-27-2002 Parallax:http://snowdeal.org/section/parallax/archives/2002_06_23_index.html#85205647

"I've been trying to get my head around the concept of "faceted classification." This topic has been discussed a bit lately on the SIGIA list, and I wanted to understand what's different about "faceted classification" from my previous understanding of "classification"... So there is value in being able to distinguish between "faceted classification" and "hierarchy" or "taxonomy" -- "faceted classification" is a more specific term -- it lends clarity to the discussion. I also like the fact that conceptually "facets" should be determined by user needs. This helps focus the information architect on the user, rather than just on the content." Kantrovich, L. 2-4-02 Croc o' Lyle. http://crocolyle.blogspot.com/2002/02/faceted-classification-example-ive.html

General discussion:

Browse beats search/combine. Smith, G. (4-15-2002) and Facets + Flash (4-29, 2003). Atomiq: http://www.atomiq.org/archives/000561.html

Talking about faceted classification: The emperor's complex clothes. Wodtke, C. June 2002. Elegant Hack: http://www.eleganthack.com/archives/002780.html

Need for clarity:

"Discussion is heating up a little and Kathryn La Barre is dropping science on us...(on the Faceted classification list) As someone who thought himself to have a very fundamental understanding of these concepts, the discussion of facet analysis and classification in the past year has done more to confuse these concepts than to clarify them in my opinion, and for that reason, I am glad that this new list was created. There seems to be a great desire to get the outcome of facet analysis – the browsable faceted interface like Flamenco, but there hasn't been a lot of discussion about how facet analysis actually takes place. The terms have not even been defined clearly enough in my opinion . . . we need the terms and the methodologies to approach facet analysis better summarized in accessible articles that can help practicing IAs. Facetted classification." Angeles, M. 12-19-2002. iaslash: http://www.iaslash.org/taxonomy/page/or/101

Scepticism:

"My complaint is that there is a lot of talk about facets, but little of any substance. Most of it won't help you build your own faceted classification scheme. It amounts to saying the grass is greener on the other (faceted) side, but fails to give you a map explaining how to get there and what obstacles you'll face along the way. And the academic literature doesn't help much either. It's too dense and I can't recommend it to the practitioner (not the stuff I've seen)." Luky, G. (2004).Get luky. http://www.getluky.net/archives/000052.html. Posted: 24 May, 2004.

Misunderstanding:

Travis Wilson (creator of FacetMap): Thread: Special vs. General Schemes: Date: Wed, 12 Mar 2003 09:14:11 +0000 http://article.gmane.org/gmane.comp.infodesign.Facetedclassification/170/ match=facet .

At the other extreme, the universal qualities espoused by Ranganathan and others just don't apply to many resources that deserve classification. The "space" facet only works in the context of resources that have physical incarnations in a spatial location; perhaps this is obvious, but it confirms that there is indeed a context -- one that many data-based resources don't share. In the end, the whole idea of a set of general facets as a "framework for facets typical of each discipline" simply limits the number of disciplines that can use FC (to those that fit within the framework). Ranganathan was really not concerned with disciplines outside of biology. I don't think that kind of limitation is appropriate for faceted classification in general, and I hope we don't impose it.

To take Phil's words to more of an extreme -- Can there even be such a thing as a general faceted schema? Facets only seem to make sense within a context.

As for Ranganathan's five-objective facet approach, I hope we can just regard that as early work and move on. While you CAN use fc based on conceptual/general categories to create facets for wine bottles. You CAN't use wine bottle facets anywhere else but for wine bottles.

Attempts at a common framework for consensus, definition and comparison:

Murray Altheim [topicmapmail] Two models of facets 18, November, 2003.
http:// www.infoloom.com/pipermail/topicmapmail/2003q4/005406.html

(1) Model A facet: (The metadata/ RDF model) or the adding of property-value pairs to a resource.

(2) Model T facet: (The faceted classification model). FC defines its subjects not by creating a set of canonical categories, but by collections of "facets". This model of defining subjects as collections of facets is all about subject identity.

Alistair Miles : Two senses of facets 3-23-2004 [public-esw-thes@w3.org.]
http://lists.w3.org/Archives/Public/public-esw-thes/2004Mar/0066.html
I have so far come across two meanings for 'faceted classification':

(Sense 1) A set of things are 'classified' according to their properties. For example (from [1]) a set of detergents are classified by 'brand name', 'form', 'scent', 'agent', 'effect on agent' and 'special property'. In this sense, each of these properties represents a 'facet' through which the set of instances can be viewed.

(Sense 2) A set of 'concepts' are grouped according to their most primitive type. For example, the concept 'marble' is placed in the 'materials' facet. The concept 'insects' is placed in the 'organisms' facet. In this sense, a 'facet' is essentially a primitive class, and every member of a facet group is either an instance or a sub-class of that class.

Aida Slavic: In reference to Miles and William Denton's Web essay: How to put a faceted classification on the Web. [http://www.miskatonic.org/library/facet-Webhowto.html] Posted: 23 March, 2004.[public-esw-thes@w3.org] http://lists.w3.org/Archives/Public/public-esw-thes/ 2004Mar/0069.html

> This is a library school essay and for me it was very useful as it clearly demonstrated how easy it is to ignore the difference between classification of objects and classification of knowledge . . . But it is very important to pay attention to this as it represents how the term 'faceted classification' is implemented in XFML and how it is understood by many people creating business portals with excellent browsing facets functionality.

In this approach "faceted classification" is classification that it fits in your Sense 1 (division according to one principle at the time, hence "faceted classification" is ANY classification that operates with sets of mutually exclusive categories of any kind). Here everything fits nicely as the term 'facet' (fr. la facette - little face) is said to be borrowed from a 'diamond' - each facet represents one side or one face of the diamond. (each property is a single face of a multifaced object). With this one gets all the advantages in managing vocabulary using an elegant relational model.

If one knows that most widely used American classifications such as Dewey or Library of Congress C. are enumerative classifications and occasionally/often? fail to consistently apply a simplest logic of division - then it is understandable why many feel necessary to make distinction between: a) messy enumerative structure b) pure taxonomy and c) something called "faceted classification" simply to emphasise that the last one is a logical and consistent in nature and in the same time helps in managing different properties of objects simultaniously [sic](and is likely to be ontologically clean in Guarino's sense and therefore easier to process by machines). Something like 'deux ex machina' on the KOS scene.

UK Classification research group, however, reserves the expression 'faceted classification' for knowledge classification only (knowledge about objects and not objects themselves). Here one obviously has more problems to sort out with facets than detergents, beer cans and bottles of wines. For CRG Sense1 is understood to be there anyway and when they attach attribute 'faceted' to some classification they think that besides this basic logical property level there must be a set of fundamental categories (Sense 2) in place.

When thesauri embraced 'facet analysis' they paid attention only to the top organizational structure in Sense 2 and ignored Sense1. The reason being the very nature of thesaurus: alphabetical indexing languages do not need detailed classificatory structure for their managment and can work with a rather rough organizational grouping as far as there is some logical principle behind it (mutual exclusiveness).

The discussion on what faceted classification is on the faceted classification mailing list last year agreed on the following (I think):

a) if one is creating a classification for objects/entities (bottles of wines, beer cans, detergents, cars etc.) then it is sufficient to have Sense 1 organization structure applied.

b) if one is producing classification to classify knowledge about objects both: facets of properties and fundametnal facets above them in order to be able to organize facets themselves. This is because of the complexity that classification of knowledge operates with, dealing with concepts as well as dynamic relationships among them.

The conclusion was that XFML is not meant and can't serve for the purpose b) and suggestion was that we should rather look into XTM in order to accommodate the kind of ontology typical for "faceted classifications of knowledge" which operate with fundamental categories (Sense 2: grouping of primitives) as well as with facets in a more technical sense (Sense1: things according to their properties).

THE UNIVERSAL DECIMAL CLASSIFICATION: A RESPONSE TO A CHALLENGE

I.C. McIlwaine

Examines the changes and trends in the developments and revisions of UDC in the context of a critique made by Neelameghan in 1972 on the need for a theoretical basis for UDC. The impact of Ranganathan's faceted approach as also his General Theory of Classification on the revision of UDC has been explained with illustrations from the recent revisions of UDC with particular emphasis on developments in the last decade.

1 INTRODUCTION

Over thirty years ago a conference was held in the former Yugoslavia on "UDC in relation to other indexing languages" (*UDC in relation to other indexing languages*, 1972). This was one of a series of such conferences, in a period when interest in the *Universal Decimal Classification* was flourishing, and among the contributors to that conference was Professor A. Neelameghan (Neelameghan, 1972). During the 1970s some twenty countries, at the very least, (Rigby, 1981) are recorded as actively interested in the classification and it was in particular seen as of potential interest for the future computerized world which was at that time only vaguely understood. From the early years of the last century India had evinced interest in the UDC and it exerted considerable influence over the development of the *Colon Classification,* not least in the name of the scheme, which is directly derived from the UDC's linking notation, the colon. So Professor Neelameghan's participation in the conference comes as no surprise.

Neelameghan's presentation "A theoretical foundation for UDC: its need and formulation" is written very much from the viewpoint of users' enquiries and makes comparisons and contrasts between the Colon Classification and the Universal Decimal Classification. This contribution to the volume paying tribute to Neelameghan's work in the field of Knowledge Organization attempts to demonstrate the ways in which the UDC has moved forward in the intervening thirty years and addressed some of the shortcomings identified in his perceptive analysis of that classification scheme.

2 HISTORICAL BACKGROUND

The UDC, developed at the end of the nineteenth century from Dewey's Decimal classification, owes much to its forefather, but it was far more ambitious in its development of the facility for listing different types of concepts separately and then providing the means of linking them by different forms of notational symbol which clearly convey the category, such as place, time, bibliographical form, language, etc. It is often forgotten that it was not for the best part of a century after its original conception that Dewey's scheme provided any auxiliary table other than one for bibliographic forms, while the first edition of the UDC (Manuel, 1907) is already equipped with an array of auxiliaries, listing place and race, time, form, languages and points of view, laying the ground for all future developments in classification, and recognizing, albeit in rudimentary form, the need to identify commonly recurring facets, both conceptually and notationally.

Twenty years after the publication of the first edition of the UDC, Ranganathan was appointed as Librarian of Madras University and went to London where he studied at the School of Librarianship at University College (now School of Library, Archive and Information Studies, University College London). There, he was greatly influenced by the teaching of Berwick Sayers and he also saw the Christmas demonstration of Meccano in Selfridges, which he speaks of so fluently as the root of his nuts and bolts to join together the various facets in his classification (Ranganathan, 1957). Much of the theory of facet analysis crystallized by Ranganathan has been put into practice in the UDC and his approach continues to inform all the developments that are taking place in that scheme at the present time.

2.1 UDC and CC

There is a very close link between these two classification schemes. Each has exerted a profound influence upon the other, and this is very clearly brought out by Neelameghan in the paper that he delivered at the Yugoslavia conference. In his paper he distinguishes the two uses to which a bibliographic classification may be put, shelf arrangement, and the indexing of "micro documents". It is the latter use which is of far greater relevance today when the challenge of searching for micro information on the Web faces those concerned with Knowledge Organization, or classification. He identifies the use of chain indexing as a major step forward in establishing a consistent subject approach, and this was a system which enjoyed widespread popularity for more than a quarter of a century from around 1950 until the advent of the computerized catalogue and the reliance upon the Library of Congress Subject headings as the preferred method of subject retrieval. He also emphasizes the need for a firm subject analysis before classifying a document – this remains a very valid requirement, and today a document may be a piece of information in any format, not necessarily something printed and held in the hand. In dealing with what was to become known as the "reference interview" he posits a "Trilogue" between the reader, the librarian and the document, so as to clarify what is required and to ensure that the right piece of information reaches the end user. Today, it is a dialogue rather than a trilogue which is the norm, and the user interacts directly with the computer to seek information, with practically no assistance from any intermediary. This lack of a middle step results in many problems, not least that of overload and it is to try to circumvent these problems that all the general schemes of classification are at the present time attempting to make themselves more amenable to direct dialogue and to provide more efficient retrieval in a networked world.

Neelameghan says: "At a given point in time, the classificationist may have to deal with only a finite universe of subjects. But if the scheme for classification he designs is to continue to be useful, he must recognise that the universe of subjects and the psychology of readers are ever-dynamic, ever-developing, and that the development of the universe of subjects is accelerating from time to time" (Neelameghan, 1972). This has become ever more evident with succeeding years as knowledge advances, but even more as ways of presenting and accessing information have multiplied and diversified. When faced with such circumstances, the analytico-synthetic classification has a great advantage over the enumerative one, since schemes like the Colon Classification and even those which are semi-faceted like the UDC have a head start over classifications such as the Dewey Decimal Classification and the Library of Congress Classification. But Dewey's scheme has learnt much from its descendants and many of the devices which were inbuilt into UDC and CC are now also being employed by it, hence the use of the term "facet" in the introduction and the discussion of citation order and the provision of "Tables indicating preference order" in the more recent editions of the scheme (Dewey Decimal Classification, 2003).

2.2 UDC and Automation

The 1970s, the decade when Neelameghan was writing, was a period when UDC was seen as having great potential for future needs. Considerable research into the possibilities for its application in automation had been undertaken in the 1960s, especially through the work of Freeman and Atherton (1969) and it was considered very seriously as a switching language when the UNISIST programme began in 1971. The retirement of Lloyd as editor in 1975 and the proliferation of committees and red tape surrounding the acceptability of revisions, together with increasing economic constraints meant that the next decade was not one to remember in the history of the scheme. It had grown very large, many sections were sadly out of date and the development was very uneven. By this time, it fully merited Ranganathan's judgement that it was too verbose (Ranganathan, 1957). In 1992 FID decided that it could no longer afford to support the scheme and the UDC Consortium was formed (FID, 1991). This resulted in the down-sized, machine-readable version known as the Master Reference File (MRF) which for the past ten years has been the authorized version of the scheme.

2.3 Developments Over the Past Decade

During the past decade much work has gone into updating the scheme and attempting to make it more amenable to the needs of the 21st Century. Current revision procedures are firmly based on the theoretical principles expounded by Ranganathan, and all revisions are fully faceted. The use of both common and special auxiliaries, inherent in the structure of the scheme, has greatly facilitated this and considerable effort in recent years has been expended in making the application of the special auxiliaries more transparent. One way in which this has been done is by introducing new common auxiliaries which incorporate a number of concepts previously listed as special auxiliaries, a notable instance being those at the beginning of class 62 – Engineering. At the present time work is being undertaken to consolidate the special auxiliaries, so that they are all clearly identified at the head of the main class to which they refer, rather than being scattered throughout that class, as happened, for example, when Class 316 – Sociology was revised in the 1980s.

Two new common auxiliaries have been introduced since the year 2000, thereby furthering the faceted structure. These are the common auxiliaries of properties and the common auxiliaries of relations, operations and processes. They are clearly notated, using -02 and -04 respectively, with the common auxiliaries of materials interposed, introduced by -03, and followed by the common auxiliaries of persons introduced by -05. These concepts are very familiar to users of the *Colon Classification*, representing the Energy Facet, the Matter Facet and elements of the Personality Facet. Phase relations are all enumerated at the beginning of the newest table, that of Relations, processes and operations, mirroring the provisions of the *Colon Classification:*

-042	Phase relations
-042.1	Bias phase
-042.2	Comparison phase
-042.3	Influence phase
-042.4	Tool phase. Exposition phase

The need for the "General Relation phase" is not felt in the UDC, because the colon, the notation that enables one part of the scheme to be connected to another, provides for this need. It was decided that works which compared subjects also differentiated between them, and consequently the comparison and difference phases of the *Colon classification* are treated together in the UDC's new table.

The order of concepts mirrors that found in the table of properties, with general processes following the phase relations, and then proceeding to processes of existence, of value, ordering and sequence, magnitude, number and degree, time, dimension, size and shape. Change of position, arrangement and movement, physical properties, states of matter follow and finally general operations and activities are listed (*Extensions and corrections*, 2003). A brief extract demonstrates the type of concept enumerated:

-044.96	Change of structure
-044.962	Construction. Synthesis
-044.963	Destruction. Deconstruction. Analysis
-044.964	Aggregation. Agglomeration
-044.965	Stratification
-044.966	Dissociation. Detachment. Separation
-044.967	Disintegration. Decay
-044.968	Rupture. Bursting
-044.969	Collapse

In the early part of his article, Neelameghan provides a detailed examination to identify those parts of knowledge which have advanced to the stage of needing radical overhaul, according to his findings when preparing the 7th edition of the *Colon Classification*. In the 1960s these included the disciplines of Astrophysics, Chemical engineering, Biochemistry, Public Health, Medical Jurisprudence and Geopolitics. This constant need to accommodate new concepts is one of the greatest problems that confront the editor of a classification scheme. Knowledge advances, new disciplines are formed and new ways of looking at time-honoured concepts occur. His list of new disciplines clearly exemplifies this problem. The mushrooming, division and joining together of previously discrete subjects places a constant strain on a classification, as well as its users, in particular if the scheme is used for shelf arrangement, as has historically been the case. This still continues today, despite the impact of "the electronic future". The more flexible a scheme is and the greater the provision for synthesis, the easier it is for the editor of a classification to cope with the situation. UDC's new schemes for Environmental Science and Biotechnology noted below are examples of this.

The problem of retrieving information on new fields of interest, especially from the World Wide Web, is lessened when one uses a classification to retrieve electronic resources, because then it becomes more like a dictionary, translating the query into the retrieval language to present the user with the information required. It also rises above the barriers of language. But custom is very pervasive and people who have become accustomed to a particular arrangement are very confused when things are changed. So, when revising a classification scheme one has to take care that the needs of users are considered, and that everything is not turned upside down in the interests of currency. One also has to remember that although a classification needs to be current, it will also have to be used to organize information from the past, which may be sought via terminology that is no longer current. Therefore, a careful balance has to be struck between excessive change and no change at all. Whichever path one follows, there will always be objections from users.

2.4 Theoretical Basis of CC and UDC

The *Colon Classification* saw many changes between editions, perhaps the most occurring in the 6th edition. These were not simply a reflection of the advances in knowledge that had taken place in the intervening years, but also of the advances in Ranganathan's thinking. The formulation of rules and the development of a theory for Knowledge Organization are matters that editors of classification schemes have to be aware of. Neelameghan's paper deals very thoroughly with underlying theory which he states arises out of (Neelameghan, 1972):

- "The difficulty of choosing a particular succession of immediate-neighbourhood-relation of remove 1, remove 2, and so on; and
- Securing a similar pattern of arrangement in the very large number of compound subjects going with different Basic Subjects"

He considers there to be very little difference between the underlying theory of Dewey's classification, and that of the UDC and this is not entirely surprising, given the historical circumstances of the UDC's genesis. Many advances in the underlying theory of Knowledge Organization have been made throughout the past century, and historically the pattern has tended to be a pragmatic approach out of which a theory has been formed, rather than a firm body of theory on which classifications or other forms of retrieval language have been based. Ranganathan was the first to propound a clear theory and set of rules for the creation of classifications. Of course, he built upon the work of his predecessors, both that of pragmatists such as Dewey and that of his virtual contemporaries such as Bliss, although his *Prolegomena* which first appeared in 1937 is essentially contemporaneous with Bliss's published works, since the second edition of his *The organization of knowledge in libraries* was published in 1939. Nevertheless, this exposition of his theory came four years after the publication of the first edition of his classification scheme, and drew heavily on his experiences in creating the *Colon Classification*.

It is certainly true that the theoretical basis of the UDC followed long after it had been put into practical application, and it was not until after the Second World War that any attempt to regularize and formulate that theory appeared in print, culminating in the publication of Perreault's work (Perrault, 1969). Since that date, firstly FID and subsequently the UDC Consortium have drawn up guidelines and rules for the revision of the classification for the guidance of those working on revision (FID, 1981; UDCC, 1993). Both the theoretical basis and hints for the practical application of the scheme are provided for in the various editions of the *Guide* to the classification. (McIlwaine, 1993; 2000). The creation of the machine-readable version led to other rules being published, but these are not related to the way in which the classification exists *per se* or to revision of the scheme's content.

Ranganathan's Five Laws of Library Science, formulated in 1928, underpinned all his thinking and base the theory of classification firmly upon the need to satisfy the wants of the user. This has not changed; the only difference in the 21st century is that those needs come in a range of formats, which could not have been predicted over seventy years ago. New ideas and new techniques that will improve the retrieval quality of a classification come with experience. This is clearly a good thing, but when implemented there is the concomitant problem of editing the past work to ensure that everything is consistent. There are countless instances of inconsistency in both the *Colon Classification* and the *Universal Decimal Classification*. One example in the UDC is with Table 1k-05: the Table of common subdivisions of persons. This began life as a special auxiliary, applicable in Class 3 – Social Sciences. Its use was later extended to class 61 – Medicine, and later still, it was thrown open for general use. In the days when it was still a special auxiliary, many disciplines needed to be extended by person, and that facet was listed as part of the class, with quite different notation. When the change to opening up the table was made, there was no careful editing to ensure that all the other notations were cancelled and the instruction to use the common table was given. A similar example in the *Colon classification* is the use of the Sectorizing Device, originally called the Octave Device. Ranganathan devised the method for extending an array by treating the digit 9 as a repeater and making it meaningless without further expansion, but there are many places in the classification where the digit 9 actually has a meaning.

2.5 Practical Application of Theory in Recent Years

Bearing these problems in mind, over the past decade revision of the *Universal Decimal Classification* has taken place in two ways. All new classes are fully faceted. These include the revision and relocation of Management at the very beginning of the classification in 005, since it was felt that Management is a general discipline which is applicable to almost every other discipline and therefore warranted a position early in the scheme. New classes for Environmental science and for Biotechnology have been developed, placed at the beginning of class 5 and class 6 respectively. These both rely heavily on combining concepts placed elsewhere in the classification, and collocating them by means of the colon.

502/504 Environmental science. Conservation of natural resources.
    Threats to the environment and protection against them.

502 The environment and its protection
- 502.1 The environment and society. Conservation and protection in general ...
  - 502.17 Protection of the environment in general
    - 502.171 Protection, rational use and renewal of natural resources
      - 502.171:531.62 Energy conservation
      - 502.171:662.997 Conservation of geothermal energy
      - 502.172 Protection of endangered living elements

502.172:502.211 Protection of endangered species. 'Red data'

...

502.2 The environment as a whole

502.21 Natural resources and energy

502.21:523.9 Solar energy

502.21:621.039 Nuclear energy

...

502.3 Atmospheric environment

502.3:504.5:621.43.064 Atmospheric pollution by exhaust fumes from traffic

502.3:504.7 Global warming of atmosphere

502.3:551.510.534:504.12 Ozone layer depletion

502.3:613.15 Air quality. Including: Clean air

...

60 Biotechnology

601 Fundamental concepts

601.2 Biological fundamentals

601.2:575.853 Cell structure

601.2:576.34 Metabolism. Metabolic design

...

601.4 Genetic Fundamentals

601.4:575.116.4 Gene mapping

601.4:575.224.4 Mutagenesis

601.4:577.212.3 DNA sequencing

...

602 Processes and techniques

602.1 Process control

602.3 Industrially important organisms

602.3:578.347 Bacteriophages

602.3:579.841.4 Methylotrophs

602.3:579.852.11 Bacillus spp.
602.3:579.873.7 Streptomycetes
602.3:582.282.23 Yeasts
602.4 Biotechnological processing. Bioprocessing
602.641 Use of viral vectors
602.641:578.826 Adenovirus as vector
602.641:578.828 Retroviruses (including lentivirus) as vectors

Perhaps the most ambitious innovation that has been produced in recent years is the new classification for Class 2 – Religion (Broughton, 2000). The entire class is totally faceted, precisely along the lines proposed by Ranganathan. In common with his scheme this classification lacks any strong Christian bias, unlike all the other classifications produced in the West. All the World's religions can be given equal treatment using a chronological order for the initial arrangement of faiths. The "big five" faiths, Hinduism, Buddhism, Judaism, Christianity and Islam have a two digit notation, the remainder having slightly longer numbers. In a manner very reminiscent of the *Colon Classification*, no combined concepts are enumerated; the class consists of lists of simple facets which are then combined according to the prescribed order, as required. The principal facets (in reverse order of citation, following the principle of inversion) are:

(Theory and philosophy) Religious concepts and ideas

(Evidences of religion) Sacred books. Scriptures.

(Agents) Persons in the subject

(Operations) Social and ritual practice and observance

(Processes) Development, decline, inter-faith relations

(Parts) Religious organizations, associations, orders, sects, and movements

(Kinds) Religions by various characteristics, e.g. Orthodox, Liberal, monotheistic

(Entities, systems) Specific religions and faiths

Equal detail can be used for each faith and as many concepts as necessary can be joined together. A similar on-going piece of work is to convert the structure of the Medicine Class in the *Bliss* Bibliographic *Classification* to form the basis of a new Class 61 – Medicine, with the intention of bringing that class into the 21st Century. There have been reports of this project in each recent issue of *Extensions and corrections to the UDC*, as well as reports at conferences, (e.g. annually at IFLA), and workshops (McIlwaine and Williamson, 2003).

In addition to total restructuring of sections of the classification, inevitably there are editorial changes and updated terminology continually needing to be added, and these are published each year in November and circulated to Consortium members and licence holders in the annually updated Master Reference File. The Editorial Team meets monthly to discuss revisions and to review changes that are needed, or are to be implemented in the near future. This is the way in which the editorial work attempts to meet the challenge of Neelameghan's statement on p.201 of his paper:

"The rate and mode of development of the universe of subjects further shows that the obsolescence rate of schemes for classification will increase in future". How true this has proved to be.

2.6 Notation

Ranganathan stated in the *Prolegomena* (p. 414) that the UDC was both verbose and not suitable for chain indexing. (Ranganathan, 1957). The reduction of its size from the so-called "full edition" to the more manageable Master Reference File of c.65, 000 classes has done much to remedy its verbosity. As to its suitability for chain-indexing (which is not something that seems to trouble people in the information world too much these days, unfortunately) this is a moot point. It has been argued that chain-indexing can be applied to any classification, but the less structured the scheme, the better indexer one has to be. The Aslib Cranfield Project (Cleverdon, Mills, and Keen, 1966) as long ago as the 1960s managed to use chain indexing with the UDC as one of the methods of indexing it tested.

Suitability for chain indexing superficially is closely connected with notation. A strong interest in an expressive notation is something that both classifications share. The *Colon Classification* can, in many respects, claim to possess the most expressive notation of any general scheme, since it is absolutely clear from the notation what type of concept or facet is denoted by any set of symbols. But the only problem is that the resultant notation is also extremely complex, and it is essential to remember the signification of each connecting symbol, be it a punctuation mark or a '&' followed by a lower case letter. The same criticism can also be levelled at the UDC. It, too, has a notation that is both very expressive and very complex. It relies on both the use of punctuation marks and on mathematical symbols, such as inverted commas, colons, curved brackets and the equals sign to signify the meaning of a digit. It is totally clear what each part of a class mark means, provided the user can memorize all these symbols, and therein lies the problem – it requires practice and familiarity and a measure of application which the average user is not prepared to invest. It is much easier just to search on words.

The UDC relies on its decimal notation to represent subordination. Ranganathan rightly points out that this practice is not consistently applied throughout the classification. This is a situation that efforts are currently being made to remedy. A notation that expresses subordination went out of fashion in the 1960s, following the publication of Jack Mills masterly exposition of classification theory in which he categorically states on pp.37-38 that the vital function of notation "is to mechanically maintain the sequence of subjects by giving each term a symbol possessing an agreed ordinal value… A theoretical function which is often assumed but whose value is now increasingly doubted is to reflect the subordination and co-ordination of the subjects symbolized". (Mills, 1960). This last doubt nowadays is no longer the case. In a networked world there are considered to be great advantages to be derived from a notation that expresses co-ordination and subordination because it greatly facilitates machine searching and enables the user to search up and down hierarchies. The UDC has always used a decimal notation and has always attempted to reflect the structure of knowledge in the notation. It has not always succeeded in doing this consistently, and many instances could be cited where this aim fails. The goal at the present time, however, is to ensure that hierarchies are clearly reflected in the notation, and one of the places where this can clearly be seen is in the more recently revised sections of the Area Table, e.g.:

(73) United States of America (USA)

...

(734) States of the north-eastern USA

...

(734.2) New Hampshire
(734.211.2) Coos County
(734.211.4) Grafton County
(734.211.6) Carroll County
(734.211.8) Strafford County
(734.213.1) Belknap County
(734.213.3) Merrimack County. Including: Concord (state capital)
(734.213.5) Sullivan County
(734.213.7) Cheshire County
(734.215.2) Hillsboro County. Including: Manchester
(734.215.4) Rockingham County. Including: Portsmouth

This example from the schedules also exemplifies clearly the UDC's response to coping with a situation where there are more than nine topics in an array. Ranganathan used the Sectorizing Device, and 9 becomes simply a repeater which is meaningless in any other sense. The UDC uses a centesimal notation, thereby expanding the available notational base from 1/9 to 11/99.

3 COMPARISON OF UDC AND CC

In his paper, Neelameghan undertakes a valuable comparison of the *Colon Classification* and the *Universal* Decimal *Classification*. He looks at the separation of planes of work into Idea, Verbal and Notational. While CC is successful on all three counts the UDC is seen to fail and especially is inhibited by its notation. This criticism to some extent remains valid, though great efforts are being put into rectifying the situation at the present time. He then compares the handling of compounds in a consistent manner and, again, the UDC is seen to fail in not clearly distinguishing facets and phase relations. This is an area where more recent revisions have improved the situation greatly, as has already been noted, especially in the provision of notation for specific types of phase relations in the most recently added Table of Common subdivisions of relations, processes and operations – Table 1k-04. The next failing to be identified in UDC compared with the *Colon Classification* is that the sequence of facets in compound subjects is not consistent across the whole of knowledge, i.e. when the same set of concepts appears in different contexts, the sequence is not always consistent. This is a valid criticism, but is now only partially true. Much effort has been expended on work to eliminate the listing of compound terms in recent years. One example is in class 72- Architecture, where building types were all listed as compound subjects. This is no longer the case, and now the colon is used to express a building for a particular purpose, linked to the notation for the subject to which it belongs, e.g. Libraries in 02, Schools and universities in 37, hospitals in 61, theatres and cinemas in 79, and so on. Similarly, in the past the special auxiliary at the head of class 7 listed many materials applied in the fine arts, irrespective of the fact that there is a Table of common auxiliaries of materials, Table 1k-03 where the same materials were listed with different notations. This has now been revised and the section removed from the Fine Arts Class.

Another problem identified in Neelameghan's paper is the facility in UDC for alternative locations, which he feels destroys the uniqueness of the class number for a subject. This does not happen in CC and it should no longer happen with the UDC where there is now a recommended citation order. Individual institutions, however, especially Special Libraries which use the scheme for shelf arrangement or the filing of off-prints have historically given their own interests precedence, and this can easily be facilitated by the reversal of numbers joined by the colon. It is no longer the recommended practice, and it makes the scheme impossible for use by co-operatives which generate classification numbers, if the rules are not adhered to. Nevertheless, individual institutions have always adopted unique practices and will doubtless continue to do so. It is only a problem for shelf arrangement. In an online situation, the UDC is so structured that it is possible to search on each element of a class mark individually, and consequently the order in which the separate elements are combined only has significance when the classification is used for filing, not when it is used for retrieval.

Extrapolation and Interpolation in Array were both found satisfactory; the use of the centesimal notation noted above, and the ability to interpolate notations which are clearly delineated at the beginning and end, normally through the use of brackets or inverted commas, are practices that the UDC maintains. Extrapolation in chain is achieved in both classifications through the use of the decimal fraction principle and hospitality between facets is also provided for by both. The final failing of the UDC that is noted by Neelameghan is the expressiveness of the class number, which only happened for place and time in 1971. This is no longer the case, and there is now far greater notational expressiveness, as the more recent revisions discussed demonstrate.

Although Neelameghan found that there was considerable incompatibility between the two classifications on the theoretical level, in an actual study of the two schemes through the series of actual examples which his paper provides, he found that in practice it was possible to construct class numbers according to the general theory of classification. He also recommends the use of the then current *Guide to the UDC* written by Jack Mills, which continues to be a valuable source for principles relating to the application of the scheme, though now very outdated in actual detail (*Guide*, 1963).

4 CONCLUSION

Neelameghan has strong words to say about the UDC. He claims that it is not based on a comprehensive and deeply founded theory, nor is it supported by explicit statements of normative principles and consequently it lacks internal dynamism. The past decade has seen considerable effort to rectify the situation. In 1989 when the Task Force for UDC System Development was set up by FID the expectation, both of FID and of the Task Force members, was that it would recommend that the UDC should cease to exist. Instead, a worldwide survey was undertaken via personal consultations and quite the reverse eventuated (FID, 1991). Much enthusiasm was expressed for the scheme, and hence the formation of the Consortium. In the past ten years much has been done to address some of the criticisms that were levelled at it a generation ago.

REFERENCES

1. Broughton, Vanda (2002). A new classification for the literature of religion. *International cataloguing and bibliographic control.* Vol. 29 (4); p. 59-61.
2. Cleverdon, Cyril; Mills, Jack and Keen, Mike. (1966). *Aslib-Cranfield research project: factors determining the performance of indexing systems.* London: Aslib.
3. *Dewey Decimal Classification and* relative *index.* (2003). Edition 22. Dublin, OH: OCLC. Extensions and corrections to the UDC. (2003). No. 25.
4. FID. (1981) *Principles of the Universal Decimal Classification and rules for its revision and publication. (FID 598).* The Hague: FID. Revised ed. 1985.
5. —. (1991) *Management Board.* Task Force on UDC System Development. Report of the Task Force on UDC System Development. (Chair: I.C. McIlwaine). The Hague: FID. Unpublished report.
6. Freeman, R. and Atherton, P. (1969). *Final report of the research project for the evaluation of the Universal Decimal Classification as the indexing language for a mechanized retrieval system.* American Institute of Physics UDC Project Rep. No. AIP/UDC -9). New York: American Institute of Physics.
7. *Guide to the Universal Decimal Classification (UDC)* (1963). (BS1000C:1963). London: British Standards Institution.
8. McIlwaine, I.C. (1993). *A guide to the use of the UDC. (FID 703).* The Hague: FID. 2nd ed. pub. 1995.
9. —. (2000). *The Universal Decimal Classification: a guide to its use.* The Hague: UDCC.
10. —. and Williamson, Nancy J. (2003). *Class 61 – Medicine: restructuring progress in 2003.* Extensions and corrections to the UDC No. 25. p. 47-65.
11. *Manuel du Répertoire Bibliographique Universel.* (1907). Brussels: IIB.
12. Mills. J. (1960). *A modern outline of library classification.* London: Chapman & Hall.
13. Neelameghan, A. (1972). *A theoretical foundation for UDC: its need and formulation.* Pp. 184-234 in UDC in relation to other indexing languages. Belgrade: Yugoslav Center for Technical and Scientific Documentation.
14. Perrault, J.M. (1969). *Towards a theory for UDC.* London: Bingley
15. Ranganathan, S.R. (1957) *Prolegomena to library classification.* (2nd ed.) London: Library Association.

16. Rigby, Malcolm (1981). *Automation and the UDC 1948-80 (2nd ed.) (FID565).* The Hague: FID.

17. *UDC in relation to other indexing languages: proceedings of the international symposium*, Herceg Novi, Yugoslavia, June 28-July 1st 1971. (1972) Belgrade: Yugoslav Center for Technical and Scientific Documentation.

18. UDCC. (1993). *Guidelines for the creation of a standard version of the UDC.* The Hague: UDCC. Typescript. Revised ed. 2004.

CONTROLLED VOCABULARIES AS A SPHERE OF INFLUENCE

Anita S. Coleman
Paul Bracke

This study presents the results of a citation study of GeoRef *articles with descriptors that represent the concept of "controlled vocabularies" a specialized area of study within Library and Information Science to understand the use of this concept in Geographic Information Science (GIS) and distinguish information science concepts from information technology. Papers with pre-selected descriptors that represented the concept of "controlled vocabularies" from* GeoRef *were selected for a citation study that used bibliographic coupling and content analysis of the article titles and abstracts to draw clusters and understand the influence of the concept of controlled vocabularies in a geo-science discipline. The results from this analysis provide one perspective of the LIS sub-domain of "controlled vocabularies" as represented in* GeoRef *and used in the context of GIS research and scholarship. Findings are used to suggest future research directions to address issues related to better understanding of the concept of "controlled vocabularies" and the provision of knowledge organization tools that will promote interdisciplinary understanding. The creation of special, more-finely grained in-depth classifications and thesauri for the concept itself, namely, "controlled vocabulary" is recommended.*

1 CONTROLLED VOCABULARIES AS A SPHERE OF INFLUENCE

This paper describes an exploratory study that examined the existence of the Information Science concept of Controlled Vocabularies in Geographic Information Science (GIS). This study is part of a larger domain analysis that is mapping the scholarly output, in Geographic Information Science from 1980 onwards, with the specific goals of distinguishing Information Science (IS) concepts from those of Information Technology (IT).

2 THE IMPORTANCE OF CONTROLLED VOCABULARIES

The NISO Z39.19 standard for the construction and maintenance of monolingual thesauri defines a thesaurus as a "controlled vocabulary of terms in natural language that are designed for post-coordination. The need to control the formation and use of terms in information retrieval systems stems mainly from two basic features of natural language, namely synonyms (different terms representing the same concept) and polysemes or homographs (terms with the same spelling representing different concepts). A controlled vocabulary is established by information specialists or lexicographers and is generally employed in indexing". (NISO, 1993) The purpose of a controlled vocabulary is thus to improve information retrieval in systems of organization. Buckland (1999) argues for the centrality of "vocabulary" in LIS. "Vocabulary" he notes, "commonly refers to the stylized adaptation of natural language to form indexes and thesauri. Much of bibliographic access, filtering, and information retrieval can be viewed as matching or translating across vocabularies. Multiple vocabularies are simultaneously present. A simple query in an online catalogue normally involves at least five distinct vocabularies: those of the authors; the cataloger; the syndetic structure; the searcher; and the formulated query". Buckland is thus extending the concept of "vocabulary" to include "the range (or repertoire) of values in any field of bibliographic description and, in a more extended sense, the range of types in a set at any level (word, field, collection, and library)". Buckland also suggest that vocabularies are central features of digital libraries.

Controlled vocabularies are thus both an IS and IT-related concept. As digital libraries have developed, the concept of controlled vocabularies and enabling true semantic interoperability and facilitating meaning across different disciplines has become increasingly important as we try to build the semantic web: "an extension of the current web in which information is given well-defined meaning, better enabling computers and people to work in cooperation". (Berners-Lee, et al., 2001) Investigating the notion of controlled vocabularies in other disciplines is thus timely. As Neelameghan (1972) has eloquently suggested, the universe of knowledge is a "turbulently dynamic continuum" with fragmentation and hybridization of disciplines frequently occurring and the study of other disciplines will help enhance our own understanding of Library Science and it's merger with Documentation or Information Science.

Domain analysis studies include citation analysis and bibliometrics (Hjorland, 2002); it has been used to document *specializations* and *modes of disciplinary growth* (Ellis et al, 1999; Hurt, 1983; White and McCain, 1998), and includes:

- Identification - for example, what is the intellectual structure of a discipline like Accounting (Bricker, 1991);
- Fragmentation among disciplines such as Management Information Science (Culnan, 1986, 1987; Teng and Galleta, 1991);
- Fusion in Medical Informatics (Morris and McCain, 1998) and;
- Specialization to identify the emerging directions and existing coherent structures of research specialties.

Citation analysis has also been used to visualize interdisciplinary fields but studies have typically not sought to isolate Information Science from Information Technology related concepts and problems. Such a distinction is of interest because IS and IT are multi-disciplinary and share many research interests and yet there is little cross citation of their literatures. Also, IS-IT is often used as a tool in other disciplines. We are curious in understanding if the role of citation networks in disciplinary growth can provide clues as to when a new IS-IT intensive discipline becomes a science and is no longer just a research method or a tool. We also wished to use citation analysis data in conjunction with content analysis data to improve the nature of our findings and to investigate the potential, problems and strengths of these methods for helping distinguish between types of concepts that can help in mapping disciplinary structures and pinpointing their growth and status.

2.1 Research Questions

- How is the concept of controlled vocabularies described in GIS literature?
- What are the relationships between articles in GIS discussing controlled vocabularies?

2.2 IS-IT Concepts as an Assumption for this Research

Anecdotal evidence suggests that basic IT concepts include components of the computer, storage, memory, processing, input, output, hardware, software, multimedia, applications, operating systems, security, ethics, and networking. Similarly, IS concepts include, human information processing, organization, storage, retrieval, and use of information, especially recorded information. In the Dewey Decimal Classification system, Table 1, the Standard Subdivisions table outlines the many Library and Information Science and Computer Science concepts that may be combined with any topic (WebDewey, 2002). Our first step in this research was to identify how a thesaurus and a classification scheme in these disciplines may show disciplinary structures. We examined the ASIS Thesaurus for Information Science (Milstead, 1998) as well as the Dewey Decimal Classification scheme for the phrase Controlled Vocabularies and made a list of the related and narrower classes, terms and phrases and came up categories of IS terms. We also briefly examined the ACM Classification for categories of IT terms for related concepts and terms (ACM Classification, 1998).

2.3 Methods Used

2.3.1 Identifying Concept Terms

We qualitatively examined both the recommended core curriculum for GIS by the NCGIA (NCGIA, 2000) and *GeoRef thesaurus* (Goodman, 2000) to identify the terms and phrases used to represent Controlled Vocabularies in these documents. *GeoRef* does not use the phrase Geographic Information Science (it uses "geographic information systems") while the *NCGIA Core Curriculum* emphasizes the discipline as Geographic Information Science and use of Geographic Information Systems as methods. Our final list of selected terms were the indexing descriptors used in *GeoRef* and these include terms such as: *nomenclature, classification, digital data*, and *spatial data*. *Nomenclature* and *classification* are clearly and closely related to the IS controlled vocabulary concept. Nomenclature covers naming conventions, and classification deals with placing entities into a normalized naming scheme based on their characteristics. Digital data and spatial data deal with issues of data standardization that allow for data retrieval and use in the GIS context.

2.3.2 Identifying Articles Dealing with these Concepts

The selected descriptors for controlled vocabularies were searched in *GeoRef* both separately and in conjunction with the term "geographic information systems". Retrieval of relevant articles was limited to English language publications and resulted in approximately 500 citations. From the resulting sets, non-journal articles (for example, books) and articles in journal titles that were not indexed in ISI's *Social Science Citation Index* or *Science Citation Index* were omitted (Web of Science, 2000) leaving us with a total of 62 citations. These limits were done for two reasons: one, to make the set size manageable and two, to limit the articles to high quality research. Selecting articles that were representative of high quality GIS research was important so that they would be representative of high quality research in the discipline. We could not pursue an original idea we had of limiting our analysis to a core set of GIS journals from ISI's *Journal Citation Reports* because coverage of these journals in *GeoRef* was highly selective.

2.4 Analysis and Results

Our test set included 62 articles and these are listed in Appendix A. Of the 62 articles, 3 contained no citations. Additionally, 19 articles contained unique citations and were not coupled with other documents in the set. The remaining 40 articles formed a network of bibliographic couplings. Articles that were cited multiple times, and thus were used to establish couplings are listed in Appendix B. A list of couplings is presented in Appendix C.

Bibliographic coupling and co-citation analysis are citation methods that can be used to identify subject relationships in articles. Figures 1 and 2 show the difference between bibliographic couplings and co-citations. In Figure 1, articles A and B are bibliographically coupled in article C. In Figure 2, we see that article F cites articles D and E.

Bibliographic coupling is a static method that establishes a relationship between articles through the presence of citations to the same articles in their bibliographies. As seen in Figure 1, if articles A and B both cite C, A and B are bibliographically coupled. This linking is based on intrinsic, immutable (in a print environment, at least) characteristics of an article – the references contained in its bibliography. Although there are exceptions, the coupling often indicates a subject relationship.

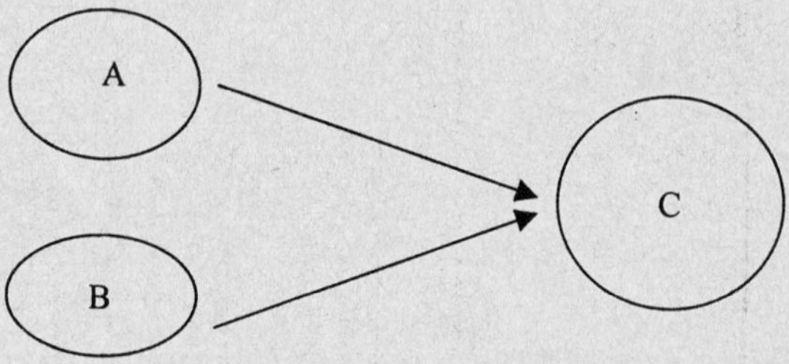

Figure 1: Bibliographic Coupling

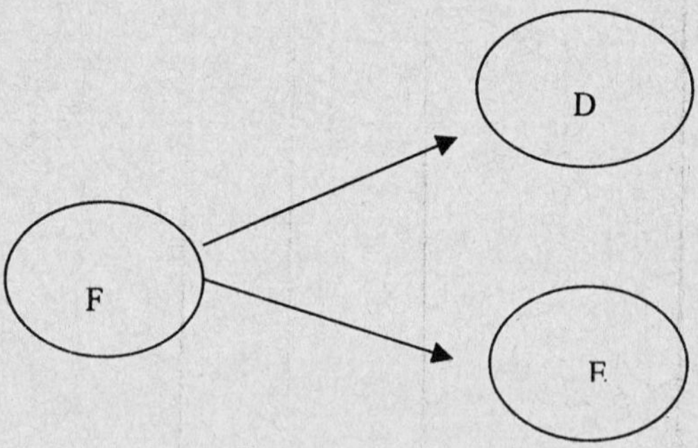

Figure 2: Co-citations

In co-citation analysis, articles become linked when they are both cited in another article. As seen in Figure 2, if articles D and E are both cited by article F, articles D and E are co-cited. This clustering is based on extrinsic characteristics, and patterns may change over time as an article gains or loses favor in a discipline, or as disciplinary lines shift. As with bibliographic coupling, co-citation analysis often indicates a subject relationship

The bibliographic couplings matrix was analyzed using MVSP 3.1. (MVSP 2002) to demonstrate statistical similarities amongst articles. The UPGMA method, Percent Similarity was used to generate the dendogram and draw the graph of bibliographic couplings. In addition to statistical cluster analysis, content analysis to overcome the limitations of citation analysis was also done. Placing titles and abstracts into categories defined, prior to analysis provides an alternative method to the bibliographic clustering analysis; the rules for content analysis are shown in Table 1. We also drew a map comparing the two clusters.

Table 1: Content Analysis Rules

Rule	Terms present	Category	Articles
1	"map*" or "cartography"	CARTOGRAPHY	J,Y,Z,AS,AZ,BJ
2.	"classification" or "classes" or "codification"	CLASSIFICATION	I,U,AB,AC,AG,BB,BE
3.	("information system" but not "GIS") or "database" of "virtual memory"	INFORMATION SYSTEM	F,L,M
4	"GIS" or "geographic* information system*" or "SDSS"	GIS AS METHOD	N,AA,AD,AE,AI,AL,AO,AT,AU,AW,AY,BC,BD,BO
5	"analysis" or "stat*"	STATISTICAL ANALYSIS	A,T
6.	"model*"	MODELING	H,R,S,V,X,AF,AH,AJ,AK,AM, AV,AX, BK,BP
7.	Name of Specific Software or "software"	SOFTWARE	C,E,G,AN,BL
8	Anything else	GEOSCIENCE	B,D,K,O,P,Q,W,AP,AQ,AR,BI, BM,BN

Five (5) clusters were generated through statistical analysis and the content analysis cluster generated eight (8) clusters. The statistical clusters related exclusively to subject-related clusters of GIS as method, model, and cartography (Table 2). There were no relationships between a statistical cluster and what we had defined as a purely IS-IT cluster (classification, software, system) with overlap of greater than 1 and the only instance of overlap with one article turned out to be with software and not classification. Articles that fell into IS-IT clusters based on title and abstract words did not correspond to the statistical clusters, indicating little or no commonality with bibliographic couplings. Table 2 shows the statistical and content analysis clusters and we briefly explain the content analysis rules used to derive these clusters.

Table 2: Statistical clusters with strongly correlating content analysis clusters

STATISTICAL CLUSTERS	CORRELATING CONTENT ANALYSIS CLUSTERS
CLUSTER 1 C,F,H,X,AG,AH,AI,AL, BI,BO	GIS AS METHOD MODEL N,AA,AD,AE,AI,AL, AO,AT,AU,AW,AY,BC,BD,BO
CLUSTER 2 J,P,AJ,AK,AU,BP	CARTOGRAPHY J,Y,Z,AS,AZ,BJ
CLUSTER 3 Q,R,V,W,AE,AV,AZ,BJ	MODEL H,R,S,V,X,AF,AH,AJ,AK,AM,AV,AX, BK,BP
CLUSTER 4 K,T,AD,AM,AN,AO,AS,AT,AY,BF,BN	GIS AS METHOD N,AA,AD,AE,AI,AL,AO,AT, AU,AW,AY,BC,BD,BO
CLUSTER 5 O,U,Y,AA,AF,AW,BD	GIS AS METHOD N,AA,AD,AE,AI,AL,AO,AT, AU,AW,AY,BC,BD,BO

"GIS as Method" was a category that only required the presence of GIS or geographic(al) information system. The phrase "as method" was added to the category name to indicate that the term almost always appeared in contexts that indicated its use as a research method. In addition, Geoscience "catch-all" category was used for titles that did not seem to form any patterns or natural groupings. Additionally, "Information System" and "Software" could easily be combined into a single category without losing much meaning. Data was not included as a rule in the content analysis because of the varieties of contexts in which it appeared. There were several references, for example, to data sets, but they were usually the object of another process. The term data was also used in the context of data structures, data processing and data handling. Although this limited the analysis of controlled vocabulary concepts in GIS, spatial data and digital data were not as core to the concept of controlled vocabulary as classification, a term that was used as a term for grouping in content analysis. More work is needed on the exact meaningful use of specific terms such as classes, ontologies, taxonomies, and arrays in the context of GIS data.

The two analyses of the sets of documents (statistical and content) thus present two different views of the documents. Controlled vocabularies seem to be well integrated with GIS-research when it is necessary in the examination of another topic but their sphere of influence in GIS based on our findings appears to be controversial and limited. Indeed Wright et al.'s argument about the "ambiguity" of GIS as science or tool is reflected in these clusters (Wright et al, 1997). Replicating the study with a larger document set for validation is necessary before other conclusions can be made.

We also find that the subject of 'controlled vocabularies" is represented very poorly and at a most superficial level in Library and Information Science thesauri and classification schemes. Interestingly, descriptive and subject cataloging along with authority control of names and titles and vocabulary control of subjects is a widespread and standard technique used to organize information resources in libraries. It is a technique that is increasingly gaining in popularity in the world of digital libraries and with the use of metadata and the advent of the semantic web. The web world, however, is chaotic and naïve in the use of many of terms and processes related to controlled vocabulary: consider for example, that large scale projects in the United States such as the NSDL (2005) or DLESE (2005) both of which use flat, short lists of terms and call them a controlled vocabulary use this phrase in the most narrow sense. The small vocabularies (lists of controlled values is a better way to describe them) have few relationships of limited hierarchies; they in no way represent the richness and depth that a true controlled vocabulary that a thesaurus potentially offers. A distinction must be made between simple and complex vocabularies, such as thesauri and ontologies, which have varying types of relationships between terms and can number in the thousands for even a small concept.

A controlled vocabulary, as any LIS professional knows, includes a range of knowledge organization tools. Both of these, a list of equivalent terms in the form of a synonym ring or a list of controlled or preferred terms in the form of Authority Files can be called a controlled vocabulary. Additionally, a range of methods can be used to build the controlled vocabulary. For example, faceted classification structuring may be used in a thesaurus, which is another form of a controlled vocabulary, making it a faceted thesaurus. Two modern faceted thesauri are the Art & Architecture Thesaurus (A&AT) (http://www.getty.edu/research/....., 2005), and Medical Subject Headings (MeSH). MeSh is part of the Unified Medical Language System (UMLS, 2005), referred to as an ontology. Figure 3 graphically shows how controlled vocabularies should be placed on a continuum of simple to complex.

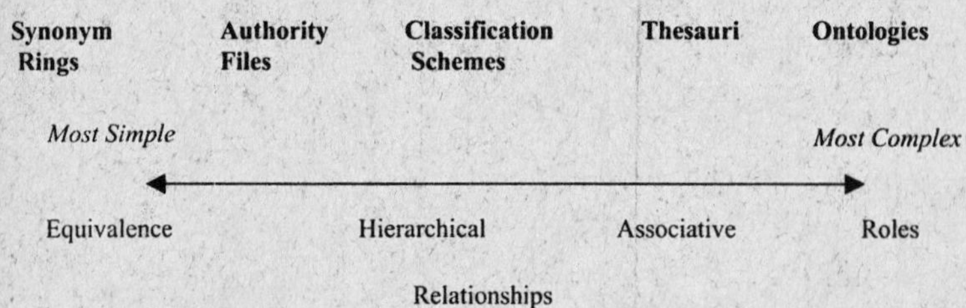

Figure 3: Types of controlled vocabularies

Simple vocabularies such as preferred lists of terms have long been proved to be clearly insufficient for efficient information retrieval. The do not represent the range of relationships among terms and phrases. The new NISO Z39.19 standard just released (2004) tries to help increase understanding about the concept of a "controlled vocabulary" and the creation of a true end-user thesaurus (Bates, 1986). If controlled vocabularies are to become a major sphere of influence that LIS exerts on other disciplines, and for LIS professionals to continue to be accepted as the experts in this area by new entrants into the field such as ontologists, taxonomists, knowledge managers, and information architects, we need to do two things: 1) an in-depth and finer-grained controlled vocabulary of the concept of "controlled vocabularies" itself with definitions of terms and their scope and context of all relationships (in particular the equivalence relationships of synonyms and using qualifies and polyhierarchies), and the many disciplines that are now engaged in this area must be created. This could be represented as a classification scheme or a thesaurus but adapted from currently existing ones; and 2) The newly developed controlled vocabulary should be used to replicate the study reported herein in order to examine our sphere of influence – both to see how this important topic has infiltrated other disciplines and how it is being used in others disciplines. Using machine classification methods on the full-text of the articles may also yield a different picture of the influence of this important concept on IT and specific disciplines.

REFERENCES

1. A&AT. *Art & Architecture Thesaurus Online.* (2005). Retrieved 15 March 2005 from http://www.getty.edu/research/conducting_research/vocabularies/aat/
2. ACM *Classification. (1998).* Top Two Levels of the ACM Computing Classification System. Retrieved 15 March 2005 from http://www.acm.org/class/1998/overview.html
3. Bates, Marcia. (1986). Subject access in online catalogs. *Journal of the American Society for Information Science.* Vol. 37(6); p. 357-376.
4. Berners-Lee, Timothy; Hendler, James; and Lassila, Ora. (2001). The Semantic Web. *Scientific American*, May.
5. Bricker, Robert. (1991). Deriving disciplinary structures: Some new methods, models, and an illustration with accounting. *Journal of the American Society for Information Science.* Vol. 42(1); p. 27-35.
6. Buckland, Michael. (1999). Vocabulary as a central concept in library and information science. **In** Arpanac, T. et al. (Eds.), *Digital libraries: Interdisciplinary concepts, challenges, and opportunities. Proceedings of the Third International Conference on Conceptions of Library and Information Science* [CoLIS3], May 23-26, 1999, Dubrovnik, Croatia, p. 3-12. Zagreb: Lokve. Retrieved March 15, 2005, from http://www.sims.berkeley.edu/~buckland/colisvoc.htm
7. Culnan, M. (1986) The intellectual structure of management information systems, 1972-1982: a co-citation analysis. *Management Science.* Vol. 32(2); p. 156-172.
8. —. (1987) Mapping the intellectual structure of MIS, 1980-1985: a co-citation analysis. *MIS Quarterly.* Vol. 11(3); p. 341-353.
9. DLESE. *Digital Library for Earth System Education.* Retrieved March 15, 2005 from http://ww.dlese.org/

10. Ellis, D.; David, A. and Wilson, T. (1999) Information Science and Information Systems: Conjunct subjects disjunct disciplines. *Journal of the American Society for Information Science.* Vol. 50(12); p. 1095-1107.
11. Goodman, Barbara, Editor. (2000). *GeoRef Thesaurus.* 9th edition. AGI.
12. Hjorland, Birger. (2002). Domain analysis in Information Science: Eleven approaches – traditional as well as innovative. *Journal of Documentation.* Vol. 58(4); p. 422-462.
13. Hurt, C.D. (1983). A comparison of a bibliometric approach and an historical approach to the identification of important literature. *Information Processing and Management.* Vol. 19; p. 151-157.
14. MeSH. *Medical Subject Headings Home Page.* Retrieved 15 March 2005 from http://www.nlm.nih.gov/mesh/
15. Milstead, Jessica L. Editor. (1998). *ASIS Thesaurus of Information Science and Librarianship.* 2nd edition. Medford, N.J.: Information Today.
16. Morris, Thodore A., and McCain, Katherine W. (1998). The Structure of Medical Informatics. *Journal of the American Medical Informatics Association.* Vol. 5; p. 448 – 466.
17. MVSP (2002). *Multi-Variate Statistical Package.* Retrieved 15 March 2005 from http://www.kovcomp.co.uk/mvsp/
18. NCGIA. (2000). *NCGIA Core Curriculum in GIScience.* Retrieved March 15, 2005 from http://www.ncgia.ucsb.edu/education/curricula/giscc/
19. Neelameghan, A. (1972). Systems approach in the study of the attributes of the universe of subjects. *Library Science with a Slant to Documentation.* Vol. 9(4); p. 445-472.
20. NSDL. *National Science Digital Library.* Retrieved March 15, 2005 from http://nsdl.org/
21. Teng, James, and Galleta, Daniel. (1991). *MIS Research Directions: A Survey of Researcher's Views.* Database.
22. UMLS. (2005). *Unified Medical Language System.* Retrieved 15 March 2005 from http://www.nlm.nih.gov/research/umls/umlsmain.html
23. *Web of Science.* (2000). Retrieved with subscription March 15, 2005 from http://www.isiknowledge. com/
24. WebDewey. (2002). *Dewey Decimal Classification.* 21st edition. Dublin, OH: OCLC. Retrieved with subscription March 15, 2005 from http://connexion.oclc.org/
25. White, H.D. and McCain, K.W. (1998). Visualizing a discipline: An author co-citation analysis of Information Science, 1972-1995. *Journal of the American Society for Information Science.* Vol. 49(4); p. 327-355.
26. Wright, D.J.; Goodchild, M.F. and Proctor, J.D. (1997). Demystifying the persistent ambiguity of GIS as "tool" versus "science". *Annals of the Association of American Geographers.* Vol. 87(2); p. 346-362.

APPENDIX A

Document Set Used in Study

A	Bourgault, G, A G Journel, J D Rhoades, D L Corwin, and S M Lesch. "Geostatistical Analysis of a Soil Salinity Data Set". Advances in Agronomy 58 (1997): 241-92.
B	Steel, Kevin, and Bette L Beswick. "Getting the Big Picture". Canadian Mining Journal 118, no. 1 (1997): 6-7.
C	Bivand, Roger S. "Using the R Statistical Data Analysis Language on Grass 5.0 Gis Database Files". Computers and Geosciences 26, no. 9-10 (2000): 1043-52.
D	Dong, Pinliang. "Implementation of Mathematical Morphological Operations for Spatial Data Processing". Computers and Geosciences 23, no. 1 (1997): 103-07.
E	Knox, Robinson Carl M, and Stephen J Gardoll. "Gis-Stereoplot; an Interactive Stereonet Plotting Module for Arcview 3.0 Geographic Information System". Computers and Geosciences 24, no. 3 (1998): 243-50.
F	McCormack, J E, and J Hogg. "Virtual-Memory Tiling for Spatial Data Handling in Gis". Computers and Geosciences 23, no. 6 (1997): 659-69
G	Wulder, M A. "The Prediction of Leaf Area Index from Forest Polygons Decomposed through the Integration of Remote Sensing, Gis, Unix, and C". Computers and Geosciences 24, no. 2 (1998): 151-57.
H	Townsend, Philip A, and Stephen J Walsh. "Estimation of Soil Parameters for Assessing Potential Wetness; Comparison of Model Responses through Gis". Earth Surface Processes and Landforms 21, no. 4 (1996): 307-26.
I	Host, George E, Philip L Polzer, David J Mladenoff, Mark A White, and Thomas R Crow. "A Quantitative Approach to Developing Regional Ecosystem Classifications". Ecological Applications 6, no. 2 (1996): 608-18.
J	Lathrop, Richard G, Jr., John D Aber, and John A Bognar. "Spatial Variability of Digital Soil Maps and Its Impact on Regional Ecosystem Modeling". Ecological Modelling 82, no. 1 (1995): 1-10.
K	Nathanail, C P, and M S Rosenbaum. "Spatial Management of Geotechnical Data for Site Selection". Engineering Geology 50, no. 3-4 (1998): 347-56.
L	Cook, Jerome S, Michael P Fahy, and Frank Tian. "Profile in Gis; Construction of Water Rights Database at El Paso Water Utilities". Environmental and Engineering Geoscience 3, no. 4 (1997): 588-94.
M	Bartsch, H U, J Kues, J Sbresny, and J Schneider. "Soil Information System as Part of a Municipal Environmental Information System". Environmental Geology 30, no. 3-4 (1997): 189-97.
N	Doerfliger, N, P Y Jeannin, and F Zwahlen. "Water Vulnerability Assessment in Karst Environments; a New Method of Defining Protection Areas Using a Multi-Attribute Approach and Gis Tools (Epik Method)". Environmental Geology 39, no. 2 (1999): 165-76.

O	Nogues, J, J Herrero, Ochoa R Rodriguez, and J Boixadera. "Land Evaluation in a Salt-Affected Irrigated District Using an Index of Productive Potential". Environmental Management (New York) 25, no. 2 (2000): 143-52.
P	Turner, Graham W, Rod M C Ruffio, and Mark W Roberts. "Comparing Environmental Conditions Using Indicators of Pollution Hazard". Environmental Management (New York) 21, no. 4 (1997): 623-34.
Q	Zhang, Minghua, Shu Geng, Susan L Ustin, and Kenneth K Tanji. "Pesticide Occurrence in Groundwater in Tulare County, California". Environmental Monitoring and Assessment 45, no. 2 (1997): 101-27.
R	Corwin, Dennis L, Peter J Vaughan, and Keith Loague. "Modeling Nonpoint Source Pollutants in the Vadose Zone with Gis". Environmental Science and Technology, ES and T 31, no. 8 (1997): 2157-75.
S	Tsanis, I K, C Valeo, J Wu, and S Boyle. "Managing Contaminated Sediments Using a Hydrodynamic Model and a Gis". Environmental Technology 17, no. 8 (1996): 877-83.
T	Dolan, David M, Shaarawi Abdel H El, and Trefor B Reynoldson. "Predicting Benthic Counts in Lake Huron Using Spatial Statistics and Quasi-Likelihood". Environmetrics 11, no. 3 (2000): 287-304.
U	Lark., R M, and P H T Beckett. "A Regular Pattern in the Relative Areas of Soil Profile Classes and Possible Applications in Reconnaissance Soil Survey". Geoderma 68, no. 1-2 (1995): 27-37.
V	Tim, U S, D Jain, and H H Liao. "Interactive Modeling of Ground-Water Vulnerability within a Geographic Information System". Ground Water 34, no. 4 (1996): 618-27.
W	Shukla, Sanjay, Saied Mostaghimi, Vernon O Shanholt, Michael C Collins, and Burton B Ross. "A County-Level Assessment of Ground Water Contamination by Pesticides". Ground Water Monitoring and Remediation 20, no. 1 (2000): 104-19.
X	Endreny, T A, E F Wood, and D P Lettenmaier. "Satellite-Derived Digital Elevation Model Accuracy; Hydrological Modelling Requirements". Hydrological Processes 14, no. 2 (2000): 177-94.
Y	Zakir, F A, M H T Qari, and M E Mostafa. "A New Optimizing Technique for Preparing Lineament Density Maps". International Journal of Remote Sensing 20, no. 6 (1999): 1073-85.
Z	Wood, William B. "A Jeffersonian Vision for Mapping the World". Issues in Science and Technology 14, no. 1 (1997): 81-86.
AA	Navas, A, and J Machin. "Assessing Erosion Risks in the Gypsiferous Steppe of Litigio (Ne Spain); an Approach Using Gis". Journal of Arid Environments 37, no. 3 (1997): 433-41.
AB	Barnhardt, Walter A, Joseph T Kelley, Stephen M Dickson, and Daniel F Belknap. "Mapping the Gulf of Maine with Side-Scan Sonar; a New Bottom-Type Classification for Complex Seafloors". Journal of Coastal Research 14, no. 2 (1998): 646-59.
AC	Cooper, J A G, and S McLaughlin. "Contemporary Multidisciplinary Approaches to Coastal Classifi-cation and Environmental Risk Analysis". Journal of Coastal Research 14, no. 2 (1998): 512-24.

AD	Chiueh, Pei Te, Shang Lien Lo, and Chin Dee Lee. "Prototype Sdss for Using Probability Analysis in Soil Contamination". Journal of Environmental Engineering 123, no. 5 (1997): 514-19.
AE	Siddiqui, Muhammad Z, Jess W Everett, and Baxter E Vieux. "Landfill Siting Using Geographic Information Systems; a Demonstration". Journal of Environmental Engineering 122, no. 6 (1996): 515-23.
AF	Cheng, Qiuming. "Spatial and Scaling Modelling for Geochemical Anomaly Separation". Journal of Geochemical Exploration 65, no. 3 (1999): 175-94.
AG	Verdin, K L, and J P Verdinb. "A Topological System for Delineation and Codification of the Earth's River Basins". Journal of Hydrology 218, no. 1-2 (1999): 1-12.
AH	Wang, Xinhao, and Zhi Yong Yin. "A Comparison of Drainage Networks Derived from Digital Elevation Models at Two Scales". Journal of Hydrology 210, no. 1-4 (1998): 221-41.
AI	Desmet, P J J, and G Govers. "A Gis Procedure for Automatically Calculating the Usle Ls Factor on Topographicaly Complex Landscape Units". Journal of Soil and Water Conservation 51, no. 5 (1996): 427-33.
AJ	Arnold, J G, R Srinivasan, R S Muttiah, and J R Williams. "Large Area Hydrologic Modeling and Assessment; Part I, Model Development". Journal of the American Water Resources Association 34, no. 1 (1998): 73-89.
AK	Srinivasan, R, T S Ramanarayananan, J G Arnold, and S T Bednarz. "Large Area Hydrologic Modeling and Assessment; Part Ii, Model Application". Journal of the American Water Resources Association 34, no. 1 (1998): 91-101.
AL	Blaszczynski, Jacek S. "Landform Characterization with Geographic Information Systems". Photogrammetric Engineering and Remote Sensing 63, no. 2 (1997): 183-91.
AM	Chung, Chang Jo F, and Andrea G Fabbri. "Probabilistic Prediction Models for Landslide Hazard Mapping". Photogrammetric Engineering and Remote Sensing 65, no. 12 (1999): 1389-99.
AN	Varekamp, C, A K Skidmore, and P A B Burrough. "Using Public Domain Geostatistical and Gis Software for Spatial Interpolation". Photogrammetric Engineering and Remote Sensing 62, no. 7 (1996): 845-54.
AO	Whitman, Dean, Timothy Gubbels, and Linda Powell. "Spatial Interrelationships between Lake Elevations, Water Tables, and Sinkhole Occurrence in Central Florida; a Gis Approach". Photogrammetric Engineering and Remote Sensing 65, no. 10 (1999): 1169-78.
AP	Newson, M D, and C L Newson. "Geomorphology, Ecology and River Channel Habitat; Mesoscale Approaches to Basin-Scale Challenges". Progress in Physical Geography 24, no. 2 (2000): 195-217.

AQ	Duncan, Christopher C, Andrew J Klein, Jeffrey G Masek, and Bryan L Isacks. "Comparison of Late Pleistocene and Modern Glacier Extents in Central Nepal Based on Digital Elevation Data and Satellite Imagery". Quaternary Research (New York) 49, no. 3 (1998): 241-54.
AR .	Li, Zhen, Wenxin Sun, and Qunzhu Zeng. "Measurements of Glacier Variation in the Tibetan Plateau Using Landsat Data". Remote Sensing of Environment 63, no. 3 (1998): 258-64.
AS	Frangi, J P, and D Richard. "Heavy Metal Soil Pollution Cartography in Northern France". The Science of the Total Environment 205, no. 1 (1997): 71-79.
AT	Korre, A. "Statistical and Spatial Assessment of Soil Heavy Metal Contamination in Areas of Poorly Recorded, Complex Sources of Pollution; Part 2, Canonical Correlation Analysis and Gis for the Assessment of Contamination Sources". Stochastic Environmental Research and Risk Assessment 13, no. 4 (1999): 288-316.
AU	Sharma, K D, M Menenti, J Huygen, and A Vich. "Modeling Spatial Sediment Delivery in an Arid Region Using Thematic Mapper Data and Gis". Transactions of the ASAE 39, no. 2 (1996): 551-57.
AV	Tim, U Sunday. "Emerging Technologies for Hydrologic and Water Quality Modeling Research". Transactions of the ASAE 39, no. 2 (1996): 465-76.
A W	Adamus, Christine L, and Martinus J Bergman. "Estimating Nonpoint Source Pollution Loads with a Gis Screening Model". Water Resources Bulletin 31, no. 4 (1995): 647-55.
AX	Julien, Pierre Y, Bahram Saghafian, and Fred L Ogden. "Raster-Based Hydrologic Modeling of Spatially-Varied Surface Runoff". Water Resources Bulletin 31, no. 3 (1995): 523-36.
AY	Correia, Francisco Nunes, Maria da Graca Saraiva, da Silva Fernando Nunes, and Isabel Ramos. "Flood Plain Management in Urban Developing Areas; Part Ii, Gis-Based Flood Analysis and Urban Growth Modelling". Water Resources Management 13, no. 1 (1999): 23-37.
AZ	Zhu, A Xing. "Mapping Soil Landscape as Spatial Continua; the Neural Network Approach". Water Resources Research 36, no. 3 (2000): 663-77.
BA	Adamus, Christine L, and Martinus J Bergman. "Estimating Nonpoint Source Pollution Loads with a Gis Screening Model". Water Resources Bulletin 31, no. 4 (1995): 647-55.
BB	Delong, Michael D, and Merlyn A Brusven. "Classification and Spatial Mapping of Riparian Habitat with Applications toward Management of Streams Impacted by Nonpoint Source Pollution". Environmental Management (New York) 15, no. 4 (1991): 565-71.
BC	Eash, David A. "A Geographic Information System Procedure to Quantify Drainage-Basin Characteristics". Water Resources Bulletin 30, no. 1 (1994): 1-8.
BD	Hammen, John L, and Philip J Gerla. "A Geographic Information Systems Approach to Wellhead Protection". Water Resources Bulletin 30, no. 5 (1994): 833-39.

BE	Heinzmann, Uta, and Gaby Zollinger. "Validation of Representativeness with Relief Parameters Based on the Comparison of Two Landuse Classifications". Catena (Giessen) 24, no. 1 (1995): 69-87.
BF	Julien, Pierre Y, Bahram Saghafian, and Fred L Ogden. "Raster-Based Hydrologic Modeling of Spatially-Varied Surface Runoff". Water Resources Bulletin 31, no. 3 (1995): 523-36.
BG	Lark, R M, and P H T Beckett. "A Regular Pattern in the Relative Areas of Soil Profile Classes and Possible Applications in Reconnaissance Soil Survey". Geoderma 68, no. 1-2 (1995): 27-37.
BH	Lathrop, Richard G, Jr., John D Aber, and John A Bognar. "Spatial Variability of Digital Soil Maps and Its Impact on Regional Ecosystem Modeling". Ecological Modelling 82, no. 1 (1995): 1-10.
BI	Mitchell, James E. "The Influence of (X,Y) Uncertainty on Prediction Error and Contour Lines from a Three-Dimensional Surface". Water Resources Bulletin 29, no. 5 (1993): 863-70.
BJ	Odeh, Inakwu O A, Alex B McBratney, and David J Chittleborough. "Fuzzy-C-Means and Kriging for Mapping Soil as a Continuous System". Soil Science Society of America Journal 56, no. 6 (1992): 1848-54.
BK	Orzol, Leonard L, and Timothy S McGrath. "Summary of Modifications of the U. S. Geological Survey Modular, Finite-Difference, Ground-Water Flow Model to Read and Write Geographic Information System Files". Water Resources Bulletin 29, no. 5 (1993): 843-46.
BL	Richards, Christopher J, Honesto Roaza, and Roaza Ruth Montgomery. "Integrating Geographic Information Systems and Modflow for Ground Water Resource Assessments". Water Resources Bulletin 29, no. 5 (1993): 847-53.
BM	Spaling, Harry. "Analyzing Cumulative Environmental Effects of Agricultural Land Drainage in Southern Ontario, Canada". Agriculture, Ecosystems and Environment 53, no. 3 (1994): 279-92.
BN	Stein, A, C Varekamp, Egmond C van, and Zoest R van. "Zinc Concentrations in Groundwater at Different Scales". Journal of Environmental Quality 24, no. 6 (1995): 1205-14.
BO	Tachikawa, Y, M Shiiba, and T Takasao. "Development of a Basin Geomorphic Information System Using a Tin-Dem Data Structure". Water Resources Bulletin 30, no. 1 (1994): 9-17.
BP	Tim, U S, S Mostaghimi, and V O Shanholtz. "Identification of Critical Nonpoint Pollution Source Areas Using Geographic Information Systems and Water Quality Modeling". Water Resources Bulletin 28, no. 5 (1992): 877-87.

APPENDIX B

Articles Establishing Couplings (cited by at least 2 articles)

BOGGY CREEK WATER QU 1987
CELL BASED MODELING 1992 DISTRICT WATER MANAG 1994
FL DOT55001000lA DEP 1985
NATIONAL ENG HDB 1972
PHASE I REPORT MASTE 1992
STATISTICAL ANAL SYS 1985 URBAN STORMWATER ANA 1990
*FAO FAO SOILS B 32 1976
*NAT RES COUNC GROUND WAT VULN ASS 1993
*SAS I INC SAS STAT US GUID VER 1686 1990
*USDA NAT SOIL HDB 1983
ABBOTT MB J HYDROL 87 61 1986
ABER JD ECOL MODEL 67 37 1993
ABER JD OECOLOGIA 92 463 1992
ADAMUS CL I ST JOHNS RIV WAT M AKIMA H ACM T MATH SOFTWARE 22 362 1996
ARNOLD JG J HYDROL 142 47 1993
ARNOLD RW SSSA SPEC PUBL 28 1 1991
ARONOFF S GEOGRAPHIC INFORMATI 1989
AYDIN K IN PRESS J APPL METE 34 1995
BAILEY T INTERACTIVE SPATIAL 1995
BAND LE ECOL MODEL 56 171 1991
BECKETT PHT J SOIL SCI 22 466 1971
BECKETT PHT SOIL FERTILIZERS 34 1 1971
BEVEN KJ HYDROL SCI B 24 43 1979
BLISS NB J SOIL WATER CONSERV 44 30 1989
BONHAMCARTER GF GEOGRAPHIC INFORMATI 1994
BRESLER E WATER RESOUR RES 24 381 1988
BURGESS TM J SOIL SCI 31 315 1980
BURKE IC BIOSCIENCE 41 685 1991
BURKE IC LANDSCAPE ECOL 4 45 1990
BURROUGH PA J SOIL SCI 22 368 1971
BURROUGH PA THESIS U OXFORD 1969
BURROUGH PA PRINCIPLES GEOGRAPHI 1986
BURROUGH PA J SOIL SCI 43 193 1992
BURROUGH PA J SOIL SCI 40 477 1989
BURROUGH PA SSSA SPECIAL PUBLICA 48 19 1996
BUTLER BE SOIL CLASSIFICATION 1980
CHANDRASEKAR V J APPL METEOROL 32 1288 1993
CHANDRASEKAR V J ATMOS OCEAN TECH 7 621 1990
CHOI GW WATER RESOUR RES 29 321 1993
CHOW VT APPL HYDROLOGY 1988
CHOW VT HDB APPLIED HYDROLOG 1964
CHRISMAN NR CARTOGRAPHICA 21 79 1984
CLINE TJ THESIS COLORADO STAT 1988
CLINE TJ WATER RESOUR BULL 25 641 1989
CRESSIE N ENV MODELING GIS 414 1993

CRESSIE N MATH GEOL 17 563 1985
CRESSIE NAC STAT SPATIAL DATA 1991
DELREGNO KJ LAKE RESERVOIR MANAG 4 17 1988
DEUTSCH CV 18 GSLIB GEOSTATISTICAL 340 1992
DEVANTIER BA J WATER RES PL-ASCE 119 246 1993
DICKINSON WT 25 COL STATE U HYDR 1967
DOE WW 7TH P ANN GRASS US C 91 1992
DOE WW THESIS COLORADO STAT 1992
DRAPER NR APPL REGRESSION ANAL 1981
EVANS BM J SOIL WATER CONSERV 45 242 1990
FEDRA K IAHS PUB 211 1993
FISHER PF INT J GEOGR INF SYST 5 193 1991
GERSMEHL PJ CARTOGRAPHICA 18 79 1981
GOODCHILD MF ENV MODELING GIS 1993
GOODRICH DC WATER RESOUR RES 27 995 1991
GORGUCCI E J ATMOS OCEAN TECH 11 586 1994
GUSTAFSON DI ENVIRON TOXICOL CHEM 8 339 1989
HAINING R SPATIAL DATA ANAL SO 1990
HALL FG LANDSCAPE ECOLOGY 2 3 1988
HALL GF SSSA SPEC PUBL 28 9 1991
HARLIN JM GEOGRAPHIC INFORMATI 1993
HARPER HH ESTIMATION STORMWATE 1992
HE CS WATER RESOUR BULL 29 891 1993
HESSION WC J SOIL WATER CONSERV 43 264 1988
ISAAKS EH INTRO APPL GEOSTATIS 561 1989
IZUNO FT J ENVIRON QUAL 20 608 1991
JAMES WP WATER RESOUR BULL 26 587 1990
JARVIS MG SOILS OXFORDSHIRE 1 1982
JENSON SK PHOTOGRAMM ENG REMOT 54 1593 1988
JETT SC P HYDR TRANSP S ST J 127 1979
JOHNSON BE USGS934018 WAT RES I 9 1993
JOURNEL AG MATH GEOL 18 119 1986
JOURNEL AG MINING GEOSTATISTICS 600 1978
JULIEN PY CER9091PYJBS12 COL S 1991
JURY WA VADOSE ZONE MODELING 245 1986
JURY WA J ENVIRON QUAL 12 558 1983
JURY WA J ENVIRON QUAL 16 422 1987
KELLOGG RL J SOIL WATER CONSERV 49 294 1994
KHAN MA ENVIRON MANAGE 13 233 1989
KLAZURA GE B AM METEOROL SOC 74 1293 1993
KNISEL WG 26 USDA CONS RES 1980
KOVAR K IAHS PUBLICATION 211 1993
LARK RM IN PRESS INT J REMOT 1995
LASLETT GM J SOIL SCI 38 325 1987
LEENHARDT D EUR J SOIL SCI 45 293 1994
LEONARD RA T ASAE 30 1403 1987
LOAGUE K FIELD SCALE SOLUTE W 175 1990
LOAGUE K J CONTAM HYDROL 8 157 1991
LOAGUE K J CONTAM HYDROL 5 171 1990

LOAGUE K J CONTAM HYDROL 5 405 1990
LOAGUE K J ENVIRON QUAL 25 475 1996
MACLEAN AL PHOTOGRAMM ENG REM S 59 223 1993
MAIDMENT DR ENV MODELING GIS 147 1993
MANDELBROT BB FRACTAL GEOMETRY NAT 1982
MARCUS KB 2 DIMENSIONAL FINITE 1991
MARSMAN B SOILS SHEET SP30 W 2 1973
MCBRATNEY AB J SOIL SCI 43 159 1992
MCBRATNEY AB COMPUT GEOSCI 7 331 1981
MCCORMACK JE INT J GEOGR INF SYST 7 263 1993
MEEKS YJ J WATER RES PL-ASCE 1!6 693 1990
MEIN RG MODELING INFILTRATIO 43 1971
MITCHELL CW TERRAIN EVALUATION 1973
MITCHELL JK WATER RESOUR BULL 29 833 1993
MOORE ID HYDROL PROCESS 5 3 1991
MULLA DJ J ENVIRON QUAL 25 419 1996
NASH JE J HYDROL 10 282 1970
NIELSEN DR HILGARDIA 42 215 1973
OCALLAGHAN JF COMPUT VISION GRAPH 28 323 1984
ODEH IOA GEODERMA 47 93 1990
ODEH IOA SOIL SCI SOC AM J 56 505 1992
OGDEN FL J HYDROL 158 1 1994
OGDEN FL THESIS COLORADO STAT 1992
OGDEN FL WATER RESOUR RES 29 2584 1993
OLOUGHLIN EM WATER RESOUR RES 22 794 1986
PECK AJ WATER RESOUR RES 13 348 1977
PELLETIER RE J SOIL WATER CONSERV 40 332 1985
PETIT AN APPL STAT 42 185 1993
PICKUS J GEO INFO SYSTEMS NOV 50 1992
PRESTON FW ECOLOGY 43 185 1962
QUINN P HYDROL PROCESS 5 59 1991
RAO DV SJ891 ST JOHNS RIV W 1989
RAO PSC ENV IMPACT NONPOINT 23 1980
RAO PSC P SOIL CROP SCI SOC 44 1 1985
RAWLS WJ T ASAE 25 1316 1982
RAWLS WJ J HYDRAUL ENG-ASCE 109 62 1983
REYBOLD WU J SOIL WATER CONSERV 44 28 1989
RIFAI HS CIVIL ENG 63 44 1993
ROGOWSKI AS WATER RESOUR RES 8 1015 1972
ROWLANDS NJ MATH GEOL 9 383 1977
RUNDQUIST DC GEOCARTO INT 2 51 1991
RUNNING SW ECOLOGY 70 1090 1989
SACHIDANANDA M J ATMOS OCEAN TECH 4 588 1987
SAGHAFIAN B THESIS COLORADO STAT 1992
SCHAAKE JC THESIS J HOPKINS U B 1965
SCOTT RM LAND SYSTEMS ATLAS W 1971
SHARMA ML J HYDROL 45 101 1980
SHARMA ML WATER RESOUR RES 15 1567 1979

SKIDMORE AK INT J GEOGR INF SYST 5 431 1991
SRINIVASAN R WATER RESOUR BULL 30 441 1994
SRINIVASAN R WATER RESOUR BULL 30 453 1994
TAYFUR G J HYDRAUL ENG-ASCE 119 51 1993
TESO RR J ENVIRON QUAL 25 425 1996
TIM US J ENVIRON QUAL 23 25 1994
TIM US WATER RESOUR BULL 28 877 1992
VANDEURSEN WPA PC RASTER PACKAGE 1992
VENTURA SJ WATER RESOUR BULL 29 189 1993
VIEUX BE HYDROL PROCESS 5 101 1991
VILORIA J THESIS U OXFORD 1989
VOLTZ M J SOIL SCI 41 473 1990
WARRICK AW WATER RESOUR RES 13 355 1977
WEBSTER R NATURE 219 680 1968
WEBSTER R STAT METHODS SOIL LA 1990
WEBSTER R SOIL SURVEY TECHNICA 12 1979
WISCHMEIER WH USDA AGR HDB 537 1978
WOOD EF J HYDROL 102 29 1988
WOOLHISER DA T ASAE 12 460 1969
WOOLHISER DA UNSTEADY FLOW OPEN C 2 1975
YOUNG RA 35 USDA CONS RES 1987
ZAWADZKI I ATMOS OCEAN 20 158 1982
ZEVENBERGEN LW EARTH SURF PROCESSES 12 47 1987
ZEVENBERGEN AW INT J REMOTE SENS 9 495 1988
ZHANG WH WATER RESOUR RES 25 2019 1989

APPENDIX C

Bibliographic Couplings

Please note that BH (J), BG (U), BA (AW), and BF (AX) were duplicates and have been removed; no citations: B, L, Z; no couplings: D, E, G, I, M, N, S, AB, AC, AE, AP, AQ, AR, BB, BC, BE, BK, BL, BM

A,K	A,AT	F,AH	H,AG
A,R	C, AI	F,AL	H,AI
A,U	C,AL	F,BO	H,AJ
A,AD	C,AT	H,J	H,AL
A,AN	F,H	H,R	H,AZ
A,AS	F,AG	H,X	H,BI

H,BO	R.AN	X,AZ	AL,BO
J,R	R,AS	X,BO	AM,AO
J,T	R,AT	Y,AF	AM,AU
J,U	R,AV	AA,AV	AM.AY
J,AN	R.AZ	AA.AW	AN,AS
J,BJ	R,BD	AD,AM	AN.AT
K,R	R.BJ	AD,AN	AN,BJ
K,AD	T,AM	AD,AS	AN,BN
K,AN	T,AN	AD,AT	AN,BP
K,AS	T,AS	AD,AY	AO,AU
K,AT	T,AT	AG.AL	AS,BN
O,AA	T,BN	AH,AI	AU,AV
P,R	U,AT	AH,AK	AU,AX
P,AK	U,BJ	AH,BO	AU,BO
P.AU	V,W	AI,AJ	AU,BP
P,AV	V,AJ	AI,AL	AV.AW
P,AW	V,AK	AI,AU	AV.AX
P,BP	V,AN	AI,BO	AV,AY
Q,V	V,AU	AI,BP	AV,AZ
Q,W	V,AV	AJ,AK	AV,BO
Q,AN	V,AX	AJ,AU	AV,BP
Q,BN,	V,BD	AJ,AV,	AX,BO
Q,BP	V,BJ	AJ,AX	AX,BP
R,T	V,BP	AJ,AZ	AZ,BJ
R,U	W,AD	AJ,BP	BJ,BN
R,V	X,AI	AK,AU	BJ,BP
R,W	X,AJ	AK,AV	BN,BP
R,AD	X,AL	AK,BP	

ALIGNING SYSTEMS OF RELATIONSHIPS

Rebecca Green
Carol A. Bean

The lateral relations of Neelameghan and Raghavan are mapped to their closest correspondents in FrameNet. Analysis of this alignment highlights important characteristics of each system of relationships and reveals varying degrees of compatibility between them.

1 INTRODUCTION

Part of the celebration appropriate to a Festschrift contribution is recollecting how one came to know the honouree and acknowledging the influence the honouree has had both on the field generally and specifically on one's own thinking. It was only in 1998, at the 5th international conference of the International Society for Knowledge Organization (ISKO), that we first met A. Neelameghan. Or perhaps we should say that that is when he first met us, for our acquaintance with the work of Professor Neelameghan reached back more than 20 years earlier. As graduate students at the College of Library and Information Services (now College of Information Studies) of the University of Maryland in the 1970's (RG) and 1990's (CAB), each of us developed an intense interest in the semantics of relationships, with a particular interest in syntagmatic relationships in the context of indexing and searching. In our investigations into such relationships, we found that they had not received a great deal of attention, but we also discovered an oasis in the desert in the form of Neelameghan and Maitra (1978). Here we found a list of 39 non-hierarchical, associative relationships. When we subsequently chose to address the relative inattention to relationships in library and information science with the publication of an edited volume on the subject, we were delighted that Professor Neelameghan accepted our invitation to contribute a chapter, which included a revised list of non-hierarchical or lateral relationships, specifically relating them to the spiritual and religious domains (Neelameghan, 2001). This past year, he shared with us a manuscript including a newly revised taxonomy of lateral relations (Neelameghan and Raghavan, 2004).

It is this latest set of lateral relations to which we refer in the present paper. Trying to understand the character of a set of relationships simply by examining it on its own is doomed to fall short from the outset. Understanding will come only through comparison, on the one hand, and through use, on the other hand. Using the relationships in the context of real systems and real searches may seem the obvious best source for developing such understanding. But we run up against the same problem when assessing the quality of a set of semantic relationships by examining the results of its use as we do when assessing the quality of a thesaurus by examining the results of its use. In neither case do we know what the ideal results consist of. For example, consider a retrieval set based on the use of a specific thesaurus. We may well have a sense of what we retrieved but should not have retrieved. We rarely have a complete sense of what we did not retrieve but should have retrieved. One semi-effective way of gauging the effectiveness of the thesaurus begins by comparing its results with the results of using other thesauri. The comparison gains in effectiveness as it is extended to investigate directly how the thesauri are like or unlike each other. In this way we get a fuller picture of both thesauri. In a similar way we can begin to get a meaningful picture of the character of Neelameghan's relationship set by comparing it with another set of relationships. Such a comparison starts by developing a mapping between the two sets of relationships. This endeavor parallels other efforts to align vocabularies (e.g., the Unified Medical Language System [UMLS] of the U.S. National Library of Medicine) or ontologies (Euzenat, et. al, 2004).

In this context, we are not mapping concepts, as has been the focus in most other alignment processes, but are aligning relationships. For this purpose, we have chosen FrameNet, an inventory of frame semantic relationships that is outwardly quite different from Neelameghan's lateral relations. At the same time, FrameNet's general-purpose nature and broad scope are similar to the basic nature and scope of Neelameghan's lateral relations, making the two relationship systems comparable.

(Neelameghan and Maitra, 1978) an initial view of the issues encountered in the alignment of the two sets of relationships. The first outcome gives us insight into the character of the individual relationship sets compared, while the second outcome gives us insight into the degree of compatibility we may anticipate between any two sets of relations as well as the nature of their incompatibilities.

2 RELATIONSHIP SETS

2.1 Neelameghan's Lateral Relations

The current taxonomy of lateral relations consists of 34 top-level binary relationships. A handful of these are further specialized, with from three to seven relation subtypes enumerated. Additionally, dozens of subtypes are recognized for the spatial relationship, but they are given no identifying notation as other relationship types and subtypes are given. That only binary relationships are listed reflects one of the primary intended uses of the set of relationships, namely to give definition to RT links in thesauri. This means, in turn, that the relationships are generally conceived as applying between descriptors. However, Neelameghan and Raghavan distinguish between lateral relations that are "near permanent," which would normally be reflected paradigmatically, and lateral relations that are context-dependent and ad hoc, which would normally be reflected syntagmatically.

Lateral relations relate concepts. In the Neelameghan and Raghavan taxonomy, a significant number of kinds of concepts are specified, including the following: meanings, language, names, statements, actions, activities, processes, events, Deity, persons, corporate bodies, devices, materials, situations/conditions, disciplines, attributes, space/location, and time. In many cases, the concepts that are related are stated generally in terms of "entities," which might be naturally occurring or artifactual, abstract or concrete, dynamic or static, etc. Some lateral relations are stated simply in terms of the concept types related, without specifying the nature of the relationship.

Consider, for example, the Process and Property-of-entity-associated-with-the-Process Relation (19) and the Activity/Process and Person-usually-associated-with-the- Activity/Process Relation (20). In other cases, the concept types that are related are not fully explicated, but are identified by the nature of the relationship. Such is the case with the Implication Relation (Neelameghan and Maitra, 1978), which is the relation between "an intended meaning/purport of the action or statement of one entity vis-à-vis another entity [that] is not explicit or evident but can be inferred".

2.2 FrameNet

A semantic frame is a relational structure that characterizes an entity, a (static) situation, or a (dynamic) event. Associated with a frame are one or more (usually from two to five) frame elements, that is, aspects of the entity, situation, or event being described. In the case of situations and events, frame elements correspond to semantic roles filled by the participants (both animate and inanimate) in the situation or event. For example, the HIRING frame includes as frame elements an Employer, who hires an Employee and pays him/her Compensation to fill a Position or to perform a Task; employment takes place in a Field. A HIRING event is expressed by identifying specific values for (some or all of) the frame elements.

The FrameNet project has developed a semantic frame lexicon, which characterizes semantic frames by enumerating their underlying frame elements and identifying specific lexical units that evoke the frame (as specific senses of *commission, employ, hire,* and *sign* evoke the HIRING frame). Sentences from a corpus are then annotated to show how various frame elements show up in specific linguistic contexts. On the one hand, this annotation effort informs any necessary revision of the frames; on the other hand, the annotation effort also validates frames. FrameNet is ultimately a linguistic venture, studying how lexical units and syntactic structures are combined to carry semantic meaning. The point of the frames is to standardize how the semantic meaning is characterized.

At present, some 600 frames have been defined (including a few that define entities). Frame-to-frame relationships have not yet been fully worked out, but include hierarchical and compositional relationships. In hierarchical frame relationships, subordinate frames inherit the frame elements of the *super-ordinate* frame; further specification comes either in defining the inherited frame elements more narrowly or in adding new frame elements. For example, the COMMITTING_CRIME frame includes Crime and Perpetrator frame elements and is inherited by the ARSON frame. Frame elements of this frame are an Event, which further specifies the Crime frame element of its super-ordinate, a Perpetrator, and an additional frame element, a Victim. In compositional frame relationships, the super-ordinate frame consists of sub-frames that describe sub-events of the overall process. For example, the CRIME_SCENARIO frame has three sub-frames: COMMITTING_CRIME, CRIMINAL_INVESTIGATION, and CRIMINAL_ PROCESS; the CRIMINAL_PROCESS frame is in turn composed of ARREST, ARRAIGNMENT, TRIAL, and SENTENCING frames.

3 ALIGNING LATERAL RELATIONS AND SEMANTIC FRAMES

3.1 General Comparison

There are several obvious differences between Neelameghan's lateral relations and FrameNet's semantic frames that stem from the differing contexts in which they have arisen. Perhaps the most obvious of them is the difference in *arity*: Neelameghan's lateral relations are binary relationships, having been developed with the need to show thesaural relations between two descriptors. FrameNet's semantic frames are n-ary relationships, having been developed with the need to show the semantic interrelationships. From here on, we will be concerned mainly with situation and event frames (www.icsi.berkeley.edu/~framenet) between a predicate (typically a verb) and all its arguments (typically noun phrases); thus it gathers all the participants of a situation or event into a single multifaceted relational unit. On a conceptual level, the *arity* difference is not as critical as it may appear on the surface. For example, Neelameghan and Raghavan note that in a sentence like (Euzenat, et. al, 2004) there are many binary relations involving any two of the Doctor, Treatment, the Hospital, the Patient, Tuberculosis, and Streptomycin. A semantic frame solution might posit a TREATMENT frame with frame elements for Physician, Patient, Medical_condition, Drug, etc. To make the two approaches equivalent would require only some way of binding together binary relations that are part of the same situation or event gestalt (both concretely and in the abstract) (Euzenat, et. al, 2004). The doctor is treating the hospital patient suffering from tuberculosis with streptomycin. The two relationship sets also differ with respect to size. It is desirable that the set of relationships used in a thesaurus be as small as possible, while at the same time making necessary distinctions. But it is desirable that the set of semantic frames used in representing meaning be as informative as possible, while at the same time unifying into the same frame the multiple linguistic expressions that convey the same meaning.

The size difference between the two relationship sets is reflected as well in a difference in generality. Many lateral relations are stated generally and then are applied in more specific settings. Semantic frames also need to express general relationships, but often include kinds of situations and events at a level of specificity outside the range appropriate for thesaural relationships. Especially because of the size differences between the two sets of relationships, the most appropriate way in which to approach their alignment is to use the set of lateral relations, which is the smaller of the two, as a starting point. The alignment proceeds by finding the semantic frame(s) in FrameNet most nearly equivalent to each lateral relation type and subtype, as given in Table 1. Many FrameNet frames are overlooked in this process.

Table 1: Alignment of Lateral Relations with Closest Corresponding FrameNet Frames

Notes: Major elements of FrameNet's semantic frames are indicated with initial capital letters (e.g., Speaker, Message, Topic, Medium, Addressee).

When the right column lacks an entry, no frame corresponding to the lateral relation has been found in FrameNet

LATERAL RELATIONS	FRAMENET FRAMES
1. **EXPLANATION/DESCRIPTION RELATION:** The relation between a concept and its definition, description, illustration, explanation, commentary, scope note, etc.	
a. Description/Explanation Relation Statement:	A Speaker addresses a Message on a Topic using some Medium to an Addressee
b. Interpretation/Commentary Relation	**Performers_and_roles:** A Performer has a certain role in a Performance of a certain

LATERAL RELATIONS	FRAMENET FRAMES
	Type and plays their part by following the directions in the Script for that particular Role. **Text_creation**: An Author creates a Text, either written, such as a letter, or spoken, such as a speech, that contains meaningful linguistic tokens, and may have a particular Addressee in mind.
c. Enumerative Definition Relation **d. Definition Relation**: The relation between a term and its definition	**Categorization:** A Cognizer construes an Item as belonging to a certain Category on the basis of certain Criteria
e. Case Study/Model/Example Relation	**Instance** Instances of Types of entities or events. **Beyond_compare:** Compared to its Competitors, a Standard is at the high end of a scale with respect to some Variable.
2. **IMPLICATION RELATION:** The relation that arises when an intended meaning / purport of the action or statement of one entity vis-à-vis another entity is not explicit or evident but can be inferred	**Coming_to_believe:** A Cognizer comes to believe some Content, sometimes after a process of reasoning. This change in belief is usually initiated by a person or piece of Evidence
3. **COLLABORATION/COOPERATION RELATION:** Relation arising from a person or corporate body (including country) working (or joining) with another person or corporate body. A variety of collaboration relations can exist between two entities. For example the types of relations between two countries can be political, military, cultural, economic / commerce/trade, cultural, scientific and technological, commonality of race, language, religion, etc. Similarly with other entities. Such association between two entities results when one entity joins with, interacts with, depends on, another entity	**Collaboration:** Partner_1 and Partner_2 or a group of Partners work together in some Undertaking.
4. **ACCOMPANY RELATION**: Relation that arises when an entity goes with, follows or is attached to, another entity	**Co_theme:** A Theme, frequently a living being, moves in relation to a second moving object, the Cotheme, along a Path or within an Area

LATERAL RELATIONS	FRAMENET FRAMES
5. **APPLICATION RELATION:** Relation arising from the application of an entity (used as a tool) in the study/manipulation of another entity	**Usefulness:** An Entity is suitable for some Purpose, i.e. it aids in the successful completion of the Purpose
6. **IMPACT/INFLUENCE RELATION:** Relation arising between two entities when one of them influences the other or there is a mutual influence	**Causation:** A Cause, animate or inanimate, causes an Effect
7. **EVALUATION RELATION:** Relation arising between two entities when one entity is evaluated / assessed / criticized from the point of view of the second entity.	**Assessing:** An Assessor examines a Phenomenon to figure out its Value according to some Feature of the Phenomenon. This Value is a factor in determining the acceptability of the Phenomenon. **Evaluative_comparison:** A Profiled_item is compared to a Standard_item, often with respect to some Attribute
8. **STRUCTURAL/FUNCTIONAL RELATION:** A function is the natural, required or expected activity of a person [as determined by his/her position, profession, or employment] or thing. **a. Organizational Relation:** Functional relations include the different types of relation that arise between person and person, person and corporate entity, person and event, and corporate entity and corporate entity in the performance of such functions. **b. Affiliation Relation:** Relation arising from a connection or association of a person or corporate entity with another person, a corporate entity, a movement, a party, a club, etc. **c. Service Provider – Client or Recipient Relation**: The Service Provider may be an Attorney, Doctor, Teacher, Priest, Consultant, Coach, etc; the Service Provider may be an individual, or a corporate entity. The Client may be an individual, or a	**Being_employed:** An Employee has a Position doing work in a particular Field, or doing work on a particular Task, for which an Employer gives Compensation to the Employee.

LATERAL RELATIONS	FRAMENET FRAMES
corporate entity. In a corporate entity, the Service Provider may be external or internal to the corporate entity.	
9. PROPRIETARY/OWNERSHIP RELATION: Relation arising between the owner and the entity owned. as in the case of ownership of Software, Patent, Trademark, etc. by an individual or corporate entity. The ownership is generally confirmed by law or by assignment	**Possession:** An Owner has (or lacks) a Possession. (This does not include body parts or medical conditions, but does include intellectual property, etc.)
10. ORIGINAL-VARIANT RELATION: The similarity/dissimilarity between entities may be identified by comparison/ differentiation studies of the entities	**Similarity:** Two distinct Entities, which may be concrete or abstract objects or types, are characterized as being similar to each other. The similarity may be based on some Dimension, such as appearance, physical or other properties of the two entities
a. Variation (Variant) Relation: Variation implies change or deviation or difference in some way -- form, condition, quality, appearance, extent, etc., from the original of the same kind. or from the usual state or former standard	
b. Transformation Relation: The relation arising from a change either in external form or in inner nature, in function, etc. of an entity and the changed entity or variant as may occur during a developmental process	**Transformation:** An Agent converts the Initial_entity into the Final_entity.
c. Copy/Imitation Relation: Copy: thing made just like another, imitation of an original; full reproduction or transcript, duplicate, replica, clone, fake, counterfeit, mimic, simulate, echo and cognate ideas. Also includes Robots that imitate/simulate a human or another machine actions. The relation arising between an original and the copied or duplicated entity	**Duplication:** A Creator makes a duplicate, the Copy, of some Original entity.
d. Entity-Shadow Relation: The relation between an entity and its shadow. Unlike a copy etc. the shadow exists only if the entity of which it is the shadow exists	

Green; Bean

LATERAL RELATIONS	FRAMENET FRAMES
e. Mirror Image/Echo Relation: The relation between the real entity and its image in a mirror (or echo of a sound). Like the shadow, the mirror image exists only if the entity of which it is a mirror image exists	
f. Antonymy/Dissimilarity Relation: The relation between two entities that can, in a given context, be viewed as opposites.	**Word_relations:** One linguistic unit, Sign_1, has a relation to another linguistic unit, Sign_2. This relation may be semantic, phonological, orthographic, or distributional in nature. **Similarity**: Two distinct Entities, which may be concrete or abstract objects or types, are characterized as being similar to each other. The similarity may be based on some Dimension, such as appearance, physical or other properties of the two entities
11. REPRESENTATION/IDENTIFIER RELATION: The relation that arises between two entities when one entity is standing in for another entity, or one entity is an identifier of another entity. Includes Proxy, Surrogate, Imposter, Pretender in particular contexts.	**Imitation**: A Creator makes an imitation or fake (the Copy) of some Original entity. **Sign**: One phenomenon, the Indicator, exists as an indication of another phenomenon, the Indicated. The Indicated can be a past, present, or future entity or eventuality. The relationship between Indicator and Indicated is not one of symbolization or iconicity. Rather the Indicator is an index of the Indicated
12. EQUIVALENCE/SYNONYMY RELATIONSHIP: The semantic relation that holds when two terms, in a given context, expresses the same meaning	**Word_relations:** One linguistic unit, Sign_1, has a relation to another linguistic unit, Sign_2. This relation may be semantic, phonological, orthographic, or distributional in nature. **Similarity:** Two distinct Entities, which may be concrete or abstract objects or types, are characterized as being similar to each other. The similarity may be based on some Dimension, such as appearance, physical or other properties of the two entities

LATERAL RELATIONS	FRAMENET FRAMES
13. **NEAR-EQUIVALENCE RELATION:** A certain concept (and the name for it) of a particular cultural group may not have exact equivalent in another cultural group; however a near-equivalent term/phrase may be used (and accepted, with explanation)	
14. **PRECURSOR/CAUSE/INSTRUMENT– EFFECT RELATION**: An entity that is a forerunner/ harbinger/cause of another entity	**Omen:** One phenomenon, Phenomenon_1 is an indication of the current or future existence of another phenomenon, Phenomenon_2. Optionally, an Outcome identifies how Phenomenon_2 is expected to turn out based on the evidence of Phenomenon_1. **Causation:** A Cause, animate or inanimate, causes an Effect
15. **CO-OCCURRENCE/SIMULTANEITY RELATION**: The relation that arises when one entity invariably occurs (in time) when another entity occurs	
16. **CONTAINER--CONTAINED ENTITY RELATION**	**Containing**: A Container holds within its physical boundaries the Contents
17. **ENTITY AND ITS PROPERTY RELATION**: The entity may be a concept, discipline, physical body, an attribute, a process, action, an event, space, or time	
a. Physical entity (thing) and its Attribute Relation	**Dimension:** An Object has a position on a scale, its Measurement, with respect to some attribute, its Dimension
b. Attribute and its Attribute Relation	
c. Action and its Attribute Relation	
d. Event and its Attribute Relation.	**Duration:** An Eventuality (event, state, time-period) has Duration
e. Space and its Attribute Relation	**Shapes:** A Substance has a dimensional extent and Shape. **Measure_volume:** Some Stuff's volume is Count number of Units.
f. Time and its Attribute Relation	**Measure_duration:** Some Process's duration is Count number of Units

LATERAL RELATIONS	FRAMENET FRAMES
18. ACTION/PROCESS AND ENDRESULT/ PRODUCT/YIELD RELATION	**Activity_done_state:** An Agent has completed an Activity. **Causation:** A Cause, animate or inanimate, causes an Effect
19. PROCESS AND PROPERTY OF ENTITY ASSOCIATED WITH THE PROCESS RELATION	
20. ACTIVITY/PROCESS AND PERSON USUALLY ASSOCIATED WITH IT RELATION	**Activity_ongoing:** An Agent is performing the portion of an Activity in which there is dynamic stability **Activity_done_state:** An Agent has completed an Activity
21. ENTITY (PHYSICAL) AND ITS APPLICATION OR USE RELATION	**Usefulness:** An Entity is suitable for some Purpose, i.e. it aids in the successful completion of the Purpose
22. ENTITY (PHYSICAL) AND THE MATERIAL OF WHICH IT IS MADE RELATION	**Part_whole:** A Whole has one or more Parts. **Artifact:** An Artifact is deliberately made or modified by an intelligent entity to be put to a certain kind of Use. Various properties of the Artifact may be specified, such as its Creator, Time_of_Creation, Name, Type, and the Material of which it is composed
23. ENTITY AND ITS PARTS RELATION: The relation between the whole and its parts (natural or artificial)	**Part_whole**: A Whole has one or more Parts.
24. ENTITY AND ITS MEASURE RELATION	**Measure_volume:** Some Stuff's volume is Count number of Units **Measure_duration:** Some Process's duration is Count number of Units. **Measure_area**: An Area/region has area of Count number of Units. **Measure_linear_extent**: Some Stuff has linear extent.of Count number of Units. **Measure_mass**: Some Stuff has mass of Count number of Units

LATERAL RELATIONS	FRAMENET FRAMES
25. **MEASURE AND DEVICE USED TO MEASURE RELATION**	**Artifact:** An Artifact is deliberately made or modified by an intelligent entity to be put to a certain kind of Use. Various properties of the Artifact may be specified, such as its Creator, Time_of_Creation, Name, Type, and the Material of which it is composed
26. **ENTITY AND ITS USUAL PLACE OF LOCATION OR MANIPULATION RELATION**	**Locating:** A Perceiver determines the Location of a Sought_entity within a Ground.
27. **PERSONS INTERACTING WITH EACH OTHER IN A SPECIAL CONTEXT RELATION**	**Education_teaching**: A Teacher instructs Students in a Subject at an Institution. The Students are seeking a Qualification
28. **SITUATION OR CONDITION AND WHAT HAPPENS IN THAT SITUATION RELATION**	**Change_of_state_scenario**: An Event occurs in which an Entity punctually or continually changes in the direction of the End state for some Reason
29. **CONTIGUITY RELATION**: One concept entails the other	**Categorization**: A Cognizer construes an Item as belonging to a certain Category on the basis of certain Criteria
a. **Contiguity based on Definition**	
b. **Contiguity based on Empirical Knowledge**	
30. **FAMILY LINE/KINSHIP RELATION** (other than parent-sibling relation)	Kinship: Alter has a kinship relation to Ego.
31. **SPIRITUAL RELATION**: In religion, relation conceived between human being and God or Ultimate Reality	
32. **FIGURE OF SPEECH (TROPE) RELATION**: A figure of speech is language used in a non-literal or figurative sense	
a. Simile relation: The relation implied in a statement that expresses a resemblance between entities of different kinds, usually formulated using words such as 'like' or 'as'	

LATERAL RELATIONS	FRAMENET FRAMES
b. Metaphor relation: The relation implied when an expression is used to refer to some entity that it does not literally denote in order to suggest a similarity	
c. Irony relation: The relation implied when an expression presents an incongruity between what might be expected and what actually occurs	
d. Oxymoron relation: The relation implied when contradicting terms are joined together	
e. Metonymy relation: The relation implied in an expression when the name of an attribute or feature is substituted for the name of the thing itself	
f. Personification relation: The relation implied when an abstract quality or idea is represented as a person or creature	
g. Synecdoche relation: The relation implied in an expression where a more inclusive term is substituted for a less inclusive one or vice versa	
33. SPATIAL RELATION: Relations among entities pertaining to or involving or having the nature of space	**Locative_relation:** A Figure is located relative to a Ground location. The location of the Figure may be further specified by its Distance from a reference location (generally, the deictic center) and the Direction in which the Figure lies from a reference location (generally, the deictic center)
34. TIME-RELATED (SUCCESSIVE LINKS) RELATION	Relative_time: Event_1 is located relative to Event_2

3.2 Alignment Patterns

Several patterns emerge in the effort to align FrameNet with the set of lateral relations. The most common or salient of these patterns are: 1) No match, 2)

Exact or near match, and 3) Level of generality difference. In addition, there are a number of less frequently occurring and more idiosyncratic alignment relationships.

No match: Even though the set of lateral relations is a much smaller inventory of relationship types, it includes relationships not included in FrameNet, which is as yet incomplete. For example, FrameNet has no coverage in the spiritual/religious realm and thus lacks any correspondent for lateral relation #31, the spiritual relation between a human being and God (or Ultimate Reality). Similarly, FrameNet has only limited coverage or relationships involving language as an entity and thus lacks correspondents for the general figure of speech relation (#32) and all of its specific types. Other No match examples include #13 (near-equivalence relation), #15 (co-occurrence/simultaneity relation), and #19 (process and property-of entity- associated-with-the-process relation).

The existence of a No match is indicated in Table 1 by an empty entry in the right hand (FrameNet Frames) column.

Exact or near match: Exact matches between a lateral relation and a FrameNet frame can only occur where the frame has two frame elements, as all the lateral relations are binary. Several exact matches occur, including the relationships between an owner and a possession (#9), a container and its contents (#16), a whole and its parts (#23), and two persons linked by a kinship. Note how a ternary relationship gets turned into a binary relationship! (#30). Near matches occur where the same conceptual relationship underlies both a lateral relation and a FrameNet frame, but the frame includes additional frame elements, as in #3, where the binary lateral relation between two collaborators is supplemented by the undertaking of the collaborators in the corresponding FrameNet frame. Similarly, FrameNet's LOCATIVE_RELATION between a Figure and a Ground is the same as the lateral Spatial relation (#33), except that the frame admits of optional Distance and Direction frame elements.

Level of generality difference: Lateral relation #10c between an Entity and a Copy/Imitation is almost a near match with FrameNet's DUPLICATION frame, which includes not only Original and Copy frame elements, but also a Creator frame element. However, the lateral relation involves more than copies duplicating the original entity; imitations, fakes, counterfeits, mimics, and robots that simulate humans are also among the derivative entities. This greater inclusivity is symptomatic of the top-down, theory- driven approach behind lateral relations, contrasting with the data-driven, bottom-up approach behind FrameNet. The greater generality of the lateral relations approach is evident also in the mapping of the single *Entity-and-its-Measure* lateral relation (#24) to five FrameNet frames, each of which measures a different variable (e.g., volume, duration, mass). At the same time, the FrameNet frames not only relate an Entity (or Stuff) to a Unit of measure, but also permit specification of the number of units; this distinction reflects the difference between stating an abstract relationship (as is appropriate to relationships between thesaural descriptors) and making a concrete assertion (as is appropriate to relationships between lexical units within a sentence). Further examples of generality differences show up in lateral relations #1b, 4, 10f, 12, 14, 17, 18, 19, and 27; in many of these instances, additional factors also come into play.

Additional sources of difference: Further insights into the similarities and dissimilarities between Neelameghan's lateral relations and FrameNet's semantic frames come through examining several of the mappings in greater depth. For this purpose, we will look at the subtypes of lateral relation #1, the Explanation/ Description relation, described as "the relation between a concept and its definition, description, illustration, explanation, commentary, scope note, etc." We note, on the one hand, that this relation generalizes over several means of clarifying a concept, most of which are verbal. FrameNet is more likely to have frames that correspond to particular means of clarifying concepts than to have a frame that generalizes over all of them. On the other hand, the taxonomy of lateral relations specifies four subtypes of the Explanation/Description relation, which FrameNet is more likely to include correspondents for. The first of these subtype relations is the Description/ Explanation relation, in which a verbal product (e.g., an essay, a lecture) describes or explains a concept (e.g., a place, an event, an artifact). FrameNet has a STATEMENT frame for making assertions, which would include descriptions and explanations. The Medium and Topic elements of this frame correspond to the verbal product and concept within the Description/Explanation relation. The STATEMENT frame also includes Speaker, Message, and Addressee frame elements. Thus, the semantic frame tends to assume the explicit involvement of human communicators, while the lateral relation makes them part of the background. The second of these subtype relations is the Interpretation/Commentary relation. The typical use of this relation is to bind a person (the interpreter) and an artistic work (e.g., an opera, a religious text). The creator of the work is again backgrounded in the lateral relation, while FrameNet makes possible a way to make the creator explicit, at least in the case of a text. FrameNet also has a frame that binds Performers of various media to their Roles. Here FrameNet backgrounds the interpretation that is implicit in a performance, while the lateral relation foregrounds it.

The third and fourth subtypes of the Explanation/ Description relation concern relations between a concept and its definition, in one case using an extensional/enumerative approach and in the other case using an intensional/ analytic approach. The closest correspondent in FrameNet is the CATEGORIZATION frame, which includes a "Cognizer [who] construes an Item as belonging to a . . . Category on the basis of certain Criteria." The basis of this mapping is the assumption that definitions give the criteria for membership in the category named by the word being defined. The Enumerative Definition relation (#1c) can then be seen to link the Item and Category elements of the CATEGORIZATION frame (that is, a Category is defined by enumerating the Items that are members of it), while the Definition relation (#1d) links the Category and Criteria elements of the CATEGORIZATION frame (that is, a Category is defined by the Criteria that its members must meet). But it is not simply an issue of the CATEGORIZATION frame including more frame elements than either the Enumerative Definition or the Definition lateral relations. While we may see a connection between definitions and categories, defining and categorizing are different activities with different intents and different foci. At the same time that the CATEGORIZATION frame is the closest correspondent to the definition relations, it is not accurate to suggest that FrameNet currently has a good way of expressing these relations. The final subtype of the Explanation/Description relation is the Case Study/Model/ Example Relation. We see again in its name that the lateral relation has a broad scope. FrameNet responds with two frames corresponding to different portions of that scope. The INSTANCE frame is FrameNet's version of the Type-Token relationship, which corresponds to the relationship between a Concept (the Type) and an Example (the Token). While any member of a class may be an example of the class, typically only some members of the class make good Models. For models, we may want prototypical instances or paragons. The BEYOND_COMPARE frame, which includes an entity that is seen as a Standard among Competitors, is how FrameNet reflects a Paragon.

4 CONCLUSIONS

The work reported here has produced a partial alignment between Neelameghan's lateral relations and FrameNet, mapping the much smaller set of lateral relations types and subtypes to their closest correspondents in FrameNet. In some cases, no good mapping was found. This may simply be a case of FrameNet's incomplete state or may reflect different relational perspectives in the two systems of relationships. Some of the mappings linked fully equivalent relationships, while others failed to be fully equivalent because of the binary relationships constraint adopted in the inventory of lateral relations. A significant number of the mappings linked lateral relations that were of a more general nature than the closest corresponding frame(s). Although various types of differences have been enumerated, these mapping patterns (other than those where no good mapping was found) reflect significant compatibility between the lateral relations and FrameNet. At the same time, in the mappings from the Explanation/Description lateral relation subtypes to FrameNet we have seen examples of more subtle relational patterns. Across closest correspondents there may be a difference between what a relationship foregrounds and what it backgrounds, or a difference in focus and intent. These kinds of differences reflect various degrees of incompatibility between the two sets of relationships. This suggests that as further work in aligning systems of relationships is undertaken, we are likely to find that relationship alignment has all the complexity encountered in the alignment of concepts.

REFERENCES

1. Euzenat J., Le Bach T., Barrasa J., Bouquet P., De Bo J., Dieng R., Ehrig M., Hauswirth M., Jarrar M., Lara R., Maynard D., Napoli A., Stamou G., Stuckenschmidt H., Shvaiko P., Tessaris S., Van Acker S. and Zaihrayeu I. (2004). State of the art on ontology alignment. http://www.starlab.vub.ac.be/publications/kweb-223.pdf. [21 January 2005].
2. Neelameghan, A. and Maitra, Ranjita. (1978). *Non-hierarchical associative relationships among concepts: Identification and typology*. (FID/CR report; no. 18, part A). Bangalore: FID/CR Secretariat Documentation Research and Training Centre.
3. Neelameghan, A. and Raghavan, K. S. (2004). *Semantics of relations in knowledge organization: Lateral relations*. (Manuscript)
4. Neelameghan, A. (2001). Lateral relationships in multicultural, multilingual databases in the spiritual and religious domains. **In** C. A. Bean and R. Green (Eds.), *Relationships in the Organization of Knowledge*. Dordrecht: Kluwer Academic Publishers. p. 185-198.

TERMINOLOGIES, ONTOLOGIES AND INFORMATION ACCESS

Widad Mustafa El Hadi

Ontologies have become an important issue in research communities across several disciplines. This paper discusses some of the innovative techniques involving automatic terminology resources acquisition are briefly discussed. Suggests that NLP-based ontologies are useful in reducing the cost of ontology engineering. Emphasizes that linguistic ontologies covering both ontological and lexical information can offer solutions since they can be more easily updated by the resources of NLP products.

0 PREAMBLE

I am pleased to contribute this paper related to natural language processing technologies which has applications in knowledge organization, a field in which Prof. Neelameghan (AN) is not only interested but has also made significant contributions. I first met AN in Lille, France, when he participated in the 3rd International ISKO Conference in 1998. Recently I came to know about AN's assistance missions to Sudan, my home country, and about his four-year visiting professorship at the University of Addis Ababa, Addis Ababa, Ethiopia, a country I have been visiting frequently.

1 INTRODUCTION

Terminology is concerned with scientific attempts at organizing knowledge. It deals with specialized vocabularies for different fields of knowledge within and across linguistic boundaries. It contributes to translation, documentation and information science. Terminology intervenes moreover in the development of reference vocabularies for increasingly diversified applications in information access: thesaurus for automatic indexing, structured indexes for hyper-textual technical documentation, reference terminologies for technical writing systems, reference terminologies for technical data management systems, ontologies for the memories of companies/organizations, computerized decision-making systems, information extraction systems, reference glossaries, etc.

2 CORPUS-BASED TERMINOLOGY PROCESSING

Extracting and building terminologies from machine-readable corpora increasingly uses natural language processing (NLP) techniques. As a result of the growing interest in this type of approach to computational linguistics, a number of roducts aimed at term recognition and extraction have been developed. Early application of automatic term extraction and recognition were developed in the context of Information Retrieval (IR). While this research can be traced back to the late 1950s, automatic term extraction aiming at building reference tools for translation, technical writing or knowledge-based systems or linguistic ontologies is a recent trend (Oaks and Paice, 2001). IR work shares with terminology the assumption that a certain type of lexical units can express concepts or topics without ambiguity. Term recognition and extraction for IR purposes has been well documented in the literature;[1] we will not dwell on it. We will instead focus on the innovative techniques in terminology processing and in particular on NLP-based ontologies as a computational linguistic activity, explaining the growth of linguistic ontologies and NLP-based ontologies research. Ontologies have thus become an important issue in research communities across several disciplines in relation to terminology processing and information access[2]. We will see ontologies in detail in the following sections.

We are witnessing the growth of terminology extraction activities necessitated by the spread of new technologies and the constant expansion of interdisciplinary research. Term extraction deals with two main activities: term acquisition, i.e. covering of a domain, which includes discovering new terms, (Jacquemin, 1997), and indexing. The purpose of term acquisition is the construction of terminological resources, such as controlled vocabularies. Thesauri are used for assisting information access through query expansion for cross-lingual information retrieval (CLIR) or for thesaurus-based querying. In this domain, automatic thesaurus construction is a well established tradition and studies have focused either on the discovery of terms or on the discovery of semantic relations (Jacquemin, 1997 for a detailed review). Bilingual term extraction tools (Dagan and Church, 1994) based on part-of-speech tagging and word alignment technologies to extract candidate terms and their translations can be used for both tasks. The monolingual part of this type of system can be used for indexing and for term extraction while the bilingual component can serve both for translation and for IR in multilingual text collections. Although this type of system was initially created for term extraction and translation, it was later reused and adapted for indexing as well, as reported by Landauer *et. al.*. (1990), quoted by Dagan *et al.*, ibid. Term extraction designers should keep in mind these new requirements (i.e., translation and IR in multilingual text collections) when designing such systems because the need for them are becoming increasingly evident.

3 EMERGENCE OF NEW TERMINOLOGY RESOURCES AND TECHNIQUES APPLIED TO INFORMATION ACCESS

Here we briefly account for some of the innovative techniques involving automatic terminology resources acquisition which is a basic component of information access. Coarse extraction techniques, as Bourigault, *et. al.*. (2001) pointed out, tend to produce huge lists of undifferentiated terms that are of little use for efficient document indexing and retrieval. To be of use, these types of lists must be subject to structuring, which is an important step towards exploiting extraction results. Some efforts were undertaken to avoid the over-productivity of terms. Peter (2001) suggests selecting only faceted terms, i.e. terms that pertain to the domain of the query. Hongyan and Tzoukermann (2001) suggest solutions to terminological disambiguation in order to avoid conflating morphologically related terms with no semantic relationship. These two methods have allowed for accurate indexing and enhanced precision in document retrieval. (Bourigault, et. al. 2001). In the same direction Jacquemin *et. al..*, (1999) and Jacquemin (2001) suggested an approach of automatic indexing over controlled vocabulary which accounts for term variation. The approach, considered by the author as rich indexing[3] combines a part of speech tagger, a generator of morphologically related forms and a shallow transformational parser. The FASTER system has been applied to both English and French languages. Evaluation of this tool on indexing tasks has produced encouraging results (cf. Jacquemin *et. al..*, ibid) as far as improvement of indexing through variant extraction was concerned. Moreover, Jacquemin *et. al..*, (ibid) have pointed out the importance of exploiting lexical and terminological data as a key to success in such approaches.

From a general point of view, the tools we have evaluated in our previous work[4], especially term extraction ones, only have a limited interest for indexing tasks, although this is not the case with other tools such as semantic relation extractors. Some of the semantic extraction tools have been adapted to indexing tasks. (IOTA and LORIA, for instance, Mustafa, 2001).

Other techniques aim at improving term and environment extraction quality. Studies in this area deal with collocations and specialized verbs (L'Homme, 2000) and relational adjectives (Daille 2001). Other techniques are used in CLIR. One of the requirements is access to multilingual data with CLIR connections between terms and their equivalents in other languages. Akiko and Kageura (2001) show how bilingual keywords lists frequently found in scientific journal articles can be used to build multilingual keywords clusters. Such clusters can be used for query expansion in CLIR and even for monolingual query expansion (Bourigault, et. al. 2001). Other significant contributions in bilingual term extraction are reported in Hull (2001), Bisson (2001) and Gaussier (2001).

4 ONTOLOGIES

Ontologies have emerged as one of the most popular means of modelling the knowledge of a domain. The meaning of this term varies in the literature, but as (Bontcheva, et. al., 2001) pointed out:

> *"it is minimally a hierarchical taxonomy of categories, concepts and terms of a domain. Ontologies can act as an index to the memory of an organization and facilitate semantic searches and the retrieval of knowledge from the corporate memory as it is embodied in documents and other archives".*

For Poli (1996),

> *"an ontology is not a catalogue of the world, a taxonomy or a terminology. If anything, an ontology is the general framework within which catalogues, taxonomies and terminologies may be given suitable organization (...). reality is organized into diverse levels and there are sophisticated dependencies among these levels and within them. An acceptable ontology should be able to model all these relations of dependencies".*

Though they are different from concept lexicon, classification schemes and thesauri, their inter-relationship is still obvious. This is why we do think that terminology resources are the basis for this type of organization. We assume that a hybridized approach for ontology elaboration (a formal and linguistic one) is necessary (cf. relevant experiences below).

Ontologies can be seen as databases with information about categories and/or concepts of a domain of knowledge as well as their relations. They are seen as "enriched" thesauri since they include definitions and semantic relations. Their role is to reduce conceptual and terminological ambiguities by identifying and properly defining a set of relevant concepts characterizing a domain. They can solve semantic ambiguity, a core problem in text understanding. In this respect, machine translation (MT) is increasingly seen as an important element of success in CLIR, an activity, which involves elements of both MT and IR. There are many other uses mentioned in the literature, but the most relevant ontology models as far as our approach and interest in this subject are concerned, are GALEN (for its multilingual terminological module), CYC (especially for the levels enabling natural language understanding and generation) and MIKROKOSMOS (for MT application). Moreover, this type of ontologies could be useful in MT environments and consequently in CLIR.

4.1 Comparing Linguistic Ontologies with Formal Ontologies

The increasing interest in ontologies for many natural language applications has led to the creation of ontologies for different purposes. Magnini and Manuela, (2002) accounted for the main differences and similarities between linguistic and formal ontologies. The former are large-scale lexical resources that are supposed to cover most of the words of a language such as WordNet. They provide at the same time an ontological structure where the main emphasis is on the relationships between concepts. Linguistic ontologies can thus be seen both as a particular kind of lexical database and as a particular kind of ontology. Two features seem to differentiate formal ontologies from linguistic ontologies as Magnini and Manuela, (ibid.) pointed out: linguistic ontologies differ from formal ontologies as far as their degree of formalization is concerned. Linguistic ontologies do not reflect all the inherent aspects of formal ontologies. As Guarino and Masolo (1999) points out, WordNet's upper level structure shows no distinction between types and nodes. To give a further example the authors comment that WordNet's hierarchical structure lacks information about disjointedness. Moreover, what distinguishes linguistic ontologies from formal ontologies is their size: linguistic ontologies are very large (WordNet, for instance, has several dozen thousand synsets), while formal ontologies are generally much smaller. Linguistic ontologies are language-dependent on the linguistic level like electronic dictionaries, glossaries and all other linguistic resources. Conversely, if we consider the semantic level we can see that concepts denoted by different words in different languages can be shared, as it happens with the concepts in formal ontologies (*see* Magnini and Manuela, 2002 for more details on this comparison).

4.2 Uses of Formal Ontologies

Recently, ontologies have been used in the context of the Semantic Web. Ontologies can be employed to associate meaning with data and documents found on the Internet thus improving different applications of retrieval systems. We give here some of the examples drawn from the literature on these specific uses: Erdmann and Studer (1999), quoted by Magnini and Manuela, (ibid.) use an ontology to access sets of distributed XML documents on a conceptual level. Their approach defines the relationship between a given ontology and a document type definition (DTD) for classes of XML documents. They are able to supplement syntactical access to XML documents by conceptual access. Other researchers suggest a set of HTML Ontology extension to manually annotate Web pages with ontology-based knowledge, which performs at high precision level but is very expensive in terms of time. ONTOSEEK (Guirano *et. al.*. 1999) is also based on content, but uses ontologies to find users in large classical databases of Web pages.

Some drawbacks have been however noticed in the use of ontologies for information retrieval. Guirano *et. al.*. (1999) reported on the limited scope of their use given their insufficient broad coverage and the necessity to constantly update them. This is why linguistic ontologies covering both ontological and lexical information can offer solutions since they can be more easily updated by the resources of NLP products, i.e. glossaries, tailored terminologies, lexical databases, etc.

4.3 Uses of Linguistic Ontologies in Information Access

4.3.1 Ontologies in Information Retrieval

Ontologies can act as an index to the memory of an organization and facilitate semantic searches and the retrieval of knowledge from the corporate memory as it is embodied in documents and other archives. Linguistic ontologies are used for content-based indexing where semantic information is added to the classic word-based indexing (Magnini and Manuela ibid). Other uses are reported in the literature: Mihacea and Moldovan (2000) quoted by Magnini and Manuela, (ibid. 44) designed an IR system, which performs a combined word-based and sense-based indexing exploiting WordNet. The inputs to IR systems consist of a query and a set of documents from which the information has to be retrieved. They added lexical and semantic information to both the query and the documents during a pre-processing phase in which the input question and texts are disambiguated.

Other experiences: Desmontils and Jacquin (2001) quoted by Magnini and Manuela (ibid. 44) suggest an approach where linguistic ontologies are used for information retrieval on the Internet. The indexing process as the authors pointed out is divided into four steps: i) for each page a flat index of terms is built; ii) WordNet is used to generate all candidate concepts which can be labelled with a term of the previous index; iii) each candidate concept of a page is studied to determine its representativeness of the page content; iv) all candidate concepts are filtered via an ontology, selecting the more representative for the content of the page.

4.3.2 Ontologies for Knowledge Management Applications

Companies and organizations develop more and more applications, such as, "organization memories", which can be described as databases whose objective is to disseminate knowledge among the employees of the enterprise. The function of these knowledge bases is to make permanent the knowledge and the know-how of the employees of the enterprise. That requires a perfect control of the terminologies used. When these knowledge bases give access to textual documents such applications can be compared to informational and documentary systems. Ontologies, be they linguistic or formal, are used in these new applications (Maybury, 2001).

4.3.3 Ontologies for Knowledge Engineering

Uschold, quoted by Vickery (1997) points out the need for ontologies:

> "*Knowledge engineering suffers from lack of formal tools for understanding domains of interest. Domain conceptualization is a necessary part of knowledge acquisition for a knowledge-based system. There is need for knowledge-level analysis, a requirement for the development of knowledge-based systems*".

The majority of methodologies aimed at developing systems containing knowledge, advocate an analysis of the field in the phase known as "knowledge acquisition". This stage performs the characterization of the relevant concepts of the field and thus establishes a list of the terms indicating these concepts. In this case, the tools assisting terminology acquisition are essential, in particular when part of the information is distributed in large volumes of texts. Knowledge acquisition is the field of application selected to validate the results of certain term extractors (cf. LEXTER, for example, Bourigault, 1992). This is why we think that terminology resources can be of help in building linguistic ontologies.

4.4 How can Terminology Resources be directed towards Building Ontologies?

Most of the methods used in building ontologies are rather empirical. Two main research trends are seen: the linguistic approach, which is represented by the research done by Terminology and Artificial Intelligence teams (Biebow and Sulman, 2000) and the formal one (Gomez-Perez, 1999). As far as the former approach is concerned, terminology acquisition tools, (an expression which covers respectively, term extractors, classifiers and semantic relation extractors), can be used in building ontologies (Velardi, et al, 2001). Term extractors produce as output, holistic lists of terms, drawn from a representative corpus, that characterize and describe a field of knowledge. In order to be of any use, this type of lists must be subjected to a structuring which is an important step towards exploiting extraction results. Terminology resources are hence increasingly seen as structured data - i.e. as a network of terms organized by relations. Pure alphabetical lists can hardly be used except for bilingual reference tools or by specialists in the relevant fields, which makes it a rather constraining process. Structuring lists of terms by semantic relations or in classes has been useful in the following applications: index-making for on-line technical documentation; browsing, information access and retrieval, building thesaurus and ontologies for information systems and more recently, for text summarization.

The first step in building ontologies is to acquire terminological resources from corpora in different languages. In our case, the idea is to use available terminology acquisition tools. This means an agreement of the designers who participate to the evaluation exercise conducted by our team at the University of Lille 3. If the tools cannot be, for any reason, made available for our ontology project we have to resort to industrial products of the same type (for a complete account of the tools tested in our two research projects, Mustafa, 2001, 2004).

4.4.1 Term Extractors, Classifiers and Semantic Relation Extractors: Cooperative integration of Tools

Many applications and extraction methods relevant to these tools have been described in the literature. But the systems tested within the framework of our evaluation exercises are geared towards a variety of applications, ranging from rough semantic relation extraction through indexing, thesaurus construction, to knowledge-based system modelling.

The outputs of the systems diverge but can, in some cases, be complementary. In fact the results drawn from the two evaluation exercises have led us to consider the feasibility of trans-systemic integration for strengthening their automatic terms identification capabilities. The idea is to combine two or three different types of systems in order to specify various integrated production processes. Systems could increasingly be seen as parts of these integrated production processes.

The formal level of the ontology will be built either by integrating a tool or by conceiving from scratch an inference engine. Thus the type of ontology we are suggesting would be semi-formal (*see* the definitions given by Uschold, 1996). In fact, part of the organization would be expressed in natural language.

4.5 Relevant Work and Similar Experiences

NLP-based ontologies are used to reduce the cost of ontology engineering. Using the existing term extraction and recognition tools together with semantic relation extraction tools and classifiers can be compared, though the procedure will be different, to several endeavours in the field of ontology constructions. It follows the path of comparable work in the field of NLP applications to MT such as the SENSUS-based ontology (for more details and relevant examples, *see* Fenandez Lopèz, 1999); TERMINAE (Biebow and Sulman, 2000) a tool for generating ontologies from specialized corpora. It uses lexical and terminological tools to build the terminological and conceptual data enriched by definitions drawn directly from the relevant corpus. The tool used enables contextual feedback in order to pick up definitions and check their validity. The process of validation and normalization of terms and definitions are carried out by a domain specialist. The final and formal layer is based on ALNR, logic description language as the designer of the systems mentioned (Biebow and Sulman, 2000).

Other experiences are related to building ontologies for knowledge management and knowledge sharing. SYMONTOS (Veraldi et. al.. 1999) a symbolic ontology management system is an example of this family of tools. The system uses OPAL (Object, Process, and Actor modelling language), a methodology for the modelling and management of a company knowledge-base. It enables the representation of the semi-formal knowledge. SYMONTOS gathers terms denoting concepts, definitions explaining (in natural language) the meaning of concepts and a set of relationships.

5 FUTURE DIRECTIONS

We are currently conducting a research project dealing with linguistic ontology design based on two types of resources. The first resource is the existing thesaurus, covering about a hundred fields of knowledge, constructed by our students at the University of Lille 3, since 1992. The second one will be the output of term extractors, semantic relation extractors and classifiers we are currently evaluating in the framework of CESART project (*see* above for details). The quality and good coverage of ontology will depend on the representativeness of the corpus used in acquiring the terminological resources (terms, semantic relations and concept definitions). In some cases ontology designing will use existing ontologies or thesaurus, manually created ones, which can be enriched thanks to increasingly common term and semantic relations acquisition tools. The first step would be the selection of a representative corpus covering a field of knowledge, and the selection of an existing thesaurus or an ontology. The second step would be to choose among the tools we are testing the most relevant ones for an integrated production of terms, semantic relations and classifications. It is important to choose tools that will allow contextual feedback in order to pick up definitions and check their validity, an essential element of the ontology. The formal layer of the ontology is under study.

REFERENCES

1. Akiko. A. and Kageura, K. (2001). The Automatic Construction of Faceted Terminological Feedback for Interactive Document retrieval. **In**: Bourigault, D. Jacquemein, Ch. & L'Homme, MC. (ed). (2001). *Recent Advances in Computational Terminology*. John Benjamins, p. 1-28.

2. Béguin, A.; Jouis, Ch and Mustafa el Hadi, W. (1997). Evaluation d'outils d'aide à la construction de terminologie et de relations mantiques entre termes à partir de corpus, *Actes des Premières Journées Scientifiques et Techniques* (JST'97), FRANCIL, AUPELF-UREF, Avignon, avril 1997, p. 419-426.

3. Biebow, B. ; Sulman S. (2000). Terminae, Une approche terminologique pour la construction d'ontologies à partir de textes. *Actes du colloque de Reconnaissances de formes et intelligence artificielle*, (RIFIA' 2000). Vol. 11; p. 81-90.

4. Bisson, F. (2001). *Méthodes et outils pour l'appariement de textes bilingues*, thèses de doctorat de l'université Denis Diderot Paris 7, en Information Scientifique et Technique, Présentée et le 12 Janvier 2001.

5. Bontcheva,. K. ; Bewster, Ch. ; Ciravena, F. ; Cunningham, H. ; Gutherie, L. ; Gaizauskas, R. and Wilks, Y. (2001). Using HLT for Acquiring, Retrieving and

Publishing Knowledge in AKT: Position Paper. **In** *Proceedings of ACL 39th Annual Meeting. Proceedings of the workshop HLT and KM*, July 6th –7th, 2001.

6. Bourigault, D. (1992). Lexter, vers un outil linguistique d'aide à l'acquisition des connaissances. *Actes des 3èmes Journées d'Acquisition des Connaissances*, Dourdan, avril.
7. —; Jacquemin, Ch. and L'Homme, M-Cl. (eds) (2001). *Recent Advances in Computational Terminology*. John Benjamins.
8. Dagan, I. and Church, K. (1994), "Termight: Identifying and Translating Technical Terminology" in Proceedings of *4th Applied NLP Conference*, p. 34-40.
9. Drouin, P. (2002). *Acquisition automatique des termes: l'utilisation des pivots lexicaux spécialisés*, Thèse de doctorat, Université de Montréal.
10. Fenandez Lopèz, M. (1999). Overview of Methodologies for Building Ontologies. **In**: *Proceedings of IJCAAI-99 Workshop on Ontologies and Problem Solving Methods*, Stockholm, Sweden, August 2, 1999.
11. Gaussier, E. (2001). General Considerations on Bilingual Terminology Extraction. In: Bourigault, D. Jacquemein, Ch. & L'Homme, MC. (ed). (2001). *Recent Advances in Computational Terminology*. John Benjamins, pp. 167-184.
12. Gomez-Perez. (1999). Développements récents en matière de conception, de maintenance et d'utilisation d'ontologies. **In** *Terminologies Nouvelles*. Rint 19. Actes du Colloque Terminologie et Intelligence Artificielle.
13. Guarino, C. and Masolo, Vetere G. (1999). OntoSeek: Content-based access to the Web. *IEEE Intelligent Systems and their Applications*. Vol. 14 (3); p. 70-80.
14. Hongyan, J. and Tzoukermann, E. (2001). Determining Sematinc Equvalance of Terms in Information Retrieval: An Approach Based on Context Distance and Morphology. **In**: Bourigault, D. Jacquemein, Ch. and L'Homme, MC. (ed). *Recent Advances in Computational Terminology*, John Benjamins, p. 245-260.
15. Hull, D. (2001). Extracting Useful Terms for Pratical Expressions by Combinaning Simple Rules and Statistaical Measures: A Compartive Evalulation of Bigram Satatics. **In**: Bourigault, D. Jacquemein, Ch. and L'Homme, MC. (ed). (2001). *Recent Advances in Computational Terminology*., John Benjamins, p. 209-224.
16. Jacquemin, C. (1997). *Variation terminologique: Reconnaissance et acquisition automatiques de termes et de leurs variantes en corpus*, Mémoire d'habilitation à diriger des recherches en informatique fondamentale, Université de Nantes.
17. Jacquemin, Ch. (2001). *Spotting and Discovering Terms through Natural Language Processing*. MIT Press, Cambridge, Mass.
18. —; and Tzoukermann, E. (1999). NLP for Term Variant Extraction: Synergy between Morphology, Lexicon and Syntax. **In**: Strzalkowski, T. (ed). *Natural Language*

Information Retreival. Text, Speech and Language Technology Series, Kluwer Academic.

19. Kageura, K.; Yoshioka, M. and Takeuchi, K. (2000). Recent Advances in Automatic Term Recognition : Experiences from the NTICR Workshop on Information Retrieval and Term Recognition. *Terminology*. Vol. 6/2; p. 151-171.

20. L'Homme, MC. (2000). Understanding Specialized Lexical Combinations. *Terminology*. Vol. 6/1; p. 89-110.

21. Maybury, M. (2001), "Human Language Technology for Knowledge Management. **In**: *Proceedings of ACL 39th Annual Meeting. Proceedings of the workshop HLT and KM, July 6th –7th*.

22. Magnini, B. and Manuela, S. (2002). Merging Global and Specialized Linguistic Ontologies. **In** *Workshop Proceedings of Ontolex'2: Ontologies and Lexical Knowledge Bases*, LREC 2002, Las Palams de Gran Canaria, 27th of May 2002, p. 43-48.

23. Mustafa El Hadi, W.; Timimi, I. and Dabbadie, M. (2004). CESART: Campagne d'Evaluation des Systèmes d'Acquisition de Ressources Terminologiques e Traduction Automatique. *Actes du Colloque LREC*. p. 515-518.

24. –; –; Béguin; and A. Debrito. M. (2001). The ARC A Project: Terminology Acquisition Tools: Evaluation Method and Tasks. **In**: *Evaluation Methodologies for Language and Dialogue Systems Workshop*, ACL/EACL, Toulouse, 6-7 Juillet 2001, p. 41-50.

25. Oaks, M.P. and Paice, Ch. D. (2001). Term Extraction for Automatic Abstracting. **In**: Bourigault, Ch. Jacquemin and M.-Cl. L'Homme (eds). *Recent Advances in Computational Terminology*. John Benjamins, p. 353-370.

26. Peter, A. (2001). The Automatic Construction of Faceted Terminological Feedback for Interactive Document Retrieval. **In**: Bourigault, Ch. Jacquemin and M.-Cl. L'Homme (éds). *Recent Advances in Computational Terminology*. John Benjamins, p. 29-52.

27. Poli, R. (1996). Ontology for Knowledge Organization. **In**: R. Green (ed.) *Proceedings of the Fourth International ISKO Conference: Knowledge Organization and Change*, Washington, Library of Congress, July 1996, *Advances in Knowledge Organization*, Vol. 5, INDEX Verlag, Frankfurt/Main, p. 313-319.

28. Uschold, M. *Building Ontologies: Towards a Unified Methodology. Presented at Expert Systems '96 Conference*. ftp://ftp.aia.ed.ac.uk/pub/documents/1996/.

29. Velardi, P.; Missikoff, M. and Basili, R. (2001). Identification of Relevant Terms to Support the Construction of Domain Ontologies. **In**: *Proceedings of ACL 39th Annual Meeting*. Proceedings of the workshop HLT and KM, July 6th –7th.

30. Vickery, B. (1997). Ontologies. *Journal of Information Science*. Vol. 23(4); p. 277-286.

END NOTE

1 Kageura *et al.* (2000), Bourigault *et al.* (2000), Drouin (2002) have given a state of the art overview of automatic term recognition and retrieval.

2 We are using the term "information access" in a wide sense since it involves multiple technologies: traditional IR techniques, cross-language information retrieval (CLIR), text summarization, information extraction, automated question and answering, machine translation in IR environments, document understanding, and multimedia document and image retrieval.

3 Rich indexing is opposed to simple indexing. The former means extraction of multi-word term occurrences and the latter means extraction of multi-word term occurrences without considering variations (Jacquemin *et. al.*, 1999: 69).

4 We are referring to a research project conducted within the framework of a program sponsored by the "Association des Universités Entièrement ou Partiellement de Langue Française" (AUPELF) - an international association whose mission is to promote the dissemination of French as a scientific medium. This research aimed to evaluate software capabilities in automatic terminology building from corpora in French. Systems submitted to this evaluation are conceived by French and Canadian research institutions (National Scientific Research Centre and Universities) and/or companies: EDF (French Electric Company) among others. These systems have been described in our previous works (*see* Béguin *et. al.* 1997, Mustafa el Hadi, *et. al.* 2001). We are currently conducting another evaluation project, CESART 2003-2005, dealing with assessing automatic terminology processing. It is the logical continuation of our first research project (*see* Mustafa el Hadi, *et. al.* 2004).

SATSAN AUTO-MATRIX VERSION 1: A COMPUTER PROGRAMME FOR SYNTHESIS OF COLON CLASS NUMBER ACCORDING TO THE POSTULATIONAL APPROACH

B. G. Satyapal
N. Sanjivini Satyapal

Describes the features and capabilities of the software SATSAN AUTO-MATRIX version 1 for semi-automatic synthesis of Colon Class number (CCN) for a given subject according to the Postulational Approach formulated by S.R. Ranganathan. The present Auto-Matrix version 1 gives the user more facilities to carry out facet analysis of a subject (simple, compound, or complex) preparatory to synthesizing the corresponding CCN. The software also enables searching for and using previously constructed class numbers automatically, maintenance and use of databases of CC Index, facet formulae and CC schedules for subjects going with different Basic Subjects. The paper begins with a brief account of the authors' consultations with and directions received from, Prof. A. Neelameghan in the course of developing the software. Oracle 8 and VB6 have been used in writing the programmes. But for operating SATSAN it is not necessary for users to be proficient in VB6 and Oracle 8 languages. Any computer literate with the basic knowledge of Microsoft Word will be able to use this application software.

1 INTRODUCTION

Classification is a tool for knowledge organization (KO). SATSAN AUTO MATRIX is a program for synthesizing Colon Class (CC) number. In two earlier papers we have described the use of SATSAN for synthesis of CC number following Dr. S. R. Ranganathan's Postulational Approach (Neelameghan, 1997; Ranganathan, 1967). In designing and developing a KO tool there are two major aspects – the semantic dimension and the collaboration dimension (Ranganathan, 1987). In this paper we focus on the collaboration dimension.

2 THE PROCESS OF CLASSIFYING

The process of classifying a subject is divided into three Planes of Work: (1) the Idea plane; (2) the Verbal plane; and (3) the Notational plane as SRR explains.

Most of the work (95 %) in the Idea plane is essentially intellectual. It begins with determining the specific subject of the document in hand, and its component ideas. Beginning with the tile of the document, it may be necessary to examine the list of contents, the introduction or even some chapters or several pages to arrive at the specific subject. From this step on, it is possible for the machine to check the schedules and/or the index to identify and pick-up the numbers corresponding to each of the idea components, organize them in the required sequence and synthesize the class number. This has been discussed in another paper (Satyapal and Sanjivini Satyapal, 2002).

The Alphabetical Index to the schedules of CC Ed. 7 (unpublished), in machine-readable text format was available. In the manual method, after arriving at the specific subject of a document, there are three approaches to using CC in assigning class number to the subject:

1. Use of the schedules of CC;
2. Use of the Index to CC; and
3. A combination of the above two.

Approach 3 is the preferred one in the manual method.

3 ANALYSIS OF THE INDEX TO CC SCHEDULES

We found that with appropriate programming it is possible to use the CC index (approach 2 above) in arriving at the CCN after determining the specific subject of the document, that is, after completing step 2 of the Postulational Approach.

The following examples show the structure / format of an entry in the CC index:

1. Basic Subject only

   Astrobiology – [BS}, BYG, p. 58
   Astronomy- [BS], BX, p. 58
   Biology – [BS], G, p. 59

Each of the terms – Astrobiology, Astronomy, and Biology – represent a Basic Subject [BS], followed by the corresponding notation, and the page number in CC Ed. 7 where they are listed

2. Isolate term from a schedule of Common Isolates:

If the term is one that occurs (that is, enumerated) in one of the schedules of Common Isolates, then it will be so indicated. For example:

> Canada [SI], 72, p. 85
> India [SI], 44, p.77

where [SI] indicates that the terms 'Canada' and 'India' are enumerated in the common schedule of Space Isolates; the digit combinations 72 and 44 are the Isolate Numbers (IN) that is the notation for Canada and India respectively; p. 85 and p. 77 indicate the page number in volume 1of CC Ed 7 where the terms Canada and India respectively occur.

Abnormal reflection, (CMPI), cM24, p. 100, where (CMPI} indicates that the term 'Abnormal reflection' is enumerated in the schedule of Common Material Property Isolates and is represented by the notation cM24.

Acquire, (CEI), w5, p. 94, where (CEI) indicates that the term 'Acquire' is enumerated in the schedule of Common Energy Isolates and is represented by the notation w5.

Sanskrit, (LI), 15, p. 68, where (LI) indicates that the term 'Sanskrit' is enumerated in the schedule of common Language Isolates and is represented by the notation 15.

Desert, (ED), Uk2, p. 55, where (ED) indicates that the term 'Desert' is enumerated in the common schedule of Environment Divisions and is represented by the notation Uk2

3. Other isolate terms: If the term does not occur in any of the schedules of Common Isolates, then the structure of the entry is as follows:

Aberration - C5C,[MP],7,p. 168
Aberration, Spherical - C5C,[MP],74,p.1 68
Abdomen - G,[1P1],14,p. 204
- L,[1P],14,p. 229

In these entries C5C, G, and L respectively represent the notation for the Basic Subject to which each of the isolate ideas – 'Aberration', 'Aberration, Spherical', 'Abdomen' is assigned.. It may be noted that the term 'Abdomen' occurs in the schedules for G (Biology) and L (Medicine).

[MP], [1P1], and [1P] denote the Fundamental Category (FC) of which the preceding isolate idea is deemed to be a manifestation (MP = Matter Property; 1P = Personality, first Round; 1P1 = Personality, First Round, First Level)

4. Speciator

Ability, Intellectual – SYS, [SP to MP]. -bT811, p. 234
Abasement – SYS, {SP to 1P1], -H2E5, p. 267
Absolute Monarchy – W, [1P to E], -754, p. 313

[SP to] denotes that the term is a 'Speciator to' another isolate, namely, to an MP (Matter Property isolate, 1P1 (Personality isolate in Round 1, Level 1, and E (Energy isolate) respectively.

A Basic Subject (BS) may also have Speciators as indicated in the following index entries:

Ayurveda – [BS], L-B. p. 61
Child Medicine – (BS), L-9C, p. 60

Thus, for a given term, using the Index to CC, it is possible for the computer programme to identify:

1. The Basic Subject(s) to which it belongs;
2. Whether it occurs in one of the schedule of Common Isolates; and

3. Whether it is a Speciator and, if so, to which isolate it is a Speciator and in which facet, and which Basic Subject.

If it is neither (ii) nor (iii) above, then the Basic Subject(s), the facet, and its notation. In the index entries the common words among the subsequent lines were removed except in the starting term line. The missing words were annotated and copied using Excel. Still the terms were not unique. To reduce manual effort, we developed a programme to identify the non-uniqueness of the terms. There were about 35,000 terms in the CC Index. We used Oracle for creating the databases as it facilitates easy access to the terms. Therefore, databases created with Excel were transported to Oracle. VB (Visual Basic) was used as the front-end to access the databases. Output reports were prepared to assess the uniqueness of the terms in all the CC Schedules. As many as 75% of the terms were found to be repeated and many of them more than three times. As suggested by Professor A. Neelameghan we used the next hierarchical term for the purpose and checked the output. The result was quite satisfactory.

CC uses several Devices – Subject Device, Chronological Device, Environmental Device, Alphabetical Device, etc. Directions as to where any of these devices is to be used are given in the schedules. The rules, with examples, for applying each of the Devices are given in the main chapters of CC. These are not reflected in the Index. For this and other reasons it was necessary to generate the CC schedules of isolates of each of the facets for each of the Basic Subjects. The databases of the schedules were generated from the information given in the Index.

Other considerations were: Anteriorizing Common Isolates with different facet structures; Phase Relations between subjects in Complex Subjects (general, bias, comparison, differentiation, application, influence); between facets of subject going with a Basic Subject, between isolates in the same array, etc.

4 CHOICE OF SOFTWARE

We retained the same softwares used in the pilot project (training module) as we felt that the programs would be simple, fast and the databases could be evaluated efficiently. Since there were a large number of rules to be adhered to for each of the Schedules of the different subject fields, the databases had to be sharpened. As a first step an electronic worksheet was developed which contained matrices for use by the user for introducing the various criteria. This electronic worksheet was agreed to by A. Neelameghan when its use was demonstrated; and he also explained additional features needed to make it more useful.

5 TRAINING MODULE

Using the electronic worksheet, programs were developed with examples to amplify all aspects of the postulates, and rules of facet analysis and synthesis on which CC is based. This electronic worksheet allows users to synthesize the CC numbers. This can be achieved by following the Step-by-Step method elaborated by S. R. Ranganathan, the user being enabled to work out all the steps of the Postulational Approach effectively for which help lines were provided. The complete explanation of the programme is available in another paper (Satyapal and Sanjivini Satyapal, 2002). This programme can not only be used by libraries for synthesising CC numbers, but it can also be used in training. A. Neelameghan named this software as "Sat-San Matrix".

Having accomplished automatic synthesis of CC numbers using a variety of subjects involving different facets, A. Neelameghan advised us on other features to be introduced, such as use of Speciators, Devices, Chemistry Rules, Phase Relation, Anteriorising Common Isolates, etc. For this purpose many more programs were written. He also outlined various other features to make the programme more automatic. This needed the Databases to be reclassified. For this purpose his suggestion to bring all terms under each of the PMEST Categories was implemented. The idea was a brilliant one. Databases were modified on this basis and the terms of all the Schedules were also brought into one database called "Term Index" with more fields for easy understanding by the users. With additional programming it was possible to reduce user's intervention to find the class number using CC (*see* Section 6 for details). The program was further sharpened and many additional features were incorporated to make it almost automatic. (*see* Section 6 for details).

The software SATSAN AUTO-MATRIX version 1 is an improvement over the earlier SATSAN MATRIX. The present Auto-Matrix version 1 gives the user more facilities to achieve freely facetted analysis preparatory to synthesizing Colon Classification (CC) number. In short the purpose of this software is to integrate computer aided method of arriving at CC number, keeping the nuances in Postulational Approach to classify documents. The steps of the Postulational Approach are conformed to in deriving the class number beginning with the Raw Title of a document. Other features such as searching Titles in Subject Index for composing Class Number, Maintenance of Subject Index database, reading Subject Index database records as a part of Reference Service for retrieval of micro-subjects for specialist users, Facet formula and maintenance of Colon Classification schedules and their indexes are also provided.

6 APPLICATION OF SATSAN AUTOMATRIX VERSION 1

6.1 Scope

The software is best used by those trained and have experience in classifying subjects by applying Dr. S.R. Ranganathan's postulates and principles of freely facetted analytico-synthetic methodology of which his Colon Classification scheme used here is an example. In the following paragraphs the features and application of the software are explained.

6.2 New Features of SATSAN-AUTO MATRIX Version 1

The following table shows the new features of SATSANAUTOMATRIX ver.1 compared with those of SATSAN MATRIX (Satyapal, 2001):

Sl. No.	Satsan-Matrix	Satsan-auto Matrix Ver. 1
1.	Semi-automatic	Fully automatic requiring minimal intervention of user
2.	Generalised facet structure	No difference
3.	Facet analysis can be adopted to any classification scheme	No difference

Sl. No.	Satsan-Matrix	Satsan-auto Matrix Ver. 1
4.	Matrix is presented for the user to carry out facet analysis in detail by using steps enumerated in the CC	Matrices are presented to the user with a difference wherein the user's involvement is much less
5.	User needs to operate Schedule, Data and Index Grids to check for Standard terms, Basic Subject, Fundamental category. The IN, FCs etc had to be transferred to the main matrix.	Only Term Index Grid needs to be consulted by user to check for Standard terms. Additional information on Basic Subject, Fundamental category and Comments if any is also provided in this grid. After authentication of standard terms in the Expressive title, FCs and INs appear in the Matrix for facet analysis and final Synthesis
6.	Cross-reference from one schedule to another needs to be done to get Terms, INs, etc.	The new formation of databases does away with cross-reference.
7.	The terms are dragged to the various matrix boxes for arranging them in the facet sequence	Software itself performs sequencing of facets
8.	FCs are annotated manually for every Term	FCs appear with standard terms and are changed if required by user after facet analysis. For this purpose software allows for a quick method without having to annotate them manually
9.	Application of Speciators, Devices, Chemistry Rules, Phase Relation, Anteriorising Common Isolates, etc. is time-consuming	The application is straightforward with minimal intervention by the user.

Sl. No.	Satsan-Matrix	Satsan-auto Matrix Ver. 1
10.	Facet Formula is not indicated	Facet formula is indicated and can be consulted while synthesising.
11.	Subject Index formats available	Subject Index along with additional facility for the Title Check is available.

6.3 Steps in Class Number Synthesis

The classification of documents is discussed under the following headings:

1. **Stage 1.** Title check
2. **Stage 2.** Compound Subjects NOT Requiring User Inputs for Facet Analysis.
3. **Stage 3.** Compound Subjects Requiring User Inputs for Facet Analysis.
4. **Stage 4.** Use of Two Matrices for Complex Subjects, subjects involving Phase Relation

6.4 Forms and Features of the Software

Main Form

The main form called 'Auto Classify' has all the elements of operative buttons for use of postulates and principles of the analytico-synthetic methodology on which CC is based. The form is shown in Fig. 1 in the Appendix. The Form is divided into two main matrices. The second matrix is usually not visible; it only comes into operation during synthesis of complex subjects involving Phase Relation. The first Matrix is the one used by the classifier for all simple and compound subjects. Above this Matrix are the text windows: one relates to 'Raw Title' and the other to 'First Expressive Title'. The 'Expressive Title' is entered in its window and the kernel terms are checked for Standard Terms. '*Formation of Class number*' button is then clicked. A nine-column matrix will come into view. The first three columns will have the boxes showing the Fundamental Category (FC) of each isolate, corresponding isolate terms and isolate numbers respectively without apparatus words. Clicking on the button '*For order change*' will activate the next three columns bringing the terms in the PMEST sequence. '*Press to order*' button, when clicked, the next three matrices will have the information for the final analysis by the user before arriving at the Class Number (CN). Clicking on '*Total Class Number*' button will result in the CN appearing in its Text Box, each of the Focal Numbers (FN) being separated by the corresponding Indicator Digits (ID). The Standard terms and Focal numbers will also appear in their respective boxes in the right-hand corner of the form. The second matrix at the bottom comes into effect when the user clicks on the 'PR' combo box list. It has similar mirror buttons as explained above. The details of analysis etc. are discussed separately.

On the right hand top corner, there are Combo Boxes namely - 'SP and Others', 'PR', 'Oxides and Salts' and 'Devices'. The user operates them for facet analysis if required. Below these combo boxes, there are command buttons and text windows namely, '*Facet Formula*', '*Title check*', '*Exit/Continue*', '*Term Index*' and '*Close Index*' buttons.

Facet formula:

Clicking on the *Facet formula* button activates a message box requiring Basic Subject Name. After entering it and clicking on '*OK*' the Facet Formula for the desired schedule will appear in the window.

Term Index:

The classifier has to check the Standard Term for each of the Isolates in the Expressive Title. The user selects (highlights) the Kernel Term in the Expressive Title window and clicks on the *Term Index* button. A list containing the 'String' will appear in a Combo Box for the user to transfer the desired Standard Term to Expressive Title text window. The record has Term, FC, Schedule Name and Comments. By clicking on the record, apart from change of Term in the Expressive Title window, comments will appear in the Comments window.

Buttons in the Bottom Right hand Corner of the Form:

The Major buttons are: '*Subject Index*', '*Save Data*', and '*To Maintenance*'.

Subject Index: The 'Subject Index' database is formed when, after completing the final step, that is, 'Subject Total Class Number', '*Save Data*' button is clicked. A message '*Enter Comments on the Subject*' will appear. The user may insert comments on the factors that are considered while classifying or may also insert other related information. After pressing '*OK*' in the Message Box, the data from the fields 'Raw Title', 'Expressive Title', 'Standard Terms' in their text windows along with the respective FC and 'Class Number' will be recorded in the Subject Index database. This index is useful for reference work and can assist the reference librarian for retrieving even in-depth subjects in order to advise the enquirer about the document in which the special subjects can be found. In addition, this database is referred to for carrying out Title Check, wherein the CN of the subject can be found directly.

Reading and Updating Subject Index: Provision has also been made in the form for reading the records in the Subject Index. This is done by clicking on the '*Subject Index*' button. The 'Subject Index Read Form' will be displayed. This form has windows for all the fields of the Subject Index database. In addition, two more windows, namely, 'Select Key Words' and 'ClassNo' text windows are provided. The keyword string is entered in the 'Key Word' text window. Search string is not case sensitive. Clicking on the '*Read Subject*' button, the first record where the string matches in the 'Standard Term' field, will appear on the screen. A message '*Want to continue*?' will be displayed. User can also use the CN as the query. Even the combination of both keyword and the CN will select all records, which satisfy both the query conditions. This form has the facility to Add, Delete and Edit/Update the records. The 'Subject Index Read Form' is shown in Fig. 2 in the Appendix.

6.5 Databases

CC Schedules: The databases are based on the existing CC7 Schedules. Apart from this, an Index including all the above databases called 'AutoIndex' is available. This index is activated by clicking on '*Term Index*' button to search for the Standard Term of the highlighted Kernel Term in the Expressive Title Window. A Combo Box lists the records containing the 'String' of the highlighted term for the user to select the desired standard term. Clicking on the standard term in the list will replace only the highlighted term in the Expressive Title Window.

Clicking on the '*Formation of Class Number*' button removes all the apparatus words. Each term is subjected to a search in the databases of CC schedules and of Common Isolates to identify its FC and Isolate Number. The term, its FC and Isolate Number are projected in a format. The next search is on the term to its right. The rows of the matrix will be as many as the number of Standard Terms. The matrix has nine columns; the first three contain searched details of FC, Term and IN. These may not be in the facet-sequence. The next two buttons i.e. '*For Order Change*' and '*Press To Order*' will bring the terms in the desired facet-sequence. Here the user may change the sequence depending on the Facet Analysis and the Facet Formula of the Subject. The synthesized CN is then obtained by clicking on the '*Total Class Number*' button, each of the Focal Numbers being connected by the appropriate Indicator Digit of CC. Some difficulty may arise in this search mode. For example, the same term may occur in two or more schedules. Such concepts/terms must, therefore, be made unique. In our work the uniqueness was achieved by the addition of the super-ordinate term This aspect is being further examined.

6.6 Stages in Arriving at Subject Class Number

Stage 1: Title Check: The 'Subject Index' database formed by the records either worked out by using the 'Autoclassify' form or by entering records directly by using the 'Subject Index Read Form' consists of the 'Raw Title' field. The program allows the user to get the intended CN of the subject of the document directly if the Raw Title of the book corresponds to what is in the database when the following actions are carried out:

* Click on '*Title Chec*k' button
* A message box will appear asking the user to 'Enter Keyword/s of the 'Raw Title'

* Enter the Keyword/s - (as far as possible, enter unique keyword of the title).
* Click on *OK*

The first title containing the Keyword/s will appear in the Raw Title text box. Its CN can be seen in the 'Total Class Number' text window. Also a message box asking the user 'Want to Continue?' will appear. Click 'No' if the title in the Raw Title window is the same as what the user is looking for. Note down the CN. Click 'Yes' if the title is different. In case the title contains the key word, the details will appear, if not, it means that the database does not contain the 'Title', which the user is looking for. In that case go to the next stage.

Stage 2: Compound Subjects NOT Requiring User Inputs For Facet Analysis:

* Enter Raw Title in the Raw Title Text Window, e. g. "Wine growing in India: a guide to viniculture"
* After the study of the document and the Raw Title, include the missing concepts / terms:
  - Name of the Basic Subject, if it is not mentioned in the Raw Title it means that the Basic Subject is missing. In the above example Basic Subject is 'Agriculture'. If in doubt, find details through 'Term Index' Help procedure using the term 'Grape'.
  - Implied Missing Term, if any. In the above example, Wine is from Grape and the document deals with 'Cultivation'. Hence the terms 'Grape' and 'Cultivation' should be included in the Title.
  - Time period. In this case it is 1986. So enter 1986.
  - The resultant title 'Expressive title' will be - "In Agriculture cultivation of grapes in India in1986"
* Enter this title in the 'Expressive Title" text window. For every Kernel Term, use 'Term Index' Help procedure to ascertain the corresponding Standard Term. Now click on the '*Formation of Class Number*' button. All the 'Apparatus Words' will be removed. 'Fundamental Categories (FC)', 'Kernel Terms (Terms)' and the 'Isolate Numbers (Iso-No)' of the terms will be displayed in the first three Matrix Boxes vertically. The resultant Matrix is as shown below:

FC	Term	Iso-No	I-Order	I-Term	I-IN	Order	Term	Focal No
BS	Agriculture	j	BS	Agriculture	j	BS	Agriculture	j
E	Cultivation	g3	P	Grape	374	P	Grape	374
P	Grape	374	E	Cultivation	g3	E	Cultivation	g3
SI	India	44	S	India	44	S	India	44
T	1986	N86	T	1986	N86	T	1986	N83

* It can be seen from the first three columns that the PMEST facet-sequence is yet to be derived.
* Click on the buttons - '*For Order Change*' and '*Press To Order*'. The next six-column Matrix will show the terms in the correct PMEST sequence. These six columns are offered for users to analyse the facets and change the facet sequence if necessary. The next stage of operation explains the procedure for it. In this example the sequence is unaltered.
* Click on the '*Total Class Number*' button. The Class Number of the subject appears in its text window as J,374:g3.44'N85

The Standard Terms in the Standard Term Text Window and Focal Nos in the Focal No text Window will appear.

Note: The above procedure can also be used when Terms involving Anteriorising Common Isolates (ACI) are part of the subject.

Stage 3: Compound Subjects Requiring User Inputs for Facet Analysis:

The aspects needing user inputs to arrive at the Class Number are explained below:

* In Chemistry, Oxide and Salt Compounds: The Rules demand changes in the digits of CN depending on the type of Oxide and Salt
* Speciators in general
* Use of Devices

Oxides and Salts

Procedure for arriving at CN for Chemical Compounds containing Oxides and Salts is as follows:

i Enter Basic Subject General Chemistry and the element of the compound in the Expressive Title Text Window. Ascertain their Standard Terms by using Term Index procedure;

ii Click on '*Formation of Class Number*' button. The Matrix with the FC, Terms and Isolate Numbers will be formed in the first three columns of the Matrix;

iii In the row of the element term where the Oxide or Salt to be added, click on the text window of the second (Term) column;

iv Activate '*Oxide and Salt*' combo box, select the desired oxide or salt. This results in changes in the second column i.e. 'Term' column and the Isolate Number in the third column appropriately as per the rules; and

v Click on '*For Order change*', 'Press *to Order*' and '*Total Class Number*' buttons. The CN will appear n the 'Subject Class Number' text window. Standard Terms of the subject and Focal Numbers can also be seen in their Text Windows.

Speciators

A 'Speciator' is a qualifier to an Entity (a Basic Subject or an Isolate Idea). An isolate idea may have two or more qualifiers applied in sequence. Here we discuss the arrangement of speciators according to Principles of Helpful Sequence. For example, consider the following Raw Title:

"Summer Fever caused by KFV carried by Monkeys"

The Expressive Title is:

"In Medicine, Disease of Lungs caused by Virus KFV carried by Monkeys and manifesting as Fever during Summer Season"

In the above Expressive Title we note that symptom of the 'Disease' is 'Fever' which occurs in 'Summer'; the 'Fever' is caused by the agent 'Virus'; the type of Virus is 'KFV' and the virus is carried by (vector) 'Monkey.' The Isolate 'Disease' is qualified by 'Fever' (as symptom) occurring in 'Summer', 'Virus' (as agent) and KFV as the type of virus and 'Monkey' as carrier of the virus. These four speciators are to be arranged in a helpful sequence by applying the Principles for Helpful Sequence such that the same sequence can be arrived at consistently by different classifiers in similar contexts. We may apply the 'Wall-Picture Principle' by taking two of the speciators at a time. Alternatively, we can *correlate* each of the speciators to one of the FCs. It may be noted that the speciator idea 'Virus' cannot be correlated with either Time, or Space, or Energy, or Matter Property. Hence it is correlated with Personality. The speciator idea 'Fever' is a symptom and can be correlated with Matter Property. The speciator idea 'KFV' is a type of virus and hence it should be attached to 'Virus' idea. The speciator idea 'Summer' is easily correlated with Time. The speciator idea 'Monkey' as carrier can be correlated with Personality (as in the case of Virus). Note that we have two speciator ideas Virus (as causative agent) and Monkey (as carrier) associated with Personality.

Applying the PMEST sequence to the speciators will give:

Disease-Virus (P-correlated)=KFV-Monkey (P-correlated) -Fever (MP-correlated) -Summer (Time-correlated)

KFV can be an array division of Virus obtained by applying the characteristic of division 'By type of virus'. If KFV is treated as a speciator to the speciator Virus (as in the present context) then it will be a Speciator of Kind 2. In this case KFV will be attached to Virus by double hyphen (equal to sign).

By applying the Wall-Picture principle between Virus and Monkey (both correlated with Personality), in the context the present subject, the concept behind the carrier (Monkey) will not become operative unless the concept behind what is being carried (KFV Virus) is conceded first. Hence the sequence given above.

Satsan Auto-Matrix Version I

A program has been formulated to facilitate the user to automatically obtain the correct sequence of speciators to any of the isolates having more than one speciator, and their sequence has been determined by applying the Principles of Helpful Sequence including the Principle of Correlation to the Fundamental Categories as discussed above. They are represented in the List contained in 'SP and Others' Combo Box. The relevant notations for this task are explained under each FC below:

[P]	[M]	[E]	[S]	[T]
"[P-P-Sp]"	"[M-P-Sp]"	"[E-P-Sp]"	"[S-P-Sp]"	"[T-P-Sp]"
"[P-M-Sp]"	"[M-M-Sp]"	"[E-M-Sp]"	"[S-M-Sp]"	"[T-M-Sp]"
"[P-E-Sp]"	"[M-E-Sp]"	"[E-E-Sp]"	"[S-E-Sp]"	"[T-E-Sp]"
"[P-S-Sp]"	"[M-S-Sp]"	"[E-S-Sp]"	"[S-S-Sp]"	"[T-S-Sp]"
"[P-T-Sp]"	"[M-T-Sp]"	"[E-T-Sp]"	"[S-T-Sp]"	"[T-T-Sp]"

Each FC column is divided into similar sequence of PMEST, the first symbol being common in each column, which gets attached to the main FC. That means the first notation is 'P' under FC [P].

The procedure for this, using the above example is as follows:

* After entering the Raw Title in its text window, enter the Expressive title in its Text window;
* Each of these terms is to be tested for Standard Terms with the help of 'Term Index' procedure. Here all are standard terms except the term 'Lungs' for which the schedule term is 'Lung' and for 'Monkeys' there is no Standard Term for it, but it is a 'Primate' the term of which is existing in the Zoology schedule as 'Primates' and its IN is suffixed with the alphabet 'M'. There is no Standard Term for KFV in the schedule. So we use it as it is (as with the Alphabetical Device); and

* Click on the '*Formation of Class Number*' button. The result is a nine-column matrix and first three of this matrix will contain FC, Term and Iso-No of the above title in the same order represented in the Exp Title Window leaving out all apparatus words. FC and Iso-No Columns will be blank in KFV row; type KFV as shown below:

FC	Term	Iso-Nop	I-Order	I-Term	I-IN
BS	Medicine	L	BS	Medicine	L
[P]	Lung	45	[P]	Lung	45
[1MP1]	Disease	4	[1MP1]	Disease	4
[M-P-SP]	Virus	23	(SPI)	Virus	23
[M-M-SP]	KFV	KFV	(SP2)	KFV	KFV
[M-E-SP]	Primates(M)	9797M	(SP1)	Primates(M)	9797M
[M-S-SP]	Fever	14	(SP1)	Fever	14
[M-T-SP]	Summer	962	(SP1)	Summer	962

Next click on '*For Order Change*' button. This results in all the terms being arranged in the PMEST sequence, those which have common FCs will be grouped together as given above namely I-Order. I-Term and I-IN columns.

Click on the 'Virus' row of I-Order Column. Activate 'SP and Others' combo box and select '[M-P-SP]'. It gets transferred to the I-Order column of the 'Virus' row. Similarly insert '[M-M-SP]' in the KFV row of the I-Order Column, '[M-E-SP]' in 'Primates' row, '[M-S-SP]' in 'Fever' row and '[M-T-SP]' in 'Summer' row. This action will keep the sequence of the terms of [MP] category. Next click on '*Press To Order*' button. The changes made in all the rows of I-Order column will be turned to '(SP1)' and the sub FCs will have the same PMEST sequence. The result will be as shown below.

I-Order	I-Term	I-IN	Order	Term	Focal No
BS	Medicine	L	BS	Medicine	L
[P]	Lung	45	[P]	Lung	45
[1MP1]	Disease	4	[1MP1]	Disease	4
[M-P-SP]	Virus	23	(SP1)	Virus	23
[M-M-SP]	KFV	KFV	(SP2)	KFV	KFV
[M-E-SP]	Primates(M)	9797M	(SP1)	Primates(M)	9797M
[M-S-SP]	Fever	14	(SP1)	Fever	14
[M-T-SP]	Summer	962	(SP1)	Summer	962

™chpbx column

Note: The (SP1) of the Order row of KFV has been changed to (SP2) by using transfer method in the 'SP & Others' combo box as its ID must be '=' (double hyphen).

* Click now on the '*Total Class Number*' button. The following class number of the Subject will appear:

  L,45;4-23=KFV-9797M-14-962

The "Standard terms" and "FocalNumber Text" windows will also be filled with their respective details.

Devices

The Program deals with the following Devices:

* Chronological Device;
* Alphabetical Device;
* Geographical Device; and
* Subject Device.

Chronological Device

Example: Raw title: "Psychoanalysis and discourse"

Kernel Terms: Psychology (BS). Psychoanalysis System (System Speciator to BS)

The term Psychoanalysis is a System of (BS) 'Psychology' and is obtained by Chronological Device, which, in this case is (1890). This is added to the (BS) by Speciator kind 1. The procedure is as follows:

* Enter 'Raw Title' and 'Expressive Title' in their respective windows. Expressive Title is 'Psychology Psychoanalysis'. Highlight (Select) 'Psychoanalysis'.
* Click on the '*Devices*' combo box and select CD. Message box asking the user to 'enter the chronological year in four digits' when it appears. Enter 1890 and click on '*OK*'. The term 'Psychoanalysis' will change to '1890'.
* Click on the '*Formation of Class Number*' button.

Following will appear in the first three columns of the Matrix:

FC	**Term**	**Iso-No**
BS	Psychology	s
TI	1890	M9

* Click 'For Order Change' and 'Press to Order' buttons. The result will be same as above;
* Click on the 'Devices' Combo Box and select 'CD';
* Click on the 'Term' Box 8th Column and '1890' row i.e. on the term '1890'. This changes the term to 'Psychoanalysis (1890)' and the order column i.e. (TI) to (SP1); and
* Click on the 'Total Class Number' button, which results in "S-M9" in its text window. The information of Standard terms and Focal Numbers will

appear simultaneously in their respective windows. In the Standard Terms Window 'Psychology (BS) Psychoanalysis (1890)' will appear.

Alphabetical Device

The Alphabetical Device (AD) consists in using the first two, or the first three, etc. letters (all in caps) of the name of an entity, existential or conceptual, for the formation or the subdivision of an isolate and applying (AD) to a binomial name, the two (AD) components in this multinomial (MUL) are connected by the Indicator Digit "+"

The procedure is as follows:

* Enter Raw Title: 'Milton's Paradise Lost' in the Text window.
* Enter Expressive Title: "Literature English Poetry John Milton Paradise Lost" in its text Window. Select Term 'John Milton'. Click on Devices Combo Box and select 'CD'.
* A Message box 'Enter Chronological Year in four digits' will appear. Click on 'OK'. In the Expressive Title Window '1608' will appear in place of 'John Milton'
* Click on 'Formation of Class number' button. Following will appear:

FC	Term	Iso-No
BS	Literature	o
[1P1]	English	111
[1P2]	Poetry	1
[TI]**	1608	K08
#	Paradise	p*
@	lost	L

- Type 'P' and 'L'
  ** Change it to [1P3] from 'SP & Others' List
  # Change it to [1P4] from 'SP & Others' List
  @ Change it to [P-Sp] from 'SP & Others' List
- Click on 'For Order Change' and 'Press To Order' buttons. Finally it will appear in the same format as per changes made above.
- Correct the last row containing '[P-P-Sp]' in 'Order' column by inserting '(MUL)' from the 'SP & Others' List.
- Click on the 'Devices' combo box. Select 'CD-LIT (Form)' and click on 'K08' box in the 8th column of the matrix. This removes the '[P-P-Sp]' from the Order column of the same row. As per rules there should not be any ID between the Form number and the CD.
- Click on 'Total Class Number' column. The following will appear in its text window:

  O,111,1K08,P+L
- The Standard Term Window will contain 'John Milton (1608) as one of the terms.

Geographical Device:

Example:

Raw Title: Studies of 18th century British art.

Exp Title: Fine-arts, United-Kingdom, 18th century (Division by GD and CD).

- Enter Terms in Exp Title Text Window;
- Check their Standard Terms using 'Term Index' procedure;
- Click on 'Formation of Class Number'. Following will result:

FC	Term	Iso-No
DS	Fine-Arts for Style	N(...)*
[SI]@	United-Kingdom	56
[TI]#	18th Century	L

* Click on '*For Order Change*' and '*Press for Order*' buttons;
* In the last three columns of the Matrix, change the various ordinal numbers for the (BS) to Na- (N(...) for the other styles of Fine arts in general);
* Click to activate the '*Devices*' combo box. Select 'GD+CD'. Click on the *FN* box column and the row which consists of IN of the Geographical Area. Brackets with changes in the order boxes can be observed;
* Click on the 'Total Class Number' button. The result will be "Na-(56, L). The latter part is the result of applying both (GD) and (CD); and
* There can be other situations where only (GD) may be used. They can be dealt with in a similar manner.

Subject Device

Example: Mysticism Zoology United-Kingdom

The Class No of the above subject is: MZ (K).56

The method of 'Bracketing' is inserted by selecting 'SD+Braces' in the Devices Combo List and clicking on *Focal No* column of the row i.e. on 'K' itself.

6.6.1 Use of Two Matrices for Complex Subjects in Phase Relation

Generally, while working with a compound subject a single Matrix is used to arrive at Class Nos. Subjects involving 'Phase relation' (PR) (given in the help procedure) call for working with two phases, presenting Inter-subject relation. The first subject is 'Phase1', and the second is 'Phase 2'.

While working with one compound subject, the other matrix is not visible. It comes into view when the user clicks on the PR list in the combo box at the top right-hand corner of the form. Clicking on it the user will see the second 'Exp Title' text window at the bottom of the form and the standard terms for Phase Relation will also appear in this Title window. The second phase subject can now be entered in this window and all steps to find its class number can be carried out. This means operation of all the typical command buttons is carried out as in the first phase subject matrix. This is as explained above but with one difference, that is, when the '*II Class Number*' button is clicked, the final CN of both the phased subjects will appear in the 'Total Class Number' text window as per rules stated in Phase Relation chapter of CC7.

The operation in the second Matrix is the same as that of the first, but with the difference that the second matrix is used only for the Phase Relation.

7 MAINTENANCE OF DATABASES OF CC SCHEDULES

A facility for maintenance of Databases has been provided in this Application Software. The Form 'Maintenance of Schedule' can be activated by clicking on the '*To Maintenance*' button in the 'AutoClassify' Form. The types of Maintenance facilities provided are: *Data Listing*; *Editing/Updating*; *Deleting and Adding records* in the databases of schedules. Apart from this the other buttons are '*Back To Auto*' to go back to '*AutoClassify*' Form and '*Continue/Exit*' button for continuing the maintenance and for ending the programme. The '*Help*' facility gives the details of its operation. The form is as shown as Fig. 3 in the Appendix.

8 SOFTWARE REQUIREMENTS

This Application Software uses Oracle 8 at the back end and Visual Basic 6 at the front end. With these two Softwares, the concept of Network Computer Architecture is feasible. As the CC grows in size and *complexity* in this age of information technology, the base software is adequate for this task and to adequately cover the current and future trends towards more users, more data, better performance, high reliability and greater scalability. *For operating SATSAN it is not necessary for the users to be proficient in VB6 and Oracle 8 languages. Any computer literate with the basic knowledge of Microsoft Word will be in a position to operate this Application Software.*

9 ACKNOWLEDGEMENT

We would like to recount how our work for preparing a software package for the synthesis of CC Number (CCN) started. I am a retired Air Vice-Marshall. The adage 'behind every successful man there is a woman' is widely known. My wife and co-author Sanjivini obtained her library science degree from the Isabella Thoburn College for women, Lucknow. She was of the first batch of women candidates in this field that year from that college. Dr S.R. Ranganathan (SRR) was highly respected by all students of her class. They wrote a letter of appreciation to him regarding CC. Sanjivini still keeps Dr Ranganathan's reply to her letter.

As I browsed through her copy of the CC and got interested in it, we thought that constructing a CCN for a subject by using a computer program would be a great challenge. Our next stop was at DRTC, Indian Statistical Institute, Bangalore, where Dr. I. K. Ravichandra Rao informed us that there was an earlier attempt to synthesize CCN and to some extent it was successful, however it could not meet all requirements of the Postulational Approach. He then advised us to contact Prof. Neelameghan at the Sarada Ranganathan Endowment for Library Science, (SRELS), for further discussion.

Prof. Neelameghan was kind enough to give us the time and also encouraged us to undertake the project and offered all help. He explained the analytico-synthetic methodology in classifying a subject and the resulting architecture of a subject expressed in the verbal plane to form the basis for assigning the notation from the CC schedules, i.e. arriving at the class number. I, being a novice with CC, he took pains to explain the related postulates and principles, and the Postulational Approach (Postulational Approach) to subject analysis and representation. With my wife's assistance I studied every aspect of the Postulational Approach and the steps involved. I also examined the CC schedules for different subject areas and the related facet formulae.

REFERENCES

1. Neelameghan, A. (1997). S. R. Ranganathan's general theory of knowledge classification in designing, indexing, and retrieving from specialised databases. **In** *S. R. Ranganathan's Postulates and Normative Principles*, Compiled by A. Neelameghan, Bangalore, Sarada Ranganathan Endowment for Library Science. Chap.5.

2. Ranganathan, S.R. (1967). *Prolegomena to library classification*. Ed. 3. Assist. by M.A. Gopinath, Bangalore, Sarada Ranganathan Endowment for Library Science.

3. —. (1987). *Colon classification. Ed. 7 (Basic and Depth Version)*. Revised and edited by M.A. Gopinath, Bangalore, Sarada Ranganathan Endowment for Library Science.

4. Satyapal, B.G. and Sanjivini Satyapal, N. (2001). Classifying documents according to Postulational Approach. 1. SATSAN-MATRIX: a computer based learning package. *National Seminar on Classification in the Digital Environment*, Bangalore, 9-11th August, 2001 Paper N, p.133-146.

APPENDIX

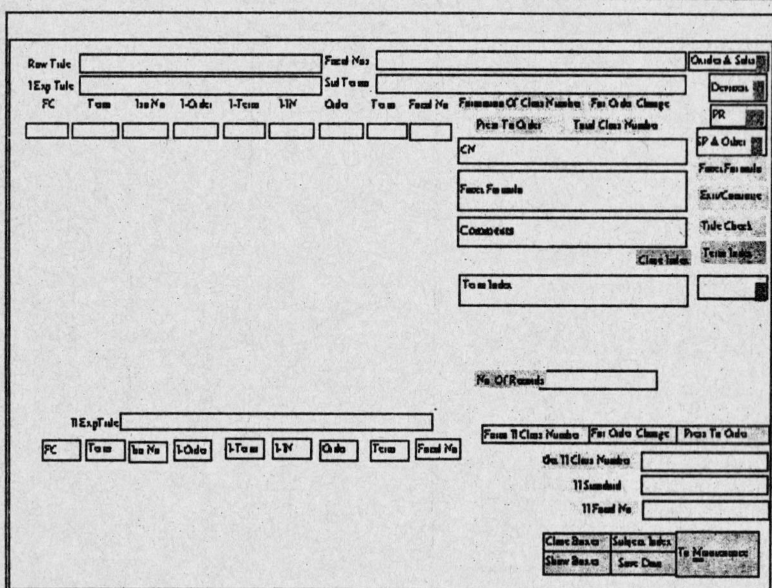

Fig. 1: Auto Classify Form

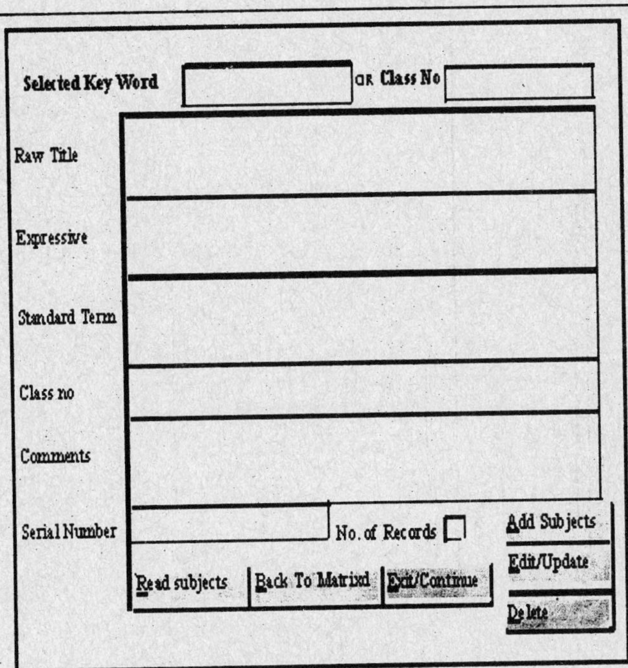

Fig. 2: Subject Index Form

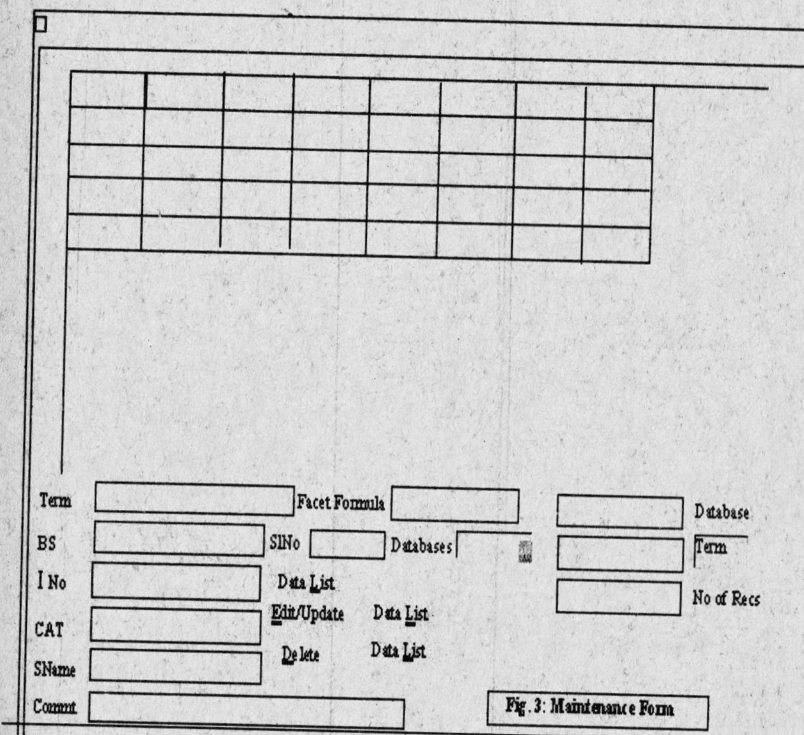

Fig. 3: Maintenance Form

INTEROPERABILITY, DIGITAL LIBRARY AND INFORMATION RETRIEVAL

INTEROPERABLE INSTITUTIONAL DIGITAL RESEARCH REPOSITORIES AND THEIR POTENTIAL FOR OPEN ACCESS AND RESEARCH KNOWLEDGE MANAGEMENT

T.B. Rajashekar

Discusses various aspects of institutional repositories from the perspective of academic institutions. There is growing interest among individuals and organizations - academic and research organizations in particular - to make innovative use of the digital medium of the Internet and the World Wide Web to reach their constituencies. Researchers and scholars in these are exploring novel ways of disseminating their work, to supplement traditional scholarly communications. The growing number of personal web pages, institutional and organizational websites indicate this trend and the realization by many organizations of the need for developing support systems at the institutional level for capturing, organizing, preserving and disseminating their intellectual output and to leverage on this knowledge capital. Defines institutional repositories, enumerates their features, and discusses their contents, design and development as well as benefits. Open access institutional repositories created and used in institutional environments may have different contents coming from different sources, on different platforms and metadata sets for description, the question of interoperability and enabling ease of access to and use by different categories of users with different information needs, is an important consideration. Several technical and non-technical parameters have a bearing on the success of inter-operable institutional repositories. These include: convincing researchers for content submission and usage of the institutional repositories; defining and managing appropriate content quality; digital rights management (publisher and researcher copyright; and access management); defining and implementing digital preservation strategies; assignment of persistent identifiers to repository items; development of aggregated repository services at consortia/ regional and national level; and development of semantic interoperability schemes. Briefly describes the institutional repositories scenario in India.

0 PREAMBLE

Prof. A. Neelameghan (AN) was one of my teachers in the post-graduate course in documentation and information science of 1976-78 at the Documentation Research and Training Centre, ISI, Bangalore. We did a very interesting software project in developing a referral directory database and search service under his guidance in DRTC, helping me to get an early start in the use of computers. We corresponded frequently when I was working with the National Informatics Centre (NIC), New Delhi. The work with NIC further strengthened my interest in and knowledge of computer-based information systems. In December 1986 when AN returned from UNESCO, he brought with him CDS-ISIS version 1.0. He assisted me in installing the software on a PC XT and experiment with it. We tried to extend the capability of the software with Pascal programs. An aspect that interested me was the exchange of records (interoperability) between CDS-ISIS databases. This led to using international standard record formats such as, UNESCO's Common Communication Format (CCF), International Standard Bibliographical Description (ISBD) etc., and to examine the structure of ISO 2709, the frame for importing records into a CDS-ISIS database. In consultation with AN, my proposal for developing a frame for converting the record structure of any database to the ISO2709 format, applying a Pascal program, was approved for my doctoral programme.

In 1998, AN assigned a project for developing a web-enabled multimedia database to a small team in NCSI under my direction. This project (OM Database Service) was exciting and gave us insight into various aspects of multimedia databases including audio and video components with an integrated database of three different databases developed with CDS-ISIS. The team had interactions with AN at every stage of the project.

1 INTRODUCTION

There is growing interest among individuals and organizations to make innovative use of the digital medium offered by the Internet and the World Wide Web (WWW) to reach out to their constituencies. This is most evident in academic and research organizations. Researchers and scholars in these organizations are exploring novel ways of disseminating their research findings, to supplement traditional scholarly communication mechanisms. The growing number of personal web pages, department and organizational websites are an indication of this trend. This has led many organizations to realize the need for developing support systems at the institutional level for capturing, organizing, preserving and disseminating their intellectual output and to leverage on this knowledge capital. Over the past few years a novel scholarly publishing and communication model has emerged in the form of 'Institutional Repositories'. Open access institutional repositories in academic institutions have the potential to provide improved visibility to the research findings and also supplement the traditional publishing systems, such as, periodicals. In addition, by bringing together the intellectual output of the institution, they also serve the purpose of improved research knowledge management.

This paper discusses various facets of institutional repositories from the perspective of academic institutions.

2 WHAT IS AN INSTITUTIONAL REPOSITORY?

According to SPARC (Scholarly Publishing and Academic Resources Coalition) position paper on institutional repositories, an institutional repositories is "a digital archive of the intellectual products created by the faculty, research staff, and students of an institution and accessible to end users both within and outside of the institution, with few if any barriers to access" (SPARC, 2002). Another useful definition of institutional repositories by Clifford Lynch says: "University-based institutional repository is a set of services that a university offers to the members of its community for the management and dissemination of digital materials created by the institution and its community members" (Lynch, 2003). These definitions reflect the current focus on creating institutional repositories in institutions of higher education. However, institutional repositories can be set up by any institution, including public and private R&D laboratories, interested in collection, organization, preservation, and dissemination of their research output. Usage of institutional repositories could be limited to internal knowledge management or information management requirements of an organization, without opening access to external users. We however do not discuss this aspect in this paper.

At the most basic level, academic institutional repositories support the following functions:

* Provide interface for online submission of research publications, typically on the institutional intranet;
* Archive and preserve the content;
* Provide online access to the content, at metadata and full publications level; and
* Share metadata with other institutional repositories through an appropriate interoperability mechanism (e.g. the OAI-PMH protocol of the Open Archives Initiative, discussed in a later section).

This is shown in Fig.1. Details of institutional repositories functionality are discussed in a later section.

An institutional repositories system consists of hardware (e.g. repository server), software (e.g. institutional repositories management software), staff for managing the institutional repositories and the institutional repositories content itself. Impetus for development of institutional repositories has come from several quarters. From a technology point of view, the networked infrastructure offered by the Internet and the dropping storage and computer costs have been major factors. Early establishment of discipline-based archives, such as, Arxiv (www.arxiv.org) provided experience in setting up and operating preprint submission and access services. We mentioned earlier researchers' interest in using the digital medium to experiment with new ways of dissemination. Developments in digital library technologies, including information retrieval, multimedia storage and retrieval, metadata standards, interoperability protocols (e.g. OAI-PMH protocol) and preservation strategies contributed to the development of repository software with requisite functionality. More importantly, interoperable institutional repositories were conceived as a key approach for supporting open access to scholarly material, by agencies like SPARC http://www.arl.org/sparc) and PLoS (Public Library of Science http://www.publiclibraryofscience.org/), and such initiatives as BOAI (Budapest Open Access Initiative http://www.soros.org/openaccess/and OAI (Open Archives Initiative http://www.openarchives.org/).

Figure 1. Basic institutional repositories functionality

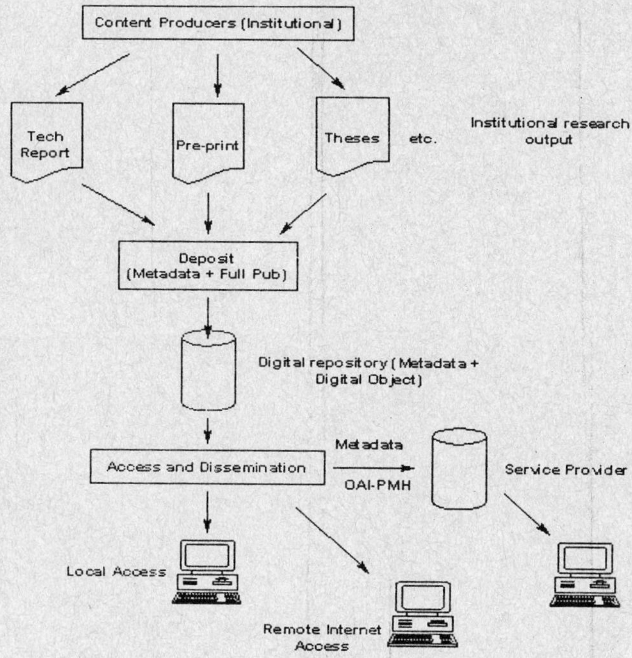

3 CONTENT IN INSTITUTIONAL REPOSITORIES

An institutional repositories essentially contains the research output of the institution. This could include:

* Published material (e.g. papers in periodicals (post-prints), book chapters, and conference papers);
* Unpublished/gray research material (e.g. pre-prints, working papers, theses and dissertations, technical reports, progress/ status reports, and committee reports); and
* Supporting research material (e.g. data sets, models, and simulations).

Actual content captured and preserved in different institutional repositories depends on the criteria adopted by each repository. For instance, SPARC Institutional Repository Checklist and Resource Guide (SPARC, 2002) suggests the following content criteria for institutional repositories of academic institutions:

* Scholarly: research / teaching oriented;
* Produced by an institution's research community;
* Non-ephemeral work: work in complete form, ready for dissemination; and
* Perpetual license: author grants the right to the institution to preserve and distribute the work via the repository.

4 EXAMPLES INSTITUTIONAL REPOSITORIES

Close to two hundred institutional repositories are believed to be operational in mid-2004 across the world. The registry at the Open Archives Initiative (www.openarchives.org) provides a complete listing (and links) to all repositories that have registered with OAI. The following are some examples of institutional repositories:

* Australian National University (http://eprints.anu.edu.au/);
* University of Montreal (Canada) (http://papyrus.bib.umontreal.ca/);
* University of Essen (Germany) (http://miless.uni-essen.de/);
* Indian Institute of Science, Bangalore (http://eprints.iisc.ernet.in/);
* CERN scientific information service (http://cds.cern.ch/);
* University of Glasgow (UK) (http://eprints.lib.gla.ac.uk/);
* Caltech (USA) (http://coda.caltech.edu/); and
* MIT (USA) (http://hpds1.mit.edu/index.jsp).

Apart from such institutional level efforts, several national level initiatives have been launched recently in Netherlands (DARE - The Digital Academic Research) and UK (FAIR - Focus on Academic Institutional Resources).

5 BENEFITS OF INSTITUTIONAL REPOSITORIES

Along with open access journals and discipline-based open access archives, such as, Arxiv and RePEc, institutional open access repositories constitute the third model in support of the re-formation of scholarly communication system. A useful definition of open access is provided by this European Science Foundation Policy Briefing: "Open access to scientific articles [literature] means online access without access-charge to readers or libraries. Committing to open access means dispensing with the financial, technical, and legal barriers that are designed to limit access to scientific research articles to [only] paying customers"* (European Science Foundation, 2003). Institutional repositories aim to support the open access cause through self-archiving of research publications by researchers and provision of open access to the archive. Institutional repositories also have the potential to bring significant benefits to institutions and individual researchers. At institutional level they have the potential to bring together research output of the institution which otherwise gets distributed over several publishing channels; demonstrate the quality, and scientific, social and economic relevance of an institution's research; increase the institution's visibility, status and public value; and facilitate improved research knowledge management. institutional repositories have the potential to bring several benefits to individual researchers: help them in establishing priority for their research findings (made possible by date stamping and publication identifier); provide wider access and visibility to their research publications and thereby improve impact; share unpublished ideas and know-how's with their peers and obtain their feedback; and support long-term preservation of their research papers. More importantly, institutional repositories are an organizational level response to support faculty seeking innovative approaches to research dissemination; otherwise they would have tended to explore and experiment on their own.

6 INSTITUTIONAL REPOSITORIES SOFTWARE AND THEIR FUNCTIONALITY

A key component of an institutional repositories is the repository management software. A recent OSI commissioned study indicates availability of several institutional repositories system software packages under open source license

***** ***(Note: text inside brackets is mine)***

(Open Society Institute, 2004). These packages are also compliant with OAI metadata harvesting protocol (see below). Available repository system software include ARNO, CDSWare, DSpace, Eprints, Fedora, i-Tor and MyCore. Most of these operate on Unix/Linux operating system platform.

Although specific features and functionality vary across these systems, most of them support key functionality required in an institutional repositories. Typical functions supported by these systems include the following:

* Registration of institutional users (authors) for document submission and other privileged use;
* Document submission, including user authentication, metadata assignment, license approval and document uploading;
* Approval/moderation of submitted documents, including metadata and format approval and peer review;
* Archiving, including date stamping, identifier assignment, preservation support, indexing and storage;
* Dissemination, including provision of search and browse front-end, OAI registration and compliance (see below) and rights management; and
* Administration, including definition and management of document formats, metadata, licenses, and submission policies.

Figure.2 below depicts the major features supported by institutional repositories software.

7 OAI INTEROPERABILITY FRAMEWORK

As varieties of open access repositories (open access journals, discipline-based archives and institutional repositories) mushroom across the world, a key concern is their interoperability. How can users access content, both at metadata and

Figure.2 IR Software Features

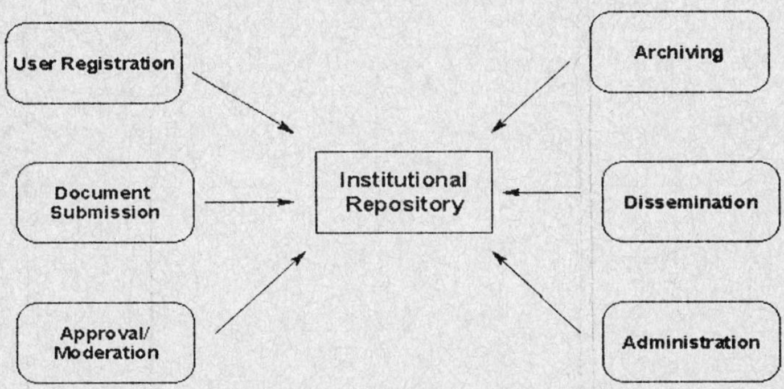

resource level, in related repositories in a seamless manner? In other words, a key requirement is enabling different repositories to share their content. While Z39.50 (a TCP/IP based standard protocol for information retrieval) has been a popular protocol for distributed searching of repositories, it has been shown that it does not scale well. Since 1999, the Open Archives Initiative (OAI, see http://www.openarchives.org/) has developed and promoted a low-barrier, easy-to-implement interoperability standard that aims to facilitate the efficient dissemination of content. The OAI Protocol for Metadata Harvesting (OAI-PMH) defines a generic mechanism for harvesting XML-formatted metadata from repositories. It is a technical standard to share data across platforms. As such, it has broad relevance in opening up access to a range of digital material. The protocol has already been taken up enthusiastically by many institutions. As a result, a distributed infrastructure of open access digital archives is now being built as a new instrument for scholarly communication. All the open source institutional repositories software mentioned in section 6 above are OAI-compliant.

The OAI-PMH protocol for metadata harvesting enables different repositories to expose their metadata for purposes of automatic metadata extraction from all participating institutional repositories and build various services, including a central metadata index and search system as illustrated in Figure-3. Such a metadata index enables users to quickly identify and select appropriate research material held in all participating institutions, and download specific publications online from the specific institutional repositories.

Figure 3. Institutional repositories interoperability through OAI protocol

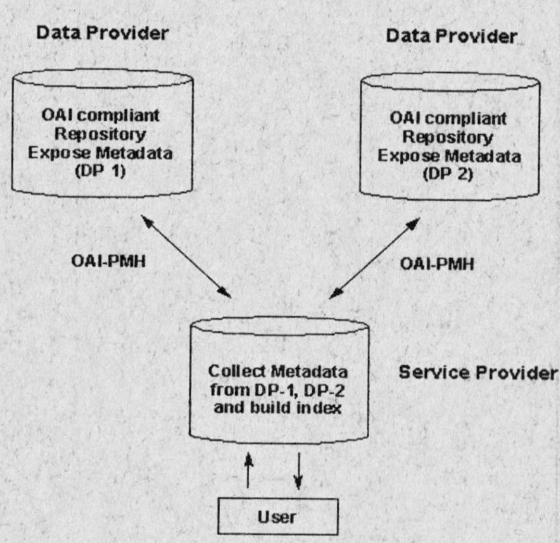

There are two key players under the OAI model - Data Providers and Service Providers. Data providers are repositories that support the OAI-PMH as a means of exposing metadata. A data provider (e.g. a corporate entity) registers with OAI and publicizes the fact that it has adopted the OAI-PMH. Service Providers issue OAI-PMH requests to data providers and use the metadata as a basis for building value-added services (e.g. central metadata index). They also register with OAI. ARC is an example OAI service provider (http://www.arc.cs.odu.edu/). ARC service provides a single point access, at metadata level, to content of all registered archives. The concept of inter-operable distributed institutional digital repositories is rapidly gaining ground today among the community of digital library developers.

8 IMPLEMENTATION AND DEPLOYMENT OF INSTITUTIONAL REPOSITORIES

How to implement an institutional repositories? Experiences and lessons from several pilot institutional repositories projects are only now becoming available (Penfield, 2002; Johnson, 2002; Nixxon, 2002). Key resource requirements include: management commitment and financial support for initial establishment and long term operation; infrastructural resources like repository server with support for fault tolerant operation and adequate network bandwidth; manpower for installation, configuration and administration of the repository software and server; and manpower for content management and collection development. Key processes include:

* Development of policies related to document types and formats; submission and approval policy; user permissions / license; and rights management;
* Development of metadata, cataloguing and subject scheme specifications;
* Selection, installation and configuration of repository system software;
* Promotion and advocacy;
* Collection development and content management;
* Dissemination and service provision; and
* Administration and maintenance.

Several technical and non-technical challenges have a bearing on the success of inter-operable institutional repositories as an effective scholarly publishing and communication model. These include: convincing researchers for content submission and usage of the institutional repositories; defining and managing appropriate content quality; digital rights management (publisher and researcher copyright; and access management); defining and implementing digital preservation strategies; assignment of persistent identifiers to repository items; development of aggregated repository services at consortia/ regional and national level; and development of semantic interoperability schemes.

9 RELEVANCE OF INSTITUTIONAL REPOSITORIES IN INDIAN CONTEXT

There is significant scope for applying the interoperable open access institutional repositories model for improving access to Indian science research, given the large number of state supported universities, institutions of higher learning and research laboratories in the country. There were an estimated 2,900 organizations involved in R&D in the country in 2001, in both commercial and non-commercial sectors. These include a very large number of R&D laboratories under governments; science agencies in various domains (industries, defense, agriculture, health sciences, biotechnology, environment, science and technology, Information and communication technologies space, energy, ocean development, etc.). In the academic sector there are close to 300 universities and institutions of higher learning, with graduate and research programmes. In 2001 there were an estimated 400,000 teachers in the country (National Science and Technology Management Information System, 2001).

These organizations produce a sizable number of research-based publications, including technical reports, manuals, guides, progress reports, presentations, etc., apart from pre-prints and post-prints of papers in refereed periodicals and conferences. These publications contain very valuable and often detailed information, such as data, observations, conclusions, analysis, best practices, etc. In some sense these publications constitute the core of research output and 'intellectual capital' of these organizations and of the country. Only a very small portion of this research gets published in formal media such as, periodicals and conferences proceedings. This has resulted in a situation in which not only an organization does not have an integrated view of its 'intellectual capital', but a much more significant limitation is the inability of an Indian researcher to access the collective pool of research publications available in all related organizations. Inability to efficiently and effectively capture, preserve and access the output of research can have significant negative impact on R&D productivity of researchers in Indian academic and R&D laboratories. The establishment of inter-operable institutional digital repositories will help in overcoming many of these shortcomings.

10 CONCLUSION

Inter-operable institutional repositories model as an effective means for improving scholarly communication is at present in its formative stage. Experiences and lessons from various pilot projects implemented in recent years indicate the significant potential of this model. Key requirements for further success probably lies in the implementation of content rich institutional repositories and development of value added services, including aggregation services, made possible by the inter-operability framework.

REFERENCES

1. European Science Foundation (2003). Open access: Restoring scientific communication to its rightful owners. *European Science Foundation Policy Briefing*. No. 21, April 2003. http://www.esf.org/
2. Johnson, Richard K (2002). Institutional repositories: Partnering with faculty to enhance scholarly communication. *D-Lib Magazine*. Vol. 8(11); November 2002. http://www.dlib.org/dlib/november02/johnson/11johnson.html
3. Lynch, Clifford A. (2003). Institutional repositories: Essential infrastructure for scholarship in the digital age. *ARL Bimonthly Report*. 226; February 2003. http://www.arl.org/newsltr/226/ir.html
4. National Science and Technology Management Information System (2001). *Directory of R&D institutions*. (NSTMIS), DST, Govt. of India.
5. SPARC (2002). *The case for institutional repositories: A SPARC position paper. Release* 1.0, 2002. http://www.arl.org/sparc

6. Nixxon, William. (2002). The evolution of an institutional e-prints archive at the University of Glasgow. *Ariadne Issue.* Vol. 32; 8-July-2002. http://www.ariadne.ac.uk /issue32/eprint-archives/intro.html

7. Open Society Institute (2004). *A guide to Institutional Repository Software.* 2nd edition. January 2004. http://www.soros.org/openaccess/software

8. Penfield, Stephen, et al. (2002). Setting up an institutional e-print archive. *Ariadne Issue.* Vol. 31; 11-April-2002. http://www.ariadne.ac.uk/issue31/eprint-archives/

9. SPARC (2002). *Institutional Repository Checklist and Resource Guide.* Release 1.0, Nov 2002. http://www.arl.org/sparc/IR/IR_Guide.html

BOUNDARY OBJECTS AND THE DIGITAL LIBRARY

Michael Shepherd
Carolyn Watters

'Boundary objects are entities shared by different communities but used differently by each group. The paper explores the multi-faceted aspects of boundary objects in digital libraries. The issue of semantic interoperability from the perspective of 'communities of practice' and 'communities of interest' has been explored. While the concept of boundary objects holds some promise of resolving this problem, an efficient solution depends on how knowledge is represented so that it can be shared among various participants in a meaningful manner. Classification schemes can be used as a standard to implement boundary objects to bridge access to shared information resources for different users. The value and utility of adoption of "Absolute Syntax" for representation of subjects as a framework for boundary objects needs to be explored.

0 PREAMBLE

The authors first met Professor Neelameghan in 1972 when he was a visiting professor at the School of Library and Information Science, the University of Western Ontario. Subsequently, we had the privilege of studying at the Documentation Research and Training Centre from September 1973 through January 1974. Meeting Professor Neelameghan and his colleagues and students opened another whole dimension for us on the organization of knowledge.

1 INTRODUCTION

Semantic interoperability across digital libraries has been defined as, "...the ability of a user to access, consistently and coherently, similar (though autonomously defined and managed) classes of digital objects and services distributed across heterogeneous repositories with federating or mediating software compensating for site-by-site variations." (Lynch and Garcia-Molina, 1995). If we assume that digital libraries are built to serve a particular community or communities in which the members are involved in similar activities and share similar values, then the meaning of any set of terms can be evaluated only in the context of those communities (Wenger, 1999). Thus, semantic interoperability is tied directly to communities of practice and to the negotiation of meaning that occurs within them and "... the degree of interoperability between information systems may be dependent on the distance between communities whose information systems attempt to interact" (Friesen, 2002).

Ostwald (2004) defines such communities of practice as, "A group of practitioners involved in a common activity, albeit performing different roles. Essential characteristics of communities of practice are: 1) they are not defined by organizational mandate (e.g., the "org chart"), but rather by the ways people actually work together, 2) they involve many different roles, as opposed to a flat structure, and 3) they experience an ongoing flux of community members, who enter the community from the periphery and gain status as knowledgeable members through participation in the community of practice".

Figure 1 is an example of a community of practice brought together for the diagnosis and treatment of patients, where the electronic health record is the object that brings the three groups together into a community. The roles are different but the activity and purpose is common to the three groups. Communities of interest are made up of various communities of practice that may have an overlap of interests and the need to share information, but may have different activities and purpose.

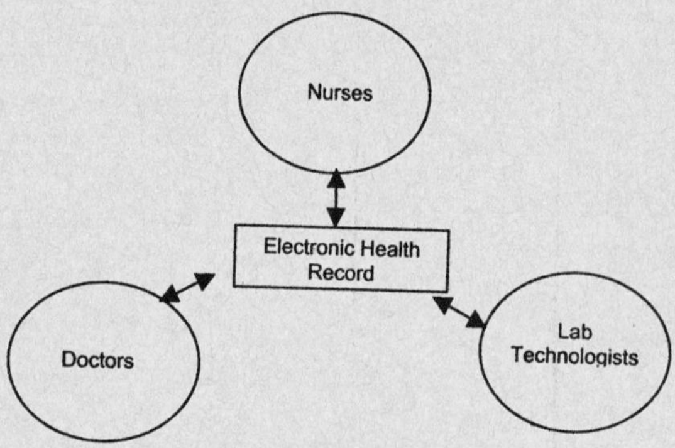

Fig. 1. Community of Practice

In Figure 2 for example, a community of practice of health practice and a community of practice of health policy come together to form a community of interest, brought together through an electronic health record repository. These concepts of communities of practice and of communities of interest are not dissimilar to the Moen's (2001) concepts of extended communities and of extra communities. Complex collaborative activities are typically solved by individuals who may or may not be members of a single group. Communities of practice form when practitioners work as a community in a certain domain doing similar work, with shared background and experience to some extent, even though within such communities individuals may have specific expertise. For example, the doctors, nurses and lab technologists of Figure 1 form a community of practice that may be short-term or long-term. Communities of interest are similar to communities of practice, but differ in the fundamental way that the participants typically do not share common backgrounds and expertise. Rather the participants bring in diverse perspectives to tackle a particular problem of common concern. For example, the health practice community and the health policy community may work together to establish health policy that directly effects how health care is practiced. As another example, parents, teachers, school boards may work together as a community of interest related to specific educational concerns in their community. Communities of interest may bring together different communities of practice representing groups of practitioners from different domains. In this paper we address the issue of interoperability that is relevant to both groups.

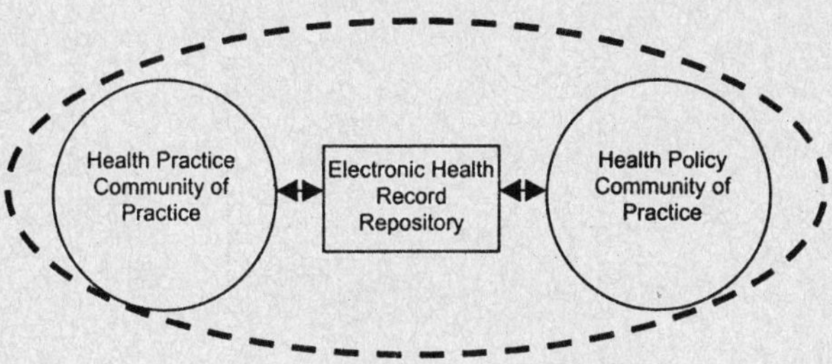

Fig. 2: Community of Interest

A fundamental challenge facing communities of practice and communities of interest is the building of a shared understanding where this does not exist initially (Arias and Fischer, 2000). Typically, in practice, this an incremental and very individual process that emerges in the generation of external artifacts, often documents. For the communities to be effective, the members must be able to communicate with and learn from others who have a different perspective and perhaps a different vocabulary for describing their ideas to establish a common context. This is more complicated in communities where participants use the same vocabulary but assign different meanings to that vocabulary. For example, a "failure" for the life insurance actuary is a person who has not died as predicted by the life-expectancy tables while a "failure" for the physician is a person who has died.

There are two levels of knowledge sharing in such communities; contributory and formative. All communities are *contributory* to the degree that each participant contributes his/her own expertise in framing the solution. For example, a school board may lobby government, teachers may propose new curricula, and some parents may provide legal or technical advice. While the participants contribute according to their core expertise, their expertise is not necessarily changed and they continue as before. Communities may then become *formative* where the process of working on the shared objectives changes the expertise and fundamental understanding of the participants. For example, a community working on an environmental issue must first establish a base of shared understanding and then may use that understanding to inform and change the legal, technical, and social perspectives of the participants, perhaps even leading to the birth of a new discipline.

The question for semantic interoperability is how to facilitate communication across these communities. According to Schatz, while the Grand Challenge for digital libraries of the 1990s was semantic interoperability across digital collections (Lynch and Garcia-Molina, 1995), the Grand Challenge of the 2000s will be "conceptual navigation across community repositories". (Schatz, 2004) The question will be how to navigate effectively across different collections of different objects represented by different communities at different levels.

Each community holds some knowledge but real world problems transcend the knowledge of individuals and specific groups, resulting in a "symmetry of ignorance" (Symmetry of Ignorance, Online 2004) among the communities that must be overcome. In order to respond to this challenge, we must be able to identify objects that serve as interfaces among different communities of practice. Boundary objects (Bowker and Star, 1999) are entities shared by several different communities but viewed or used differently by each of them. They necessarily contain sufficient detail to be understandable by both parties however neither party is required to understand the full context of use by the other party. Boundary objects may be interpreted differently by the different communities, but it is the acknowledgement and discussion of these differences that enables a shared understanding to be formed (Boundary Object, Online 2004).

An example of a boundary object is the electronic health record as shown in Fig. 1. It is used by doctors, nurses and lab technologists to care for the patient with a community of practice of health practitioners. The repository of electronic health records of Figure 2 is a boundary object that brings together multiple communities of practice into a community of interest. Each community of users will have a slightly different view of and understanding of the boundary object, but the boundary object serves an interface among these communities.

2 SEMANTIC INTEROPERABILITY

Semantic interoperability is a focus of research within the World Wide Web community as well as within the Digital Library community. Within the World Wide Web community, semantic interoperability research has been focused on the development of the Semantic Web, which "... is not a separate Web but an extension of the current one, in which information is given well-defined meaning, better enabling computers and people to work in cooperation." (Berners-Lee, *et. al.* 2003) The key phrase within this definition is "... information is given well-defined meaning ..." as this has been a goal of indexing and classification since knowledge was first classified. Attempting to give well-defined meaning to information is far more difficult to do automatically than to do manually and, assuming that it is given meaning, there still remains the problem of sharing this representation to better enable computers and people to work in cooperation. The sharing of representations for cooperation requires *interoperability*, i.e., the ability of one system to communicate and interact with another system. While progress has been made on the sharing of metadata (syntactic interoperability), the problem of semantic interoperability, i.e., the sharing of the meaning of terms and how they are used, is much greater.

The meaning of any set of terms, and the significance and utility of any taxonomy, can be evaluated only in the context of a community whose members are involved in similar activities and share similar values (Wenger, 1999). In short, semantic interoperability is tied directly to communities of practice and to communties of interest, and to the negotiation of meaning that occurs within them (Friesen, 2002).

Digital libraries allow for the independent development of information resources that can be shared by users in innovative and efficient ways. Digital libraries allow access to distributed and heterogeneous information to provide support for semantic interoperability (Paepcke, *et. al.* 1998) across communities. That is, users from a variety of backgrounds and disciplines may access appropriate information and contribute information to the shared digital library. At the user-interface level it is possible to create different user interfaces for the different communities, as users interact with the resources in a variety of contexts. Alternatively, a common look and feel or meta-level interface may be preferred that is above the individual native interfaces as a unifying artifact to capture the essence of the emerging community.

Interoperability is a central concern when building digital libraries as these libraries are often collections of independently developed components. Semantic interoperability requires the development of semantic representations and indexes of resources. Semantic representations, such as metadata, classification schemes, and indices, allow and even encourage semantic interoperability and the use of agents to select context appropriate resources, to communicate with each other, and to merge resources written from different perspectives. True interoperability would ensure that knowledge could pass between agents (and between agents and their users) in a transparent manner, allowing search agents that could reply to the user's semantic intentions (not just keywords), based on the user's domain, context, and possibly user and/or community profile.

There are two general approaches to achieve interoperability (Paepcke, *et. al.* 1998) in this context; the use of standards and the use of mediation. One of the oldest approaches to achieving interoperability among heterogeneous components is to agree on a single standard that drives a limited amount of homogeneity among them. Examples are ISO 802 for network connections and Z39.50 for information retrieval. Alternately, communities may agree on a family of standards, such as the OSI and e-commerce payment standards, from which component designers have the choice of implementing one or more from the shared set of standards.

Mediation provides a higher level of autonomy for component designers by providing functionality outside of the participating local systems that mediates between components. Mediation may include the translation of data formats as needed between systems. For example, network gateways operate as mediators to facilitate interconnectivity in heterogeneous networks, like the Internet. Mediation may be either *a priori* or *ad hoc*. That is, the mediation may be based on some prior agreement using a family of standards and identifiers or wrappers to facilitate the exchange of the component. When the interoperability is achieved by describing the semantics and structure of the data and operations as part of the component, often as metadata, the components can be used without prior arrangement and potentially without the help of third-party mediators. Rather the mediation is achieved *ad hoc* directly by the receiving system using information contained in the component.

3 BOUNDARY OBJECTS

Boundary objects are entities, which may be linguistic, physical, or digital, which serve to facilitate communication and information exchange among various constituencies. That is, boundary objects occur in situations where individual constituencies have only partial knowledge or control over the interpretation of the object. For example, the interpretation of a health record differs from patient, physician, lab technician, and administrator. Boundary objects are artifacts that often perform a brokering role involving translation, coordination and alignment between the perspectives of specific communities. The effectiveness of boundary objects in providing these functions depends on the levels of competency, motivation, and experience of the participants.

Boundary objects can serve two major purposes. They can serve *directly* as objects that support interaction and collaboration among different communities, where shared understanding is needed. Second, they can serve *indirectly* as objects around which new shared understandings are developed within the multiple constituencies. In either case, boundary objects are entities that provide a foundation for effective communication among disparate communities. Without boundary objects, these communities cannot create the necessary shared understanding to be effective in the framing and resolution of the common goal and not all stakeholders would be empowered to engage fully in the process.

3.1 Boundary Objects in Digital Libraries

Digital libraries are a key mechanism for shared understanding and semantic interoperability among communities of practice and among communities of interest. The usability and effectiveness is affected when designers, content providers, and users have very different backgrounds, both cultural (Theng, *et. al.* 1999) and domain expertise. As such, digital libraries must provide both direct and indirect boundary objects to support this role, including classification schemes and digital documents. Whether boundary objects are to serve directly or indirectly, they may be implemented either as standards or as mediators. For instance, classification schemes such as the Dewey Decimal Classification can be used as a standard to implement boundary objects to bridge access to shared information resources for users from different cultures. In this instance, all repositories are mapped *a priori* into the Dewey Decimal Classification. However, the Dewey Decimal Classification scheme may also be used as a mediator as in the Renardus project (Day, 2001) in which it is used as a switching language to map to other classification schemes.

Within digital libraries, boundary objects occur as classification schemes, digital documents and as digital libraries themselves.

Classification Schemes: Classification schemes provide an organized view of shared resources, where these resources are part of a larger and possibly distributed knowledge set. Classification schemes can function both directly and indirectly as boundary objects. A shared common classification scheme allows different communities to access the same resources without presupposing that the users fully shared a definition or understanding of either the classification scheme or the resource. Shared classification schemes are flexible enough that each participant can interpret the semantics sufficiently well for its needs within his or her community. Simultaneously, they are robust enough to maintain a commonality across sites.

Boundary Objects and the Digital Library

Within the context of digital libraries, the direct use of classification schemes as boundary objects can be achieved in two ways: *imposed* and intentionally created. Standard classification schemes, such as the Library of Congress or the Dewey Decimal Classification, can be imposed on the digital library *a priori*. All participants, regardless of background, are required to map resources and queries onto this standard. In this case the classification scheme itself operates as a boundary object to facilitate semantic interoperability.

Communities can facilitate collaboration by first agreeing explicitly on a shared vocabulary and a classification scheme that reflects the intended shared semantic organization. In this case, boundary objects are explicitly and intentionally created and again become part of the resultant digital library.

Classification schemes can also act as indirect boundary objects when they are discovered *post hoc*. That is, an analysis of the semantics of the combined set of resources could be used to generate a unique classification scheme that reflects the reality of the contents. In this case, the classification scheme is an indirect boundary object as it reflects a new shared understanding of the contents of the digital library and itself becomes a new resource in the digital library.

Digital Documents as boundary objects: A key change from a traditional library to a digital library is the flexibility of the representation of the content, which provides the potential for multiple simultaneous views of the structure and content of the resources. Digital documents play a significant role as boundary objects, objects of practice and reifications of practice (Wenger, 1999; Wenger and Snyder, 2000); indeed, one document may take on all of these roles.

An important role then for documents is as boundary objects -- inanimate brokers and translators among constituencies and among participants. Documents as boundary objects are plastic enough to support disparate individual needs and robust enough to maintain a common and shared meaning. Documents moving among constituent groups act as information conduits and a means to coordinate practice. Documents can also "patrol and control", reinforcing the community's perimeters.

As objects of practice, digital documents provide the information necessary for the flow of the work. With their greater interpretive flexibility, digital documents help members negotiate sustainable adaptations of messy reality to the artificially clean and ordered structure of codes, classifications, databases, work flows, and forms. To this extent, documents may both structure practice as objects that demand attention of a certain nature, and de-structure practice when the documents do not match the canonical reality assumed in the work.

As reifications of practice, documents serve to anchor practice and to make the work visible, both within and outside the community. Documents that are created outside the community to assert authority over practice (e.g., government or regulatory policies) are, however, not reifications of practice. Even though a document is shared within a community, we cannot assume that the meaning is shared by everyone. Wegner (1999) states that by, "... providing a shared context for constructing meaning, documents are the beginning rather than the end of the process of negotiation".

Digital library as composite *boundary object:* A digital library system itself can function as a composite boundary object. For example, the digital library with or without shared classification schemes, can be the common point for all users by providing messaging systems, FAQs, and links to resources by which users and content providers can easily exchange information. Visualization techniques, including self-organizing maps and graphical browsers, can be used to dynamically generate structure and content maps that can be manipulated directly by users.

Boundary objects provide an opportunity for participants to learn about other perspectives. The digital library interface, however, needs to facilitate this learning environment for it to be effective. For example, the digital library should provide facilities that help end-users and content providers explore related resources by the use of intelligent intermediaries, mentoring, hints, and access to multiple views and perhaps online thesauri.

The Digital Library can provide support for participants to create boundary objects. Giving end-users the opportunity to articulate and exchange their ideas and current difficulties may leverage cross disciplinary solutions. Even Chat Rooms and shared memos facilitate discussion and debate from different approaches. Digital libraries can also provide users with an awareness of which resources are most widely used, hot spots of shared activity.

4 SUMMARY

This paper has attempted to explore the multi-faceted aspects of boundary objects in digital libraries. In order to overcome the semantic interoperability problem and solve the grand challenge for digital libraries (Lynch and Garcia-Molina, 1995; Schatz, 2004), we must approach the problem from the perspective of communities of practice and communities of interest. While the concept of boundary objects does hold some promise of resolving this very difficult problem, it boils down to how the knowledge is represented so that it can be shared among various participants in a meaningful manner.

An approach to this is the adoption of an "absolute syntax" for the description of subjects (Ranganathan, 1967) as a framework for boundary objects. Neelameghan (1971) defines absolute syntax as the sequence of the component ideas in a subject helpful and acceptable to majority of users where the structure denotes logical form and the parts, properties or aspects are in some manner related to each other.

REFERENCES

1. Arias, E. and Fischer, G. (2000). Boundary objects: Their role in articulating the task at hand and making information relevant to it. *International ICSC Symposium on Interactive and Collaborative Computing (ICC'2000)*, University of Wollongong, Australia, ICSC Academic Press, Wetaskiwin, Canada, p. 567-574.
2. Berners-Lee, T.; Hendler, J. and Lassila, O. (2003). The Semantic Web. *Scientific American.* May 17, 2001. Available April 18, 2003. http://www.scientificamerican.com/print_version.cfm?articleID=00048144-10D2-1C70-84A9809EC588EF21
3. *Boundary Object.* Available July 2004. http://webguide.cs.colorado.edu:9080/entwine/Concepts/Concept210/viewDesc
4. Bowker, G.C. and Star, S.L. (1999). *Sorting things out: Classification and its consequences.* Cambridge, Massachusetts: The MIT Press
5. Day, M. (2001) *Renardus DDC classification mapping - a summary of work in progress.* Available July 2004. http://hilt.cdlr.strath.ac.uk/Dissemination/Workshop%20documents/Renardus%20Report.doc
6. Friesen, N. (2002). *Semantic interoperability and communities of practice.* Available July 2004. http://www.cancore.ca/documents/semantic.html

7. Lynch, C. and Garcia-Molina, H. (1995). *Interoperability, scaling, and the digital Libraries research agenda: A report* on the May 18-19, 1995, IITA Digital Libraries Workshop, August 22, 1995.

8. Moen, W.E. (2001). Mapping the interoperability landscape for networked information retrieval. **In** *Proceedings of First ACM/IEEE-CS Joint Conference on Digital Libraries*, Roanoke, VA, June 24-28, 2001. p. 50-52. http://www.unt.edu/wmoen/publications/MapInteropJCDLFinal.pdf

9. Neelameghan, A. (1971). Sequence of component ideas in a subject. *Library Science*. Vol.8; paper Q.

10. Ostwald, J. (2004). *Knowledge construction in software development: The evolving artifact approach*. Available July 2004. http://www.cs.colorado.edu/~ostwald/ thesis/glossary.html

11. Paepcke, A.; Chang, C.; Garcia-Molina, H. and Winograd, T. (1998). Interoperability for digital libraries worldwide. *Special Issue on Digital Libraries, Communications of the ACM*. Vol. 41(4); April 1998.

12. Ranganathan, S. R. (1967). Hidden roots of classification. *Information Storage and Retieval*. Vol. 3; p. 399–410

13. Schatz, B.R. (2004). *Navigating the Distributed World of Community Knowledge*. Available July 2004 [http://www.sis.pitt.edu/~dlwkshop/paper_schatz.pdf]

14. *Symmetry of Ignorance*. (2004). Available July 2004 http://webguide.cs.colorado.edu:9080/entwine/Concepts/Concept178/viewDesc]

15. Theng, Y.L.; Duncker, E.; Mohd-Nasir, N.; Buchanan, G. and Thimbleby, H. (1999). Design guidelines and user-centred digital libraries, *Third European Conference ECDL'99*, Abiteboul, S. and Vercoustre, A.(Eds.), Springer. (1999), p. 167 - 183.

16. Wenger, E. (1999). *Communities of practice: Learning, meaning and identity*. Cambridge University Press.

17. —. and Snyder, W. (2000). Communities of practice: The organizational frontier. *Harvard Business Review*. January-February 2000; p. 139-145.

A PFT-BASED APPROACH TO MAKE CDS/ISIS DATABASES OAI-COMPLIANT

Francis, Jayakanth
Lalitha Aswath

CDS/ISIS is a powerful and popular software package for managing computerized bibliographic data. It is developed and maintained by UNESCO since 1985. It is free software available in binary form for MS-DOS, MS-Windows, Unix, and Unix-based operating systems like Linux. It is used by many libraries and organizations in many countries to maintain their Online Public Access Catalogues (OPACs) and other bibliographic databases. With the advent of the Internet and Web technologies, publishing the content of databases on the Web provides a round the clock access to the content from any PC with Internet access. Some CDS-ISIS databases are published on the Web, but many are still on standalone systems or on local area networks. Interoperability is the key for the efficient dissemination of information to end-users. The Open Archives Initiative Protocol for Metadata Harvesting (OAI-PMH) provides a technical framework for interoperability of OAI-compliant digital libraries (UNESCO. 2004). However, CDS/ISIS databases are not OAI-compliant. In this paper, we describe a simple approach, to make CDS/ISIS OAI-compliant. It is based on printing CDS/ISIS records in an OAI static repository format.

1 INTRODUCTION

When Prof. Raghavan of the Madras University invited me (Jayakant) to contribute a paper to the Festschrift volume being brought out in honour of Prof. Neelameghan (AN), we readily accepted the invitation. Indeed, it is a great privilege and honour for us to be contributing a paper for the volume.

CDS/ISIS software package is one amongst the many areas of Professor Neelameghan's interest and specialization. He has contributed extensively to the application of this package and conducted a large number of training programmes on CDS/ISIS to many library and information personnel in many developing countries worldwide. He has also been a designer and a consultant for a number of national and international projects involving applications of this package. I (Jayakant) have been associated with him in a couple of projects and training workshops related to CDS/ISIS.

I was on a six-month fellowship at the Old Dominion University, Norfolk, Virginia, USA, during Aug 2004 to Feb 2005. During this period, I was working on my proposal related to "Approaches to make CDS/ISIS databases OAI-compliant". I had several e-mail exchanges with Professor Neelameghan seeking clarifications and advice related to CDS/ISIS. He would always promptly respond to all my queries and shared his knowledge of CDS/ISIS. In our present work, thanks to him for providing us with a sizable sample of records in MARC21 format from CDS-ISIS databases for testing and other advice by which we could eventually succeed in implementing our PFT-based approach to make records from a CDS/ISIS database OAI-compliant.

2 SCOPE OF THE PAPER

CDS/ISIS is an advanced non-numerical information storage and retrieval software developed and maintained by UNESCO since 1985 to satisfy the need expressed by many institutions, especially in developing countries, to be able to streamline their information processing activities by using modern (and relatively inexpensive) technologies (UNESCO, 2004). It is available as free software in binary form for different operating systems like MS-DOS, MS-Windows, Unix, and Unix-based OS like Linux. Many libraries and organizations across the world are using this package for managing their online public access catalogues (OPACs) and other bibliographic data. The growing popularity of this software package can be inferred by the fact that UNESCO, upon requests, has distributed more than 5,600 copies of this software in the last twelve months to different individuals and organizations around the world (UNESCO, 2005). With such a large user base, it is quite likely that some would like to share at least their metadata with the rest of the world. Web enabling of databases makes it possible to access the content from any of the computer systems with Internet connectivity. However, not many of the CDS/ISIS databases are Web-enabled and for the ones that are Web-enabled, the end-users will still have to locate and visit these databases individually, which is not an efficient way of information retrieval. A better way of delivering distributed information resources, with related content, is by way of automatic federation, i.e. gathering of metadata automatically from the distributed databases and building a single central index.

Recent efforts, such as the Open Archive Initiative (OAI), specifically address the issue of federatiing distributed OAI-compliant digital libraries (DLs). To take advantage of OAI, it is necessary to make the CDS/ISIS databases OAI compliant. This will greatly help database developers and users in two ways; one, it will become easier for the community to exchange records with each other, and secondly, it will be feasible to build a federation of distributed databases.

There are two approaches to make existing CDS/ISIS databases OAI-compliant: static and dynamic. In the static approach, the existing records in a database are exported to a file conforming to the OAI static repository file format and the OAI static repository file is made OAI-compliant. The major limitation of this approach is that any new record added or any changes made to the existing records will not be automatically reflected in the exported file. In the dynamic approach, an OAI software layer acts as an intermediary between the CDS/ISIS databases and the OAI service provider. The OAI layer interacts with the database in real time to generate responses. This approach has the advantage that the OAI responses always reflect the current state of a database. This is the recommended approach. This however, requires installation and maintenance of a full-fledged web serving software. Both these approaches are discussed in detail in two earlier papers (Jayakanth, *et. al.* 2004; Jayakanth, *et. al.* 2005). In this paper, we discuss an approach to create an OAI static repository file for the database records based on directly printing the records in the OAI static repository format rather than exporting the records and converting the exported records to OAI static repository format.

3 CDS/ISIS DATABASE

CDS/ISIS is specifically designed to handle textual data efficiently. It has a flat file structure representing data in non-tabular fashion. The data elements of a CDS/ISIS database can be repeatable and can have sub-fields as well. Every data element has a corresponding tag number associated with it. The tag numbers can be any numeral in the range 1-32767 but it is preferable to use tags conforming to ISO 2709 or tags prescribed by the MARC family of formats.

The formatting language of CDS/ISIS is quite powerful and is basically used for two purposes - defining the template for displaying / printing the data elements of the records and, for the generation of flexible indexes, based on inverted file structure. A good understanding of the formatting language of CDS/ISIS is the key for its efficient usage.

The search language of CDS/ISIS uses Boolean and proximity operators. It also has a powerful sequential search engine called the free text searching for complicated search queries expressed through the formatting language.

Non-availability of standard Open DataBase Connectivity (ODBC) or Java DataBase Connectivity (JDBC) drivers is a hindrance to interact with the CDS/ISIS databases programmatically. This makes it difficult even to publish databases on the Web. There are several freeware common gateway interface based programs available on the Internet. These programs serve as servers for the CDS/ISIS databases in the Web environment. WWWISIS, developed by BIREME, the Pan American Health Organization based in Brazil, is one such gateway program (BIREME. WWWISIS, 2005; BIREME. Wxis, 2005).

4 THE OPEN ARCHIVES INITIATIVE (OAI)

E-prints are scientific or technical documents circulated electronically to facilitate peer exchange and scientific advancement. These generally include pre-publication drafts of journal articles (preprints), scholarly papers, technical communications, or similar documents relaying research results among peer groups (Office of Scientific and Technical Information, 2005). The computer servers, which store and disseminate e-prints, are popularly referred to as e-print servers, e-print archives, or e-print repositories. The first and the foremost amongst the e-print archives is the arXiv.org (2005). The arXiv e-print service covers the fields of physics, mathematics, non-linear science, computer science, and quantitative biology. Some of the other notable e-print archives are CogPrints covering the fields of Psychology, Linguistics and Neuroscience, NCSTRL covering the field of computer science research reports, NDLTD covering thesis and dissertations, and RePEc covering the field of economics. The rapid growth of e-print archives has resulted in a certain amount of scattering of information. As a result, the users have to visit several individual servers to locate research information related to their fields of study. Exploring the possibility of interoperability of distributed e-print archives resulted in the establishment of the OAI (2005a). Interoperability is the ability of multiple systems with different hardware and software platforms, data structures, and interfaces to exchange data with minimal loss of content and functionality (National Information Standards Organization, 2005). Thus, the origins of the Open Archives Initiative lie in the growth of a number of e-print archives (Herbert and Sompele, 2000) and the challenges posed by such a growth. The technical framework for interoperability developed by the OAI is known as the Open Archives Initiative Protocol for Metadata Harvesting (OAI-PMH).

The OAI-PMH is a low-barrier and non-intrusive protocol. It is an HTTP-based request-response transaction framework for communication between a harvester and OAI- compliant data providers (Lynch, 2001), (OAI, 2005b). The data providers maintain OAI-compliant repositories, expose their metadata according to a metadata standard, and register their base URLs with an OAI service provider like Arc. Arc is an open source OAI service provider (Liu, *et. al.* 2001). The service providers extract the metadata from the registered data providers and build a federation service that will make the union of all the holdings available for searching and retrieving. Thus, an end-user can access one interface, enter a query and find results from all participating databases combined into one result set that will be presented through a browser interface.

The interaction between OAI data providers and an OAI service provider is illustrated in Figure 1.

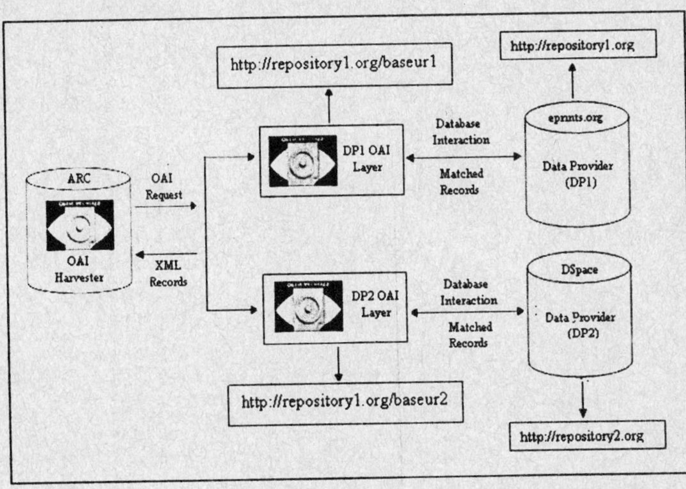

Fig. 1: Interaction between Data Providers and OAI Service Provider

5 THE NEED FOR INTEROPERABILITY OF LEGACY DATABASE SYSTEMS

A major barrier for information dissemination to a user community is that many digital libraries and bibliographic databases, legacy or contemporary, use heterogeneous technologies inhibiting interoperability. From the users point of view, such heterogeneous systems necessitate users to visit the systems individually and also get acquainted with multiple user interfaces. This can be quite time consuming and also intimidating. If such heterogeneous or legacy systems can be made interoperable, then it becomes feasible to build federated search services. The federation makes it convenient for the end-users, and they no longer need to search the individual repositories. Over the years, thousands of databases have been created using CDS/ISIS. Some of these databases are accessible on the web, but a good majority of them are still on standalone systems or on a local area network. Even if the databases were to be available on the Web, the end users need to visit these distributed databases individually. This is not an efficient way of information dissemination. And, for such of those databases not accessible on the Web, the possibility of end users not being aware of their existence is quite high. This could result in duplicating the work done in the past and, the knowledge contained in such 'hidden' databases could go unused.

Interoperability is the key for the efficient dissemination of information to end-users. The Open Archives Initiative Protocol for Metadata Harvesting (OAI-PMH) provides a technical framework for interoperability of OAI-compliant digital libraries. To take advantage of OAI-PMH technical framework, legacy bibliographic/database systems need to be made OAI-compliant.

6 MAKING CDS/ISIS DATABASES OAI-COMPLIANT

6.1 A PFT-Based Approach

Reference has already been made to both the static and the dynamic approaches. In the static approach, a data provider makes a metadata collection available as a XML file in a specific format – an OAI Static Repository –, which becomes OAI-PMH harvestable through the intermediation of OAI Static Repository Gateway software (Hochstenbach, *et. al.* 2003). An OAI Static Repository must comply with the conformance rules specified in the specification for an OAI static repository and OAI static repository gateway document (OAI, 2004). To create the XML file conforming to the OAI Static Repository, the methodology we had proposed in our earlier paper was to export the records from a database on to a file and to convert the file containing the exported records to an OAI static Repository using any of the high level programming languages. Using a programming language to carry out the required conversion gives good control while performing the conversion. However, not every database manager will be knowledgeable is using a high level programming language to do the required conversion. Moreover, the formatting language of CDS/ISIS lets us print the records in any desired format. So, we experimented with it and were successful in printing database records directly in OAI Static Repository format. This method is more efficient in that it eliminates the process of exporting the database records and also the usage of a programming language to carry out the conversion. The PFT file used by us to generate the OAI Static Repository from a sample database is given in the Appendix. This is a generic file, which can be used by databases using tag numbers that conform to MARC21 standard.

An OAI Static Repository thus created can be made OAI-compliant by either importing it into a kepler archivelet or through the intermediation of static repository gateway.

6.2 OAI Static Repository and OAI-Compliance

An OAI Static Repository is nothing but a XML file adhering to the schema specified in the specification document. It can be made OAI-compliant by importing it into kepler archivelet or through the intermediation of the static repository gateway. Kepler archivelet is a self-contained, platform independent and lightweight software package that allows one to create and maintain an OAI-compliant repository (Maly, *et. al.* 2001). The static repository gateway approach requires the installation and configuration of static repository gateway software. Figure 2 shows a screenshot of a kepler archivelet containing records exported from a CDS/ISIS database.

Fig. 2: Screenshot of a Kepler Archivelet with Records from a CDS/ISIS Database

7 CONCLUSION

Making the CDS/ISIS databases OAI-Compliant will help the CDS/ISIS community to exchange data easily with each other, building services based on federation of CDS/ISIS databases, and CDS/ISIS databases can participate in the interoperability of DLs based on harvesting. The OAI Static Repository approach is ideal for database records not exceeding 5000 and that the records are more or less static in nature. It is also a good approach for institutions and organizations, which can not afford to have a full fledged OAI system.

NOTES AND REFERENCES

1. UNESCO. (2004). *CDS/ISIS for Windows*. [Online Revised 06-09-2004] http://portal.unesco.org/ci/en/ev.php. URL_ID=5330&URL_DO=DO_TOPIC&URL_SECTION=201.html [Accessed on 01 Feb 2005].

2. —. (2005). *5,600 copies of UNESCO's CDS/ISIS Distributed During Last 12 Months.* [online 21 Jan 2005] http://portal.unesco.org/ci/en/ev.php. URL_ID=18069&URL_DO=DO_TOPIC&URL_SECTION=201.html [Accessed on 01 Feb 2005]

3. Jayakanth, F.; Maly, M Zubair and Aswath, L. (2004). *Approaches to make CDS/ISIS Databases OAI-compliant with other Digital Libraries*. http://www.unesco.org/isis [Accessed 07 Feb 2005]

4. —; — and —. (2005). *Interoperability of Legacy Bibliographic Database Systems over Internet – A case Study with CDS/ISIS.* http://www.unesco.org/isis [Accessed 07 Feb 2005]

5. BIREME. (2005). *WWWISIS.* http://productos.bvsalud.org/product.php?id= wwwisis& lang=en> [Accessed on 01 Feb 2005]

6. —. (2005). *Wxis.* http://productos.bvsalud.org/product.php?id=wxis-modules&lang=en [Accessed on 01 Feb 2005]

7. Office of Scientific and Technical Information. *Research Communications for Scientists and Engineers.* (2005). [online 30 Jan 2005] http://eprints.osti.gov/ [Accessed on 02 Feb 2005]

8. Cornell University Library. (2005). *arXiv.org e-Print archive.* http://arxiv.org/ [Accessed on 02 Feb 2005]

9. *Open Archives Initiative (OAI).* (2005a). http://www.openarchives.org/ [Accessed on 02 Feb 2005]

10. National Information Standards Organization. (2005). *Understanding Metadata.* http://www.niso.org/ [Accessed on 02 Feb 2005]

11. Herbert Van de; and Sompel, Lagoze C. (2000). The Santa Fe Convention of the Open Archives Initiative. *D-Lib Magazine.* 4(2). http://www.dlib.org/dlib/february00/ vandesompel-oai/02vandesompel-oai.html [Accessed 01 Feb 2005]

12. Lynch, Clifford A. (2001). Association of Research Libraries. Metadata Harvesting and the Open Archives Initiative. *ARL Bimonthly Report 217* [online August 2001]. http://www.arl.org/newsltr/217/mhp.html [Accessed 03 Feb 2005]

13. Open Archives Initiative (OAI). (2005b). *The Open Archives Initiative Protocol for Metadata Harvesting* [online 12 Oct 2004] http://www.openarchives.org/OAI/ openarchivesprotocol.html [Accessed 03 feb 2005]

14. Liu, X.; Maly, K. and Zubair., M. (2001). *Arc – An OAI Service Provider for Digital Library Federation.* Vol. 7(4). http://www.dlib.org/dlib/april01/liu/04liu.html [Accessed 12 Feb 2005]

15. Hochstenbach, P.; Jerez, H.; Sompel, H. and Van de (2003). *The OAI-PMH Static Repository and Static Repository Gateway.* http://public.lanl.gov/herbertv//papers/ jcdl2003-submitted-draft.pdf [Accessed 10 Feb 2005]

16. Open Archives Initiative (OAI). (2004). *Specification for an OAI Static Repository and an OAI Static Repository Gateway.* http://www.openarchives.org/OAI/2.0/guidelines-static-repository.htm [Accessed 10 Feb 2005]

17. Maly, K.; Zubair, M. and Liu, X. (2001). *Kepler – An OAI Data/Service Provider for the Individual.* Vol. 7(4). http://www.dlib.org/dlib/april01/maly/04maly.html [Accessed 11 Feb 2005]

APPENDIX

```
if a(MFN) then
'</Repository>'
fi
if val(mfn)=1 then
'<?xml version="1.0" encoding="UTF-8"?>'
'<Repository xmlns="http://www.openarchives.org/OAI/2.0/static-repository"'
        ' xmlns:oai="http://www.openarchives.org/OAI/2.0/"'
        ' xmlns:xsi="http://www.w3.org/2001;XMLSchema-instance"'
        ' xsi:schemaLocation="http://www.openarchives.org/OAI/2.0/static-repository'
        'http://www.openarchives.org/OAI/2.0/static-repository.xsd">'
'<Identify>'
'<oai:repositoryName>PubsSR</oai:repositoryName>'
'<oai:baseURL>"http://dhcp-200.cs.odu.edu:9117/cgi-
bin/gateway/gateway.cgi/dhcp-200.cs.odu.edu:9117/gateway/pubsrf.xml" </oai:baseURL>'
'<oai:protocolVersion>2.0</oai:protocolVersion>'
'<oai:adminEmail>franc@cs.odu.edu</oai:adminEmail>'
'<oai:earliestDatestamp>2004-09-15</oai:earliestDatestamp>'
'<oai:deletedRecord>no</oai:deletedRecord>'
'<oai:granularity>YYYY-MM-DD</oai:granularity>'
'</Identify>'
'<ListMetadataFormats>'
'<oai:metadataFormat>'
'<oai:metadataPrefix>oai_dc</oai:metadataPrefix>'
'<oai:schema>http://www.openarchives.org/OAI/2.0/oai_dc.xsd<
/oai:schema>'
'<oai:metadataNamespace>http://www.openarchives.org/OAI/2.0/
oai_dc/oai_dc.xsd</oai:metadataNamespace>'
'</oai:metadataFormat>'
'</ListMetadataFormats>'
fi
'<ListRecords metadataPrefix="oai_dc">'
'<oai:record>'
'<oai:header>'
```

```
'<oai:identifier>oai:cdsPubs:ncsi-iisc/mfn-' mfn '</oai:identifier>'
"<oai:datestamp>" v5 '</oai:datestamp>'
'</oai:header>'
'<oai:metadata>'
'<oai_dc:dc
 xmlns:oai_dc="http://www.openarchives.org/OAI/2.0/oai_dc/"
  xmlns:dc="http://purl.org/dc/elements/1.1/"
  xmlns:xsi="http://www.w3.org/2001/XMLSchema-instance"
  xsi:schemaLocation="http://www.openarchives.org/OAI/2.0/oai_dc/ http://www.openarchi
ves.org/OAI/2.0/oai_dc.xsd">' mhl,
if p(v245) then
 '<dc:title>' v245 '</dc:title>'
fi
 (if p(v100) then
 '<dc:creator>' v100 '</dc:creator>'
fi),
 (if p(v600) then
 '<dc:subject>' v600 '</dc:subject>'
fi),
 if p(v520)then
 '<dc:description>' v520 '</dc:description>'
fi,
 if p(v260^c) then
 '<dc:date>' v260^c '</dc:date>'
fi,
 if p(v260^b) then
 '<dc:publisher>' v260^b '</dc:publisher>'
fi,
 if p(v7) then
 '<dc:type>' v7 '</dc:type>'
fi,
 if p(v856^q) then
 '<dc:format>' v856^q '</dc:format>'
fi,
 if p(v856^u) then
```

```
'<dc:identifier>' v856^u '</dc:identifier>'
fi,
 if p(v786)then
 '<dc:source>' v786 '</dc:source>'
fi,
 if p(v41)then
 '<dc:language>' v41 '</dc:language>'
fi,
'</oai_dc:dc>'
'</oai:metadata>'
'</oai:record>'
'</ListRecords>'
 if val(mfn)=9 then
'</Repository>'
fi
```

THE CHANGING LANGUAGE TECHNOLOGY AND CDS\ISIS: UNICODE AND THE EMERGENCE OF OTF

K.H. Hussain
J.S. Rajeev

Language technology is undergoing a great change and within a few years languages of the world will embark on OTF (OpenType Font) Technology. Major operating systems have already started embedding Asian languages using OTF. Being a major bibliographic DBMS, CDS\ISIS cannot ignore these developments that have taken place in text processing. This paper looks at the ideas behind Unicode and OTF and examines future developments of multilingual information systems. The Unicode is a minimalist encoding which includes currently all major scripts in use and allows easy migration from an existing encoding scheme to it. Indic language computing will be tremendously benefited from the development of OTF in compliance with Unicode. CDS\ISIS should be made Unicode compliant by utilizing the shaping and encoding engine on various operating systems so that it can be effectively utilized to develop and distribute local information systems using vernacular scripts. The source code of CDS\ISIS may be made available under a free software license, allowing the evolution of the package in a free and socially useful manner.

1 INTRODUCTION

CDS\ISIS, a bibliographic DBMS developed by UNESCO, is known for its efficiency in handling large volumes of textual data. It is one of the most used documentation packages in the world. Libraries in India started automating in the eighties using CDS\ISIS, thanks to NISSAT. The curriculum of Library and Information Science programmes in practically every university includes the study of CDS\ISIS. In 1997 WINISIS was launched with the technical help from BIREME (Latin American and Caribbean Centre on Health Science Information) and since then a lot of utilities have been developed. In India, packages like 'DELISIS' (for general search and retrieval), 'Nitya' (for digital archiving) (Ravindran Asari, 2000; Hussain, *et.al.* 2002) and M-Isis (for search and retrieval using Malayalam script) (Hussain, 2004) were developed in Windows environment. At the same time its popularity as a library automation system is waning due to its inefficiency in handling non-documentation operations such as periodical control, circulation control, etc. Other packages such as LibSys, Alice, SOUL, etc, have acquired major installations in university and research libraries in India. Still the limitations in handling Indian language scripts pose major hurdles for these packages. Even after a decade of library automation, all of the libraries in Kerala develop their electronic catalogue of Malayalam collections in the Roman script by transliterating titles and other bibliographic data.

While CDS\ISIS is successfully exploring new areas of applications by adapting to local languages for publishing bibliographic CD-ROMs and digital archives of local documents, the whole language technology (i.e. Font technology) is undergoing a sea change. Within a few years almost all the languages of the world will embark on a new technology called OTF (OpenType Font) Technology. Major operating systems like GNU\Linux and MS Windows have already started embedding local languages using OTF. CDS\ISIS cannot stay away from these developments. The good thing about OTF is that it is well suited for Unicode compliance and the task of developing information systems in local scripts will be easy and as natural as in English, if the package is capable of handling OTF. This paper looks at the ideas behind UNICODE and how the new font technology OTF is compliant with Unicode concepts. The paper also examines how this emerging language technology is going to result an entirely different kind of environment suitable for developing multilingual information systems and suggests major considerations for revising CDS\ISIS in the age of free software and OTF.

2 UNICODE

The Unicode is a universal encoding format designed to represent the symbols and script elements of the world in a uniform manner. In order to understand the Unicode, it is necessary to see the extant systems using which multi-lingual systems were made.

In the beginning was the ASCII encoding, designed for English text representation and interchange. Until then, there was no standard for the representation of text elements and this led to problems in interchange of documents and computer messages. The ASCII solved this problem by assigning to each script element and control words, a unique number which would be interpreted the same way on all systems. The ASCII was a 7-bit code, and it quickly became ubiquitous in all computing frameworks. Maximum number of characters and control words, collectively called code-points, encodable according to the scheme was 128 (i.e., 2^7). Later, the 8-bit processor architectures prompted many computer equipment manufacturers to utilize the extra bit for encoding additional characters. An extra bit would mean a doubling of the code space i.e., from 128 possible code points, to 256 code points (i.e. 2^8). This new encoding was known as extended ASCII (EASCII). It included various accented characters for European languages as well as additional non-script characters useful for building text based user interfaces. However, the same problems as the pre-ASCII time emerged, i.e., the inability to properly interchange documents and messages because of the lack of standardization of code point assigned to a particular character\shape. In order to solve this problem, the concept of code-pages was invented. In a document, which utilized extended ASCII code points, there would be an additional code called the code-page. The code-page number could be used to specify which encoding scheme is being used in the extended-ASCII code space. The manufacturers were now free to develop their own encoding, as long as they also applied for a code-page number allocation. This was not without problems. One notable problem was the integration of data from multiple sources, which used encodings in more than one codepage for the same language script. Elaborate systems were used to combat this problem. The emergence of the global Internet and World Wide Web only compounded the problem further. The codepage in use could not be understood from the data alone (say for incorrectly encoded data), and this even went to the extent of devising probabilistic and statistical models for predicting the code page.

It was in response to this (and other issues such as Chinese/Japanese/ Korean unification), that the Unicode was born. Starting from research in this area at XEROX PARC, interest grew in a universal encoding format for all scripts for the purposes of computing. At the culmination of around five years of intense collaboration among world-renowned organizations such as Apple, Microsoft and others, the Unicode Consortium was incorporated in January of 1991 to formalize these ideas. The Unicode is a minimalistic encoding which includes currently all major scripts in use. The basic principle "encode the characters, not the glyphs" denotes the minimalism of the Unicode encoding. By encoding only abstract characters to code points, the encoding would be able to reflect the semantics of the script rather than represent a mere number. This simplifies higher level processing, such as EASCII to Unicode conversions and, text stream to visual rendering.

In short the advantages of Unicode are:

* It is a minimalistic encoding designed to represent all other encodings;
* Along with the OTF layout it allows development of languages with complex visual rendering requirements;
* It allows easy migration from an existing encoding scheme to the Unicode; and
* The determination of script \ code page can be done automatically in the Unicode, since each script is allocated a unique code block.

3 EMERGENCE OF OTF (OPENTYPE FONT)

Fonts are the means by which characters in a language can be rendered visually on the screen or in print. It is one of the basic subsystems of computer text processing. Initially, fonts were bitmap fonts, i.e., each character consisted of a 2-dimensional matrix of pixels with each element being a single bit indicator whether the screen is dark or light at that pixel. Soon, for the purposes of digital typography, fonts were designed with Bezier curves, which allowed arbitrary scaling of the font without loss in quality. The abstract curve representation of a character is also known as a glyph. Irrespective of the type of font, each character representation was also assigned a number for unique identification. This number also corresponded to the code-point for the shape in the ASCII. As mentioned earlier, the concept of ASCII quickly evolved into EASCII and code-pages scheme. The font had to be designed with the code-page in mind.

For new languages that entered the computing arena, like Indian languages, the encoding and font design went hand in hand. Typically, the encoding was dependent entirely on the font making rendering on the screen easy as long as a single code-page was used throughout. This scheme came to be known as font encoding, and the data is encoded based on the positions of characters in the font. Still, the number of code-points that can be represented without changes to the rendering system would remain the same at 256 code-points. This imposed constraints on the number of glyphs that could be designed in any given font. Combinations of basic characters known as ligatures or conjuncts could be designed and used by allocating a code-point to it. But the space available would remain as low as 256. This forces incomplete and disintegrated implementation of various languages (or families) like Indic languages, which need a lot more than 256 code-points to represent the entire repertoire. This is what happened in the case of Malayalam language when attempts were made to accommodate its nearly 1000 traditional characters.

OpenType Font (OTF) is the new technology with a variety of features that allow complete implementation of Indic languages satisfying all their peculiar characteristics. It was introduced jointly by Microsoft and Adobe in 1997 to meet the requirements of complex scripts and multi-lingual /multi-script documents, as well as new techniques in rendering (such as in auto-hinting). Although OTF can be used with a variety of encoding, it is best implemented with the Unicode. For each Unicode encoded character, the font designer can design glyph shapes for that character. The designer may also design glyphs in the so-called unencoded slots. Total number of shapes in the encoded and unencoded slots may come to around 65,000 glyphs (i.e. 2^{16}). The unencoded set contains glyphs for combinations of encoded characters. In this way, an Indic language text that contains mostly conjuncts can easily be represented and accordingly a font can be designed accommodating any number of glyphs. An OTF can only be used advantageously in conjunction with a shaping engine (rendering engine) that is usually implemented in the OS or the windowing toolkit. The shaping engine provides text layout services, which transform a piece of text into glyphs from both the encoded and unencoded sets. This meets the complex shaping requirements for conjuncts in Indic languages with the use of basic abstract characters of the Unicode.

This process of shaping occurs as follows:

* The text is analyzed and broken down into segments. Segmentation is done at cluster boundaries;

* Then the string is mapped to a set of glyphs representing the basic characters;

* The basic glyphs are then further transformed on the basis of OTF features. OTF features are special tags associated with the unencoded-glyph shapes, which establishes correspondence between complex shapes and their basic components. The application of features can happen either by substituting the complex shape with a sequence of basic shapes, or by positioning the shapes over the existing shape;

* The final sequence of glyph shapes is laid out according to the requirements of the software.

For speed, interoperability and simplicity of laying out fonts, the system applies several optimization techniques. In general, the position of the OTF layout process is in the OS. For highly specialized applications that require fine use of text visuals, it may also be re-implemented for the particular system. Needless to say, the process should be standard on all systems, so that there are no different input methods and different visuals for the same text.

4 OTF IN MALAYALAM

Indic language computing will be greatly benefited from the development of OTF technology. That the limitation of 256 slots is left behind by the 65000 code points alone makes OTF receptive to conjunct-rich Indic scripts. An example of the application of OTF in Malayalam script will explain conjunct and its Unicode representation clearly.

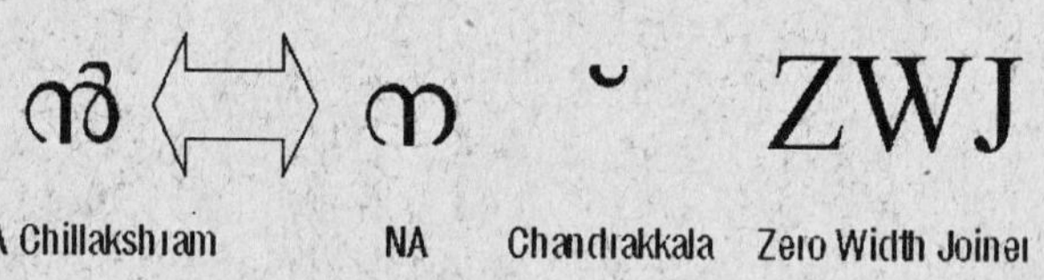

Consider the *NA Chillaksharam. NA* is represented by a single basic character in the Unicode block. As per the philosophy of the Unicode, glyphs that may be represented by sequences of basic characters will not be allocated a specific code point. So, the *NA Chillaksharam* is not given such a code point. In order to allow rendering of the chill form, the OTF provides a "Halant" feature. According to the Unicode standards, the *Na* Chillaksharam form is represented in the encoding by the sequence

NA + Chandrakkala + ZWJ

All the three characters that constitute this sequence are basic characters in the Unicode. The Halant feature is tagged on the *NA* Chillaksharam glyph that is placed in an unencoded slot and this is applied to *NA + Chandrakkala + ZWJ* glyph sequence. Such a sequence is indeed transformed into the *NA* Chillaksharam form when rendered on screen.

5 THE UNICODE AND LEGACY ENCODING

In Malayalam there exist two different character sets namely '*Traditional*' (Original/Old) and '*Reformed*' (Typewriter) character sets. '*Traditional*' is the exhaustive character set consisting of all the conjuncts and archaic characters in Malayalam which may number around 1000. '*Reformed*' character set designed for use in typewriters in 1970 consists of nearly 100 characters containing only a few conjuncts of original Malayalam. Most of the Malayalam fonts and word processing applications like ISM-Gist and SreeLipi use *Reformed* character set where as 'Rachana' a word-processing package to create text in original Malayalam uses *Traditional* character set. Considering these different character sets of Malayalam, an understanding of the Unicode encoding model can be derived easily from the following example:

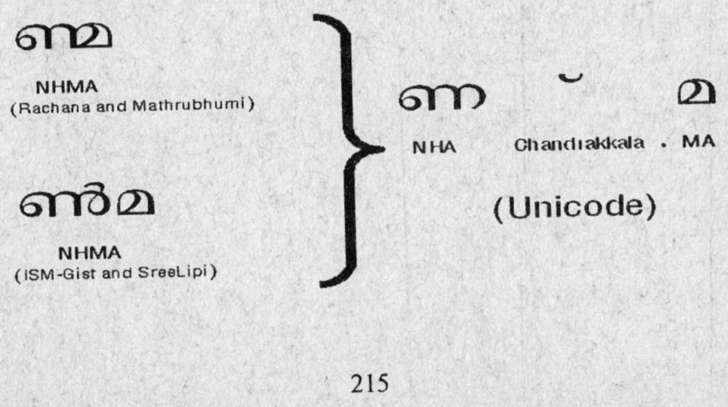

A common non-minimal encoding is the 'Mathrubhumi' encoding which is used to print and publish 'Mathrubhumi' newspaper and weeklies. In this encoding, for example, there exists a single code-point for the representation of *NHMA*, where *NHMA* is

NHA + Chandrakala + MA

'Rachana' uses the same encoding for *NHMA*. In another encoding for Malayalam such as ISM-Gist and SreeLipi, no code-point exists for this character. Instead the character is rendered as the combination of three basic characters

NHA Chandrakala MA

Unicode solves this problem by encoding only the basic minimal characters from which the compound characters are generated. *NHA, Chandrakala* and *MA* have individual code-points and the complex shape *NHMA* is encoded as the basic code-point sequence such as:

NHA (followed by) Chandrakala (followed by) MA

Rachana / Mathrubhumi and other encodings can easily be encoded using the Unicode. Along with appropriate OTF fonts and layout tables, it is possible to provide the exact rendering encoding schemes of both *Traditional* and *Reformed* character sets. OTF can reuse glyphs developed for older systems and allow migration to the Unicode system. In time, all documents using either encoding can be converted and the users can be fully migrated from legacy encoding to the Unicode. Of course all this would depend on proper encoding scheme for various features of the Indic script under consideration, and this requires a complete understanding of the linguistics of that script and language. In some cases, this is easy, and in others it may be difficult as in the case of Malayalam. Peculiar properties of some characters may even be highly disputed making implementations nearly impossible or highly volatile. Malayalam has been allocated a code-block within the Unicode, but various issues have been discovered regarding the script and it's encoding. Many of these issues are also dependent on a disputed area of the linguistic properties of the script, along with technical difficulties in other areas.

6 NEW POSSIBILITIES OF CDS\ISIS APPLICATIONS

Only recently the Library of the Government Brennen College, Thalassery, Kerala achieved the first digital catalogue in Malayalam by publishing a searchable reference CD of its holdings of 21,000 Malayalam books. M-ISIS, the front end of this CD that employs search and retrieval using Malayalam script is the Malayalam adaptation of CDS\ISIS. 'Nitya', a package programmed using ISIS32.DLL for digital archiving has already demonstrated the strength of CDS\ISIS in retrieving scanned images. 'Nitya' explores potential of CDS\ISIS in CD-Publishing of databases and full texts.

These experiments and events show that:

* Though applications of CDS\ISIS in Indian libraries are declining, its superiority as a textual database and documentation package is undeniable and it can be effectively utilized for publishing bibliographic data on CD. Its ability to handle several million records and its speed of retrieval are still unrivaled by modern RDBMS. Its specific structural design to handle bibliographic information is still unique.

* Adapting CDS\ISIS to Indian languages is possible and it can be successfully employed in developing and distributing local information systems using local scripts.

Creation of M-ISIS based on the 8-bit TTF (True type Font) technology brought forth many problems in accommodating the 1000 characters of original Malayalam. Similar problems may have to be confronted in adapting the package to other Indic languages. If CDS\ISIS / WINISIS is revised to accommodate OTF and comply with Unicode, tremendous possibilities will be opened in developing local information systems in the same script using which people think, talk, read and write. Since the architecture of CDS\ISIS is heavily based on documentation principles and cataloguing practices, it will excel in developing and distributing digital archives of palm leaves and other local documents in Indian languages. For example, in the event of such a development, the *National Bibliography of Indian Literature* published by the Sahitya Akedemi can be efficiently produced and distributed in CD with bibliographic records in the original languages and scripts using CDS\ISIS better than in any other software currently available.

7 CDS\ISIS IN THE AGE OF FREE SOFTWARE AND OTF

It is high time to assimilate what is achieved in the language technology front, without which no software, especially those meant for text processing and textual databases can survive and achieve progress. It is necessary to set priority in revising CDS/ISIS to make it Unicode compliant by utilizing various shaping and encoding engines on various operating systems. (On Windows, the Uniscribe shaper, and various Unicode related data APIs; On GNU\Linux, various choices are available for shaping such as PANGO, QT etc).

Supporting Unicode and supporting legacy encoding are not mutually exclusive. It is possible to make mappings between the legacy encoding and the Unicode encoding, which will allow the vast amount of data already available in CDS/ISIS databases to be reused in the new Unicode model. The source code of an international resource such as the CDS\ISIS may be made available under a free software license such as the FSF/GNU licenses GPL (General Public License) or LGPL (Lesser/Library General Public License). It is also possible to offer CDS\ISIS under both licenses at the same time, allowing the evolution of CDS\ISIS in a free and socially useful manner.

Free licenses on the source code will not only open new fronts of application and customization in library and documentation activities, but also lead to widespread use of WINISIS on the most advanced network-oriented operating system. Several packages available on the GNU/Linux operating system provide choice to developers who may not be used to a particular system for deployment. The choices are available in windowing toolkits (Motif, GTK, Qt, etc), in network servers (Apache, Tomcat, etc), web application frameworks (Webware, Zope, PHP, etc) and languages which can easily connect with native libraries (Python, Perl, Ruby, Scheme, Java, Objective-C, C/C++, etc). This allows easy use of CDS\ISIS in many applications. Furthermore, the wide usage of CDS\ISIS will allow it to evolve further and attain greater heights. Coupled with the high customizability of the GNU/Linux platform, it will also be possible to implement high-performance specialized applications, leading to further growth.

8 POSTSCRIPT

It was in 1987 that I (Hussain) first met Prof. A. Neelameghan. Two years later, I went again to Bangalore, this time to attend classes on CDS\ISIS. The teacher was Prof. Neelameghan and I began my decade long romance with CDS\ISIS. His classes were marvelous and he used CDS\ISIS to explore the whole range of information system development beyond the bibliographic information system. Subsequently I met him occasionally at workshops and conferences, and he always enquired about my experiments with CDS\ISIS. Accomplishments of M-ISIS (Malayalam ISIS) and 'Nitya' (for digital archiving) can be traced to the enthusiasm he showed in my work. A couple of years ago he asked me to contribute a paper on 'Nitya' software. Recently he asked me to present a paper on M-ISIS in the 'National Seminar on Digitization: Practical Experiences', August 2004, sponsored by Sarada Ranganathan Endowment. Future evolution of CDS\ISIS is closely related to what is happening on the language technology front. Hence the theme of this article will be dear to this great teacher.

9 ACKNOWLEDGEMENTS

We would like to thank Mr. Joseph Sebastian (BTC Engineering, Kuwait), Mr. R. Chitrajakumar (Leader of Rachana Linguistic Campaign) and Dr. Varghese Paul (Cochin University of Science and Technology, Kerala).

REFERENCES

1. Hussain, K.H; Raman Nair, R. and Raveendran Asari, K. (2002). Importance of search and retrieval in CD-ROM full text publishing: Experiments using PDF documents and 'Nitya' archival system. *Information Studies*. Vol. 8(3); p. 173-180

2. —. et al. (2004). *Creation of digital archives in Indian languages using CDS\ISIS: Development of M-ISIS (Malayalam ISIS) and 'Nitya'*. National Seminar on Digitization: Practical Experiences. 9 - 12 August 2004, Bangalore, India

3. Ravindran Asari, K. (2000). *Nitya Archives: A Solution for Organizing Digitized Content in Agriculture*. Agricultural Information Systems: Vision 2020. Thrissur, IASLIC Study Circle, 2000.

4. —; Hussain, K.H and Raman Nair, R. (2002). Nitya Archives: Innovative blending of techniques for selective access to information from digitally organized text (SAIDOT). **In**: Parthan, S (Ed.) *Proceedings of the National Conference on Information Management in e-Libraries*, 26-27 February 2002 IIT, Kharagpur. Allied Publishers Limited, New Delhi, p. 275-285.

WEB REFERENCES

1. Unicode Consortium. http://www.unicode.org

2. OpenType Specifications. http://www.microsoft.com/OpenType/OTSpec/

3. CDS\ISIS. http://portal.unesco.org

4. Rachana OTF. http://www.stendekrnd.com/rachana/rachana.html

ADDITIONAL READING

1. Sulochana Devi, L. (1997). Information System for Research in Sanskrit and Indology. **In** *the Proceedings of the National Conference on Vedic Sciences*. Madras, JGRCVS.

TEXT MINING IN BIOMEDICINE: CHALLENGES AND OPPORTUNITIES

Padmini Srinivasan

Text mining is about making serendipity more likely. Serendipity, the chance discovery of interesting ideas, has been responsible for many discoveries in science. Text mining systems strive to explore large text collections, separate the potentially meaningful connections from a vast and mostly noisy background of random associations. In this paper we provide a summary of our text mining approach and also illustrate briefly some of the experiments we have conducted with this approach. In particular we use a profile-based text mining method. We have used these profiles to explore the global distribution of disease research, replicate discoveries made by others and propose new hypotheses. Text mining holds much potential that has yet to be tapped.

1 INTRODUCTION

It is widely acknowledged that biomedical knowledge is growing at an astounding pace. This creates an enormous challenge for scientists trying to keep pace with developments in their field. At the same time these vast collections of published works offer an excellent opportunity for text mining, i.e., the automatic discovery of new and interesting hypotheses that might ultimately contribute to the growth of biomedical knowledge. Text mining is similar to data mining (Agrawal and Srikant, 1994; Fayyad and Uthurusamy, 1996) in its goal. But instead of mining well-structured databases, text mining operates on semi-structured text collections. In both cases the emphasis is on postulating hypotheses that require further scientific study and verification.

Text mining in the biomedical domain has attracted the attention of many researchers, e.g. Andrade and Valencia (1998); Feldman, *et. al.* (1997); Masys *et. al.* (2001); Smalheiser and Swanson (1996); Smalheiser and Swanson (1996b); Srinivasan and Wedemeyer (2003); Srinivasan and Libbus (2004); Swanson (1986, 1988); and Swanson *et al.* (2001). Recently Blagosklonny and Pardee (2002) referring to text mining as conceptual biology outlined its importance in hypothesis driven biomedical explorations. Examples of recent text mining applications include automatically identifying viruses that may be used as biological weapons (Swanson et al., 2001), proposing therapeutic uses for thalidomide (Weeber, 2003) and finding functional connections between genes (Chaussabel and Sher, 2002; Shatkay, *et. al.* 2000).

In essence, text mining is about making 'serendipity', the chance discovery of interesting ideas, more likely. We know from history that serendipity has often shaped the pathways of science. Classic examples include Fleming's observations of a culture of Staphylococcus dissolving when the plate was accidentally contaminated with a blue-green mold. This discovery of penicillin eventually led to the development of antibiotics. The serendipitous discoveries of artificial sweeteners Saccharine and Aspartame, although possibly not as momentous, resulted when scientists accidentally tasted spills in their research labs. Serendipity may be influenced by several intangibles including researcher intuition, prior experience and knowledge, and the ability to creatively span multiple disciplines.

Text mining systems are designed to enable such serendipitous discoveries and in effect make them less serendipitous. Clearly such systems would have to separate the potentially meaningful connections from a vast and mostly noisy background of random associations. Given their emphasis on texts, such systems strive to simultaneously analyze the published literature from multiple disciplines, sift through the evidence, identify implicit connections that have potential, and then ensure that these are novel in that they have not yet been explicitly addressed. Our goal, along with those of others in this field, is to design and evaluate algorithms that can support such text-based functions. In this paper we summarize our profile-based text mining approach (Srinivasan and Wedemeyer, 2003; Srinivasan and Libbus, 2004) and also outline a few of the experiments that we have conducted. The reader is referred to these articles for full details.

2 PROFILE-BASED MINING

Given a particular topic of interest, our procedure begins by first building a profile from an appropriate text collection. A topic is any subject of interest such as *treatment of hypertension* or *ATM gene*. A profile is essentially a representation of a topic that is derived from the text collection being mined. When using MEDLINE as the database to mine, our topic profiles are vectors of weighted Medical Subject Headings (MeSH). These terms belong to a controlled vocabulary and are manually assigned to each MEDLINE document by trained indexers at the National Library of Medicine. Given a topic, our algorithm first retrieves relevant MEDLINE documents. MeSH terms are then extracted from these documents and their weights are calculated. These weighted terms form the profile vector for the topic. We discuss the method for calculating weights below.

The table in Figure 1 (a screenshot from our prototype system) shows the vector of terms for the topic: CDKN1A. The second column labeled MeSH Term lists the extracted terms from documents that are about the topic. We also exploit the fact that MeSH terms have been classified using 134 UMLS (Unified Medical Language System)[1] semantic types as for example *Cell Function*, *Sign or Symptom*. Each MeSH term is assigned one or more semantic types. For example, interferon type II falls within both *Immunologic Factor* and *Pharmacologic Substance* semantic types. More generally, semantic types represent 'categories' that have been used to classify the MeSH metadata. Semantic types are useful because depending on the nature of the discovery goal we may adopt a particular *view*, i.e., we may restrict the discovery process to consider only certain semantic types. In these cases the topic profiles are restricted to MeSH terms belonging to semantic types specified by the view. The table shows in column[1] the semantic types corresponding to each term in the profile for CDKN1A. As an example, the table also indicates how one may restrict the profile to a view consisting of just a couple of semantic types.

We calculate term weights for the MeSH terms. Term weights are a slight modification of the commonly used TF*IDF scores. Since a MeSH term typically occurs once in a MEDLINE record, here TF_i (term frequency) equals the number of documents in which the MeSH term t_i occurs within the retrieved document set. IDF_i (inverse document frequency) is log (N/TF_i) where N is the number of documents retrieved for the topic. Weights are normalized as shown below for term t_i. This vector of weighted MeSH terms forms the topic profile

1 http://umlsks.nlm.nih.gov

$$weight(t_i) = v_i / \sqrt{v_1^2 + v_2^2 + ... + v_r^2} \qquad (1)$$

where

$$v_i = TF_i * \log(N / TF_i) \qquad (2)$$

and there are r terms in the profile. The third column of Table 1 shows the calculated weight while the last column displays the rank of each term within its semantic type.

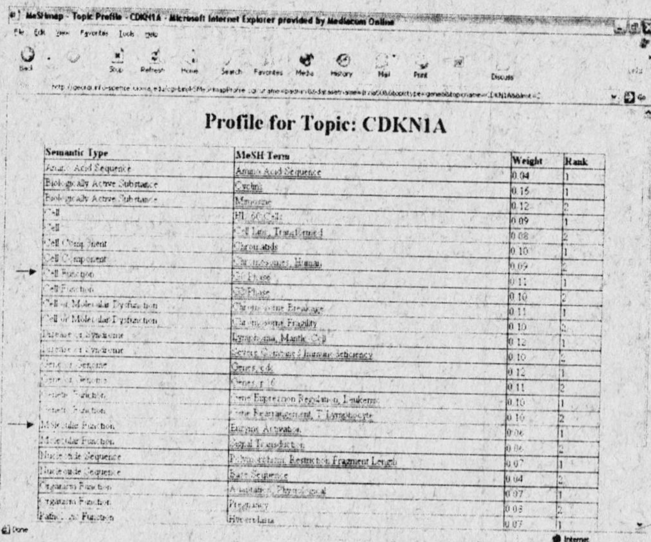
Profile for Topic: CDKN1A

Semantic Type	MeSH Term	Weight	Rank
Amino Acid Sequence	Amino Acid Sequence	0.04	1
Biologically Active Substance	Cyclins	0.15	1
Biologically Active Substance	Mimosine	0.12	2
Cell	HL-60 Cells	0.09	1
Cell	Cell Line, Transformed	0.08	2
Cell Component	Chromatids	0.10	1
Cell Component	Chromosomes, Human	0.09	2
Cell Function	G1 Phase	0.11	1
Cell Function	G2 Phase	0.10	2
Cell or Molecular Dysfunction	Chromosome Breakage	0.11	1
Cell or Molecular Dysfunction	Chromosome Fragility	0.10	2
Disease or Syndrome	Lymphoma, Mantle-Cell	0.12	1
Disease or Syndrome	Severe Combined Immunodeficiency	0.10	2
Gene or Genome	Genes, cdc	0.12	1
Gene or Genome	Genes, p16	0.11	2
Genetic Function	Gene Expression Regulation, Leukemic	0.10	1
Genetic Function	Gene Rearrangement, T-Lymphocyte	0.10	2
Molecular Function	Enzyme Activation	0.06	1
Molecular Function	Signal Transduction	0.06	2
Nucleotide Sequence	Polymorphism, Restriction Fragment Length	0.07	1
Nucleotide Sequence	Base Sequence	0.04	2
Organism Function	Adaptation, Physiological	0.07	1
Organism Function	Pregnancy	0.03	2
Pathologic Function	Hyperplasia	0.07	1

Fig. 1: Profile for the Topic: CDKN1A

3 EXPLORING INDIVIDUAL PROFILES

Although our main goal is to explore implicit connections between topics through their profiles, these profiles are useful in their own right. We may also explore individual profiles for trends of interest. We demonstrate this notion by exploring individual disease profiles. Consider a user who is interested in studying the global prevalence of research on mental diseases. Using our text mining function a profile is built for this topic by first retrieving MEDLINE documents that are about mental disorders. Since the focus is on the global prevalence of research, this profile is restricted to the metadata category represented by the semantic type *Geographic Area*. (Note that this semantic type has nothing to do with the geographic affiliations of the authors of the corresponding documents or the location of the organization(s) to which they belong. Rather, geographic MeSH terms are applied when the study explicitly pertains to the geographic region). The resultant profile is then a set of weighted country names where the weights are computed as shown in equation 1. These weights reflect the relative emphasis of mental disorders research in the context of the corresponding nation. We can thus rank the nations by their weights and when this data is fed into appropriate visualization software such as a GIS the user may see output as shown in Figure 1. In the figure the colour changes from green to red as the relative research emphasis on the disorders increases. Regions coloured white are not included in the analysis. Regions coloured blue have zero emphasis on such research. Thus our user can visually explore the global distribution of research on diseases of interest.

Similar profiles and figures may be generated for any other disease. Further, these may be restricted to any time period such as a particular decade of interest, by limiting the retrieved set of documents appropriately. Such profiles may also be the basis for further research. Table 1, for example, summarizes one form of analysis that is based on disease profiles. It shows for each group of high, middle and low income nations, the two most studied diseases. It provides this information for each of 4 decades. For example, mental disorders have been the most frequently studied class of problems in the high-income nations across all decades. In the decade of the 60s for 19 out of 52 high-income nations this entry was at rank 1. Although this family of problems does not rate high for middle and low-income nations, a World Bank Study on the Global Burden of Disease, found mental disorders to be the leading cause of disability in the world for 1990[2]. The question may be asked: why are the middle and low-income groups not showing greater research emphasis on mental disorders? This is in fact an issue that has generated

2 World Health Organization. The Global Burden of Disease. A Summary. (http://www.who.int/msa/mnh/ems/dalys/intro.htm).

much attention. For example, in developing countries mental health is viewed as secondary to the more life threatening infectious diseases. Lack of awareness, stigma and discrimination against the mentally ill are also some of the barriers[3].

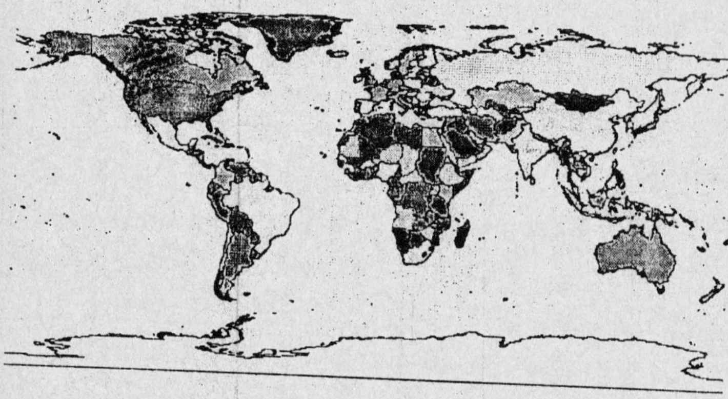

Fig. 2: Global Prevalence of Research on Mental Disorders

Examining Table 1 again, we now look at malaria. It is the most or close to the most frequent top ranked disease for the low and middle-income groups while it is absent from the high-income group for any time period. This pattern is consistent with the fact that malaria is predominantly a tropical disease occurring in Asia, Africa and South and Central America[4]. Several other diseases are also present only in the middle and low-income groups such as Schistosomiasis and nutrition disorders. Tuberculosis, the second most frequent top ranked disease in the 60s for a significant portion of the world becomes less frequent over time and is totally absent from the top ranking

3 World Health Organization. The Global Burden of Disease. A Summary. (http://www.who.int/msa/mnh/ems/dalys/intro.htm).

4 National Institute of Allergy and Infectious Diseases (US Department of Health and Human Services).Malaria. NIH Publication No. 02-7139. September 2002. (http://www.niaid.nih.gov/publications/malaria/).

pool of the high-income group for the decade of the 90s. These trends are also consistent with global occurrence patterns for the disease[5]. High income countries such as France and Finland have reduced their numbers of tuberculosis cases over the decades, while in many of the low-income nations, these numbers are on the rise. For example, in Malawi the number went from about 5,300 in 1985 to about 19,000 in 1995 and we observe that it has remained a top ranked disease in research for this nation.

Overall, the low and middle-income groups are more similar to each other in their top ranked diseases while being quite distinct from the high-income group. Trend analysis supports our intuition that changes in the prevalence of a disease over time may generate similar changes in the prevalence of research on the disease. The exceptions, as in mental disorders are revealing in their imbalance and consistent with external evidence regarding the emphasis on the disease. A complete version of this study is available in Srinivasan and Wedemeyer, 2003).

Table 1: Top Ranked Diseases in Research Emphasis

Disease/Disorder	1960s	1970s	1980s	1990s
High Income: 52 countries				
Mental Disorders	1 (19)	1 (19)	1 (18)	1 (15)
Tuberculosis, Pulmonary	2 (11)	7 (2)	9 (1)	n/a
Neoplasms	2 (1)	5 (5)	4 (7)	3 (13)
Substance-Related Disorders	4 (6)	2 (12)	6 (5)	11 (1)
Acquired Immunodeficiency Syndrome	n/a	n/a	2 (16)	2 (12)
Middle Income: 90 countries				
Malaria	1 (8)	2 (11)	1 (17)	4 (9)
Nutrition Disorders	1 (8)	3 (9)	10 (3)	11 (2)
Chagas Disease	2 (7)	10 (2)	8 (5)	5 (8)
Tuberculosis, Pulmonary	2 (7)	1 (12)	5 (8)	7 (6)
Chronic Disease	7 (1)	1 (12)	7 (12)	12 (1)
Leishmaniasis	7 (1)	9 (3)	2 (11)	5 ??

5 World Health Organization. Tuberculosis. Strategies, Operations, Monitoring and Evaluation. (http://www.who.int/gtb/Country_info/

Disease/Disorder	1960s	1970s	1980s	1990s
Occupational Diseases	2 (7)	4 (8)	3 (10)	8 ??
Acquired Immunodeficiency Syndrome	n/a	n/a	4 (9)	1 (22)
Mutation	7 (1)	n/a	n/a	2 (13)
Low Income: 64 countries				
Malaria	1 (10)	1 (18)	1 (34)	1 (27)
Schistosomiasis	2 (8)	2 (15)	4 (8)	3 (4)
Acquired Immunodeficiency Syndrome	n/a	n/a	2 (9)	2 (26)

4 EXPLORING IMPLICIT RELATIONS BETWEEN PROFILES

Some of the really interesting discoveries involve identifying novel relationships between a pair (or larger group) of topics. For example, one may seek genes related to a given disease or want to identify dietary factors that influence a disease. Swanson and Smalheiser initiated this kind of effort in a series of papers (Smalheiser, 1996a; 1996b; Swanson, 1986; 1988). In essence they designed two discovery processes. The first an open one in which the user provides only a single input topic and the goal is to discover novel associations between this and other topics. The second is a closed process in which two topics are provided as input and the goal is to discover novel associations between them. The closed discovery relies on a user's intuition about which two topics to pursue while the open is exploratory to a higher degree.

Our topic profiles readily support such open and closed explorations. In fact our profile-based implementation of the discovery procedures give us several advantages as described in (Srinivasan, 2004). A classic example of a discovery made by Swanson is that fish oils may be useful in treating Raynauds disease (Swanson, 1986). This discovery was later verified (DiGiacomo, Kremer and Shah, 1989). Swanson also predicted 11 different pathways between Migraine and Magnesium (Swanson, 1988). The hurdle in their procedures is the need to manually examine, comprehend and select phrases at different steps. Others (e.g. Lindsay and Gordon, 1999) have succeeded in reducing but not eliminating the need for manual intervention during the process. In our algorithms we only expect the user to specify the input and the semantic metadata categories of interest.

To summarize briefly Swanson's path of discovery, he first observed that Raynaud's syndrome is exacerbated by high platelet aggregability, high blood viscosity, and vasoconstriction. He also observed that these phenomena are reduced by dietary fish oils. Moreover, the literatures on Raynauds and fish oils had no overlap. By reading the titles in these two literatures, Swanson was able to suggest that fish oils may be beneficial to patients with Raynauds. We now demonstrate our ability to replicate his discovery with our profile-based text mining function.

Raynauds disease as the input topic initiates our open discovery algorithm. Essentially we first conduct a PubMed search to obtain the documents that are about Raynauds. The Raynauds search is limited to human studies in the time period 1960 to 1985 (since Swanson's discovery was made in 1986). We then build a profile from the retrieved documents. This profile is limited to a view defined by eight functional semantic types *Cell Function, Finding, Molecular Function, Organism Function, Organ or Tissue Function, Pathologic Function, Phenomenon or Process* and *Physiologic Function*. We chose these 8 functional semantic types under the assumption that the user has an interest in factors that influence the functional aspects of the disease. We then select a single top ranking MeSH term from the Raynauds profile for each of the 8 semantic types. The selected (top ranking) terms are:

Cell Function: platelet aggregation

Finding: scleroderma, systemic

Molecular Function: antibody specificity

Organism Function: aged

Organ or Tissue Function: regional blood flow

Pathologic Function: thrombosis

Phenomenon or Process: recurrence

Physiologic Function: blood viscosity

Observe that key aspects such as platelet aggregation and blood viscosity appear on this list. Again through a process of retrieval we build independent profiles for each of these 8 terms. Retrieval is conducted from the same publication time period again constrained to human studies. These 8 profiles are then merged to obtain a single combined profile. A combined weight is calculated for each term and these are ranked within each semantic type. Were a real user present, these ranked lists would be shown to this user who may then select particular semantic types to browse. Since Swanson was interested in dietary factors the appropriate semantic types to examine at this point would be *Element, Ion, or Isotope, Vitamin* and *Lipid*. Out of these three the results are most interesting for the *Lipid* type. These are shown in Table 2 which lists the ranks of the top 20 terms that are novel in that they do not already co-occur with the Raynauds, our initial topic. It may be observed that 5,8,11,14,17-eicosapentaenoic acid, is an important polyunsaturated fatty acid found in fish oils. It is also the active ingredient in it. Thus we see that the concept of fish oils is indicated within rank 7. The MeSH term "fish oils" itself is ranked 19th. The other entries are also meaningful. For example, lipoproteins have been studied in association with fish oils as seen for instance in a 1985 document (PMID: 3903563) which indicates the reduction of plasma lipids and lipoproteins by marine fish oils. To complete the logical connection, oxidation of low-density lipoproteins has been recently studied in conjunction with Raynauds (PMID: 7639801, a 1995 publication). Also a 1999 study explores the effect of Probucol, an antioxidant that influences low-density lipoprotein oxidation time lag, on Raynauds (PMID: 10378706).

Table 2: Top 20 Lipid Terms Indirectly Related to Raynauds

Rank	MeSH Term	Rank	MeSH Term
1	Lipoproteins, LDL	11	Glycolipids
2	Oils	12	Chylomicrons
3	Lipoproteins, HDL	13	Linolenic Acids
4	Lipoproteins, VDL	14	Glycerides
5	Platelet Activating Factor	15	Lipid Peroxides
6	Phosphatidylcholines	16	Butyrates
7	5,8,11,14,17-Eicosapentaenoic	17	Sodium Tetradecyl Sulfates
8	Lysophosphatidylcholines	18	Cardiolipins
9	Gangliosides	19	Fish Oils
10	Iodized Oil	20	Liposomes

Having demonstrated the potential in our profile-based mining methods by rediscovering the Raynauds-fish oils connection and successfully replicating several other discoveries, work that is reported in detail in (Srinivasan and Wedemeyer, 2003), we turn our attention to the problem of suggesting new hypotheses. In particular we have used our open discovery procedure to suggest novel uses for Curcumin Longa (turmeric) (Srinivasan and Libbus, 2004). Our interest in curcumin was sparked by the fact that this spice is widely used in Asia and is highly regarded for its curative and analgesic properties. These include the treatment of burns, stomach ulcers and ailments, and for various skin diseases. Curcumin is also used as an antiseptic, in alleviating symptoms of the common cold as well as a depilatory. A number of MEDLINE records have reported on the anti-cancer and anti-inflammatory properties of curcumin (PMIDS: 12680238, 12678737, 12676044[6]) Our open discovery goal is aimed at determining whether there are novel disease contexts in which curcumin could prove beneficial, and to propose evidence-based hypotheses that can be experimentally verified.

PMID numbers within parentheses such as these refer to PubMed record ids. The reader may enter these directly into the PubMed interface to retrieve the corresponding records.

We started with a search on *turmeric OR curcumin OR curcuma*. A total of 1,175 PubMed documents were retrieved[7]. The majority of these publications (1,043, 89%) are relatively recent, being published in 1990 or later. This indicates a surge in scientific interest in the health effects of this spice, which has long been valued in Asia for its medicinal properties. Using these documents we built a profile for curcumin. Focusing on the three semantic types *Gene or Genome; Enzyme;* and *Amino Acid, Peptide or Protein* we selected the top 10 MeSH terms from each of these semantic types. Example terms include: ras, bcl-2, myc, MAPK, Glutathione Transferase, Protein Kinase C and Prostaglandin-Endoperoxide Synthase. Once again, following our open discovery strategy, we retrieved documents for each of these terms and built their profiles. The resulting profiles were all combined and combined weights calculated for each term. Restricting our attention in this combined profile to terms in the semantic types *Disease or Syndrome* and

6 PMID numbers within parentheses such as these refer to PubMed record ids. The reader may enter these directly into the PubMed interface to retrieve the corresponding records

7 (done on November 15, 2003)

Neoplastic Process we find the following top listings: Retina, Spinal Cord, Cystic Fibrosis, Amyotrophic Lateral Schlerosis, Crohns disease, Laryngeal Neoplasms, and Choriocarcinoma.

Exploring the literature further regarding some these suggestions, we find good rationale for suggesting connections between turmeric and several of these top entries. For example, we see that genes such as IL-1beta, COX-2, TNF-alpha, JNK, ERK, NF-kappaB are involved in regulating cell proliferation and leukocyte attachment and the breakdown of the blood-retina barrier, which are early signs in diabetic retinopathy. Interestingly, curcumin is capable of inhibiting the activity of these genes. Thus we hypothesize that curcumin may have therapeutic value in preventing or ameliorating diabetic retinopathies. Similarly curcumin may prevent retinal pathologies including ocular inflammation and glaucoma.

Crohn's disease, characterized by a chronic relapsing intestinal inflammation, along with ulcerative colitis (both are irritable bowel syndromes or IBD), are commonly classified as autoimmune diseases, implicating a number of inflammatory cytokines in the process of pathogenesis. The balance between pro- and anti-inflammatory cytokines, particularly between the pro-inflammatory interferon IFN-gamma (IFN-gamma) on the one hand and the anti-inflammatories IL-4 (interleukin-4) and transforming growth factor (TGF-beta) activity, is believed to control chronic intestinal inflammation (11994418). Curcumin inhibits a number of these genes and cytokines. For example, it inhibits NF-kappaB activation and in turn suppresses TNF- alpha signaling and its target transcription factors (PMIDS: 11753638, 11506818, 12878172, 12578124, 7786295, and 12825130). Curcumin also influences MAPK based pathways which have a role in intestinal inflammation. For example, it inhibits JNK (PMIDS: 12957788, 12854631, 12582006, 12130649, 12105223, and 9674701). Curcumin also influences TGF-beta: in wounds, which involve inflammation, the observed beneficial effect of curcumin treatment was attributed to an increase in TGF-beta (PMID: 9776860). Curcumin significantly inhibited IL-12 leading to decreased IFN-gamma induction and increased induction of IL-4 (an anti-inflammatory) (PMID: 10510448). Given the roles of these genes in IBD in general and Crohn's and ulcerative colitis in particular, we hypothesize that curcumin may have beneficial effects on both Crohn's and ulcerative colitis. Full details are available in (Srinivasan and Libbus, 2004).

5 OPPORTUNITIES AND CHALLENGES

Text mining is a field that has relatively recent beginnings. Its importance in bioinformatics as an area that fuels hypothesis generation and exploration has been recognized. Even in other fields such as accounting and finance, text mining has been explored as for example to discover relationships between companies. For example Kloptchenko *et. al.* (2002) analyze the textual portions of companies' financial statements to see if future performance can be predicted. They use an approach based on self-organizing maps to cluster financial ratios of companies on one side and the textual reports on the other. A similar study by Back et al. (2001) found for example that companies tend to exaggerate their performance in their financial reports. Looking across developments in different application areas we observe that we are presently at a point where new and innovative methodologies for knowledge discovery via text mining are still being developed and tested.

From our experience in text mining we see that one significant challenge is that we do not yet know how to recognize a 'good' text mining problem. What are the properties of such a problem? Text mining has sometimes been referred to as the process of finding 'a needle in a haystack'. However, we suggest that we first need to know if there is a needle in the haystack. Otherwise the mining effort could be wasteful. Our closed discovery process offers users a chance to explore connections between any two topics. But which two topics would be reasonable to explore? Obviously user expertise and intuition would be key in answering this question, i.e., in selecting appropriate haystacks. But as text mining researchers it might be useful to think about general models that serve as guidelines. For example, looking for new *disease* contexts in which particular *substances* may be involved either beneficially or negatively, could be one overall framework. This is indeed what underlies our turmeric example. The model could be considered in reverse where we start with a given *disease* and look for *substances* that are related in some way. Instead of *substances* we could look for *microorganisms*. In this way, it would be interesting to see if it is possible to build a constrained set of models that might be useful to both designers and end-users of text mining systems.

Our experience in text mining tells us that simple methods can go a long way. Using a profile based representation with standard term weighting strategies from information retrieval, involving well known ranking methods, making use of standardized vocabularies; these in combination have allowed us to build a text mining system that has been used successfully to replicate the many discoveries made by Swanson and Smalheiser and with less manual input involved in the process. As expected text mining is now beginning to be applied in the context of the Web. However the excellent potential for text mining in this domain has barely begun to unfold. Continuing with the emphasis on discovering novel and interesting ideas from text collections is one that is likely to yield excellent returns.

6 ACKNOWLEDGEMENTS

The author acknowledges National Science Foundation grant no. IIS-0312356 that partly funded this research.

REFERENCES

1. Agrawal, R. and Srikant, R. (1994). Fast algorithms for mining association rules. **In**: *Proceedings of VLDB, International Conference on Very Large Data Bases*, p. 487-499.

2. Andrade, A. and Valencia, A. (1998). Automatic extraction of keywords from scientific text: application to the knowledge domain of protein families. *Bioinformatics*. Vol. 14(7); p. 600-607.

3. Back, B. *et. al.* (2001). Combining Numerical Data and Text Information from Annual Reports using Self-Organizing Maps. *International Journal of Accounting Information Systems*. Vol. 2; p. 249-269.

4. Blagosklonny, M. V. and Pardee, A. B. (2002). Unearthing the gems. *Nature*. Vol. 416; p. 373.

5. Chaussabel, D. and Sher, A. (2002). Mining microarray expression data by literature profiling. *Genome Biology*. Vol. 3(10); research0055.1-0055.16.

6. DiGiacomo, R.A.; Kremer J.M. and Shah, D.M. (1989). Fish oil dietary supplementation in patients with Raynaud's phenomenon: A double-blind, controlled, prospective study. *American Journal of Medicine*. Vol. 8; p. 158-164.

7. Fayyad, U.M. and Uthurusamy, R. (1996). Data mining and knowledge discovery in databases (Introduction to the special section). *Communications of the ACM*. Vol. 39(11); p. 24-26.

8. Feldman, R. *et. al.* (1997). Maximal association rules: A new tool for mining for keyword co-occurrences in document collections. **In**: *Proceedings of KDD, International Conference in Knowledge Discovery and Data Mining*, Newport Beach, CA., August 14-17, 1997, p. 167-170.

9. Kloptchenko, A. *et. al.* (2002). Combining Data and Text Mining Techniques for Analyzing Financial Reports. *Eighth Americas Conference on Information Systems*.

10. Lindsay, R.K and Gordon, M.D. (1999). Literature-based discovery by lexical statistics. *JASIS*. Vol. 50(7); p. 574-587.

11. Masys, D.R. *et. al.*. (2001). Use of keyword hierarchies to interpret gene expression patterns. *Bioinformatics*. Vol. 17(4); p. 319-326.

12. Shatkay, H. *et. al.* (2000). Genes, Themes and Microarrays. Using information retrieval for large-scale gene analysis. **In**: *Proceedings of Intelligent Systems for Molecular Biology*, La Jolla, California, p. 317-328.

13. Smalheiser, N.R. and Swanson, D.R. (1996a). Indomethacin and Alzheimer's disease. *Neurology*. p. 46:583.

14. —, and —. (1996b). Linking estrogen to Alzheimer's disease: An Informatics approach. *Neurology*. Vol. 47; p. 809-810.

15. Srinivasan, P. (2004a). Text Mining: Generating Hypotheses from MEDLINE. *Journal of the American Society for Information Science and Technology*. Vol. 55(5); March 2004; p. 396-413.

16. —. and Libbus, B. (2004). Mining MEDLINE for Implicit Links between Dietary Substances and Diseases. To appear in *Bioinformatics* (ISMB Supplement).

17. . and Wedemeyer, M. (2003). Mining Concept Profiles with the Vector Model or Where on Earth are Diseases being Studied? **In**: *Proceedings of Text Mining Workshop*. Third SIAM International Conference on Data Mining. San Francisco, CA.

18. Swanson, D.R. (1986). Fish oil, Raynaud's syndrome, and undiscovered public knowledge. *Perspectives in Biology and Medicine*. Vol. 30; p. 7-18.

19. . (1988). Migraine and Magnesium: Eleven neglected connections. *Perspectives in Biology and Medicine*. Vol. 31; p. 526-557.

20. ; Smalheiser, N.R. and Bookstein, A. (2001). Information discovery from complementary literatures: categorizing viruses as potential weapons. Journal of the American Society for Information Science. Vol. 52(10); p. 797-812.

21. Weeber, M. *et. al.* (2003). Generating hypotheses by discovering implicit associations in the literature: A case report for new potential therapeutic uses for Thalidomide. *Journal of the American Medical Informatics Association*. Vol. 10(3); p. 252-259.

POSTSCRIPT

I have long been interested in the foundational classification and knowledge organization research of Dr. S. R. Ranganathan, Prof. Neelameghan (AN), Dr. Gopinath and others. The analytico-synthetic approach was truly ahead of the times. AN's contributions are prolific both in extending as well as demonstrating the feasibility of these. I first met AN at the 2nd ISKO Conference in Chennai, India, in 1992. Subsequently he invited me to be on the Advisory Board of the periodical *Information Studies*. Recently I learnt of another dimension in AN's profile, an interest in medical information, medical bibliometry, and medical historiography with published papers as early as 1954. Five decades later he continues to flourish in this direction. A recent paper with Dr. Ravichandra Rao, presents an analysis of the books, tracts, etc. on communicable diseases by members of the (former) Indian Medical Service (IMS) (1615-1930) including correlations with the incidence of such diseases in India. I may also refer here to a paper on text mining, knowledge products and discovery by Haravu and Neelameghan (2003), and another on information organization and knowledge discovery by Neelameghan and Hemalatha Iyer (2003). It pleases me to observe that I can connect my research interests to AN's work. My paper in this volume shows strong connections with his research on communicable diseases. The knowledge organization, and information retrieval community to which I belong is forever indebted to the research trails that AN and others have carved ahead of us.

DETERMINING AUTHORSHIP OF WEB PAGES

Timothy C. Craven

Assignability of authors to Web pages using either normal browsing procedures or browsing assisted by simple automatic extraction was investigated. Candidate strings for 1000 pages were extracted automatically from title elements, meta-tags, and address-like and copyright-like passages; 539 of the pages produced at least one candidate: 310 candidates from titles, 66 from meta-tags, 91 from address-like passages, and 259 from copyright-like passages. An assistant attempted to identify personal authors for 943 pages by examining the pages themselves and related pages; this added 90 pages with authors to the pages from which no candidate strings were extracted. Specific problems are noted and some refinements to the extraction methods are suggested.

1 INTRODUCTION

One way or the other, titles can be identified for the great majority of Web pages. Around 88%-96% of pages have been found to contain a *title* element (Craven, 2003). Apparent titles (titles as they would appear to be from viewing the beginning of the page in the browser, often coded as *h1* elements) are almost as common as tagged titles; and a recent study of 16 Web bibliographies (Craven, 2002), found that the latter were almost always preferred in citations.

Other constituents of conventional bibliographic description, however, may be considerably harder to determine. For example, the date is often not indicated on a page, or an indicated date does not correspond to the actual date of the contents; examining the HTTP header may or may not yield a date for the file, depending on the configuration of the server.

Authorship or responsibility is also often unclear. Even when authorship may be deduced, the context in which an author is named is quite unpredictable. A meta tag may be employed for this purpose, but this technique is not widely known, and common experience suggests that it is rarely applied. Authorship information is sometimes included in the *title* element. Sometimes, the responsible party may be inferred from a mailing address. What is most commonly recommended is for a phrase indicating responsibility to be included in the footer of the page, along with a date and contact information. Beginners are advised to look at the top or bottom of the page for author information (Savage, 2003). If the author is named nowhere on a page, it may be possible to deduce an answer by examining related pages on the same site; for example, by following a "Home" or "About us" link.

If the advice of Estivill and Urbano (1997) is followed, one should look first for authorship information, as for other bibliographic information, at the main rendering of the page and only if nothing is found there proceed to other sources, such as the *title* element, meta tags, or other pages.

Land (1998) suggests allowing nicknames and e-mail addresses as Web page authors, but only when other sources of information, such as following links, have been exhausted.

The present study is concerned with quantifying, in a preliminary way, the extent to which pages can be assigned possible authors using either normal browsing procedures or browsing assisted by simple automatic extraction of likely candidates.

2 METHODOLOGY

An existing page capture and analysis tool used in earlier research was modified to extract four different types of candidate strings that might identify a page's author or authors.

The first kind of string was extracted from the page's title element. The full title was analyzed for cue sequences suggesting an authorship statement. These included prefixes ("school of ", "society of ") and suffixes ("'s", " located in ", " welcome", and others), which were stripped off; beginnings ("city of ", "institute for ", "village of ", "association for "), which were retained while stripping everything that preceded, and middles (" school of ", "society of "), which served only to mark the sequence as author-like. The remaining author-like sequences were then output as the first kind of candidate string.

The second kind of string was extracted from meta tags; specifically, meta tags with name equal to "author", "owner", or "copyright". The values of the content of these tags were reduced by removing multiple spaces and punctuation and any of a number of common phrases and symbols associated with copyright statements ("copyrighted by", "copyright", "&#169", "©", and so on).

The third kind of string was derived by looking for text sequences that looked like mailing addresses. These sequences were identified by looking for address cues (" box ", " p.o. ", " street ", etc.) in conjunction with numerals; the immediately preceding text was then extracted, stripped of multiple spaces, punctuation, and copyright phrasing, and made into the candidate string.

The fourth kind of string was a product of searching for copyright-like statements elsewhere in the text of the body of the page. A passage was identified as copyright-like if it contained a strong copyright cue (the copyright symbol) or if it contained a weak copyright cue ("copyright", "(c)", or "[c]") combined with a number in the range 1900-2100. Text following such a cue was stripped and made into the candidate string.

The program was then run on 1000 random URLs from Yahoo!'s random page service, with the URL and candidate strings being logged for each.

A separate file of just the 1000 URLs was produced and a research assistant was assigned the following task: using a standard browser, to visit each URL in turn; to try to determine the author of the page; to place the answer next to the URL in the file ("0" if the page could not be accessed, "x" if the author could not be identified"); and to add an asterisk if it was necessary to go to another page or pages to determine the author.

3 RESULTS

Title-based candidate strings were the kind most commonly produced, with a total of 310 or 31.0% of the pages. Most commonly, they appeared to be properly formatted corporate names, such as "Madison Area Bicycle Club" or "Dayspring Homes Inc". The name might be abbreviated through use of an acronym, as in

"NY Renegades" for "New York Renegades". Names might be too short for unique identification, such as "BAHAI" for the site of the Bahá'í Community of Irving, Texas or "FIC" for that of Financial Institutions Consulting, Inc. One case was observed of both the acronym and the full form being included: "SAAA Scottish American Athletic Association". Some names looked like parts of URLs, but might in fact be actual corporate names; for example, "pharmacy.ca Canada" or "www.carpethouseinc.com". There were cases of extra material on the end that was not part of the name, as in "www.asecondbyte.com Coming soon" or "Kelly Menswear Ireland Experts in Made to Measure Men". Geographical location was appended to the name proper in "Toad Hollow Vineyards Sonoma County California". Sometimes, descriptive matter was included before the actual name, as in "Mardi Gras Kingcakes from the King of King Cakes Gambino" or "Security Risk Management and Vulnerability Assessment Software from RiskWatch Inc". Examples were also noted where cue prefixes and suffixes produced inappropriate results: in "good grooming shaving & styling products", only descriptive matter was extracted rather than the corporate name "ChiselChin"; the suffix "home" caused "Vacation" to be extracted from "Vacation home rental in Orlando Florida, condo rental", where the actual corporate name is "Orlando Vacation Homes"; in "Chicago", the use of "'s" as a suffix cue produced a bizarre result from the page title "Chicago's premier dance and wedding band for a decade - The Stay Tuned Orchestra"; similar, though less puzzling, were such strings as "Henley Women" for "Henley Women's Regatta" and "Hall" for "Hall's Carpet". Reasons for some anomalous extractions could not be determined because of changes to the pages in the interval between the original program run and subsequent analysis.

The second longest string extracted was "city of wind catchers IranYazd Touring&Tourism Organization.Yazd with ancient culturehistorical and religious places is the city of wind catchers", which in fact is the whole title, just short enough to fit into a typical caption bar. The longest was:

> *Harrison Cove Lodge Barkley Sound BC Fishing* Westcoast *Fishing Wilderness Hiking Caving Sea Kayaking Nature Cruises Canadian West Coast Lodges Canadian Nature Cruises Canadian Sea Kayaking*

> *Canadian HeliHiking BC Sea Kayaking BC Nature Cruises BC Fishing BC Fishing Lodges Vancouver Island Fishing Resorts BC Rain Forests A yearround luxury wilderness resort and home base for Soft Adventure.*

This is almost all the title, missing only an inexplicable final "s".

Candidate strings from meta-tags were extracted from only 66 pages (6.6%). Again, these were mostly corporate names, though there were five personal names by themselves (for example, "Mark Hudson", "Tony Wilson"), one with a title added ("Rep Sanford Bishop"), and two in combination with a corporate name ("Lisa Verkley Goldwing Communications", "NETWORKING NEWSPAPER C.SHEAHAN"). Three corporate names took the form of domain names ("officerspcatamesideglossop.org.uk", "Beachhotelsharjah.Com", "ooraingallery. co.uk"). One name appeared to be a code name ("wms owner" for a page mounted by Abilene Christian University). In a couple of cases, unanticipated copyright phrasing was not stripped ("Code Design and graphics are AmeriCal Floral", "De Africaserver is een initiatief van Maarten Rens Fons Geerlings Rene de Ree en Marco Legemaate en is een geregistreerde handelsnaam van Maarten Rens Produkties Maarten Rens Produkties"). In one instance, some date information was left unstripped ("Lighthouse Colorprint 01 May").

Candidate strings from passages that looked like mailing addresses were slightly more common, with a total of 91 (9.1%). Well-formed corporate names were often extracted (for example, "Jegge Team", "Whiteworks Christening Gowns"), including three in the form of domain names ("vailvalleylodging.com", "guysharpe.com", "BenGlassLaw.com"). One personal name with title was found ("Steve Nielsen President"). A title by itself also occurred ("Executive Director"). Extraneous material was included in six (for example, "Carriage House.The Apple Inn where memories begin"). Some of the names extracted may not have been of page authors, but of places of business or subjects of the page contents; for example, "COSTA VERDE PLAZA" was extracted from the page of Bissell Architects, and "chancery" was extracted from the CIA page on the Seychelles. Two instances were noted of extraction of a suite number (as in "Suite 209"), one of a generic division designation ("Corporate Office"), one of a specific division designation with part of the corporate name ("Inc Kona Facilities"), two of "Mailing Address", one of "Address", one of "contact us at", one of "MEETING PLACE", one of "Founded 1893", one of "Established in", and one of "A PROFESSIONAL ARCHITECTURAL CORPORATION". Treating too many different special characters as breaks resulted in eleven truncated extractions (for example, "Breakfast" from "Captain Briggs House Bed and Breakfast"). In ten instances, part of one address was extracted because another street or post office box number followed immediately; part of a URL was extracted once for the same reason, as were parts of three telephone numbers, one word out of hours of business, and the phrase "Site Map". One extraction was from an address-like passage that was not actually an address ("You can also take a look at our new office on Hwy 98"). Again, some anomalies could not be explained because the pages had changed.

Candidate strings from copyright-like passages, at 259 (25.9%), were almost as common as those from titles. Eight were in the form of domain names (including "uPUBLISH.com" and "Planetbr.com"). Rather generic was "Cabinet". Again, there were a relatively few personal names (for example, "Ann Wong Randi Pritchard Melissa Taylor"). Extraneous trailing material was included in 39 candidate strings (for instance, "Eagle Painting Last modified July 26", "Ray and Pat Jegge No reproduction of any kind of text or", and "Theta Nu Xi Multicultural Sorority Inc Website created by"); not included in this total were a couple of instances of appended character entity references, such as " ". Leading extraneous material was noted in six (including "03 DEXTER FAMILY PRACTICE" and "s and ER8858 Pte Ltd"). Both leading and trailing extraneous material was found in three (including "property of Rebellion   All the arrows and other graphics" and "&copy Room 413 Pty Ltd A.C.N 081373640"); in a further related instance, the name was enclosed in quotation marks ("" Seaside Motel & Resort ""). Only extraneous material was seen in "Powered by Firework", "Please read our" (where the author name preceded the copyright symbol), "All photographs herein are the property of the photographer", "MMIII News Sources" (the only observed instance of a date in Roman numerals), "Site design by" (where a link containing the author name follows), "Please email me at", "Privacy Statement", and "Web and Graphic design". One candidate string repeated the information ("Town of North Elba Town of North Elba"). Inclusion of a link on the second author's name caused truncation in the case of "Henley Women's Regatta &". On four pages, use of Big5 encoding caused the Roman alphabet name of the author to be garbled. One instance was noted where a passage was incorrectly identified as copyright-like because it contained a year and a weak copyright cue ("Founded in 1981, the Scottish American Athletic Association (SAAA) is an independent educational, non-secular, non-profit 501 (c) (3) corporation").

In only 12 instances did the candidate string from the title match the candidate string from the copyright-like passage exactly: "Teck Chai Contractor", "Applied Air Systems Inc", "Connector Technology Inc", "OBrien Corporation", "Dance Classics Inc", "Lakeview Performance Marine & Recreation Ltd", "Safe Security Inc", "Advanced Technology Solutions Inc", "Parkside Magnetic Resonance Center", "Victoria University", "Bog Trotters Mountain Bike Club", and "Roscoe & Swanson Accountancy Corporation". The match rate is somewhat higher for the title string as the beginning of the copyright string (31) and for the copyright string as the beginning of the title string (20).

Of the 1000 pages, 461 (46.1%) had no automatically extracted candidate strings of any kind.

The assistant attempted 943 of the URLs. Of these, 26, or 2.8%, were unavailable; 727, or 77.1%, were available but the author could not be determined (the assistant was looking only for personal authors). This left 190, or 20.2% of the URLs attempted, for which authors could be determined; for 148 of these, or 15.7% of URLs attempted, the authors were apparent from the pages themselves; for 42, or 4.5%, external sources of information were required. Two of the author names identified by the assistant were exactly the same as names extracted automatically from titles; four more were extracted from titles, but with some extraneous matter; there were also several partial matches, such as a given name "Debbie" extracted from the title where the assistant recognized the fuller name

"Debbie A. Carriere". Two of the assistant's author names were identical with candidate strings extracted from meta-tags, apart from capitalization, punctuation, and diacritics; one other was extracted from meta-tags, but with other material; and there were other partial matches. Three of the assistant's names were found in candidate strings from address-like passages; there was also one partial match. Three assistant names exactly matched candidate strings from copyright-like passages, capitalization aside; six others were contained within candidate strings from copyright-like passages; and there were six further partial matches.

The assistant missed no personal author names that were presented in title-based candidate strings or in copyright-like passages (some other personal names were found in titles, but as parts of corporate names). The same generally held true for candidate strings from meta-tags; a exceptions were pages with the author meta-tagged as "Lisa Verkley", with the copyright holder tagged as "NETWORKING NEWSPAPER C.SHEAHAN", and with both copyright and author tagged as "Mark Prado"; there was one long copyright statement that gave four personal names, but the actual copyright holder was apparently a corporate entity. Since mailing addresses were not necessarily those of page authors, some candidate strings based on address-like passages did name persons who were not identified as authors by the assistant.

The assistant's personal name assignments provided authors for 90 out of 435 pages from which no candidate strings had been extracted automatically, or 20.7%.

4 DISCUSSION

A combination of the four different extraction methods would likely produce useful candidate strings for about half of a population of Web pages similar to that produced by the Yahoo! random page service. Combination of automatic extraction with human page scanning, including scanning of related pages where necessary, would raise the total appreciably. From this study, it might appear that the success rate might rise only to around 60%, but it must be remembered that the assistant was looking only for personal author names, while corporate names seem in fact to be more common. Once corporate authors are included, a much higher combined success rate is to be anticipated.

The automatic methods could clearly be refined somewhat more. The use of "'s" as a suffix cue seems especially problematic. Some more unusual styles of dates might be added for stripping, as might further stock phrases like "Last modified". In addition to the lists of cue beginnings and middles, a list of cue endings, such as "Inc" and "Ltd" might also be invoked.

The method of using address-like passages is probably the one with the least overall utility. Even so, it might be improved somewhat by refining it to avoid extraction of common phrases such as "Mailing address" which are obviously not names, as well as strings that look like parts of telephone numbers or alternate addresses.

Some automatic reconciliation procedures might be designed for cases in which more than one automatic method produces results; for example, where one form is apparently an acronym of another the longer form might be preferred.

The possibility of automatic extraction from related pages might also be explored. Nevertheless, the correctness of names extracted from other pages as authors of the original page is likely to be less assured. It may therefore be wiser to leave pages that do not themselves identify their authors as anonymous. On the other hand, the fact that nearly a quarter of the assistant's assignments of personal author names were achieved by examining related pages suggests that this possibility should not be summarily dismissed.

None of the automatic methods performed particularly well at extracting personal authors' names, as compared with the assistant's manual identification. Where author names are meta-tagged, however, automatic extraction might be a useful assistance for someone identifying authors manually, since the meta-tagged information is awkward to get at and easily missed.

5 ACKNOWLEDGMENTS

Research reported in this article was supported in part by the University of Western Ontario Office of Research Services with funds provided by the Natural Sciences and Engineering Research Council of Canada.

The extensive assistance of research assistant Craig Huffman in data gathering is also acknowledged.

REFERENCES

1. Craven, T.C. (2002). What is the title of a Web page? A study of Webography practice. *Information research.* Vol. 7(3). http://InformationR.net/ır/7-3/ paper130.html.

2. . (2003). HTML tags as extraction cues for Web page description construction. *Informing Science Journal.* Vol. 6; p. 1-12. (http://informingscience.org/Articles/Vol6/v6p001-012.pdf).

3. Estivill, A. and Urbano, B. (1997). *Cómo citar recursos electrónicos.* http://www.ub.es/biblio/citae-e.htm.

4. Land, T. (1998). *Web Extension to American Psychological Association Style (WEAPAS)* (Rev. 1.6). http://www.beadsland.com/weapas/; http:// www. beadsland.com/weapas/

5. Savage, A. (2003). *TekMom's Citation Page.* http://www.tekmom.com/cite/

KNOWLEDGE MANAGEMENT IN SPECIALIZED AREAS

INFORMATION SYSTEM FOR KNOWLEDGE MANAGEMENT IN THE SPECIALIZED DIVISION OF A HOSPITAL

M.C. Vasudevan
Murali Mohan
Amit Kapoor

Information systems are essential support for knowledge management in all types of enterprises. This paper describes the evolution and development of a specialized hospital information system. The system is designed to integrate for access and retrieval from databases of patients' case records, and related images - CATSCAN, MRI, X-Ray – and to enable online access to full text of relevant papers on the Internet/WWW. The generation of information products and services from the system is briefly described.

1 VHS AND PROF. NEELAMEGHAN

We are pleased to contribute this paper describing an evolving information system in the design and development of which Prof. Neelameghan has been closely associated. This association with the VHS Hospital, Chennai and more particularly its Dr. A. L. N. Neurological Centre, began in the late 1980s, although the late Dr. B. Ramamurthy, the former Head of the Centre, knew the professor from his years with the Madras Medical College and Madras General Hospital in the early 1950s.

A demo/lecture presentation about Unesco's CDS-ISIS software version 1.0 was organized for a few invited doctors at the TB Hospital in Chetpet, Chennai. Dr. Ramamurthy and other senior doctors attended the demo on how an integrated information system consisting of databases of case records of patients, of syndromes, bibliographical references, profiles of institutions, experts and projects can be built-up, indexed and relevant information from all of the databases can be retrieved simultaneously. Dr. Ramamurthy was impressed and so were the other participating doctors. Subsequently, workshops organized by the University of Madras, Department of Library and Information Science in collaboration with the Computer Science Department were attended by, among others, interested doctors from a couple of hospitals in Chennai.

In the meantime, VHS Neurological Centre acquired a couple of PCs (XT), and had Prof. Neelameghan to assist in the installation of CDS-ISIS, design the databases, and provide hands-on training to staff members of the Department (now Centre). From that time on, over the decade we had the professor assist us from time to time for debugging, installing new versions of the CDS-ISIS and for advice. The evolving system described in this paper is a result of this collaborative endeavour.

2 KNOWLEDGE MANAGEMENT AND ENTERPRISE MANAGEMENT

It is now well recognized that effective and efficient knowledge management (KM) is an integral component contributing to the successful management of an enterprise.

Knowledge is embodied in natural objects, in man-made artifacts, various types of documents (in conventional and in digital forms), discourses, video conference products, notes, letters, case histories, discussions, phone conversations, websites, virtual group exchanges, databases, and most importantly in people (tacit knowledge) within and outside the enterprise. These knowledge resources, individually and collectively, constitute the *Enterprise Knowledge Base.*

KM in an enterprise generally involves:

- Identifying, selecting and cataloguing / mapping all information resources pertinent to the enterprise's needs (Knowledge Yellow Pages of the enterprise);
- Identifying information flow patterns among individuals and among groups (units, departments) – finding out who asks what questions; what information is obtained from which sources, what types of information is not easily available and/or accessible; and
- Designing and developing user-friendly systems for access of and retrieval from, the enterprise's knowledge base, particularly interlinking and integrating knowledge resources (internal and external) to meet current and anticipated needs of the different categories of users and those associated with them externally vis-à-vis the enterprise's activities (Hsinchun Chen, 2001; Haravu, 2002).

3 KNOWLEDGE-BASED PRODUCTS: GENERAL FEATURES

Even in the emerging digital societies the printed document or an electronic version of it influences the way people perceive information. However, the convergence of media technologies facilitates the representation, storage, presentation and delivery of text, audio and video files, enabling the development of truly knowledge-based products and services. Such a product is expected to have at least some of the following features: It should

- Have captured the *tacit knowledge* of experts in a domain of study or practice;
- Promote and be the result of, *collaboration* between domain / subject experts, information specialists and users;
- Be *rich in content* and have a wide reach within the potential user communities,
- Enable *quick and easy access* to required data and information;
- Be possible for users of the product to *learn new skills* or improve skills, gain insights and *assist knowledge discovery* in the target domain;
- Facilitate flow and access to information and inter-personal dialogue, *across cultures and linguistic boundaries*, where necessary and possible; and
- Continuously *evolve* with new inputs from the interactions with the users, and developments in information and communication technologies.

Research on better methods of KM and search for knowledge discovery tools are mutually synergizing. The factors influencing KM may be grouped as follows:

- *Collaborative Dimension,* drawing upon the tacit knowledge of domain specialists and experts by obtaining their recommendations and advice in the design of the system, particularly in content development and organization to meet the needs of users
- *Symbolic and Semantic Dimension*, covering resource descriptions and knowledge organization, and communication. Resource descriptions and

indexing entail the use of cataloguing rules, metadata, taxonomies, subject classification, clustering and categorization schemes, knowledge mapping, indexing techniques, table of contents, subject headings, and authority files control variant forms of key information, such as, names of geographic areas, personal and corporate entities, well structured vocabularies, including thesauri, ontologies, and coding schemes; and less traditional tools like semantic networks, self-organizing maps, and word nets. Symbolism and semiotics may be influenced by culture, traditions, conventions, and experiences, mostly tacit knowledge influencing interpretation of messages.

- Environmental/Contextual Dimension, for instance, a charitable organization Essentially service-oriented vis-à-vis a profit driven enterprise; or a rural environment vis-à-vis an urban, metropolitan and cosmopolitan environment.
- Organizational/Structural Dimension, that is, the hierarchy, control and decision centres; information flow pattern, top-down, bottom-upward, spiral; intermediary intervention, impact of information and communication technologies (ICTs), policies and directives. The structure and/or policies may facilitate or be an impediment to accessing knowledge and its flow, and
- Technology Dimension covers such aspects as the appropriateness, accessibility to and affordability of, the technology to be used.

In a particular context or enterprise environment, for example, hospital environment, some of the above factors may be more predominant than others.

4 ORIGINAL SOURCES AND DIGITIZATION

Designing appropriate databases and imputing data/information – text, image, sound or a combination of these – is a preliminary step. This is to be based on an understanding of the needs of the potential users of the system. The creation of the electronic records or digitization involves the conversion of source records (text, image, voice), recorded on different media – print on paper, tape, phono-records, etc - to computer-readable form and format, necessary for storing the records and enable fast, easy access and retrieval of the desired information/ records to meet the needs of users. Digitization is, obviously, an integral part of *content development* in the design and development of databases in information systems. The original received in machine-readable form may be retained in the form and format as received/accessed, but the software used for information retrieval should be able to call or provide links to them as and when necessary or be capable of searching and retrieving information from them directly.

The records in machine-readable form can be stored in the computer's hard disc, and on CD, magnetic tape, etc., all of which can be used by the computer. The objective may be the preservation of the original records which otherwise may suffer from wear and tear of frequent use, or from other environmental factors, and at the same time the information content may be more easily retrieved. The retrieved information / records can be used for a variety of purposes. They may be disseminated to users directly or online via networks (e.g. intranets and extranets - the Internet/WWW) in convenient forms and formats. This applies to current records as well and even if the objective is not long-term preservation. The CDs and diskettes can be used almost anywhere, for instance, on desktop PC and laptop. The machine-readable form (which may be in compressed format) enables significant saving in storage space. Multiple copies of the records can be made as backup. What kinds of information products and services are expected to be generated from the database(s) created is another important factor.

For the system described in this paper the objective is both preservation of the original case records of patients and related images and also to provide access to their information content for a variety of current uses.

5 THE SYSTEM

5.1 Components

The knowledge base and products, the development of the contents of which is briefly discussed in this paper, are those of a special division of a hospital (referred to here as VHS/NS. The core competence of VHS/NS is *neuro-surgery* especially of *tumours of the brain.* The total system is designed to eventually integrate several components:

- Bibliographic databases (library catalogue, index to papers, etc.);
- Profiles of experts and institutions,
- Complete case records of patients,
- CATSCAN, MRI, and other images,
- Teaching / learning CDs, and
- Links to web resources.

These components have evolved over a decade in parallel with the hardware and software used. This paper discusses the digitization involved in creating the database of case records of patients, database of CATSCAN and other images, and indexing and interlinking these components among themselves and with web resources. *The doctors (users) consider the patients' case records and associated images as core information support components.*

5.2 Types of Query and Use

The content of the databases, organization of records in each of the databases, files and folders, the indexing and interlinking among them are designed to facilitate the system's response to the queries of doctors of VHS/NS. Some of the sample queries which the system can respond to are mentioned here:

- Find case records and related image files of:
  a. Female patients, of age group 20-30 years, diagnosed for meningioma
  b. Male patients, involved in particular occupation, resident of a particular location, diagnosed for Neuroblastoma
  c. Patients diagnosed for Arachnoid's Cyst, subjected to chemotherapy and surgery, and died within a year
  d. Patients with meningioma, subjected to a particular surgical procedure and those who received only chemotherapy

- Is a particular patient a new admission/second, third... readmission?
- Various reports providing quantitative data
- Video-clips and other images on CD for teaching/learning

Among other things, the image files can be used for projection (in teaching, learning, and discussion sessions). The link to web documents facilitates access to a wider range of related information sources.

6 PATIENTS' CASE RECORDS DATABASES

6.1 Input Forms and Formats

The databases of case records of patients had been developed much earlier to the idea of linking image files to the corresponding records of patients was thought of. The patients' records database (TMR1), demo database VHSM) was designed and developed using Unesco's CDS-ISIS software. The software has powerful indexing and fast retrieval capabilities (*See* section 4.2). And the databases are portable on to the successive versions of the software and also the Windows version (WINISIS). Therefore, the products output by the digitization process, (the form and formats) should be compatible with and usable by WINISIS, that is convertible to WINISIS database record structure (ISO 2709) and so also the image file formats (BMP, GIF, JPG), formats of voice recordings should be acceptable to WINISIS. The generation of information products and services depends in a large measure on these factors and also on the environment – digital library and/or conventional library – within which the information products and services are to be generated, disseminated, and used.

There are separate databases for tumours of the brain, pituitary, spine, and vascular system and for trauma cases.

Partly based on the existing printed case record forms, the doctors enumerated some 180 attributes/parameters for the brain tumour database (TMR1). (*See* Annex 1 on which data/information and comments are recorded. The 180+ parameters/fields of TMR1 may be broadly grouped as covering:

a) History of the patient
b) Examinations and findings
c) Investigations
d) The course in the hospital and the treatment given.

Each attribute constitutes a field in the database record; one record for each patient, with links to related images and full texts of papers. In brief the data input worksheet (fields) is a near mirror image of the case record form. In many instances information on: Whether a surgical procedure was followed or not?; whether certain treatment was given or not? (i.e. Yes or No) is indicated and if 'yes' then the details are provided. Negative results are also to be recorded; so also the presence or absence of a feature of the tumour.

The data entry operator enters the basic details of the case sheet into the appropriate fields of the database TMR1. The Surgical Operation notes for current cases are directly typed into the corresponding fields of the database.

In the case of backlogs, the operation notes are directly scanned using a HP Scanner, in '*editable text*' format, and not an image of scanned text to support its search and retrieval. After scanning, the Operation notes are copied and pasted into the respective fields of the corresponding WINISIS database (TMR1) record.

To facilitate easy entry of the backlog records, which have fields that do not correspond to the TMR1 database fields, we have added new fields for the Discharge Summary in the Field Definition Table and the corresponding Worksheet. These summaries are scanned, corrected and pasted or are directly typed into their respective fields of the database. The Discharge Summary is directly typed into the corresponding fields of the database at the time the patient is discharged. For experienced persons, scanning and pasting proves to be a much faster procedure than keying-in the data. However, the latter is less expensive and easier for some of the data entry personnel.

Some patients get readmitted to the hospital; some of them may have the same problem they had suffered/were treated for earlier, while others may have new problems. In either case a new case record is created and the above steps are followed. The number of such readmissions is indicated in the original case record, which can be searched.

The content of almost all the fields is indexed. Certain amount of vocabulary control is exercised. International Disease Index, MESH (NLM/Medical Subject Headings) and similar standardized vocabulary lists have been helpful.

7 IMAGE FILES

All radiological images, clinical pictures and other documents including EEG recording, audiogram etc., are either photographed using digital camera or are scanned and output in JPEG format. Relevant and necessary images from the other Clinics/Hospitals brought by patients are also digitized and are stored in a chronological sequence. These photographs are then edited using Adobe Photoshop version 7 and reduced to smaller customized files, which are linked to the relevant records of the related WINISIS databases. Storing all these images data on a single hard disk is neither appropriate nor necessary. Therefore, when the case records database size reaches about 600 MB, they are written on to a CD containing the WINISIS database files and all the related scanned images and documents in a separate folder.

The sample studied consists of over 1250 case records (including readmissions) of some 150 patients. The image files on CD hold over 2000 images obtained as mentioned above. Initially when the database of patients' case records was designed, the images were not considered, except that a file/image number was entered in the related record. There may be one or several images per patient. A single picture, in most cases, contains one image, but there are several each containing two or more images (of the same patient). For the purpose of identification some textual information also forms part of most of the images – Name of the patient, gender, age, names or initials of the doctors concerned, the source of the picture, where it was made. Additionally, in some pictures other technical data about dimensions, position, and medical/surgical features of the tumour are included. Many of the images include icons for zooming, printing, and mailing. The images have been ported on to CD in JPEG format for use in the information system.

As a direct search in the picture folders is relatively less convenient, a reference database has also been prepared. A WINISIS record for an image has fields for Tumor category, Name of the patient, Gender, Age, Date, Link specification, and Notes (name/initials of the doctors concerned, where the picture was received from/made, whether it is a video-clip, whether it may be used for teaching/ leaning etc.). An index to this data enables quick identification and retrieval of relevant record(s), and clicking on the cue connects to the related image files.

The pictures relating to a patient are used together with the detailed case record. Images may be used, for instance, in comparative studies, of the type of brain tumor. Hence the VHS/NS case records are linked by the tumour category (e.g. Meningioma). They may be linked by the code number assigned to each patient and entered in the related files and records.

7.1 Organization of Images on CD

As images can also be used independently of the case records, the preferred arrangement of image files is as follows: At the top level a folder for each type of tumour (arachnoid cyst, chordoma, craniopharyngioma, ependymoma, glioma, hemangioblastoma, meningioma, etc.) is created; within each folder the images are organized alphabetically by patient's name. Thus, when a tumour folder is retrieved independently or called from a patient's case record, the user can open the file of images for each patient for study and examination. This arrangement was preferred by the doctors (users).

8 OUTPUT PRODUCTS / SERVICES

In addition to responding to queries such as those mentioned in Section 4.2, some printouts are also generated. Printouts of the Discharge Summary and the Operation notes are required to be handed over to the patients and are also filed in the hospital files. Separate print formats have been designed for these purposes using WINISIS formatting facility and the printouts taken at the time of discharge of the patient.

9 ACCESS TO WEB RESOURCES

Case records can be linked to related Internet resources via the corresponding URL. The web resources are categorized as:

* General overview and information on brain tumors
* Comprehensive information sources
* Recent research
* e-Journals and papers
* Discussion forum
* Cancer info network
* Info sources with links to sites around the world

10 OPENING PAGE

The opening page displays the menu to link to: 1) Patients Case Records Databases; 2) Image files [on CD]; 3) Training CDs; and 4) Internet/Web Links (*See* Annex 2).

8 CONCLUDING REMARKS

The development of the system has been a joint effort on the one hand of the doctors who have the domain expertise and who are also the end users of the system, and information specialists (IS). To begin with, VHS/NS doctors and researchers, in discussion with the information specialist, decided on the several components (databases, records, etc.) of the system. The doctors/surgeons defined the type of products and services expected from the system, selected the case history records and (later) the images, and prepared much of the inputs to the system. The collaborating IS planned the database systems, selected the software - WINISIS 1.4 – (Unesco, 2002), set up the pilot testing system, obtained feedback of users, upgraded and scaled the system, and trained the junior assistants to prepare inputs, indexing, searching etc. The s*emantic dimension* involved decisions on fields to be indexed, the type of indexing technique to be employed, vocabulary control, inter-linking of the files, etc. Although each case record is uniquely identified with a particular patient, the users (doctors and surgeons) are predominantly interested in the features of the disease (tumour), comparing a case with several others having the same type of tumour. Hence the preferred arrangement of the pictures in the folders/files is by name of tumor and within each category by name of patient. This is also a reason for establishing links between case records and images by the type of tumour rather than by name of patient. Of course both in the case records and the image folders retrieval by name of the patient or other parameters is possible.

REFERENCES

1. Hsinchun Chen. (2001). *Knowledge management systems: a text mining perspective*. Tucson, Arizona, USA: knowledge Computing Corporation.
2. Haravu, L.J. (2002). Knowledge management: paradigms, challenges and opportunities. *Sarada Ranganathan Endowment Lectures, 22*, 2000. Sarada Ranganathan Endowment for Library Science, Bangalore.

ANNEXURES

Annex 1: List of fields of database TMR1 (Brain Tumours)
Annex 2: Screen prints of demo databases

***Demo Databases*:**

VHSP! Main Opening Page. Menu lines linked to corresponding databases mentioned below.

VHSM Database of Patients' Case Records. Demo contains 1220 case records. Linked to Image records database (VHSTP on CD)

VHSTP Catalogue of Image records. 105 records. Linked to:
Image folders in VHSTP on CD
Patients' case records in VHSM

VHSUR Opening Menu page to Internet/Web sites. Menu lines linked to corresponding sites through the URL

ANNEX 1

Fields and Data Elements of TMR!

Institution
Head of institution
A.L.N.C. No.:
Name
Address
Brought by
Referred From/By
Receiving Person
Contact (s)
Age r range
Sex:
Admission*: adse
Readmission1* adse
Readmission2* adse
Readmission3 >* adse
Disease Index No.:
Personal history
Family history
Final Diagnosis:
Symptoms Onset:
Symptoms Progression:
Complaints:
Consciousness:
Memory:
Glasgow Coma Scale:
Speech:
Lobar Function*
Visual Acuity*
Color Vision ub
Visual Fields: ub
Visual Acuity Right:
Visual Acuity Left:
Diplopia ub
Ptosis ub
Nystagmus:
Internuclear Ophthalmoplegia:
External Ophthalmoplegia: ub
Pupil Changes ub
Fundus:
Anosmia ub
5th Nerve:
5th Corneal ub
5th Sensory: ub
5th Motor ub
6th Nerve ub
7th Nerve: ub
7th Nerve (Upper/Lower):
8th Nerve: ub
8th Nerve (Hearing Loss):
9th Nerve:
10th Nerve:
Swallowing:
Phonation:
11th Nerve:
12th Nerve ub
Hemiplegia:
Paraplegia:
Quadriplegia:
Monoplegia:
Upper Limbs (Spinal Motor): ptwcub
Lower Limbs (Spinal Motor): ptwcub
Reflexes (Upper Limb): ub
Reflexes (Lower Limbs): ub
Personal History*
Family History*

Extensor Plantar: ub
Sensation (Upper Limbs) ub
Sensation (Lower Limbs) ub
Sensation (Trunk):
Sphincters:
Urinary Continence Tof
Rectal Continence:
Gait shao
Associated Illness:
Treatment*
Pathological Diagnosis:
Post Operative Complications*
Result:
Time Of Death:
Cause Of Death*
General Examination:
Blood Group:
ECG:
Cardiovascular System:
X-Ray Chest:
X-Ray Skull:
X-Ray Spine:
Four Vessel Angiogram:
Carotid Angiogram:
Carotid Angiogram Description:
CT Scan Head:
CT Scan Description*

CT Scan Spine:
NMR*
Pneumoencephalogram*
Myelogram:
Myelogram Description*
Previous CNS Surgery*
Operative Complications*
Post.Op. CT Scan*
Operative*
Advice*
Ventriculogram*
Post.op. Follow-up*
Recurrence:
Surgery For Recurrence:
Pathology Altered*
Operated More Than Twice:
Readmission:
Prolactin:
GH:
LH:
T3:
T4:
TSH:
FSH:
Testoterone:
Cortisol:
Remar

Attributes marked with an asterisk (*): Multiple data may be entered; or the data may be extensive and broken into convenient sentences and paragraphs.

Attribute name followed by sub-field indicators in lower case letters: The data may be divided or delimited into sub-fields. For example:

u = Unilateral. b = Bilateral p = Power. t = Tone. w = Wasting. c = Coordination

ANNEX 2

Screen prints

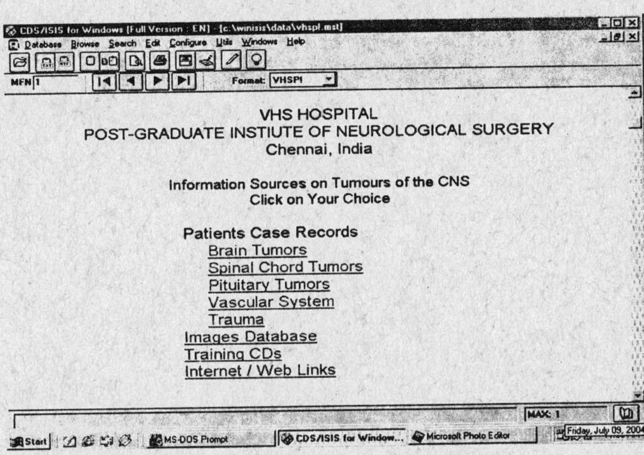

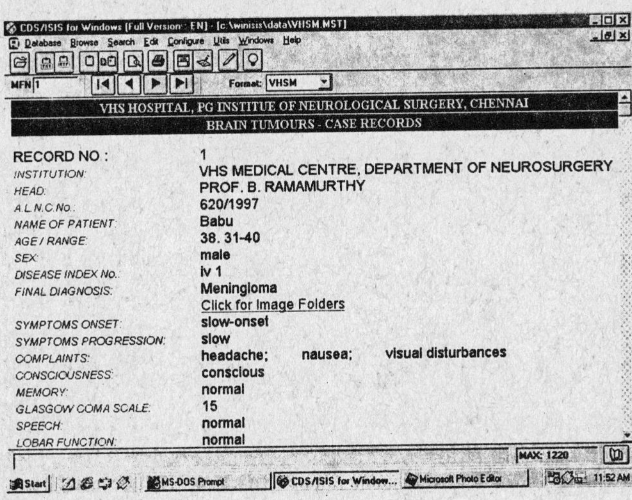

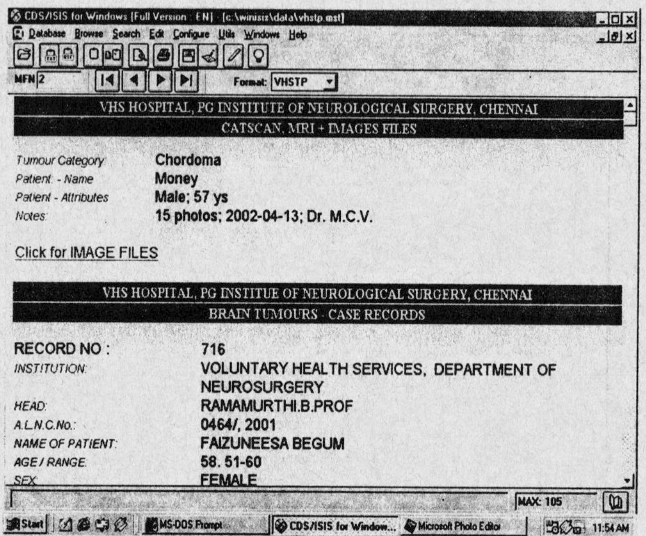
CDS/ISIS for Windows [Full Version : EN] - [c:\winisis\data\vhstp.mst]
Database Browse Search Edit Configure Utils Windows Help
MFN 2
Format: VHSTP
VHS HOSPITAL, PG INSTITUTE OF NEUROLOGICAL SURGERY, CHENNAI
CATSCAN, MRI + IMAGES FILES
Tumour Category: Chordoma
Patient - Name: Money
Patient - Attributes: Male; 57 ys
Notes: 15 photos; 2002-04-13; Dr. M.C.V.
Click for IMAGE FILES
VHS HOSPITAL, PG INSTITUE OF NEUROLOGICAL SURGERY, CHENNAI
BRAIN TUMOURS - CASE RECORDS
RECORD NO : 716
INSTITUTION: VOLUNTARY HEALTH SERVICES, DEPARTMENT OF NEUROSURGERY
HEAD: RAMAMURTHI.B.PROF
A.L.N.C.No.: 0464/, 2001
NAME OF PATIENT: FAIZUNEESA BEGUM
AGE / RANGE: 58. 51-60
SEX: FEMALE
MAX: 105
Start
MS-DOS Prompt
CDS/ISIS for Window...
Microsoft Photo Editor
11:54 AM

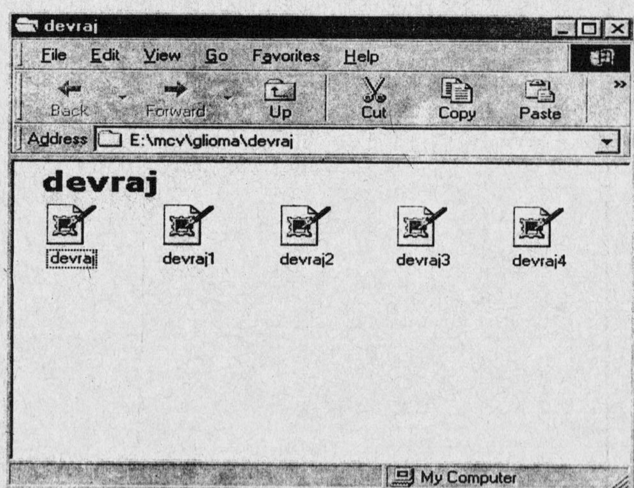
devraj
File Edit View Go Favorites Help
Back Forward Up Cut Copy Paste
Address E:\mcv\glioma\devraj
devraj
devraj
devraj1
devraj2
devraj3
devraj4
My Computer

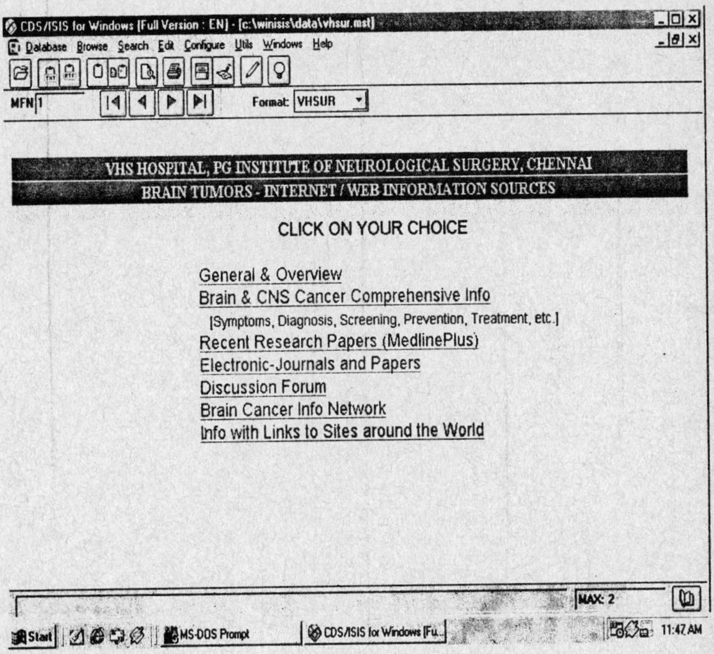
CDS/ISIS for Windows [Full Version : EN] - [c:\winisis\data\vhsur.mst]
Database Browse Search Edit Configure Utils Windows Help
MFN 1
Format: VHSUR
VHS HOSPITAL, PG INSTITUTE OF NEUROLOGICAL SURGERY, CHENNAI
BRAIN TUMORS - INTERNET / WEB INFORMATION SOURCES
CLICK ON YOUR CHOICE
General & Overview
Brain & CNS Cancer Comprehensive Info
[Symptoms, Diagnosis, Screening, Prevention, Treatment, etc.]
Recent Research Papers (MedlinePlus)
Electronic-Journals and Papers
Discussion Forum
Brain Cancer Info Network
Info with Links to Sites around the World
MAX: 2
Start
MS-DOS Prompt
CDS/ISIS for Windows [Fu...
11:47 AM

FIVE LAWS OF INFORMATION SERVICE AND ARCHITECTING KNOWLEDGE INFRASTRUCTURE FOR EDUCATION AND DEVELOPMENT

K.R. Srivathsan

The key principles and organizational aspects of information systems needed to build efficient knowledge management systems designed to assist groups engaged in knowledge intensive services for creation of wealth and value are discussed. Highlights the core principles of knowledge management that help understand the interplay between information systems and the dynamics of information and interaction that results in effective ways of knowledge based wealth creation.

1 COMPLEXITY OF EMERGING INFORMATION SHARING ENVIRONMENT

Traditionally libraries and publishing industry handled the acquisition and dissemination of generic knowledge in the form of books, journals, reports, etc. These are more in the nature of study and reference materials. With the Internet and electronic form of storing and distributing knowledge, libraries have begun offering some of the generic body of knowledge in the form of objects databases. New information suppliers such as database designers, aggregators and distributors have emerged. Journals and databases in diverse fields such as commerce, economics, agriculture, statistical data, health information and multimedia content are increasingly becoming available in electronic form. These are challenging and complex new developments in several ways for the library community for several reasons:

a) IT (Information technology) today is still evolving in both technology and management sense. Such issues as security, privacy, fair use, and intellectual property issues like copyright and ownership, virtual organizations management, etc. remain open.

b) There are emerging needs to support virtual knowledge driven enterprises where members from different organizations pool together the requisite information and competencies to offer services of value over the web to users. These call for appropriate methodologies to manage information resources generation and utilization. We may call them, as explained later, as thematic communities.

c) The user of information ultimately gains value from such services provided it is the *right information* available at the *right time, in the right place and in the right context* as and when he/she is engaged in knowledge intensive work. Hence effective value proposition goes with efficient organization of knowledge-related activities like interaction, group collaboration, messaging services, etc.

d) The Internet and IT world itself is swiftly changing over from the client – server interactions to seamless peer-to-peer interactions over web-accessed information and interaction services. Users may access information from anywhere independent of the client systems they use.

e) With ever increasing proportion of information in complex multimedia and digital form, there are immense challenges ahead concerning archiving and retrieval of the same. With sophisticated technology needed for access and playback of the information, the world is yet to intelligently grapple with preservation of human heritage over the coming decades. This calls for reinvention of computer systems and information presentation devices such that the technology may evolve to a good extent reasonably independent of modalities of knowledge creation and its utilization in society.

In the above context, we have to consider not only the information sharing aspects *per se*, but need to look at the dynamics of how this information is put to use by the users of the same. Here it will be useful to identify as to how we use information in the real world when we are engaged in knowledge driven activities. This aspect is developed in the next section.

The economist Laski stated that the cost of money is that much we forego by not using it in the best possible alternative ways. If we change the word money to information, this statement is as much valid in the context of knowledge-enabled wealth creation. Here we use the term information as that which when received by a person or a system either changes, or has the potential to change the state of the system. Hence wealth creation or development in the coming knowledge era is about how effectively the members of working groups or organizations use such opportunities created by information and create value. It is in this context that

Peter Drucker states: "Knowledge has become the key economic resource, and the dominant – and perhaps even the only source of competitive advantage". In this paper we look into some key principles and organizational aspects of information systems needed to build efficient knowledge management systems that assist groups engaged in knowledge intensive services to create wealth or value.

2 FIVE LAWS OF INFORMATION SCIENCES AND INFORMATION DYNAMICS

S.R. Ranganathan stated the classic five laws (Ranganathan, 1999) of Library Science as the guiding spirit behind architecting and managing the libraries of the 20th Century as knowledge supermarkets. The same may be rephrased as given below with somewhat different relative emphasis to guide us in architecting and managing emerging information systems of the 21st Century:

a) Information is for use

b) To every user, the information he/she seeks

c) Information of value to go to the user who may benefit from it

d) Save the time of the user

e) The information sources, the organization of the information and delivery system and beneficiaries of information are one integral organism

In much the same way Ranganathan uses his five principles to drive the classification and management of printed information and libraries, we shall attempt to arrive at frameworks and structures that will help us build future information systems. There are fundamental changes in the way information is generated and used in this networked era. Some of the conspicuous ones are:

i. In volume, information is becoming explosive. Presentation of information therefore needs to be specific to the needs of the user or the group that uses it.

ii. The dynamics of generation and usage of information has increased tremendously. The original objective of library as a knowledge aggregator and disseminator needs to be enhanced to include links between the way users or groups' workflow needs and the knowledge base they need to refer to during the course of the work. Understanding such information workflow interactions over applicable organizational behavior framework will lead to the right type of information dynamics that has to be built into the information systems.

iii. Users need protection from the information flood and glut, and need systems that help them stay focused while working in knowledge intensive activities.

iv. Unlike the traditional long-life library institutions, we may set up *ad hoc* information systems and close them on need basis. As an example, an information system for disaster management may be set up at short notice for a target focused group for a particular type of calamity, and afterwards wound up with due archival of knowledge generated and audit of activities.

A great deal of work has been done and continues to be done in Data Warehousing, Artificial Intelligence (AI) based search/access techniques and Software Agents. Google and other popular search engines are fine examples of such AI tools. They, together with Net Crawlers, Semantic Web and 'Know-bots' (Knowledge Robots) help in building smart query and attributes driven filtered view of the open global information space accessible over the web. In a limited way they provide some features for personalized systems for custom view access of the open information. These add efficiency by reducing the information glut to more manageable volumes of information that we seek and work with. However, they are mostly passive and do not address information generation and efficient utilization issues.

So we build compound information systems by adding component systems of value such as search engines, digital libraries, document and workflow management systems, e-publications and distribution, Groupware and collaboration tools, etc. Enterprise Knowledge Management Systems and Enterprise Applications Integration are good examples of such systems. However, the present approach to building such enterprise systems is mostly *ad hoc* and shaped by contingent needs of the concerned organization. In this paper, we highlight certain core principles of knowledge management that help us understand the interplay between information systems organizations on the one hand, and the need to support the dynamics of information and interaction that results in effective ways of knowledge based wealth creation.

2.1 Information Infrastructure for Virtual Knowledge Enterprises

Given the scenario of the emerging web-accessed information world, we address the kind of informatics framework of architecting and managing information systems of the future. Today in most portals, the information management and access facilities are largely dictated by local expediencies and internal workflow needs. There appears to be ever increasing need to adopt open architectures that are driven by data/metadata standards and protocols of information exchanges. A brief review and requirements of some of the efforts towards standards of information organization is given here. Firstly, let us look at the need for different types of classification and associated data structures. There are the following four broad functions in information classification.

i. *Organization of generic body of knowledge*: The Dublin Core metadata standard is currently popular to organize, manage and access digital libraries. Dublin Core is a 'scalable' metadata standard in that we may expand the metadata tree to include pointers to small units of information with subtopics. There are a few others in broad subject areas. For example, ACM recommends a classification scheme for Computer Science-related subjects.

ii. *Subject specific Knowledge Maps*: Every subject area comes with its own technical classification or taxonomies. Examples are industry specific classification of records, classifications in Botany, Zoology, etc. We need to expand such standards to include subjects like Law, documents classification in E-Governance, Economics and Statistics in different areas, etc. Each classification system has to be supported by corresponding open generic information systems made available widely for data exchanges over open standards, possible across globally distributed members from working groups in different organizations. The classification will serve best if it closely corresponds with the kind of knowledge questions the users will frequently ask in the subject area.

iii. *Workgroup specific documents generation and publishing*: Every activity today is increasingly driven by knowledge. The engine for driving this knowledge space is with workgroups that access, generate and publish information relevant to their function or business. Members of any workgroup or strategy group need tools for regulated generation of information. The document versioning tools are one such example. Publishing and Groupware software tools provide controls like versioning. They also need support for workflow processes to monitor, control and release of information publications. These are increasingly becoming available in platforms for Enterprise Applications Integration and Knowledge Management that are getting adopted in and adapted to, an increasing number of organizations.

iv. *Capturing information regarding events and related knowledge generation*: When information systems are juxtaposed and used with enterprise systems, we get new facilities that were not available hitherto. Enterprise systems are to be equipped to provide alerts to real world events and also capture logs of such events and appropriate actions taken. Alerts may be generated by pre-specified conditions or through smart agents. The organization of necessary data structures for events capturing and alerts is not that well studied in traditional information sciences, but is well understood in the area of Network Management. For example the metadata structures like Abstract Syntax Notation –1, (ASN-1) for building records of events and actions are used to form the Management Information Base in networks. They are also of value in enterprise systems like the Virtual Enterprise information system model shown in Figure 2 for logging of events and alerts.

The organization and architecture of information systems are influenced very much by the way we design the metadata frameworks for each of the above four component areas. How they influence the architecture may be understood better if we visualize that the environment in which any knowledge worker needs as having the four component areas as shown in Figure 1. Organization of generic information pertains to (i) above. It traditionally has been well exposited under the metadata organization as in Library Sciences and classification principles like

Dublin Core, or Ranganathan's facet classification. However the dynamic and strategic information organization in the second quadrant of Figure 1 needs considerable study and global efforts in standardization. To a considerable extent it is conditioned by the kind of knowledge questions the system has to ask in applying the information for knowledge-driven functions.

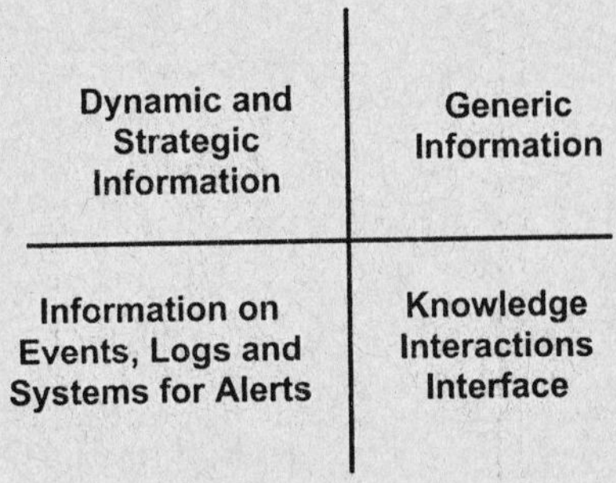

Fig. 1: Component Information – Interactions Systems for Virtual Enterprises

As a strategy, we need to look beyond information generation, aggregation and dissemination functions. We have to ask how the information systems will result in value addition to the users when juxtaposed with their work environment. Such integrated information systems combined with workflow processes of any group engaged in knowledge-based services may be modeled as shown in Figure 2. The assumption behind the model here is that every knowledge intensive service is driven by a close-knit group of users. They need their associated or custom knowledge base for reference and study purposes while they are engaged in their work. An earlier paper by the author (Srivathsan, 2004a) made the case that in a Knowledge Society the 'citizen' (or K-Citizen as referred to) is the focused group of knowledge workers that drive specific services of value. Such a view helps in architecting the knowledge driven information infrastructure of the kind shown in Figure 2. It shows the typical knowledge interactions environment that every K-Citizen or Knowledge Services Group lives in doing a variety of tasks. The environment may be referred to as Virtual Knowledge Driven Enterprise, or simply as Virtual Enterprise [VE]. Every VE has the following attributes.

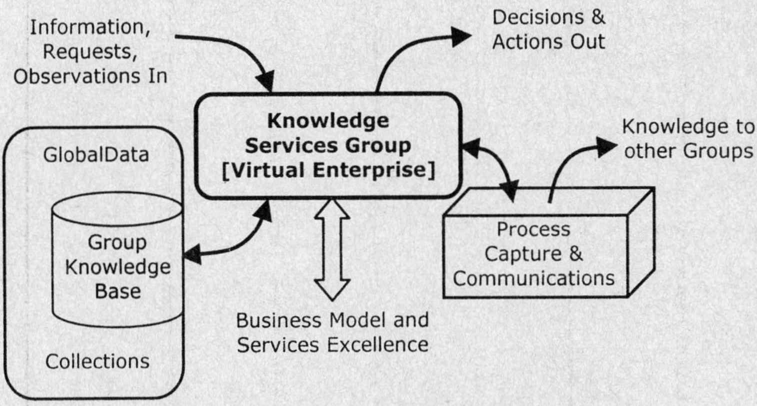

Fig. 2: Knowledge Services Group Work Environment

a) The members of the VE may belong to different organizations, or, to different groups within a large organization.

b) The VE gets inputs in the form of requests, observations, alerts and information that requires attention. The VE uses its own business workflow, as it executes its tasks.

c) Every VE needs its own focused knowledge base partly consisting of a filtered view of the global data / information collections of relevance for the business or services that are rendered to its customers. We call it the Group Knowledge Base.

d) Such Group Knowledge Base (GKB) has both generic (relatively static, validated) and dynamic information components. The generic part is characterized by the capacity to manage as per traditional library practices that includes the subscribed digital information components.

e) The dynamic part of information of the GKB pertains to current active data or information that is strategic to the VE's business or services delivery. For example, in agriculture, this may be weather, market and information concerning farm inputs. Future information systems need to co-link dynamic information that is strategic to the related generic information space. This will add much value like the Decision Support System for the work(s) the VE is engaged in.

f) During the course of VE functions in servicing the customers, or, engaged in their own activities, they create information by way of reports, logs of decisions taken, events, and alerts. It is important to have coherent reports and analysis of the logs of such information. Such reports serve in two ways. First is that they have the potential to provide knowledge inputs to other VEs or thematic communities. Second is that they serve to direct the organizational learning for the VEs own needs.

g) Lastly, the complex mix of such functions as given above needs effective user interfaces. We call it as the Knowledge Interaction Interface as stated in another paper (Srivathsan, 2004a).

h) The above mix of information and interaction functions for the VE architecture of Figure 1 is shown in Fig. 3 below. Every VE needs systems that support the relatively slow changing generic knowledge base as supported / provided in conventional libraries, except that this may be the relevant part of the Digital Library of interest for the group. In real-life real-time working environment, the same group has to constantly deal with faster changing dynamic and strategic information. For example, a group engaged in agriculture commodity trade will need relevant market information, crop predictions, implications of weather on productivity and prices, futures trading that are strategic. Every group arrives at decisions based upon information inputs, requests, and observations through its own workflow. They need to capture the workflow process in arriving at decisions in the form of events log, alerts and intermediate steps. Such captured process builds accountability and helps the group learn from its past. It helps build the organizational learning culture.

Each group or VE needs a Knowledge Interaction Interface [KII] as part of some Enterprise Integration Portal to deal with the information space outlined in Figure 1. In (Srivathsan, 2004a) a generic structure for typical KII was developed. The same is reproduced in Figure 3. The explanations for the components of KII in Figure. 3 are given in another paper (Srivathsan, 2004a). The Indian Institute of Information Technology and Management – Kerala (IIITM-K) has developed a class of Enterprise Portals that are now deployed in several organizations. The efforts to enhance their features are being continued.

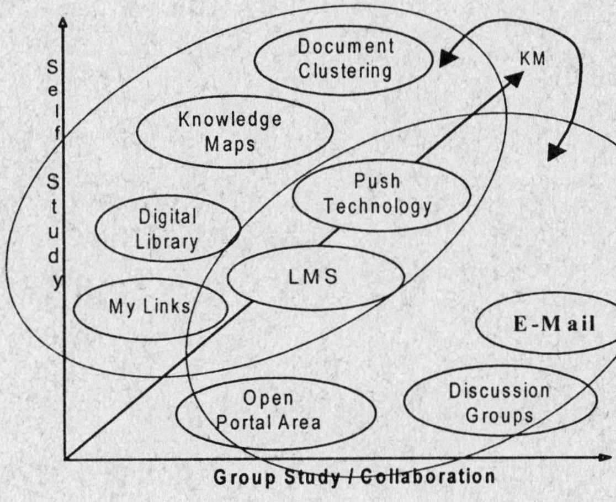

Fig. 3: Personal and Group Interface for Knowledge Interactions

In the next section, we give sample case studies of building the future Knowledge Infrastructure on how the thematic community or VE model is implemented. These are based on the KISSAN (Kissan Information Systems, Services and Networking) - Kerala and Education Grid projects.

3 CASE STUDIES

3.1 KISSAN-Kerala

The KISSAN-Kerala Project aims to provide the 'Right Information at the Right Time to the Right Persons (the farmers and agriculture related industry and trade related persons) in their Right Places and in the Right Context". The project targets the entire State of Kerala. As explained in (Srivathsan, 2004b), the methodology is based upon the following four component activity areas.

a) A central interactive Kerala Agriculture Portal (ww.kissankerala.net) that serves as the meeting ground of institutions, programmes, farmers, traders, scientists and related government officials. The portal, besides being a source of growing and rich quality content is becoming a way to disseminate locale-specific information and advisories, market information and opportunities, etc., it serves thematic communities (or VEs) in different strategic studies and advisory areas.

b) A popular weekly TV serial Krishideepam in Malayalalm over a commercial TV channel with wide reach. It attracts more than 10 million viewers and the KISSAN Project management gets a large number of queries after each episode. The episodes deal with validated agriculture information of current interest, success stories of individual farmer's initiatives and interests, opportunities awareness, and similar topics that address farmers' concerns.

c) Hosting the secondary level Agriculture Call Centre services that handles queries from farmers and others coming over the telephone, portal or email. Useful questions are aggregated and made accessible over the portal under the FAQ section.

d) The project will soon be launching the Virtual University for Agriculture Trade (VUAT) that will build awareness among the farmers, agriculture-based industry, traders, and farm inputs suppliers. The issues will concern with the productivity and profitability of the State's largely plantation crops dependent agriculture and keep enhancing the global competitiveness of the State's agriculture.

Based upon the experience in developing the technologies and running the programmes related to the KISSAN-Kerala project, the need for building a 'Scientific Portal for Agriculture' has been identified. This is briefly stated in the following subsection.

3.2 Scientific Portal for Agriculture

A major problem in giving knowledge empowerment to any farmer is that he/she needs timely and correct information, with expert interpretation as needed and from many sources on a continuing basis. He/she needs the support of experts who are able to give right decision inputs and guidance to take the right steps that enhance his/her sustainability, productivity and marketing concerns, thereby leading to better employment security. Further, with the WTO regime, bio-safety and environmental concerns, modern farmers need larger awareness of global issues of concern that will have deep impact on trade security and sustainability. Here we propose the concept of a Scientific Portal for Agriculture being built by the KISSAN-Kerala research team. This portal is designed to provide for farm or farmer specific information along with support for his/her educational and enterprise needs.

The proposed architectural view of the Scientific Portal is shown in Figure 4. An objective of the Scientific Portal is to present to each user (e.g., a farmer) mainly those components of relevance and interest to him in the context of his farm and farming needs. Such total information has several components each of which may come from different organizations or sources. The architecture is scalable and allows for any number of farmers and other interested stakeholders to build their own knowledge interaction spaces as illustrated in the VE model of Figure 1. There are several issues related to technology and standards that need to be examined in developing the VE information environment shown in Figure 1. We need development of XML schemas and profiles like the E-Portfolio definition for farms and farmers. These will be addressed as and when relevant VE services get configured and commissioned.

A multi-institutional project to develop and commission the Scientific Portal for Agriculture with capacity to configure and service large number of VEs is being proposed. The project is coordinated by the IIITM-K with the Kerala Agricultural University, and the Computer Science Department of the Kerala University. The Documentation Research and Training Centre of the Indian Statistical Institute at Bangalore is being consulted for the design of effective schemas and metadata frameworks needed for driving the dynamically configurable portal functions.

3.3 Multiple Communication Approaches for Kissan-Kerala Services

The Five Laws of information sciences clearly imply the need for a dynamic feedback for any successful IT enabled service. The KISSAN-Kerala project provides the service by integrating four types of systems as given below.

a. The central KISSAN portal (www.kissankerala.net) that provides several interactive and dynamic information services. These include daily information related to market, weather, crop advisories, virtual market, etc. It is also a place to send questions with attachments for expert answers and collections of answered questions that are of much help to any one visiting the portal. Some innovative interfaces like the GIS map driven access to location specific advisories are supported.

b. The weekly Krishideepam TV serial program over popular commercial TV channel provides selective information dissemination for current awareness, best practices, innovations and success stories adopted by individual farmers, etc.

c. Call centre services to take queries and request for services from farmers from anywhere and respond to the same through different modes of advice and actions.

d. A Virtual University for Agriculture Trade related awareness building among farmers, small and medium agriculture related industries and others.

The four together constitute a comprehensive and effective delivery of timely information and empowerment services of significant value to the farmers of Kerala. This is borne out by the considerable enthusiasm for the projects' services and over 10 million regular viewers for the TV serial. Further, the project already services a fair number of queries (about 20 to 30 per day) for a variety of services and soliciting information of diverse kinds. Experts from a variety of organizations (as indicated in Figure 4) provide inputs for the different services.

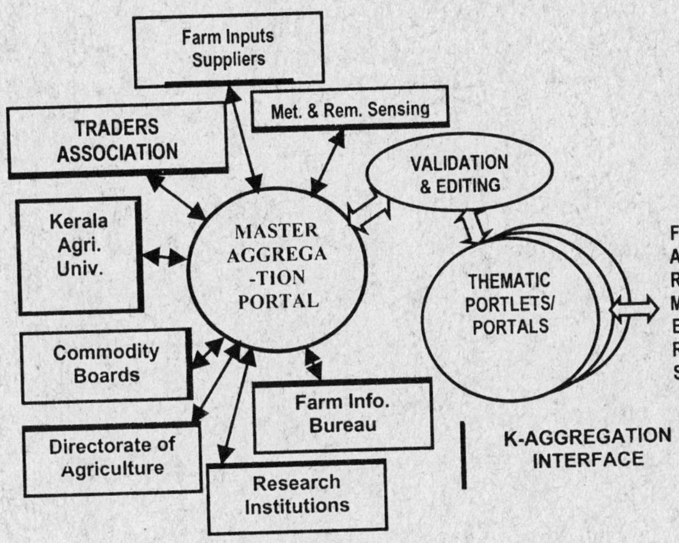

Fig. 4. Information Aggregation and Flow Management in Scientific Portal for Agriculture

3.4 The Kerala Education Grid Project

This project is in several ways complementary to the KISSAN-Kerala project. The spirit, approach and methodology of this project are discussed in another paper (Srivathsan, 2003). The project aims at enhancing the quality of education through collaboration across networked institutions. While the Scientific Portal provides the Knowledge Infrastructure for supporting multiple VEs, Education Grid enables academicians and experts from multiple institutions form distributed communities of practitioners in different subject areas. The approach to maintaining such communities in Education Grid is shown in Figure 5. It is assumed that each participating college has state-of-the-art education servers that have Learning Management System, Group Collaboration support and ways to organize and access their digital collections like a Digital Library.

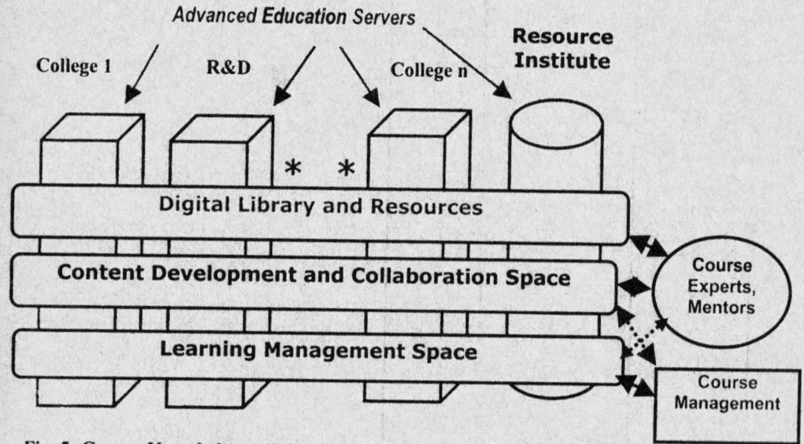

Fig. 5: Course Knowledge and Collaboration Spaces over Education Grid

In each subject, one of the premier institutions is given the responsibility as a resource institute. The Resource Institute maintains the Digital Library and Resources relevant to the concerned subject. The teachers in the subject and experts in the resource institute along with identified mentors or experts from other places form the community like a VE for the subject. They compile the e-courseware, conduct teacher training and release approved content for use in the different colleges. Processes to monitor quality of the content and effective learning delivery are being developed and being put in place. The Kerala Government is considering formalizing the Education Grid as the Virtual Institute of Science, Technology and Arts [VISTA] and making it a cooperative knowledge sharing forum across the colleges. An advanced research and management school in Informatics will drive the core of VISTA's programmes and services. The

Education Grid will be augmented by adding educational satellite services, computational portals in different subjects located at institutions that can best maintain and run them.

4 SUMMARY

Building the Knowledge Infrastructure for socially relevant areas like Education, Agriculture, Health, etc. requires innovation, collaboration structures and distributed processes supported by relevant strategy groups with members from different organizations. It also needs a refreshingly different look at the value propositions of the services provided in the light of the five laws of Information Sciences. This in turn needs several new information systems organization and management practices facilitated ably by modern enterprise portals supporting web-services enabled group specific activities.

The concept and requirements of Scientific Portal emerges out of the above considerations. IIITM-K in its KISSAN-Kerala and Education Grid projects has built the early prototypes and commissioned such advanced knowledge management systems. Over these portals pilot services for agriculture and education sectors have been commissioned.

REFERENCES

1. Ranganathan, S.R. (1999). *Five Laws of Library Science*. Sarada Ranganathan Endowment for Library Science; Bangalore.
2. The Abstract Syntax Notation – 1, Available in the *RFC documents Series of Internet Standards*.
3. Srivathsan, K.R. (2004a) The 'I' in 'IT' – A Pancha Kosha View, *Global Journal of Flexible Systems Management*. Vol. 5(1).
4. —. (2004b). et. al. Strategy focused IT facilitation of Agriculture Extension Services – The KISSAN-Kerala Approach. Presented at the *National Workshop on Alternative Approaches in Agriculture Extension Services, held Feb. 2004* at Mitraniketan Krishi Vigyan Kendra, Vellanad, Trivandrum District.
5. —. (2003). Management of Refereed Content Generation and Utilization in Formal Higher Education. *Global Journal of Flexible Systems Management*. Vol. 4(1-2).

DOCUMENTATION OF COMPOSITIONS IN CARNATIC MUSIC: NEED FOR AND UTILITY OF, A COMPUTERIZED DATABASE

K. S. Nagarajan

Carnatic Music is one of the two major classical systems of music of India. The task of building databases and Documentation of Carnatic music poses several challenges. Mentions the need and motivation for undertaking the work. Briefly elucidates certain aspects of Carnatic music relevant to database design. Points out with examples the usefulness of the system for a variety of purposes and clientele. Describes the structure of the different databases of the system – music compositions, tunings, audio-recordings; ancillary files, such as, for alternative versions of songs, raagamalikas, pallavis, music for South Indian dances; and derived files that list musical pieces grouped according to type or form of Music. Highlights some of the problems in collecting data for the contents of the databases. Concludes with a note on future plans.

0 PROLOGUE

I am pleased to contribute a paper to this festschrift volume. I have been engaged in this labour of love, sporadically though, for more than a decade. I have great personal admiration and regard for Prof. A. Neelameghan's work during most of his career, particularly after he joined the faculty of the Documentation Research and Training Centre, Bangalore in the early 1960s. He has been rightly considered as an 'alter ego' to the late National Research Professor Dr S.R. Ranganathan. Neelameghan has made significant contributions to the area of 'Knowledge Organization', going much beyond the confines of Colon Classification pioneered by his mentor. His contributions to the formulation of course contents, teaching/training methodology and building-up of institutions for training in information science and management in the Philippines, Ethiopia, Venezuela and China (PR) and advice to several national governments and non-governmental organizations in many countries, during his nearly decade-long tenure at UNESCO are well known and appreciated. He has assisted in the design and development of a number of databases – bibliographic and non-bibliographic - in India and in other countries, and he maintains several personal databases on varied subjects including the humanities. We have had discussions about my project on music documentation from time to time. I consider it a privilege to be part of a diverse group of people, whose articulated contributions are intended to be a tribute to the lifetime of dedicated, scholarly work by this remarkable person in the field of information science and technology on his Platinum Jubilee.

1 INTRODUCTION

1.1 Motivation for the Work

During the past four decades and more machine-readable databases have proliferated in the various branches of science and technology and in the social sciences and humanities as well. Later developments have ushered in databases that are designed for dynamic use in business and industry. The area of performing arts appears to have received relatively less attention, at least in India. I have been an avid listener (*rasika*) of classical Indian music, especially of the Carnatic or South Indian stream, for over 50 years. In parallel I have participated and managed documentation work and service in CSIR (Council of Scientific and Industrial Research, Government of India) institutions (National Aerospace Laboratories, and the Indian National Scientific Documentation Centre) for over two decades. Against this background, it occurred to me: "why not take up a documentation project to cover, in depth, all music compositions on a scale never perhaps conceived of before?"

1.2 Carnatic Music

Between the two major forms of classical music of India mentioned above, the Carnatic stream is renowned for a plethora of musical compositions in a wide variety of forms and languages. Several thousands of compositions (lyrics with music) have been ascribed to saint poets or ecstatic devotional singers of the 15th

and 16th centuries, e.g., Vyasaraya, Purandaradasa, Kanakadasa (in Kannada), Annamacharya (in Telugu and Sanskrit) and many others in later times, especially by the Trinity: Muthuswamy Deekshitar, Shyama Sastry and Thyagaraja (18th and 19th centuries). The Tamil Trinity (AruNaachala Kavi, Mutthudhaandavar, Maarimutha PiLLai) and Swathi Thirunal, [a 19th century Maharaja of Travancore] have created a treasure trove of musical works. These together can be considered as the quintessence of 'sahityas' for Carnatic music. The works of scores of other composers who flourished from the 17th-18th century onwards have further enriched these. On a rough count there appears to be an impressive list of about 900 gifted people who have been either *vakgeyakaaras* (i.e. those who have created both the lyrics and the music for them) or lyricists (leaving it to others to give musical shape to their creative production) and, in very recent times, some who have created abstract musical pieces without any verbal lyrics to go with them. Nobody, even among well-known musicologists and senior musicians, seems to have an accurate idea of the total number of compositions available, and fit for presentation, in classical music concerts; guesstimates vary from 10,000 to a few hundred thousands.

1.3 Usefulness of Computerized System

A database to be really useful for a variety of purposes and user needs, must go beyond the skeletal data that are usually furnished when items in a concert are announced in the electronic mass media (radio and TV) or when a programme is printed (as in the case of the annual conference and festival of the Music Academy, Chennai). These skeletal data are confined to the name of the composition preceded by the starting word(s) or first line of the composition (or SAHITYA), the RAAGA (or the melodic mode) and the THAALA (or the rhythmic structure). Other parameters, such as: TYPE (e.g. *Krithi/Keerthanai, VarNam, PadhavarNam, Swarajathi, Padham, Javali, Thillana*, etc.); LANGUAGE (of the lyric); THEME (devotional / philosophic, didactic, patriotic, romantic/erotic, on Nature, in praise of a king/patron or a guru (*Narasthuthi, Gurusthuthi*), etc.; DEITY to whom dedicated or in praise of which god/goddess--in case of songs with a devotional theme; SET TO MUSIC or tuned by whom; NOTATION, if any, furnished by whom; PUBLICATION (or a MSS.) wherein the full text of the *sahitya* has been/ is/can be found; AUDIOGRAPHIC reference (in case of the not-so-well-known songs, if any of these has been found in a commercially released cassette, LP disc, or a CD) are also important and useful fields for specific search and/or end-uses. This main database or file is named CARMUCOM for Carnatic music compositions.

It is attractive to extend such an ambitious documentation effort to compile at least two more concurrent or parallel databases: a bibliographic database of all publications and unpublished manuscripts and typescripts that contain full versions of the *sahitya*, with or without notations in the relevant languages (all the South Indian languages plus Sanskrit); and to extend this even further, to prepare a union catalogue of the holdings of such material in various libraries--notably those associated with the Music Departments of major Universities, cultural bodies such as the Music Academy, 'Sampradhaya', Kalakshetra, etc. in Chennai; the Swathi Thirunal Academy/College of Music, Thiruvananthapuram; the SN Akademi, New Delhi; and other schools and colleges of eminence in the field of classical music all over the country.

A database of all the available/accessible audio-recordings of Carnatic music: archival or commercial, whether existing as EP or LP discs; on tape (reels or compact cassettes) or as CDs will also be similarly useful. An extension of this exercise would involve the 'data capturing' of the title and type of each song, its composer, *raaga* and *thaaLa*, the person who had tuned the piece (if other than the composer), as contained in each cassette/LP/CD with information on its title, producer / publisher, marketing code number, year of recording or issue etc. Such a machine-readable catalogue / directory will enable serious students of music, researchers, guides, teachers, musicologists and others, to take up comparative assessment or evaluation of the rendering of the same song or piece of music by different vocalists or on different instruments or by the same artiste in different years or by those belonging to different schools of learning (*shishya parampara* or *paataanthara*' or *gharana*).

Let us imagine a possible scenario when a user has access to four such related databases, with appropriate indexes, mentioned below:

- Compositions,
- Composers/lyricists/tunesmiths,
- Books, pamphlets, journals and manuscripts containing full texts of the compositions (indicating whether 'with' or 'without' notation and in the script of which language) – may be extendable to include all books in any language dealing with any aspect (aesthetical, theoretical, historical, biographical, comparative, etc.), and
- All available/accessible audio graphic (sound) recordings of such compositions by several composers.

The user can then do any, some, or all of the following searches for information and obtain outputs:

- Find any particular composition (hereafter referred to as *sahitya*) given its starting word(s), and the output sorted out and arranged according to *Sahitya* or by any other parameter;
- Find all compositions of a particular type (e.g. *JavaLis, or Krithis or VarNams*), and the output alphabetically arranged by name of *raaga* or of composer or *thaala* or other parameter;
- Find *jaavaLis* in a given *raaga* by any composer, or by particular composer; or
    - those in a combination of a given *raaga* AND *thaaLa* or
    - of a given *raaga* and *theme;* or
    - all *krithis* devoted to a chosen deity (say, *Vinaayaka*) in all languages (of the lyric) or only those on *Vinaayaka* in Sanskrit or Kannada or Tamil or Telugu, and so on.
- The combinations of parameters are virtually endless!
- When teaching or learning a composition in a certain *raaga*, say *Chaarukesi* or *Sunaadhavinodhini*, find titles of other compositions (whether by the same or other composers) in the same *raaga* to help elucidate different passages in those compositions that highlight the spirit or the mood of the same *raaga*, as handled by different composers or even different tunesmiths (those who have set to music the lyrics penned by others). This facility will also help in planning a workshop or lecture-demo or series of mini-concerts,

each one on one *raaga*, and in selecting songs to be presented by different artistes in the same *raaga*, but by different composers and/or in different languages and different types of composition, on the same platform;

- Select compositions in a given *thaaLa* or
  - those by the same composer in different thaaLas, or
  - those in one selected *raaga* but in different *thaaLa*s –
- Such retrieval facilities can assist learning/teaching rhythmic (percussion) instrument-playing or for rendering improvised KALPANASWARAs, to conform to different t*haLaas*, or for lecture-demos devoted only to *laya* or *thaaLa* aspects;
- for performing musicians, professional or amateur, to get help in enlarging their repertoire or for choosing the musical pieces to be sung to suit a given occasion, say, in different festivals, in praise of different deities: e.g. *Rama Navami*, *Gokulashtami*, *Vinaayaka Chathurthi*, *Navaaraathri, Shivaraathri, Hanumajayanthi*, etc.
  - For variety, songs by different composers and in different languages of the lyrics can be chosen though all, or most,
  - of them can be in praise of one chosen deity – the computer makes such tasks easy and quick;
- as an aid to memory, even for very senior musicians, music teachers and musicologists, preparing for a concert, lecture, discussion etc. to search for examples of musical pieces to illustrate a particular point at issue; one may vaguely remember one relevant piece by a particular composer but had forgotten the starting line of the *sahitya* or vice versa. Knowing any one or two of the parameters pertaining to a song, one can search the entire database and list on the screen all the items indexed under this one or the other parameter (or a combination of the two) to get at what one had in mind but could not instantly recall.
- for a would-be composer, on the verge of a creative effort, say of creating a *thillana* in a certain *raaga*, to search
    - the database to select all the existing *thillanas* in that chosen *raaga*, to help recall these so as to avoid inadvertent
  - duplication of musical ideas or to decide on taking up some other *raaga*. Similarly, while creating a *krithi* or

- tuning the same after finalising the lyric, to examine other existing *krithis* in the same *raga* composed by others to

  - avoid repetition of the tune (or *varNamettu*) that may already exist for another song, access to such a database
  - will help tickle the memory and possibly can avoid wastage of time and effort.

➢ While most publications of texts of lyrics are arranged composer-wise (a few are anthologies e.g. *Thillaanaas* or *Jaavalis* by several composers, or a compendium of select works of a few composers) many of these are out of print and certainly not all such publications are available with one institution or individual, in one place. The proposed database can retrieve all compositions by any given composer, as a checklist, though only the starting line would be available indicating the title(s) of the books in different languages, containing the full text of the compositions. If a union catalogue of printed material on Carnatic music is also available as an adjunct database, the required source can easily be located and even electronic copy obtained.

➢ The multi-indexed catalogue database of audio-recordings can be very useful not only for listening to music, lecture demonstrations etc., but also to artistes, producers, distributors, vendors of commercially produced audio-records (CDs and cassettes). Here are a couple of illustrative instances.

1) A recording company approaches a musician-artiste to record, suggesting a theme and/or contents of the CD/cassette or leave the choice to the artiste. In either case one would like to ascertain whether the same or some other artiste has already recorded the particular song(s) thought of. Or if a song in a particular *raga* is thought of, then it will be useful to find out what other songs in the same *raga* have already been recorded and produced / marketed so as to avoid duplication and / or copyright problems. Similarly, with songs pertaining to a particular theme, say on, God *Vinayaka* or Goddess *Saraswathi*, or patriotism, etc.; or songs by a particular composer or in a specific language

2) Now, consider from the selling or retailing outlet point. A customer interested recordings of classical music. He/she may seek either a particular album of a preferred artiste or a cassette or CD recorded by that artiste. If the customer requires a recording based on a composer

(e.g. by Purandaradasa, or Kshetragna) or a recording containing a specific song (e.g. the *Kalinga Nardhana thillaana* by Oothukkadu Venkatasubba Iyer), the seller's usual catalogue of music or audio recordings or the arrangement of the recordings in the store will not help Similar problems will arise if the potential buyer is a student or teacher of music seeking for all recording of Lalgudi Jayaraman or Balamurali Krishna, or those containing *alapana* of selected *ragas* by particular artiste(s). On the other hand, with a multi-index database one can quickly identify the required items. Such a catalogue database can also serve several purposes for the vendor (stock analysis and inventory management, ordering of items, gain better knowledge of customer requirements, etc.).

With a one-time data entry, covering the various parameters relating to each musical composition, the system can give several outputs, indexed and arranged according to any parameter(s); and list songs according to desired parameter(s). The possibilities are virtually endless:

Such a machine-readable database is quickly updatable and thus supplements any print-on-paper publication (an anthology, an index or a catalogue) or an annotated guide to musical compositions. It also facilitates easy transport and exchange of the contents. It can give rise to several mini-databases like: compositions only in one language, or those known to have been created in a given century or period, or only of one structural type (like *Krithis, Padhams, JaavaLis, Varnams,* etc.) or all songs that are on a philosophical or romantic or a patriotic theme or those devoted to the praise of one deity. The idea of mini-databases can be extended to obtain from the master database of all compositions, known to exist (either in print or as MSS.), select short lists on the following lines, given as illustrative examples:

1) List all VRNs (="*thaanavarNams*") in Telugu language,
2) List all VRNs, in any language, in *ATa thaaLa*,
3) List all VRNs by "so-and-so" composer,
4) List all VRNs in *Bhairavi / Thodi* (or any other) ragaa,

5) List all SWJs (="*swarajathis*") arranged alphabetically, by the name of the composer
6) List all PLVs (="*pallavis*") in *Khanda Thriputa thaaLa*,
7) Is there any composition in *KaedhaaragowLa raaga* and in *Simhanandana thaaLa* ? If so, by whom and where can one find it (if published) or who has got it as a mss and in which language / script ?
8) Is there a book containing all/most compositions of Vidvan Balamuralikrishna in more than one script (say, Devanagari, English, Tamil and Telugu); If so what is its title and price? Who is its publisher and when was it published?
9) List all PDMs (="*padhams*") in Tamil devoted to Nataraja, venerated as the Lord of the Cosmic Dance, composed before the 20th century.
10) List all PDMs in Telugu in a romantic (='*sringara*') *rasa*
11) List all compositions of Ghanam Krishna Iyer in two formats: one arranged alphabetically according to the starting word and another according to the *raaga.*
12) List all compositions in Kannada language devoted to Lord Krishna, except those by the Haridasas.
13) Is / are there any VRN ("*thaanavarNam*") or JVL ("*jaavaLi*") in *raaga Dhwijaavanthi*; if so, who is/are the composer(s)?
14) I heard a '*tharangam*' by sage NaraayaNa Theertha on the radio in the *raga Valaji*. I could not catch the starting words. How does this song begin and who has tuned this piece?
15) I listened to a delightful '*ragamaalika*': "*RaagathilchiRanda raagamedhu*?" I could not keep track; how many and which are the *raagas* and who composed?

2 DATABASES

2.1 Database of Music Compositions

VADEYKAR.DBF is a database of musical compositions. The Sanskrit word *Vaak-geyakaara* connotes a person who has created a song or written the lyric or musical piece. The fields for this database include: NAME (a 14-character alpha code); ATTRIBUTE (the State and any grouping, such as *Haridasa*s of Karnataka, *Azhwaars* or vaishnavite saints of Tamil Nadu, to which he/she belongs; CENTURY when alive or when the musical composition was created; fields for language(s), type(s) and number of compositions; MUDRA (or *ankeetha*) the pseudonym or 'signature' of the poet-composer occurring in the songs, in most cases; TITHONORS for any significant title(s) / honour (s) bestowed on the composer; CLASSIFICN or Category, whether V or L or T or T (for *Vaakgeyakara*' or Lyricist or Tunesmith or both - V + T); PUBLYRICS to indicate title(s) of publication(s) containing the lyrics composed; BIOGRAPHY, again to indicate book(s) containing biographical information on the person; and a single-character field for the 'composer group' to indicate *ad hoc* groupings: (1 to 5 OR A to E) for pre-17th century; 17-19th century composer-titans or legendary names; lesser-known 18-19th century names; outstanding 20th century composers; and lesser-known ones of the 20th century.

The database on books – MUSBOOKS – is meant to list all books, related to Carnatic music including biographical, historical and comparative studies, besides those containing texts of lyrics, with or without notation for *swaras* or musical notes.

2.2 Documentation of Audio Recordings

Two databases as a pilot project have been created, viz., AUDRECAM (AUDio RECordings of CArnatic Music), and CONTAREC (=CONTents of Audio RECordings). These have 3 or 4 inter-linking common fields. The former contains a bibliographic catalogue pertinent to the recordings:

2.2.1 Fields in AUDRECAM

(a) Type of recording LP (for Long-Play disc record) / AC (for audiocassette) / CD (for audio only or multi-media CD) [this can be extended to include media that require a TV receiver or a computer-monitor for playback].

(b) Duration of the record (in minutes)

(c) System / Stream and Medium of Music -- (say, CV for Carnatic Vocal or HI for Hindustani Instrumental and name of instrument (main, solo), likewise HV or CI and .so on.

(d) Number of Main Artistes (S (for single) / D (for Duo) / T (for Trio or M (for Multiple, or more than 3 performing together)

(e) Name(s) of Main Artiste(s);

(f) to (j) Names of Accompanying artistes (melodic and rhythmic)

(k) Title of Audio Record

(l) Producer (Company / Institution) of the Audio Record

(m) Code No../ ID No. of the recording, given by the producer

(n) Name of the composer, if exclusively devoted to musical works of just one composer

(o) Type of composition, if exclusively containing music of only one type (say, only PADHAMs, or only VARNAMs, or only THILLANAs or only SWARAJATHIs or only DEVARANAMAs or only DAASARAPADHAgaLu

(p) Year released/published for sale

2.2.2 Fields in CONTAREC

(a) *Sahithya* (=title or starting line of song)

(b) Type or Form of composition (a 3-charac.code is used)

(c) *Raaga*

(d) *ThaaLa*

Presence of improvisory/creative (*manodharma*) elements (an indicative one-character field: Yes or No, for

(e) *Alaapana*

(f) *Thaanam,* these two features, if present, that precede the rendering of a song; and then 3 other features that are linked to a lyric during its musical rendering, namely

(g) *Neraval*

(h) *Kalpanaswaram*

(i) *Chittaswaram* (this feature could have been 'built-in' by the original *vaakgeyakara* or subsequently added to the lyric by a tunesmith or a teaching/performing musician)

(j) Composer (4-ch.code for)

(k) Tuned (or set tomusic) by (4-ch.code for name)

(l) Audio Record Number (unique number for the commercially released or archival recording containing the song, in the AUDRECAM.dbf)

(m) Sidenitem = side (A or B OR 1 or 2 and Item number in the cassette / CD

(n) Duration (of this song / musical unit in the recording)

Data entry for this file CONTAREC requires the involvement of someone, if not the compiler of data, who is musically knowledgeable and who actually listens to the recording, to identify and note the musical parameters (and note the duration of rendering, with a timer !).

3 TUNINGS. DBF

In this database, an attempt has been made to identify, establish and authenticate the person(s) responsible for the musical shape or value (or '*dhaathu*') of each lyric (or '*maathu*'). This will apply only to those songs for which both the lyric and the music have not been created by the same person; in other words, songs which are not the creations of a *vaakgeyakara.* Rarely is the tunesmith given credit, or acknowledged or publicized, when he/she is different from the lyricist, in the context of concerts and recordings of Carnatic music. While in the world of film music, the term 'composer' refers to the person who has set the lyrics to music, invariably in the classical Carnatic music milieu a composer means the lyricist, whether or not the latter has also created the music for his/her lyric.

3.1 Tunesmith

In the collective repertoire of Carnatic musicians, past and present, are hundreds of songs each of which exists because of the combined creative efforts of a tunesmith who is distinctly different from the lyricist; and the two need not be contemporaries. Lyrics by AruNagirinaathar, Annamacharya, AaNdaaL (and other vaishnavite *azhwaars*), Jayadeva, Narayana Theertha, Sadashiva Brahmendra, Basavanna, Jothi Ramalinga Swami or latter-day Ambujam Krishna or Periasami Thooran have been set to music, by scores of musicians of the 20th century, captivated by the lyrical or poetic beauty or the devotional fervor of the lyrics. The role of the tunesmith in giving musical life / existence to a lyric that can be sung, is as important to the listeners, as the authorship of the lyric. Hence this database will be a value added feature of the entire exercise of building up of a comprehensive digitized catalogue of musical works in the Carnatic genre.

To cite a classic example, there is this exciting song in Sanskrit by the 19th century King of Travancore State, Maharaja Swathi ThirunaaL that starts with the line *Bhaavayaami Raghuraamam,* originally composed to be sung in the *raaga Saavaeri*. It got transformed into an exquisite *raagamaalika* (a song in a garland of *raagas*) when re-tuned by the late great musician Semmangudi Srinivasa Iyer. However, whenever this song is broadcast in the media, or labeled for a disc/cassette/CD or a programme containing the song is printed, credit is never assigned to the great musician-tunesmith, whose creative talents made this song a delectable piece with melodically much-enhanced value. It is usually labeled as a composition by Swathi Thirunaal. This feature that a tunesmith can be a person different from the lyricist has also given rise to the phenomenon of multiple musical versions of the same lyric in several cases. Different musicians have found it desirable or attractive to 'tune' the same lyric to different *raagas* and/or *thaaLas*, at different times. Thus we find various musically different versions existing for the same song (in *different raagas*), the lyric for which had been 'composed' by Purandaradasa or any of the other Haridasas, or by Annamacharya or the *thiruppugazhs* of AruNagirinathar or the *thiruppaavai* by the saint-poetess AndaaL (or Godha Devi), and so on.

4 ANCILLARY FILES

4.1 File ALTVERS

The feature discussed in preceding section necessitates certain Ancillary Files. ALTVERS (Alternative Versions of the same song), in this project, is one such.

To illustrate, in the spiral-bound, printed "Alphabetical Index to Karnatak Songs" by Lakshman Ragde (in Canada), we find 3 entries for a Purandaradasa song *Kande karuNaanidhiya*, in 3 different *raagas – Suratti*, *KunthalavaraaLi*, and *Naadanaamakriya*; another song by Bhadrachala Ramadas, who lived before the famous Thyagaraja, *O Raama ni naamam* has 4 listings with *ragas*, namely, *KalyaaNi, Kaamavardhini, PoorvikalyaaNi* and *Yadhukulakaambhoji.* This may lead an uninformed ~~seeker~~ of musical information to wonder whether the devotee-composer had created that lyric but ~~sang the~~ same in 6 different *ragas*. Efforts are being made to trace the authorship of the different tunes ~~and give credit~~ to them in the TUNINGS file and the ALTVERS file. This is one of the difficult aspects of collecting data. Whereas the ALTVERS file will contain data only on those songs that have more than one melodic version, the TUNINGS file will contain data on all songs that have the tunesmith different from the lyricist. The file structure for both is identical to that of the main file CARMUCOM.

Other ancillary files planned or created on a pilot scale are mentioned in the succeeding sections

4.2 File RAGMALIK

The file: RAGMALIK, contains data on *Raagamaalikas*. These are songs each one of which is in a garland or sequence of *raagas*, which are either created as such by a *vaakgeyakaara* or single-*raaga* pieces converted into *raagamaalikas* by latter-day musicians. While the file structure is basically the same as that for CARMUCOM, the *raaga* field has to be supplemented with another field (RAGNAMES), much longer in order to accommodate the names of multiple *raagas*; in *the raaga* field, only the expression RAAGAMAALIKA (x) is written, 'x' representing the number of *raagas* present in that item. This separate file RAGMALIK is warranted mainly to save the disk-space of the main file; and it needs to be referred to only by those who are keen to know the names of the *raagas* covered by each *raagamaalika*.

4.3 File PALLAVIS

The file PALLAVIS lists all pieces of the form or type: *pallavi* considered to be a highly evolved type of composition giving scope for the display of the musician's grip of the different facets of music: *raaga* (the melodic), *thaaLa* (the rhythm), tempo or gait (calculated rendering at double/triple or fractions of the standard speed) of a specially conceived short segment of *sahitya*. Ability to render a *pallavi* in complex *thaaLas* or those in complicated combinations of tempo is considered to be a hallmark of an academically well-accomplished musician. Most *pallavis* are created by the musicians themselves, sometimes on the spot, to display their competence in this aspect, vouching for their abilities or *manodharma*, among fellow-musicians and very knowledgeable *rasikas*; there are also many *pallavis* created by maestros handed down in the *gurukula* lineage, and published. There are some books (especially one by a medical doctor and S. Pinakapaani) containing texts and notation of about 150 *pallavis* while many other books contain selections of these, as composed / conceived by different experts. The computer file on these is almost similar to that of the main file CARMUCOM, except that this has a couple of extra fields to provide for *nadai* or gait of the *thaaLa,* the phase difference (sometimes it is 'zero') between the start of the *thaaLa* and of the *sahitya* (called *athitha, or anagaatha* or *eduppu*) and the duration of the lull or silence zone (*kaarvai*), that characterizes each *pallavi*. This file is of interest mainly to the serious students of music, teachers, examiners, analysts, critics and researchers. A reference to this file can be valuable not only for academics in music but also for the performing musician while preparing for a lecture-demonstration or workshop as a resource person.

4.4 File MUSDANCE

The file MUSDANCE [Music for Dance] provides information on the two classical South Indian dance forms, viz. *Bharatha Natyam* (or *Nrithyam*) and *Kuchipudi*. Certain types or forms of musical compositions are designed for dance; certain others can be sung or played on an instrument at a music concert as well as can be danced to, after suitably choreographed (body movements, hand gestures and facial expressions appropriately conceived and arranged according to the grammar of the dance genre, to suit the meaning and import of the lyric and music). Some types of compositions are not suitable for dancing. All *padhavarnams* and *chowka varnams*, a few *thanavarnams*, all *padhams* and *jaavaLis* and most *thillanas* are fit for dancing; so are some of the krithis, keerthanams and *bhajans*, whose meanings have been understood by the choreographer or dance master, who can make the piece danceable. Senior dancers, dance gurus and professional choreographers need to be contacted to obtain a list of musical pieces that they have perfected for dancing and taught to performing dancers. A beginning has been made by obtaining the list of musical pieces in the dance repertoire of noted dancer and guru V.P. Dhanjayan of Bharatha Kalaanjali, Chennai; some 50 to 60 others like him, at different locations, have to be contacted. Here again the file structure would be only slightly different from that for CARMUCOM, in order to provide for the name of the choreographer, name of the dancer and the place and date where the item was first staged or danced to.

5 DERIVED FILES

There are, several derived files or these can be created as and when needed. These are lists of musical pieces grouped according to type or form (like *varNams, krithis, swarajathis, padhams, javaLis, ugabhogas / viruthams, bhajans* etc.); according to *raaga*, according to the composer or lyricist or tunesmith, according to language, according to the theme (philosophical, didactic, patriotic, panegyric, devotional — on Divine deities or on holy, venerable persons, like spiritual gurus — on nature, on childhood, womanhood, on music, etc.) and if devotional on different deities (using a controlled vocabulary). These can be temporarily created, copied/printouts made and used and the files can be erased, to be re-created on the computer, when needed again. Such derived files can also be of select list(s) of musical compositions meeting the requirements of a given occasion, needing songs based on a desired combination of parameters. For example:

a) List of songs on Lord Krishna, in Kannada language by all composers except those by Vyasaraya, Purandaradasa and Kanakadasa

b) List all *thaana-varNams* in *Dhwijaavanthi raaga*, giving name of the composer, *thaaLa* and the language of the lyric;

c) List *thillanas* in the 5 specified *raagas*, and indicate for which of these audio-recordings have been published as cassettes or CDs [*Raagas* desired: *Khamaas, Dhaesh, Vaasanthi, Sivaranjani and Hamsaanandhi*];

d) List compositions of Mysore Sadashiva Rao, Mysore Vasudevachar, Papanasam Sivan, Harikesanallur Muthiah Bhagavathar and G.N. Balasubramaniam on Devi (Parvathi), indicating language of the lyric, *raaga* and *thaaLa;*

e) List songs on Muruga / Subrahmanya: at least 10 by Koteeswara Iyer, and 4 each by Periasaami Thooran, VaaNi Jayaram, Cuddalore Subramanyam, D. K. Pattammal & M.M. DhandapaaNi Desikar, not duplicating the *raagas* used.

f) List krithis, each composed in multiple languages (=*maNiparavaaLa*) by Muthuswami Deekshitar and Swathi ThirunaaL.

6 UTILISATION OF DATA

Even before the compilation is completed and brought out for public use, there have been several queries from musicians/students of music/connoisseurs, answers for which could be furnished by searching the database. Some of these queries pertained to:

(a) Verifying the authorship of a particular song;

(b) List of *krithis* or *varNams* in a particular speficied *raaga*;

(c) All songs in a given *raaga* in a specified language;

(d) Songs created by a specified composer dedicated to a particular deity, with information on the shrine or *kshetra* kept in view or venerated.

These queries have been from well-known musicians or music pedagogues. Such interactions and queries also helped in the design and development of the system. Problems arise mainly due to gaps in information pertaining to one or more facets of the lyrical and musical values of the songs, in most of the published sources of information. Experienced performing musicians, pedagogues, musicologists, students of music have been and are being contacted to fill these gaps. Many cases of ambiguity (e.g. doubtful authorship of a lyric, name of the *raaga* or the deity to whom/or the shrine to which the song has been dedicated, etc.) necessitate recording multiple and divergent values of data and the respective sources of information. In respect of unpublished works of certain composers, the problems are more acute and revolve around identifying contact persons (among the descendants or disciples of the deceased composer or of his friends/ contemporaries).

7 FUTURE PLANS: PRODUCTS AND SERVICES

It is envisaged to publish the databases on CD-ROMs by the end of 2005. It is hoped that not only students and teachers of music, professional musicians, critics and connoisseurs, researchers and authors on music, planners and producers of musical audio-recordings and reviewers thereof, would all benefited by using what is hoped to be a reliable and up-datable database. The launching of these databases on a web-site has been suggested.

7.1 Acknowledgements

Venerable music gurus and musicologists have been of great help. Nearly 60 to 70 senior musicians (including those listed earlier, who have seen a demo of the work have gifted copies of their books on music, some containing the text of many of their own compositions. Most of them have unstintingly given data on their lyrics and/or tunings. Other top-ranking musicians have lent (or given away spare copies of) books from their personal collections, containing musical compositions that they had learnt / taught others. Among other musically involved friends have helped by acting as referral centres and/or actually collecting data from books and human resources. Started nearly a decade ago, with very little infrastructure, this project has been helped substantially through the award of a Senior Fellowship by the Department of Culture, Ministry of Human Resources Development, Government of India, during 1996-98 and from early 2004 through a substantial grant from the India Foundation for the Arts, Bangalore-560 080. The author is grateful to these agencies for their generous support and encouragement.

SAINT TYAGARAJA CD: A MODEL FOR KNOWLEDGE ORGANIZATION AND PRESENTATION OF CLASSICAL CARNATIC MUSIC

T. N. Rajan

Describes a CD multimedia product on Saint Tyagaraja as a case study in knowledge organization and presentation. Gives a brief background on Carnatic music (South Indian classical music) delineates the main features and facilities of the multimedia CD.. A methodology for creating such multimedia information sources has been evolved with the experience gained in this effort.

0 PREAMBLE

When I received an invitation from Dr. K.S. Raghavan to write a paper for a festschrift to Prof. A. Neelameghan (AN), I was doubly pleased. It gave me an opportunity to describe a collaborative work resulting in a knowledge product – the Tyagaraja CD – fulfilling my long-standing desire on the one hand, and to recall my association and friendship with AN since the early 1950s.

As a descendant of Saint Tyagaraja lineage, I had special interest in Indian classical music and had discussed with AN from time to time, the application of information organization techniques and tools – classification, indexing, vocabulary control - to organizing, classifying, indexing and retrieving information on Indian classical music. However, it was only during the past five years or so it has been possible to apply information technology to prepare knowledge products of Indian classical music thanks to the collaborative effort with musician B.S. Iyengar and information specialist L.J. Haravu.

My association with AN goes back to 1951 when he was librarian of the Vivekananda College in Chennai. He used to spend a few hours at our home in Royapettah, Chennai, on some Sundays. I was then not quite sure of the prospects of librarianship as a career, but AN said I should not be hasty to move out of the library profession to seek other pastures. In November 1951 on his suggestion, I applied for and joined the library of the Vivekananda College as he moved out to join the Madras Medical College. Soon after I was called to the National Library, Calcutta, where the late Prof. B.S.Kesavan was National Librarian. After a few years there, with the experience gained, I was called to join the Indian National Scientific Documentation Centre (ISDOC), CSIR, in Delhi, where Prof. Kesavan was Director. Starting as a lecturer, then promoted to Reader (Associate Professor) and then Professor and Head of INSDOC's postgraduate professional course in information science. During this period, AN used to make official visits to INSDOC, to attend INSDOC's Advisory Committee meetings, staff selection meetings, and to present lectures to the participants in the training course. On almost every such occasion AN would spend time with me, discuss professional matters, often over a meal or a cup of coffee at our home. We had common interests in classification, indexing, thesaurus, and other knowledge organization tools. After a long gap of many years we met in Delhi at an IGNOU (Indira Gandhi National Open University) meeting on formulating a syllabus and preparation of course materials for the proposed Masters course in information studies. He mentioned about his enjoying the multimedia CD on Saint Tyagaraja. Thus, for more than one reason, I thought it appropriate to contribute a paper about the preparation of the CD to the festschrift.

1 INTRODUCTION

Saint Tyagaraja, an outstanding exponent of classical Carnatic Music, exploring new grounds, was a great trend setter. In a paper entitled *Text mining and data mining in knowledge organization and discovery* Haravu and Neelameghan (2003) briefly describe the multimedia CD on the compositions of Saint Tyagaraja, as an example in preparing knowledge products. In another paper, Neelameghan and Hemalata Iyer (2002) describe the contents of and facilities provided for using, the Tyagaraja CD and consider it as an example of "information presentation, organization, and indexing for communication across cultures and faiths".

This paper briefly describes the design and development and the contents and components of the multimedia CD, highlighting its conceptual framework and salient features, exemplifying a new approach to knowledge organization and presentation. A brief introduction to Carnatic music and life-sketch of Saint Tyagaraja are given to facilitate better understanding of the CD contents in the proper context.

2 MUSIC APPRECIATION AND ENJOYMENT

Music is an abstract fine art and a performing art. Music performance, in fact, gives a form and content to the subject in a more concrete manner which can be enjoyed by even lay persons irrespective of any music system. However, a knowledge of the attributes of the music system would enable a listener to understand its subtleties, appreciate and enjoy the nuances of the fine art in full measure. A learner, a connoisseur, a teacher, a practitioner, a critic or a scholar will all benefit from a presentation of the music content and its rendering, if the audio, visual and text matter are presented in tandem. Multimedia technology provides a unique opportunity to achieve this integration. A brief account of the salient features of Carnatic music follows.

3 CLASSICAL CARNATIC MUSIC

Classical Carnatic music is a system of music practiced in the southern parts of India. It has a well founded theoretical base, highly scientific in its structure and ramifications.

Carnatic music has a hoary past. In the last two hundred years and more, it has acquired an amplitude and depth, both in theory and practice, that this period is considered as its period of renaissance.

The *Raga system* (melodic matrices or patterns) of Carnatic music is its main feature and its very foundation. Every *raga* is a distinct music entity by itself and possesses well-defined characteristics. A classification system of 72 parent *ragas (Melakarta* system) was designed and developed in the 18th century, through a process of permutation and combination of the twelve notes of the octave. This *Melakarta* system, constituting the basis of Carnatic music, affords almost limitless avenues for *raga* development. From the parent scale (*Janaka Ragas*) any number of derivative *ragas* (*Janya Ragas*) can be formulated. Every *raga* has a separate aesthetic form and can be easily recognized by a trained ear. Singing and performing *raga* exposition (*raga alapana),* demands a very high degree of musical training, culture and creativity.

Musical_compositions are concrete forms of the abstract *raga* which manifest the various facets of the *raga*. In other words, while the beauty underlying a *raga* is very subtle and delicate to grasp its full aesthetic value, musical compositions present a more concrete form of the *raga*, making it easier to understand its scope and dimensions.

The rhythmic pattern (*Tala*) is another important feature of the classical Carnatic music system. Its function in musical compositions is to maintain the balance of their music. It is another aspect of performing music that gives immense enjoyment to a listener.

There are different types of compositions, of which the *kriti* is the most appealing with lofty contents of lyrics and music. The *kriti* is the most highly evolved amongst art musical forms. It is also the more important of the melodic group of compositions. The elastic nature of this form, provides ample scope for a composer for displaying his/her creative capacity. There is considerable freedom for a composer to choose the *raga*, the rhythm (*tala*), gait, tempo, style and theme for his/her composition.

Kirtana is another form of composition, mostly devotional lyrics, singing/ praising the glory of the Lord Supreme.

In *kritis*, the lyrical content is set to music. The choice of the *raga*, *tala*, etc. has to .express the contents of the composition in such a way that the music and the lyrics blend harmoniously. This demands a high level of expertise, both in creation of lyrics and setting it to music. Such a musician-cum-composers is called a *Vak-geyakars* , *Vak* meaning literary text and *Geya* musical setting. The equipment and qualities set for this genre of composers are far superior than those who write only the lyrics or those that merely set music to already written lyrical text.. Saint Tyagaraja was one of the greatest of *Vakgeyakaras*.

4 SAINT TYAGARAJA (1767-1846)

Tyagaraja was born in Tiruvarur, a small township in Tanjore District in Tamil Nadu, South India. His forefathers had migrated to Tamil Nadu after the fall of the Vijayanagar Empire. Tyagaraja's father later shifted to Tiruvaiyaru, a village nearer to the Royal Patrons in Tanjore. Tyagaraja lived in this village till his death.

As a child Tyagaraja was precocious and learnt all that is to be learnt in Carnatic music at a very early age. He learnt Telugu (his mother tongue) and Sanskrit very well, in which he became a scholar. He also studied the Ramayana and the Mahabharata, the *puranas* and scriptural literature. Devotion to Sri Rama was another trait he inherited from his family surroundings. With this initiation in his early years, he became an ardent devotee of Sri Rama which intensified his faith as he grew. All his compositions, *Kritis* and *Kirtanas* were primarily of the devotional mode; the *kriti* was taking the art forms of music with a few lines of lyrics while the *kirtanas* were more elaborate in lyrical content.

Tyagaraja never courted wealth using his expertise in music and music composition. He deliberately chose a path of simple living and high thinking. *Nadopasana* (spiritual elevation through music) was his life's mission.

Tyagaraja adopted the 72 *Melakarta* scheme for his compositions. He followed the three part *kriti* pattern namely., *Pallavi*, *Anupallavi* and *Charanam* which was established prior to Tyagaraja, for setting his lyrics. The *Kriti* or *Kirtana* opens with a *pallavi* with an idea, the *anupallavi* and *charanam(s)*, develops this opening idea and elaborates them further with other contributory ideas, similes, illustrations and incidents that demonstrate or justify the leading idea of the song.

Tyagaraja, it is said, composed a few thousands of *kritis* and *kirtanas*, of which only about 700 are currently available. While devotion was the core theme of his creations, Tyagaraja has handled a variety of subjects in his compositions which include graphic descriptions of the Supreme Lord, musicology, poetic imagery, apt similes and metaphors, illustrations and analogies, humour and satire, vagaries of human behaviour, worldly sayings and wise observations on human life, and paths to spiritual development.

Tyagaraja's lyrics and music are equally of the highest quality. *Kritis* get enriched by musical elaborations, known as *sangatis* an integral and indispensable part of a composition.. These are variations on a musical theme, developed step by step. Each one of them is an evolution from the preceding one and makes an improvement upon it. These variations are introduced either for emphasizing certain delicate and latent shades in the meaning of the lyrics or for bringing out the colourful and varied aspects of the *raga bhava*. Tyagaraja was the innovator of the concept of *sangati*.

The 700 compositions of Tyagaraja include the art forms, *Utsava Sampradaya Kirtanas* (traditional ritual worship), *Divyanama Sangkirtanas* (sacred names of the Lord), and two dance dramas, 'Prahlada Bhakti Vijayam' and 'Nauka Chaaraitram'.

All these compositions are either in Telugu or Sanskrit.

5 CONCEPTUAL FRAMEWORK OF THE TYAGARAJA CD

5.1 Overview

In planning the database for the Tyagaraja multimedia CD, the primary objective was to integrate voice, text and image. It means that a user while listening to the *Kriti* being sung, should have the option to see on the computer screen, the image indicating the theme of the *kriti*, the text of the *kriti*, or any one of the following elements of the *kriti*, namely, Word by Word Meaning, Summary, Notes, Special Commentary. The product should be a unique one that would help each of the targeted audiences.

Students can use the CD as a learning kit, carefully follow the text while learning to sing any *kriti*, try to understand its summary meaning, or get an insight into the significant aspects of the lyrics, and how the raga and tala are blending with the *kriti*, as described in the Special commentary, or see the Notes section explaining some of the special aspects of the lyrics, etc. These facilities are generally not available to a student while learning, as most of the printed materials, audio cassettes, CDs, etc. deal with only one aspect of the *kriti*.

Similarly a teacher can use this CD as a teaching aid, highlighting different aspects of a *kriti*, its music, lyrics, the significance in terms of the music, *raga*, the tempo and others.

A practicing musician, a music critic, a scholar or a lay listener interested in the *kritis* of Tyagaraja should find this CD a useful reference source on many aspects of the *kritis* in one source.

Keeping this primary objective in view, in selecting the compositions of 108, out of the 700 compositions available, certain criteria were adopted to give a fair representation to all the different types of compositions. The *kritis* (which includes the kirtanas) represent

Different themes (e.g. musical aspects, divine form devotion, passionate appeals, etc.)
Art models (e.g. the Kriti title: *Chakkani Rajamargamu*)
Divyanama and Utsava Sampradaya Kirtanas
Kritis from Tyagaraja's Dance Drama *Prahlada Bhakti Vijayam*
Different *ragas* (79 *ragas* are represented)
Variety of *Kriti* structures and t*ala*
Anecdotes, personal references in the *kritis*
Compositions alluding to epics and *puranas* in the *kritis*
Popular *kritis*

The compositions were sung by well known musicians, (both female and male artists, a few front-rank artists, young and upcoming artists and a veteran, a Sangita Kalanidhi awardee, the highest award in classical Carnatic music), without any accompaniments such as the violin or the *mridangam*. The primary purpose is to draw the full attention of the listener to lyrics and the *raga bhava* of the *kritis* which are usually lost when sung with accompaniments. The CD has the provision to let users listen to *kritis* with or without the Special commentaries. the narrations of which were also recorded.

The text matter comprises of text of *kritis*, in Telugu language and script and also the text, transliterated into Tamil, Devanagari and Roman scripts. Telugu words, transliterated into Roman script with meanings in English, summary meaning of each composition, notes indicating, for example the context in which the *kriti* was composed, any allusion to the epics or *puranas* etc., and Special commentary highlighting the lyrics and the musical aspects which include

Their musical subtleties

Their nuances in structure and rhythm

The emotions and feelings that underlie the compositions

Suggestions regarding place and time for *kriti* in a concert

Suggestions for *neraval* and *swaraprastharas*, constituting the *manodharma sangita* part of a concert

The pictures representing the themes of the compositions, were specially drawn by a musician-cum-artist. Some temple icons of the deities are also presented to indicate the deity on whom the song was composed.

The language of the CD is in English to cater to a wider audience, nationally and internationally.

A summary of the features of the CD are given in section 5.1.

5.2 Components and Facilities for Use

The multimedia CD presents a unique portrayal of selected 108 Tyagaraja devotional songs *(kritis*). It attempts to especially foster understanding and appreciation of the *kritis* across linguistic borders within India. In addition, the presentation also promotes interest in Carnatic music for international audiences. The CD has several features that foster communication across linguistic boundaries in India and to some extent even internationally.

The 108 kritis included in the product represent different themes, *ragas*, *talas* and art models used by Tyagaraja. Instrumental rendering of 35 kritis: on veena, violin and flute separately 10 or 12 by each instrument, is included to augment the entertainment value of the CD. Users may listen to vocal or instrumental music selectively, in a continuous mode, choosing their favourites.

The opening screen has icons for:

Help
Searching database by title, theme, *ragam*
talam (beat), and other fields
Browse *kritis* database
Record by record
See lyrical content
See summary
See commentary
See text of *kritis*
Index to kritis
See list of titles
Sort index by *Raga*
Sort index by *Tala*
Select kriti *to view*
Listen to music
Listen to commentary
Index to deities
See *kritis* on deities
Select *kriti* to view
Open Internet browser
Browse articles
Link to websites
Print text of *kritis*
Index to all lyrical content word
Or index to common errors in articulation of
content words
See meaning of words
Select *kriti* by content word
Slide show on quantitative analysis
See distribution of *kritis* by *ragas*
and other tables
Slide show on Tyagaraja
Early life
Adult life and middle life
Works
Tyagaraja literature
Premonition and final end
Tyagaraja Aradhana festivals

The music menu options include:

Select and play *kriti* (vocal)
Select and play *kriti* (instrumental)
Play title music
Stop title music
Continuous play
Favourites

Database Searching: The databases can be searched by title, theme, *raga, tala* and other fields, such as, keyword, deity, vocalist and lyrical content. Every composition is provided with a special commentary, lyrical text, summary, notes, and the text in four languages / script: English / Roman (default), and the Indian languages, Telugu, Tamil, and Devanagiri. Further help is provided through a linked glossary accessible from the summary, lyrical content special commentary, and notes sections of the CD.

The Lyrical Content section shows a table of all Telugu lyrical content words/phrases and their meanings in English

The Summary section provides a gist of the contents. Since many of Tygaraja's compositions draw from the events in the Indian epic, Ramayana, and other Hindu scriptures, the less known stories alluded to, are presented in detail. This is particularly helpful to those unfamiliar with Indian culture, and also for Indians and people of Indian origin who may wish to gain more knowledge of the cultural heritage conveyed through the epics and scriptures.

The Index to Common Errors in Rendering of Content Words: This section presents an alphabetical listing of words / phrases from Telugu lyrics along with its meaning in English. It provides guidance on where the word should be split and how it should be pronounced while the song is musically rendered. A list of such common errors along with how it aught to be sung is also demonstrated. (For an example see Note 2)

Commentary: This section allows users to view the text in four languages while music/commentary is played or heard.

Special commentary: presents information that fosters music appreciation, such as, the impact of raga, basic music technicalities etc. Users can choose to play just the music, or music with commentary, or just plain commentary. For example, search by the theme 'gratitude' retrieves the kriti 'Dasarathe ni momu.' The special commentary provides insight into the deployment of the raga, the use of swaras and their effect, thereby promoting music appreciation. Though the technical terminology used in the commentary may prove a barrier to lay-users in music, the glossary of terms can be accessed for meaning of these terms.

Specially commissioned articles in HTML format on the Uniqueness of Tyagaraja, the Ghana Raga Pancharatnas, and Disciples of Tyagaraja. The articles contain links to other web pages and/or music clips on web sites. A selected index to web sites on Carnatic and Tyagaraja is included.

The Index to Kritis allows users to sort the database by the *kriti* title, *raga* and *tala*. Thus for instance, by selecting a particular *raga*, 'Todi,' all the kritis set to this raga can be retrieved.

Quantitative Analysis of Saint Tyagaraja's Compositions: A slide show presents a quantitative analysis of his 688 compositions. The distribution of kritis by melakarta ragas indicates that out of the 72 *Melakarta ragas*, Tyagaraja used 51 ragas. This is further analyzed into *melaragas* with *janya*, *melaragas* without *janya*, and *janyas* only. The distribution of the *kritis* based on several criteria, such as, by the raga groups, by *shuddhamadyamam* and *prtimadhyamam swaras*, etc. is presented in the slide show. This feature of the CD is especially of interest to Carnatic music scholars.

Life-sketch::The biographical sketch of the saint is provided by means of a Power-Point presentation titled 'Saint Tyagaraja's life and works'.with the following features - Early Life, Adult and Middle Age Life, and Works.

The feature, Tyagaraja on the Internet provides links to specially commissioned articles, text of kritis, index to web sites and select bibliography on Tyagaraja. These are educative to both national and international audiences.

The Annual Thiruvaiyaru Aradhana Festival. This is an annual feature of the past several decades, when musicians of all categories vocalists, instrumentalists, young and old, men and women, congregate to pay homage to the Saint Composer, singing in chorus the *Pancha Ratna Kritis* of Tyagaraja (Five gems of Tyagaraja's compositions).

6 DEMOS AND FEEDBACK

At various stages of the development of the CD, there were consultations with experts in Carnatic music and Tyagaraja specialists, to enlist their views and getting proper feedback. While the work was in progress, demonstrations were organized and conducted to find the reactions of various groups of persons including practicing musicians, music scholars, students and teachers, connoisseurs and lay persons. The feedback was encouraging and modifications suggested for improving the quality of the CD were implemented. The demos held: four at Hyderabad, two at Chennai and one at Bangalore.

7 THE PROCESS

The CD product is a 3-year effort of three specialists, one a musicologist-musician-critic-writer, another a musicologist-vanika-information specialist, the third an information management specialist-IT-software specialist.

Musicians were specially commissioned for this CD and their singing the kritis were recorded at various stages. during the progress of the work. The narration of the commentaries by the team members, were also recorded at different stages.

The preparation of the kriti texts in different scripts, the summary meaning, the Notes and the Special commentary, etc. required considerable research and study. The special commentary for each kriti is an innovative contribution.

The pictures were also specially drawn for this CD. by expert artists.

The additional features of the CD were incorporated to make the CD more useful.

To integrate all these involved considerable experimentation. Writing the software, inputting all the data into the system and creating the multimedia database were indeed challenging.

The product is a unique one in many ways. Several features of the *kritis* of Tyagaraja have been strung together that give full scope for understanding, appreciating and enjoying his *kritis* by listeners.

8 SUMMARY AND CONCLUSION

Summing up, the features of the Multimedia CD:

- Kritis included in the product represent different themes, art models, *ragas*, *talas*, etc. used by Tyagaraja;
- Integrates the music, meanings, summaries, and text of the *kritis* with special commentaries and images;
- The *kritis* have been rendered specially for the product by well known vocalists;
- Renderings of 35 kritis on the veena, violin and flute included;
- A database of kritis that can be browsed record by record;
- The database can be searched by several keys;
- Index to *kritis* that can be sorted by title, raga and tala;
- Index to deities;
- Specially commissioned articles in HTML format providing also links to other web-based resources on Carnatic music and Tyagaraja;
- Index to lyrical contents i.e. Telugu words or phrases in each of the 108 *kritis* with their meanings in English;
- Index to common errors in rendering lyrical content with suggested rendering of such words and phrases;
- Slide shows on Tyagaraja life and Works;
- Slide show on quantitative analysis of Tyagaraja's compositions; and
- Facility for continuous play of vocal and instrumental renderings.

The experience gained in planning and producing the multimedia CD on Saint Tyagaraja has resulted in a well documented methodology for such productions.

It is possible to provide such a product for all the compositions of Tyagaraja and two other members of the Great Musical Trinity, Muthuswamy Dikshitar and Shyama Sastri or even extend it other Vakgeyakaras of later periods. These constitute excellent material for very many research studies.

REFERENCES

1. Haravu, L J and A. Neelameghan. (2003). Text Mining and Data Mining in Knowledge Organization and Discovery: the Making of Knowledge- based Products. *Cataloging & Classification Quarterly*. Vol. 37(1/2); p. 113-130.

2. Neelameghan, A. and Hemalata Iyer. (2002). Some patterns of information presentation, organization, and indexing for communication across cultures and faiths. *7th ISKO International Conference,* Challenges in Knowledge Representation and Organization for the 21st Century: Integration of Knowledge Across Boundaries Grenada Spain, 10-13 July, 2002; p. 539-545.

THE NATIONAL TUBERCULOSIS INSTITUTE, BANGALORE: RECENT DEVELOPMENTS IN LIBRARY AND INFORMATION SERVICES

Sudha S. Murthy

Briefly describes the information products and services, the related databases, development of digital library and web-resources and web-based services, vocabulary control tools, networking, and other projects of the Library of the National Tuberculosis Institute (NTI), Bangalore. Acknowledges the involvement of and advice and assistance provided by Prof. A. Neelameghan to these programmes and projects.

1 INTRODUCTION

My association with Dr S. R. Ranganathan, father of library movement in India, and Prof. A. Neelameghan (Prof. AN) dates back to 1966, when I was a student at the Documentation Research and Training Centre (DRTC), Bangalore. I have been a silent admirer of both of them, their scholarly work and as teachers and guides. I also had the good fortune of learning and receiving advice from Dr. M.A. Gopinath, Dr. S. Seetharama and Dr. G. Bhattacharyya of DRTC. In my professional work their guidance and advice from time to time enabled me to transform the Library of the National Tuberculosis Institute (NTI), Bangalore, into an information resource centre, applying information and communication technologies to generate and provide access to various information products and services to satisfy the information needs of users both within the Institute as well as outside it, for example the field workers, other institutions and the public. By way of this essay I express my indebtedness to these scholars and teachers not only for what knowledge I gained from their teaching but also for their continued advice and assistance. I feel honoured to record my reminiscences, and especially the advice and guidance received from Prof. AN in my professional work and career.

2 INTRODUCTION OF NEW SERVICES

The NTI is a premier institution set up by the Government of India, Ministry of Health and Family Welfare to conduct community wide applied research and development of Nationally applicable Control Program for the Prevention and Control of Tuberculosis (TB). I joined the NTI in September 1967, after completing my professional studies, and I could count on the DRTC for advise and support in my work, putting into practice what I had learnt. Soon after my joining NTI, a current awareness service - *Periodical Abstracts Bulletin* - was introduced. So also user education in the form of orientation of new entrants to the training courses. These professionals – researchers and field workers - with different academic background come from different work centres. For them a specially designed list of suggested readings and a *Selective Dissemination of Information Service* was started. Bibliographies were compiled on demand and in anticipation on the multidisciplinary aspects of community-wide research, prevention and control of TB. Today all these together constitute the database of information sources for responding to users' queries.

3 COMPUTER APPLICATIONS

3.1 Use of MEDLINE

Guidance was sought for searching the MEDLINE service of the National Library of Medicine, Bethesda, MD. USA when it was first brought to India in 1976. In 1993, the Library at NTI, Bangalore, was one of the first in the country to apply computers for information storage and retrieval. With DRTC's advice on system configurations and technical specifications, proposals were drawn up for procuring hardware and software. Even to this day the systems and software procured then provide good support.

3.2 Creation of Databases

Soon after installation of the equipment, I was deputed to attend a 6-week course on computer applications in Library and Information Science at DRTC. In 1993, a collaborative project was proposed by the Foundation for Research in Community Health, Bombay, in collaboration with the NTI, Bangalore, for identifying the resources in and to prepare a document on the "Sociological aspects of Tuberculosis". This collaborative project involved the selection, collation and compilation of source materials dispersed and located in many government, and non-government / private, academic and research organizations locally, nationally and internationally. NTI was to create a database of all these resources and the Library had UNESCO's CDS/ISIS database application software. Prof. AN assisted in creating a structured database using Common Communication Format (CCF) and controlled vocabulary. The database had approximately 300 validated records of extended abstracts. The thesaurus was specially developed on the sociological aspects of TB. The online retrieval facility and the printed document have been extensively used. The database for the document 'Sociological Aspects of Tuberculosis', published by the NTI in 2002, was developed using WINISIS (CDS/ISIS for Windows), which was used also for hosting it on the intranet and the Internet.

4 HEALTH INTERNETWORK (HIN) INDIA - TB - PILOT PROJECT - WHO PROJECT

The NTI, Bangalore was identified as the Nodal Centre for the Health InterNetwork (HIN) India - TB - Pilot Project, a public-private initiative launched by Dr Kofi Annan, the UN Secretary-General, to bridge the digital divide in health (Health InterNetwork India Project .. 2003-2004; Ravishankar, 2003; Chandrasekharan, 2003). This lead given by the WHO (World Health Organization, 2001) brings together international agencies, governments and NGOs, and country partners under the principle of ensuring *equitable access to health information.* The focus of HIN is on improving the information environment of health personnel - professionals, researchers and scientists, and policy makers. The objective is to bridge the digital divide between the developing and developed countries and enable global access and use of health data. The NTI, through the WHO, sought and secured the technical consultancy of Prof. AN for the project. Prof. AN's guidance in framing the academic profiles of the professional candidates for the project work and in their selection was appreciated by NTI and WHO. The HIN Project was initiated in 2002. Given below are some of his specific contributions.

4.1 Initiation of the Project

UNESCO's open source software WINISIS available free of cost to non-profit organizations in Member States was recommended and used in the project for designing the database structure, content development and information retrieval

4.1.1 Union Catalogue of Core Periodicals in TB and its hosting on NTI website

Prof AN advised on the selection of fields for the database of Union Catalogue of Core periodicals in TB (UCCTB) from the National Union Catalogue of Scientific Serials in India (NUCSSI) developed by the Indian National Scientific Documentation Centre (INSDOC), New Delhi, porting of data of details of journals from the JNL database (in FoxPro) to the WINISIS database (TBSER) using conversion FST and Ref and Refl functions for navigation within and across databases.

4.1.2 Analysis of NUCSSI

The NUCSSI has 59 FoxPro databases. Six related databases were identified for extracting data and importing into UCCTB.

1. **HD.dbf** : Database of Libraries (425 records);
2. **TF.dbf** : Database of Journal Titles (38063 records);
3. **TFC.dbf** : Database of Current Titles (17989 records);
4. **HF.dbf** : Database of Holdings (2,22,162) records);
5. **SKW.dbf** : Database of Subject of the Journal (# of records : 1398); and
6. **PD.dbf** : Database of Country of origin of the Journal (114 records).

4.1.3 Conversion of Data

The data in NUCSSI, as mentioned above, is distributed in six databases. In this format data could not be conveniently ported on to the Web. Therefore an intermediate and integrated database was prepared using WINISIS for launching on the Internet. The steps to convert data from NUCSSI to WINISIS database were:

* Copying of NUCSSI databases into a separate directory;
* Creation of six databases with the corresponding data structure in WINISIS;
* Changing the Field Selection Table (FST) file appropriately in WINISIS; and
* Using DB3ISO Pascal program for converting the FoxPro databases into ISO 2709 files for importing into the WINISIS databases.

Finally, it was decided to have three databases for the UCCTB, viz., TBPERS (holding the details of TB core periodicals), LIBCOD (for collecting details of host libraries in India) and UNCAT (giving details of holdings of particular journal(s) in a library). A template worksheet was created for data entry for each of the databases.

The fields in the databases are as follows.

LIBCOD Database

Tag	Field Name	Tag	Field Name	Tag	Field Name
1	Title_Code	1	Library_Code	1	Title_Code
2	Serial_Title	2	Institution	2	Library_Code
3	Title_History	3	Address	3	Holdings
4	Publisher	4	Tel_Fax_Gram		
5	Place_of_Pub	5	Last_Updated		
6	Country_of_Pub	6	State		
7	Starting_Year				
8	ISSN				
9	Periodicity				
10	Website/ E-mail				
11	Subject				

Initially, TBPERS database had only five fields Title_Code, Serial_Title, Place_of_Publication, and Country_of_Publication. The new fields Title History, Publisher, Starting_Year, ISSN, Periodicity, Website, and Keywords were introduced and necessary changes made to accommodate these fields in the data entry worksheet, indexing parameters, etc. All records (73) of TBPERS database were checked manually and data for the newly introduced fields were taken from different sources such as:

- Ulrich's International Periodicals Directory;
- NLM Classification; and
- Journals available in NTI library.

Necessary cross-references from previous titles of periodicals, where necessary and applicable, are given. Downloaded holdings data corresponding to the title codes of the core periodicals (1518 records) and updated UNCAT database. NTI's data is updated periodically.

Discussion on Delphi ISIS to host information on web: Instructions for user-friendly search strategies were developed. Finally, the Union Catalogue of Core periodicals was hosted successfully on the NTI website with assistance from the National Informatics Centre (NIC), Bangalore. Some screenshots are given in the annexure.

4.2 Common Webportal for National Health Information Collaboration (NHIC)

4.2.1 Need Assessment Survey

The Foundation for Research in Health Systems, Bangalore (2002) carried out the Information Needs assessment survey at the 2 project sites - rural Bangalore in Karnataka and Deogarh district in Orissa. The survey was an attempt to elicit the information requirements of different health care professionals, policy makers, and academics with different professional backgrounds working at various workstations and who were involved with the TB and Tobacco control programmes. In addition it attempted to assess the e-readiness of the pilot sites in terms of availability of hardware, electricity, telephone, skills of the users at the pilot sites, etc. The information obtained from the survey provided the base for content development, which is the corner stone of the HIN project for bridging the digital divide in health information and the gaps between health research policy and practice. .

4.2.1 Templates of NHIC Database

The creation of this web portal was a component of the HIN project. Advice was sought on the templates for various types of data entry developed by M/s Indegene systems, Bangalore, and transmitted the suggestions and guidelines to the developers of NHIC.

4.2.2 Searchable and Interoperable Database for Full Text Articles

A detailed database using metadata techniques with local variations was developed for better information organization and management. In this each article has search facilities and link for retrieval of full text. A screenshot of the Web portal is given in the Annexure.

4.3 Thesaurus on TB

Prof. AN briefed on the importance of using a vocabulary control tool, such as a thesaurus and the various inputs required, the principles and procedures to be followed and on terminological sources. The available specialized thesauri and terminologies, such as, BIOTHES (an online thesaurus of biological terms, developed using WINISIS), MeSH, International vocabulary for Diseases and Surgery, and WordNet were examined and. the practical aspects of constructing the thesaurus were demonstrated. A researcher in TB was associated in the thesaurus project as a Medical Consultant. During the period detailed discussions were held with the Medical Consultant on appropriate terminology to be used especially for Non-Medical Subject Headings (Non–MeSH terms). The importance of local concepts and related terms were highlighted. Using the guidelines the Medical Consultant selected local Non-MeSH, providing scope notes, standardizing the vocabulary and structured the list similar to the MeSH list. The rules to be followed in assigning Subject descriptors while indexing documents, the advantages of applying facet analysis, identifying facet relations and structuring of subjects accordingly in formulating index terms and search expressions for searching and retrieval from databases were briefed. The following is a sample list of Non-MeSH terms with scope notes:

Descriptor: Short course chemotherapy

Scope note: Standard combination of anti-TB drugs containing isoniazid and Rifampicin given for a duration of not less than six months.

Descriptor: State TB centre

Scope note: Responsible for running TB control program in the state in addition to its own case finding, treatment and training activities.

Descriptor: State TB officer

Scope note: Medical officer from Government who is in charge of TB control activities in the entire state

Descriptor Supervised treatment

Scope note Anti TB medicine doses administered to a patient under the supervision of a health worker or a designated person.

Descriptor Suspect case

Scope note A patient with tuberculosis diagnosed by X-ray examination and not confirmed bacteriologically by sputum examination

Descriptor Symptom screening

Scope note Screening of persons with symptoms of cough for more than three weeks for evidence of tuberculosis

Descriptor Symptomatics

Scope note Persons with symptoms suggestive of tuberculosis, e.g. cough for more than three weeks duration

4.4 Proposed Tree Structure for the non-MeSH Terms within the MeSH tree

All MeSH Categories
Biological Sciences Category
Environment and Public Health
Public Health
Public Health Practice
Communicable Disease Control
TB control Programme
National TB control Programme
National Tuberculosis Institute
Tuberculosis Association of India
District TB Programme
District TB centre
State TB centre
PHIs
Primary Health Centre
Chest symptomatics
Case finding
Case holding
Defaulter
Case fatality
Case, index
All MeSH Categories
Analytical, Diagnostic and Therapeutic Techniques and Equipment Category
Investigative Techniques
Epidemiologic Methods
Tuberculosis
Tuberculin test

Annual risk of infection
All MeSH Categories
Analytical, Diagnostic and Therapeutic Techniques and Equipment Category
Therapeutics
Chemotherapy, tuberculosis
Drug regimen
Compliance
Defaulter
Case holding

5 DIGITIZATION

Prof. A.N. advised on prioritization and selection of documents for digitization, and important issues to be taken into account in digitizing documents, especially full texts. These issues included intellectual property right and copyright issues and the need to obtain prior permission from the copyright holders.

5.1 Documents on CD for TB Programme Workers

Relevant documents on Control Programme and Health Education segregated on the basis of activity, knowledge, skills and professional background of the medical and paramedical programme workers at the District and Primary Health Centre level, were made available on 2 CDs, which were easy to use and had auto run facility. These documents were such that they could be used as resource documents in:

* Day to day functioning;
* Health education;
* CME programmes;
* Making programme workers computer savvy with minimum effort;
* Printing of the documents for mass distribution; and
* Preparation of summaries in local languages.

6 DIGITAL LIBRARY

The developments mentioned in the preceding sections constituted the initial steps toward building up a digital library. Prof AN assisted in monitoring the development of the digital library at NTI, which included guidance on category of users, formats for data entry, user-friendly outputs and search parameters.

HIN Awareness Meets were important events when NTI Library staff met face to face and discussed with information users, faculty members and researchers, NTI management, representatives of other TB institute libraries participating in the network, experts / consultants, vendors, etc. Prof. AN and other experts explained the benefits that could be derived from the HIN e.g. by researchers and field workers on TB, leading research institutions and making available the national data on TB to the periphery as well as to the global community. His participation in the national level workshop of resource institutions for content development held at NTI, Bangalore on 14th Nov 2002 provided technical guidance, among other things, on various copyright issues in producing the published literature on electronic media.

Prof. AN's basic guidelines to the forum during discussions on the existing listservs available at IISc, Bangalore and administrative rules and regulations to be followed has benefited the NTI in preparing the initiative on discussion groups. Constructive suggestions on Journal Custom Content for Consortia (JCCC) in respect of content segregation and subject classification as also useful and creative inputs that could go into on-line publishing and its importance on free access -- "Any time, anywhere and any place" were received. A more detailed account of our experience in digitization appears in another publication (Murthy, 2004). The database of publications of NTI has been ported on to the Internet and is also accessible on the intranet of NTI.

For the future, Prof. AN has suggested several other products and services to constitute a wider knowledge base including databases of profiles of Experts,

Institutions, Ongoing Research in TB and multimedia information resources for use in the field.

7 CONCLUDING REMARKS

In this brief essay I have outlined the various information activities, projects, products and services, digitization and networking at the NTI, Bangalore. I wish to conclude that the involvement of and encouragement received from Prof. AN in most of these does not end with this script. It is seamless. He is a true "Karmayogi " doing and assisting in, the work he is called upon or takes up himself and does not expect anything from anybody in return but only the joy of being able to be of service to someone or some institution. He has an abundance of patience and is always ready to help any one from any corner of the world who seeks his help. His constant encouragement has enabled me disseminate the results of HIN project and the widespread popularity of the NTI library and Information services is a result of this. His interest and ability to absorb new developments in the field at his age is remarkable and is a good example to young information professionals to emulate.

DOCUMENTS USED

1. World Health Organization, Geneva. (2001). *UNF/UNFIP Project document; Health Internetwork (India* Pilot) 12th June.
2. Foundation for Research in Health System. (2002). Ahmedabad. Health information needs assessment: highlights of the survey of pilot sites Health InterNsetwork (HIN) Project.
3. Murthy, Sudha S. (2004). Digitization: a practical experience. *Papers. National Seminar on Digitization: Practical Experiences, Bangalore, 9-11 August 2004.* Paper G. Bangalore: Sarada Ranganathan Endowment for Library Science.
4. Health InterNetwork. (2003-2004). India Project Tuberculosis. *Report on technical consultancy.* Vol.1,2 & 3.
5. Ravishankar, Lakshmi: (2003) Health Inter Netowrk India Project on Tuberculosis: Work Report of Project Assistant: Sept 2002 – February 2003
6. Chandrasekharan, Sujatha (2003): Health InterNetowrk India Project Tuberculosis: Work report on Medical Consultancy – January 2003 to July 2003

ANNEXURE

Webshots

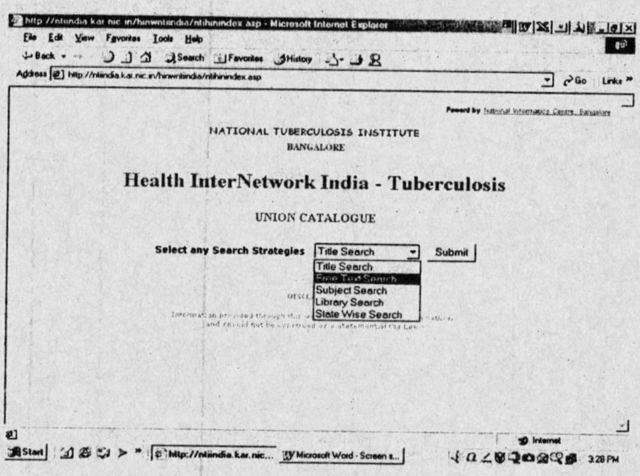

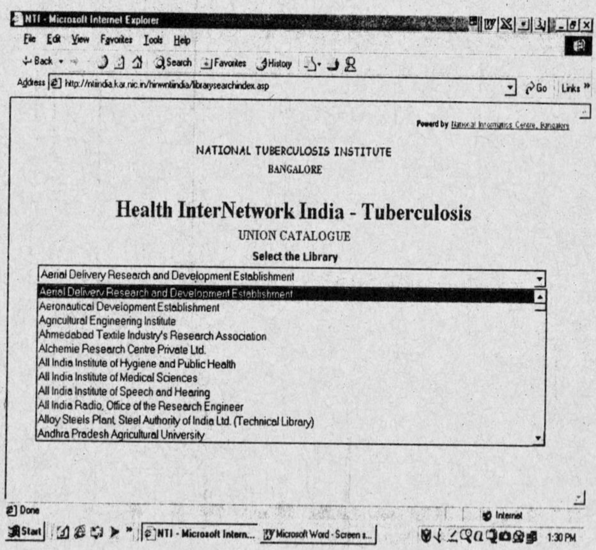

TITLE : AMERICAN REVIEW OF TUBERCULOSIS

Name of the Institution	Library Holdings		
	Subscription Period (+ indicates continued subscription)	Not Available Volumes	Incomplete Volumes
INSDOC, National Science Library	149-52, 1994-95		
Vallabhbhai Patel Chest Institute	149-163, 1994-2001+		

TITLE : AMERICAN REVIEW OF TUBERCULOSIS AND PULMONARY DISEASES

Name of the Institution	Library Holdings		
	Subscription Period (+ indicates continued subscription)	Not Available Volumes	Incomplete Volumes
INSDOC, National Science Library	149-52, 1994-95		
Vallabhbhai Patel Chest Institute	149-163, 1994-2001+		

TITLE : BRITISH JOURNAL OF TUBERCULOSIS

Name of the Institution	Library Holdings		
	Subscription Period (+ indicates continued subscription)	Not Available Volumes	Incomplete Volumes
Lady Hardinge Medical College and Smt. Sucheta Kripalani Hospital	1994+		
National Medical Library (DGHS)	83, 1989+		

Health InterNetwork India - Tuberculosis

UNION CATALOGUE

LIBRARY NAME : B.J. Medical College

Title Name	Library Holdings		
	Subscription Period (+ indicates continued subscription)	Not Available Volumes	Incomplete Volumes
ACTA CYTOLOGICA	34, 1990+		
ACTA NEUROLOGICA SCANDINAVICA	28-88, 1973-93	32-35,65-72,85-86	
AMERICAN JOURNAL OF EPIDEMIOLOGY	81, 1965+	102,108,120,124,126,129-30,135-36	
CHEST	39, 1961+	71,87,95-96	
CLINICS IN CHEST MEDICINE	5, 1984+	5-6,10-11,13	
JOURNAL OF CLINICAL GASTROENTEROLOGY	11-12, 1989-90		
JOURNAL OF CLINICAL MICROBIOLOGY	5, 1977+	7,29-30	

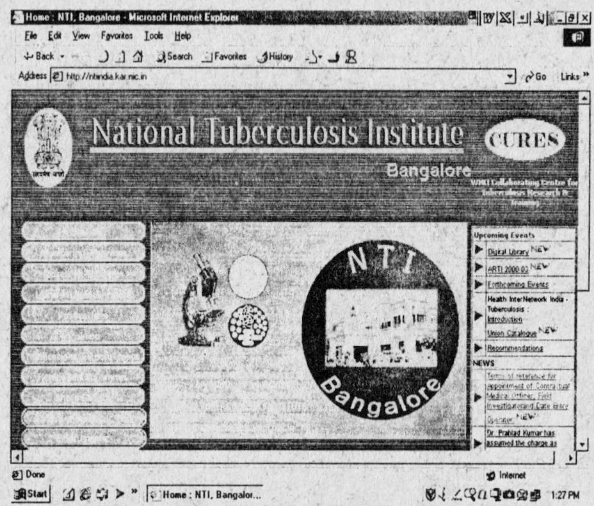
Home : NTI, Bangalore - Microsoft Internet Explorer
File Edit View Favorites Tools Help
Back Search Favorites History
Address http://ntiindia.kar.nic.in
Go Links
National Tuberculosis Institute
CURES
Bangalore
NTI
Bangalore
Upcoming Events
Digital Library NEW
ARTI 2000-02 NEW
Forthcoming Events
Health InterNetwork India - Tuberculosis : Introduction
Union Catalogue NEW
Recommendations
NEWS
Dr. Prahlad Kumar has assumed the charge as
Done
Internet
Start
Home : NTI, Bangalor...
1:27 PM

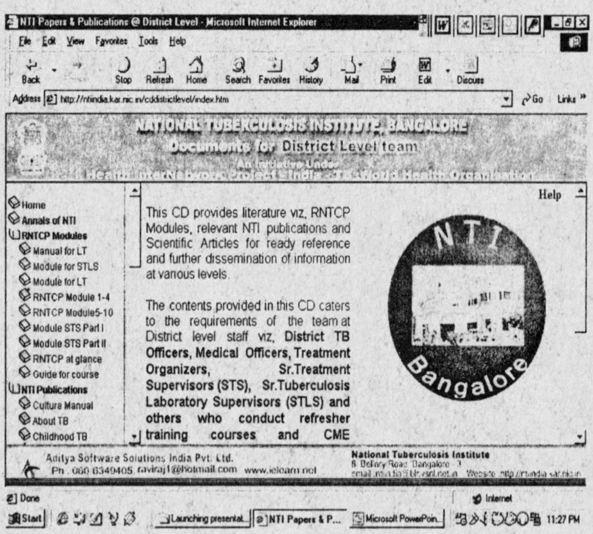
NTI Papers & Publications @ District Level - Microsoft Internet Explorer
File Edit View Favorites Tools Help
Back Stop Refresh Home Search Favorites History Mail Print Edit Discuss
Address http://ntiindia.kar.nic.in/cddistrictlevel/index.htm
Go Links
NATIONAL TUBERCULOSIS INSTITUTE, BANGALORE
Documents for District Level team
An Initiative Under
Home
Annals of NTI
RNTCP Modules
Manual for LT
Module for STLS
Module for LT
RNTCP Module 1-4
RNTCP Module5-10
Module STS Part I
Module STS Part II
RNTCP at glance
Guide for course
NTI Publications
Culture Manual
About TB
Childhood TB
Help
This CD provides literature viz, RNTCP Modules, relevant NTI publications and Scientific Articles for ready reference and further dissemination of information at various levels.
The contents provided in this CD caters to the requirements of the team at District level staff viz, District TB Officers, Medical Officers, Treatment Organizers, Sr.Treatment Supervisors (STS), Sr.Tuberculosis Laboratory Supervisors (STLS) and others who conduct refresher training courses and CME
NTI
Bangalore
Aditya Software Solutions India Pvt. Ltd.
National Tuberculosis Institute
Done
Internet
Start
Launching presental...
NTI Papers & P...
Microsoft PowerPoin...
11:27 PM

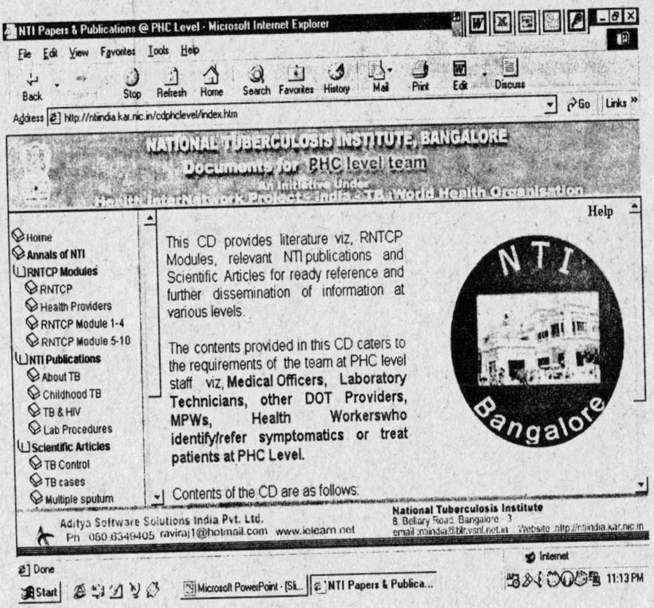
NTI Papers & Publications @ PHC Level - Microsoft Internet Explorer
File Edit View Favorites Tools Help
Back Stop Refresh Home Search Favorites History Mail Print Edit Discuss
Address http://ntiindia.kar.nic.in/cdphclevel/index.htm
Go Links
NATIONAL TUBERCULOSIS INSTITUTE, BANGALORE
Documents for PHC level team
An Initiative Under
Health InterNetwork Project - India - TB : World Health Organisation
Help
Home
Annals of NTI
RNTCP Modules
RNTCP
Health Providers
RNTCP Module 1-4
RNTCP Module 5-10
NTI Publications
About TB
Childhood TB
TB & HIV
Lab Procedures
Scientific Articles
TB Control
TB cases
Multiple sputum
This CD provides literature viz, RNTCP Modules, relevant NTI publications and Scientific Articles for ready reference and further dissemination of information at various levels.
The contents provided in this CD caters to the requirements of the team at PHC level staff viz, Medical Officers, Laboratory Technicians, other DOT Providers, MPWs, Health Workerswho identify/refer symptomatics or treat patients at PHC Level.
Contents of the CD are as follows:
NTI
Bangalore
Aditya Software Solutions India Pvt. Ltd.
Ph 080 6549405 raviraj1@hotmail.com www.ielearn.net
National Tuberculosis Institute
8, Bellary Road, Bangalore - 3
Done
Internet
Start
Microsoft PowerPoint - [Sl...
NTI Papers & Publica...
11:13 PM

SRI RAMAKRISHNA MATH LIBRARIES: COMPUTER APPLICATIONS

D.N. Nagaraja Rao

Briefly describes the developments in computer applications to create catalogues of information source materials in the Sri Ramakrishna Math (RM) Libraries in Bangalore and Mysore and the association of Prof. A. Neelameghan in these endeavours. Presents as a background the objectives of the RM and the means of dissemination of the Maths' philosophy, the related value systems, the studies and researches thereof, and the discourses of Sri Ramakrishna Paramahamsa, Swami Vivekananda, Holy Mother Sarada Devi and their followers, world-wide. In recent years RMs have taken advantage of developments in computer and communication technologies to create websites and CDs further facilitating the dissemination of information locally and globally. The creation of databases of RMs' library resources is perceived as an important information support to learning, studies, and research.

0 PREAMBLE

This essay briefly narrates the association of Prof. A. Neelameghan (AN) with the units of the Sri Ramakrishna Math (RM) in Bangalore and Mysore since 1993. However, AN tells me that he has been associated with RM even earlier. In 1951 during his short stint as librarian of the Vivekananda College in Mylapore, Chennai, he with some other teachers of the College used to visit, on some weekends, the RM in Mylapore to do 'social work'. As one residing in the student's hostel of the College, he was also responsible to wake up the students every morning by 5 am, assemble them in the hostel common hall for prayer and recitation of devotional *slokas*. Later in the early 1960s at the Documentation Research and Training Centre (DTRC), Bangalore, this practice was followed with the difference that the teachers and students resident on the DRTC campus would accompany Dr.S.R.Ranganathan (SRR) for morning walk for about an hour discussing library and information science topics!

AN also informs me that about 1965, the RM, Bangalore, sought SRR's guidance in the organization and cataloguing of its library materials, mostly dealing with religion, philosophy, and related subjects. SRR and AN visited the Math. Colon Classification (CC) has a substantial list of such classics arranged according to CC numbers. At SRR's request one of the swamijis prepared a classified list of additional source materials in Indian philosophy, etc. Subsequently, the swamiji presented the completed list and also gave a discourse on the subject at DRTC.

SRR, I understand, had prior acquaintance with Swami Ranganananda and other senior swamijis of the RM. When Swami Ranganananda visited the Bangalore Math, SRR invited him to present a lecture in DRTC. The public response to the lecture announcement was so overwhelming that the lecture had to be arranged in the more spacious Seva Sadan hall in Malleswaram, Bangalore.

1 THE RM AND DISSEMINATION OF VEDANTA PHILOSOPHY

1.1 The Beginnings of Ramakrishna Order

Moona (2004) describes the beginnings of the Ramakrishna Order and the Maths thus: "Inspired by Sri Ramakrishna Paramahamsa, the prophet of religious harmony and universalism, in 1886, the Ramakrishna Order was organized by his sanyasin disciples headed by Swami Vivekananda with two fold objectives:

Creation of a band of monks devoted to self-realization and spreading of the universal principles of Vedanta among people.

Carrying on, in co-operation with lay disciples and workers of service in various fields – spiritual, moral, cultural, educational and social – looking upon on all men and women, irrespective of caste or class, creed or colour, as veritable manifestations of the divine.

"For fulfilling these objectives, Swami Vivekananda strted in 1897 the Ramakrishna Mission Association and in 1899, the Ramakrishna Math at Belur, Kolkata. For the last one hundred years the Ramakrishna Mission through its hundreds of Centres in India and abroad has been engaged in the sacred task of showing the right path of life to the general public". Obviously, one of the objectives of the RM is to disseminate the essence of Vedanta and the related philosophy of life and value systems throughout the world, in all levels of society. This dissemination and exchange has largely been through:

* Discourses and lectures by the monks of the Maths and invited scholars, in several countries of the world;
* Papers in the Math's journals *Prabuddha Bharata* and *Vedanta Kesari* as well as in other national and international periodicals, and conference proceedings;
* Presentations at conferences, seminars and symposia;
* Books and cassette recordings;
* Discussions and exchanges during Retreats (Nagaraja Rao, 2004);
* Training courses for aspirants; and

The *Vidya Salas* (schools) associated with the Maths (Sri Ramakrishna Vidyashala, Mysore, 2004)

The Maths and other associated institutions maintain libraries generally used by the inmates as well as visiting scholars. Vrajaprana (1998) describes how, in recent years, developments in information and communication technologies (ICTs) have been taken advantage of by the RMs – to create websites on the Internet to disseminate Vedanta philosophy, information about the work of the Ramakrishna Order, and of the Maths, their publications, etc. The paper also lists URLs of several related websites.

Full texts of the writings, discourses, sayings, photo gallery, etc. of Swami Vivekananda, and Sri Ramakrishna Paramahamsa, and Holy Mother Sarada Devi are now available as searchable multimedia. CD. Voice recordings of such personalities as Swami Ranganananda are included in the CDs. (Swami Vivekananda: life, works and research…, 2001; Bhagavan Sri Ramakrishna and Holy Mother Sri Sarada Devi…, 2004). It is within this broader context of attempts to apply ICTs to create sources of information to support and facilitate more effectively and efficiently the study, learning, research and dissemination of information on RM's Vedanta philosophy that the application of computer to create online catalogues in some of the Math libraries briefly described here should be viewed.

2 EXPERIMENTS WITH CDS/ISIS AND WINISIS

In 1993, at the Sri Ramakrishna *Vidya Shala* (SRKVS) Library, I was attempting to create a resource database using CDS/ISIS software package which we had received along with the manual from NISSAT (DSIR), Delhi. The SRKVS management had made available a PC, and sanctioned two apprentices (under the Board of Apprentice Trainee scheme of the Government of India, Chennai) for data entry work (Nagaraja Rao, 2001). However, there were some problems in using the software. The information professionals I contacted in Mysore could not help me. About that time I learnt that AN was presenting lectures to library professionals attending a Refresher Course, at the Academic Staff College (ASC), Mysore University, Mysore. The message I received from CFTRI also provided some information about AN, and his special interest in CDS/ISIS. I contacted him in the University guesthouse and brought him to the Vidya Shala library in the evening after the lectures. He diagnosed the problem, suggested using the then current version of the software. AN installed the later version and the problems were solved. He also demonstrated the various search options and the use of Boolean operators. Also advised on certain points so as to avoid getting into trouble again.

Later in the evening we made a courtesy call on the Swamiji in-charge. AN expressed appreciation of the effort of the Vidya Shala to develop computerized catalogue and suggested utilizing CDS-ISIS for various other functions in the library to derive maximum benefit. On our way back to the guesthouse he advised me that continuous hands-on-experience will enable mastering the capabilities of the software, implying "practice makes a man perfect". Subsequently, there was no problem, and our efficiency gradually improved in retrieving information about our resources; circulation also increased, and the progress was very smooth – speedy, reliable, and flawless when compared to the earlier manual practices.

AN's first visit to Vidya Shala, and his help and advice greatly encouraged me to take up new database projects. RM's collaboration with AN in the computerization of the catalogues of information materials in the various Math libraries has led to productive results. Thereafter, I had calls from other libraries of RM centres for introducing computer application to create online catalogues of their collections. I did venture to install and create databases suitable to their local needs. In some Centres, we have switched over from DOS version to the Windows version of CDS/ISIS or WINISIS. We have created separate databases for circulation and serial control, in addition to our online library catalogue. In the Bangalore RM, there are separate databases for books, audiocassettes, and CDs. We have won the approbation of our regular members and devotees of the Math. Our volunteers have all been trained and given hands-on experiences. The Swamijis of the Math greatly appreciate AN's guidance and service on site and over the phone in the application of computers in the library. With the experience gained in the Mysore and Bangalore centres, I have been able to introduce CDS/ISIS applications in the libraries of RMs in Vishakapatnam, Delhi and Mumbai.

3 PLAN FOR INFORMATION RESOURCE CENTRE ON YOGA

During 1998 I had an assignment of reorganizing the library of the Vivekananda Kendra, located at Prashanti Kuteeram, about 35 kms from Bangalore city. The Director desired to create 'a Central Information Centre for Yoga and Allied Subjects' which should serve yoga centres, not only in Bangalore but also those in other places. A meeting was convened to draft a proposal for submission to the Government of India, for financial assistance. On my request AN and Dr. T.B. Rajashekhar, Associate Chairman, National Centre for Science Information (NCSI), Indian Institute of Science (IISc), Bangalore, visited the Kendra on 3 February 1999. After discussions a project proposal for setting up a "National Information Centre for Yoga and Allied Sciences (NICYAS)", at Vivekananda Kendra Yoga Research Foundation, Prashanti Kuteeram, Bangalore, was prepared and discussed with the Director of the Kendra. The 5-year plan document provided details of the types of information sources to be acquired, their organization, types of information services, networking with other centres in the subject, ICT equipment (hardware and software) and facilities and personnel required. The total cost of the proposed project was about Rs. 41.2 lakhs.

4 VIVEK DB TO OM DB

AN maintains a set of databases of extracts and quotations, life sketches, glossary etc. relating to the spiritual field. It may be interesting to know as to what triggered this project. As a token of our gratitude for his visiting the SRKV school, in Mysore, in 1993 and rectifying the library catalogue database, I gifted AN with a set of the *Complete Works of Swami Vivekananda*, Mayavati Memorial edition, (Calcutta: Advaita Ashrama), then in 8 volumes. A couple of months later AN called to tell me that each of the printed Vivekananda volumes has a separate index and that he wished to create a single computerized index to the 8 volumes using CDS-ISIS. I thought it was a good idea and mentioned AN's proposal to the senior swamijis of the *Vidya Shala* in Mysore. They were pleased with the project but suggested that AN should first examine the printed concordance to the works published by the Ramakrishna Mission Institute of Culture, Kolkata. I sent a copy of the concordance – *Pearls of Wisdom* – to AN. A month or so later he reported that he has created a VIVEK database and index of some 3000 entries based on the concordance. AN then went on adding extracts from the discourses of Sri Ramakrishna Paramahamsa and of the Holy Mother Sarada Devi to the database and extended the scope to include extracts from the writings and discourses of other spiritual leaders and scholars covering major religions of the world.. The VIVEK database was renamed OM database. He also added a bibliographic database of the source documents. The database was demonstrated and its usefulness explained at a library conference in Bhuvaneshwar, Orissa. Privately AN spoke to Dr. Murthy, then Director, DESIDOC, Ministry of Defense, (also attending the conference) about his desire to add further to the contents of the OM database (about 8000 extracts then) and also to create a database of life sketches of some of the seers, saints, and scholars. It would appear that Dr. Murthy was interested in the project and explained that the extracts in the databases would be useful to the executives of the Defense department for stress relief, reference, etc. and that DESIDOC would provide partial support for the project. A part of the DESIDOC funded project was assigned to NCSI, Bangalore (Dr. T.B. Rajashekar et al) specifically to port the database(s) on to the Internet. In the meantime AN increased the number of records in the OM database to over 14,000, and the OMBIO database contained over 70 life sketches some with pictures. Devotional music audio clips were added. An introduction (voice recording) to Indian spiritual heritage and usefulness of the databases was provided by Shri C. Subramaniam (now deceased), and a technical introduction on the content of the databases by AN was added. Subsequently a multimedia CD was prepared and submitted to DESIDOC. AN maintains and updates the databases – the main Extracts database OM02 now holds about 17500 extracts records, 120 life sketches in the OMBIO database; an online glossary (GLOS database) of over 5000 spiritual terms (Sanskrit, Pali, Arabic / Persian and English), and a bibliographic database (OMBIB) of the source documents used in the preparation of the contents of the other databases. The scope is broad covering most of the major religions of the world, *and includes about 5,000 extracts from the writings and discourses of Swami Vivekananda, Sri Ramakrishna Paramahamsa and Holy Mother Sarada Devi.* The databases are hypertext linked; the CDs mentioned above can be run from the related records in the OM02 and OMVIO databases; and records relating to Mysticism are hyper linked to a related website.

Earlier I had created a VIVEK database on the Vidya Shala PC and downloaded the extracts from the works of Swami Vivekananda (from the OM database) given by AN. I demonstrated to the teachers and students how to retrieve records responding to specific queries. Gradually the system gained popularity. During January 1994 there was a rush for display of quotations for writing articles, or essay writing for the annual magazine, and the demand peaked just before 12th January, being observed annually as "National Youth Day" (Swami Vivekananda's birth day). Until our Advaita Ashram, Calcutta, brought out a CD of 'Swami Vivekananda's Complete works' there were frequent searches in the VIVEK database for quotations, and passages for recitation, articles for magazines, etc.

In updating the OM databases AN has used many of the books that I have gifted him in addition to the many others he had procured on his own.

5 KARNATAKA POLICE ACADEMY, MYSORE, LIBRARY

I had been called to advise on the creation of a database of the catalogue of the Police Academy. At my request, AN visited the Karnataka Police Academy (KPA) in Mysore, on 8 Feb. 2002, installed WINISIS (CDS/ISIS for Windows) and transferred the records of KPA database (catalogue of library resources) from the DOS version. The then Director of KPA, Sri H.N. Satyanarayana Rao, IPS honoured AN that day evening at a "Get-together" of the IPS Officers, Faculty Members, Special invitees, dignitaries and a large contingent of Trainees for Sub-Inspectors Cadre.

6 CONCLUSION

It is a matter of pride for me to have been associated with Prof. Neelameghan and to have benefited from his professional guidance. To an appreciable extent he is responsible for acquainting me with newer techniques, molding my thinking, and sharpening my professional skills. His affection, guidance and support have enabled me to remain in the profession and enjoy the work. I am still actively serving our Mission centres, because of his backing and support. I sincerely pray the Almighty, to bestow upon him a long and healthy life.

It would be appropriate to conclude with the masterly pronouncement of Swami Vivekananda (*Collected Works*, .v.3, p. 195).

> *"Teach your selves, teach every one his real nature,*
> *call upon the sleeping soul and see how it awakes.*
> *Power will come, glory will come, goodness will come,*
> *purity will come, and every thing that is excellent will come*
> *when the sleeping soul is roused to self-conscious activity"*

REFERENCES

1. *Bhagavan Sri Ramakrishna and Holy Mother Sri Sarada Devi: an integrated e-book* . (2004). Kolkata: Ramakrishna Mission Ashrama.
2. Moona, Suresh. (2004). Ramakrishna Math, Bangalore – 100 years. *Centenary commemorative souvenir*, 1904-2004, Bangalore: Ramakrishna Math, 2004 December 25. p. 1-4.
3. Nagaraja Rao, D.N. (2001). *Sri Ramakrishna Vidyashala library – its growth and achievements: reflections of a retired librarian*. Mysore: The Author. (unpublished script)
4. —. (2004). *Role of retreats to wards enhancement of human values. etc.* Mysore: The Author (unpublished script)
5. *Swami Vivekananda: life. works and research (Multimedia CD)*. (2001). Calcutta: Advaita Ashrama
6. Sri Ramakrishna Vidyashala, Mysore. (2004). Swarna smriti; *golden jubilee souvenir*. Mysore: The Vidyashala
7. Vrajaprana, Pravrajika. (1998). Vedanta on cyberspace: the Vedanta movement and the electronic frontier. *Prabuddha Bharata*. Vol. 103; January 1998; p. 91-103.

SAVE THE TIME OF THE GODLY: INFORMATION MEDIATOR'S ROLE IN PROMOTING SPIRITUAL AND RELIGIOUS ACCOMMODATION

Mohamed Taher

Dedicated to Professor A. Neelameghan, a mentor of my mentors, and whose single outstanding contribution to the Multi-faith world in an electronic document, OM Information Service (OMIS), overshadows all that is catalogued in the present article.

Information mediating – as practised by the library profession -- links information seeker with information source and helps in saving the time of the faithful. In the age of Internet, librarians are trying their best to satisfy the information needs of the users, with vast variety of resources (both print and online). The article highlights spiritual and religious questions received at the library's reference desk. Web-based reference transactions are increasing the use of libraries and providing seekers with greater access to resources. Moreover, Internet helps enhancing skills and competencies as well opportunities for learning this sort of mediation. While most librarians may or may not know that they are a valuable source for fostering spiritual and religious accommodation, there are, nevertheless, many ways to illustrate this social good performed by the information mediators. In line with their professional duty they are also into building taxonomies and bases for knowledge management even in the spiritual domains. This paper provides samples of best practices and facilitates assessing return-on-investments.

1 INFORMATION MEDIATION PERSPECTIVES IN EVERYDAY LIFE OF THE FAITHFUL

Dr. S.R. Ranganathan formulated his Five Laws of Library Science in the 1920s (Ranganathan, 1963).

* Books are for use
* Every reader his / her book
* Every book its reader
* Save the time of the reader
* Library is a growing organism

These laid the foundations of library and information service in all environments to all types of clientele. He also declared that Reference Service was the *summum bonum* of library service and the user/information seeker should be welcomed and treated as a faithful devotee would treat if the Supreme Being visited his/her home as a guest (Ranganathan, 1961). This calls for certain moral and ethical qualities in the host, the reference librarian [59c, 59d].

Today spirituality and religion receive considerable attention, from both markets and consumers. This is obvious from the fact that secular institutions are, more than ever, trying to accommodate diversity in workplace. And libraries are in this process attending to socio-religious queries, building their resources and expanding their own capabilities to handle the increasing demands from those interested in religious and spiritual matters. Public libraries may receive queries of information seekers who probably primarily need such information for personal reasons. Academic libraries receive requests primarily (from students, researchers, faculty) for academic reasons, and secondarily for private/personal reasons too. A detailed study is required to look at such intentions and use patterns. Such a study is not attempted here.

Information mediating service is based on either an existing demand or on potential needs of the faithful seekers. In both scenarios librarians use the technique of reference interview with the information seeker, directly or indirectly. In other words, information mediators are facilitators in saving the time of the Godly and this facilitation process is achieved in more ways than one:

* Personalized or direct help offered to the information seekers in locating, right information, at the right time, from any maze;
* Mediating (reference-interview) in an online reference desk – such as, real-time Ask-A-Librarian, or e-mail-based reference service; and
* Adopting value added services, such as, outreaching the community in providing information in printed and/or electronic formats.

Input of collected raw information, its throughput by way of processing and appropriate storage and output in the desired format resulting in organization of information as a customized product, called as knowledge information. The uniqueness of a professional role is more so in the mental activities of this practice, which centres on representation of information rather than knowing information (Bates, 1999).

For over a century librarians have donned the mantle to help information seekers, as a professional commitment resulting in 'Reference Service' becoming the most important interface for public relations. What is done during reference work is either of the two: a) facilitating direct access, that is., linking the information seeker with an information source; or b) directing, that is, identifying pin-pointedly a relevant source which might be of value to the information seeker. How this process began makes interesting reading. "The father of the American reference process, Samuel Green, instituted the first formal reference service at the Worcester Public Library in Massachusetts in 1876. He emphasized the importance of personal aid to people requesting information. Until Green made his policy statement, the tendency of librarians was to look upon themselves as keepers of archives rather than as activists in providing information for the public." (Katz, 1978). The reference process is not always simple:

> *"Lest you think that all librarians have to do is look up once and a while and say Shush!, here are some of the actual questions they have been asked: ... I need a photocopy of Booker T. Washington's birth certificate .. I need to find out Ibid's first name for my bibliography. ... I am looking at a list of laws that I can break that would send me back to jail for a couple of months."(Davis, 2001)*

With the coming of telephone at the reference desk, the reference desk had an expanded territory and thereby the utilization of the reference desk and its facilitator increased. What all could have transpired on telephone-based reference transactions? The answer to this is not altogether left to imagination. *The Book of Answers* (Berliner, 1999) compiled based on The New York Public Library's Telephone Reference Service lists at least 37 questions, under the category Religion. Break up of the 38 questions reveal the sub-facets that are dealt herein, namely, a majority of these questions/answers are relate to Christianity (22); other faiths - Judaism (4); Islam (4); Hinduism (5); Buddhism (2). A glance at one or two questions from the book gives a feel of the pulse:

* **What is nirvana? Is it anywhere near Valhalla?** "Nirvana is not a place but a state of bliss to which Buddhists aspire. In Sanskrit it means the 'going out' of a light. Early Buddhists used the word to describe the extinction of the fires of cravings. Valhalla, in Norse mythology, is the heavenly hall of slain heroes. It also represents a state of bliss—but one in which the dead feast and fight each other for sport."
* **Who founded Hasidism?** "The Jewish spiritual movement was founded by Israel ben Eliezer, now better known as the Ba'al Shem Tov (Master of the Good Name). He was a healer and holy man who lived in the Ukraine (c. 1700-1760.)"

By a thematic analysis, these 37 questions can be categorized under the following: history (8); worship (6); geography (2); scriptural (8); and theology (13). This book on Telephone reference transactions (that went on for 20 years in one state library system) contains one line question and the related response, for thousands of cases. Surfing these pages provides a great insight into the truly converging faith-based environments, which exists in the cosmopolitan New York. To safeguard the personal rights of the involved parties, the book does not name the librarian or the inquirer. Unfortunately, however, there are limitations making a more meaningful analysis difficult. The book does not provide information on:

* Time when these questions were posed – faith based questions may be seasonal or occasional;
* The inquirers – age, gender, location inquirer, educational and other status;
* Whether the responses were provided by librarians, or the help of experts was sought; and
* The percentage of queries/answers that were of 'quick reference' type, and what percentage was research-based.

This telephonic reference albeit, heralded an era of communication between the librarian and the information user, and was a landmark achievement in saving the time of the user. The reference process progressed to include other telecommunication tools, such as, fax, computerized online databases and E-mail. While many libraries offered email-based reference services, a few have made available the actual contents of the request and the response. The recording of these transactions, as transcript is available on the Internet, and one such example is from an American academic library (University of South Florida, 2004):

* What training does the Dalai Lama go through once declared the Dalai Lama?
* I need to find current articles (magazine or newspapers) on the Kosovo crisis, and I do not know how to do it.

Electronic formats that are being used by information professionals now have advanced considerably, and include the Web-based tools. In fact adapting the Web-based interactive tools, libraries have opened their doors to visitors around the globe. While e-mail provided the ability to handle the questions, Web-based capability does the same handling, but here the transactions are in real time. Real-time refers to direct personalized interface based on the library's Website. The Website visitor can submit a question; the question is then instantly handled by a human intermediary; and this human intermediary provides an answer directly to the information seeker. The reference process had value added by 'reference interview.' Reference interview, then in Web context can be defined as: 'A real time or non-real time, Web-based – text, and sometimes voice and/or video - communication between the reference interviewer and interviewee.' An extensive article on real-time reference interview that is emerging in the Web-based environments, as well as real-time reference interview tools, is dealt in my recent publication (Taher, 2002).

Table 1 shows how the results of the reference interviews between the respective librarians and myself. This test enabled demonstrating the real-time scenario, which exists for the Website visitors.

Table 1: Real Time Interactive Reference Interview (Taher, 2002)

Library	Link	Questions Asked	Transaction Time	Service Timings	Satisfaction	Follow up
Pasadena Public Library	Inactive / changed*	5	10 min.	24 /7	4**	None
Cornell Univ. Library	Active	7	12 min.	Mon - Fri (1-5 p.m.)	5	None

Library	Link	Questions Asked	Transaction Time	Service Timings	Satisfaction	Follow up
Boston Public Library	Active	6	10 min.	24/7	. 5	None
Duke Univ. Library	Active	8	10 min.	Mon - Fri (1-5 p.m.)	6	Once

*New address: www.247ref.org/portal/access2.cfm?lib= Pasadena

**1-10, 1 is very low 10 very high

Web-based reference service took over from email, and the reference process has come to a stage of live interaction. Ask-A-Librarian is the generic name of this process. A quick glance at the prevailing patterns in offering Ask-A-Librarian services is as follows:

Religion To send a reference question or e-mail to a library area click on Ask a Librarian. To send a comment or question about the web page contact Web0@mail.clarke.public.lib.ga.us

Religion and Philosophy

For Information or to Ask a Reference Question: Ask A Librarian Or, Call 704-INFO (704-4636) in the Olympia area or 1-800-562-6022

Non-violence

Pearl A. Wanamaker Library Ask a Reference Question

Ask a Librarian

Multicultural Multifaith Resource Collection
Sandwell Libraries and Information Service

Librarians do contribute in this online interaction primarily with the information seekers, and secondarily with colleagues and peers, through many ways. Furthermore, library professionals are continuously adding content to the Web. For example, Dr. John L. Gresham, has continuously expanded his Webliography (or Web-based bibliography): Finding God in Cyberspace: A Guide to Religious Studies Resources on the Internet. The current theme is Religion in/and Cyberspace: The encounter between religion and digital culture. The page has list of a) articles/papers; b) Conferences; c) Church statements and other documents, includes Church related sources and others (with no items under this category); d) Books; e) Book reviews; f) Courses; and g) Websites.

Obviously, in these roles a librarian and his/her mediation with the end-user gets a humane touch, and this is an interesting factor in an otherwise totally mechanized visualization process. Moreover, this human-computer mediation is done in a professional manner, ignoring – as humanly as possible - the personal choices of faith or spirituality. This consideration and inclusiveness is important in the Faith-based perspectives. Realistically, it is pertinent to mention that it is impossible to separate mind and spirit while making the ends meet in everyday life. Then the question which can be raised, but deliberately unanswered here - dealt at length elsewhere in library literature- is whether one can appropriately balance between one's faith and professional responsibility. A similar question may also prop up – while we are constantly dealing even with materials, not just humans – that is, how much of neutrality by the practitioner is possible in dealing with pro-choice/ anti-choice resources. Are there any options available in handling such obvious 'inhuman' scenarios? Instead of totally bypassing, an answer to this subject of co-existence and religious accommodation is not dealt with here.

2 OBSERVATIONS FROM A LIBRARIAN AT THE REFERENCE DESK

We have in the following two narratives of information professionals, indicating how they look and feel about Online worship in terms of their respective work environments.

Background

> I am a Reference Librarian and Web Administrator for a regional campus library of a state university. In addition to my other duties, I am the bibliographer for the Philosophy and Religion Departments. Rutgers Camden is in an urban setting. While our primary mission is to support the courses taught at our institution, we also serve our local community. We are the county seat for and we are often used by city and county workers as well as the legal professionals from the county courthouse. Since many citizens of Camden are dependent upon public transportation and we are geographically closer to their homes than the public library, we

are used regularly by high school students and as well as regular folk pursuing their own research interests.

Questions that Get Asked about Religion at the Reference Desk

The Rutgers students that approach the Reference Desk are almost always working on an assignment for class. The questions that pertain to Religion are generally related to a Comparative Religions class where they have to compare and contrast an issue or theme across different organized religions. As a Reference Librarian, it is my job to question-negotiate and help them locate the materials that they need. As bibliographer for the Religion Department, it has been my goal to make sure that the collection is as representative as possible for all denominations.

Sometimes students in an English Composition class will approach the Reference Desk for help regarding a religion-based topic that they have chosen for their theme. It is my experience that the students who, when given a choice, choose to write about religion are those students for whom religion is a key factor in their life, i.e. people whose religion is deeply meaningful to them as individuals. These students are from across the entire spectrum of beliefs. I have worked with Evangelical Christians, Roman Catholics, Muslims, and Zoroastrians, among many, many others.

The local citizens tend to use the library in its more traditional role - that of a quiet haven for reading and reflecting. The community folk who approach the Reference Desk often have questions about religion. They ask for help finding concordances, explicatory materials, reference works, or copies of sacred literature. As do all reference librarians, I strive to be respectful of every patron that approaches the desk. I try to be especially sensitive in the question negotiation process in religious research. The query that the patron comes to me may have a deep and personal meaning.

Religion and *Web Administration*

As Web Administrator, part of my duties is to create and maintain guides to the library resources available to our users both in print and on the Web. On these guides, I try to include as many free resources, including full-text versions of sacred texts, that are available electronically that I can find. I also try to include links to authoritative religion sites on the Web so that our users will have reliable on-line resources.

As mentioned previously, many community members do come to our library to read, think, and access the Web. These patrons also use the

Internet to research their topics and to access religious-themed message boards and discussion groups. For example, there is a group of young Latter Day Saint missionaries stationed in Camden who visit the library regularly in order to get Web access. The faculty and staff of the Paul Robeson Library feel that it is important to serve our neighbors. We try to make the library as welcoming and user-friendly as possible.

Final Thoughts

On a personal note, I do not belong to an organized religion. I consider myself a seeker. I enjoy my role as Religion Bibliographer for I have the professional responsibility to investigate the print and electronic resources that will best serve our users. In addition, I get the opportunity to have interesting conversations with students, faculty, staff, and community members on issues of philosophy and religion. As I help patrons on their intellectual quests regarding religion, they are also helping me on mine (Personal communication, 2003a).

Another instance is worth documenting, as reported from personal interactions:

Some limitations:

I am agnostic...point of entry for discourse on Faith is very nebulous. Discourse is very superficial too. My major clientele is aged 25 on an average..:very rarely do they articulate their faith. No formal queries related to Faith.

Some observations:

However, there is discussion on yoga, Indian classical music, pilgrimage (rooted in religion?) --- mostly in the form of exchange of interesting websites (URLs) - information about spiritual centres; spiritual teachers / groups. I have helped connect people with similar interests. This may lead to exchange of books / tapes among them. Play the referral function; chain e-mails with religious images / animated worship artifacts

The Web does not seem to be the preferred source of info./ inspiration among my clientele (although it is for professional info).

Anecdotes:

Have an ex-student (Certificate course in LIS), Waghmare who is keen to develop a library of Buddhism ...Helped him plan a physical library- esp.

with bibliographies. Perhaps I should encourage him to compile resources available on the Web on his interest. (Personal communication, 2003b)

Within such an existing professional scenario of a librarian, John Trotti finds an analogy in the performance of a priest. In this analogy the librarian is both acting as mentor and minister, in the information seeking process, and thus states:

"The ministering library is not a warehouse, a monument to learning, a repository of antiquarian curios, or a substitute for the campus bookstore. On the contrary, it is basically people-centered." (Trotti)

Internet Question Box (Christian index, calls itself as The Nazareth Resource Library):

What Is This Page About?

As the main page says, its mission is to be Bringing quality Christian literature to the World Wide Web. Because my areas of specialization are in the areas of apologetics, the Bible, and theology, these are the kinds of files I put up here. I also have a specialization in the early Church Fathers, and I plan on adding files from them too.

Who Runs This Page?

My name is James Akin, and I am an apologist working for a ministry named Catholic Answers, where I am also a contributing editor to This Rock magazine (The Nazareth Resource Library, 2004).

Reference Questions at Stumpers-L (faith-based index):

The Stumpers list is a place for librarians (and others) to discuss reference questions, which they are unable to answer using available resources, including the Internet and local interlibrary loan capabilities.

This site contains information about the list, including how to subscribe to the list, how to send questions to the list, frequently asked questions from and about the list, and some links to list-related resources in other places (Frequently Asked Questions From Stumpers, 2004).

Search results for 'Worship':

26 questions, in the year 2001; A few examples of questions asked:

* Looking for words and music gospel song;
* Earliest non-Christian references to Jesus;

* War stories / divine intervention;
* Hymn sheet music;
* Burial custom, ancient Egypt; and
* Hanukkah worship music.

10 questions, in the year 2002; A few examples of questions asked:

* Preaching resource;
* Music question;
* Children's book - Caroline on Sunday; and
* Órúnmìlàism: the Basis of Jesuitism.

One sample from the questions, to see the pattern:

If anyone has access to a Worship resource such as "Word and Witness" I have a last minute fill-in request for a church this week. The nearest seminary "Wesley" will not take an ILL request even with promise to pay. I would really like to have just a page: with hymn suggestions / call to worship/prayer of confession like word and witness does. I can work up a sermon on the Hebrews 34 text by Sun. but need the bulletin done by tomorrow for the church secretary.

In short, libraries and today's Webmasters do receive questions that are also about spiritual and religious care.

Database-Driven Web Sites: In a competitive age libraries are faced with a threat of being sent to oblivion. Today's endangered species, that is., libraries, are facing real threat from virtual competitors, such as, Google, Kartoo, Excite, and Northern Light. Being on such a competitive edge, libraries are trying to survive as well as add value to their services / products by adapting Web-based tools. Among these services, there are many that meet the online worship needs. An illustration of this developmental perspective is visible for all subjects on the Web, and in a case that is our concern, it is quite significant. The Judaic Studies resource, as a tool that is supported by an online database, is accessible from Web site of the University of California, San Diego. A glance at the website provides a variety of details that directly help the information seeker. Discussing the Browser by Subject or Type, Laura Galvan-Estrada in an article 'Moving

Towards a User-Centered, Database-Driven Web Site at the UCSD Libraries', states:

> "The initial screen of a subject (read here, Judaic) browse displays featured items for that subject. For any subject added to a record, the author can specify whether the resource is major or minor within the subject, and can tag them as featured to display first. The list of types for any resource sort alphabetically in a table of contents on the right side of the display, with the number of resources next to each type" (Antelman, 2002)

3 ETHICS, COPYRIGHTS, AND INTELLECTUAL FREEDOM

Does the proactive role of a Web-based librarian deal with issues of character, aesthetics, rights and responsibilities? The answer is one word is, YES. But that is at the same time NO, too. This paradox is just to state the true colours of the Web domains, that allows religious virtualization at one end in, say democratic environments, to blocking, filtering and knocking out of such virtual space in, say other than democratic environments. A glance at the trends in this sort of perplexing scenario will make the point clear.

Empirical Analysis of Internet Filtering in Saudi Arabia (http://cyber.law harvard.edu/filtering/saudiarabia)

Empirical Analysis of Internet Filtering in China (http://cyber.law. harvard.edu/filtering/china)

Political Regulation Of Internet Use: Examining The Role Of Fear. Justin Peart (http://marketing.byu.edu/...)

Steve Watters, "Teachers in Focus: See No Evil" (http://family.org...)

While the Web-based trends are obvious from the above, professional bodies such as the American Library Association, has its guidelines: 'Code of Ethics.'(www.ala.org...)

Where and how to find the right information at the right time? This question can be answered first by understanding who does what in thc information handling industry. In today's trillion dollar information industry – going by any standards of the economy, be it first world, second world or third world -- some are destined to be gold collar professionals and some are blue collar jobbers. The former get paid for cutting cakes, latter do the donkey jobs. Let us take a quick walk around and see what this means by defining the jobs that the two main category of professionals do in this prime industry.

The purpose of discussing professional definitions and their areas of interest is not to divert the subject of online worship. It is just to pinpoint who does what in the facilitation process. The role of librarians as an information provider is primarily related to the content, rather than to the networks and wiring the sacred cyberspace. Librarians have the skills to manage information content by providing direct interfaces – Meta tags, catalog the resources, classify the documents, store the texts, etc. This does not mean that information technology professionals (Web masters, software and hardware developers, media and other tool managers, etc.), are less important in this facilitation business in the cyberspace. The latter have no way – rather no time or need - to go into the intricacies for an understanding of information seeking and information retrieval processes. It is appropriate to quote a librarian who intrinsically understands both these type of information professionals:

> "Only the librarian has the ability to manage the traditional library system as well as the evolving bionic library in which the traditional organic enterprise is extended by and merged with the new. The librarian is educated and trained to deal with the selection, acquisition, organization, service, preservation, and training activities that are required in the print-on-paper information model as well as the digital one.
>
> On the other hand, those computing and other information professionals, who are quite important to the digital platform on which electronic information flows, have no reason or means to learn how knowledge seekers are likely to approach this fresh mixture of the old and new systems to find the information they need. Neither are these specialists likely to learn the culture, methodologies, or management requirements of the traditional information system. Establish a rational, comprehensive information-selection program? Order a book or journal? Catalog and classify it? Process, house, service, and preserve it?; only the librarian.

> Select for users a new, valuable source from the host of data on the Internet, much of it only loosely describable as "information"? Attach descriptors and access and retrieval pointers? House the system; provide a menu and interface that information seekers will understand; and train users in the skills required to make effective use of these new capabilities? Surely the librarian" (Billings, 2002)

The bottom line is librarians mostly deal with information (content managers in the Web parlance) and hence appropriately called information-mediators ("We will always need interpreters...) or infomediaries (One should not confuse this information...) whereas all other information professionals (ISPs / Information technologists / techies) lead in providing service – that is, technology-based, access to / connect to / platform - that facilitates access to the information content, and hence appropriately called service providers.

What librarians do is yet another detailed note, given the competitive edge they are today standing on. One gets a greater understanding of their strengths by reading the following 3M Innovation's ad: "The trouble with the Information Superhighway is there are no road maps, no marked exits and too few drivers who know where they're going." The fine print at the bottom of the page lets us read: 'But having vast amount of information available and actually finding what you're looking for, as any librarian knows are two different things.'(For more details on information seeking..., 2004)

This is to say that information finding – more so in the Web-based scenario - has become a major task for librarians and other information providers. If this informational research job is offered to the commercial / business agencies in the markets, they do find the required information, may be even within the timeframe the results are ready to go. These agencies do perform information mining in all possible sources, and have been running their business very skillfully, making substantial profits. They even sell their products, not because it is always easy (as beautifully packaged and door-delivered), rather because of their strategic marketing skills; added to this is the susceptible human behaviour: convenience is what it's all about. But the cost - for this 'at your door step service' or charge - the information seekers would pay for this 'information search' is quite high. (COST)

It is one thing for the corporate to be billed for information research, and another to the individual. Whereas, if libraries continue to provide the same services there are chances that end-users would be saving substantially. Library services in corporate sectors, as well would find better return on investments. (Outsell's analysis of data from... 2004; Jupiter Research Forecasts...2004) Such a debate on fee-based information service, or 'free information for all' will never end. So also there is an unending research to prove or otherwise, if libraries are going to be bypassed by the big business, and takeover the traditional primary role of information mediation from libraries (Kenney, 2003).

4 TOOLS OF THE TRADE

Although the network concept dates back to 1969, only in 1990, the Internet was opened to the public. Between 1990 and 1995 there were many developments in terms of Internet finding its own place in everyday life of the people. E-mail, bulletin boards, and other online platforms in operation much before, had already facilitated traffic of ideas and inspiration of the holy type. But with the spread of the Net as a common source for all, the magic, with synchronous connectivity was totally different. So quick was the evolution that neither the people nor the media seriously felt the emergence of online worship. However, in 1996 appears the first detailed news story about signs of diversity in faith-based perspectives. Reporting about religious activity in May 1996 Lois Abraham of The Canadian Press reported in a provincial news daily, The Windsor Star as follows:

> "Tod Maffin, 25, of Vancouver launched his Anglicans Online! web site about a year ago.
>
> Tod says, ``One day I posted a message in the Christian discussion group on the Internet saying that I had these resources on the Internet they could check out. Within two hours the web site was swamped. I went from what was previously generating three or four visits a week to between 800 and 1,000 visits in a day. It just exploded! And I had no idea that that was a resource that people were after. ``It created a responsibility for me.' (In May 1996...)
>
> The news writer makes a specific remark, and that is interesting in terms of how the Church considers this non-traditional activity: "Most clergy view the Internet as an adjunct to personal interaction."

A glance at the neighbours among the diverse faith community the situation is not any different. While the debate on cyberspace being Kosher (theologically permissible) or not continues, there are other ways that the faithful find utility of the Net. A causal effect for Jewish interest in being present online is obvious from the following:

Connection is also what the latest Jewish phenomenon is all about: the explosion of Jewish dot-coms

"A lot of people are looking for a connection with the Jewish community and not finding it," says Harry Nelson, 32, CEO of allthingsjewish.com, an e-commerce site. That, he says, is where the Internet has successfully stepped in, to help younger Jews stay connected with Judaism outside the federation and synagogue world, which has little meaning to them.

"What do they want?" asks Nelson of Washington. "They want more passion in their Judaism. They don't want a bloodless Judaism. They want a Judaism of song and dance." Of course they also want someone with whom to share their newfound Jewish passion. (Cultural, affiliated, dot.com.., 2004)

Further, the above cited news report, in The Windsor Star, mentions activism among the other faiths, namely,:

- Judaism 101: Has links to Israel and Jewish resources (http://shamash. org/trb/judaism.html)
- Dunya, the CyberMuslim Information Collective: The basics of Islam, the Koran and links to newspapers (http://www.uoknor.edu/cybermuslim)

Among the non-Christian worship resources, Hinduism, has much to offer, with a slant towards inclusive worship space for its cousins:

Hurry OM: **Nidhi Taparia**

There are many me-too versions. Like ePrarthna.com launched in April 2000, which claims to be the only site offering pujas at over 1300 temples in India. The aim is to add every little temple on the street in India and abroad on its list. CEO, N. Nambi , explains, "As a user, I would rather offer prayers to a small Ganesh temple near my house, which I visited daily, than perform a puja at a big temple I have never visited."

There are added benefits, like an online mall offering books, cassettes, CDs, idols and more, along with virtual pujas, image galleries comprising over 3,000 images of gods, goddesses and temples, daily panchangas, and even a reminder service for those who do not want to miss their daily ritual no matter where they are.

Most Web sites on religion offer similar content and prices. Online Darshan has a facility of being able to find all aartis for different deities, or important slokas for different occasions. Seva Puja has online remedial prayers along with information on temples and how to get there, minutiae on fasts, epics, and stories in most religions ranging from Hinduism and Buddhism to Jainism and Sikhism (Hurry OM: Nidhi Taparia).

Along with the Web technology, developments in software have taken leaps that were inconceivable earlier. Web has an intrinsic ability to provide a base for a variety of technologies to integrate and converge, all at the same time. A significant integrated tool for a variety of religious practices is (for a price) available on the Web, under the catch phrase, 'plug and pray'. One instance of Hinduism from this site is worth mentioning:

Plug-pray - Hinduism Kit: (www.plug-pray.org…)

Do you need to change religion to grab the chance for a career outlook? Are you going to work abroad? Getting a new customized god is easy with Plug'n'Pray. A new spirituality and a new respectability can be yours at a mouse click.

Religious Gurus from all over the world compiled these kits for you. Religious and cultural habits are fully illustrated: audio and video files will teach you everything about prayers, mortification and purification rituals, as well as ready to use supplications, special formulas and sacred functions (Plug-pray.., 2004).

In short, what is obvious from the above description is that worship related matters are emerging, not just among the Christian groups (examples among the Christian sites in this news story refers to Anglican Websites: http://www. anglican.ca.anglican, and www.ecunet.org/ecunet/ecuhome.htm; Salvation Army's e-mail traffic, and an online Confession booth: http://anther.learning.

cs.cmu.edu/priest.html), but also among other faith groups. Absent in the story is the fact that there are no clues about similar Internet activities of other faiths. A review of the continuum, or otherwise, that the Internet promises is more appropriate here. In such a review one can see if these faith-based Web activities improved gloriously, remained the same as segmented information services, or contrary to this did these services reduced their activity, diversified or got washed off in the wake of the .com depressions. Statistically speaking, people have shown a constant level of interest in at least one segment of Online worship – membership in religious organizations- between 1995 and 2000. To quote: "There was no difference between Internet users and non-users in rate of membership in religious organizations, in either 1995 (about 63 percent) or 2000 (about 56 percent). However, in 2000, users who spent more hours online per week were slightly more likely to belong to more religious organizations."(Katz, 2002). Such religious activities and involvement has grown, is evident in another study. While the population that is covered in the study is limited to one small – albeit electronically connected – university town in Virginia's Blacksburg, the trends are really representative of an emerging pattern among the faithful:

"Residents of Blacksburg were significantly more likely in 1999 to use the Internet to communicate with local family members, church members and members of informal social groups (such as baby-sitting and sports clubs) than in 1996." (Kavanaugh, 2002a)

Another voice from the Islamic corner:

> Mustafa Hussein of the Islamic Society of Greater Kansas City said some people log onto the group's Web site seeking information about Islam. Also, some Muslims seek information about the Kansas City Muslim community before moving here (Gray, 2001).

How do people react to such offers is the more interesting feedback, which the survey provides:

> "When people discover that their church, or their child's teacher or soccer team, or Boy Scout troop is distributing news and inviting discussion via the Internet, they have a direct interest in using that service. Furthermore,

as with telephone networks, computer networks provide increased access to members of a person's social circle, including members of the same group or organization. The acceleration of Internet adoption by organizations ratchets up the adoption by members affiliated with those organizations. By fall 2001, over a hundred and twenty non-profit organizations in the community were annual subscribers of these bundled Internet services offered by BEV in 2000" (Kavanaugh, 2002b).

5 CONTENT AND CATEGORIZATION OF THE WEBSITES THAT PROVIDE LINKS

What do Websites identify as a resource for online worship, especially in a religious diversity perspective? Categorization of the Faith Groups: Analyzing a faith and its denominations help in a better understanding of the services, products and this facilitates an easy way to get a clear picture the respective community as a whole. Such a classification of faith groups, within its own circle and from a comparative view, helps also in developing better conceptual maps of what is a religion, sect, cult, and so on. In terms of best practices, a very detailed analysis of the classificatory practices is provided on the following Website: adherents.com/classify.html

One finds here a classification and a clear annotation of the respective knowledge:

- What constitutes a Religious body?
- What is a Sect?
- What is Denomination?
- What is the meaning of the term Church?
- What does congregation mean?

It also recommends this model, wherever possible, to be applied to non-Christian faith groups. Further, adapting the knowledge management and taxonomic skills, the market today provides sufficient advanced mechanism for handling information even in faith-based environments. One case, for illustration, is the customized product developed by Digital Brain < digitalbrain.com > that can be used by any person, lay or scholarly, in utilizing the state-of-the-art resources for information storage and retrieval.

Virtual Rituals: A Website with a title 'Virtual Rituals' lists the following as the opening statement to describe its contents: "The following are examples of sites that facilitate online religious practice. Most of them represent well-known religious traditions in the "real world" but offer "virtual" places of prayer, worship, study, or meditation" (Virtual Rituals). Evidently, its focus is probably on being comprehensive in its coverage of the term Online worship, as it covers: a) Cyber-based places of worship, b) worship, c) study and d) meditation. Whereas, the Websites mentioned under each faith group are very meager, and are neither representative sample, nor a good systematic set of resources. It covers the following religious traditions: Buddhist (2 links), Christian (6 links), Hindu (6 links), Jewish (2 links), Muslim (3 links) and Zoroastrian (1 link). Among the items listed on this Website, with a separate heading, the next category is: Miscellaneous Non-Traditional, New Age, or Techno (5 links). The listed Websites represent non-traditional and New Age, but also includes a Website called Cyber Church – probably included under the heading: Techno. There is a third category of listing on this Web site, with a heading, Psychology and Spirituality (3 links).

The above description of a Website indicates that there are Websites that try to catalogue or create an organized scheme to present Religious diversity resources. Nevertheless, it also indicates a problem with categorization. One needs to know the basic taxonomy or classification to be able to place each religion / spirituality in a suitable category (Broughton, 2000).

Lectures, Sermons, religious discourses with inspirational content, and in Full-text are now available on the Websites – some are free for download and some can be heard from the Website. Faith groups do have their own Web sites that list the sermons. Some libraries attached to religious academies have developed thematic indexes that facilitate finding information by respective faith groups. Analytical information about such Web-based content is also available (Abel-Kops, 2003). Further the following instances illustrate focused and useful samples:

> *Interestingly, on the Internet there is extensive material provided by the faith groups themselves, even in the case of sermons. Not only one can find sermons, there are discussions that deal with ifs and buts of handling online sermon / preaching. "Ever preach in a chat room?" is a article in*

the online magazine, New Wineskins: The Believers Magazine (http://www.wineskins.org...). What makes this news story worth reading is its slant on discussing the new emerging roles for the mediator of faith in the online environment.

Other examples are:

* Vanderbilt Divinity School Library, Nashville, Tennessee (http://divinity.lib.vanderbilt.edu...)
* Wabash Center for Teaching and Learning, Wabash Centre for Teaching and Learning in Theology and Religion, Wabash College, Crawfordsville, Indiana (http://www.wabashcenter.wabsh.edu...)

6 CHANGING ROLES OF THE INFORMATION PROVIDERS:

6.1 Changing Paradigms

There is a growing knowledge base on (a) how information is viewed by the consumers; (b) how consumer expects information; and (c) the responsiveness of the market to these virtual dimensions – all because of the belated dawning of the fact that information and its perception - as useful or otherwise - actually lies in the eyes of the beholder. Given these changing paradigms information seeking as well as information provision is also undergoing a vast change in the last few decades (Bruce and Todd, 1993).

Testing Faith in the Market God (http://marty-center.uchicago.edu…., 2001)

Increased reliance on the Internet is also changing and will change the power structure of congregations by pushing previously "marginalized techies" into new leadership roles such as "church webmaster". In addition, the maintenance of these sites puts public relations responsibilities in the hands of members who previously might not have played a role in constructing and retaining a congregation's image.

Thumma wondered to what extent some churches might construct online identities designed for broad appeal that would misrepresent to some degree a church's core mission. "Will congregations fabricate a public persona, and then have trouble living up to the HTML image it has created for itself?" he asked. "Perhaps in five years, we'll know".

6.2 Teach Me How to Become a Online Worship Facilitator

All said and done, if Online worship is considered as just a new method to do the traditional process of praise and prayer in a new setting, then online worship as a new device calls for training the trainer and training the masses. While what this amounts to surrounds technology and practice / knowledge of technical skills, but this is not be all, and end all. There is more than what meets the eye. Hence, this new methodology requires adding new skills to reach the divine, and these skills can be summarized as human capital, knowledge capital and communications.

Human capital comprises of two sub-facets: a) the spiritual caregiver and b) the spiritual seeker. Knowledge capital includes a) infomediaries, b) content development, and c) technical know-how of the Web architecture. Communications includes a) the four Ps of marketing (product, promotion, placement, and price), b) marketing strategies, c) e-culture and d) digital economy. Spiritual caregivers are getting ordained through formal education by attending regular schools, as well as informal education online. The seeker can either join a regular (faith / spiritual) group and gain the required insight to reach divine on Cyber space or look for online methods – at one's own pace- to be initiated into online worship. To be up-to-date with current practices and current trends the caregivers need to be constantly online and surfing for newer trend (Continuing education in just…). In so far as building technical know-how and content of the Knowledge capital, there are four different levels of education and training: a) Web wise understanding the language and culture of the Web (including anatomy, physiology, psycho-socio-linguistics, morphology, syntax and semantics, and all other segments that encapsulate Web architecture); b) holistic exposure to virtually religious and spiritual Web domains (comprehensive, pinpointed and exhaustive comprehension of their online / virtual presence); c) web related certification and training programs (incorporating both infostructure and infrastructure, and maintaining a just balance in education that cares for use and abuse, with course orientation such as, ethical hacking, legal testing, moral censorship, family-friendly firewalls, intellectual copyright protection, etc.); and d) practical experience with electronic knowledge management systems (within the context of knowledge creation, acquisition, transfer, sharing, application, utilization, storage / archiving, retrieval and dissemination) (Adekunle…., 2003). Interestingly, one has to be aware that Knowledge capital as a whole has become the crux of the Web economy. Despite this value that the knowledge explicitly holds in the messier modern world, there is little concerted effort to "… explore the evolution of information and content pluralism and a more cosmopolitan approach to online content" (Skrzeszewski, 2002). Further, "the quest for ROI on knowledge and content services has become the mantra. Yet human factors, a critical link in the e-content value chain, are still all but missing from the radar of enterprise priorities" (Casey, 2002). Whereas this talk about infomediaries brings us back to the subject mentioned earlier – a return to square one, in order to demonstrate that whoever mediates in information seeking Is a special breed of person and has to have special skills in enabling reaching the deep Web. For those who need a clearer perspective of the deep Web and its associated paradox in finding online worship's Websites the following lines, from a Web service provider, are self-explanatory (Campbell, 2004):

> 1996 -- So... like there are 5 million stinkin' web pages out there.
>
> Used to be you logged in and you could find your way around pretty easily. No more.
>
> For instance, you may web surf for years and yet never find out about the historical accomplishment that is the Sea Monkey Worship Page!!!
>
> -- http://haven.uniserve.com/~ sbarclay/seamonk.htm .
>
> Made right here in Canada.
>
> We at eyeNET believe such an oversight of such an ubersite would be a crime. And we at eyeNET will not allow it to happen.

Deep Web, then presents a three dimensional mirage, namely, Web information seeking information use and information need satisfaction, gets created due to many reasons. We may, however, highlight the four main reasons: a) hidden Web sites that are not visible (on the Web that is by its nature nonlinear) to the Web surfer –Web sites are hidden either because of lack of recognition by search engines or lack of marketing the Web site by the respective Web masters; b) scatter (or we may as well call, spread) of the Web. That is, for instance, information by a religious / spiritual organization, or church (or about it and for) is all totally dispersed. This dispersal is so intense that it is easy to say one hand really does not know what the other hand is doing. Added to this confusion is the fact that there are official and unofficial Web sites of many organizations. And then there are proponents and opponents of this very body. And then there are those who review these and link these, all stand unconnected—in the so called wired world; c) lack of single or even a systematic index (do not ever think of having a user-friendly type of index as in a book or a library catalogue); d) Most Web sites get noticed either by a referral (word of mouth, banners, browsing Web directories, via e-mails), or indirect (serendipity or accidentally, rather than by choice, from non-Web resources such as media, flyers, books, etc.); e) Additional issues are probably due to, indirect Web site addresses (or URL), the privately owned (by and large free) versus corporate (with chances of it having restricted access, or fee-based) Web, etc. Such being the profile of the Web, is in fact a world that is more so horizontal, in its architecture, and goes on spreading everywhere without gathering any mass or being easily categorizable into a vertical set of resources.

6.3 Build Your Own Toolkit or Strategy for Survival

What best practices can help in developing the required basic and advanced skills? What are the agencies that can be approached for this purpose? These are fundamental skills or strategies for assisting the traffic on virtual religious and spiritual routes. Furthermore, if one is ready to get, set and acquire these skills, one must be sure that the pre-requisites are also given the due consideration. Such pre-requisites are, seemingly basics, but vital concrete tools just-in-time, as well avoid confusion later:

* Define your priorities – Among the various categories, such as, prayer, praise, scripture, sacrament, etc. which are essential, e-commodity, budget-wise, community's need wise
* Your strategy could make or break you – each technological discovery and / or adaptation for the Web-based environment is just based on a primary factor called, risk. Not all the technological advances are accepted on the face value, rather there is unlimited Web-phobia (going in line with media-phobia, technology-phobia, computer-phobia), and one has to learn to differentiate myth from fact in such situations (The Open Source

Philosophy, 2004). This then calls for a clear grasp of five significant facets: end-users, e-context, e-content, e-commerce, and infra- (as well as info) structure. A deeper look at these facets reveals that it necessitates a clear estimation of the type of audience among the end-users (are these pessimists or optimists; confident or scared; beginners or Netizens; investors or window shoppers; insiders of the community or outsiders; dissenters or integrators). Similar issues in the case of contextually are vital (leads the customer or diverts; links the surfer with user-friendly interfaces of the Web or otherwise; realizes its own value and potential or insensitive to the realities of the volatile Web). So also about the content (end-user's need based or hodgepodge; communicable or design less). Again, on the commerce side value-wise (is it a value added site for sustaining itself and the user interest, or totally heedless of the market interface). And finally, the infra- and infostructure that goes in making the site dynamic and interactive Webwise (state-of-the-art technology or archaic; uses a technology that can converge with other multimedia systems or is a stand alone stale ancient machine that supports the otherwise constantly shifting gears mechanism of the Web.). This is not the end-all of the stratagem!!! Importantly, because not all the interactive tools of Online worship made and marketed in one go. Be aware that you are surfing in a boat that is full of darkness and with rocky terrain and inhabited, not just by user-friendly angels. Rather, the Web is a mixture of those who care for the public good, and those who care for other ends. And the latter includes even creative souls who care nothing whatsoever about family values (In any society even today..., 2003).

* Simplify processes by adapting appropriate solutions to recurring hurdles – Managing time, as well as, the tools that are evolving each day as state-of-the-art technology and these taken with a proper dose of organizing skills may prove we are all trying to stay on top-of things. (Join and participate, 2004).

* When deciding goals, mission and vision keep it simple and original – Thinking locally and acting globally, dawned to many that it is as important as, thinking globally and adapting locally. Web started horizontally, but Web service market soon found that on the surface there is just the mirage, and that much is skin deep. Learn to navigate in one focused direction, rather than be-all and be-nowhere. As advised

elsewhere, adapt proper strategy to map within thematic areas or categories, such as, faith-wise, community-wise, region-wise, time-wise, etc.

* Online worship/digital religion and e-prayer are popular, so assume there is a lot of cut-throat competition and be prepared for the worst. There are as many producers of content in the sacred cyberspace, as there are competing distributors, service providers, and Webservants even in this market populated by religious and spiritual communities.
* Creative visualization is as essential in Online worship as is inspiration about content, format, tools, and the market. While Web screens are able to get the end-user touch screens, audio, and visual aids, they must also find means to enable achieving a sense of actualization (or call it self immersion). This actualization may lead to fulfillment of desires through imagination and affirmation. And this is not to say that such actualization is limited to Online worship alone, it could happen all the time even in a real world. What is important about the Web-based solution is --empathy of serene and calm atmosphere - equally essential for the soul to transcend. Thus, the designer, developer and the facilitator must be consciously taking part (in building virtual sanctuary), as such a positive result cannot be achieved in a stand-alone situation.

Becoming a Online worship specialist is then, a task of jack of all and master of none (You may not get..., 2004). It is a missionary position requiring compatibility of being highly skilled as one who is cyber savvy, tech guru, prayer facilitator and faithful to every seeker in this World Wide Worship. Such an infomediary (See note # 22) must be willing to walk an extra mile, as information mediator has come a long way from being a mere street corner help to being a virtually blessed bandwidth and along the way has learnt to take the heat off the hot seat.

Cautionary note: There is no end to guiding, teaching and mentoring. You need to be familiar with Web architecture, its coding, functions, design, as well as, the basic sensibilities of respective faith groups. One has to be a graduate, both mentally and skill wise, in these areas otherwise it may tend to be spoon-feeding. After all, if you are the online worship facilitator you will have those basic skills, including temperament, attitude, and more than all compassion.

7 LITURGY AS A NEW MANTRA FOR ALL INFORMATION PROVIDERS

> **Surf Print – Accommodation in Practice**
>
> "So whereas Christians regarded the invading Arabs as God's rod for their chastisement, many Jews saw them rather as God's instrument for their deliverance" ('Non-Muslim Conceptions of Islam').
>
> Mohammed, like the biblical prophets, had a distinctive role in turning people (Jews, Christians, and Arabs) from their idolatrous practices back to faith in the one, true, nonmaterial God of Abraham, Isaac and Jacob. His zeal against idol worship had its effect on both Christianity and Judaism. Not much has been written on this aspect of the Prophet's ministry. Rabbis Maimonides (twelfth century C.E.) and Sholome (thirteenth century) both acknowledge Mohammed's contribution to faith and dependence upon God and not idols." (Help for Church Webmasters..., 2002)

To add a philosophical, ethical, spiritual dimension this article takes a unique step by highlighting the oft-forgotten liturgy of Librarianship. What? Liturgy? Where did this idea come from? Is this spiritual or mundane in character? How does this liturgical perspective fit into the scheme of a profession, which seemingly just concerns itself with cataloguing 'books' and doling out the 'documents at the circulation desk'?

One moment please. Let us put the cart behind the horse, and then see the truth about this information profession. The profession has one of its professed goals of providing 'information for all.' In meeting this goal it remains neutral to the possible extent. In this neutrality lies the liturgy. Does this have religious or spiritual sanctity? The answer is, yes. For instance the Muslims believe that human intellect is endowed with the capacity to judge between good and bad, evil and wicked, satanic and angelic – the choice to select is individual adult's own decision (Al-Quran: Chapter 90, Verse 10). Information professional then follows the dictum of providing access to all, free for all, open for all. In a context of diversity in faith traditions, we do find information about how a profession finds for itself some means to get divine inspiration. It is generally accepted by all faith groups that by and large there is a need to spread the good word to all (or disseminate as is professed by the library fraternity). This is not evangelically speaking, or even to impose on others what we think is right. Rather it is by way of creating a religious accommodation in a world torn today in worst ever known personal and collective attacks. The liturgy of librarianship, to quote an information professional from Christian frame of reference, is:

> "Balancing a spirituality that mandates 'witnessing' with the neutrality ethics of librarianship can be tricky, but the best sharing of anyone's faith is the simple living of it in front of others. Your life is the best testimony as to the value of your faith, and no faith is worth its salt when imposed by mandate or bullying. Each of us has reached our point in faith by a journey, and others must make their own. One of librarianship's strongest faith statements is that information has value, librarians must impart that value to patrons, and that they must then build their own belief system out of that imparted information" (Wessles, 2003).

In the context of free for all information-access environment there is a full-fledged plan of action, called the Five Laws of Library Science propounded in 1931 by the Indian library guru Dr. S. R. Ranganathan [59a]. These Laws, mentioned at the beginning of this essay, represent eastern philosophy of information dissemination. Recalling these Five Laws here:

* Books are for use;
* Every reader his / her book;
* Every book its reader;
* Save the time of the reader; and
* Library is a growing organism.

Many information specialists have re-worded these to suit the changing dimensions of the information environment. For example, to suit the Web-based Reference Service Marilyn Moody modified the second law: "Every Reader His or Her Access..."(Moody, 1999) Furthermore, the most crucial and architecturally powerful component of the Internet is the bandwidth – the width of the information superhighway using which either you download or upload any bit or byte, irrespective of the size of the file/resource. So great is the power of bandwidth even in today's post .com era, that great giants who provide Internet Service are eventually likely to control all the free pathways of the cyberspace and may make you pay through the nose. There is a direct inference drawn from the Fourth Law, and suggests that Internet service providers and Webmasters must care for user-friendly bandwidth. George McMurdo Says:

> All five laws are worthy of re-examination for emerging nuances of contemporary relevance, with the changing dynamics of publishing and information discovery on the Internet and the World Wide Web. However, the fourth one, Save the time of the reader, is quite prosaically relatable to some of the issues mentioned above, to do with the size of graphic image files, and their consequent 'bandwidth friendliness' and effect on loading-times of web pages (Clickable image maps.., 2004).

Similarly, to suit the reference interview process in the context of real-time – or synchronous Ask-a-Librarian activity in reference services- Taher re-phrased the Five Laws as follows (Taher, 2002):

* Information is for Use;
* Every Interviewee his / her Information;
* Every Information its Interviewee;
* Save the Time of the Interviewee; and
* Information is a Living Organism.

Analogous to the need to create user-friendliness environments an open source expert reiterates that Five Laws as best practice principles would add value to the information society:

> "Recognizing Ranganathan's five laws of Library Science and their underlying concepts as powerful inspirations for social change, I would

> like to analyze the open source software, as defined by the Open Source Initiative (OSI), and its congruency with the five laws. If the underlying concepts upon which the five laws are built had such profound impact on our society, then the proponents of the open source movement can learn a thing or two" (The Open Source.., 2004).

While the above open for all liturgies still remains here the focus of the discussion, let us glance at the derivatives that have evolved in the information profession. From a meditation point of view, Walt Crawford and Michael Gorman offered Five New Laws of Library Science – amending the original Laws of Prof. Ranganathan, as follows (Our Singular Strengths.., 2004)

* Libraries serve humanity;
* Respect all forms by which knowledge is communicated;
* Use technology intelligently to enhance service;
* Protect free access to knowledge; and
* Honor the past and create the future.

Some prefer to view these as principles of best practices, rather than as 'laws' (one needs to still keep in mind that the law giver, Ranganathan's favorite list is not limited to laws alone, he has many related terms: canons, principles, etc.). To illustrate this best practice idea we may cite 'On Principles of Librarianship' by Huang Jungui:

> "The author thinks that the first four laws among Shiyali Ramamrita Ranganathan's Five Laws of Library Science have guiding significance and eternal vitality, while they have also limitations. However, Ranganathan didn't substantially explain the fifth law, i.e. "A Library is a growing organism". M. Gorman's Five New Laws of Librarianship are innovative, but they are not a development of Ranganathan's Five Laws. Neither Ranganathan's Five Laws and Gorman's Five New Laws are laws of library science. They are actually laws of library practices. Then, the author proposes that principles for library development should include five main aspects of library practices and librarianship, such as adaptation to economic and technological developments, national adaptation, reader

> enteredness, sustainable development and the objective of library profits" (Huang, 2004).

A recent publication on Judaism by Douglas Rushkoff (2002) continues this tirade to make the information access more open and liberal. Under the section on 'Open Source Judaism, he states:

> "An open source religion would work the same way as open software development: it is not kept secret or mysterious at all. Everyone contributes to the codes we use to comprehend our place in the universe.

Perhaps in the end the open-source culture will triumph not because cooperation is morally right or software "hoarding"' is morally wrong (assuming you believe the latter, which neither Linus nor I do), but simply because the closed-source world cannot win an evolutionary arms race with open-source communities that can put orders of magnitude more skilled time into a problem. Eric S. Raymond, "The Cathedral and the Bazaar" (Raymond).

> We allow our religion to evolve based on the active participation of its people. We internalize and engineer Jewish laws and ideas as adults, rather than following them by rote, as children. We come to realize that the writings and ideas are not in stone, but invitations to inquire, challenge, and evolve. Together, as a community, we define Judaism as the ongoing resolution of our individual sensibilities (111-112)".

In short, such an inclusive liturgy of librarianship in religious diversity perspective makes it useful for the faithful to co-exist. It enables, on the one hand, as a blessing in disguise to avoid colour blindness and on the other, fostering harmony among all citizens of the global village.

NOTES AND REFERENCES

1. Bates, Marcia J. (1999). The Invisible Substrate of Information Science. *Journal of The American Society For Information Science.* Vol. 50(12); p. 1043-1050,

http://topology.eecs. umich.edu/archive/bates_99.pdf (18 Feb 2004); and C. W. Choo. "Information Science Taxonomy." http://choo.fis.utoronto.ca/IStaxonomy (18 Feb 2004)

2. Katz, William A. (1978). *Introduction to Reference Work. Volume 1*. Basic Information Sources, New York, NY: McGraw Hill Book Co. p. 5-6.

3. Davis, Mitzi (2001), *You Can't Tell a Book*, January 1, 2001. http://circlesmart.com/article.cfm?article_id=3101 (6 Mar. 2002)

4. Berliner, Barbara. (1999). *The Book of Answers: The New York Public Library's Telephone Reference Service's Most Unusual and Entertaining Questions*. New York, N.Y.: Prentice Hall.

5. University of South Florida (2004). *University of South Florida - E Mail Reference Questions*. http://www.lib.usf.edu/ref/ifrank/refquestions.html (18 Feb 2004)

6. Taher, Mohamed. (2002). The Reference Interview Through Asynchronous E-Mail and Synchronous interactive Reference: Does it Save the Time of the Interviewee? *Internet Reference Service Quarterly*. Vol. 7(3); p. 22-34.

7. *Ask a Librarian*. http://www.timberland.lib.wa.us/religion.asp

8. *Non-violence*. www.tacoma.ctc.edu/library/sites/nonviolence.shtm

9. *Ask a Librarian*. www.lea.sandwell.gov.uk/libraries/mmrc.htm

10. Personal communication (2003a). *Observations about Librarians and Religion*. Vibiana Bowman, Reference Librarian and Web Administrator, Paul Robeson Library, Rutgers – The State University, Camden, New Jersey. Email: bowman@camden.rutgers.edu October 18, 2003.

11. Personal communication (2003b). *Manazhiyil Kesavan Prasanna*. Information Officer, Motorola, Somajiguda, Hyderabad 500 082 India, Email: mkprasanna@mihy.mot.com November 14, 2003

12. Trotti, John B. The Theological Library: In Touch with the Witnesses. **In**: *Christian librarianship: Essays on the integration of faith and profession*. Edited by Gregory A. Smith. With a Foreword by Donald G. Davis, Jr. Jefferson, N.C.: McFarland & Co., Publishers; 48. http://bookweb.kinokuniya.co.jp/htmy/0786413298.html

13. *The Nazareth Resource Library*. http://www.cin.org/users/james/index.htm (18 Feb 2004)

14. *Frequently Asked Questions From Stumpers*. (2004). http://domin.dom.edu/depts/gslis/stumpers/faqf.htm / (18 Feb 2004)

15. Antelman, Kristin. Ed. (2002). *Database-Driven Web Sites*. New York, N.Y.:Haworth Press. p. 57-58.

16. *Empirical Analysis of Internet Filtering in Saudi Arabia.* http://cyber.law.harvard.edu/filtering/saudiarabia

17. *Empirical Analysis of Internet Filtering in China.* http://cyber.law.harvard.edu/filtering/china

18. Peart, Justin. *Political Regulation of Internet Use: Examining the Role of Fear.* http://marketing.byu.edu/htmlpages/ccrs/proceedings99/peart.htm

19. Watters, Steve. *Teachers in Focus: See No Evil.* http://family.org/eforum/teachermag/features/a0010733.cfm

20. *While the Web-based trends are obvious from the above, professional bodies, such as the American Library Association, has its guidelines: 'Code of Ethic'.* www.ala.org/alaorg/oif/1981code.html

21. Billings, Harold. (2002). *Magic and Hypersystems: Constructing the Information-Sharing Library.* Chicago, Ill: American Library Association, p. 76.

22. "We will always need interpreters, evaluators, and guides, even when the whole Western and Eastern cultural patrimony has been mounted in a digital chip ... the need for explanation, interpretation, and conversation will remain, and it will not met by machines," said Prof, David Hoekema, Academic Dean and Professor of Philosophy at Calvin College, quoted in Billings, Magic & Hypersystems, p. 81

23. One should not confuse this information mediation role with the term 'Infomediary,' as used elsewhere. Infomediary is an Elsevier's journal title in the field of library science (published between 1985 and 1993). Nevertheless, the present work will use information mediators and infomediary as interchangeable terms. Two books deal at length with this perspective of infomediation: John Hagel and Marc Singer. Net Worth: Shaping Markets When Customers Make the Rules. (Boston, MA. Harvard Business School Press, 1999); and Don Tapscott and others. Digital Capital: Harnessing The Power of Business Webs. (Boston, MA. Harvard Business School Press, 2000): 180 - 82).

24. For more details on information seeking see, Barbara Quint, "Inside a Searcher's Mind: The Seven Stages of an Online Search", Online, May and July 1991; Glenda Myers and P.A. Van Brakel, "A Web-Based Evidence Based Model Information-Seeking Model," www.shef.ac.uk/~scharr/eblib/GMabs.htm (18 Feb 2004); Colleen Cool, Soyeon Park, Nicholas J. Belkin, Jürgen Koenemann, Kwong Bor Ng, "Information Seeking Behavior in New Searching Environments," http://www.scils.rutgers.edu/tipster3/colis.html (18 Feb 2004)

25. COST: "Google Answers currently allow users to set a price for answers between $2.00 and $400.00... Early versions of the tips for users on the Google Answers site suggested using an hourly rate of $25.00 for factoring appropriate prices for questions based on anticipated time to complete the answer. Although it may seem logical that Google Answers researchers would be less likely to take on questions that would require more work than they would be compensated for, there is no explicit measure to evaluate.

Hobbyists who serve as Google Answers may well take on a question for the challenge... Like a number of expert services and unlike Google Answers, the librarian provides an estimate for the user before undertaking the work." in Keeney, Google Meets eBay, 9.

26. Outsell's analysis of data from 4,700 respondents showed that when corporate end users got beneficial data from their information centers, they either boosted revenues by an average of $801,585, cut costs by an average of $2,549 or saved an average of 12 hours... The lesson here is not that every interaction with the corporate library is a moneymaker or a dollar-saver, but when people do turn to the library to support their decisions, quite often, a lot of money is on the line," says Outsell researcher Mary Corcoran. Cybrarians: Office Libraries Check Out (2001, May 14). http://www.computerworld.com/roi/may/0,3277,STO60308,00.html (18 Feb 2004)

27. Jupiter Research Forecasts 50% Growth in Paid Search Will Drive Online Advertising Recovery to $6.3 Billion in 2003, www.internet.com/corporate/releases/03.07.03-newjupresearch.html (18 Feb 2004); "For Paid Search, Feedback is essential," www.internt.com/bus-news/article.php/2034071 (18 Feb 2004);

28. Kenney, Anne R. et al. (2003). Google Meets eBay: What Academic Librarians Can Learn From Alternative Information Providers. *D-Lib Magazine.* June 2003; p. 1-14. www.dlib.org/dlib/june03/kenney/06kenney.html (18 Feb 2004)

29. *In May 1996 Lois Abraham of The Canadian Press reported in The Windsor Star* (an Ontario provincial newspaper)

30. *Cultural, affiliated, dot.com Jews seek meaningful connection,* April 7, 2000/2 Nisan 5760. Vol. 52(31). www.jewishaz.com/jewishnews/000407/dotcom.shtml (10 Feb 2004)

31. *Judaism 101: Has links to Israel and Jewish resources.* http://shamash.org/trb/judaism.html

32. *Dunya, the CyberMuslim Information Collective: The basics of Islam, the Koran and links to newspapers.* http://www.uoknor.edu/cybermuslim.

33. *Hurry OM: Nidhi Taparia.* http://www.rediff.com/netguide/2000/dec/26god.htm

34. *Plug-pray - Hinduism Kit.* www.plug-pray.org/ENG/KitHinduist.html (10 Feb 2004)

35. Katz. (2002). p. 130.

36. Kavanaugh. (2002a). p. 336.

37. Gray, Helen T. (2001). *Worship On The Web: Religion sets its sites along information superhighway.* The Kansas City Star, 18 May 2001, 22:15, www.kcstar.com/item/pages/printer.pat,fyi/3accaf37.518,.html (10 Feb 2004)

38. Kavanaugh. (2002b). p. 331

39. *Virtual Rituals.* http://www.clas.ufl.edu/users/gthursby/rel/electron.htm

40. Broughton, Vanda. (2000). A New Classification for the Literature of Religion. *66th IFLA Council and General Conference*, Jerusalem, Israel, 13-18 August, 2000. www.ifla.org/IV/ifla66/papers/034-130e.htm

Latest Revision: May 12, 2000 (12 Jan 2004). This paper makes an extensive attempt to present the existing bias, remedies that can be adapted in a non-christian (we can call it multifaith) context. Despite its bias towards one classification scheme, its taxonomy proposed on faceted classification model for UDC is of great value for others to adopt:

National Center for Charitable Statistics. "NCCS--National Taxonomy of Exempt Entities – Core Codes – Definitions: Religion." http://nccs2.urban.org/ntee-cc/x.htm (12 Jan 2004); Polis Denominational Taxonomy. "Denomination Taxonomy: 1990 Denominations as Listed by Glenmary Research Center." www.polis.iupui.edu/RUC/Research/Glenmary_by_Polis_Types_as_table.htm (12 Jan 2004); Anton Karl Kozlovic. "Seven Logical Consequences of Interreligious Dialoguing: A Taxonomy of Praxis Possibilities." Marburg Journal of Religion, 8 (1) Sept 2003, 1-24 www.uni-marburg.de/religionwissenschaft/journal/mjr/kozlovic2.html (12 Jan 2004). It is worth mentioning that Google has five facets to explain its googlism. More on building metadata to capture information at "Visual Resources Association's Delivering Digital Images," www.tasi.ac.uk/advice/delivering/metadata.html; See also digital metadata bibliography at www.taher.cjb.net

41. Abel-Kops, Chad P. (2003). *What has straw in common with wheat*? A Selective Review of Bibliographical Control in the Field of Homiletics. http://firstmonday.org/issues/issue6 _7/abel/index.html (18 Aug, 2003): 6

42. *Ever preach in a chat room*? New Wineskins: The Believers Magazine. http://www.wineskins.org/content.asp?CID=48182

43. *Vanderbilt Divinity School Library*. Nashville, Tennessee. http://divinity.lib.vanderbilt.edu/bibs/homiletics.htm

44. *Wabash Center for Teaching and Learning, Wabash Centre for Teaching and Learning in Theology and Religion*. Wabash College, Crawfordsville, Indiana. http://www.wabashcenter.wabash.edu/Internet/preach.htm

45. Bruce, Harry and Todd, Ross. (1993). Cultural Dimensions in Reference Services: Is There Unity in Diversity?" **In**: *Infobridges: Linking Australia and Asia*. Proceedings of the Second National Reference and Information Service Section Conference, Darwin 9–11 July 1993. Edited by Murray Maynard. Darwin, N.T., p. 85-95. Australian Library and Information Association.

46. *Testing Faith in the Market God*. (2001). http://marty-center.uchicago.edu/sightings/archive_ 2001/sightings-110501.shtml

47. Continuing education is just the inspiration required to sustain the spirit. Rev. Ken Blank and John W. Campbell. *Current Research: A Survey of Responsibilities and Time*

Allocations, Including Supervisors and Administrative Tasks... www.cpeokc.org/ curretnsearch.htm (18 Feb 2004) ; Instances of faith-based initiatives for a Christian audience is visible in Worship.com's venture between Passion Conferences and WebMatters New Media: http://worship.com/us.htm; from a Muslim perspective in the (probably now defunct annual program) Islamic Internet Conference, 1999.

48. Adekunle Olusola Okunoye. (2003). *Knowledge Management and Global diversity: A Framework to Support Organisations in Developing Countries. Doctoral thesis.* (Fin., Finland, University of Turku, 2003), 86. www.cc.jyu.fi/~adeokun/e-papers/Dissertation 2003.pdf (18 Feb 2004)

49. Skrzeszewski, Stan (2002). *Feedback. Information Highways.* Vol. 9(5);5 Jul-Aug 2002; p. 7.

50. Casey, Vicki (2002). People Seeking Information: E-content's Human Face. *Information Highways.* Vol. 9(5); 5 Jul-Aug 2002; p. 14-17.

51. Campbell, K.K. (2004). *To The Barricades! Content Over Chrome on the World Wide Web.* http://www.kkc.net/eyenet/1996/net0118.htm (18 Feb 2004).

    What it implies is the need for a special eye to look not just far, but also deep at the same time. Based on the complexity of the problem, service providers have come up with solutions, one of these is "Search Engines / Data Bases." http://cmhosting.net/access/ 20data.shtml (18 Feb 2004); the other attempt to undo the problem is by individuals to gather and categorize (Sermon & Lectionary, A Holy Easter, Grief and Loss, Connections, Heaven, Pastor's ...and the mundane) Web sites, such as, "Charlene's Special." http://www.spirit-net.ca/charlene/special.html.bak (18 Feb 2004); and another sample is of a browsable multifaith guide form Zensearch database, which fits not only many religions, it also has diversity in its samples for each faith: www.zensearch.com/e-shopping/society_culture_philosophy_religion_1.shtml (18 Feb 2004)

52. In any society even today, despite it being considered the worst in morality by some, there are sensible people who wish to have family-friendly Internet. An infomediary must know what sources exist on the Web for such friendly gestures, either free or for a price. Check the following sources for some guidelines, trends, and information: "Most Americans Do Not Understand How Websites Use Information About Them: New Annenberg Research Finds that Americans Misunderstand Purpose of Internet Privacy Policies." June 25, 2003, www.upenn.edu/researchatpenn/article.php?686&tch (2 Feb 2004); "Online Chat Safety: The Christian Chat Quick Start Help." www.thechristianchat.net/safetyhelp.html (31 Oct 2003); Learn to read the fine print, even in not-so-fine spaces:

    "This site can be blocked by installing any of the filtering software... Please prevent access of this site to minors by using filtering software" and the software are:

> "Surfwatch" http://www.surfwatch.com/ (18 Feb 2004)
> "Netnanny" http://www.netnanny.com/ (18 Feb 2004)
> "Cyberpatrol" http://www.cyberpatrol.com/ (18 Feb 2004) See:
> http://www.bambili.com/top/top17.asp (24 Jan 2004);

In a faith perspective, one finds concerns in yet another segment:

> Islamic academics call for common guidelines on use of Internet:
>
> CAIRO, Dec 3 (AFP) - A Saudi-sponsored academics' organization called for standardized religious guidelines Thursday to govern the use of the Internet in the Islamic world. Following a meeting here this week, the League of Islamic Universities recommended "unifying the fatwas (religious rulings) issued on the use of the Internet in order to avoid contradictory viewpoints on the subject".

53. *Join and participate in Virtual Worlds Explorer, at Centre for Advanced Learning Technologies*. The CALT Virtual Worlds. www.calt.insead.edu/VirtualWorlds (21 Jan 2004)

54. You may not get the title of master, because you will be later competing with so many self-declared virtual meta-masters. Read the following to understand how these meta-masters get themselves, presumably, the status of creators, destroyers and sustainers: Steve Grand. "Confessions of a Cyber-God." www.cyberlife-research.com/articles/confessions.htm (22 Jan 2004)

55. *See* notes and references # 22

56. *Help for Church Webmasters: Internet Users Get God*. (2002). Issue 9, 01/02/02. http://www. downeychurch.org/BackIssues/Issue9.html

57. Wessles, Mike (2003). Faith at the Front Desk – Spirituality and Patron Service. *American Libraries*. Vol. 34(5); May 2003; p. 43

58. Ranganathan, S.R. (1963). Five Laws of Library Science. 2nd ed. Bangalore, **In** *Sarada, Ranganathan Endowment for Library Science*. 1st ed. 1931.

59. Ranganathan, S.R. (1961). *Reference service*. Ed. 2., Chapter E, Sec. 412.

Pristine Purity of Reference Service

"All stain of egoistic choice, of hankering after personal profit, and of self-regarding desire must be extirpated from the reference librarian while effecting contact between reader and book. There must be no demand for fruit and for seeking for reward; the only fruit is the fulfillment of establishing contact between books and readers; the only reward is a constant progression towards the attainment of the ideals set up by the Laws of Library Science. The reference librarian should allow nothing to creep in to stain the purity of the self-giving. His only object in action should be to serve, to fulfill, and to become a manifesting instrument of the Divine Sakti in her works. There must be no pride of the instrument, no vanity, no arrogance. The books constitute Purusha as Akshara Brahma (Scriptal form of God). The readers constitute Prakriti manifesting itself as Manushya Prakriti (human manifestation of nature)."

60. Moody, Marilyn. (1999). Every Reader His or Her Access: The First Law of Library Science. *Internet Reference Service Quarterly*. Vol. 4(3); p. 1-3.

61. *Clickable image maps*. (2004). jimmy.qmuc.ac.uk/jisew/ewv23n2/PART4.HTM (18 Feb 2004)

62. Taher, Mohamed (2002). The Reference Interview Through Asynchronous E-Mail and Synchronous interactive Reference: Does it Save the Time of the Interviewee?" *Internet Reference Service Quarterly*. Vol. 7(3); p. 22-34.

63. *The Open Source Philosophy*. (2004). www.kmentor.com/socio-tech-info/archives/cat_ the_open _source_ philosophy.html (18 Feb 2004)

64. *Our Singular Strengths: Meditations for Librarians..American Library Association*, 1997. lib.law.washington.edu/hazelton/Talk-People-LawLibshipFuture.htm (18 Feb 2004)

65. Huang, Jungu. (2004). *On Principles of Librarianship*. www.nlc.gov.cn/newpage/publish /xuebao/2001_2.htm (3 Feb. 2004)

66. Rushkoff, Douglas. (2002). *Nothing Sacred: The Truth About Judaism*. New York, N.Y.: Crown Publishers.

67. Raymond, Eric S. *The Cathedral and the Bazaar*. http://www.firstmonday.dk/issues/ issue3_3/raymond/

ADDITIONAL READING:

[Please contact the author]

WEBLIOGRAPHY

1. Abel-Kops, Chad P. (2003). *What has straw in common with wheat*? A Selective Review of Bibliographical Control in the Field of Homiletics. http://firstmonday.org/issues/ issue6_7/abel/index.html (18 Aug, 2003)

2. *Business intelligence - What is it?* (2004). www.cmis.csiro.au/bi/what-is-BI.htm (10 Feb 2004).

3. Understanding Intelligence (1995), In: Leonard M. Fuld's *The new competitor intelligence*; John Wiley & Sons, 1995. http://www.fuld.com/Tindex/CIbook/chap01. html (10 Feb 2004);

4. *BusinessiIntelligence gap.* (2004). www.antarctica.net/bigap.html (21 May 2004)

5. *CIA, Inc: Espionage and the craft of business intelligence.* (2004). www.earth-religions.com/CIA_Inc_Espionage_and_the_Craft_of_Business_Intelligence_1574883887.html (24 Mar 2004)

6. *Content filtering technologies and Internet Service Providers enabling usercChoice* (2000) http://www.cs.dal.ca/~shepherd/filtering/ISPweb.htm#Examples (22 Mar 2000)

7. Deep into the Bone... (2004). **In**: *Re-inventing Rites of Passage.* www.gracecathedral.org/enrichment/experts/exc20010516.shtml (10 Feb 2004)

8. Dodge, Martin. (2001). *Mapping how people use a website: Ben Fry's anemone visualization.* Map of the Month, Mappa Mundi Magazine, June 2001, http://mappa.mundi.net/maps/maps_022 (23 Dec 2003): Fry's ultimate dream map of the Net would apply the organic information design paradigm to smoothly summarize the vast richness and complexity of online activity, providing an almost omnipotent overview of the whole

9. Freston, Sean D. (2004). *CI challenges in Southeast Asia.* www.imakenews.com/eletra/mod_print_view.cfm?this_id=88894&u=scip2&issue_id=000019276 (24 Mar 2004).

10. Graef, Jean L. (2004). *Using the Internet for Competitive Intelligence.* www.cio.com/CIO/ arch_0695_cicolumn.html (10 Feb 2004);

11. *Internet marketing reference.* (2004). www.marketingterms.com/dictionary (24 Mar 2004)

12. Neelameghan, A. (1999). Lateral Relations and Links in Multicultural, Multimedia Databases in the Spiritual and Religious Domains: Some obervations. *Knowledge Organization.* Vol. 26(2); p. 74-79. 2 refs.

13. O'Neill, Edward, T. and Chan, Lois Mai (2004). FAST (Faceted Application of Subject Terminology): A simplified LCSH-based vocabulary. Paper presented at *World Library and Information Congress, 69th IFLA General Conference and Council,* 1-9 Aug 2003, Berlin. www.ifla.org/IV/ifla69/papers/01e-Oneill_Mai-chan.pdf (22 Apr 2004)

14. Rajashekar, T.B.; A. Sreenivasa Ravi, and A. Neelameghan. (1998). *Designing a multimedia information service for the Internet and CD-ROM.* http://itt.nissat.tripod.com/itt9802/ois.htm

15. *Rapid ROI: How top companies are leveraging Web data to keep customers, improve content and maximize profit (2004).* www.internetworld.com/webseminar/archives (10 Feb 2004)

16. *Religion web sites surge amid spiritual holidays and extensive news coverage, according to Media Metrix* March 2002 Internet ratings. (2004). http://www.comscore.com/press/release.asp?press=277 (23 May 2004)

17. *Research outlet and integration: The 4Cs for WWW information professionals - content, context, control, and continuity*. (2004). http://www.twurl.com/roi-4cs.htm (24 Mar 2004)

18. *Researching companies online – a tutorial*. (2004). www.learnwebskills.com/company /index.html (10 Feb 2004)

19. *Roundup: Off-the-shelf market research on the Web*. (2002). The Information Advisor, April 2002. www.informationadvisor.com (10 Feb 2004)

20. *Six Ways to Measure Performance and Create Success*. http://www.webmomz.com/ Business-Articles/business-business-metrics.shtml ; Melody Y. Ivory (2003) Automated Web Site Evaluation: Researchers' and Practitioners Perspectives. Boston, Kluwer Academic Publishers.

INFORMATION SOCIETY

INFORMATION SOCIETY, INFORMATION NETWORKS AND NATIONAL DEVELOPMENT: AN OVERVIEW

P .B. Mangla

Highlights the growing importance of information and information institutions in the socio-economic development of a country. Emphasizes the fact that the value of information is not intrinsic but lies in the use and applications to which it is put. In this context, the need for an effective and efficient national information infrastructure making innovative use of the available ICTs has been brought out.

1 FRAMEWORK

The vital role information institutions - libraries, documentation centres and information centres - play in education, spread of literacy, research and overall socio-economic development of a country or a society is now well recognized. Information, whether in the form of empirical data, or, in the developed form called knowledge is therefore being rightly regarded as a vital national resource, as essential to the nation's well being and security as any other resource, such as, land, water, minerals, etc. Beyond the frontiers of a country it provides an important basis for international relations, cooperation, peace, prosperity and overall development of nations. The wealth of popular, intellectual, scholarly and research resources in libraries, information centres and information systems of a country is, therefore one of the greatest assets of that nation. But like several natural resources information or knowledge resources, if unexploited or untapped and also unsupported and uncoordinated in growth and usage, would certainly be in danger of being wasted and inefficiently as well as ineffectively utilized. At the same time information is different from several other resources in the sense that it is dynamic in growth and inexhaustible.

Historically a substantial part of human knowledge and culture have been handed down to successive generations in the form of recorded knowledge. This resource consists of documents such as clay tablets, books, journals and other categories of texts: of audio and visual materials and of other units of information or data that can be processed and handled by a computer. In recent years these records have become increasingly varied through technological extensions of written words, pictures and sounds. For example, a significant part of a country's information resources is today recorded on films, magnetic tapes, video-cassettes, CD-ROMs, DVDs and in computer files. As the nation's knowledge grows and the number of these records increases our dependence upon them also increases proportionately and the need to gain access to them becomes more even more crucial. It has been rightly said that 'no society can advance beyond a certain point without effective access to its collective memory of records, or, conversely, an advanced society that loses control of the record will regress'*.

Information is created, stored, processed and distributed or disseminated by a vast array of diverse information activities in the private and public sectors both at the national and international levels, by employing thousands of specialists and spending large sums of money, and by using a wide range of technologies to achieve equally widely varying objectives. For example, the publishing industry, the bibliographic database industry producing indexing and abstracting and other access services, the telecommunication media and private and public information services are just a few of the many and varied elements that make up the rich mosaic of the contemporary scene. Libraries, information systems, information networks and other information facilities are certainly among the most important custodians and disseminators of these records of cultural heritage. They must therefore be adequately equipped, organized, financed and inter-connected if their resources are to be made accessible and available to all the people of a country. Norms of equity and justice demand it. In any country this is possible only with the active support of the government(s) and the public and private agencies and institutions.

It hardly needs to be emphasized here that right information provided when it is needed, where it is needed and in the form in which it is needed, improves the capability of an individual, a business, a government agency and various other organizations, to take informed decisions and achieve the targeted goals

---

* *(Note: The term 'Information' is used here in a generic sense, and is often used interchangeably with 'knowledge'. The term 'Information Systems' is used in a wider sense to include libraries, documentation centers, information centers and all such institutions involved in information processing and dissemination. Library Schools include all such institutions engaged in the education and training of all categories of Library and Information professionals.)*

effectively and efficiently. The need for relevant and authentic information has become all the more essential today with the spread of democracies simply because no democratic system can function efficiently and effectively without proper information support. It is undoubtedly true that 'access to information and ideas is indispensable to the development of human potential, the advancement of civilization, and the continuance of self government'.

2 EMERGENCE OF INFORMATION SOCIETY/KNOWLEDGE SOCIETY

Traditionally, over the years, human society has generally been categorized with designations such' as 'open' or 'closed', 'agrarian' or, industrial', democratic' or 'totalitarian', and 'socialist' or 'capitalist' which served as useful indicators of the kind of society being discussed or talked about. In the present times, however, in view of the essential need for information and easy access to information resources, societies are being designated as 'information societies' or 'knowledge societies'. Since the 1970s rapid developments in Information and communication technologies (ICT) have brought in vast changes in economic, industrial, cultural and sociological spheres and ushered in an era, which could even be described as a 'revolution'. The revolution we are concerned with here is not yet complete; it is evolving and has been at the same time less obvious and more far reaching than a mere change of regime or political system. It has been a revolution in our ways of living, working and communicating which directly or indirectly have affected every one of us on this planet. In a way 'information' is all around us, in the air, under the oceans, and in outer space. Its presence gets recognized not just because of the media or professional futurologists but also as a necessity in all walks of human activity.

A glance through the published literature on the subject, however, indicates that the term 'information society' has been widely used rather in a general or even somewhat unscientific manner and that the sociologists have yet to construct a proper theory about it. Several authors such as Kochen, Mashelkar, Machlup, Cronin (1986), Peter Drucker, Alvin Toefler (1980), and Marc Porat have published commendable studies on this subject. While Dizard has used the term 'information age', Daniel Bell calls it 'post-industrial society' which in a way is being used as synonymous with the term 'information society' (Bell, 1986). Bell sees modern industrial countries in the stage of transition into the last of a three-stage sequence of economic evolution. According to him, first there is pre-industrialism, an economy based mainly on extractions from nature such as mining, fishing, lumbering or agriculture. While today there are still several developing countries whose economies are totally pre-industrial, yet even several developed ones such as USA, Japan and UK still engage in these types of activities, but they are not the major areas of growth. The next stage is industrialism, which is based on fabrication of nature, the production of goods, in other words it is a manufacturing economy. Finally, the post-industrialism is an economy based on growth and application of new knowledge including applications in the delivery of services. This, according to him, is the economy of 'knowledge worker' wherein intellectual technologies replace machine technology. This change from an industrial society to a post-industrial society leads to a growing percentage of white-collar workers, especially of professional and technical nature, in the work force. Bell further rightly emphasized that the revolution in science and technology required by the post- industrial society cannot be led by the working class and that the new emerging society would have the dominance of the professional and technical people. McGarry (1993) discusses the changing context of information vis-à-vis the society.

Some may comment that information in some form or the other has always existed and has been valued in every age and by every society. It was essential to the march of progress in the pre-industrial times and during the industrial revolution and it remains so today. So what is the need to characterize the present and future society as 'information society'? Well, to some extent this question is quite valid and reasonable. But it becomes evident that the emerging society is indeed different when we take into account the various developments such as, vast amount of information being produced today, the sheer amount of R&D activity that underpins all those advances in computers and telecommunications that are taken for granted, communication satellites, the electronic office, the home delivery of computer-based information and entertainment services. These developments and several other related ones give us ample justification to call it as 'information society' as such which is a much wider concept, encompassing developments in science and technology, economy, politics and administration, and several other aspects of sociological or human studies. In such a society T.S. Eliot's anguish that 'Where is the wisdom that is lost in knowledge, and where is the knowledge that is lost in information 'would sound to be just a poetic lamentation. Information today is an essential ingredient for acquiring knowledge and possibly even 'wisdom'.

On the basis of the available literature and general usage of the term and also by taking into account the various developments in the developed countries an 'information society' may, therefore, be defined as the one in which the quality of life and also the prospects for social change and economic development depend increasingly on information and its exploitation. In such a society, the living standards, patterns of work and leisure, the education systems, R&D activities, the market place are all influenced markedly by information. This is evidenced today by an increasing array of information-intensive products and services, produced and communicated through a wide range of media, many of them electronic in nature. Developments in countries such as Japan, USA, UK and Germany amply demonstrate the viability of this generalized framework of such a society.

It may be relevant to point out that during the recent past several studies have been conducted to measure the different aspects of this emerging information society by using indicators such as 'amount of information', 'expenditure on information in the context of the GNP of a country', 'information industry', 'information machines', 'information services', 'information manpower', and 'communication media'. In one such measure it was found that the information workforce in the USA rose from 12.8% (1900) to 46.6% (1980) and in UK from 12.4% (1900) to 38% (1980). Today it is estimated to be around 60% in these two countries and more than 70% in Japan. The situation in several developing countries is also changing rapidly.

3 INFORMATION SYSTEMS, INFORMATION NETWORKS AND NATIONAL DEVELOPMENT

It is essential to reiterate here that the value of information is not intrinsic, but lies in the uses to which it can be put. From these uses advantages can be derived that are beneficial to its owner and other users. Developing systems and mechanisms that facilitate awareness of and access to information sources have been two major areas of concern to library and information professionals, information policy makers, managers, and others. These have been discussed and debated in seminars, conferences and several other forums both at the national and international levels. In India, for example, these have been discussed at the conferences of the professional associations, and in the meetings of various working groups appointed by the Planning Commission (Government of India), Council of Scientific and Industrial Research (CSIR), University Grants Commission (UGC) and several other governmental and non-governmental organizations (NGOs). At the International level, inter-governmental organizations, such as UNESCO, and other UN agencies and such other organisations as IFLA, ICA and ICSU have been keen to find universally acceptable solutions to several trans-national issues. Some of these issues include access to information (UAP), right to information; freedom of information, on-line access to remote data- bases, facsimile transmissions, language barriers, intellectual property rights, copyright, censorship, privacy, confidentially of information and various other related and even legal issues.

Information systems dealing with government policies and programmes, educational systems, social security programmes or science and technology programmes have also been developed to contribute to the socio-economic and cultural development of all individuals in the society (whether rich or poor, young or old, men or women, literate or illiterate, urban or rural), and to enable the nation make industrial, scientific and economic progress. Globally speaking, they would further assist the nation make its distinctive contribution to world peace and prosperity, and maintain its identity and personality in the comity of nations.

In several situations it has also been noticed that many developing countries do not have information even on less expensive but equally suitable technologies developed in other developing countries. Therefore, international programmes such as Technical Co-operation among Developing Countries (TCDC) and several others strongly stress the need for these developing countries to widely disseminate and exchange information on their technology developments among themselves, and with others. Agencies, such as, the specialized organs of the United Nations and NGOs, such as IFLA, FID and funding agencies such as IDRC of Canada and DSE of Germany have assigned priority to the need for making this flow of information less expensive and wherever possible, even free of cost.

4 INFORMATION TRANSFER: THE ROLE OF ICTS

Developments in communications have often been at the centre of changes in the society. Since Gutenberg, the printed text has become the principal medium of sharing information and knowledge the world over. As early as in 1947 the famous historian Arnold Toynbee in a lecture at London University entitled *'The Unification of the World'* laid much emphasis on his basic thesis that 'developments in transport and communications have created- or would create, a single planetary society'. Fifty years ago that was an unusually farsighted view; the phrase 'Global Village' still lay few decades in future, and Marshal McLuhan had yet to herald the dawn of electronic culture. More recent breakthroughs in communications –telecommunications, satellite technology - have brought about profound social and economic changes in the present day society .To day new technologies can transfer vast amounts of information almost anywhere in the world in a matter of seconds.

The advances in ICTs would enable the establishment of whole new societies in cyberspace, linking easily individuals with common interests to share views and opinions. These new technologies from e-mail to cellular telephony to teleconferencing let more and more people share knowledge without having to be in the same place. Sharing information through computers interlinked through telephone lines such as through INTERNET is becoming commonplace in industrialized countries and is becoming so in many developing countries as well. To quote Al Gore, the former Vice-President of the United States, 'Gutenberg's invention which so empowered Jefferson and his colleagues in their fight for democracy seems to pale before the rise of electronic communication and innovation from the telegraph to television to microprocessor and the emergence of a new computerized world - an information age'.

It is worth pointing out here that in several developing countries the use of ICT, though growing fairly rapidly, is still limited in applications. The governments in some of these countries have in recent years given the use of ICTs high priority because ICTs hold enormous potential for driving the economy and accelerating social development. These countries are also realizing the inherent dangers that Digital Divide entails. Today people in remote communities the world over can have access to information and knowledge beyond the dreams of anyone even in the industrial countries a quarter century ago. To quote the UN Secretary General Kofi Annan, 'the digital revolution has unleashed an unprecedented wave of technological change. Used responsibly it can greatly improve our chances of defeating poverty and better meeting our other priority objectives'. To quote further, 'Ten years ago getting information from or to the developing world was costly and more time consuming. But today the World Wide Web is changing that. We can now read newspapers on-line from every comer of the world within seconds of their publication. We can find and download information from national government departments, leading overseas research institutions and key non-governmental organizations just as quickly' (Annan, 2000).

5 NATIONAL INFORMATION SYSTEMS INFRASTRUCTURE

The national capabilities for making knowledge and information accessible for wider use are often referred to as a country's national information infrastructure.

Pauline Atherton has identified the following seven elements of such an infrastructure (Atherton, 1977):

- A nucleus of physical information resources (libraries, documentation centers, information analysis centers, etc);
- A supply of trained information personnel;
- Linkages to personnel information sources, i.e. to technical consultants, scientists, engineers, and technologists in higher education, research and development establishments, technological institutes and other technical units;
- Linkages to significant decision making bodies, government agencies, economic sectors, educational institutions, research and development establishments and technological institutions;
- Two-way communication channels with users;
- An organizational system that brings together and energizes these resources, personnel, and linkages; and
- National policies that promote the systematic development of the infrastructure.

It may be added here that in the developing countries 60- 70% of population lives in rural areas and their level of literacy is rather low. The national information systems and infrastructures in these countries need to develop programmes and activities especially geared to meet the information needs of their rural communities. Without going into details it may be sufficient to mention that the role of A V materials, TV, radio, person-to person contacts, community television programmes, etc. should be given due recognition in these programmes and activities.

National information systems must not, however, be limited to libraries, documentation centres and information centres. They constitute an important component in the gamut of all those organizations and institutions concerned with generating, collecting, storing and disseminating information and knowledge. The

IT infrastructure, the network of tele-centres and extension centres, mass media, etc should also be viewed as a necessary component of the total national information system. All these are closely inter-related it is essential that the 'information sector' be viewed in totality so as to eliminate unnecessary duplication and thus develop a well-coordinated system of information and communication services in a country.

6 EXAMPLES FROM SOUTH EAST ASIA

Our basic hypothesis that there is indeed a close relationship between information and development is proven to be true when we study the information systems and their role in some developed and developing countries, If, for example, we look at the successful economies of countries, such as, Japan, Singapore and South Korea, we find that they are indeed countries in which economic and scientific information is widely and easily accessible. In all these three countries, information technology has been developed and exploited to a high level of sophistication. This has led not only to the more effective management of enterprises and institutions, but also to major structural changes in economic activities. In the newly industrialized countries more widespread benefits have accrued because of the key role of information and the effective use of information technology in government and business as also in the development of new products, in the redesigning of the existing products and in the creation of new systems of manufacturing and distribution of goods. Information systems in these countries also support the vital service sectors such as banking, media, education and research. Actually, in several ways, these countries are today comparable to technologically advanced countries of the West. South Korea, for example, has also been a pioneer in implementing a national information plan to provide centralized resources and information services to support industry. Even in Indonesia, the development of library and information services has been clearly incorporated into national planning and this has received considerable support from the World Bank and the Asian Development Bank.

7 THE INDIAN SCENARIO

Regarding the scenario in library and information systems and services (LISS) in India there is a fair amount of literature, such as books, periodical articles, reports, seminar/conference proceedings and research monographs published during the past 50 years or so. Seminal contributions made by S.R. Ranganathan are well recognized and have put India in a prestigious position in the world. Successive national governments have given adequate recognition to the vital role that LISS can play in the overall socio-economic development of the country as can be seen in the Five Year Plans, government reports and other documents. As a result, a fairly large infrastructure of LISS has been developed during the past five decades or so, in terms of national libraries, academic libraries, scientific and research libraries and public libraries. Indian National Bibliography, started in 1958, aims at providing a bibliographic control over the Indian publications, and documentation services at the national level are provided by documentation centres, such as, the National Institute of Science Communication and Information Resources (NISCAIR) (constituted with the recent merger of INSDOC and NISCOM), DESIDOC, NASSDOC and NISIET. Information systems and programmes such as those of INFLIBNET, NISSAT and ENVIS are in operation, as also metropolitan area networks such as DELNET, CALIBNET and MALIBNET have been established. Several institutions such as the Bhaba Atomic Energy Research Centre (BARC), Mumbai and the Indian Council of Agricultural Research (ICAR), New Delhi, function as input centres for global information systems such as INIS and AGRIS, respectively. Collaborations with several global information programmes and databases such as ASTINFO, APINESS, and several others have developed so as to provide access to information resources at the international level. Access through information networks such as NICNET, ERNET, etc is being utilized by the LISS in the country. More than 125 educational institutions are conducting L&IS educational programmes at various levels. Library Associations both at the national and state levels have been established. Organizations such as UGC, CSIR, ICSSR, RRLF are active in developing LISS in the country. Digitization activities such as the

Traditional Knowledge Digital Library (TKDL) project of NISCAIR (CSIR) are progressing (Mashelkar, 2002). Indian Digital Library in Engineering Services Technology (INDEST) provides for access to electronic resources to about 38 institutions in S&T, Engineering and Management in the country. CSIR also provides its network of laboratories with access to e-journals. A National Mission for Manuscripts sponsored by the Department of Culture (Govt. of India) has been launched by the Hon'ble Prime Minister on February 8, 2003.

While these are significant developments, there are several gray areas that need attention. The country is yet to adopt a National Policy for LISS (Mangla, 1997). The use of information technology has yet to gain wider acceptance and use even in fairly large sized libraries and information centres. While our planners, decision makers and LIS professionals continue to emphasize that priority be given for the further development of LISS in the country, the whole exercise should not continue to remain a matter of mere rhetoric. Instead action should be based on an understanding of the utility and value of information and information systems in national development. There is much to learn from the positive experiences of several countries in South East Asia and, of course, those of the developed world.

8 INFORMATION MANPOWER

Information professionals function as intermediaries between information sources, information systems and information users. They are designated variously as information brokers, information providers and information gatekeepers. In a way the traditional librarian is also expected to perform similar functions. The term 'librarian' is even used synonymously with, 'information professional' in general parlance, with emphasis that the latter is more modern and forward looking than the former. This emphasis is seen more prominently almost everywhere since the late 1970s because of the application of ICTs in library and information services. Developments, such as, on-line public access catalogues (OPAC), access to databases whether online or off-line, increased use of computers in house-keeping operations and for user services, access through global networks such as the Internet, use of audio-visual media, etc necessitate the availability of a new breed of information professionals who have the required education and training, motivation and orientation. Library schools must, therefore, not only give a fresh look to redesigning the LIS curricula but also take concrete steps to implement them. Library and Information Science being an interdisciplinary subject of study requires a multi-disciplinary faculty (core and guest-faculty) for proper education and training in the real sense. Since most of the library schools are part of the respective university systems they are indeed in a good position to draw subject specialists from other faculties or teaching departments for this purpose and make optimal use of the infrastructural facilities available in the parent organization.

9 CONCLUSIONS

In the present information age developing and strengthening of a country's information systems and infrastructure should receive high priority in the programmes for national development. Innovative use of technology – adaptation of technology developed elsewhere as well as application of indigenous technology, can solve many problems more quickly and certainly at a lower cost than by initiating and conducting its own research projects. Several countries, in particular the developing ones, must give special attention to the development of their information infrastructures as very often they get flooded with research information and knowledge that they would otherwise find difficult to disseminate to their users. A well-organized information system supported by an equally efficient information infrastructure would certainly promote effective and efficient information transfer and utilization. Developing a well conceived and planned National Information Infrastructure (NII) would greatly help in narrowing the gap between the developed and developing countries. This may look like a 'utopia' today but I am sure, that with the rapid pace of development of ICTs and better understanding growing among nations this would not just remain a dream. The whole world thus emerges as a real Global Village and the future slogan should be *Global Vision-Local Touch*, with inherent diversities but with connectivity.

REFERENCES

1. Annan, Kofi A. (2000). *We the peoples: The role of the United Nations in the 21st century*. New York: United Nations.
2. Atherton, Pauline (1977). *Handbook for Information systems and services.* Paris: UNESCO.
3. Bell, D. (1986). *The coming of post-industrial society..* New York: Basic Books.
4. Cronin, Blaise.(1986). The information society. *Aslib Proceedings*, 38; p.121-129.
5. McGarry, Kevin (1993). *The changing context of information: an introductory analysis.* London: Library Association Publishing.
6. Mangla, P.B. (1997) National policy on libraries, information systems and services in India: An overview. *The New Review of Information and Library Research*, 3; p.155- 74.
7. Mashelkar, R.A. (2002) Protecting India's traditional knowledge, *Employment News*, March 16-22; p. 1-3.
8. Toefler, A. (1980). The Third Wave. London, Collins.

DIGITAL DIVIDE IN INDIA - NARROWING THE GAP: AN APPRAISAL WITH SPECIAL REFERENCE TO KARNATAKA

K.N. Prasad

This paper presents a report of the projects and programmes for narrowing the digital divide in India with special reference to the State of Karnataka. The various endeavours of the governments and non-government organizations in the country in creating awareness in rural areas especially through information kiosks are highlighted. Such activities and programmes in the State of Karnataka are briefly described.

1 INTRODUCTION

1.1 Definition

'Digital divide' is defined as the disparity between individuals (and classes of people) with and those without access or ability to use computers, communication technologies, and networks, such as, the Internet. This applies to all segments of population. Digital divide may exist between those who reside in urban areas and those in rural areas; between the educated and the uneducated or illiterate; between economic classes; and between the industrialized/technologically advanced and the less developed or developing nations. Digital divide may also exist among institutions in an area, that is, those who use information and communication technologies (ICTs) and those unable to use them. However, the focus of attention has been on segments of population seen as underserved or socially disadvantaged – low income, rural and multicultural communities and women (Rogos and Latta). The term 'digital divide' is of recent origin but the 'divide' or disparity among classes of population has existed for centuries.

1.2 Organization of the Paper

Following the introduction section, the paper discusses how digital divide manifests among classes of people, e.g. the urban and rural residents. The efforts – programmes and projects – to bridge the digital divide at the national / all India level, are briefly described followed by short descriptions of similar programmes and projects in the State of Karnataka.

1.3 Prof. Neelameghan's Interest

Prof. A. Neelameghan (AN) has been interested in information support to socio-economic development since the early 1970s when he was called upon by UNESCO to collaborate in the preparation of the UNISIST II background / working document. Again, he contributed to the preparation of the background document and initiation of DEVSIS by the International Development Research Centre (IDRC) Canada, in 1975. Subsequently he has been involved in the regional DEVSIS projects, e.g. at the Marga Institute, Colombo; in OECD's International Development Information Network (IDIN) especially in ADIPA/APDC in Kuala Lumpur, in Indonesia's NGO network (women empowerment, legal aid to the poor, technology transfer), South-Pacific Regional Development Information Network (SPARDIN) and others.

Most of the programmes, projects and activities that AN has been involved in during his tenure with UNESCO and subsequently (1978-), and even at present, are related to the introduction of computer applications and networking and training of library and information personnel in developing countries, to enhance their capacity to use ICTs, thus contributing to bridging the digital divide. He has several papers on development communication and problems of information access and use in developing countries. Being closely associated with the work of the Sarada Ranganathan Endowment for Library Science, I have been drawn into studies and discussions on 'digital divide'.

2 MANIFESTATIONS OF DIGITAL DIVIDE

2.1 Improving Skills to Use ICTs

The rapid developments in ICTs and their applications in many sectors of the national economy are ushering in a knowledge-based society and rapid globalization. The latter, in particular, is leading to blurring of geographical and political boundaries in peoples' interactions, commercial transactions, and development interventions (healthcare delivery, educational opportunities, etc.), at the local, national and international levels. At the same time there is apprehension that ICTs may widen the digital divide between the ICT '*haves*' and the ICT '*have-nots*'. Because of this digital divide represents an important social issue as well as a business challenge. However, the solution is influenced by several parameters and not just by market forces alone.

Information is the key to democracy for efficient governance. It has become possible for even the common man to access information globally as well as obtain locally relevant information enabling the citizen's intelligent participation in the democratic process and governance. Even so for tens of millions of people around the world the Internet is still not such a friendly place. That is so because many of the world's writing systems still are not encoded in software which means millions of people can not write e-mail, build Web sites, or search databases in their native scripts. Modern information and communication facilities can contribute considerably to resolving the problems of a rural society. The major factor that has prevented rural areas from benefiting fully from the potential of ICTs has been the low penetration of telecommunication services into rural areas. Although recent developments and cost reduction in wireless communication including both local loop and satellite communication extend access and use of telecom services in rural areas, there is still a long way to go.

This situation calls for the provision of a highly sustainable, cost effective, shared community facility, capable of servicing most of the requirements of the rural society. Such a centre could be the community library of the future supporting the goal of universal access to the emerging Information Society. The Multipurpose community telecentres can support basic telecommunication and office administration services, such as providing telephone, fax, e-mail, Internet access, word processing and photocopying, etc. in rural areas. They can also facilitate access to library and information services, utilizing their own document holdings and national and worldwide information banks in support of literacy campaigns, basic and non-formal education, government programmes and other public service activities. They can facilitate traditional rural media for providing outreach activities (Rose, 2000).

India, like most other developing countries, has three-fourths of its population of over 1 billion, living in villages. They constitute a vital base of the national economy - for the production of raw materials of food, clothing, shelter, etc. and of democratic system. They live close to nature and hence are concerned and involved with its nurture and conservation as they are with the variegated native knowledge systems, cultures, arts, and languages. Hence development programmes must give priority attention to rural development. People at the grassroots are handicapped in several ways. Being barely literate they are susceptible to economic, social, political, and technological exploitation and manipulations. This together with other factors leads to their failing to receive appropriate basic education facilities, health care delivery, employment, and other social and economic benefits. These factors individually and in combination increase the vulnerability of the people in the rural areas and widen the economic gap between them and the urban communities.

Rural and remote areas exhibit one or more of the following characteristics:

- Scarcity or absence of public facilities such as, reliable electricity supply, water, roads and transport;
- Scarcity of technical personnel;
- Difficult topographic conditions, e.g. lakes, rivers, hills, mountains or deserts which render the construction of telecommunication networks very costly;
- Severe climatic conditions that make critical demands on the equipment;
- Low level of economic activity mainly based on agriculture, fishing, handicrafts, etc.;
- Low per capita income;
- Underdeveloped social infrastructure (health, education, etc.);
- Low population density; and
- Very high calling rates per exchange line, reflecting the scarcity of telephone service and large numbers of people rely on a single exchange line (Yasuhiko).

These features make it difficult to provide public telecommunication services of acceptable quality by traditional means at affordable prices, while also achieving commercial viability for the service provider (Yasuhiko).

Rural communities and individuals need to be empowered by enhancing their capacity to access, select and use information as a basis for and in tandem with all other development efforts whether they relate to literacy, food, health and family welfare, population growth, enviornment, trade, employment, or whatever. There are three distinct but inter-related aspects to be taken note of in considering information support to grassroots level development. These are:

1) Provision for and communication of, pertinent data and information to support rural people's efforts for their own development be it in agriculture, literacy, health, housing, employment, natural resources conservation, or environment matters;
2) Rural people possess a fund of valuable native knowledge - food, health, and medicine related, plant and animals, social and cultural value systems, ethno music and arts etc. which need to be recorded, processed, disseminated and utilized on a much wider scale. A good part of such information may not be in written or printed form but transmitted orally; and
3) Information required for preparing development plans at the national and sub-national (state, district, block, village) levels - data on demographic aspects, agriculture and other economic activities, human settlements, health and family welfare, etc. to be provided to the planners, plan implementers, and supporting agencies (Neelameghan, 1998).

When it comes to the digital divide, literacy is an issue that is often overshadowed by access. Unless all citizens are able to learn and apply a side set of literacy skills, mere access to technology will mean very little to them. ICTs are evolving at a rapid rate. It is, therefore, becoming increasingly important for people's skills to evolve with it. It is also important that citizens are provided ample opportunities to learn these skills, especially considering the fact that within the next few years, half of all jobs will either be in the IT industry or will require IT-related skills. Therefore, government must continue to explore strategies for improving literacy and learning opportunities. If we cannot cultivate these skills, the digital divide will persist.

2.2 Factors Affecting Digital Divide

Factors that affect digital divide include the following:

- Economic, geographic and educational inequalities between developed and developing countries/areas within the country (rural-urban);
- 85% Internet content is in English whereas only 10% world's population speaks English. A large number of Indians are fluent in English but the overall percentage of Indians knowing English remains a miniscule;
- Hesitation in / resistance to, accepting new technology. This is not a major constraint in India;
- Lack of awareness regarding new technologies or lack of motivation from the society/family/educational institutes. This also is not a major constraint in India;
- Cost of the new ITC equipment: It is very often the recurring expenditure that is the bottleneck than the one time investment;
- Technological barrier such as deficiencies in infrastructure or training. It is the support system, which is often not geared to meet the challenge. For example, irregular electricity supply prevents viewing of television or inefficient telephone lines hamper the use of Internet.

Stated simply, the "digital divide" is the gap between the technology haves and have-nots. There are people who have Internet access at home and there are people who do not even have computers at home or even skills to use computers. There are other inequities – times and places where things are not equal and fair. Rural households are less likely to have computer and Internet technology than urban households. The young could be haves, the old and disabled are have-nots.

3 BRIDGING THE DIGITAL DIVIDE: GENERAL SCENARIO

3.1 Variety of Services

More than 3 billion people or over 50% of the world's population live in rural and remote areas of developing countries. Today, a wide variety of services, such as, e-mail, e-commerce, tele-education, health/ telemedicine, among others, have made interactive multimedia services important for rural and remote communities. The Valleta Action Plan (VAP) formulated at the Second World Telecommunication Development Conference in Malta, in March 1998 sought to promote universal access to basic telecommunication, broadcasting and Internet as tools for development in rural areas (Yasuhiko). The Internet Website *itu.int/itudfg7* was established to gather and exchange information on the development of communication technologies that meet the needs of rural areas of developing and developed countries.

The World Bank defines 'rural development' as a strategy to improve the economic and social life of specific groups of people, the rural poor. It involves extending the benefits of development to the poorest among those who seek a livelihood in the rural areas. S. Giggey defines a rural community information centre as a place where members of the community can (Upadhya and Ravichandra Rao, 2001):

- Get information about subjects of their interest;
- Take part in economic activities;
- Discuss and share knowledge, information concerned with extension work and with other members of the community, planners, and administrators;
- Find materials that help them maintain and update their literacy and skills;
- Meet to organize and work together on community projects;
- Use equipment to produce their own information materials;
- Enjoy cultural and leisure activities; and
- Seek and use information as an aid to their work and adopt it under new conditions.

3.2 E-governance

E-governance is the application of IT to the processes of government functioning to bring about Simple Moral Accountable Responsive and Transport (SMART) governance that works better, is transparent, costs less and is capable of fulfilling the citizen's need as never before. E-governance usually consists of four stages. In the first stage called 'E-foundation' the basic infrastructure is set in place; also, primary applications like LAN are implemented and information (content) is created. The second stage called 'E-facilitation', involves participation of the stakeholders, the government employee and the citizen. The Third stage, 'E-business' involves desk-based transactions on the web. The fourth stage is 'E-commerce'. E-governance implies a new set of responsibilities for the executive, legislature and citizenry.

Thus, e-governance entails the use of ICTs for:

1) Efficient delivery of government services to citizens and business,
2) Better dissemination of government information,
3) Improved efficiency of government information, and
4) Improved revenue collection and budgetary controls.

The benefits of e-governance include:

1) It provides integrated government services through a single window by re-engineering government processes;
2) It enables speeding up of transactions and transparent functioning;
3) It reduces procedural and postal delays involved in current manual system. This helps control of corruption and increase participation of people in policy-making and decision processes by improving communication between government and the public; and
4) It ensures overall governance with minimum red tape and zero corruption.

According to an assessment by the National Council of Applied Economic Research on e-readiness, Karnataka, Andhra Pradesh, Maharashtra and Tamil Nadu are the leaders in e-readiness, whereas Delhi, Chandigarh, Gujarat and Goa are the aspiring leaders. It follows a three-phase approach: Publish, Interact and Transact. In 'Publish', the access to the government information is expanded by using ICT, 'Interact' focuses on the broadening of civic participation in the government by involving the citizens in government processes at all levels, whereas 'Transact' is to make the government services available online. The e--governance services are further classified as improved services to citizens, improved services to business and enhanced government administration and all these services could be provided at the municipality level, state level or the central government level.

3.3 E-Commerce

E-commerce (Electronic Commerce) consists of the buying, selling, marketing and servicing of products or services over computer networks. E-commerce may also be viewed as the conduct of business, commercial communications and management through electronic methods, such as electronic data interchange and automated data collection systems. E-commerce involves the electronic transfer of information between business entities.

Several factors have a role in the success of any e-commerce venture. These include providing 1) value to customers; 2) service and performance; 3) an attractive website; 4) incentive for customers to buy and to return; 5) personal attention; 6) a sense of community, discussion boards, chat rooms etc.; 7) reliability and security; 8) a 360-degree view of the customer relationship. It may also enable 9) owning the customer's total experience; 10) streamlining business processes; 11) helping customers to do their job of consuming; 12) constructing a commercially sound business model; 13) engineering an electronic value chain; 14) operating on or near the cutting edge of technology; and 15) setting up an organization of sufficient alertness and agility to respond quickly to any changes in the economic, social and physical environment (http://www.vanviiweb.com...).

3.4 E-learning

E-learning (Electronic learning) covers a wide range of applications and processes such as Web-based learning, Computer-based learning, Virtual class rooms, and

Digital collaboration. It includes the delivery of content *via* Internet/Extranet (LAN/WAN), audio – and videotape, satellite broadcast, interactive TV, and CD-ROM (The three views of e-Learning). The term is not without different interpretations. Cisco defines it as the online delivery of information by a server or host computer that is connected to the World Wide Web (WWW). E-learning is a method for the delivery of a learning package. Its advantages over other more traditional forms of instruction include scalability at low cost, reduced peer effects, self-paced learning, and just-in-time delivery of training. Its disadvantages include a lack of moderation or mentorship, a tendency to provide `one size fits all' and a loss of the peer and time pressures (The three views of e-Learning).

3.5 Improving Telecommunications

Extending telecom services to rural areas is crucial to providing access to information to the very large number of socially and economically disadvantaged rural masses. With the view to bringing Internet services to rural areas the following solutions are envisaged:

1) Wireless access systems, such, as FWA (Fixed Wireless Access) and VSAT are effective means of establishing infrastructure in rural areas since they are less costly and easier for installation over the wired systems;
2) IP (Internet Protocol) based network is more economical and flexible than circuit switched network;
3) Packet-based wireless access technologies, such as, IMT-2000 and wireless routers, are being designed to deliver wider range of traffic types more efficiently than traditional wired and cellular telephony network;
4) Linking suppliers and implementers on the web by providing the comprehensive catalogue with contact information is the useful means for the equipment procurement with less cost;
5) Shared use concept is used for making ICT terminals and facilities at Multipurpose Community Telecentres available at affordable cost in rural areas;
6) The financing scheme and / or special funding mechanism for the start-up of the rural and remote area services may be necessary for the accelerated improvement of the rural and remote accessibility;

7) Collaboration for promotion of rural projects among multi-actors such as Governments, UN Agencies, PTOs, and NGOs etc. should be encouraged; and

8) Participation of women and the youth for the promotion of information access for rural community should also be promoted.

4 DIGITAL DIVIDE: INDIAN SCENARIO

4.1 Information Kiosks

From being useful for delivery of e-governance initiatives to building brands, kiosks are increasingly gaining importance in the country. And they are now being looked at as a possible solution to help India bridge the digital divide. The 'Gyandoot' project, for instance, which won the CSI-TCS National Award for 'Best IT usage of the year 2000, carried out by the Madhya Pradesh government, kicked off with the installation of a low-cost rural intranet covering 20 village information kiosks in five blocks of a district. Information vital to the farmer, like agricultural produce rates, land records and grievance services has proved to be the most popular feature of the kiosks. The initiative has been of great use, not only in doing away with red tape, but has also generated employment for village youth trained to use such kiosks - appropriately called *Suchanalayas*. Another successful example is the Warana village in Maharashtra where sugarcane farmers receive payment slips from the village information kiosks.

Information Kiosks in Rural India: Over the past decade the Internet has been touted as a powerful engine that could raise living standards in poor and remote communities of rural India. It is opening up new avenues for education, commerce and participatory democracy. But the reality is a growing digital divide that is preventing from showing the benefits of the information age. The gap between digital *haves* and *have-nots* is very wide in India. The new approach seeks to bridge this gap with a national network of owner-operated computers with Internet access. It takes advantage of low cost wireless technology that eliminates the need for telephone lines. It is predicted that there will be thousands of information kiosks across the country, providing the poorly educated rural community with direct access to government officials and records as well as online services such as, banking and medical consultations.

In many ways India is the perfect laboratory for adapting the Internet to development needs, bringing together abundant technological expertise with an estimated 700 million people in 600,000 villages. Although telephone lines are not necessary, electricity is, and unreliable power supplies leave many villages without electricity for all but few hours a day. With 22 telephone lines and 3 computers per 1,000 people, India has a very poor basic information and communication infrastructure. Even though this infrastructure is highly concentrated in urban areas, Internet access via the telephone is still difficult and expensive in urban areas. In rural India, more than half of India's villages lack telephone connectivity, let alone Internet access. This lack of information and communication infrastructure results, in people having to waste time and money chasing information and government officials. Lack of clarity in processes, and corruption and mismanagement in systems and operations is rampant. The inaccessibility of information affects the rural poor more than other sectors of the community. Similarly, lack of market information (on commodity prices, various input suppliers, etc.) leads to loss of income and exploitation of rural entrepreneurs by middlemen. Such exploitation and losses further marginalize small and marginal farmers and village artisans. In this context, ICTs can play a significant role in making information available at a reasonable cost and also help find innovative solutions to the problems of poverty and inequality by accelerating development and introducing transparency into systems and operations (http://www.main. edc.org ...).

4.2 Other Programmes and Projects

Gyandoot: One clear reason for the success of rural projects like *Gyandoot* is that the use of kiosk is totally independent of a person's knowledge of computers. Says Sonali Chowdhry, Netcomm Labs' Chief Executive: "Ease-of-use is seen as the sole reason for the popularity of kiosks among the masses. The government sector has seen optimum utilization of kiosks since they can be easily used by an average person". Additionally, the plus point for kiosks is the fact that they can be deployed in the language of the region. Looking at the potential for kiosks as an information medium, the national IT Task Force has recommended the use of kiosks in community centre projects for rural areas.

Community Radio: Communication is the means by which people create their identity, both individual and collective. Community radio favours oral expression, vernacular languages and direct dialogue. It promotes human rights, empowerment, democracy and active citizenship. Community radio has a unique role to play in bridging the digital divide. As an interface with the Internet it can connect people into a global dialogue while providing the means to place that in a local context. For the community radio participant it can provide access to information technologies as tools for creative communication in which traditional barriers of literacy and of perception are, if not removed, at least significantly reduced. Community radio has the potential to make a strategic contribution to education and social development but a sustainable approach to its contribution to education and social development requires firm foundation (Buckly).

ICT4D: ICT4D stands for Information and Communication Technology for Development, and it has become a fashionable buzzword as multilateral agencies, national governments, and non-governmental organizations worldwide seek to bridge the digital divide. One person who has consistently cast a skeptical, yet interested eye on this trend is Kenneth Keniston, Andrew W. Mellon Professor of Human Development in MIT's Program in Science, Technology, and Society also Director of the MIT India Program, has been spending two to three months every year in India, which arguably has the largest number of ICT4D projects in the world. He says:

1) Cheap information kiosks are helping India bring computing power to the masses, providing a model for how to bridge the digital divide; and
2) The lessons learned in India may be relevant to the rest of the world.

Billions of dollars are being spent on ICT4D - but if it crashes, people may feel that the money is better spent on something else. To prevent that we need to know what works and what does not work, how costly it is, and who can pay for it.

Information Kiosks: One tactic that particularly interests Keniston has been the deployment of community information centres in India - kiosks where villagers can pay a few rupees for accessing land records, market prices, and other information. India is host to a large number of community information centre experiments, including private-sector initiatives like *Drishtee*; government-to-citizen initiatives like the *Bhoomi* project, which has computerized 20 million land records; and the deployment of community information centres by Indian agriculture business giant ITC, an effort that improved the efficiency of the company's supply chain.

Special Issues: India is not only a very large country with a population of over a billion and diversity of languages, geographical climates, religions, cultures and so on (eCENSUSIndia, 2002), it is also a country of stark contrasts. It is said that whatever is true of India, the exact opposite of it is also true of India. For example, India houses the highest number of illiterate persons (302 million) in the world. At the same time India has a very large pool of highly skilled IT professionals and has the third largest scientific manpower in the world. There are districts in the country where illiteracy has been completely wiped out. However, there are also some remote rural areas where literacy rate is just about 10% or so especially amongst the females. (Census of India, 2001, eCENSUSIndia, 2002).

India with its 18 official national languages has a very special problem standing in the way of adoption of software. The problem is that the ISCII [Indian Standard Code for Information Interchange] is not widely used. Organizations such as the Centre for Development of Advanced Computing, National Centre for Software Technology, and the Technology Development in Indian Languages Programme of the Government of India have ended up creating a tower of Babel where no two systems can talk to each other. One important recent development has been the growth of advocacy groups that favour UNICODE, based on ISCII. There is also the lively, but fragmented IndLinux group, as well as the Free Software group.

ICT application in rural development may be classified as those that: provide decision support to public administrators for improving planning and monitoring of development programmes; improve services to citizens and bring in transparency; empower through access to information and knowledge and help in training to improve the functioning of developmental organizations and expand employment opportunities in rural areas (Bhatnagar and Schware, 2004).

Community Information Centres: There are several models of Community Information Centres. In Madhya Pradesh, for example, the Gyandoot project had the backing of the deputy district collector but was designed to be largely self sustaining. In Warana, the big impetus came from the Maharashtra government, the sugarcane cooperatives, and the National Informatics Centre. Then we have the ITC, which has set up a vast operation with 800 Community Information Centers operational and increasing to 2000 kiosks soon. Soybeans, shrimp, and coffee are transacted through these kiosks, and they have a very carefully thought out revenue model. By bypassing the middleman, ITC saves eight to ten percent of the purchase of soy, which is very impressive. In Warana, enough savings are generated from the kiosks to sustain and maintain them.

From the point-of-view of sustainability, the *Drishtee* Community Information Centers and the Sustainable Access in Rural India (SARI) projects are similar. They plan to offer a variety of services through the Community Information Centers to recover initial investments and operating expenses. We do not know the degree to which these projects are self-sustaining, but it's perhaps too early to say. Then there are the *Bhoomi* and records project in Karnataka, the government of Andhra Pradesh's various e-government projects, the National Informatics Centre's efforts to computerize the district collectors' offices across India, and the efforts of Chhattisgarh to computerize the state's functions. There is the case of the SARI project's collaboration with the Aravind Eye Hospital, Madurai, where the retinas of people were photographed and the doctors identified cataract patients among them, but one doesn't know how sustainable that is. India probably has more ICT4D projects than any other country in the world, but there are no studies on their impact on the common man.

When implementing these systems in rural areas, anything may go wrong. Computers break down, viruses bring down the systems, and impact studies are lower down in the priority list. Then there are projects that have a low impact, and therefore there is no motivation to do impact studies. There are two aspects to an impact study: impact and sustainability. To study the impact, one should live in the villages, and talk to everyone in there. We also need to take a very hard look at sustainability and understand what are the expenses in building, maintaining, and sustaining the infrastructure. What are the possible sources of revenue? We know that if you pour enough money, you will be successful. But NGOs get tired of pouring money, and they eventually pull out. One positive example is that of using the kiosks to teach children the use of computers. This has made some money for the kiosk operators.

Bhoomi Project: In India, the lives of 700 million people are connected in some way or other to land. In this, the Bhoomi project in the state of Karnataka really stands out – it has comprehensively computerized land records. Rajiv Chawla, who headed the project, enlisted an army of people to check and recheck the records - some of them illegible, some of them in ancient Kannada, some on bad paper that is falling apart, and some of them contested.

Hole-in-the Wall: Providing the under-privileged access to ICT is a major challenge facing developing countries, such as India. NIIT, New Delhi, has come out with an interesting solution of minimally invasive education especially for the semi-literate slum-dwelling kids. The project called the Hole-in-the-Wall Project is the brainchild of Dr. Sugata Mitra, Scientist, NIIT, New Delhi (Bhatia Parteek and Bhatia Sanmeet 2004).

Simputer: The Simputer Trust, a Non-Profit Organisation conceived and designed the Simputer in November 1999. It has developed *Dhwani*, a text-to-speech system for Indian Languages. It has LINUX software and operates on three AAA batteries. It has a text-to-speech conversion capacity with which it can voice communicate to the users in English, Hindi and Kannada and soon in Tamil, Telugu, Bengali and Marathi. Several applications like e-mail, playing MP3 music files and video clips and small business accounting can be done through it. Simputer would also help to speed up the money order transactions of the postal department wherein a smart card costing around Rs.50 could be used by the rural folk for money transaction using the postman's Simputer.

Agmarknet: Various state agricultural boards (APMCs) have formed an agricultural marketing information network (Agmarknet) by hosting a portal site called www.agmarknet.nic.in. This Website links the various mandis, major mandis and APMCs of the country and provides computerized market data, market fees and charges, arrivals, dispatches, sales, transport, losses and wastage along with other issues such as APMC infrastructure and taxes. These commodities have been divided into seven categories: cereals, pulses, fibers, spices, fruits, vegetables and oilseeds, which help the farmer to surf for the commodities mandi-wise. It is aimed to create a nationwide network for the speedy collection and dissemination of market information, which reduces intermediary costs, and bring benefit to a wide cross-section of farmers and consumers.

Escotel's 'Grameen Phone Seva': Escotel provides rural phone services to 2500 villages of the country covering 110 towns on major highways and 7.5 million people. It helps the villagers to stay in touch with the world, the market, train schedules and reservations, avail the emergency services while for the local government it provides connectivity with the remote areas. Escotel has subsidized the handset as well as the usage cost by 50% for the operator (one per village). The advantage to the villagers is that they can contact anyone in the whole world, anytime (24 hours) at a very nominal cost i.e. around Rs. 7.50 per minute. The response was overwhelming resulting into about 500 installations in 8 months.

CorDECT: The Telecommunications and Networks (TeNet) Group (www.tenet. res.in) of the Electrical Engineering Department of IIT, Chennai, have developed this low-cost Internet access technology called CorDECT. It has been used in France, Brazil, China and in the Indian districts of Kuppam (AP) and Madurai (Tamil Nadu). It has also been launched now in Hyderabad, Patiala and Delhi. TeNet is providing seamless integration of both voice and Internet services (35170 Kbps) and n-Logue Communications, its business model developed with the help of local entrepreneurs includes a public kiosk, telephone instruments, 100 MHz Pentium PC, 16-hour power backup with telephone, 4-hour backup for PC and an STD pca meter and is provided at a very economical cost of Rs. 35,000 to the entrepreneurs.

Shiksha India: To bridge the digital divide in India, a group called Shiksha India was formed at the 16th World Economic Forum (WEF). In partnership with BCG, it is working for the success of the five C's, namely Computers, Connectivity, Content, Coaching and models of Commercial sustainability in schools of Delhi and Kolkata. The project strives to extend education, increase earning capacity and promote entrepreneurship. These are easy methods of education through CDs and provide free supply of course materials to schools. The Department of Information Technology will coordinate this project through ERNET. The present scenario: 'Schools Online' has provided several computers to schools of Delhi and Intel has already started coaching in these schools. Content on subjects like mathematics, science, humanities and value-based Indian culture has been outlined. Several commercial test models are worked at presently, where computers would be used after schools hours and various cyber cafes and adult literacy centres would be fabricated. Recently, Microsoft has announced $20 million assistance to this project that would aid in training of 80,000 teachers and 3.5 million students in about four to five years (Social initiatives – Shiksha India ...).

Fourth R India - Computer Education in the Villages: Fourth R India aims at providing free computer education to one million students/children in the age group 3-19 years, all over India in the next two years. They have formulated their own curriculum, which gives equal emphasis to theory and lab modules whereas the schools would provide the infrastructure. Their 'popular curriculum' uses freeware like the Star Office and Shareware using low-end machines, making the curriculum to work on any machine. Till now 20 schools have been covered. They have training provision for the teachers too, where any teacher from a recognised school can get 15 hours free training at any of its centres in the country.

World Links' Project in India: World Links, the Washington DC-based international NGO, has launched a program to train secondary school teachers of 125 schools in Delhi, Karnataka, Kerala, AP, Punjab, Gujarat and Tamilnadu, in the classroom application of IT by providing school connectivity (connecting Indian schools with the schools around the world), basic computer literacy and professional training. With the help of local partners, Intel Corporation and Schoolnet India, and engaging 35 master trainers, it will provide four phases of award-winning teacher professional training programme to reach 1,500 teachers and 30,000 students in about three years. This project is partially funded by the Dutch Government and the World Bank grants funds, and will leverage $3 million in partner-financed ICT-in-education investments in India.

TARAhaat.com for Rural India: TARAhaat.com designed by the Development Alternatives Group, TARAhaat (Technology and Action for Rural Advancement), a not for profit business, markets environmentally sound technologies for livelihoods and basic needs. Haat is a village market, a bazaar, held periodically (once a week) in rural areas in India.

The Website is developed as a 'one-stop shop' for India's rural community to access information on matters ranging from education to market prices. By using graphics, animation and voice-overs, the designers have allowed the site to reach its core audience, many of whom are illiterate, non-English or Hindi speaking and who have never used a computer before. Illiteracy is high especially among rural minority groups such as women, the Scheduled Castes and Tribes making text-based medium inadequate. Information, therefore, has to be presented in an easily understood and in an unambiguous manner. Language posed a huge barrier because of the 24 recognized languages and their many dialects to address the various issues, TARAhaat decided to make the website as graphics-intensive as possible in order to guide users to the information they needed regardless of the language or literacy level. To simplify the navigation process, the designers have added sound and animation to the web page. As the user moves the mouse over the different elements, text boxes would appear with a listing of the information found in the next sub-level. A voice-over of the listing is also added allowing users who could not read to understand the contents of the box.

Despite its success at allowing almost universal access to the site, there are still a few issues that TARAhaat need to address to continue improving accessibility. One such need is to expand the language selection to reflect the diverse users of the site.

Activating higher levels of production and consumption in rural markets is urgently needed to build fast growing, globally competitive and resilient economies in developing nations. Despite the explosive growth of the Internet world wide, the benefits of ICTs have yet to reach the Third World Village. The slow penetration of IT into the rural economy underlies a serious threat to a global sustainable development, accelerating it may well be the most effective means for overcoming the threat.

TARAhaat is a window to the World connecting to local and national resources, access to world wide information, to health services, matrimonial and mailing services; for the farmer it will offer a weather forecast service for planting, land ownership certificate, facility to order seeds or machinery parts, monitor food grain prices and negotiate rates with buyers; and for the youth, it will offer career counseling, admission forms, educational opportunities, distance learning courses, job options, entertainment, etc (http://www.sden.org…). Ashok Khosla (2003) has described in detail the TARAhaat approach for transforming the rural marketing system.

E-choupal: ITC's International Business Division has launched the e-choupal initiative in rural India to empower farmers. This is the single largest information technology based intervention by a corporate entity in rural India. The e-choupal Website (www.echoupal.com) provides agricultural inputs, information about the products and services to enhance farm productivity, scientific farming practices, market prices of crops-home and abroad, and the weather broadcast - all in local (Hindi) language. It even maintains four crop-specific Websites for Soya, Coffee, Aqua and Wheat. The full contents of the Websites are available to the registered Choupal Sanchalaks (lead farmer) only who act as the interface between the system and the farmers and these lessons are implemented by the farmers with the assistance of the ITC workers. This movement is reaching 6,50,000 farmers of 6000 villages through 1,020 kiosks and in the coming decade is planned to cover 15 states, 1,00,000 villages and 10 million farmers by installing 20,000 e-choupals.

CVC's Anticorruption Experiment: The Central Vigilance Commission (CVC) in India has begun to share with citizens a large amount of information related to corruption. The CVC website has published the names of officers from the elite administrative and revenue services against whom investigations have been ordered or penalties imposed for corrupt practices.

Computerization of the Indian Railway's Passenger Reservation System: It has significantly increased the efficiency of the reservation process, increased the morals of the railway staff and the quality of customer service. It also gave Indian Railways (and India more widely) a more modern image, and it helped to build information age capabilities within the country (Khosla, 2003).

Owner-operated Computer Centres: The National Survey conducted in 2002 reveals that less than 1 percent adults access Internet in India. The new approach in bridging the digital divide is the national network of owner-operated computer centres with Internet access-part cybercafes, part digital town halls. The use of low-cost wireless technology eliminates the need for telephone lines.

Grameen Sanchar Sewak: This project aims to provide telecom services to rural people using. WLL (Wireless Local Loop) technology. The project has been conceptualized to provide accessibility of public telephone to rural population at their doorsteps by using WLL technology. The scheme would be implemented through the Grameen Dak Sewaks (Postman), Delivery agents of the Department of Posts (DoP). These agents would work as the franchisees of Bharat Sanchar Nigam Ltd. (BSNL). For this pilot scheme, the existing rural WILL infrastructure would be used and the Grameen Dak Sewak who will now be called Grameen Sanchar Sewak will be provided a Fixed Wireless Telephone with display facility. The pilot project will cost up-to Rs.3 crores. When the Grameen Sanchar Sewak goes to a house to deliver a letter, he will carry the Fixed Wireless Telephone with him. Since the Sewak reaches practically every house, the scheme will enable the phone services to be made available practically to all the citizens in his area. In the initial phase of the pilot project 1800 Grameen Dak Sewaks would cover about 8000 villages in 21 telecom circles covering all the States except Andaman and Nicobar Islands, Haryana and Punjab.

Infosys Foundation, Bangalore: Infosys Foundation (E-mail: foundation@infy.com) was established with the objective of supporting the underprivileged in India. Promoted by Infosys Technologies Limited, the Foundation began its activities in Karnataka in 1996 and now extended to Tamil Nadu, Andhra

Pradesh, Maharashtra, Orissa and Punjab. The Foundation primarily aims at improving the health, learning and education and basic facilities, benefiting a large number of individuals and institutions.

The Foundation has undertaken 'A Library for Every School' programme, one of the largest education programmes in the country. So far, more than 6500 libraries have been set up in the government schools in rural Karnataka. A minimum of 200 books, depending on the strength of the school, is provided (http://www.infosys.com…).

Azim Premji Foundation, Bangalore: The Azim Premji Foundation focuses on universalization of elementary education and works along with the government and non-governmental organizations. The Foundation started functioning in January 2001 with a corpus of around Rs.1.5 lakh WIPRO shares. It has already spent around Rs. 50 million on this initiative. It runs its educational initiative in Karnataka and Andhra Pradesh. The concept of computer assisted learning centre was conceived in response to the needs of the people in rural Karnataka. Their immediate objectives were: Attracting children to schools; creating excitement in and around the school; simplifying difficult concepts, thereby making learning exciting and fundamentals strong; and sound foundation to IT literacy. The programme is aimed at making students think critically, view things creatively, solve problems in a group, learn multi-tasking and peer group interaction (http://www.azimpremjifoundation.org ..).

Aditya Birla Foundation: Set up in 1999, the Aditya Birla Foundation spends about Rs.540 million every year on activities ranging from rural development schemes to social reforms. All of this is to provide self sufficiency to the down-trodden by helping them with formal and vocational education *(http://www.azimpremjifoundation.org…)*.

NICNET: The National Informatics Centre's Network connects district level and rural level government offices to government secretariats in the state capital.

NCST and IITs have developed Hindi and Tamil language systems based on the Linux operating system.

5 DIGITAL DIVIDE: KARNATAKA

5.1 Bhoomi: Online Delivery of Land Titles

As briefly mentioned earlier, under the "Bhoomi E-Governance Project" of the Government, all 20 million land records of 6.7 million land owners in 176 taluks of Karnataka have been computerized by the Department of Revenue. This system works with the Software called "BHOOMI" designed fully in-house by the National Informatics Centre, Bangalore. The project is largely funded by the Government of India, but some critical components are funded by the State Government. The BHOOMI software provides for printing of land records as and when required. It incorporates process of online updating to ensure that the RTCs [Record of Rights, Tenancy and Crops] provided to the farmers are in sync with the time.

The software enables the administrators to generate various reports based on type of soil, land holding size, type of crops grown, etc and thereby facilitates informed policy decisions. Residents of some 2,000 villages will soon be able to obtain land records and host of other information related to their lives at their doorstep.

Buoyed by the success of decentralization of BHOOMI project through two pilot projects underway in Mandya and Maddur taluks, where some 42 kiosks, operated by private entrepreneurs, have been disbursing land records at the village level, the government is extending this initiative to 2,000 more villages.

In addition to land records, some 42 other services like issuance of caste and income certificates, soil types, weather patterns, market prices, etc. can also be loaded on to kiosks and utilized commercially.

Prior to computerization, farmers had to seek out the Village Accountant to get a copy of the Record of Rights, Tenancy and Crops (RTC) - a document needed for many tasks such as obtaining bank loans. There were delays and harassment. Today, for a fee of Rs.15, a printed copy of the RTC can be obtained online at computerized land record kiosks (Bhoomi centres) in 140 taluk offices.

The highlights of BHOOMI are:

- Fully online system to carry out computations on land records data;
- Fingerprint biometrics authentication to ensure fool proof authentication system and to enforce the concept of non-repudiation. Facility to scan the field mutation order passed by revenue authorities and the notice served on the public;
- Land record centre in each taluk office for public interface;
- Synchronizes with the regular fieldwork done by Village Accountants and Revenue Inspectors;
- Provision for interfacing of Touch Screen Kiosk at taluk office; and
- The above features helps in bringing total transparency in land records management with the added advantages of security and reliability (Bhoomi).

The BHOOMI kiosks across the State are not just for land records but they have become the nerve centres of information for the farmer. Everything related to farming and the rural community like mandi prices, weather changes, soil types, among other things, are available at the touch of a button. BHOOMI is now moving to urban centres and adding on more functions, aimed to make government functioning transparent and easy for citizens. If BHOOMI has dramatically changed the lives of farmers and the rural community, a silent revolution is happening in the urban centres, Kaveri, or Karnataka valuation and e-registration, is attempting something similar in urban centers. The Department of Stamps and Registration is bringing down registration time from more than a month to less than 30 minutes through computerization. The novelty in this project is that it is being done without any government investment, on a build-operate-transfer basis (Bhoomi).

5.2 Computerized Gram Panchayat

Bellandur in Karnataka is probably the first village in the country to have computerized panchayat records in 1996. There are five villages under the Bellandur Panchayat and land and property records are digitally stored. Whenever a meeting is organized it is posted on its website **www.egovindia. com/bellandur**. The proceedings of the meetings, action plans and accounts are all posted on the website. It is proposed to issue identity cards to the villages to help check criminal activities. Delegations from the U.N., BBC, Cambodia and Nepal and ministers and bureaucrats from several States have visited the panchayat (http://www.egovindia. com/billandur).

5.3 Other Programmes

Transport Department: In the Transport Department, obtaining a learner's and driver's license is now done fast. All government circulars and orders will shortly be up on the Intranet. As part of its transparency drive, government tenders are put on the respective departmental websites, to ensure the public is aware of every step the government takes (http://www.egovindia.com…).

Primary Schools: The Karnataka government has chalked out an ambitious programme to introduce computer education in 1,000 higher primary schools from 2004-05. The government is planning to appeal to corporates and IT giants to donate used computers for the programme. The funds will be taken from the resources set aside for the Sarva Shiksha Abhiyan (SSA) programme and generated through community participation. However, there are more than 20,000 government higher primary schools to be covered under the programme. This will be in addition to the already existing computer education programmes *Mahiti Sindhu* in 1,000 government high schools, a centrally sponsored programme in 238 government secondary schools and the Government-Azim Premji Foundation joint programme in 135 higher primary schools. "With the latest drive, the Government wants to introduce computer education in fifth and sixth standards – preferably in Urdu schools and in extremely backward districts". Each school will be provided with five computers. Corporates, who donate the machines, will be allowed to display their name board within the school premises and are being encouraged to adopt schools of their choice (http://www.azimpremji foundation.org…).

Vahini, Nondini, Khajane, Therige, etc. are some of the other e-governance initiatives of the State. The silk exchange (Bangalore) has computerized the whole silk process since 1985 where the auction and the transaction details like the rate, buyer, seller, actual weight, etc. are recorded onto a card as well as the system. Services, such as, online registration and scanning of the documents, encumbrance certificates are also available in the sub-registrar's office, Bangalore.

Kria (Karnataka Right to Information Act) *Katte,* the umbrella forum of organizations involved in ensuring that the Right to Information Act is followed, has managed to wrest an agreement from the Chief Secretary and other Secretaries to the Karnataka Government. In this arrangement, if one is unable to get access to information that is in the public domain, a copy of the relevant records can be had against cash payment. The government has agreed that payments below Rs.200 need not be remitted by a demand draft. It has also been agreed that the fee charged should not exceed the actual cost of supplying the Information and this will apply to maps or sketches as well (Government agrees…, 2005).

The Chairman, Public Affairs Centre, the organization behind Kria Katte was assured that all government departments and utility agencies will make available all relevant information about their functioning and how a citizen can have complaints attended to.

There will be posters and notice boards on office premises and the FM radio and websites will be used to guide citizens.

Vidya Vahini project has been initiated to provide computer literacy to the rural schools of the state. Belgaum district has been identified as the pilot district, where 20 schools will be provided computer literacy along with the complete infrastructure. 'Gnana Vahini' project on similar lines has also been proposed for the universities.

E-tappal: An e-mail and messenger services in Indian languages has been launched with the objective of taking IT-enabled service to the common people. Initially, the e-mail service will be available in English and Kannada and will be followed by other Indian languages (E-tappal, 2002).

Project TelNek by Anchorage at Bidadi: Some 200 women at Bidadi, these days, think themselves an empowered lot because of the commercial emancipation a computer can offer, thanks to a community-centric initiative. In 2000, an NGO called Anchorage was established to expand and further leverage ICT (Information and Communication Technologies) for social empowerment. The scope of technology to enhance the small and medium companies was never better felt.

Under the project TelNek, women are working on coreldraw, designing websites of metro clients. So why a small town like Bidadi, a few kilometers from IT Capital Bangalore? Says Surbhi Sharma, Trustee, Anchorage: "Bidadi has proximity to a developed place but by itself has no access to infrastructure. The youth and other job-seekers had to go till Kengeri to even print CVs. The ICT premise is basically for newer tools to benefit people in rural areas, so we zeroed in on Bidadi" (Community more e-mpowers ...., 2004).

6 CONCLUSION

It has been reported that there are more failure stories than successful ones. One key factor that emerges from various case studies is the attitude and action of senior public officials, both politicians and manages. In Andhra Pradesh, it seemed like a sudden jump to hi-tech governance when the State Government launched e-Seva centers to enable the common man to pay all bills under one roof. Flooded with technical snags and server problems, people are now back to where they were-long queues (The Week, 2005). It is heartening to see many NGOs coming forward to make Gandhiji's dream of Gram Swaraj come true. However, the government involvement in making rural population information rich is both imperative and important. For bridging the digital divide in India concerted efforts is required in the following areas:

- *Technological barrier*: Though the Internet revolution has gripped the country and India has emerged as a world leader in Information Technology, the fruits of this revolution have yet to reach a vast section of the population. With a density of nearly 0.1% of Internet access, a long road lies ahead before Internet access reaches each and every village of the country. Bandwidth availability is another problem. To effectively reach the rural poor and have-nots a concerted effort is required for community-based access to Internet services through kiosks. Through a multitude of technologies ranging from fiber optics network, VSAT to cable TV, it is possible to cover the entire length and breadth of the country. Efforts are required in this direction for the process of information dissemination to be really successful.
- Socio-psychological *barrier*: A significant proportion of the population belongs to the traditionally backward communities and a process of computer education, particularly focused on these groups is required before an adequate demand and usage of Internet services can be created. Women, in particular need special attention. Computer education and learning centres may be opened all over the country for women.
- Database *creation* and automation: Though a sizeable amount of information exists about various physiographics, demographics, ecological and economic characteristics of the country, a detailed micro-level data, particularly in automated form is not available. A process of such data collection, compilation and automation is required to fully exploit the potential of Information and Communication technologies for development purposes.

- Targeting the *future* generation: The new economy based, as it is on usage of computers and communications, the upcoming generation i.e., school going children need to be made fully conversant with this. Computer literate children would also promote environment protection and sustainable development through better access to information (http://sdnp.delhi.nic.in…..).

REFERENCES

1. Bhatia, Parteek and Bhatia, Sanmeet. (2004). The hole in the wall: Bridging the digital divide. *Information Technology*. Vol. 13(7); p. 26-27.
2. Bhatnagar, Subhash; Schware, Robert. Ed. (2004). *Information and communication technology in development: Cases from India*. 2004, Sage Publications India Pvt., Ltd., New Delhi.
3. Bhoomi. http://www.revdept.01.kar.nic.in/bhoomi/home.htm
4. Buckly, Steve. *Community radio - the new tree of speech*. http://www.infundo.digitalbrain.com/ infundo/web/tech/documents/kb19/ kb19.pdf?verb=view%20
5. Community more e-mpowers bidade's women folk. (2004). *The Times of India*, Bangalore, Monday 15 November 2004.
6. Electronic Commerce. http://www.vanviiweb.com/articls/e/1/Electronic_commerce.html.
7. E-tappal to bridge digital divide. (2002). *Business Line (Internet edition)*. Jan. 18, 2002.
8. Government agrees to make access to records easy. (2005). *The Hindu*, Bangalore, Tuesday 4 January 2005.
9. Information kiosks in rural India. http://www.main.edc.org/mosaic/mosaic7/india.asp.
10. Khosla, Ashok. (2003). TARAhaat.com: An Internet-enabled rural market place. *Information Studies*. Vol. 6(4); p205-232.
11. Neelameghan, A. (1998). Information technology and rural development. *Information Studies*. Vol. 4(1); p. 55-61.
12. Rogos, Amanda and Latta, John. *Digital divide*. http://www.fourthwave.com/Digital Divide.htm.

13. Rose, John. (2000). Lessons from the establishment of multipurpose community telecentres. *Information Studies*. Vol. 6(1); p. 5-28.

14. *Social initiatives – Shiksha India.* http://www.ciion/ino.org/social-initiatives/483/default.asp.

15. *TARAhaat.com: Designing for rural India.* http://www.sden.org/webworks/cases/usability _da1.htm

16. *The three views of e-Learning.* http://www.nwlink.com/Ndonclark/hrd/elearning/define.html

17. *The Week* – (2005). Feb 6, p. 28.

18. Upadhya, Padma V and Ravichandra Rao, I.K. (2001). Rural Community development informaiton service and related aspects: A literature review. *Information Studies*. Vol. 7(3-4); p. 191-250.

19. Yasuhiko, Kawasumi. *New technologies and solutions for rural accessibility.* www.telecor.gob.ni/BCS/societal-issues/58/58.pdf.

20. http://www.azimpremjifoundation.org/html/clc.htm

21. http://www.egovindia.com/billandur

22. http://www.infosys.com/infosys-foundation/about.html

23. http://sdnp.delhi.nic.in/resources/digital-divide/old.main.home

FUTURE OF THE BOOK WILL THE PRINTED BOOK SURVIVE THE DIGITAL AGE?*

K.A. Isaac

Discusses the factors, especially developments in information and communication technologies (ICTs) that influence the access and use of information by a person – as student at various levels, researcher, on the job, and for general purpose. Concludes that books and libraries will continue to be with us and are in no danger of being replaced by the products and services that are ITC-based. There will be changes in the nature and size of library holdings and library services. Books of recreation and books of inspiration will continue to appear in the conventional form Acquisition of books of information will be confined to the essentially required for continuous reading. For the other books and journals in each field, full text databases accessed online will have to be depended on. Reference books and costly books and journals required can be acquired in CD-ROM at a fraction of the cost of the printed versions. So the future library will be a combination of the conventional books and IT products in varying degrees or a hybrid library, depending on the types of library. The Impact of ICTs will be highest on research libraries.

0 PREAMBLE

I have known Prof. A.Neelameghan (AN) since 1952 when we met at the All India Library Conference held in Hyderabad that year. Our close contact started after he joined the Documentation Research and Training Centre (DRTC), Indian Statistical Institute, Bangalore. I used to visit DRTC periodically for delivering lectures and for other purposes and AN used to visit our Department and the Vikram Sarabhai Space Centre (VSSC) in Trivandrum. We have also met at conferences, seminars, workshops, etc. There were occasions when we used to interact on professional matters especially the developing trends in LIS. Our contacts became less frequent after he joined the UNESCO.

The broad area of AN's work and contributions are in the areas of Knowledge Organization and applications of IT for organization and dissemination of

---

* Based on the author's paper, *The future of the book* forming a chapter in his book 'Glimpses of Library and Information Science'. New Delhi: Ess Ess Publishes; 2001.

information, in its varied aspects. In the emerging digital age and knowledge society, what will be the future of the printed book is an important subject for consideration.

1 INTRODUCTION

The invention of printing in the middle of the fifteenth century, which led to the production of books in multiple copies, was a revolutionary development. It paved the way for the democratization of knowledge. Earlier, when books had to be produced through the laborious and time-consuming process of writing by hand the emphasis was on their preservation rather than on their use, which was restricted to the privileged few. Today there are facilities for accessing books by all those who can read and understand them. The influence of books on the human race is unmatched. They provide people education, information, sense of values, culture, intellectual stimulation, and recreation; in short, everything that enriches and elevates their lives. Books have served as powerful instruments for improving the quality of life of people. Nothing else has influenced and determined the course of human history, whether it be in the realm of religion, philosophy, economics, politics, culture or science and technology as books have. Books have been so much a part of our lives and very being that life without them is unthinkable for us. This being the relationship between human beings and books, the talk that we often hear today of the possible extinction of books and their being replaced by the electronic media is a matter of concern and anxiety for all. Forecasts were made in the 1970s by Library and Information scientists like F.W. Lancaster and others, on grounds that cannot be dismissed as not wholly valid, of the withering away of books and libraries and the emergence of a 'paperless society' where the electronic media will reign supreme, by the turn of the century. This has not happened so far and we have to examine whether it is likely to happen in the future.

2 ELECTRONIC MEDIA

What are the electronic media, which are predicted as having the potential of replacing books, i.e. all forms of print-on paper sources of information? The radio and the T.V have been long with us and they will continue to play their role of providing information and entertainment. But they pose no threat of replacing books. What, therefore, we mean by electronic media in this context are the products and services of modern information technology (IT), which have made breathtaking strides of development since the early 1980s. The basic achievement of these developments has been to facilitate universal availability of information and speedy access to information for supporting all human endeavors. Today there is no area of human activity, which has not been impacted by IT. The major components of IT are the computers and telecommunications. The library was one of the institutions where IT made its early appearance. This was in the early 1960s. First introduced for performing certain routine housekeeping operations more efficiently than was possible manually, the computer, in combination with telecommunication technology has grown to such proportions as to take over the entire functions of books and libraries. Computer technology has now acquired the capability of processing and storing large volumes of information and the developments in communication technology have made it possible for this information to be transmitted to anyplace in the world whatever the distance. Another development is that computers are becoming smaller, but more powerful and their costs are coming down bringing them within the easy reach of institutions and individuals even in developing countries. This trend of increasing sophistication and efficiency of computer and telecommunication technology is steadily continuing and further revolutionary developments are in the offing.

The discovery that telecommunication channels could be harnessed for carrying digitized information facilitated computer networking globally. The different computer networks have now been interconnected to form the Information super Highway or the INTERNET which has revolutionized the communication and information / data transfer process.

The result of these developments is that numerous databases pertaining to each discipline or group of related disciplines have been set up all over the world. Initially they were bibliographic databases guiding people to the location of the information sought by them. Now there are several full text databases also from which the information required can be directly accessed. There are full text databases of many learned journals, monographs and reference books like encyclopedias etc. This means that a person possessing a personal computer with INTERNET connectivity will be able to retrieve the full text of the information that he/she needs directly without having to depend on physical access to books and libraries.

Another important development affecting libraries is the invention of CD-ROM (Compact Disk Read Only Memory) in 1983, which revolutionized the publishing process. Information is stored in the CD-ROM by the Laser Optical Technique. At present a CD- ROM can hold matter equivalent to 2,50,000 pages. Bibliographies, catalogues, abstracts, indexes, reference books, etc are increasingly being published in this medium.

Yet another IT-based development is the multi-media. The multi-media content of CD-ROM can integrate different forms and formats of information presentation - text, graphics, animation, music and video into a single e-document and can be displayed and played simultaneously through hypertext linking.

User-friendly communication protocols make INTERNET a means of global communication. The most important turning point in this direction was the development of the World Wide Web (WWW). In addition to text and numerical data, WWW facilitates accessing graphics, animation and sound. The lag in communicating research results can now be eliminated if the matter to be communicated is ported on to a web site. In fact an author's paper can be accessed worldwide as soon as he/she keys in the matter on the Internet.

These developments in IT have various impacts on and implications to the various kinds of books normally acquired by a library.

3 DIFFERENT TYPES OF BOOKS

Books are of different types - books of recreation, books of inspiration, books of information and books for learning. Novels and other forms of literature, works of art, travelogues, biographies, popular magazines etc fall in the first category. Classics like religious and philosophical books, books propounding a theory or an ideology and other books of permanent value blazing new trail of thought inspiring people to high ideals in life and, inculcating values in them are all books of inspiration. In the category of books of information and learning fall books dealing with various subjects at the macro or micro Level like textbooks, monographs, reports, standards, patents, journals, conference proceedings, dissertations, annual reviews etc. Secondary sources of information meant for accessing the contents of primary sources such as indexing and abstracting journals and other bibliographies and reference books also fall in this category.

As far as books of recreation are concerned, even the staunchest of the advocates of the supremacy of the electronic media do not forecast any radical changes in their continued appearance in the conventional book form and their being used by readers in that form although they will be supplemented by the electronic media. The kind of hospitality that these books, which contain light and recreational reading matter, offer to their readers in respect of convenience and flexibility of use cannot be matched by any other medium. A person would like to read them at his/her convenience and pace, may be at the dining table, on the bed, while traveling or wherever else, although e-books in the shape and format of conventional books are available.

As regards books of inspiration also, although they constitute more serious reading materials, the mode of reading them will be much the same as in the case of books of recreation. The impact of the electronic media in their case also is likely to be marginal.

Now we come to the third category of books - books of information and leaning - which are the most important ones in education, research, professional pursuits and all other human endeavors, which have to be supported and sustained by information. These are the types of books that Lancaster and others anticipated, will be replaced by the electronic media. The users of these books are students, teachers, researchers, professionals, scientific and technical personnel and other educated classes. They use them for the information that they need to improve their knowledge and competence in the diverse endeavors and enterprises that they are engaged in. They also depend on and make use of the information available through the electronic channels for this purpose. The dominance of books versus the electronic channels for information transmission for the purpose of its acquisition by people in the future will depend on the likely changes in the use pattern of information.

4 LIMITATIONS OF PRINYRD BOOKS IN INFORMATION TRANSMISSION

There are various developments that reduce the relevance and usefulness of books and other printed media as channels for the prompt, effective and precise transmission of information. They are: 1) increasingly large volumes of information are being produced and the consequent proliferation of literature embodying it which has crossed the level of its amenability to effective bibliographic control and retrieval for use by conventional methods; 2) high specialization of research and inter-disciplinary research leading to wide dispersion of information of interest to a specialist and the resulting difficulty in locating the required information; 3) the steady increase in the cost of books and journals which make them beyond the reach of individuals and some of them even beyond the reach of many libraries; and 4) the delay in getting a research paper published in a standard journal which is the most popular medium for scholarly communication.

These developments threaten to impede access to information. The implication of the increase in the volume of information produced in each branch of knowledge is that a specialist or researcher in that field is required to read much more than the time at his/her disposal would permit and thus he/she would miss a good percentage of information of interest to him/her. So he/she is forced to do selective reading by retrieving the - essential information of relevance to him/her from a computerized database with the help of appropriate search tools or engines.

The phenomenon of the dispersal of information required by a specialist in a variety of sources makes its location extremely difficult by conventional manual methods. The information concerned may be published in a totally unsuspected source where it will not be normally looked for. It is also likely to elude the attention of those who are responsible for the compilation of secondary sources like indexing and abstracting journals and other bibliographies in their relevant field. . Here again if such scattered information is indexed or entered in a database its retrieval will be easier.

The escalating cost of printed sources compels libraries to confine their acquisition to the essentially required ones and depend on programmes of resource sharing for accessing the ones not so frequently required. Continuous runs of several secondary sources and full texts of many journals are now available for online search. Also many of these are available in CD-ROM and materials, which are not frequently required or are required for libraries in that format at can acquire reference much less cost.

In scholarly communication, quick dissemination and access are of great importance. The results of research should be transmitted as expeditiously as possible. This is now hindered by the delay in the publication of research papers in standard journals. The delay can be minimized, as mentioned above if the text of the paper is ported on to the WWW for universal accessibility, from anywhere at any time as were, by a person with personal computer with INTERNET connectivity.

5 IMPLICATIONS

The question to be examined in the context of these developments is whether there will be a complete takeover of the conventional media of communication by the electronic media. Some professional futurologists hold the view that the present trends unmistakably point to the inevitability of a substantial, if not complete, replacement of the conventional media by the electronic media. Even if this turns out to be an imperative need, many people will have reservations regarding the desirability of such a situation emerging because of their strong bond with books and the convenience of using them. In this context the pattern of acquisition of knowledge by an individual during the period of education, period of occupation and also later in life as learning is a life long process, has to be examined.

School education is characterized by the primary dependence of students on classroom teaching and the teacher. This is so particularly in the early stages of school education. At the later stages, especially the secondary and higher secondary levels, classroom learning is marginally supplemented by self-learning through reading. The reading is confined to the prescribed textbooks and occasionally it goes beyond them and extends to other books dealing with the subjects to be learned. Such reading helps the students to be mentally and intellectually more involved in the learning process and enables them to gain a thorough knowledge of the subjects concerned. When they enter undergraduate education, self-study through reading will become even more necessary, thanks to the increased quantum of knowledge that they will have to acquire at this stage. Those who join professional courses will also have to do it, perhaps in a larger measure. At the postgraduate level of education the emphasis shifts substantially to reading and self-learning with the role of the teacher and the classroom reduced to providing guidance to the students. The students would draw up lists of the core books and journals in their respective fields for regular and sustained reading aimed at gaining a through grounding in the subjects of their specialization. But there will be other sources also in which information of interest to them would be available. For knowing about them and gaining access to them bibliographic databases are very helpful. So at the post-graduate level of education both regular reading of selected core literature and of literature that can be accessed through IT channels is necessary.

At the research level the path to the original literature to be read is primarily through secondary sources and for this, dependence on IT channels considerably increases. The library that is regularly used by a scholar holds in the area of his/her specialization would be only a very small percentage of the total volume of literature that he/she will have to consult. Therefore for accessing the bulk of literature of relevance the researcher is dependent on the electronic media.

Those who are in various occupations particularly the learned professions like education, law, medicine, engineering etc. the need to update the knowledge through continuous exposure to the current developments in their fields is indispensable and for this they will have to depend on their own libraries as well as on the IT channels, perhaps more on the latter. The pattern of acquisition of knowledge by a professional after he/she ceases to hold a formal job is likely to be much the same as during his/her active professional career. As regards the general public who would like to keep themselves generally knowledgeable about various matters, books and libraries will continue to be the main prop although a good deal of information of day to day use may become available online, information kiosks and the like.

So in education, research, occupation and life in general acquisition of knowledge is a main concern of people and reading is the most important means for the purpose. It is through regular and sustained reading that the real development of an individual takes place and his/her mental and intellectual faculties get sharpened. For such essential and sustained reading it is doubtful if books can be substituted by any other media. But for peripheral reading and for reference purposes particularly at the higher stages of education and research the products and services of IT will play an increasingly important role.

6 CONCLUSION

From the preceding discussion it seems safe to conclude that books and libraries will continue to be with us and are in no danger of being replaced by the products and services of the fast expanding information technology. But there are bound to be changes in the nature and size of library holdings and library services. Books of recreation and books of inspiration will continue to appear in the same form as at present and form part of the holdings of libraries. Acquisition of books of information will be confined to a select few of the most important ones, which are essentially required for continuous reading. For the other books and journals in each field which are not frequently required computerized full text databases from where they can be retrieved online will have to be depended on. Reference books and costly books and journals required only occasionally can be acquired in CD-ROM at a fraction of the cost of the printed versions. So the future library will be a combination of the conventional books and IT products in varying degrees depending on the types of library. The Impact of IT will be the maximum on research libraries and the minimum on public libraries. The thought that books will not totally disappear but will continue to be with us sharing the responsibility of knowledge dissemination with the products of IT and enriching our cultural heritage is soothing indeed.

ROLE OF TRADITIONAL LIBRARIANSHIP IN THE INTERNET/DIGITAL ERA

A. Ratnakar

Emphasizes the importance of the principles, techniques and tools of traditional library services such as, users needs study, classification, etc. in the digital era. Education and training of library and information professional to fit into the emerging information society and digital era should include both conventional (or traditional)knowledge organization theories and methodologies as well as the application of information and communication technologies.

0 PREAMBLE

The role of a teacher in imparting knowledge and moulding the student to reach his potential and become a useful member of the society that he is part of, is an important ethos in the 'Guru-Shishya Parampara' of Indian culture. The teacher becomes a role model to his student by his exemplary devotion and commitment to his chosen field of activity. To this class of teachers belongs Prof. A. Neelameghan who is known among library and information professionals all over the world as a saint, philosopher and a guiding light to youngsters entering the library profession. A devoted librarian who practiced the profession before venturing into teaching what he practiced, carried the tradition of Prof. S.R. Ranganathan at DRTC as well as other national and international organizations, which he helped in formulating policies and programmes. While being a strong advocate of new technology, Prof. Neelameghan firmly believes that 'Users Requirements' is of utmost importance. This article is dedicated to him as a salutation to his contributions to L&IS, especially classification and documentation.

Since the time Ptolemy laid the foundation for the ancient library in Alexandria around 288 BCE libraries have undergone changes and continue to do so. As the media for communication changed with time – from hieroglyphics, representation through language and scripts, recording on different media (papyrus, parchment, palm leaves, etc) there has also been a continuous development in the technology for the production of the written material. The printing press of the 15th Century represents one such major development. The print-on-paper is now one among the many channels of information such as audio, video and digital forms. In the following paragraphs we shall briefly examine the implications of these changes for the librarian and for teaching programmes in library schools.

Technology has played a significant role in the development of Internet. However, while assessing the development of Internet, one has to consider how much of it helps in meeting the requirements of the traditional functions of a library. From inception of library services at Alexandria, classification of documents played a significant role in organizing the collection of the library. In India Dr. Ranganathan laid the foundation of library services with many standardized procedures and tools to meet the demands on library functions. These included tools for classification and cataloguing, information retrieval and dissemination, collection development and precise methods for helping a reader with his requirements by way of reference service. His perception of the relationship between a book and a reader is brought out succinctly in the Five Laws of Library Science. In the present era, all he said still hold good and perhaps the only required change is to replace the term 'book' by 'information'. His concept of analytico-synthetic system of classification is very much made use of in the organization of information on the Internet.

While it is important to gear up to any changing scenario by proper planning, it is necessary to take stock of the existing conditions in any particular environment. This is true even with respect to the 'Changing Role Model of Librarians and Library and Information Profession in Digital Era'. While training the coming generation of librarians for the Digital Era, we cannot afford to ignore or minimize some of the fundamental (traditional) functions of a librarian for which sufficient and necessary training is to be imparted. Library and information profession is a '*service oriented*' profession and this aspect should be borne in mind while training professionals in this field. Drawing an analogy from the medical profession where doctors are there because patients are there, librarians are there because of the readers. If there were to be no readers, then there is no place for a librarian. Users needs come before any other consideration. Some of the traditional functions of library profession, which helps in meeting the "users requirement", are:

- Recommend/acquire information products;
- Classify/catalogue documents;
- Prepare bibliographies, guides and indexes;

- Facilitate interlibrary exchanges of documents;
- Documents preservation programmes;
- Assist users in accessing information and library materials;
- Plan physical facilities;
- Public relation activities; and
- Orientation programmes for users.

Though technology can certainly be used for discharging more efficiently some of these functions, it is important to realize that many of them require human intervention. The most important point to be considered and examined dispassionately (without getting awed by the power of technology) is the *contents* of a library and the content of a document. There are two aspects to be taken into account with regard to content:

- Thought content of the document; and
- Quantity of information available.

While there have been attempts for long for automatic machine classification, a stage has not yet been reached where machines can totally replace the traditional classifier/classificationist. Dispensing with or diluting the importance of classification will not be possible where the concept of '*Open Access*' libraries is practised. And open access libraries have been recognized by both scholars and librarians as the most helpful means for browsing the literature available. Hence the role of teaching classification in detail in library schools is essential even in the era of Internet and technology based libraries/information centres. Another important aspect of *content* is: how much of it is presently available on the Internet in a particular discipline, particular geographical location, particular language and particular time period. Bulk of the information available on the Internet today is in languages that employ the Latin script (English, French, German and other European languages) and negligible amount in other languages and very little in Indian languages (0.3% at most). This is for a country where there are 18 languages written in some 12 scripts including Arabic and Latin. It is estimated that around 22% of world population (including those of Indian origin) speak languages written in Indic scripts. So we see how little material is available for non-English speaking Indians residing in India for using Internet effectively. In addition to this, the Indian content (even in English language) available for researchers is, to say the least, minimal. There are not more than 100 to 125

Indian scientific and technical journals available full text on the Net. Even this is a very generous estimate. The numbers with respect to social science and humanities journals is almost negligible. Though Internet does help medical professionals with several databases of medical literature, information pertaining to Indian systems of medicine and information based on Indian traditional knowledge is almost negligible. So even those pursuing research in medicine get very little Indian content on the Internet. One has to keep in mind that library users in India come from different backgrounds, different age groups, with different levels of education, different vocations and having different information needs and with limitations in terms of language abilities. Libraries have to serve not only the well educated but also the *not so well educated.*

Another vital issue to be borne in mind is technology itself. Though knowledge of technology is spreading fast in India, the availability of the same in a country like India is very disproportionate with respect to different cities, institutions in the same city and different types of libraries (however there are some exceptions to this). The upgradation of technology is another issue to be borne in mind. It will not be easy for all libraries to upgrade the technology at the same speed as the technology made available by the industry. This will cause some limitations in using the hardware/software, which is not supported by the manufacturers. Granted that things are improving on all these fronts, it will not be before another decade at least before one can confidently say that new technology will meet most of the demands of the users.

The library and information professional in India has to be trained to meet the demands/requirements of varied types of clientele. He/she has to be well grounded in traditional librarianship as well as new trends in library services. Hence, in this situation, for a long time to come, library schools have to pay equal emphasis on teaching and training professionals in traditional functions along with the new skills required to meet the requirements of the digital era. We should certainly train the new generation of librarians to meet the challenges of digital/internet era without diluting the academic curricula, which covers traditional methods of librarianship. This of course will mean library schools having enough qualified human resources and sufficient time to cover the traditional curricula and the new fields of subjects included to meet the developing trends in the library and information field.

A NEW PARADIGM OF EDUCATION SYSTEM FOR REACHING THE UNREACHED THROUGH OPEN AND DISTANCE EDUCATION WITH SPECIAL REFERENCE TO THE INDIAN INITIATIVE

S.B. Ghosh

In the process of transition towards Knowledge Society, development of educated citizens is of prime concern for all nations of the world. The problem becomes acute for those with sizeable population with diversified culture, background and economic condition. Methodologies for provision of education are undergoing a sea change and are in a transitory phase of development with technology acting as an agent for change. It is in this context that a new method of education - Open and Distance Education (ODE) plays a vital role. The various methods followed in ODE system and the initiatives taken in India are discussed here, with particular reference to the role of the Indira Gandhi National Open University (IGNOU).

0 PREAMBLE

I felt honoured when I received an invitation to contribute a paper for a Festschrift volume being brought out to honour Professor A. Neelameghan who has made substantial contributions to various aspects of Library and Information Science (LIS). Though initially I was in a dilemma in choosing the area of my contribution, I chose to write on education system in general which has been so near and dear to him. Methods of provision of education is changing giving rise to open and distant learning method. This contribution is to pay my deep regards and respect to a person - a teacher, par excellence. Prof. Neelameghan has been advisor/ consultant to a number of IGNOU courses in library and information science and has edited and prepared several course materials. He has also been closely associated with and assisted in the development of the Web enhanced Training Programme on WINISIS, an e-learning initiative taken under the ODL system.

1 NEED FOR A VIABLE ALTERNATIVE FOR EDUCATION SYSTEM FOR ALL

An educated nation is the backbone of any society. Eradication of illiteracy has been taken as a priority programme by every country in the world. Many programmes have been initiated by Governments, inter-governmental organizations and private bodies to help making education at all levels - basic and higher education - accessible to all sectors of society with the primary objective of developing educated manpower. Higher the percentage of educated manpower of a country, higher is its index of socio-economic development. In the changing scenario of globalization and economic liberalization, there is an obvious need and demand for quality education at all levels. It is not only the provision of quality education as a one time measure but also sustaining it for life long learning. Different methods have been tried and being experimented over the years. Developments in computer, communications and multimedia technologies are ushering in a new era to bring education to the doorstep of the hitherto un-reached. It is in this context that the Open and Distance Education system (ODE) assumes great importance.

2 OPEN AND DISTANCE EDUCATION

The emergence of distance education system is the outcome of the technological developments particularly the Information and Communication Technologies (ICTs). The system envisages provision of education everywhere. The open education adds a further dimension to it, that is, openness - any one and any time. The open education philosophy is to make available education to all sections of society irrespective of age, caste and creed. "The societal mission implied by the term open and distance learning system reflects a commitment to reaching out to individuals end groups in our societies that otherwise would not be able to benefit from post-secondary education" (Cookson, 2002). Though the ODE system as we see today is a new method of delivery, the concept is not new. Of course, it is true that the ODE system has gained momentum particularly since the last decades of the twentieth century, mainly due to the significant developments in computer and communication technologies. In Germany, two educationists - Charles Thuzo and Caustov Longjiensidth established the first distance education centre to teach English language through postal system. In 1892, thirty nine different courses were started by the Harvard University under the guidance of William Rainie, which may be considered as initiation of distance education system in the modern sense (Ghosh, 2001). At present there are around 1130 institutions all over the world offering 40,000 courses/educational programmes through the distance mode in a variety of subjects. The popularity of ODE system has gained ground more in developing countries. Over 40 Open Universities have been established throughout the world, of which India has 10. The entire idea of Open University is based on the cafeteria system of education wherein each one can take whatever he/she wants without any hindrance (Venkatasubramanian, 2001). The '*learner-centeredness*" is key to the open education system, which guides the structure and process for implementation through distance education mode.

2.1 Generations of Open Distance Learning - From Correspondence Courses to E-learning

The distance education, which was started through correspondence course mode adopted different methods or combination of methods from time to time utilizing the technology available. It is said that open and distance learning (ODL) is passing through the fifth generation or models of development. Why such transitions are witnessed? It is because of requirements for providing flexible education with openness - anyone, anywhere, and any time vis-a-vis the technological developments. These models/generations are based on the nature of the physical medium available at a particular point of time that facilitates learner's access. The phases through which these models have passed may be categorized as follows:

- Correspondence courses;
- Use of audio tape, video tape, computers, broadcasting through radio and television, individually or in combination;
- Tele-learning with interactivity feature;
- Use of multimedia, Internet, computer mediated communication; and
- E-learning/Web-based learning.

Modern distance education system, which was initiated through the model of correspondence courses underwent changes due to developments in technologies, particularly ICT and media technologies such as audio, video, computer, radio and television, augmenting the process and capability of delivery of instruction. The lack of interactivity in these technologies resulted in the next generation/model - the tele-learning model comprising of interactive radio and audio-video conference. The progress in ICT particularly its interactive capabilities resulted in delivery of instruction through multimedia, Internet, computer-mediated communication. Broadcast radio and television was used for a long time in distance education. Developments of Internet and Web technology have ushered in a new era with ODL systems moving towards virtual classroom and e-learning. The input, processing, output capabilities of ICT are used now to develop computer-based tutorials - a feature of e-learning system. The present scenario is, thus seen both as a supplement to the '*face to face*' classroom and in some cases as a replacement for that. In fact, this model is in use already in USA, New Zealand and some other countries as a supplement to the conventional classroom system. The various models used so far are to satisfy the following features of ODL system:

- Development of need based courses;
- Development of usable study material based on learners' abilities and reach;
- Provision of study materials regularly;
- Provision of regular seminar/workshop;
- Timely and regular updating of the curricula and study materials;
- Developing infrastructure/methods for counseling;
- Provision of appropriate mechanism to link learners and teachers; and
- Conducting examination at learners' choice and maintaining punctuality of results announcements.

3 INDIAN SITUATION

In the Indian scenario, the educational system includes about a million schools covering primary, secondary and higher secondary levels, 13,000 general colleges and more than 2000 professional institutions. Further, there are about 2000 training institutes and polytechnics. The higher and professional education systems together host nearly nine million students. An additional enrollment of about 4.8% of the present strength every year is expected in the coming years. Looking closer at the issues facing higher and professional education systems, it is clear that the increasing demand for quality education would need infusion of massive new infrastructure, a proposition extremely difficult to accomplish through conventional approaches. It is against this backdrop that open-distance education and learning assumes importance (Kasturirangan, 2004).

In India, with a population of more than 1billion and a literacy rate of about 60%, the ODE was seen as a viable system as early as in 1986 in the National

Education Policy document, which stated that "the future thrust will be in the direction of open and distance learning". This obviously includes basic and higher education. The establishment of the National Open School, Indira Gandhi National Open University (IGNOU) and several Open Universities at state level are pointers in this direction.

Institutionalized higher education in India through the distance mode was initiated by the University of Delhi in 1962 with the opening of its School of Correspondence Courses. The first ODE institution was started with the opening of the B.R. Ambedkar Open University (Andhra Pradesh Open University) in Hyderabad in 1982. IGNOU was established in 1985 through an Act of Parliament. Many state Open Universities have been established in Andhra Pradesh, Bihar, Gujarat, Karnataka, Himachal Pradesh, Maharashtra, Orissa, Rajasthan, Tamil Nadu and West Bengal. Some others are in the process of being established. Apart from these, there are around 104 Universities and some private institutions offering programmes in the distance mode. These institutions offer programmes/courses at various levels from certificate to Ph.D. not only on basic disciplines but also on applied, skill oriented and professional disciplines, such as, Management, Computer Science, Health Sciences, Engineering, Education, Library and Information Science etc.

4 HYBRID MODEL

Keeping pace with the developments in technology, though various models are available or developed in ODL system the mode of delivery (model) is dependent upon the societal pattern of a country. In a country as diverse as India having communities/people with varied backgrounds, literacy levels, economic conditions and technology accessibility, it is not feasible to follow a uniform model. The IT action plan of the Task Force of the Government of India envisaged one PC per 50 persons with universal access to Internet/Intranet connection by the year 2008. According to NASSCOM, the number of Internet connections in 2002 was 8 million. With the planned growth in the telecom sector, the total number of telephones by the end of October 2004 was 88.6 million (Statesman, 2004). Though a large number of Internet Service Providers and increased number of telephones will penetrate different sections of the society in the near future, still the accessibility and adaptability of technology will take some time. The various initiatives of the Government of India for tele-education have given a major boost for ODL system in the country. The first Satellite based Instructional Television experiment (SITE) in 1975-76, followed by Training and Developmental Communication Channel (TDCC) initiated by ISRO for interactive training and education are milestones in this development. TDCC employs one-way video and two-way audio. The dedicated educational TV Channel *Gyandarshan* uses this technology for tele-education. The dedicated radio channel *Gyan Vani* is used for two-way radio counseling. These channels are used not only by the institutions of the ODL system but also by other formal educational institutions. The recently launched dedicated satellite for education - EDUSAT - is unique in the world to facilitate extensive nationwide outreach of educational programmes. In the context of the present scenario, the delivery method is a combination of various methods from print material to e-learning method. While the dual mode universities follow correspondence model based on print media, the open universities are adopting print media to electronic mode of delivery in combination. The State Open Universities are offering courses in their respective languages.

5 ASSURING QUALITY EDUCATION

As significant steps have been taken to develop technological infrastructure for ODL, the maintenance of standards, coordination and promotion of ODL system is monitored by Distance Education Council (DEC), the counterpart of University Grants Commission for distance education. DEC provides support to distance education institutions for development of infrastructure, institutional reforms, academic improvement, staff development and improvement of quality education and accreditation.

6 EXTENT OF OUT REACH THROUGH ODL SYSTEM

The ODL has witnessed tremendous growth in respect of access to education in India. There has been a 24 percent increase in the number of learners per year during 2002 and 2003 in Open Universities and 9.5 percent in dual mode institutions. The ODL system at present is providing education to 22 percent of the total number of students in the higher education system of the country. The Government has set a target of reaching 40 percent by the end of the 10th Plan period (Dixit, 2004). The growth rate of ODL is set at about 10 percent and 5-10 percent in the formal system.

7 IGNOU INITIATIVES

IGNOU has already emerged as an internationally recognized role model to provide learner-centric quality education to large target groups of learners (Dixit, 2004). As the National Open University of the country, it acts as an apex body in ODL, provides support and collaborates in the development of ODL system in the country. IGNOU is also providing education to students in 26 countries of the world. For delivery of the courses, IGNOU adheres to the hybrid model with a combination of print and electronic media. While the Bachelor of Information Technology (BIT), Advance Diploma in Information Technology (ADIT) are offered as Virtual Campus Initiatives (VCI), the Web-enhanced delivery of courses such as Web enhanced Training Programme on WINISIS package is an e-learning initiative taken under the ODL system.

The Delivery of courses through print media is supplemented by face- to- face counseling, teleconferencing (one way video-two way audio) through the dedicated TV Channel *Gyan Darshan* and interactive radio counseling through dedicated radio channel *Gyan Vani*. IGNOU is the nodal agency for their operation.

7.1 Diversity of Subjects

The credibility and acceptability of ODL system is reflected through a total enrollment of 3,34, 415 students in the July 2003 and January 2004 sessions of IGNOU, at various levels. IGNOU is offering 88 programmes on different subjects at different levels, as listed below:

Certificate Level	-	23	Bachelor's Degree	-	14
Diploma Level	-	11	Master's Degree	-	12
Post Graduate Diploma	-	17	Ph. D.	-	8
Advanced Diploma	-	3			

These courses cover not only the basic subjects Arts, Commerce, Sciences, and Humanities but also, as mentioned above, professional and skill oriented disciplines like Computer Science, Engineering, Management, Education, Health Science, Tourism, Library and Information Science and Hospitality and Hotel

Administration. Additionally, based on the importance of contemporary issues, short courses are offered for specific groups of learners.

8 FUTURE OF ODL

With technology continuing to develop at a fast pace, the delivery of higher education system will change in the future. The distance education system is expected to grow further with more openness. In the context of emerging networked society, it is noted that the Internet is being used more and more for a variety of purposes from business and commerce to governance. The society is gradually moving towards a system where it will be possible to perform most of the work from home. This will be true of learning and education also. "As a result of use of WWW, online learning will be on the increase, many more institutions will become involved in delivery of instruction and the line which separates traditional on-campus education from ODL will become very blurred indeed (Tam, 2000).

REFERENCES

1. Cookson, Peter. (2002). Access and Equity in Distance Education. *15th Annual Conference of the Asian Association of Open Universities*, New Delhi, Feb. 21-23, 2002 (Keynote address).
2. Dixit, H.P. (2004): Vice-Chancellor Report. *15th Convocation, IGNOU*, 2004.
3. Ghosh, S.B. (2001) Reaching the Unreached for Library and Information Science Education. Paper. *IFLA Conference*, Boston (USA), 2001
4. IGNOU Profile, 2003 & 2004.
5. Kasturirangan, K (2004): Convocation Address. *15th Convocation, IGNOU*, 2004.
6. Statesman. (2004). Tele-density touches 8.2% in October. Statesman, Dec. 8, 2004 (Business & Finance Supplement).
7. Tam, S.W. (2000): Managing Learner-Centeredness. *ICDE Asian Regional Conference*, New Delhi, November 3-5, 2000.
8. Venkatasubramanian, K. (2001): Valedictory Address. *7th Annual Conference of Indian Distance Education Association*, New Delhi, April 27-29, 2001.

KNOWLEDGE WORKERS OF THE NEW MILLENNIUM: AN INSTANCE OF INTERDISCIPLINARY EXCHANGE AND DISCOVERY

Michael Medland

Dr. Michael Bancroft Medland is involved in research on meta-cognitive tools for improving learning skills of young children - the potential knowledge workers of the 21st century, as he calls them. He is interested in Dr. S. R. Ranganathan's facet analysis and synthesis in knowledge organization, and in teaching this mode of thinking to young children. This paper presents are extracts from e-mail correspondence between Dr. Medland and Professor A. Neelameghan in 2002 and from Medland's research proposal on the subject[2] in which he incorporates aspects of analytico-synthetic approach in meta-cognitive tools for learning.

1. In February 2002 Dr Michael Medland was on an assignment in Korea. He wrote (e-mail) to Neelameghan:

"...I have read your paper on Dynamism and Stability in Knowledge Organization: S.R. Ranganathan's Contributions[3]. I found it enlightening and interesting. My own work deals with developing KOTs (Knowledge Organization Tools) and teaching them to young children. I am trying to integrate the kinds of things you are saying with some of my own. I believe that the integration would be helpful to both library science and education psychology, especially, with the explosion of information that is taking place.... I am from education psychology and only discovered the most interesting ISKO text I mentioned previously in the book give-away bin in the university I taught last year".

Dr. Medland sought more information sources on facet analysis, analytico-synthetic approach to subject structuring and PMEST. He was given a list of selected references. A couple of months later he sent an optimistic report:

"I have already tried my analysis on English-speaking four-year olds. Most four-year olds have the knowledge categories already. I want to try and teach them to talk about the categories (the knowledge ontology) and use them to analyze and synthesize knowledge, to accelerate their learning about and acting on the world, individually or in groups (a value statement)".

Dr. Medland was quite enthusiastic about his research, achieving a fair amount of success, but was apparently handicapped of access to appropriate information source materials in Korea. On 24 Apr 2002 Neelameghan wrote to him:

Dear Dr Medland:

I did not receive your first e-mail with attachment. Only the 21 April letter and e-mail came through. You have mentioned that Ranganathan's Colon Classification stresses symmetry. In practical classification representing a subject with several component ideas (e.g. Antibiotic treatment of microbical lung diseases in children), the attempt is to represent those components in a sequence of concept terms or codes. This is an attempt to represent a multidimensional universe (of knowledge) in a linear (line) mode. In doing so it is near impossible to retain in the linear representation the strength of bonds (or immediate neighbourhood relations) that obtain among the component ideas in the multidimensional universe. There will not be a symmetrical representation of the multidimensional universe in the linear mode.

In Nature there is much symmetry and perhaps an equal number of instances of asymmetry (Is this in itself a case of symmetry?)

The question of Symmetry arises in another context as well. Dr Ranganathan's work is anchored on a set of Normative Principles. These operate at different levels. Therefore, for purposes of differentiation he had categorized them as follows:

- BASIC LAWS applicable to thinking in all disciplines (e.g. Law of Symmetry, Law of Impartiality, Laws of Interpretation, Law of Context, and Law of Parsimony);
- LAWS of a subject area (e.g.Laws of Physics, Laws of Library Science, etc.).applicable to a particular subject / discipline. Such Laws may be formulated as in the hard sciences; they may be Revealed Laws as in the religio-aesthetic group of subjects; or Speculative Laws as in some of the social science subjects.

- Then for a branch of a discipline the normative principles are called Canons (e.g. Canons of Classification in Library Science); and there are normative principles for a sub-branch of a branch of a discipline (e.g. Principle of Helpful Sequence in Classification).

When conflicting results are obtained in applying two or more principles (e.g. in regard to Helpful Arrangement, then we appeal to the higher laws (e.g. Law of Context or the Basic Laws) for resolution of the conflict.

Warm regards
A. Neelameghan"

Dr. Medland wrote in reply:

"Hello ANM,

Thank you for the email.

I am in Korea until May 12. I have no way to get books here. Part of the reason I will return is because of no resources that speak passable English (or more accurately, I can't afford such resources). I will read Ranganathan when I return. Your direction is helpful.

I used Ranganathan's Colon Classification as an example of how the concept of symmetry is everywhere. I was making no attempt at being precise. Symmetry problems exist at ontological and epistemological levels. If you have both levels formulated "about" right, you can determine where clarity exists or does not exist. (Clarity is reached by resolving ambiguity, contradiction, rightness, and vagueness). Each time a learner finds non-clarity there is a re-search problem. You talk of CONFLICT, not clarity. They are about the same thing. A lack of clarity could be called cognitive conflict.

Please remember I am out to teach both sides (teacher and Learner) to talk together with a common language, a language of knowledge. Does the work in library science attempt to promote a common language between database designer and user so libraries/databases can be effectively used/searched? I am

NOT out to develop a database coding system in any way. What I want to do, I think, will help users use databases, communicate their search needs, pack and unpack text (because that is what they get out of the search), and identify and resolve clarity issues (do re-search). Three and four year olds are already traveling down that road. Should we start them off with some powerful tools for analysis and synthesis of knowledge?

Take care,
Mike Medland"

2. In December 2002 Dr Medland developed a research proposal titled "*Reading. Knowledge Work, and Meta-cognitive Tools*" (2002). This document responds to literacy concerns expressed by the U.S. Government's Interagency Educational Research Initiative (IERI) Reading Team. Following a definition of what the future reader will be doing, elaborates the expected activities into seventeen applied research questions, proposing a potential solution for each. Given also is a description of a five-year research program to build the suggested solutions. This research program is expected to lead to "1) an increased knowledge of the processes that underlie reading, and 2) multimedia products that teach early literacy skills like phonemic awareness, beginning reading skills, and the support skills necessary for learning science. These latter products will simulate what scientists and technologists do when they analyze and synthesize text in order to solve problems."

In a brief background note, Dr. Medland mentions that during the latter half of the twentieth century, rapid change forced the need for a more literate America. The Federal Government responded in the 1960's with Project Head Start and Project Follow *Through.* Together, these Projects showed that students at-risk could rapidly gain basic skills when put in a planned, structured, and consistent learning environment.

As the computer-based information age emerged, it led to the global, interdependent, virtual economy. New directions to acquiring literacy and learning skills were needed. The Federal Government pooling the resources of three federal agencies pooled resources to form the IERI to fund researches that would increase knowledge in reading, science, and mathematics education.

2.1 *"What will the literate citizen be doing in the new millennium?*

Those with a futuristic bent give a very simple answer: citizens will be knowledge workers doing knowledge work Knowledge work is an individual or group process (activity) of unpacking the contents of knowledge sources (analysis) and then packing the knowledge found (synthesis) in order to answer a learning problem. What is this new literacy?

1) The new conception of literacy seeks to instill tomorrow's citizen with more than just content;
2) Reading, science, and mathematics learning are highly related in the context of the new literacy;
3) Knowledge workers will be continually learning throughout their lives; thus, they will need to learn rapidly and "enjoy" that learning;
4) Knowledge workers will participate extensively in collaborative and concurrent activities to produce knowledge; and
5) All citizens will be engaged in knowledge work to help their "enterprise" move successfully into the future.

The enterprise could be the knowledge worker's family, the community, the corporation, or the government. In addition, there is more to an American citizen than being just a knowledge worker — the values for instance. Yet developing knowledge workers, those with enough literacy to contribute, is an important task to insure the continual becoming of America".

2.2 *How can we guarantee that our children will become knowledge workers?*

Dr. Medland answers this question by breaking it into seventeen applied research questions, supplying a possible answer to each, and then outlining a five-year research project to produce the products that will begin to move all children toward becoming tomorrow's knowledge workers.

Within this framework another issue will be: ***What would a "language code" look like and do?***

A research direction can be found within the fields of artificial intelligence and information science. The artificial intelligence community has turned to the examination and construction of ontologies to deal with Gruninger and Usehold's concern with disparate backgrounds, languages, and techniques. From the practical side, an accepted ontology is a commitment to use a common language to talk about knowledge (content) in a domain. It is a way to talk about a knowledge base (domain) so its contents can be parsed, represented, searched, and expanded.

Knowledge Sharing Criterion

The artificial intelligence community begins ontology construction with a new and deceptively simple question: "What is an ontology for?" Their answer: it is for knowledge sharing and reuse. In the process of building sharable and reusable ontologies, the artificial intelligence community has taken a engineering approach to their design: evaluate them to the extent to which they promote the goals of knowledge sharing and reuse, and then revise to achieve greater effectiveness.

This is in perfect keeping with the IERI reading teams requirements. By using the ontology (a common language), users can share knowledge. From a psychological perspective, knowledge sharing is a social activity. Moreover, by using language to talk about what is known, it becomes a meta-cognitive activity. Thus, ontological language functions as a meta-cognitive tool to grasp, relate, share, and promote "knowledge."

Knowledge Reuse Criterion

Knowledge reuse refers to the ontology's ability to handle an expanding knowledge-domain. This is a helpful criterion, but incomplete for teaching and learning purposes. The educational community needs an expanded reuse criterion. It would make no sense to posit a new ontology for each subject domain. Such would just burden and muddle the "thinking" of learners; it would cripple the assimilation and accommodation of knowledge. This crippling would parallel that done by the inconsistent phonetic code of English. Therefore, there needs to be an "across-domain" criterion for the ontology. Students and teachers would learn one ontology and then apply it to all knowledge domains to expedite the teaching and learning process. We want students to make queries and assertions about what is learned, and to quickly assimilate and accommodate knowledge. This is the heart of the knowledge worker's task. Such an ontology complements the process or strategy research mentioned above (Research Question 8). Essentially, it would give muscle to the skeletal process of getting meaning from text.

Across-Domain Criterion

The fields of information science, knowledge representation, and database design have methods for knowledge-base construction, retrieval, and expansion that can help our understanding of just what an across-domain ontology must do. All libraries, or database engines, catalogue embodied knowledge. Every catalog system takes embodied knowledge and codes it for retrieval (Neelameghan, 2000). The encoding mechanism, with its categories and subcategories, is an ontology: a way to fracture the world of embodied knowledge so that it can be placed in a database and retrieved. The Dewey Decimal, the Library of Congress, and the Colon Classification Systems, to name just a few, are all ontologies. In addition, they all possess one thing in common: they have symmetry. The classification scheme is the same one used for retrieval. Ranganathan's (1963) analytic-synthetic method, as part of his Colon Classification system, stressed the importance of symmetry in the classification of knowledge. The importance of symmetry cannot be ignored. We see it in the languages of science and most clearly in the symmetric relationship between explanation and prediction. Throughout science and technology, the language tools used to analyze worlds are the same ones used to synthesize them. In the same vain, young students who analyze a text must perform a synthesis activity to place what is learned into their existing knowledge base and/or create a new text to answer the learning problem that spurred the analysis.

How can we do this? How *would* an ontology or language code 1) help the teacher / learner communication process (sharing criterion), 2) foster the analysis and synthesis of any domain of embodied knowledge (across domain criterion), and 3) handle the expanding knowledge students will encounter during schooling and beyond (reuse criterion)? The ontology should provide students with a tool during individual or group learning sessions to both assimilate and accommodate content in the context of the knowledge work. Basic comprehension questions—who, what, why, when, where, and how—do not give the student or teacher an organizational tool. The social construction of knowledge requires analysis and synthesis processes that mirror each other, that are complex enough to eventually help students handle complex text, yet simple enough to be learned and used by young children, starting at about four years of age.

Basic comprehension questions represent a weak ontology to analyze text. And being weak, this ontology cannot guide the synthesis task. We need an expanded comprehension set, a strong ontology that has a direct correspondence to the grammatical structures in text as suggested by Martin. The direct correspondence would allow for both analysis and synthesis activities. In the parlance of knowledge representation research, we build an "upper-level ontology," one that handles language as presented in text. The importance of such an ontology has not been overlooked by artificial Intelligence, knowledge representation, and information science researchers and practitioners (e.g., Institute of Electrical and Electronic Engineers, 2002).

REFERENCES

1. Reading, Knowledge, Work, and Meta-cognitive Tools (Draft). (2002). December.

2. Neelameghan, A. (2000) Dynamism and Stability in Knowledge Organization: S.R. Ranganathan's Contributions. **In**: *Dynamism and Stability in Knowledge Organization: Proceeding of the Sixth International ISKO Conference*, 10-13 July, 2000, Toronto, Canada. Edited by Clare Beghtol, Lynn C. Howarth, and Nancy J.Williamson. Wurzburg, Germany: Ergon, 2000; p. 164-169.

THE PERSON AND ASSOCIATED ORGANIZATIONS

PROFESSIONAL PROFILE OF PROFESSOR A. NEELAMEGHAN: EXCERPTS FROM INTERVIEW SESSIONS

Hemalata Iyer

0 PREAMBLE

When the festschrift volume was conceived, I was asked to contribute to the volume because of my professional association with Professor A. Neelameghan (AN), who was my teacher at the Documentation Research and Training Centre (DRTC) established by Dr S.R. Ranganathan in 1962. We have co-authored papers for conferences and periodicals and he has been a mentor for my own research. I am delighted to contribute this article based on interviews and discussions with him.

Prof. Neelameghan (AN) has had a very distinguished professional career with a broad range of interests including, library and information science education, information systems and services, information policy, management, industrial information services, database design, knowledge organization and related tools.

He joined Dr. S.R. Ranganathan in 1962 at the DRTC in Bangalore, India, where he made prolific contributions to research, especially in the area of knowledge organization.

In 1974 he was elected Chairman of the International Advisory Committee of UNESCO/UNISIST. Four years later he joined UNESCO, General Information Program (PGI), as Project Coordinator of the UNESCO/UNDP Postgraduate Training Course for Science Information Specialists in Southeast Asia (Manila, the Philippines). He continued his remarkable career working to develop specialized programmes and projects for UNESCO and other international organizations. Although AN retired from UNESCO in 1986, he continued as a consultant and resource specialist for a number of UNESCO projects and committee meetings, the League of Arab States, the International Development Research Centre (IDRC), Asia-Pacific Development Centre (APDC, Bangkok), the Marga Institute (Colombo, Sri Lanka), the Caribbean Industrial Research Institute (CARIRI, Port of Spain, Trinidad) and national governments and NGOs in many developing countries. He is currently active in the field, both on his own and through the Sarada Ranganathan Endowment for Library Science, Bangalore. He is also an Honorary Visiting Professor at the DRTC.

When I proposed this interview initially he was quite reluctant to narrate his career; he said nobody else will be interested in reading it. But I persisted and persuaded him showing him a letter I had received from one of the journal editors in the USA. He then acquiesced.

During a question and answer session, both face to face and via e-mail, AN discussed his entry into the profession, his educational experiences in the United States, his association with DRTC and Dr. Ranganathan, his international work, current research interests, and answered my questions regarding his perception of the future of classification and knowledge organization. Excerpts from the interview are given below.

His professional commitment and excellence has always been an inspiration to me and I hope this interview will serve to be inspirational to the readers as well.

AN now lives in Bangalore with his wife Lakshmi. He has two sons and two daughters, two grandsons and five grand-daughters, and a great-granddaughter.

HI: ***At the outset I want to thank you for your time. What prompted you to pursue Library and Information Science as a career?***

AN: My entry into the library profession was fortuitous. After graduating (1947) with a degree in the physical sciences from the Madras University, I got married and following a three-month stint as an apprentice in an insurance firm in Madras (now Chennai), joined the Pasteur Institute in Coonoor (a hill station in the southern State of Tamil Nadu) as Librarian. The Institute did research on rabies and produced and distributed anti-rabies vaccine.

The Institute proved to be a good learning environment for a non-professional librarian. I knew precious little about providing library service and even less about library techniques and management. But the Institute expected me essentially to assist the researchers find relevant references in periodicals, translate the titles and, sometimes, abstracts of papers published in the several

French periodicals received by the library. I had learnt French as a second language in the school in Mahe, Kerala, a former French Colony.. I was also to assist the Director of the Institute with the publication of his research papers. The experience in searching for information, sometimes joined by the researchers themselves, was interesting and, at times, even exciting. I learnt to use indexing, abstracting, and review periodicals and gained familiarity with biomedical terminology. Biomedical subjects became my field of specialization during most of my library service career. The Institute's library was accessible to users 24 hours, seven days a week! The users included besides the researchers and technicians of the Pasteur Institute but also those of the Nutrition Research Laboratories of India and Malaria Institute of India, both housed in the same building.

Frequent visits to some of the labs and workplaces of the Institute and interactions with the research and technical staff onsite were most helpful in 'understanding' something of the nature of research and techniques used which, in turn, helped in rendering useful reference service on request and in anticipation, the latter based on the current issues of journals. I continued such interactions with information seekers throughout my service career.

The researchers approved of a new simple classification scheme that I worked out and the resulting arrangement of the collection of some 5,000 books in the library! William Warner Bishop's book on cataloguing and a couple of books by Dr. Ranganathan available in the Institute's library provided me guidance in cataloguing and library service.

I also learnt some statistical analysis and data tabulation in sorting and organizing the rabies data cards that the Institute maintained to prepare annual reports on rabies. This was helpful in my later studies in the US and attracted me to bibliometrics and scientometrics..

HI: ***When and how did you acquire professional qualifications?***

AN: The experience at the Pasteur Institute drew me to library work and motivated me to acquire professional qualifications. Some of the senior technical staff of the Institute urged me, but in vain, to join them in laboratory work.

Although the Institute did not support my request for deputation to study library science, I received an excellent commendation letter from the Director and blessings of everyone else there. In mid-1949, I joined the one-year postgraduate Diploma (later Bachelor's degree) course in library science of the Madras University, Department of Library Science, established by Dr. Ranganathan in the 1930s.

Dr. Ranganathan had left the Madras University Library some four years earlier in 1945. However, from his erstwhile colleagues and co-authors in the Department (C. Sivaraman, K.M. Siinivasan, and V.Sundaram) we got a pretty good grounding in such subjects as cataloguing, classification, and reference service. We practiced Dewey Decimal Classification (DDC), Colon Classification (CC), ALA Cataloging Rules, and Ranganathan's Classified Catalogue Code (CCC). Mr. Sundaram, whom Dr. Ranganathan used to call a walking encyclopaedia, was then in service but the others had retired.

Mr. Sivaraman introduced me to the Madras Library Association (MALA). He was then maintaining MALA's library collection, which I was permitted to use in preparing for the British Library Association's Associateship examinations. I passed the examinations in Classification and Cataloguing but did not pursue it further as I left Chennai in 1950 to work as a cataloguer in the Occidental Section of the Osmania University Library in Hyderabad, Andhra Pradesh. Mr. Masood Yezdani and Mr. B.P. Shenoy were respectively the University Librarian and my supervisor, both my classmates in the Madras library science course! The library used ALA cataloguing rules and DDC.

The following year I moved to a private college library (the Vivekanananda College) in Chennai that used Dr. Ranganathan's CC and CCC. After five months of cataloguing and classifying some 11,000 books, I was looking for greener pastures. In November 1951, an opportunity presented itself. Under a programme for upgrading the libraries of the medical colleges of the Madras State Medical Services, I joined as librarian of the Madras Medical College (MMC), an old institution established in 1823. The college library served also the medical personnel of the adjoining large General Hospital and was also open to private medical practitioners in the city. The collection of over 30,000 books and bound periodicals was accessioned and catalogued for the first time. I was looking for a special classification scheme for the health sciences. I knew about Cunningham's Classification, Army Medical Library Classification now the National Medical Library), etc. but none of these schemes were available in the city! Interestingly, H. E. Bliss's Bibliographic Classification (BBC) and his works on Organization of Knowledge were available in the MMC library which I used. Perhaps no other library in India has used or is using the BBC!

Dr. D.V. Subbha Reddy, then Head of the Institute of Physiology at MMC, was Chairman of the Library Committee. He was also a pioneer on studies in the history of medicine in India. We organized a separate collection of some 1,500 books and tracts and published several joint papers on the history of medicine. I compiled an annual Bibliography on Indian Medical Historiography, published in the *Indian Journal of History of Medicine.* I started compiling a list of the works by members of the Indian Medical Service, 1615-1930 (completed in 1962), and the history of Indian medical periodicals, later published (1963) by the Indian Association of Special Libraries, Kolkata, with a preface by Dr. B.C.Roy.

HI: ***I understand that you received your Masters degree in Library Science in the US; how were the graduate programmes in the 1950s?***

AN: Late in 1952, I applied for and was awarded a Medical Library Association (MLA) fellowship for 1953 (a Rockefeller Foundation grant) to specialize in medical librarianship in USA. A Fulbright travel grant was also secured. From Bombay I travelled by steamship, along with 23 other Fulbright grantees (in various other fields), arriving New York 23 days later, with a stopover of 9 days and change of boat in Italy. After a week of orientation in Washington DC., I enrolled in library science courses, as previously arranged, at the George Peabody College for Teachers, (now part of the Vanderbilt University), Nashville, Tenn. I was also assigned daily three hours of practice work in the neighbouring Vanderbilt University Medical School library, where the late Ms Eileen Cunningham, a well known medical librarian, author of a classification scheme for health sciences, and coordinator of the MLA international fellowship program, was then the chief librarian. The practical work put me through almost all aspects of library work – from book shelving, through technical processing, reference work, circulation, working on committees, etc.

In addition to the usual courses in library science, we were required to take courses in three cognate subjects. I selected Philosophy of Science (History of Science was my first choice, but such a course was not available in the university), Audio-visual Education, and Vital Statistics.

It was a fruitful year in the U.S. I was elected president of the class, the first time a foreign student was so honoured in the Nashville school. I was also biographed in the *Who's Who of Selected Students of American Colleges and Universities* (1953-54). A paper based on one of my term papers – an analytical study of the coverage of some 4,500 medical periodicals in ten abstracting and indexing periodicals was subsequently published.

I recall three experiences novel to me at that time. The first related to reference service practice. The instructor for reference service and bibliography, Ms. Frances N. Cheney, a widely respected teacher and reviewer of reference materials, wanted us to get the experience of meeting and helping users in a real world situation. The exercise was called EOTO (Each One Take One). Left to our own wits, we positioned ourselves at 'strategic points' in the college / university library. As a user walked in one of us would approach him/her and offer help in using the catalogue, reference books, etc. Users' reactions ranged from a polite 'Thank you, I can manage' to a stern 'Will you leave me alone!' Desperate to show some good results, one of my classmates persuaded her friend who was enrolled in another course to accept help from us. When other users saw this, some of them came to us for assistance! We adopted another strategy. We met the Reference Librarian of the library and told her about our predicament. She had a knowing smile and introduced us to some of the users who came to her for help and then we were in business! So we learnt that generally users would not take help from 'strangers,' and an aspiring reference assistant needs to be introduced to users by library personnel whom users were familiar with and had confidence in!

The second and third experiences related to final tests (examinations) in the course on audio-visual education. The tests were of two types: one an objective test and the other a project.

The objective test consisted of 120 tape-recorded questions. As the tape recorder played each question was repeated once. The examinees received a magnetized answer sheet (plus a copy sheet) with corresponding question numbers and boxes with choice of answers. The duration for answering the 120 questions was exactly 60 minutes. At two questions a minute one had minimal time to think and mark. The sheets were magnetically scanned and assigned marks.

For the project I was asked to mount an audio-visual show to depict some aspects of India to the class. I was the only one from India in the class. However I was able to get help from a couple of female students from India in other courses in the college. We borrowed a cinema reel (20 min) about India's struggle for freedom from the Indian Embassy in Washington DC. As pre-planned, on the day for the show, the Indian students came into my class in their colourful native dresses. One of them did an Indian dance to taped music, another student brought some artefacts for exhibit and distributed some Indian sweets, and I operated the movie equipment. On the whole it was an enjoyable, cooperative, novel experience.

I received my Masters degree after two semesters, spent vacation time (Christmas and part of Summer) site-visiting science and medical libraries in several cities, and completed a summer course in science literature at Columbia University in New York. Based on the term paper – comparative study of German and US indexing, abstracting and review periodicals in surgery - prepared for the course, an article was subsequently published in the *Journal of Documentation* (Aslib). On the way back to India in September 1954, I visited several medical libraries in England, and attended a medical librarians conference in Leeds.

Some twenty years later in 1974, I visited the library school in Nashville on my way to Mexico from London, Ontario, Canada. The staff members had all changed, but Ms. Cheney and her husband, though retired, fetched me from the airport, remembered to provide me with *vegetarian food*, and took me to the school where they had put on an exhibit of my project reports (done there) and reprints of some of my other papers. As I was then involved in UNESCO/PGI programmes, I spoke to the students on library development planning.

HI: ***Did you join the Documentation Research and Training Centre soon after graduating in Library Science in the US?***

AN: No. To the surprise of many, I re-joined the MMC Library after returning from the US in September 1954. My contacts in the US enabled us fill many of the gaps in our periodicals collection and to receive gifts of many valuable encyclopaedic volumes and indexes to medical literature. About this time I started on some research studies and publications.

In mid-1956 I joined the library, later named Technical Information Centre (TIC) of the Hindustan Antibiotics Ltd.,(HAL), Pimpri, near Pune, one of the early public sector undertakings of the Government of India. We introduced weekly current awareness service (CAS), a fortnightly information alert service to the management, a patents abstracts service (once every ten days), a permanent exhibit of about 120 antibiotics samples, a photo gallery of production plants and a well appreciated reference service. The CAS involved selecting papers for indexing from the current issues of over 350 periodicals, company newsletters, technical reports, and issues of indexing and abstracting services (e.g. *Chemical Abstracts, Biological Abstracts, Excerpta Medica* select sections, and others) to cover papers published in periodicals not received in the library. Technical reports and some 15000 items were checked each month to select about 200 relevant ones for listing in each weekly issue. Throughout the week it brought researchers and a few engineers to peruse the current issues of periodicals. The best part was that the Works Manager (top boss of Production) would scan each new issue of the CAS on Friday morning, mark items to be perused by himself, and others that he felt particular senior technical personnel should look at and report at the next technical meeting about the relevance of the information. The persons who received such notices could not ignore them as it came from the top boss! This was excellent support to and marketing of, our CAS in particular and other services in general among the production and engineering personnel.

The HAL Technical Information Centre (TIC) was a very good experience in information service to different categories of users in a corporate environment. Isolation of new antibiotics from microorganisms was a routine research activity at the Research Centre of the company. From time to time a researcher, having obtained a crude chemical substance from a fermented broth, would give the TIC the physical and chemical properties – optical rotation, melting point range, UV spectrum peaks, etc. and some biological properties, and ask us to find out other known antibiotics with similar properties. The information could help them to answer questions or solve problems they faced. If substances with similar properties were found to be too toxic in animal and / or clinical tests, they would abandon further work on the substance; or the microorganisms may be a new source for a known substance. The researcher might also find it difficult to extract or purify the substance and may get some clues from the published documents on similar substances. By the mid-1950s, over 1,500 antibiotic substances from microorganisms had been reported, although only half a dozen were commercialized.

Our Director of Research had suggested that the library prepare a handbook on the properties of these substances to facilitate answers to such queries. A novel indexing system on properties of antibiotics was designed. It was a compact reference system. A brief report appeared on it in the *Journal of Chemical Documentation (Amer. Chem. Soc)* in 1962.

The TIC was also assigned the tasks of editing and publishing the technical bulletin of the company and organization of a series of lectures on subjects of interest to the research, technical and production staff of the company.

On several occasions the information support provided saved substantial amounts of money for the company, helped to win patent litigation, solved technical problems and secured a better image to the company and its researchers, and of course for the TIC. The TIC was always included in the company tours (often the tour started from the TIC) for important visitors – researchers and celebrities, such as, Nobel laureates E.B. Chain, Howard Florey, N. W. Pirie; heads of State, Emperor Haile Selassie, Chou en Lai, Presidents of India etc. Industrial and business information services continued to interest me and it was a course that I taught in India and abroad.

During this time I was invited to participate in some of the meetings of the Indian Standards Organization, (now Bureau of Indian Standards), Sub-Committee on Documentation, chaired by Dr. Ranganathan.

HI. ***Tell us about your association with Dr. Ranganathan and DRTC***

AN. I met Dr. Ranganathan for the first time in 1952 while participating in the Silver Jubilee celebrations of the Madras Library Association in Chennai. He was the principal speaker. I presented my first paper on library service in which the sentence 'If readers would not come to the library then the library should go to readers' caught on. Dr. Ranganathan was then organizing a collective effort for compiling a list of 'removable and irremovable attachments' to personal names of different cultural groups in India, which can be used as a source book in cataloguing. I also contributed to the list. I visited him at his home in Triplicane, Chennai. Later I met him at the All Library Conference in Hyderabad, over which he presided. He was aware of the scholarships I had received to study in the US the following year. Nevertheless he asked me, through one of his close associates, if I would like to take up a good post of librarian in a special library in Dehradun (North India). I was in a dilemma, but my friends advised me to go for studies in US. After that I had practically no contact with him until 1961. I did write him a couple letters while in Hyderabad requesting a facility for working librarians to sit the Masters degree of the University of Delhi which he had established. But that was not allowed.

In late 1961 when I was with HAL, Dr. Ranganathan enquired of me (by a postcard written in Tamil, structured and numbered in his characteristic style, if I would join as Reader (Associate Professor) in the Documentation Research and Training Centre (DRTC) he was then establishing in Bangalore, as a constituent of the Indian Statistical Institute (Calcutta, now Kolkata). I was thrilled that Dr. Ranganathan had noticed my work and publications and the unexpected invitation to work with him was most welcome. In May 1962 I joined the DRTC. Dr. Ranganathan was then Honorary Professor and Head of the Centre. I was promoted to full Professorship in 1965, when Dr. Ranganathan was appointed the National Research Professor by the Government of India. Subsequently, I succeeded him as Head of DRTC and remained there until 1978 August when I left to join UNESCO. On 27 September 1972, Dr. Ranganathan's son Mr. R. Yogeshwar (now living in Luxembourg) and I were at Ranganathan's death bed in the hospital in Bangalore.

Dr.Ranganathan considered the decade 1962-1972 the most fruitful in terms of research in classification in particular, and knowledge organization in general. I taught documentation (now information systems and services), and specialized library services (e.g. support to industries, R&D, etc). But I also audited Dr. Ranganathan's classes on classification, universe of knowledge, and cataloguing, and reported on the teacher-student exchanges in a series of papers. These reports were helpful to both the students in DRTC and to other faculty. For me it was a learning experience getting into Dr. Ranganathan's approach to teaching classification and cataloguing, elucidation of the theoretical foundations, and so on.

Dr. Ranganathan expected from the faculty (without his actually saying so) total commitment to research and teaching. Dr. Elaine Svenonius, former Professor at UCLA, who was a Visiting Professor for five months at DRTC in 1975, said in an interview for the journal CCQ in 2000: "I was curious to see what DRTC was like – it had been, and at the time still in part, run like a commune, where five faculty and ten students lived, studied, dined, and talked together incessantly about information organization".

From its very start the teachers and students of DRTC accompanied Dr. Ranganathan on his daily early morning (5:30 am) walks of about 2 km. He conversed on many things but mostly on the minutiae of information organization. The early mornings in an unpolluted, invigorating environment in Bangalore generated fruitful discussions and new ideas. This good practice was discontinued after 1965 due to Dr. Ranganathan's weakening constitution.

By 1965, I was teaching three courses, Design and Development of Schemes for Classification of Micro-documents: Theory and Practice, and Universe of Subjects: Its Structure and Development, Information Service in Specialized Centres (Industry, R&D). These added more depth to my understanding of teaching and research in information systems and services, especially to the information organization component.

Of course, Dr. Ranganathan received many visitors from all over India – students and researchers, scientists and statesmen, executives and people of various genres and even 'realized souls'. The staff and students of DRTC had the privilege of meeting some of them. There were library and information specialists from abroad too. Some of them stayed to present lectures to the students and staff.. Yet others were invited to present the Sarada Ranganathan Endowment lectures. These contacts enabled DRTC to keep step with the developments in the field and its library to receive valuable source materials.

Association with Dr. Ranganathan had an invigorating and challenging effect on the people working with him. We almost perfected the methodology for the practical design of freely-faceted depth classification for specialized subjects. DRTC students applied the methodology to designing a 'depth' classification scheme for a narrow subject in partial fulfilment for graduation. Another requirement was the preparation of either a project report on the planning and design of an information support system based on interactions with users in an R&D laboratory or an industry; alternatively, a student may prepare a substantive report on the trend of development in a specific subject.

I was personally interested in border and interdisciplinary subjects as part of the studies in Universe of Subjects: Its Structure and Development. In this context. application of statistical analysis to 'scatter and seepage' studies was found useful. Lectures in statistical analysis were introduced as regular course modules in the late sixties with assistance from external experts. However, the first DRTC annual seminar (1963) was largely devoted to such studies. About this time external experts were also invited to introduce computer and its applications in information handling to DRTC students (and staff too). This led to some interesting collaborative work on semi-automatic CC class number synthesis, generation of index strings, and consideration of issues relating to computer-based information retrieval (which Dr. Ranganathan called Doc-finder). Subsequently, Informetrics and Scientometrucs and Computer applications in information storage and retrieval were introduced as core modules of DRTC course. Subsequently, in the syllabi of the regional schools of information science I was involved in developing countries (Manila, Beijing, Caracas, Ibadan, Erthiopia) these subjects were introduced.

In the area of information organization, the modes of formation of subjects, facet syntax and Absolute Syntax, modification and extension of Chain Procedure to generate various kinds of indexes, types of relations among concept terms (e.g. in thesauri), computer applications to thesaurus construction, automatic generation of CC number and subject headings, and seminal mnemonics were among the topics that particularly interested me. Our studies in these areas pointed to applications of the findings in the design and development of information systems and services, user interfaces, etc. For instance, organizing ideas according to the concept of seminal mnemonics found a parallel in general systems analysis and application in the presentation of ideas in technical writing (content development). The findings were mainly disseminated through the proceedings of the *DRTC Annual Seminars*, and the journal *Library Science with a Slant to Documentation* (now *SRELS Journal of Information Management*), both of which were started by Dr. Ranganathan in 1963.

At the time I left DRTC to join UNESCO in 1978, Dr. G. Bhattacharyya, Dr. M.A Gopinath, Dr. S. Seetharama, and Dr. I.K. Ravichandra Rao, all graduates of DRTC, were on the faculty to continue the good work of the Centre. Subsequently they successively headed the Centre.

HI: ***You had spent a year or so in Canada. What was this Canadian connection like?***

AN: I spent a useful academic year (Sept. 1973 - July 1974) as a Visiting Professor at the School of Library and Information Science (SLIS), University of Western Ontario, London, Ontario. Interactions with Professors Elaine Svenonius, Sam Neil, Bill Cameron (the Director) and Visiting Professor Jason Farradane and others were valuable experiences. About that time SLIS was planning to introduce a Ph.D programme and a revision of the Masters Degree curriculum to support the doctoral programme, with additional emphasis on information organization, indexing, research methodology, application of statistical methods, etc. I was invited to be the chairman of the curriculum revision committee. I also handled classes on faceted classification, modes of formation of subjects, and business information service.

Interestingly, the first Ph.D. from SLIS (Dr. Michael Shepherd, currently Professor at Dalhousie University, Faculty of Computer Science, Halifax, NS, Canada) did research on the use of CC as an information retrieval tool for his thesis. He and his wife Caroline spent several months at DRTC in 1975 to learn more about CC, and they also taught computer applications courses.

At SLIS, Prof. Svenonius initiated a small discussion group, which met on Friday evenings to exchange ideas about designing an 'automated scientist,' an intelligent computer program that could evaluate an experimental scientific paper. The computer program was to be designed to examine, say, a text, and be able to judge whether the experiment reported had validity in terms of soundness of hypothesis, whether the sample size chosen was adequate, etc. The group consisted of a logician and faculty member that taught research methodology (Prof. Svenonius), a linguist (for predicate calculus), a mathematical sociologist interested in knowledge organization, and myself (on facet structuring and representation of subjects). There were other visitors who participated in the discussions. Although we did not produce an 'automated scientist' and eventually the group was dissolved as members left to join other institutions, the interdisciplinary discussions were rewarding and a good learning experience.

About that time I was also interested in Dr. Ranganathan's postulate of Absolute Syntax *vis a vis* his PMEST sequence. I had a couple of students and colleagues working on the representation of PMEST sequence in two or three Indian-languages with interesting results supporting the Absolute Syntax concept. In this context I was examining deep structure grammar, transformational grammar, linguistic universals, human associative memory, general systems theory etc. In a class discussion on the universality of the facet syntax based on Absolute Syntax (with possibility of use in inter-linguistic and inter-cultural communication), an issue was raised as to how one would communicate a concept if the concept itself did not occur in a particular culture. For example, the concept of 'past' did not figure among the concepts of a particular group of Canadian-Indians that a student had worked with. Similarly, some South-Pacific Islanders recognized only three primary colours. This issue of cross-cultural, inter-linguistic communication of ideas has continued to interest me. In a related discussion, another student pointed out that the PMEST sequence had heuristic value, more like cybernetic hunting (cf. guided missiles).

While at SLIS, I had opportunities to lecture on faceted structures, Absolute Syntax, chain indexing, etc. at the Department of Linguistics, University of Ottawa, and work with an Associate Professor in the University of Toronto,

School of Information Studies, on a project on analytical indexing of educational films in reels. During this time, on invitation, I also presented lectures at the Universities of Rhode Island, Syracuse, Pittsburgh, Vanderbilt, etc. in USA, and in Mexico.

Subsequently, Dr. Ganesh Bhattacharyya of DRTC served as visiting Professor for about 3 years at SLIS and Dr. I.K. Ravichandra Rao, also of DRTC, did his doctoral studies at SLIS.

HI: ***You were involved in the activities of international organizations, such as, FID/CR, UNESCO, IDRC, etc. What was the type of work that you were involved in?***

AN: Dr. Ranganathan was closely associated with the activities of FID, FID/CA (later FID/CR), IFLA and ISO (TC/46 particularly) through his important contributions. We at DRTC were invariably drawn into these activities. In 1967, I chaired the FID/CR conference in Tokyo, as Dr. Ranganathan could not make it. I was chairman of FID/CR from 1973-1980, taking over from Dr. Molgaard-Hansen. Reports on R&D in classification and indexing in different countries were published. The Third International Study Conference on Classification Research on Ordering Systems for Global Information Networks was organized in Bombay in January 1975. I participated in the discussions on the Broad System of Ordering (BSO, supported by FID and UNESCO) as a member of the related FID/CR Committee. On the initiative of the DRTC Alumni Association, the FID/CR instituted the international Ranganathan Award for Classification Research. The first recipient of the award was Dr. Derek Austin of the *British National Bibliography*.

In 1974 I was elected Chairman of the International Advisory Committee of UNESCO/UNISIST and during 1974-78, I assisted in different capacities with specialized committees concerned with education and training, national information policy, social science documentation, and regional issues in information. Participation in the preparation of a background document for UNISIST II was a rewarding experience. Information support for socio-economic development was a highlight of the document. Subsequently Unesco/PGI incorporated this aspect of information provision especially in developing countries, for example at the Unesco-sponsored seminar in Toledo, Spain.

I was also then involved individually and through expert groups, advising governments (including India) or other agencies in the establishment of national information system for science and technology, specialized subject centres and preparing development plans for information centres in industries, R&D establishments, etc. As member of an India-US joint committee to foster cooperative activity in the information area I led the first group of Indian information scientists to the U.S. for site-visits, seminars, and discussions with counterparts. At the final joint meeting of the teams in Washington D.C. to formulate recommendations on cooperation, Dr. M. Anandakrishnan, then Science Advisor to the Indian Embassy in Washinton D.C., advised and assisted us in the preparation of the final report. As member of a government sponsored team, I visited several countries of Europe, along with Prof. S. Parthasarathy (then of INSDOC, Delhi), and Dr.V.A. Kamath (Bhabha Atomic Research Centre, Bombay (Mumbai)), to discuss collaboration in the information field.

During 1973-1977, I participated in and contributed to, along with a representative of the Department of Science and Technology, Government of India, a few regional Unesco meetings in Asia. About this time Prof. S. Parthasarathy who was returning to India after completing a Unesco assignment in Somalia and debriefing in Paris, came to DRTC, persuaded me to apply for the Chief Technical Adviser's post of a regional training course in Asia. He brought the application form with him! This resulted in my joining, in August 1978, UNESCO's General Information Programme (PGI) as Project Coordinator (in Director's grade) of the UNESCO-UNDP Postgraduate Course for Science Information Specialists in South-east Asia, based at the Institute of Library Science, University of the Philippines, Manila. The success of this regional programme prompted other developing countries and regions to make proposals to UNESCO and other aid agencies, such as IDRC for similar national / regional schools / programmes to be established. I was closely involved in the initiation of such programmes in Beijing (China), Caracas (Venezuela), Ibadan (Nigeria), and Addis Ababa (Ethiopia). I also taught in the schools in Manila (1978-82), Ethiopia

(1990-94) and for shorter periods in Beijing, Caracas, and Port Moresby (Papua-New Guinea). These regional programmes involved securing the support, financial and other, and agreements, not only of officials and other individuals and institutions in the region but also appreciation and commendations internationally recognized experts. We have been fortunate in this respect. Prof Wilfred Saunders (Sheffield University) who was called in to assist in regional consultation seminars in Beijing and Caracas has commended the groundwork that I had prepared on behalf of Unesco/PGI. Prof F.W. Lancaster and other external experts, who were invited as examiners for the Addis Ababa Masters degree course, appreciated the high level of the teaching, students' achievements and facilities provided in the regional school. Dr. G. Bhattacharyya and Dr.G.G. Chowdhury, external experts, joined the School of Information Studies for Africa (SISA) faculty during my tenure at the institution. Just before leaving SISA, in 1994, my wife and I established the five-year Lakshmi Neelameghan Research Fellowship at the school for supporting research by Ethiopian students.

My first visit to Beijing along with Mr. Jacques Tocatlian, on behalf of UNESCO, was in 1980 to strengthen PGI's ties with China, which led to several PGI supported programmes – training, national information policy, etc. – and my visits to that country every year until 1991. On my first visit in 1980, UNESCO/PGI also asked me to visit alternative energy systems and to report on the related information support provision. This took about a couple of weeks Since, at that time UNESCO/PGI was considering supporting a feasibility study on an international information network for alternative energy, I continued such data collection for Malaysia, Singapore, Indonesia, Nepal, Sri Lanka, Thailand, Australia, etc. in the Asian region. Although no international network emerged, UNESCO assisted the production of a number of manuals on information repackaging and such repackaged resource books on inexpensive and efficient cooking ovens, etc.

In India, during 1975-1985 period, UNESCO/PGI supported a demonstration of online access to ESA (European Space Agency) databases from TIFR (Tata Institute of Fundamental Research) premises in Mumbai; assisted the National Institute of Oceanography (CSIR), Goa, for acquiring computer equipment. for data processing; the Publications and Information Directorate (PID/CSIR), New

Delhi, for computerizing the Medicinal and Aromatic Plants Abstracts (MAPA) database; the National Aeronautics (now Aerospace) Laboratory (CSIR), Bangalore, to set up online access to ESA databases and provide information services thereof, and initiation of the Environmental Information Service (ENVIS) project, in Visakhapatnam.

In mid-1975, I made a long trip starting from Bangalore: First to participate and report on a Unesco-sponsored meeting on national information policy in Herzeg Novi in former Yugoslavia; then present a paper on information service to industries at a Unesco-supported international seminar on the subject in Sofia, Bulgaria; next, responding to a long-standing invitation from Dr. Peter Lazar, presented a couple of lectures at the national documentation centre in S&T in Budapest, Hungary; in continuation, on a prior invitation by Brazil's Ministry of Education, travelled to that country to lecture on industrial information service at the University of Belo-Horizonte, Minais Gerias, and present lectures on national information system planning at an international conference in Porto Allegre; then departing from Porto Allegre back to the East to Denpassar, Bali, Indonesia, to participate in a Unesco/PGI regional meeting (8 July) on education and training of information professionals, at which I presented a related policy document. This was an important regional meeting for, it led to Unesco processing of papers for starting the Post-graduate Training Programme for Science Information Specialists in South-east Asia in Manila, the Philippines, a couple of years later. [On a lighter note, I completed my lectures in Porto Allegre on 6 July and was expected in Denpassar by 7 July evening; this could be accomplished only by flying to Rio de Janeiro (Varig) and from there by Air France Concorde (supersonic) to Paris, and continue by normal aircraft to Bangkok (Air France), Jakarta and Denpassar (Garuda)].

As a member of an USAID-supported 3-man team, I had visited Cairo in the seventies to evaluate the policies and plans for developing a science and technology information (STI) network for Egypt. Years later (1986), following a mission to Cairo, the report that Jacques Tocatlian, then Director of PGI, and I prepared for the Government of Egypt became a source document for subsequent similar policy formulations for other developing countries / regions, and for the first edition of UNESCO Handbook on national information policies. At a regional meeting in Amman, Jordan, an information policy document modelled after the Cairo document, was presented and accepted as a basis for formulating national information policies in the Arab states within the framework of ARISNET. Earlier I also participated and contributed to a UNESCO/PGI mission to Teheran, Iran, for formulating national STI policy. Much of my subsequent work in the Arab States was through projects of the Arab League Documentation Centre (ALDOC) of the League of Arab States (in Tunis and Cairo), headed by Ms Faria Zahawi.. This included assisting in the formulation of proposals and plans for development of the ARISNET (Arab Regional Information Systems Network), and preparation of manuals, guidelines, national information policy documents, project proposals and reports for UNDP etc. During my initial visit to Tunis, Mr. Abdul Rahman Kamaruddhin was adviser to ALDOC/ARISNET. When he moved to the Islamic Development Bank (IDB) in Jeddah, I was invited to visit Jeddah a couple of times to demonstrate CDS-ISIS, participate in seminars on information networks, etc.

I also assisted in the preparatory meeting of the Euro-Arab cooperation (information networking) conference and prepared the report of the main conference held in Granada, Spain.

UNESCO's CDS-ISIS software was made available for public use in December 1985. Since then, I have been a resource person in nearly one hundred workshops on CDS-ISIS in many developing countries, beginning with the first workshop in Jamaica in 1986 April for the Caribbean region. This was the first CDS/ISIS regional workshop outside Unesco, Paris.

In 1974 the Statistics Division of ESCAP (Economic Commission for Asia and the Pacific) invited me to a regional seminar in Bangkok on socio-economic development information. I contributed a paper on the scenario in India and collated the reports of various groups to facilitate preparation of the consolidated report of the seminar. Ms Kate Wild representing IDRC talked about the development information programme being initiated by Mr. John Woolston. In 1975, on IDRC's invitation I participated in a month-long expert group meeting at ILO, Geneva, on IDRC's DEVSIS (Development Information Service) programme.. I was specifically involved with the classification and organization of entries in national bibliographies on socio-economic development. Subsequently, I participated in several IDRC-supported seminars and projects on development information in Asia and Africa. Socio-economic Development information has continued to be an area of interest for me. The theme of my presentation at the inaugural Plenary Session of the IFLA Conference in Manila (1980) was "Some Issues in Information Transfer: a Third World Perspective" published in *IFLA Journal*, 7(1), 1981; p. 1-8. Several papers and a book containing some of my thoughts on the subject of information support for development planning have since been published. My interest in development information involved me in such programmes as OECD's. International Development Information Network (IDIN), its Asia component located in ADIPA (Association of Development Research and Training Institutes of Asia and the Pacific), and the Asian and Pacific Development Centre, both in Kuala Lumpur; ICLARAM, then in Manila, and the fisheries information system in Cebu, the Philippines, the NGO networks (Women empowerment, technology transfer, legal aid to the poor, etc.) in Indonesia, development information bibliography at the Marga Institute in Colombo, and several others in Asia. My participation and contribution to the development of an integrated information support system for technology transfer on conversion of bagasse to ethanol, for small enterprises, initiated by CARIRI (Caribbean Industrial Research Institute), Port-of-Spain, Trinidad, was an interesting and valuable experience.

My first training mission in Africa was to Khartoum, Sudan, in 1977, to present a UNIDO-supported IDCAS regional training programme of 2-week duration on industrial information services.

I moved from Manila to UNESCO headquarters in Paris in 1982, to head the section on Institution Building and Networking (IIN) in PGI, and retired in 1986 as Regional Advisor for Asia-Pacific. The preparatory work for launching the inter-country cooperative programme ASTINFO, for South-East Asia and Pacific, involved preparation of policy documents and agreements between UNESCO and Member States and visiting and discussing with government officials in a number of developing countries in Asia, and Australia. The successful inter-country cooperative programme was subsequently emulated in Latin America and the Caribbean. The Section also initiated and supported the international Chemical Information Network (ChIN) and I was closely associated with the Asian component. On behalf of UNESCO I undertook technical assistance and advisory missions to several developing countries (and this continued after my retirement) in the Asia Pacific Region (Iran, Pakistan, Sri Lanka, Nepal, Malaysia, Indonesia, the Philippines, China, Papua-New Guinea, etc.), Australia, Arab States, Africa (Sudan, Uganda, Malawi, Ethiopia, Ghana, Nigeria, etc), Latin America (esp. Venezuela) and the Caribbean (Jamaica, Barbados, Trinidad, etc.). Advice and assistance on formulation of national/regional information policies, planning trans-national, national or institutional information systems, teaching in short courses and workshops, mobilizing national and international resources, and preparing project proposals were some of the types of work I was involved in this position. In several instances I assisted in the preparation of reports of consultative meetings, including those of PGI Steering Committee, at headquarters and elsewhere. These were important learning experiences for me.

Unesco Secretariat staff is a microcosm of world cultures and peoples. And the types of work and missions I had undertaken to different countries necessitated interactions with people from different cultures, and view points. However, my colleagues in Unesco/PGI and from other divisions were most helpful and very understanding, and so too were the officials, professionals and consultants from and in different countries I interacted with. They all made my work worthwhile, easier and pleasant.

HI: ***What are your current interests?***

AN: During 1961-63, Dr. Ranganathan established the Sarada Ranganathan Endowment for Library Science (SRELS) as a charitable trust. One of the objectives of the trust is to promote R&D in library and information science and dissemination of research findings. Under the auspices of the Endowment we have continued to work on knowledge organization topics, indexing languages, faceted classification, thesaurus, user-interfaces, database design, and preparation of software programs, etc. The Endowment organizes annual national seminars and lectures, conducts workshops, and provides, on request, advisory/consultancy service to various types of organizations. It publishes the quarterly *SRELS Journal of Information Management*, and books and reports. I have been the honorary Secretary of SRELS from 1967-78 and again from 1996 to the present. One of my functions is to assist in the organization and overseeing of these activities and to contribute to them. I am also the Executive Director (honorary) of the Ranganathan Centre for Information Studies (RCIS), Chennai, established in 1993. I edit and publish the quarterly journal *Information Studies* of RCIS (now in its eleventh volume. You may also be aware that I regularly contribute papers to international and regional conferences and publish papers in Indian and international periodicals. We have co-authored some.

I maintain a personal digital library of bibliographies, full texts, records from different types of information systems that I have helped to develop in various types of institutions in India and abroad, instructional materials and aids, software packages and computer programs, etc. These are useful in responding to queries or request for assistance that I receive from various individuals and institutions, and in the short training courses and workshops in which I get involved. There is also a multimedia information resource system (includes several CDs and links to websites) on spiritual matters that I maintain and continue to develop.. It has also been a base for studying intercultural, interfaith communication and information exchange and development of a multilingual glossary and thesaurus.

HI: ***Do you perceive a change in the role of cataloguing and classification in the emerging digital environment?***

AN: I do not envisage any significant change in the *role* or *function* of cataloguing and classification in the digital environment. They will continue to have the same respective functions as heretofore, namely, description of work (cataloguing), embodied as text, image, audio, video, and multimedia, in information sources on CD, networks, websites, etc., and classification being used as a tool for organizing the information/knowledge content. Together they are intended to facilitate identification, access and retrieval of relevant information source records and/or information from them, in response to or in anticipation of users' needs, queries, search expressions, etc.

We may recall Dr. Ranganathan's description of the three aspects of a document/information source: (1) the Soul or the ideas embodied; (2) the Subtle Body or language and mode of expression, style, format, etc.; and (3) the Gross Body or the physical carrier. In a digitised work, aspects (2) and (3) differ from those of the conventional resource. The recording/storing medium and the means of dissemination and communication of ideas may change, as they have over the centuries – from recording by markings on cave walls, rocks, papyrus, palm leaves, paper, film, and on to the microchip, and communication through gestures, use of natural language, writing, on to electronic means for communication. We now have to handle text, images, audio, video and multimedia increasinglynin an integrated mode.

A large majority of users seek and search for the embodied ideas or content (aspect 1). I do not see a change in this. With a digital resource, aspect (2) may be in digital form, but the retrieved records and/or information needs to be expressed in a (natural) language, and in form(s) that the user is comfortable with. In respect of aspect (3), the user may get a print out, download on to another carrier, or peruse the records/information online on a screen. The newer forms of the subtle body and the gross body will influence access to and retrieval of the content.

Ranganathan's Canons of Cataloging still apply. His Five Laws of Library Science can guide cataloguing work: if each user is to get his/her information source and every user's time and effort are to be conserved, then the catalogue entry should indicate the nature of the subtle body and of the gross body and what devices and software may be used to access, retrieve and organize the information for convenience of use. The rules and codes for cataloguing digital resources, e.g. ISBD (ER), and various metadata formats for document description will continue to be developed. An aspect to be kept in mind is that a good part of the digital information on the Web, for instance, changes frequently or even disappears. The concept of 'pre-publication' cataloguing is equally if not even more valid / useful in the Web environment.

HI: ***Is classification important in the digital environment?***

AN: For a human being, classification in the sense of, firstly, distinguishing an entity from others (that is, drawing boundaries among them) by their shared and differentiating attributes and, secondly, organizing (or enabling the user to do so) the entities or information about them in a helpful sequence is a neural necessity. Just imagine not being able to recognize the boundaries between entities! It is the means of survival and advancement. In the physical world we do this from our birth, collecting data about the entities in our environment using our sensory organs (or getting that information from other sources). There is corresponding processes in intellection – the processing of concepts about the entities, abstract or concrete, comparing that information with what is already stored in the memory, noting the similarities, differences, etc. Thus, there may be incremental learning, or a whole new discovery. As long as the human brain structure and related functions continue as they have been since the first of the *Homo sapiens* on earth, classification in this sense has to continue to enable quick retrieval of relevant sources and filter out non-relevant ones. This process will be even more important in the digital environment. The Internet and intranets enable almost seamless access to loads of information sources and vast quantities and varieties of information in response to a query. Much of it may be found irrelevant to a user's *interest-at-the-moment*. This can produce information overload. As of now, library and information (LIS) professionals, and of course end-users, may have little control on what information is mounted on the networks, how it is organized, etc. However, reference interviews in person and online, query analysis and restructuring, use of tools such as classification schemes, thesauri, subject headings lists, concept maps, and other vocabulary management tools, help in retrieval of relatively more precise and qualitatively better information and effective presentation to the user. Faceted analytico-synthetic classification techniques, data exploration, data analysis and text mining using appropriate software are proving to be useful. Together they could even lead to knowledge discovery. Hypertext linking on networks enables multi-database searching on a global scale. No one information organization tool by itself will be able to give all help in all contexts – but a judicious combination of them could be more effective.

HI: ***Are Dr. Ranganathan's contributions to classification theory still relevant in the digital era?***

AN: Dr. Ranganathan has provided a sound theory for the organization of information. All his canons, principles and theories for any branch of LIS are anchored and guided by his Five Laws (equally applicable to information service in the digital era). Studies in psychology, the human brain and education indicate that the analytico-synthetic faceted approach to the processes of intellection, learning, knowledge organization, and communication appears to be innate to human beings.

Dr. Michael Medland, an educational psychologist, reports of his success with four-year olds in the faceted approach and use of categories in a personal communication. He wrote: "My own work deals with developing knowledge organization tools and teaching them to young children. I am trying to integrate the kinds of things you are saying … with some of my own…I have already tried my analysis on English-speaking four-year olds. Most four-year olds have the knowledge categories already. I want to try and teach them to talk about the categories (the knowledge ontology) and use them to analyze and synthesize knowledge, to accelerate their learning about and acting on the world, individually or in groups … you have mentioned seven categories, not five. Can you lead me to the others? I am also interested in some of the organizational principles as presently understood: Wall-Picture, Bond Strength, Facet Sequence, Isolate Sequence, etc.

"The seven are most important for now. I think with the seven, not the five, I will be able to illustrate a high degree of congruence between Ranganathan's work on absolute syntax and my upper level ontology, as well as why and how children can learn them."

The seven categories or types of concepts that Dr. Medland mentions are Dr. Ranganathan's Personality, Matter Material and Matter Property, Action (Energy), Space, Time, Speciator, and Context or Domain Specifying element.

The analytico-synthetic faceted method is equivalent to the modular approach of systems specialists (Herbert Simon, and others). The latter have affirmed that the modular approach is relatively more stable and able to perform its functions in a dynamic environment. In the ISKO6, Toronto paper we have elaborated on how Dr. Ranganathan's theories and methodologies endow knowledge organizing tools dynamism and stability to perform efficiently in the environment of a dynamic universe of subjects.

Facet structured queries have been shown to retrieve more relevant records/documents than Boolean expressions (Kwasnik, Godert, and others). Hemalata Iyer and Raghavan have shown that facet structured expressions (in different languages) of subjects *a la* Ranganathan are consistently more correctly interpreted than other structures. And as such subject structures or expressions derived according to the Postulational Approach can form the basis for generating different types of subject indexes (POPSI, PRECIS, KWAC, etc.).

HI: ***Do you visualize the library profession as being the lead players in classification or do you see computer science and other fields taking over this area?***

AN: LIS professionals and ICT experts both deal with data and information and their sources - collection, storing, processing, retrieving and serving users. ICT experts may not be aware of the theories, tools and techniques that the LIS profession has developed to achieve this with much success. They may therefore try to reinvent some of the tools, perhaps without a sound theory backing. On the other hand, as an increasing amount of information will become available in digital form, ICTs can offer powerful means of information access and retrieval. ICT specialists need to consider and apply the theories and techniques that LIS has developed and used successfully.

Information/knowledge organization methods, information source description, vocabulary management, and retrieval and service provision constitute the common ground; collaborative interdisciplinary work and research by LIS and ICT professions in association with or drawing upon appropriate work in the fields of learning, psychology, brain functioning, etc. is what is needed in the digital era. It indicates the kind of subject areas and practical knowledge and skills that LIS professionals must equip themselves with in the digital era. This is a challenge to the LIS profession in its attempt to establish an important role in the information field. ICTs can be harnessed as a powerful support. On the other hand, LIS professionals, especially those providing information service, interacting with users, and system designers need to be subject or domain specialists rather than (or in addition to) merely learning the theories and techniques of LIS and being able to use appropriate ICTs.

Networks such as the Internet and converging technologies support globalization. There is potential for almost any person to place ideas (in text, image or voice form) on the Net and disseminate them worldwide. This will be most effective (perhaps most troublesome too!) if there is only one language of communication or every person learnt and understood every other native language! But this not the case and perhaps it may never be so. At present, the English language is dominant in the digital world. However, there are many ideas, arts, cultures, and practices expressed in native languages of many different countries; there may not even be equivalents to some of the concept terms in the English language. Globalization also sparks nationalism. There is a growing trend to use native languages and scripts in ICT applications to facilitate spread of education and knowledge, and inter-cultural appreciation at the national level. Within the decade there will be vast amounts of information in such languages as Chinese, Japanese, Spanish, Hindi and other Indian languages. ICT tools will have to handle inter-language translation and interpretation. Specialists in languages, IT, communication, LIS and others can together make important contributions in this regard.

HI: ***Very often the library lingo (technical terminology) itself becomes a barrier to interdisciplinary collaboration. Do you share this viewpoint?***

AN: Each evolving discipline builds its own technical vocabulary, e.g. physics, chemistry, biology etc., and their sub-branches. Such vocabulary facilitates productive communication among the specialists and researchers in the field without wasting words. In this era of growing interdisciplinary cooperation, the participants familiarize themselves with the technical vocabulary involved. If LIS professionals need to work with computers and software, they do learn the technical vocabulary of that field; so it should be with the ICT professionals who would use the theories, tools and techniques developed in the LIS field in the interest of productive cooperation and avoiding reinventing LIS tools and techniques. Fortunately, with the spread of information technology, home use of computers and children learning their use for a variety of purposes, the future generation of information users and LIS professionals will be much more familiar with the technology and lingo of ICTs than the present generation. Should we not also introduce classification and other knowledge organization methods in the education of children if that would help them in learning, etc.? as Prof. Medland mentioned.

HI: ***Thank you once again for sharing your knowledge, experience and professional insights in this interview. It's been a pleasure.***

A. NEELAMEGHAN AND UNESCO: CONTRIBUTIONS AND REMEMBRANCES

John Rose

This paper is intended to present the very substantial contributions which Mr. Arashanipalai Neelameghan has made to UNESCO over a period of thirty years. However, in a Festschrift volume intended to provide an insight into the influence of a personality like Mr. Neelameghan, due as much to his personal character as to his assessable achievements, it would not be appropriate to leave out personal impressions and experiences. I have thus tried to bring both elements in this article, the first part treating the main contributions of Mr. Neelameghan to UNESCO, and the second the remembrances of his colleagues.

I have prepared this paper as an official UNESCO assignment, but it also includes my personal view as a colleague and friend of Mr. Neelameghan, and I therefore accept responsibility for any inaccuracies or misconceptions, which may have inadvertently been introduced. I am grateful for the contributions of other former UNESCO colleagues of Mr. Neelameghan to this endeavour, particularly Ms Susanne Ornager and Messrs Yves Courrier, Victor Montviloff, Kenneth H. Roberts and Jacques Tocatlian.

The 60's and 70's represented a period of effervescence for the United Nations System, which was established after the Second World War to promote reconstruction and cooperation among the industrialized countries, but then quite rapidly found its membership and mandate oriented towards socio-economic development. The First and Second Development Decades were proclaimed by the United Nations in 1960 and 1970. UNESCO's membership expanded from 78 (of which 49 were developing countries) at the beginning of 1960 to 140 (of which 107 were developing countries) at the start of 1980.

This period also witnessed the beginnings of a consciousness of evolution towards an information society, bracketed by the commencement of the Lockheed DIALOG online access system in 1961 and the publication of *Towards Paperless Information Systems* by F.W. Lancaster in 1978. In 1972, UNESCO, which had always had a strong information programme in support of traditional library and archival work, initiated the UNISIST Programme, also known as the UNESCO Programme for Cooperation in the Field of Scientific and Technological

Information[1]. Although UNISIST was originally concerned with information in science and technology in the strict sense, it was built on basic principles of information science and was extended within UNESCO to all fields of specialized knowledge with the merger of the UNISIST Programme into the UNESCO General Information Programme (PGI) in 1976.

Originally, the UNISIST Programme was conceived mainly to facilitate information exchange among scientists, and particularly to overcome barriers to information flow emanating from the Cold War. Assistance to developing countries was foreseen as only one of five initial UNISIST objectives (ICSU and UNESCO, 1971), and in 1972 the first expert meeting intended to advise on how UNESCO could promote development through information science (UNESCO, 1972) brought together 23 participants of which only seven were from developing countries.

Thus, in the early seventies, when Mr. Neelameghan first became involved in the UNESCO information programme, the Organization was trying both to effectively orient its activity towards support for development (including by recruitment of a representative number of staff from developing countries into its Secretariat) and to bring modern information science and information systems into one of its priority programme areas.

Mr. Neelameghan's first participation in this effort was when, as Professor and Head of the Documentation Research and Training Centre (DRTC) in Bangalore, he was invited to serve on the newly established UNISIST Advisory Committee which held its first session in February 1974. At the second session of the UNISIST Advisory Committee in May 1975, Mr. Neelameghan was elected to serve as Chairman of the Committee. He was reappointed to the enlarged Advisory Committee for the General Information Programme and elected as its Chairman when it was convened in 1977.

---

1 In the feasibility study stage, undertaken in cooperation with the International Council of Scientific Unions (ICSU, now the International Council for Science), UNISIST meant "World Science Information System" but was later renamed retaining the same acronym when it became a UNESCO programme.

During 1975 Mr. Neelameghan was member of the Study Team set up under the auspices of the International Development Research Centre (IDRC), the Organization for Economic Cooperation and Development (OECD), the United Nations Development Programme (UNDP) and UNESCO to study the establishment of an international bibliographic information system on development for policy makers, decision makers, planners and researchers, entitled DEVSIS (Neelameghan, 1975). Although this system was only partially implemented, the feasibility study had considerable influence on the nascent international movement to use information to promote development.

During the first session of the UNISIST Advisory Committee in 1975, Mr. Neelameghan chaired the Working Group which elaborated the terms of reference for the future Ad Hoc Committee on Education and Training Policy and Programme, which met regularly until 1988. He collaborated for many years with this Committee (Neelameghan, 1982), and with UNESCO's programme of activities on education and training in librarianship and information science, notably in the organization of a UNISIST Seminar on the education and training of information users in 1976 (Wilson, et. al. 1976), in preparing a policy paper on human resources development in the information field in Southeast Asia (Neelameghan, 1977), and in authoring the UNISIST policy guidelines on education and training of information personnel (Neelameghan, 1978).

In July 1978, Mr. Neelameghan joined the UNESCO Secretariat at Director level as Project Coordinator of the UNDP-financed project to establish a Post-Graduate Training Course for Science Information Specialists in Southeast Asia (RAS/75/034), located in the Institute of Library Science of the University of the Philippines (UPLIS) in Manila. This project had been studied and planned by UNESCO since 1971, at the request of several member states in the region and with important contributions from Mr. Neelameghan in terms of conception and mobilization of international support. It was intended to prepare a nucleus of professional staff needed for planning, establishing and operating national scientific and technical information systems and services in the participating countries.

Mr. Neelameghan served with the project for four years, initiating a one year Post-graduate diploma course in the academic year 1978-79, which was integrated into UPLIS post-graduate programme with possibility of continuation to a Master's degree starting in the academic year 1981-82. By the completion of the project and absorption of the course into the UPLIS programme at the end of the academic year 1983-84, 148 specialists from 14 countries of the region had earned diplomas, and many more had participated in specialized short courses and workshops (UNESCO, 1985). Mr. Neelameghan prepared a very substantial amount of the teaching materials for the project, and documented the experience in the training of librarians in computerized information services (Neelameghan, 1983b). The success of this project in jump-starting information systems and information science training in the region, and particularly Mr. Neelameghan's singular contribution, were widely acknowledged by the professional community, the participating member states, and the international sponsors.

In 1979, Mr. Neelameghan was asked to prepare, for UNESCO, a draft of the working paper for the Intergovernmental Conference on Scientific and Technological Information for Development (UNISIST II), which was convened by UNESCO in Paris in June 1979 to better orient the newly created General Information Programme towards development needs, while building on both new and traditional information techniques and infrastructure. This document, produced in a very short time (after a draft prepared by another author was rejected by UNESCO) formed the basis for the discussions at this successful conference which formulated recommendations on information strategies and action at the national, regional and international levels, subsequently adopted by UNESCO. Mr. Neelameghan also prepared that year a contribution on information science for a UNESCO series of publications on the ramifications of time in various sciences (Neelameghan, 1979).

In December 1982, Mr. Neelameghan was transferred to UNESCO headquarters in Paris as Programme Specialist in the Division of the General Information Programme, and in July 1985 was named Chief of the Section on Infrastructures/Institutions and Networking of that Division. During this period, he was responsible for building up and coordinating the UNESCO programme for assisting developing countries to introduce appropriate technologies in information work, notably microcomputers and computerized information retrieval services. This effort, which had been mandated by a recent UNESCO

General Conference, was realized through numerous activities such as advisory services, technical assistance missions, specialized conferences and training workshops, pilot projects, and mechanisms for exchange of information and technology transfer. The specific domains of action pioneered by Mr. Neelameghan within this programme included computer communication networks, geographic information systems (GIS), multimedia techniques, and networking in priority domains of scientific and technological information.

In providing conceptual and strategic support to these activities throughout the world, Mr. Neelameghan personally took charge of a number of key projects. One of these was the establishment of the first operational access in India to international online information services, launched at the National Aeronautical Laboratory (now, National Aerospace Laboratories) in Bangalore in June 1986 with support from the National Information System for Science and Technology (NISSAT), the European Space Agency (ESA) and UNESCO. Although this dedicated international data connection was discontinued as uneconomical in March 1988, it proved the importance and feasibility of online services in India and paved the way to their wide introduction in that country through other government supported schemes, initially through dial-up access (Lahiri and Sunder Singh, 1989). Other activities of this Section, on which I collaborated closely, concerned the integration of factual data services and documentary services to respond to development needs. These included the establishment of the international Chemical Information Network (ChIN) more particularly the Asian network component with its node at the University of Chulalongkorn, Bangkock, and the Regional Information Network on Medicinal and Aromatic Plants for Asia and the Pacific (APINMAP); pilot projects on the development of the data and information services of the National Institute of Oceanography (Goa, India) and of a geo-based information system for development planning in Kalutara District, Sri Lanka (in collaboration with the UN Economic Commission for Asia and Pacific [ESCAP]); and the organization of a Regional Seminar on Information Systems for Sub-national Development Planning in Visakhapatnam, India in December 1985.

One of the major responsibilities of Mr. Neelameghan during his work with UNESCO in Paris was to provide support for the establishment of UNESCO's

Regional Network for the Exchange of Information and Experience in Science and Technology in Asia and the Pacific (ASTINFO) which was launched in 1982 following a recommendation of the Second Conference of Ministers Responsible for the Application of Science and Technology to Development and Those Responsible for Economic Planning in Asia and the Pacific (CASTASIA II) held earlier that year in Manila (UNESCO, 1982). ASTINFO was conceived as a framework for intergovernmental regional cooperation and mobilization to develop infrastructure and expertise in the area of scientific and technological information[2], and soon developed under Mr. Neelameghan's guidance into an extensive programme of policy papers and consultations, training courses and pilot projects, including cooperation in promotion of science and technology in development at the grass-roots level (Neelameghan, 1983a). In January 1986, Mr. Neelameghan was appointed Regional Adviser for the General Information Programme in Asia and the Pacific, to devote full time to the organization of this project whose secretariat was provided by the UNESCO office in Jakarta. In this period he advised several Asian countries (including China, Nepal, Pakistan, the Philippines, Sri Lanka, Thailand and Vietnam) on the formulation of their national information policies, and substantially contributed to the elaboration of UNESCO guidelines in this domain.

The diversity of UNESCO's information activities during Mr. Neelameghan's service in the Secretariat are reviewed in the context of the special problems faced by developing countries in an article which he co-authored (Neelameghan and Tocatlian, 1985). He left the UNESCO Secretariat in August 1986 at the mandatory retirement age of 60, returning to Bangalore as Honorary Visiting Professor at DRTC in December that year.

In the intervening years, Mr. Neelameghan has maintained a close relationship with UNESCO, and has contributed to numerous UNESCO activities. In the late 1980's, he undertook several consultant missions to advise on the development of

2 Originally initiated by fifteen countries in the field of scientific and technological information, ASTINFO was gradually broadened in scope to cover all interests of the General Information Programme, and in 2002 it became the Asian Pacific Information Network (APIN), responsible for coordination of the activities of UNESCO's Information for All Programme in the region.

the Arab Regional Information System Network (ARIS-NET) sponsored by the League of Arab States, as well as a mission to advise on the formulation of a national information policy in Egypt (Neelameghan and Tocatlian, 1987). He also developed an application under UNESCO's CDS/ISIS package for an integrated database including information on publications, institutions, projects and personnel, which was widely adapted and used in developing countries. Mr. Neelameghan was later member of the Advisory Board for the preparation of UNESCO's *World Information Report*, published in 1997, and contributed the chapter on international cooperation in the information field (Neelameghan, 1997).

Throughout his association with UNESCO, Mr. Neelameghan has been fully dedicated to the work with which he was involved, and has been held in great esteem by all of his colleagues. When he sought input from others for specific tasks, he was diligent and persistent but always tactful, so that colleagues felt obliged to accept his requests for data or ideas as priorities. On the other hand, although he had exceptional knowledge and judgement, and was usually right, he was always ready to discuss his approach with colleagues and to modify or abandon it on the basis of a cogent argument.

Mr. Victor Montviloff, who was a UNESCO staff member responsible for information policy activities at the time of Mr. Neelameghan's service, remembers that he "was always an unlimited source of information and knowledge, which he readily shared with his colleagues. Many appealed to his capacity to provide a clear and prompt judgement regarding the information issues and to his ability to prepare, in no time, substantial written contributions. He was a real professional and a very pleasant colleague to work with". Mr. Yves Courrier, who also worked with Mr. Neelameghan at that time recalls: "Neela would never measure his time spent helping other colleagues to do their work. He was so unselfish, his only interest being to use the opportunity of being at UNESCO to assist our colleagues in developing countries. In my own case, when I was appointed Chief of the Section for Education and Training (January 1985), he 'anonymously' contributed to many activities that I was in charge of, by giving ideas and advice, and sometimes doing the work himself. In particular, he would prepare letters that I would just have to sign!" Mr. Kenneth H. Roberts, who preceded Mr. Courrier as

Chief of the Section for Education and Training, expresses in another way the universal admiration felt by Mr. Neelameghan's colleagues: "There is no figure from my UNESCO years whom I knew so little yet remember so vividly and esteem so highly".

This was also true for his relations on behalf of UNESCO with external colleagues. Mr. Neelameghan's demeanour was one of humility, almost to the point of being self-effacing, yet his interlocutors were invariably impressed by his evident sincerity and his eagerness to contribute to any effort to promote information science. Mr. Roberts has remarked in this context: "I was always struck by the respect and admiration expressed [for Mr. Neelameghan] by UN staff at various levels as well as by professional colleagues from other international organizations and national organizations and institutions".

Ms Susanne Ornager, who worked as Associate Expert for ASTINFO in Jakarta under Mr. Neelameghan's supervision from Paris, contributed the following remembrance to this paper: "Mr. Neelameghan was a very private person. He had his own very gentle/quiet style. But mind you, not subdued! I remember that when I came to [UNESCO] HQ, he had asked for one month to prepare me for my 'field work'. He never gave me an agenda for that month. The first day I sat in my office waiting for somebody to tell me what to do in UNESCO. After a half hour, I knocked on his door. I was asked to sit down, and for three hours he lectured about ASTINFO, CASTASIA II, a network for the region, CDS/ISIS, his postgraduate students from the Philippines and their whereabouts, and finally he gave me his view about political issues in the region within the information field. That repeated itself for one month and then I went to the field. I felt very much on my own at that time, but later I have realized that he provided a lot of information which I utilize even today. As a non-Asian there were many issues I didn't understand; however, in his quiet way he managed to teach me about the region, its culture, its information problems, potential solutions, where to find the reliable information people, and he introduced me to many influential persons in Asia. I am truly grateful for his support then and his follow-up afterwards. He kept in touch with me for many years".

My own personal remembrance of Mr. Neelameghan is also of selfless and committed support in guiding me towards professional growth and towards an insight into the cultures, viewpoints and aspirations of people in developing countries. He went out of his way to introduce me to leading professionals and to decision makers in his own country, India, and later helped me to undertake a study leave there which was a watershed in my life and career.

Mr. Neelameghan's strongest professional interest, and the area in which he had the greatest impact for UNESCO, has undoubtedly been that of education and training of information specialists, including missions to most regions and many countries to assist in the creation or development of post graduate programmes in information science (Beijing, Caracas, and Addis Ababa).. But Mr. Neelameghan's eclectic interests and insight have also impacted on a broad diversity of other areas. He has had, for example, a particularly important influence in fostering applications of information technologies or information in promoting the use of new technologies to meet specific needs in the life of people in developing countries (database on medicinal plants, solar stoves, safe water, etc.), and in educating people to undertake such work. In an organization like UNESCO, many issues become political. Mr. Neelameghan always avoided entering political debate, and resolutely built his contributions on reason and professional competence.

Mr. Jacques Tocatlian, former Director of the Division of the General Information Programme, affirms that "Mr. Neelameghan is one of those who has contributed the most in shaping the programme objectives, priorities and content of PGI over the years. Both as a consultant and as a staff member, he has served Member States in all regions with untiring energy, competence and total dedication". A local university staff member once expressed it in another way by describing the UNESCO information programme as becoming "an eloquent spokesperson for what were perhaps in many instances Mr. Neelameghan's ideas".

REFERENCES

1. ICSU and UNESCO. (1971). *UNISIST: Study report on the feasibility of a World Science Information System*. Paris: UNESCO.
2. Lahiri, A. and Sunder Singh, B.G. (1989). Bibliographic databases and networks: The India scenario. *Astinfo Newsletter (UNESCO Bangkok Office)*. Vol. 4(3); p. 4-14.

3. Neelameghan, A. (1975). *Discussion paper, Expert Group on a Development Information System for the ESCAP Region (Bangkok, 1975) and DEVSIS Steering Committee*, 2nd session (Paris, 28-29 April 1975). Paris: UNESCO (DEVSIS/ST.COM.II/INF.1).

4. —. (1977). *Policy on information manpower development, Workshop on Scientific, Technical and Industrial Information Services in Southeast Asia, Bali, Indonesia, 1977.* Paris: UNESCO (WORKSHOP/STII/SEA/3; SC.77/WS/49).

5. —. (1978). *Guidelines for Formulating Policy on Education, Training and Development of Library and Information Personnel.* Paris: UNESCO (PGI.78/WS/29).

6. —. (1979). Expressions of time in information science and their implications. **In** *Time and the Sciences Series,* Paris: UNESCO, p. 103-118.

7. —. (1982). *Improving the use of information systems, services and sources through user education and orientation: Some issues with reference to developing countries, Ad Hoc Committee on Education and Training Policy and Programme*, 5th session (Paris, 1982). Paris: UNESCO (PGI/E.T.V/4; PGI.82/CONF.604/COL.1).

8. —. (1983a). ASTINFO: Regional Network for the exchange of information and experiences in science and technology in Asia and the Pacific. **In**: *The Library in the Information Revolution. Proceedings of the sixth Congress of Southeast Asian Librarians*, Singapore, 30 May-3 June 1983, Singapore: Maruzen Asia, p. 259-272.

9. —. (1983b). Training in computer applications and on-line search for students of library science: A case study. *Unesco Journal of Information Science, Librarianship and Archives Administration.* Vol. 1; p. 12-22.

10. —. and Tocatlian, J. (1985). International cooperation in information systems and services. *Journal of the American Society for Information Science.* Vol. 36(3); p. 153-163.

11. —., and —. (1987). *Establishment of a national information policy and a strategy for its implementation: Egypt.* Paris: UNESCO (FMR/PGI/87/103; RP/1986-1987/VII.2.1/ Technical report).

12. —. (1997). Issues and trends: International co-operation and assistance. **In**: *World Information Report.* 1997/1998, Paris: UNESCO, p. 361-380.

13. UNESCO (1972). *Ad Hoc Working Group on Information Requirements of Developing Countries in the Framework of the UNISIST Programme, First Session,* UNESCO House, Paris, 8-9 May 1972, Final Report. Paris: UNESCO (SC-72/Conf 126/4).

14. —. (1982). *CASTASIA II: Second Conference of Ministers Responsible for the Application of Science and Technology to Development and Those Responsible for Economic Planning in Asia and the Pacific,* Manila, 22-30 March 1982, Final report. Paris: UNESCO (SC-82/CASTASIA II/5).

15. —. (1985). *Postgraduate training course for science information, Southeast Asia - (mission).* Project findings and recommendations. Paris: UNESCO (FMR/PGI/OPS/85/258(UNDP); UNDP/RAS/75/034/Terminal report).

16. Wilson, T.D.; Neelameghan, A.; Burian, K.; Sweeney, G.P.; Menou, M.J.; Evans, A.J. and Gray, J. (1976). *Final report, UNISIST Seminar on the Education and Training of Users of Scientific and Technological Information*, Rome, 1976. Paris: UNESCO (SC.77/WS/22).

STUDIES AND RESEARCH IN INFORMETRICS AT THE DOCUMENTATION RESEARCH AND TRAINING CENTRE (DRTC), ISI, BANGALORE

I.K. Ravichandra Rao
Bibhuti Bhusan Sahoo

Contributions of DRTC to informetric studies and research are discussed. A report on recent work - a quantitative country-wise analysis of software literature based on the data from two bibliographic databases i.e. COMPENDEX and INSPEC is presented. The number of countries involved in R & D activities in software in the most productive group is increasing. The research contribution on software is decreasing in developed countries as compared to that in developing and less developed countries. India's contribution is only 1.1% and it has remained constant over the period of 12 years 1989-2001. The number of countries involved in R&D activities in software has been increasing in the 1990s. It is also noted that higher the budget for higher education, higher the number of publications; and that higher the number of publications, higher the export as well as the domestic consumption of software.

0 PREAMBLE

Along with Dr. S.R. Ranganathan, Prof. A. Neelameghan (AN) has been on the faculty of the DRTC from the inception of the first postgraduate courses in documentation in May 1962. He played an important role in introducing courses and research in statistical analysis and its applications in library and information studies not only at DRTC but also in the national and regional schools for information studies, as part of his work for Unesco, IDRC and other organizations. We are pleased to contribute this paper to the festschrift.

1 RESEARCH AND TRAINING IN STATISTICAL ANALYSIS AT DRTC

In their paper *From Librametry to Informetrics*, Ravichandra Rao and Neelameghan (1992) discussed the definition and scope of librametry, bibliometrics, informetrics and scientometrics. At the Aslib Conference in Leamington Spa in 1948 S.R. Ranganathan suggested that librarians should develop "Librametry on the lines of biometry, econometry and psychometry, since "many of the matters connected with library work and services involve large numbers" (Aslib Proceedings, 1948). Quantitative methods applied to library management and services have thus come to be known as librametry. The field did not develop until the early 1970's.

Again in 1963 in a paper to the first Annual Seminar of the Documentation Research and Training Centre (DRTC), Bangalore, Ranganathan illustrated with examples the application of statistics to library work and services (Ranganathan, 1969). The scope of the practical application of librametry was outlined by Neelameghan (1969) in another paper presented at the same seminar.

The postgraduate programme in information studies at DRTC was started in May 1961. As part of its regular academic programme, DRTC introduced statistical analysis to its students through lectures by specialists invited from other institutions. From the late 1960s at least one DRTC faculty member was available to teach and guide research in statistical analysis and its applications. In the early 1960s students and staff of DRTC carried out several 'scatter' and 'seepage' studies in different subject domains to:

- Demonstrate that in interdisciplinary subjects the seepage was relatively more extensive;
- Provide a basis for periodicals selection; and
- Identify the "roots" of a new subject.

Some of these studies were reported in the first DRTC Seminar (1963) on documentation periodicals. Other studies in bibliometrics and scientometrics were initiated in the second half of the 1960s and continued thereafter. Some of the important findings of such studies by DRTC faculty members are:

- The distribution of duplication of research works in general, and in antibiotics in particular, follows a modified poisson model (Neelameghan and Buche, 1970). Application of the square-cube law to the data enables more precise predictability of duplication (Neelameghan and Gupta, 1971).
- Success-breeds-success phenomenon explains the law of scientific productivity (Ravichandra Rao, 1981);
- Negative binomial model can appropriately be applied to explain the distribution of scientific papers (Ravichandra Rao) as well as the library circulation data (Ravichandra Rao, 1981); Good fit of negative binomial distribution to the library circulation data may be found if the time gap between the current use and the last use of the documents (or by the users) is not very large;
- It is only those documents which are circulated/used are likely to be circulated/used again and again (Ravichandra Rao, 1981);
- It is only those users who borrow documents are likely to borrow documents again and again (Ravichandra Rao, 1981);
- 80-20 rule fits library use data – 80% of the documents contribute only 20% of the total use of the collection and vice-versa (Egghe, 1986), (Ravichandra Rao, 1981);
- Higher the growth of the literature, faster the obsolescence of the literature (less the half-life of documents) and vice versa (Ravichandra Rao and Meera, 1991);
- The Bradford multiplier (n) is unlikely to be a constant (Ravichandra Rao, 1997);
- Exponential distribution does not necessarily always explain the growth of the literature; depending on the subjects, period covered, kind of data, one may have to choose a model – exponential, logistic, Gompertz, linear, etc. (Egghe);
- The distribution of papers over authors, based on fractional counting, can be derived using theory of convolution under the assumption that both the

distribution of authors and distribution of papers (integer counting) confirm to Lotka's Law. (Egghe and Ravichandra Rao, 2002); and

- Statistical analysis can support studies on the pattern incidence of communicable diseases, that is, to medical historiography (Neelameghan and Ravichandra Rao, 2005).

Some of the studies were also centred around mapping of science literature, particularly in the area of engineering and software.

DRTC faculty members present lectures and guide students in bibliometrics and scientometrics in other institutions in India. Informetrics is now included in library and information studies in several Indian universities and centres such as INSDOC of CSIR (now part of NISCAIR). There are research contributions to informetrics and scientometrics from these institutions, NISTADS, M.S. Swaminathan Research Foundation, Chennai, etc. Indian journals in information studies such as the SRELS Journal of Information Management regularly publish papers in the field of Informetrics.

2 INTERNATIONAL

As part of his work with Unesco, IDRC and other international organizations in institution building and human resources development, AN laid the ground work and assisted in the development of postgraduate training programmes in information studies for Southeast Asia in Manila, the Philippines, in Beijing, China, for Latin America in Caracas, Venezuela, in the regional schools (ARCIS) in Ibadan, Nigeria, in SISA, Addis Ababa, Ethiopia, and in Port Moresby, Papua-New Guinea. In the syllabus for these programmes statistical analysis was included. One of us (Ravichandra Rao) was invited to present lectures in bibliometrics, etc. in the regional schools in Manila, and Addis Ababa (also as Master's thesis examiner) and to provide inputs to a regional seminar on curriculum design in Caracas.

DRTC organized the Third International Conference on Informetrics and Scientometrics in 1991, marking the beginning of the year-long celebrations of S.R Ranganathan's birth centenary.

With this brief introduction to the work done in informetrics at DRTC, mostly under the guidance of / supported by AN in the 1960s and 1970s, we present a brief report on the study carried out at DRTC in recent months - an analysis of the literature of software studies.

3 SCOPE OF THE STUDY

The work reported here is a study of the country-wise contribution of software literature. The main objectives are to:

(1) Examine the overall contribution of different countries' research output in the field of software studies, over a period of time;

(2) Study and compare the contribution of India's research output in software studies; and

(3) Study the growth of literature in software related topics.

4 NEED FOR COUNTRY-WISE ANALYSIS

Research activities are central to the development process of any country. It can provide tools that help alleviate the specific problems that afflict many less developed countries - to control diseases, lack of infrastructure (energy, information, transport, etc.), and to tackle the degradation of the environment, etc. Secondly, science and technology are central to the dynamics of economic development itself. Economically successful countries are those that are able to turn technical innovation into economic productivity. Effective science and technology policies are thus crucial for developing countries. The success stories of Japan, Korea, and Taiwan, are in large part, stories of a long-term strategy, focused on fostering indigenous innovation capacity. The base for productivity and prosperity of a country in any field is reflected in the research activities; carried out in that country.

Lal and Ray (1991) have examined 511 papers in horticulture from 4 leading journals during 1987-88. The analysis revealed that the contribution of Indian scientists largely appear in domestic journals rather than in foreign journals. They further observed that USA is the leading contributor (26.02%) of research papers followed by Australia (17.89%) and Netherlands (8.94%), among 25 countries. India published only 2.44% of the total research publications in the field of horticulture. This kind of statistics will further help us in analyzing:

- Why a country publishes only x% of articles in a subject; for example in the above case, we can find out why India, an agriculture-based economy, published only 2.44% of the articles? and
- The relationship between publication and socio-economic indicators, if any (Rousseau and Rousseau, 1997).

Miquel, et al (1995) have identified a publication pattern for nations that reflects its interest and potential in 18 disciplines and compared the publication patterns of 48 nations by descriptive multivariate analysis; i.e. by measuring the distance between nations in the n-dimensional system. The data set were extracted from the diskette purchased from the Institute for Scientific Information, which covered different types of publications such as articles, proceedings, papers, notes and reviews. The data is described by a three dimensional matrix -- 18(fields) X 48(countries) X 12 years (1981-92). They restricted the dataset to 48 countries, which together contributed about 97.9% of the world output. They observed that the USA published the maximum number of articles – 2.3 million articles, corresponding to about a third of the total. This is 5 to 10 times greater than its closest peers (Japan, England, USSR, FRG, France and Canada). India was in the 9th position.

Parmar et al analyse the records related to library automation in the *INSPEC (*1969 to July 2004) database. They observed that, the literature has grown linearly with a growth of about 600 items per year, since 1984. The USA is the predominant publishing country in the area of Library Automation related literature. The USA contributed 54% of the literature and the first 7 countries -- USA, UK, Germany, Netherlands, Australia, India and Hungary -- contributed 90% of the total publications. These are only a few examples of case studies of country-wise analyses.

5 DATA COLLECTION

Publication data on "software and related topics" were collected from the COMPENDEX and INSPEC database for the years 1989-2001. The data from two databases were merged into one database depending on the year of publications, using ISO export and import option in the WINISIS. Programs were written to extract the "name of the country" from the author affiliations field and also to add a field "country", in the new database. Table 1 presents data on the total number of publications in software studies for the period 1989 to 2001.

Table 1. Distribution of publications according to the Year of Publications over a period of time – 1989-2001

Year	No. of Publications	Year	No. of Publications
1990	50,414	1995	54,850
1991	47,802	1996	63,081
1992	32,538	1997	83,960
1993	34,899	1998	67,554
1994	47,595	1999	72,612
		Growth Rate	**17.85%**

***Note*:** The growth rate is computed under the assumption that exponential model fits the empirical data -- $y = ab^x$, in which case (b-1)% is the growth rate R^2 is 0.9826756; r is 0.9913518.

Table 2 Gives the distribution of papers in different counties.

Table 2: Total number of publications in different countries from 1989-2001

Sl. No.	Country/ publications	Total	Cumulative total	%	Cumulative %
1	USA	259448	259448	0.369	0.369
2	Japan	53906	313354	0.077	0.445
3	UK	49303	362657	0.070	0.516
4	Germany	35935	398592	0.051	0.567
5	China	31285	429877	0.044	0.611
6	Canada	27882	457759	0.040	0.651
7	France	26989	484748	0.038	0.689
8	Italy	21770	506518	0.031	0.720
9	Taiwan	15039	521557	0.021	0.741
10	Australia	14510	536067	0.021	0.762
11	S. Korea	14384	550451	0.020	0.783
12	Netherlands	10897	561348	0.015	0.798
13	Spain	9192	570540	0.013	0.811
14	India	7671	578211	0.011	0.822
15	Sweden	6927	585138	0.010	0.832
16	USSR	6833	591971	0.010	0.842
17	Singapore	6487	598458	0.009	0.851
18	Switzerland	6228	604686	0.009	0.860
19	Hong Kong	5900	610586	0.008	0.868
20	Israel	5524	616110	0.008	0.876
21	Belgium	5281	621391	0.008	0.883
22	Brazil	5174	626565	0.007	0.891
23	Finland	5092	631657	0.007	0.898
24	Greece	4571	636228	0.006	0.904
25	Poland	4450	640678	0.006	0.911
26	Austria	3839	644517	0.005	0.916
27	Denmark	3013	647530	0.004	0.921
28	Portugal	2781	650311	0.004	0.924
29	Norway	2458	652769	0.003	0.928
30	Turkey	2289	655058	0.003	0.931

Sl. No.	Country/ publications	Total	Cumulative total	%	Cumulative %
31	Hungary	2170	657228	0.003	0.934
32	New Zealand	1676	658904	0.002	0.937
33	S. Africa	1658	660562	0.002	0.939
34	Mexico	1586	662148	0.002	0.941
35	Ukraine	1531	663679	0.002	0.943
36	Egypt	1459	665138	0.002	0.946
37	Yugoslavia	1438	666576	0.002	0.948
38	Slovenia	1410	667986	0.002	0.950
39	Ireland	1271	669257	0.002	0.951
40	S. Arabia	1192	670449	0.002	0.953
41	Czech	1173	671622	0.002	0.955
42	Romania	1110	672732	0.002	0.956
43	Argentina	859	673591	0.001	0.958
44	Bulgaria	777	674368	0.001	0.959
45	Malaysia	760	675128	0.001	0.960
46	Thailand	708	675836	0.001	0.961
47	Iran	641	676477	0.001	0.962
48	Croatia	617	677094	0.001	0.963
49	Others	26349	703443	0.037	1.000

5.1 Observations

In Table 2, we may observe that:

- India's contribution is only 1.1% (7,671);
- USA has contributed most of the research papers and it is about 36.9% (2,59,448) of the total publications (7,03,443);
- Japan, China and Canada contributed 7.7% (53,906), 4.4% (31,285) and 4.0% (27,882) respectively;
- Contribution of European countries (including Russia) is about 31.4% (2,20,804);

- Contribution of Mexico, Brazil and Argentina amounts to 1.1% (7,619);
- Asia's (excluding Japan, China and India) contribution is 6.6% (46,709);
- Israel contributed less than a percent (5,524); and
- Other countries together contributed 6.0% (42,535).

Further, we note from Table 3 that:

- India's contribution has more or less remained constant – between 1.1% to 1.3%;
- Publications of software research output have declined from 48.8% to 29.4%, 7.5% to 6.4%, and 4.9 % to 3.4% in USA, UK, Canada, respectively;
- Publications of software research output have increased from 6.1% to 8.2%, 4.5% to 5.6%, 3.4% to 3.9%, 2.9% to 3.4% 1.8% to 9.9%, 1.20% to 2.1% in Japan, Germany, Italy, China and Australia respectively; and
- In other countries, either decline or increase is quite insignificant and very marginal.

Out of the total number of publications in the subject, 80% have come from the top 12 countries as a whole, whereas in 1989, only the first 7 countries published the 80% of the articles. Research output on software studies is growing in developing and less developed countries. The overall percentage of the contributions in software studies is decreasing in developed countries as compared to the developing and less developed countries. Data in Table 2 indicates that China's research contribution has been growing during the period. The percentage of India's contribution to the total number of contributions has remained constant. The average growth rate of developing countries is greater than the growth rate in developed countries. Hence, it would appear that research in countries like China, South Korea, Taiwan, and Singapore is growing at a faster rate than in the developed countries.

Further, we note that China has the highest growth rate; China's literature grows exponentially! South Korea and Taiwan too have higher growth rates. In Europe,

Germany had the highest growth rate. India's growth rate of software literature is quite high, particularly when compared to USA, UK and Canada.

Table 3 below shows the number of countries that published 80% of the articles from 1989 to 2001; it also gives data on the number of countries having different percentiles. Further, in recent times, there is more number of countries in the least productive group, particularly at the 95th percentile – less number of countries contribute in the most productive group (say, 95th percentile). The number of countries is however increasing in the productive group if it is up to 90th percentile.

Table 3: Percentiles of the Software literature (top 70 countries)

Year	No. of countries having following percentage of contribution					
	50%	60%	70%	80%	90%	95%
1990	1	2	4	7	21	48
1991	1	3	5	9	22	48
1992	2	3	6	10	23	48
1993	1	3	6	10	20	48
1994	2	4	6	12	23	41
1995	2	4	7	12	24	43
1996	3	5	7	13	24	38
1997	3	5	8	13	24	38
1998	3	5	8	13	23	39
1999	3	5	8	13	23	36

Table 4 gives data on publications and higher education budget. The analysis indicates that higher the budget for higher education, higher the number of publications and vice-versa. Table 5 gives data on export of software, domestic consumption in terms of money and the number of publications. We note that higher the number of publications, higher the export as well as the domestic consumption.

Table 4: Correlation coefficient for the number of publications vs Higher Education Budget and S&T budget

Year (a)	Publi-cation (b)	Higher Education Budget (c)	S & T (d)	Year (a)	Publication (b)	Higher Education Budget (c)	S & T (d)
2001	895	13142.5	3907.5	1995	612	5,355.7	1764.8
2000	853	11,690.0	3248.5	1994	510	3,940.0	1407.4
1999	828	9,999.6	2941.7	1993	399	3,147.3	1153.4
1998	619	9,684.1	2442.5	1992	260	2,619.4	929.9
1997	770	7,656.0	2004.0	1991	394	2559.0	861.7
1996	588	6,536.3	1854.0	1990	422	2316.5	758.7
	R	**0.9274**	**0.9256**				

Table 5: Correlation coefficient of number of publications vs Export and domestic use of software

Year	Publication	Export	Domestic	Total
2001	895	36500	11634	48134
2000	853	28350	9400	37750
1999	828	17150	7200	24350
1998	619	10940	4950	15890
1997	770	6500	3470	9970
1996	588	3700	2600	6300
	R	**0.81997129**	**0.833783**	

6 CONCLUDING REMARKS

This study shows that:

- USA has contributed most of the research papers. The percentage of contribution of USA is decreasing as the number of countries engaged in research in the field increased over the period between 1989 and 2001.
- India's contribution is only 1.1%, which has remained a constant over a period of 12 years.
- The percentage of contributions of developed countries is decreasing whereas the percentage of contributions of developing countries is increasing. It shows that there is an increase in the awareness of the need for research and development in software in developing countries.
- The study also indicates that higher the budget for higher education, higher the number of publications, and higher the number of publications, higher the export as well as domestic consumption of software.

REFERENCES

1. *Aslib proceedings*. (1948). Vol. 1; p. 102.
2. Egghe, L. and Ravichandra Rao, I.K. *Classification of growth models based on growth rates and its applications*.
3. —. On the 80/20 rule. (1986). *Scientometrics*, Vol. 10; p. 55-66.
4. — and Ravichandra Rao I.K. (2002). Duality revisited: construction of fractional frequency distribution based on two dual Lotka's Law. *Journal of American Society Information Science*. Vol. 53(10); p. 789.
5. Lal, Arjun and Ray, P.K. (1991). Pattern of research contribution in leading horticultural journals of the world: a comparative study. *IASLIC Bulletin*. Vol. 36(3); p. 95-102.
6. Miquel, J.F.; Ojansoo. T.; OkuBo. Y.; Paul. A. and Dore J.C. (1995). World science in 18 disciplinary areas: comparative evaluation of the publication patterns of 48 countries over the period of 1981-1992. *Scientometrics*. Vol. 33(2); p. 149-167.
7. Neelameghan, A. Librametry. (1969). *DRTC Seminar*. Vol. 7; Paper LC.
8. —.; Buche,V.V. and Gupta, B.S.S. (1970). Distribution pattern of the duplication of discoveries. *Nature*. Vol. 227; p. 1060.
9. —. and Gupta, B.S.A. (1971). Multiple production of antibiotics: distribution pattern. *Current Science*. Vol. 40(6); p. 131-132.

10. Parmar; Arvind Singh; Kumar; Sanghmitra, A.; Prakash; Thushara and Kalyane, V. *Highlights of Library Automation related documents in the INSPEC*. http://eprints.rclis.org/archive/00002525/01/parmar-08-11-04.pdf.

11. Ranganathan, S R. (1969). Librametry and its scope. *DRTC seminar*. Vol. 7; Paper DA.

12. Ravichandra Rao, I.K. (1981). Document and user distribution in transaction records of Canadian University Libraries. *Doctoral Thesis*. Faculty of Graduate Studies, University of Western Ontario, London, Ontario, Canada.

13. —. and Meera, B.M. (1991). Growth and obsolescence of literature: an empirical study. Presented at the *Third International Conference on Informetrics*, Bangalore, 9-12 August 1991.

14. —. Distribution of scientific productivity and social change. *Journal of American Society for Information Science*. Vol. 31(2); p. 111-21.

15. —. (1997). Analysis of Bradford Multiples and a model to explain law of Scattering. Paper presented at the *6th International Conference on Bibliometrics, Informetrics and Scientometrics*. 16-19 June 1997, Jerusalem.

16. Rousseau, S. and Rousseau, R. I. (1997). Data envelopment analysis as a tool for constructing scientometrics indicator. *Scientometrics*. Vol. 40; p. 45-56.

17. Neelameghan, A. and Ravichandra Rao, I.K. (2005). Bibliometric support to medical historiography: a case study of the incidence of communicable diseases in India in the 19th Century. *Information Studies*. Vol. 11(2); 2005 April; p. 79-92.

PROFESSOR A. NEELAMEGHAN

M. A. Gopinath

The presentation of a festschrift is a festive occasion. The festschrift signifies the significance, impact of the person and his/her contributions - in the past and possibly in the future as well.

Dr. S. R. Ranganathan caught me into his folds, in 1963, after my B Lib. Sc. He introduced me to A. Neelameghan (AN) who had joined the Documentation Research and Training Centre (DRTC) when it was established the previous year. Later I joined the post-graduate course at DRTC, was Research Assistant to National Research Professor in Library Science Dr. Ranganathan, taught several courses, researched and guided research, at DRTC as Lecturer, Reader (Associate Professor), and Professor and Head of the Centre A.N. was full time with DRTC until 1978.. Obviously we had daily interactions.

"Equilibrium is the game. Rhythm is life". That is how AN projected to me the work when I first met him. Within minutes he asked me to Index the papers of the oncoming DRTC Seminar (June 1963). The papers were still coming and being processed.. But some had already been mimeographed. They had numbers, and pages. A kind of partial diffraction of a potential organized text. The title of the document:: "Documentation Periodicals". Its subtitle 'Seepage, Scatter, Coverage and Time Lags'. It was a study of Documentation of Scientific and Technical papers and their dissemination. The topic was novel to me. I asked "Is there a method for preparing the index"? He paused and said "You know chain procedure". I agreed and left with a box of 5"x 3" slips. It is direction economics. That is the man I found always, throughout our time together. He puts in some thought seed. You begin to burrow, furrow, and winnow your syntaxes. He will give a time for completion. And demand the product to be placed in his hands not later than the dead line specified.

Dr. Ranganathan asked us to put blinkers to facilitate concentration. He passed away in September 1972. Then began an open management era. AN would put people around me. They had to do their work, but I had to guide them.. I had difficulty. Guiding others was new to me then.. One day I mentioned this to him. He told me to read Rutherford on R and D Management. He gāve the same problem to other people and got different results from different people. They were Research Assistants and not students. They had to resort to different methodologies. We would then discuss and compare the approaches and strategies we adopted. Afterwards, this method of guiding others stayed and played with me always.

AN is an enigma. You may not anticipate what he will do or want you to do. He will give you a galley proof of a paper to correct and ask for it to be completed by next day. It may be difficult English, difficult technology and difficult reading, but you have to proof-read. And it was training and learning for us.

AN left to join UNESCO in mid-1978 and whenever he came to India, I consulted him, on policies and programmes, methodologies, strategies, performances. I remember the verandah in his house where we had pleasant exchange of ideas, with welcome interruptions by his wife Mrs. Lakshmi with coffee and snacks. She always had a warm enquiry about my mother and wife.

Our general conversations were in 'monosyllables'. I ask a half question, he will complete with a probability "You may do so". But, it was adequate consultation certainly.

Communications were on a different level. People will come and say that Prof. A.N. wanted us to meet you. They presented their problems. I went to the job as quickly and smoothly as possible having gained experience and confidence.

AN is knowledge-giving, knowledge-setting, adventuring, venture sorting, and winnowing away the mind, matters, money, energy, space and time. His classes were interesting and scanned the world panorama.

"AN" Principles for life:

- Work is a Rhythm.
- Allotted work is your Prime concern, you have to do it, none will do it for you.
- If you go to a Seminar, do not be meek, take a lead, manage the team, prefer Quality to quantity in work and management.
- You develop yourself. Force an impact. Be 'unique' in the universals.
- Do not expect anything from anywhere. They are all thus and thus and that is it.
- Always be innovative, and make others innovative.
- Work, play and progress.

Prof. Neelameghan contributed significantly to Documentation, Medical Librarianship, Depth Classification, Reference work and service, Bibliometrics, and Scientometrics. He is an excellent teacher of these subjects.. He did contribute to a variety of information services and preparation of information products. He organized seminars, colloquia, conferences at institutional, national and international levels. He consolidates the field wherever needed.

AN contributed to the design and development of information products and services, especially of the DEVSIS type at national, regional, and international levels. He formulated and assisted in the formulation of Library and Information Education Policies and programmes, both short term continuing education courses as well as complete graduate and post-graduate programmes. He contributed significantly to UNESCO programmes in the information area from the headquarters in Paris, and national / regional higher information studies schools in Africa (Addis Ababa, Ethiopia and Ibadan, Nigeria), Latin America (Caracas, Venezuela), South-east Asia (Manila, Philippines), and China (Beijing). He has excellent perception of Third World socio-economic problems and their impact on literacy, education, and libraries..

He often used the Delphi approach to examine a problem and find solutions. It means that there is no single solution. It is a continuum. He embodies brass stacks, bench level, supervision, and managerial approach to librarianship. He is an epitome of information himself. He is consulted for advice by individuals and institutions and he is a popular problem solver. He has provided plans for several R&D and industrial information services in India and abroad.

A.N. is humble. He does not want any recognition. Least of all this festschrift. But those, who are with him, feel that it is an honour to salute a man who works very hard and provided his soul and whole to Dr. S R Ranganathan during life and after. They both played in building team-cum-relay research in Library and Information for our advantage.

When I put my thoughts to him, his name translates to "blue cloud". I used to think of "Ooty" where he was born.. Here is what Nobel Laureate C.V.Raman is supposed to have remarked to high school students: "You do not have to be Ramans to think. Be curious. Look at the sky. Think why is it blue?" I leave it at that: What 'Blue' is many to many.

My wife and son join me in expressing our good wishes to Mr. and Mrs. Neelameghan. May God bless them with good health to continue their good work.

A SALUTATION OF AFFECTION

K.S. Deshpande

There are very few among our friends, meeting whom is a great pleasure, with whom conversation is enlightening, whose very memory brings warmth to our hearts. Prof. Neelameghan is one such priceless friend of mine.

Naturally, therefore, I was transported with happiness when my friend, Dr. K.N. Prasad, told me sometime back, that a group of Prof. Neelameghan's students, colleagues and admirers, had launched the idea of bringing out a Festschrift in his honour, I thought I should not allow this opportunity of paying a tribute to him, slip through my fingers.

The very thought of Prof. Neelameghan brings to my mind a beautiful Sanskrit *slōka* of Bhartrihari*, which describes the qualities of a true gentleman. Since the *slōka* applies to him, I quote it here:

तृष्णां छिन्धि भज क्षमां जहि मदं पापे रतिं मा कृथाः
सत्यं ब्रूह्यनुयाहि साधुपदवीं सेवस्व विद्वज्जनान् ।
मान्यान्मानय विद्विषोऽप्यनुनय प्रख्यापय स्वान् गुणान्
कीर्तिं पालय दुःखिते कुरु दयामेतत्सतां लक्षणम् ॥

trsnam chindi bhaja ksamam jahi madam pape ratim ma krthah

satyam bruhyanuyahi sadhupadavim sevasva vidvajjanan|

---

* Bhartrhari-viracitam nitisatakam, English Rendering by Prof. M. K. Suryanarayana Rao, Lalitha Prakashana, 107/1, 2nd Main Road, Mount Joy Extn. Hanumanthanagar, Bangalore 560 019, INDIA, August 2000.

manyanmanaya vidviso pyanunaya prakhyapaya swan gunan

kirtim palaya duhkhite kuru dayametat satam laksanam ||

Freely rendered into English the burden of the *slōka* runs thus:

> *Cut asunder your desire. Take to forgiveness. Give up pride. Don't feel complacent in doing sinful deeds. Speak the truth. Follow the course of the virtuous. Serve the learned. Revere those who deserve reverence. Conciliate even the foes. Unfold your own (good) qualities. Retain your good name. Be kind towards the distressed. These are the characteristics of the virtuous.*

My association with Prof. Neelameghan goes back to the late fifties of the last century, when as a member of the Board of Studies of the University of Poona, I used to visit that city of culture and learning and where Prof. Neelameghan was in charge of the Technical Information Centre of the Government of India sponsored antibiotics factory – the Hindustan Antibiotics, Pimpri, a dozen km from Pune.

In 1963-64, the second year of the school of library science, at Karnatak University, I initiated publication of a professional journal on comparative librarianship, styling it as *Timeless Fellowship*, and Prof. Neelameghan was one among the stalwarts who contributed an article for the very first issue. He contributed articles for the later volumes also, enhancing the value of the journal.

In the latter half of the *sixties* when I was associated with the development of the infant Bangalore University Library, Prof. Neelameghan was already there working in the DRTC with the master of our profession – the late Dr. S.R. Ranganathan, of hallowed memory. Our meetings at the DRTC were frequent and we became closer friends.

After I had made considerable headway in the streamlining of the operations of the Bangalore University Library and putting it on firm grounds, the Vice-Chancellor, Dr. V.K. Gokak, suggested that I should sally forth into starting a degree course in Library and Information Science. It was my good fortune that I could have the expert advice of Dr. B. Anderson of Bombay University, and Prof. Neelameghan, who constituted the Board of Studies.

We drew up a modern comprehensive syllabus and submitted it to the university. With the expiry of Dr. Gokak's tenure as Vice Chancellor, our proposal was apparently shelved temporarily; and I returned to my parent institution, the Karnataka University at Dharwad.

Months rolled by into over a year when under the new dispensation of Dr. H. Narasimhaiah, the Bangalore University asked me to give the green signal for propelling forward the Degree course. Accordingly a meeting of the *Ad-hoc* Committee, which served as the Board of Studies, was convened in Dharwad in 1972 to suit my convenience. Prof. Neelameghan was my honoured Guest at Home. How modest, how unassuming was he as my guest!

Needless to add, that we updated the syllabus and requested the Bangalore University to go ahead.

Our efforts bore fruit when the Bangalore University started the M.Lib.Sc. programme, with the classes and examinations for the first batch being conducted by Prof. Neelameghan and his colleagues – Dr. Bhattacharyya, Dr. Gopinath, and Dr. Seetharama.

September 1972: Early morning. There was an urgent phone call from Bangalore. The caller at the other end was my good friend Shri. J.N. Kamalapur, the Director of All India Radio, Bangalore Station. And what he conveyed to me descended on me like a bolt from the blue. The doyen of our profession - revered Dr. Ranganathan had merged with the immortal spirit earlier in the previous night. For a moment I was speechless!

Shri Kamalapur continued and suggested that I offer my *Shraddhanjali* to the adored departed in Kannada from the Dharwad Station of AIR at 8.00 p.m. on that day. He further sought my advice as to whom he should contact in Bangalore to perform a similar service in English from the Bangalore station. Pat went my reply suggesting Prof. Neelameghan's name.

Thus it transpired that simultaneously both of us offered our tearful *pranams* to the great soul, on 27th September 1972 at 8.00 pm.

In November 1976 the UNESCO had convened in Bangalore an important meeting of the Supervisors of Library and Documentation Schools in the Asian Region and I had been nominated as the Rapporteur and Panel Member. Prof. Neelameghan was the Convener. How ably, intelligently, and modestly, did he conduct the meeting!

The story of our warm relationship goes on like this, and before I conclude I must refer to another sweet significant event. The Institute of Information Studies of the Sarada Ranganathan Endowment for Library Science, Bangalore, had arranged a two pronged programme on 12th August 1997 at which Prof. Bhattacharyya released an important book by Prof. Neelameghan and I felicitated our elder Prof. S. Parthasarathy on his completing his 80th year of an eventful life, punctuated by solid contributions both to the profession and the science.

By virtue of his numerous path-breaking contributions to Library and Information Science, Prof. Neelameghan easily adorns the status of the Stalwart in the Profession. Age has not dimmed his enthusiasm nor diminished his intellect. When some one asked Michael Angelo (1475-1564) the eminent Italian sculptor, painter, architect and poet as to what he was engaged in, late in the evening of his life, his answer was "Ancora Impara" - I am still studying.

That is the noble path, which Prof. Neelameghan is treading now. May he live waxing through a hundred autumns and springs, is all that I wish and pray for!

PROFESSOR A. NEELAMEGHAN AND THE SARADA RANGANATHAN ENDOWMENT FOR LIBRARY SCIENCE

K.N. Prasad

1 THE ENDOWMENT: FOUNDING AND OBJECTIVES

Prof. Arashanipalai Neelameghan (AN) has been associated with the Sarada Ranganathan Endowment for Library Science (SRELS) since its founding by Dr. S. R. Ranganathan (Dr.SRR) in 1961 (registered with the Treasurer of Charitable Endowments, Government of India, New Delhi, in 1963). Its aims and objectives briefly are: to improve the library and information services in India; to train library and information service personnel; to promote the provision of efficient library and information service; and to apply research results of library and information studies.

2 PROGRAMMES AND ACTIVITIES

The objectives are realized by supporting R&D in library and information science (LIS), organizing periodically a course of lectures on recent developments in LIS and other related fields by national and international experts, and publication of these lectures and of other nascent ideas in LIS. Three series of lectures organized, in alternate years, under the auspices of the Endowment: are: Sarada Ranganathan Endowment Lectures (1965-); Dr. S.R. Ranganathan Memorial Lectures (1973-); and Curzonco-Seshachalam Endowment Lectures (2001-);

3 BOARD OF TRUSTEES

In addition to Dr.SRR and AN, the other founding members of SRELS, who constituted the first Board of Trustees, were: Mr. R. Yogeshwar, son of Dr. SRR, representing the family of SRR, Shri Seshachalam Chettiar, Curzon & Co., Chennai, a close associate of Dr.SRR and member of the Madras Library Association, and Prof. P.N.Kaula. Dr.SRR, as Member-Secretary (honorary) of SRELS guided and conducted all its affairs until mid-1968. The members of the present Board of Trustees are: Prof. S. Parthasarathy, Chennai, Mr. R. Yogeshwar, Luxembourg, Mrs. Saroja V. Guruswamy, Chennai, Prof. A. Neelameghan, (Member-Secretary), Bangalore, Dr. T. B. Rajashekar, Bangalore, and Prof. K.S. Raghavan, Bangalore.

4 ENDOWMENT AND DRTC

From the beginning till about 1980 SRELS was located on the premises of the Documentation Research and Training Centre (DRTC), ISI, Bangalore. Dr SRR was one of the co-founders of DRTC and remained its Honorary Professor and Head until his death in 1972. The secretarial work of SRELS was handled by the secretarial staff of DRTC. During the first decade, 1962-1972, AN took care of the work relating to the editing, publishing, and business of the periodical *Library Science with a Slant to Documentation* (1), also started by Dr.SRR in 1963 as an organ of SRELS, maintenance of the related accounts, registers, etc. In addition to the subscriptions, each year some 100 periodicals and report series in LIS were received in exchange for the Endowment's periodical, mostly from USA, UK and Europe. These were placed in the DRTC library.

5 AN ELECTED MEMBER-SECRETARY

In 1965 Dr. SRR was appointed National Research Professor in Library Science by the Government of India, which entitled him to have his own research assistants and secretarial staff. In the latter half of 1968, Dr. SRR desired to pass on the Secretaryship of the Endowment to another member of the Board of Trustees. Thus, on 14 Oct. 1968, approving a proposal by Dr SRR the Board elected AN as Member Secretary and co-opted Dr. M.A Gopinath as member. AN served in this capacity until August 1978 when he left India to join Unesco. Dr. Gopinath was elected Member Secretary. When Dr. Gopinath migrated to USA in mid-1996, AN was again elected Member Secretary by the Board; and he continues to function in that capacity.

In mid-1980 the DRTC moved to its new premises on Mysore Road (some 15 KM from the city). SRELS remained in the city; its office moved from place to place until a more permanent location was secured in Rajajinagar in April 1989 from where it continues to function. An Executive Officer overseas the administrative work of SRELS.

6 PAST TWO DECADES

AN retired and returned from UNESCO, Paris, at the end of 1986. He brought with him the UNESCO database software CDS-ISIS, prepared a user manual, conducted a workshop in DRTC, installed the software in the Endowment's PC, and trained the project assistants to use it. An early use of the software was to create the database of the SRR bibliography, which SRELS was then compiling. This bibliography was recently published on a CD. During 1987- to mid-1990 SRELS organized several CDS-ISIS training workshops in Bangalore and Chennai with AN as the principal resource person.

From September 1990 to July 1994 AN was Visiting Professor at the IDRC-Unesco supported School of Information Studies for Africa (SISA), Addis Ababa University, Addis Ababa, Ethiopia. During this period he was also working on a couple of books and guided students to develop CDS-ISIS databases and Pascal programs (e,g, ABNCD integrated database; VOCON.PAS for online vocabulary control; SELECT.PAS for multiple database surfing and search). During term breaks from SISA he assisted in workshops and seminars and guided development of CDS-ISIS Pascal programs by the research assistants of SRELS and participants in the CDS-ISIS workshops in Bangalore and Chennai.

Dr. SRR's Birth Centenary: During 1991-1992 AN attended consultative meetings to plan the celebrations of Dr. SRR's birth centenary, provided financial support for producing the multimedia videocassette on the life and work of Dr SRR; participated in the International Informetrics Conference, Bangalore. August 1991, marking the start of the centenary celebrations; organized and edited the special issue of *Libri* (Copenhagen), v.42. 43 (Jul. – Sept, 1992) devoted to Dr. SRR; and assisted in the organization of and participated in the Second International ISKO Conference on Cognitive Paradigms in Knowledge Organization, held in Chennai, 26-28 August 1992.

On return to Bangalore in mid-1994, AN continued assisting in workshops, onsite training and installation and application of CDS-ISIS, in various institutions. AN has developed and maintains different types of databases and thesauri, used in training courses and for experimentation.

The books he started on while in Ethiopia were completed and published by SRELS. These and the Endowment lectures edited by AN have been published by SRELS. AN has guided and /or assisted in several projects undertaken by SRELS.

Prof. Neelameghan has been honoured by the American Society for Information Science/SIG III Award for promoting international cooperation in the information field. He has also been awarded the FID/CR SR Ranganathan Award for Classification Research (1982) for applying Dr. Ranganathan's normative principles and knowledge organization methodologies in database and user interface design and development. He has been honoured with "Award for Excellence" for contribution to information studies by the International Biographical Centre, UK., and with the "Seal of Honor" by the American Biographical Institute, USA. In India, he has been made a Fellow of the Society of Information Scientists.

AN's long association of over four decades with the Sarada Ranganathan Endowment for Library Science has benefited a large number of students, teachers and research workers. His contributions to the journal *Library science with a Slant to Documentation* and its later versions, and to various seminars, conferences and workshops in India and abroad have helped to promote the library and information profession and research in information studies, an objective of the Endowment. Again, the consultations he has offered, the training programmes in the design and development information systems, and databases on behalf of SRELS have helped many libraries and information centres to offer better information services to their users. AN's contributions in some other areas of his interest like library and information policies and programmes and institution building have been internationally acknowledged.

The fact that he is still being called on for advice in different areas by many individuals and organizations speaks volumes of his scholarship.

Notes:

1. The title was changed to *Library Science with a slant to Documentation and Information Studies* from Vol. 25 in 1988 and to *SRELS Journal of Information Management* from Vol. 37 in 2000.

CONTRIBUTING AUTHORS

ANANDAKRISHNAN, M.

Vice-Chairman, RCIS, Chennai. **Contact Address**: Chairman, Madras Institute of Development Studies, #79, 2nd Main Road, Gandhi Nagar, Sadyar, Chennai 600 020. E-mail: ananda1928@gmail.com

ASWATH, LALITHA

Professor, Department of Library and Information Science, Bangalore University, Jnana Bharathi Campus, Bangalore - 560 056, India. E-mail: lalitha_aswath@hotmail.com

BEAN, CAROL A.

National Center for Research Resources, National Institute of Health, Bethesda, MD USA. E-mail: cabean@mail.nih.gov

BEGHTOL, CLARE

Associate Dean and Graduate Coordinator, Faculty of Information Studies, University of Toronto, 140, St. George Street, Toronto, Ontario M55 3G6, Canada. E-mail:clare.beghtol@utoronto.ca

BRACKE, PAUL

Head of Systems and Networking, Arizona Health Sciences Library, University of Arizona, Tucson, AZ 85719, E-mail: paul@ahsl.arizona.edu

COCHRANE, PAULINE ATHERTON

Graduate School of Library and Information Science, University of Illinois at Urbana-Champaign. 501 E. Daniel Street, MC-493, Champaign, IL 61820. E-mail: pcochran@uiuc.edu

COLEMAN, ANITA S.

Asst. Professor, School of Information Resources and Library Science, University of Arizona, Tucson, AZ 85719 E-mail: asc@u.arizona.edu

CRAVEN, TIMOTHY C.

Faculty of Information and Media Studies, Middlesex College, The University of Western Ontario, London, Ontario N6A 5B7, Canada. E-mail: craven@uwo.ca

DAHLBERG, INGETRAUT

Former Chairperson, International Society for Knowledge Organization, Am Hirtenberg 13, D-64732 Bad König, Germany. E-mail: IDahlberg@t-online.de

DESHPANDE, K. S.

University Librarian and Professor (Retd.) Karnatak University, Dharwad. **Contact Address**: Ramachandra Krupa, 19/1, Mahishi Road, Malamaddi, Dharwad 580 007. Ph: (0836) 2790763

GHOSH, S. B.

Professor, Faculty of Library and Information Science, Indira Gandhi National Open University (IGNOU), Maidan Garhi, New Delhi-110068, India. E-mail: sbghosh@hotmail.com; sbghosh@ignou.ac.in

GOPINATH, M. A.

Visiting Professor, North Carolina Central University, Raleigh, NC, USA. E-mail: gopi17nath@gmail.com

GREEN, REBECCA

College of Information Studies, University of Maryland, College Park, MD USA E-mail: rgreen@umd.edu

HUSSAIN, K.H.

Kerala Forest Research Institute, Peechi- 680 653, Thrissur, Kerala, India. E-mail: hussain@kfri.org

ISAAC, K. A.

Librarian and Professor of Library Science (Retd.), Kerala University, Thiruvananthapuram. **Contact Address**: T.C./27/973(14), Vidyadiraja Nagar. Poojapura, Thiruvananthapuram – 695012, Kerala, India. Ph: (0471) 2359502

IYER, HEMALATHA

Associate Professor, School of Information Science and Policy, State University of New York at Albany, Albany, NY 12222, E-mail: hi651@albany.edu

JAYAKANTH, FRANCIS

National Centre for Science Information, Indian Institute of Science, Bangalore 560 012, India. E-mail: franc@ncsi.iisc.ernet.in

KAPOOR, AMIT

Neurosurgeon, Post-Graduate Institute of Neurological Surgery, Dr. A. Lakshmipathi. Neurological Centre, V.H.S. Hospital, TTTI Post, Taramani, Chennai 600113, India. E-mail: dramitkapoor@yahoo.com

LA BARRE, KATHERINE

The Graduate School of Library and Information Science, University of Illinois at Urbana-Champaign. 501 E. Daniel Street, MC-493, Champaign, IL 61820. E-mail: pcochran]@uiuc.edu

MANGLA, P. B.

Former Head, Department of Library & Information Science, and, Dean, Faculty of Arts, University of Delhi. E-mail: manglapb@yahoo.co.in

MCILWAINE, I.C.

Editor in Chief, Universal Decimal Classification. School of Library, Archive and Information Studies, University College London, UK. E-mail: I.mcilwaine@ucl.ac.uk

MEDLAND, MICHAEL

Department of Foundations, Research and Reading, East Carolina University, Greenville, NC 27858, USA. E-mail: mb_medland@hotmsil.com

MOHAN, MURALI

Neurosurgeon, Post-Graduate Institute of Neurological Surgery, Dr. A. Lakshmipathi. Neurological Centre, V.H.S. Hospital, TTTI Post, Taramani, Chennai 600113, India. E-mail: drmurali78@rediffmail.com

MURTHY, SUDHA S.

Senior Librarian, National Tuberculosis Institute, 8, Bellary Road, Bangalore 560003, India. E-mail: ntiindia@blr.vsnl.net.in; sudhasm@ yahoo.com

NAGARAJA RAO, D. N.

No. 5, 1st Cross, 1st Stage, Gokulam, Mysore 570003. Ph: (0821) 2516773

NAGARAJAN, K. S.

Scientist (Deputy Director) (Retd.), Indian National Scientific Documentation Centre (INSDOC), CSIR, Gocernment of India, New Delhi and Bangalore. **Contact Address**: 'Chitrakoot' Apartments, 18th Cross, Malleswaram West, Bangalore- 560055. Ph: (080) 23340922.

PRASAD, K. N.

Executive Officer, Sarada Ranganathan Endowment for Library Science, 702, 42nd Cross, III Block, Rajajinagar, Bangalore 560 010, India. E-mail: srels@vsnl.com; prasadkn@vsnl.net

RAJAN, T. N.

Head (Retd.), Training Division, Indian National Scientific Documentation Centre (now, NISCAIRS), New Delhi. E-mail: tyaganatarajan@yahoo.com

RAJASHEKAR, T. B.

Chairman, National Centre for Science Information (NCSI), Indian Institute of Science, Bangalore 560 012, India. E-Mail: raja@ncsi.iisc. ernet.in

RAJEEV, J.S.

Stendek R&D, Kalamassery, Kochi 682 017. E-mail: rajeev_jsv@ stendekrnd.com

RATNAKAR, A

Education and Training Consultant, Informatics (India) Ltd., New Delhi. E-mail: asparir@hotmail.com

RAVICHANDRA RAO, I.K.

Professor and Head. Documentation Research and Training Centre, Indian Statistical Institute, 8th Mile Mysore Road, Bangalore 560059, India. E-mail: ikrrao@hotmail.com;

ROSE, JOHN

Programme Specialist (Retd.), Information Society Division, Unesco, Paris, France. E-mail:johnrose@alumni.caltech.edu

SAHOO, BIBHUTI BHUSAN

Senior Research Fellow, Documentation Research and Training Centre, Indian Statistical Institute, 8th Mile Mysore Road, Bangalore 560059, India. E-mail: bibhuti@isibang.ac.in

SATYAPAL, B.G.

Freelance Application Programming Group 32, Esther Enclave, Jayanthi Nagar, Horamavu, Bangalore 560043, India. E-mail: bgsnsram@vsnl.com

SATYAPAL, N. SANJIVINI

Freelance Application Programming Group 32, Esther Enclave, Jayanthi Nagar, Horamavu, Bangalore 560043, India. E-mail: bgsnsram@vsnl.com

SEETHARAMA, S.

Professor and Head (Retd.), Documentation Research and Training Centre (DRTC), Indian Statistical Institute, Bangalore 560059. **Contact Address**: 17, Varadarajulu Street, Egmore, Chennai - 600 008 Ph (Mobile): 9840492150

SHEPHERD, MICHAEL

Faculty of Computer Science, Dalhousie University, Halifax, NS, Canada B3H 1W5. E-mail: shepherd@cs.dal.ca

SRINIVASAN, PADMINI

Director, School of Library and Information Science, The University of Iowa, Iowa City, IA 52242, USA. E-mail: padmini-srinivasan@uiowa.edu

SRIVATSAN, K. R.

Director, Indian Institute of Information Technology and Management-Kerala (IIITM-K) Thiruvananthapuram, Kerala. E-mail: director@iiitmk.ac.in

TAHER, MOHAMED

Information Specialist Ontario Multifaith Council, Toronto, Canada E-mail: mtaher@omc.ca. Website: www.library.omc.ca

VASUDEVAN, M. C.

Neurosurgeon, Post-Graduate Institute of Neurological Surgery, Dr. A.Lakshmipathi. Neurological Centre, V.H.S. Hospital, TTTI Post, Taramani, Chennai 600113, India. E-mails: vino_deep@hotmail.com

WATTERS, CAROLYN

Faculty of Computer Science, Dalhousie University, Halifax, NS, Canada B3H 1W5. E-mail: shepherd@cs.dal.ca

WIDAD MUSTAFA EL HADI

UFR IDIST & CERSATES (CNRS UMR 8529); Université Charles De Gaulle, Lille 3, BP 149, F-59 653 Villeneuve D'Ascq, France. E-mail: mustafa@univ-lille3.fr

WILLIAMSON, NANCY J.

Faculty of Information Studies, University of Toronto, Faculty of Information Studies, University of Toronto, 140, St. George Street, Toronto, Ontario M55 3G6, Canada. E-mail: nancy.williamson@utoronto.ca